THE
SOVIET
BLOC

UNITY AND CONFLICT

THE
SOVIET
BLOC

UNITY AND CONFLICT

By

Zbigniew K. Brzezinski

Revised Edition

FREDERICK A. PRAEGER, *Publishers*
New York · Washington · London

Frederick A. Praeger, *Publishers*
111 Fourth Avenue, New York, N.Y. 10003, U.S.A.
77-79 Charlotte Street, London W.1, England

Published in the United States of America in 1961 by
Frederick A. Praeger, Inc., Publishers
Sixth printing, 1967

The original clothbound edition of this book was published
in 1960 by Harvard University Press, Cambridge, Mass., as Study No. 37
in the Russian Research Center series and Study No. 1
in the Center for International Affairs series. The present
edition has been revised and expanded

Library of Congress Catalog Card Number: 61-17111

Manufactured in the United States of America

To
Merle Fainsod

Contents

PART I
IDEOLOGY AND POWER IN THE EMERGENCE OF THE SOVIET BLOC

THE FIRST PHASE
1945–1947
THE PEOPLE'S DEMOCRACY
INSTITUTIONAL AND IDEOLOGICAL DIVERSITY

THE SECOND PHASE
1947–1953
STALINISM
INSTITUTIONAL AND IDEOLOGICAL UNIFORMITY

THE FOURTH PHASE
1957–1959
THE COMMUNIST "COMMONWEALTH" INSTITUTIONAL DIVERSITY AND IDEOLOGICAL UNIFORMITY

Introduction

THIS volume on the Soviet bloc is jointly sponsored by the Russian Research Center and the Center for International Affairs — the oldest and the youngest of such centers at Harvard. For the Russian Center, this is number thirty-seven in a series of distinguished studies. For the Center for International Affairs, this is the first fruit of its research program, and for this reason, as its Director, I am contributing the introduction.

Wise judgments and effective action in international affairs have always required sound appraisal of the international environment, both existent and emergent. In a revolutionary epoch like our own, this task poses unprecedented demands on knowledge, understanding, and creative analysis. The vast upheavals reshaping our world so profoundly and so rapidly have no historic parallel. The impact of technology, ideology, and their manifold consequences has radically transformed the power, purposes, and status of most nations and the character of the international order. Foreign affairs have become more pervasive and more intimately linked with domestic events than ever before. Many inherited concepts and attitudes do not fit the new realities and even obscure perception of them. For the United States, its new postwar role has given special urgency to this need for greater knowledge and comprehension of the new conditions. But all nations, old or new, confront the necessity to adapt their policies and thinking to the changing environment.

The research program of the Harvard Center for International Affairs reflects this concern with understanding the structure and dynamics of our era. By its studies, the Center seeks to shed light on forces and processes of change and their effects on international relations. In several major fields work is already under way. These include studies on social and economic development, on the relation of military technology to foreign affairs, and on the emerging situation and role of Europe. Joint studies have been undertaken with existing regional centers at Harvard where research interests intersect.

This analysis of relations within the Soviet bloc, which is such a joint endeavor, should be of interest to specialists in international affairs as well as to experts on the Soviet Union. There have, of course, been many volumes on relations between the USSR and the West, but studies of relations among the members of the Soviet bloc are much less common. Yet Eastern Europe, the main focus of this study, is significant not merely for itself, but as an indicator of broader Soviet attitudes. This was the case during 1945–1948, when Soviet activities there, in violation of Yalta, Potsdam, and other agreements, gradually alerted the West to Soviet hostility and ambitions. In the same way, an understanding of the evolution of Soviet-satellite relations over the last fifteen years should help to illuminate the basic purposes of the Soviet leaders and their outlook on foreign affairs. The special value of this study lies just here. The author has not been content to sift and piece together the available data merely to recount the sequence of events from 1945 to 1959. His aim has been to find an intelligible framework for the events which reveals their pattern without forcing them; he has sought to show not only how the bloc has changed, especially since Stalin, but what has made it change. In considering the factors making for unity and conflict within the bloc, the author has examined the relation of Communist ideology to power and the interplay of both in interparty conflicts, as well as the impact of domestic developments in one Communist state on its relations with others.

In consequence, the analysis provides some insight into the much debated question of the influence of ideology in shaping current policies and actions of Soviet leaders as well as into their use of ideology as an instrument of power. The implications of the analysis throw light on some issues not pursued in the book, such as the relation of disengagement to Soviet purposes. Implicit in much of the argument over this issue was the idea that the Soviet rulers might be prepared to sacrifice Communist control of some or all of the Eastern European satellites for concessions designed to promote Soviet security interests. The evidence on Soviet-satellite relations marshaled in this study seems to offer little support for this notion. If the author's analysis is correct, the Soviet rulers after Stalin, while seeking to adapt the relations to changed conditions, never contemplated for an instant that any of these nations might be allowed to slip out from Soviet domination. Such an idea clearly could not be squared with their "two camp" concept, or with the pattern underlying their handling of the Hungarian tragedy and their dealings with Tito in 1955–1958.

At the same time this study illuminates the actual and potential stresses inherent in the structure of the orbit which could ultimately complicate control, or even disrupt it. These tensions spring partly from the variations among the satellites in their dependence on Soviet power and partly from the necessity to justify, or at least reconcile, policies in terms of ideology. In consequence, practices of those regimes, like Poland's, which emphasize "domesticism," are almost bound to embarrass others which need the reassurance of uniformity. These cleavages among the Communist elites are complicated by the risks of popular discontent which are likely to be exacerbated by the rigidity of the less self-reliant regimes. Their experience since 1953 has doubtless taught the Soviet rulers that they operate within severe limits or rigidities in holding the bloc together, given their ideological focus. If the several Communist regimes do not succeed in further consolidating their power, the burden of shoring them up in the face of popular hostility may prove increasingly onerous. And, if they are successful, the result may be greater pressures for heterogeneity within the bloc. For the West, these strains within the bloc are relevant to claims that "realism" requires the recognition of Soviet domination of these areas as final and beyond change. This study indicates that, while it is hard to foresee how the situation may evolve, it would be unwise to treat it as forever frozen.

In short, this study is valuable on two planes. Its solid research puts together the historic facts on a comprehensive basis; and its orderly analysis offers a conceptual framework that is enlightening in broader terms.

ROBERT R. BOWIE
Director, Center for International Affairs

Author's Note for Revised Edition

I am pleased that the publication by Praeger of the softcover edition has made it possible to include a new chapter on the Sino-Soviet dispute and an Appendix on "The Organization of the Communist Camp." Some minor textual corrections have also been made. I am grateful to the Russian Institute of Columbia University for its research facilities and assistance, and to Professor Alexander Dallin for his helpful comments.

Z. B.

May 1961

Author's Preface

THE events of recent years have made it plain that the Communist camp is neither homogeneous, monolithic, nor unchanging. Underneath the external façade of unity a continuing process of change is taking place through evolution as well as through the internal clash of "antagonistic contradictions," to use a popular Marxist expression. Evolution is part of life; political systems, be they states or empires, are not immune to it. A scholar's task in observing such gradual change is to determine, if possible, its direction and its likely future significance. In time even gradual evolution may produce a real discontinuity: there is a qualitative difference between a boy and a man even though they are still the very same person. Similarly with the Communist camp.

The "antagonistic contradictions" are a different problem. The Communist camp as a collective entity is guided by purposes which are said to reflect its collective interest. At the same time, within these dominant, universal objectives there are also the specific, particular interests of the component units. Occasionally, and almost inescapably, a clash between the universal and particular takes place, and much of the history of relations between Communist states has to be written in terms of such conflicts. Even with the best of intentions and even with a conscious desire on the part of its members to adjust their interests, a collective organization of states produces strains and tensions. In the case of the Communist camp the disparity between the dominant power and the dependent Communist regimes resulted from the very start in the imposition of a one-sided priority of interests which ultimately was conducive to the emergence of open antagonisms and contradictory objectives.

Some of these conflicts might have been avoided had the Soviet leaders been more skilled in managing an international empire. Initially at least, they were limited by their own inexperience. Having viewed international affairs in terms of the hostile external world ranged against the Soviet Union, they could not think of the new Communist camp in any other way except as a slightly more expanded

Soviet system. In the interwar period international Communism had become identified with the interests of Soviet power, and the Soviet leaders had become accustomed to think of Communists from other nations primarily as agents of that power. This tendency was especially marked after the purges of 1937–1938 which had liquidated many prominent foreign Communists (including almost the entire leadership of the Polish Communist Party). The majority of the survivors continued to serve the Soviet Union as employees of the Comintern or in the international branch of the NKVD. After 1945 it was difficult for Moscow to consider them as equals, especially since most of the new regimes were still largely dependent on Soviet backing. The new leaders who had come from the USSR experienced a similar difficulty in adjusting their perspectives. It was hard for many of them to think of themselves as national leaders and no longer as agents of the center.

In time, however, the reponsibility of leadership and the complexity of building Communism under specific national conditions began to assert themselves, and both Moscow and the local leaders had to learn by trial and error that organizing relations among Communist-ruled states is more intricate than running the Comintern's various national bureaus. The story of these relations is thus also the story of the education of Soviet and other Communist leaders in making "agonizing reappraisals" and in seeking new ties for inter-Communist unity.

In undertaking this study I have tried, whenever possible, to approach the question of relations among Communist states from the standpoint of the regimes concerned, either in Moscow or in the Communist capitals.* In so doing, I have assumed that the Communist leaders by-and-large are dedicated to "the construction of Communism" though, as we shall repeatedly see, that objective does not mean precisely the same thing to all of them. In attempting to construct Communism (or initially Socialism) they make political judgments which reflect their ideology as well as their special interest in maintaining their political power, the power without which the ideology would be only an empty shell. As a result, the policy of a given Communist regime involves an intricate balance between its universal ideological values and particular power imperatives. My concluding chapter attempts to develop further the nature of this interdependent relationship between ideology and power on the basis of the evidence pre-

---

* For this reason words such as "socialism" or "People's Democracy" will often be employed in the sense as used by the Communists.

sented in the book. For the moment, suffice it to say that, viewed purely from an "outside" perspective, the Communist camp is necessarily overshadowed by the steep wall dividing the Communist and the non-Communist political systems. That shadow, accordingly, obscures the many differences in approach and interpretation which manifest themselves within the Communist system. To an outsider, a particular Church may appear homogeneous until he becomes aware of the various theological or institutional conflicts which operate within the organization.

Turning more specifically to the scope and purpose of this book, let me note, first of all, that my outlook on the general problem of the Soviet bloc has been shaped in large measure by my special interest in Soviet politics. This need not be a handicap since, for a while at least, the political operations of the camp were modeled on Soviet domestic politics. I would also add that I did not approach the problems with which this book is concerned from the standpoint of the specific aspirations of the peoples of the Communist-dominated states. This study is not, therefore, an additional contribution to many useful treatises dealing with Soviet domination and/or exploitation of other states. Nor is it a study specifically of the conflict between Communism and nationalism. Since the book's frame of reference is the relationship between the ideological orientation of the Communist regimes, on the one hand, and the imperatives of their political power, on the other, nationalism must be considered as a factor which Communist leaders recognize when shaping their policies. Nationalism can even influence the perspectives of Communist leaders and make them place a greater value on particular national interests than on the "universal" requisites of the camp. However, to a Communist, the nation-state and its interests are not ends in themselves, even though they may be reflected in the policies designed to achieve the ultimate end. Traditional nationalist objectives, therefore, lose some of their importance. But as this book hopes to show, the changing nature of the relations between Communist regimes and the USSR gradually introduces into these relations the specific interests of those regimes building Communism. Nationalism thus becomes an inherent, even if not a primary, factor in policy.

My primary purpose is to examine how the Soviet bloc has changed over the years, what problems faced and continue to face its Soviet and other Communist leaders, and how they go about solving them in terms of their general ideological orientation. The book will also try to show how internal changes in the USSR affected political developments within the other Communist states and eventually changed the pattern of relations among them. In so doing, the study will point to the forces which make for unity within the Soviet bloc as well as the pressures making for diversity. To the extent possible, it will do so in terms of the Communist regimes and not in terms of the nations concerned. This book, therefore, is not meant to be either a history of the Communist take-over or of Communist rule, although some of these domestic aspects are summarized when relevant to external relations. Individual or factional struggles, as important as they are, are not extracted for the purpose of historical narrative or minute examination but are treated within the context of the general pattern of interacting domestic and external pressures, aspirations, institutions, and outlooks that at once shape the camp and change it. More hopefully perhaps, this book is meant to be a modest contribution to the study of the interaction of ideology and institutions of power of several states within the same ideological context. A general theory of ideology-institution relationships among states awaits further study and thought, but my hope is that this might provide the nucleus for some generalizations.

Before outlining the structure of the book, it might be desirable to say a word or two about sources. They fall roughly into five categories: (1) official speeches and statements of Communist leaders; (2) Communist press — books dealing with the problem of new Communist states as well as some unpublished Communist documents; (3) summaries and reports of various Western agencies, most notably of Radio Free Europe in Munich; (4) secondary sources dealing with Eastern Europe, useful particularly for the early portion of the book; (5) my own interviews with Communist officials in the Communist states or abroad, personal observations from travel in Communist states, and statements and depositions by former Communist officials now abroad. Admittedly, such sources would not satisfy the rigorous archival standards of diplomatic history, but perhaps both the subject matter and its contemporary nature might be considered as legitimate justification.

The book is organized into two parts: "The Emergence of the Soviet Bloc" and "Relations Among the Communist States." It first delineates the emergence of and describes the central characteristics of Stalinism as the early pattern for relations among Communist states; it then discusses the forces and circumstances which challenged that pattern, namely the internal developments in the USSR, Poland, and Hungary as well as the impact of the Soviet policy on Yugoslavia.

The book then attempts to analyze the Soviet and Chinese responses to those challenges; and, finally, it points to some continuing issues inherent in the pattern of Communist interstate relations. A special problem which arose in the course of writing this book was the case of China. A study such as this would be incomplete without some consideration of Sino-Soviet relations. That, however, is a subject meriting full-scale analysis; some excellent studies of the subject have recently been published.[1] Accordingly, the question of relations with China is considered whenever relevant to other problems of the camp. In the later stages of this book the Chinese role in the camp is frequently discussed, and conclusions are drawn about the problem of leadership, both political and ideological, within the camp, about the role played by the Chinese during the crisis of 1956 and after, as well as about the implications of the very presence of China within the bloc.

The first part of the book places generally known events into a framework more suitable for an analysis of the developing pattern of Soviet–satellite relations. Familiar episodes, such as the Stalin–Tito break, are treated schematically; Chapters 1 and 5 are, in effect, summations of the broad pattern of domestic developments in the area between 1945 and 1953. The second, lengthier, part of the book deals with the patterns of relations proper once the Stalinist system was undermined, shows in more detail how some of the Communist leaderships responded to new circumstances, and examines the nature of the change in the relations among them. The two parts of the book are each subdivided into major sections, which attempt to identify the general character of the relationship between ideology and power prevailing within each distinctive phase in the relations among the Communist states. The above method of organizing the material was chosen in preference to a topical division (for instance, economic relations, political relations, military relations, and such), since it lends itself more to a study of the continuously interacting factors changing the structure of the camp. In a subsequent study on "The Organization of the Communist Camp," the author plans to deal with these problems functionally and in more detail. It is freely conceded that some of the interpretations, even if cautiously stated, may require revision as more information gradually becomes available.

A final point is the matter of acknowledgments. My first debt is to my teacher and colleague, Professor Merle Fainsod, to whom I shall owe much of whatever I might contribute to the field of Soviet or Communist study. His expert comments were invaluable as was his continuing personal encouragement. To Professor Robert R. Bowie, I owe thanks for many important suggestions as well as "ideological" discussions, which helped to clarify my notions. His sharp questioning and penetrating logic were often disconcerting, but always enjoyable and valuable. To Professors Adam Ulam, Benjamin Schwartz, Ferenc Vali, and Andrew Gyorgy go my thanks for tolerating my impatience when they were reading the manuscript, and for their helpful comments. I am also grateful to several officials of various Communist states, for their willingness to discuss matters they should not have discussed with me. My special thanks go to my old friend and colleague, Professor Albert Mavrinac, who, while on a Fulbright to the southern shores of France, spent so much of his time on chapter after chapter arriving by mail from America. Each envelope returning to Cambridge and bearing his exhaustive comments was proof once again that a wise friend is a matchless asset.

In our age, personal acknowledgments must be matched by institutional ones. The Russian Research Center has been my haven for many years. Association with its various scholars has been a source of continuing stimulation to me, and its patient support for my toils is hereby gratefully acknowledged. The Center for International Affairs, the co-sponsor of this study, has provided a unique forum for testing my hypotheses against the judgment and experience of senior foreign-policy officials from a variety of countries. The Munich office of Radio Free Europe, under the able direction of Dr. W. E. Griffith, was generous in opening its files to me. The Social Science Research Council and the Inter-University Committee on Travel Grants made it possible for me to undertake several trips to the area with which my study is concerned.

Special thanks go to Mr. Peter Kolar, my research assistant, who assiduously traced obscure sources, checked footnotes, and assembled the bibliography. To my wife, but for whom this book might have appeared much earlier though with the inconsistencies and semantic monstrosities that she so unrelentingly combated through countless evenings, I owe a particular debt which I affectionately acknowledge.

ZBIGNIEW K. BRZEZINSKI

May 1959

PART I

IDEOLOGY AND POWER IN THE EMERGENCE
OF THE SOVIET BLOC

THE FIRST PHASE
1945–1947
THE PEOPLE'S DEMOCRACY – INSTITUTIONAL AND
IDEOLOGICAL DIVERSITY

Those politicians of the revolutionary class who are unable "to maneuver, to compromise" in order to avoid an obviously disadvantageous battle are good for nothing. – V. I. Lenin, *"Left-Wing" Communism: An Infantile Disorder*

CHAPTER 1

The Political Background

> To tie one's hands beforehand, openly to tell the enemy, who is now better armed than we are, whether and when we shall fight him is being stupid, not revolutionary. To accept battle at a time when it is obviously advantageous to the enemy and not to us is a crime. — V. I. Lenin

HISTORY has been playing cruel tricks on its most dedicated apostles, the Marxists-Leninists. Both their defeats and their victories have been "unhistorical": they have failed where they thought they ought to have succeeded and they succeeded where they ought to have failed. What is more, they were often defeated when acting "historically," and they often prevailed when acting "unhistorically." The revolutionary activity of industrial proletarians resulted in one failure after another, from Hamburg to Shanghai. The conspiratorial activity of the elite of the proletariat, symbolically embodying that proletariat but not actually composed of it, succeeded in largely rural Russia, compressing two separate stages of history into one. Subsequently that elite initiated the accelerated processes of industrialization which should have provided the historical foundations for their victory. Basing itself on the power of the state which it had created, that same elite then sponsored, through military occupation, the setting up of Communist governments in East Central Europe. Finally, in China, a revolution led by the Marxist-Leninist elite, but based on the peasantry, completed the process of standing "history" on its head. Historical dogma in its pristine form could not comprehend the unpredictability of the historical process.

The purpose of this chapter is to summarize the political problems which the Communists encountered in East Central Europe between 1945 and 1947. The next chapter addresses itself to the special ideological issues which arose as a consequence and which interacted with the strategic and tactical adjustments the Communists had to make in view of the East European situation. During these early years the problem of "relations between Communist states" was still, strictly speaking, nonexistent, except in the case of Yugoslavia. The new political structures of the various East European states were still only being erected. In some of the countries the Communists were acquiring power; in some they were just consolidating it; and only in one were they in a firm position independent of Soviet support. Under the protective shield of Soviet armies stationed in Central Europe, the local Communists were initiating patterns of domestic transformation: the domestic pattern was one of reform, reconstruction, and political realignment.

The Communist Involvement

The immediate objectives dictating the Soviet policy in East Europe during the war and immediately afterwards, and affecting the pattern of Soviet relations with it, may be broken down into five major areas of presumed Soviet interest. The first involved the desire to exert influence on the lands immediately west of the Russian frontier in order to deny the area to Germany — in the past a source of major threat to Russian security. There is no doubt that from the perspective of the *prenuclear* age the Soviet leaders could not feel certain that the mere defeat of Germany would ensure Soviet security and that the post-World War I situation would not be repeated. Moscow's emphasis on security was readily understood by the Western powers, especially in view of Russia's war effort. Prime Minister Winston Churchill frequently stated in the Commons during the war that the West was willing to go to some lengths to guarantee Soviet security from Germany on terms satisfactory to the Russians. As a result, the Western leaders were also inclined to grant the Soviet Union the benefit of the doubt insofar as the second broad Soviet objective was concerned: to ensure that East Europe would not be controlled by domestic elements which, while hostile to Germany, would also be hostile to the Soviet Union. Stalin encountered little difficulty in demonstrating that East Europe could not shield the USSR against a resurgent Germany if simultaneously it was unwilling to collaborate very closely with the USSR. Hence, he argued, it is essential that East Europe not only be denied to Germany but also that it be governed by regimes which were purged of all opponents of the USSR. Given the prevailing power balance, it was up to Stalin to decide what criteria would determine just who was an enemy of the USSR.

The remaining three probable Soviet objectives for East Europe seemed at the time less apparent to the West; or perhaps it was that the West simply felt unable to oppose them.[1] The first of these was to use the area for purposes of Soviet economic recovery. The war damages inflicted on the USSR by the Germans could be healed much more rapidly by extracting capital from East Central Europe through the removal of enterprises and resources. Insofar as the former Axis powers were concerned — that is Bulgaria, Hungary, and Rumania as well as Germany — the Western powers concurred and a policy of reparations was endorsed. The situation differed sharply in the case of Poland, Czechoslovakia, and Yugoslavia, all Allied powers. There could be no question of direct reparations, but at least in the case of Poland and Yugoslavia the Soviet Union extracted some economic advantages. In Poland there was the matter of the incorporation of eastern Poland into the USSR and the removal of industrial equipment from those parts of Germany assigned to Poland as compensation for the German occupation and for the loss of territory to the USSR.[2] In the case of Yugoslavia joint companies were established which, according to the Yugoslavs, the USSR found profitable.

The fourth objective, we may surmise, was to deny the area to the capitalist world since it was likely to plot hostile moves against the USSR. No doubt the Soviet leaders, even at the height of the Grand Alliance, must have considered the possibility that some day after the conclusion of the war the capitalist world would again be arrayed against the USSR. Many of the wartime Soviet suspicions about alleged British or American contacts with German anti-Nazi groups were derived from such general ideological assumptions about capitalist behavior. As a result, Anglo-American declarations to the effect that postwar governments in East Central Europe must be democratic were presumably viewed in Moscow with a great deal of mistrust. The Kremlin undoubtedly suspected that such governments were meant to be the springboard for an eventual capitalist onslaught against the USSR.

The fifth probable objective was related to the preceding one. If ideological assumptions played a role in the crystallization of Soviet defensive interests in East Europe, then it is likely that the other part of the ideological orientation, namely its offensive component, was also present. Leninist-Stalinist strategic concepts have always emphasized the importance of a strong basis for expansive operations, and it is inevitable that any accretion of territory to the base of socialism in itself was regarded as reflecting the march of socialism toward its eventual victory. It would be impossible not to relate the new political situation in East Europe to this historical process, especially since the prevailing situation was already clearly suggesting that the area had become divorced from capitalist domination in space and from the capitalist era in time. It would be inconceivable not to consider the establishment of Soviet power in East Europe as another revolutionary turning point in a process which *must go forward*.

The objectives of the local Communists were much more precise: to attain firm control over the levers of power and to consolidate that power. This achievement would relieve the Soviet Union of the obligation to maintain its influence by direct force, which might eventually provoke the West and which, in any case, was contrary to the basic Communist belief that external domination must be supported by domestic efforts to change the existing society. For this reason, East Central Europe was not to be considered as an occupied area but as a zone of eventual revolution, carried out by indigenous elements but backed, to the degree necessary, by Soviet power. The processes of obtaining domestic power were therefore linked to a series of internal programs, postulated by the Communists, to which progressive and democratic elements could not object. These programs stressed reform, political, social, and economic, for which there was great need. Indeed, enlightened public opinion could not oppose many of the measures recommended. Some of the politically active liberal elements in East Europe undertook at least partial collaboration with the Communists since it appeared that democratization went hand in hand with Communist reform programs. But what appeared to many a liberal as a desirable end was to the Communist leadership merely a means, and a means which in itself set social forces in motion toward the ultimate Communist objective. The democratic forces were further handicapped in that they often lacked defined programs which could justify explicitly their purposes and draw clear lines between them and the Communists'. This absence of clarity both in purpose and action hindered the non-Communists, as did the decisive factor of Soviet strength backing the Communist parties.

The Communist challenge to these non-Communists favoring reform amounted, in substance, to this: collaborate with us or oppose progress which you also desire. The challenge was well calculated, given the prevailing attitudes among the dominant social groups: the intelligentsia, the peasantry, and the workers. The intelligentsia, always a group of great importance in a revolutionary period, had been deeply disillusioned by what they construed to be the failure of the democratic world to evolve a clear-cut program designed to create a better life for war-torn Europe. Much of this intelligentsia, hounded by the Nazis and wooed by the Communists, had become alienated from the prewar governments because of their failure to cope with existing ills. A minority of them, drawn to Marxism sometimes by curiosity, sometimes by the appeal of a doctrine which seemed to know where history is pointing, were willing to give this ideology a chance to build a better world.[3]

To the peasants, prospects of land reform held out a vision of the fulfilment of their most cherished dream, and one much too long denied. The peasantry, while rarely politically active, was the backbone of the various peasant parties which could conceivably contest the Communist control of power, and plans for land reform forced these parties to endorse at least some part of the economic program of the Communists. It is true that fears of ultimate collectivization persisted and neutralized much of the political capital that the Communists might have hoped to gain among the peasants; nonetheless, land reform did serve to alienate the peasantry from some of the influential, landowning, anti-Communist elements in the predominantly rural areas.

The workers and industrial engineers were primarily interested in getting their factories going again. Unlike the peasants who can live off the land, the workers were especially dependent on the economic recovery programs. Their primary concern was to make certain that smoke was again pouring from the factory smokestacks. To most people in war-devastated East Europe, rapid economic reconstruction was the most vital issue, even more so than politics. And to a majority of them state planning appeared necessary and logical.[4]

The Communists, even though a small minority, were thus able to exploit a situation in which to oppose their programs of reconstruction was to engage in what amounted to sabotage of the national interest. Politically, it meant isolating oneself from the mainstream of public opinion. Faced with this dilemma, the politically active non-Communist elements split into three groups. First there were those who believed that despite everything the only course open was that of underground resistance. Between 1945 and 1947 this policy was pursued by the remnants of the anti-Nazi underground in Poland — organized into the generally liberal group "Freedom and Independence" (WIN) and the right-wing "National Armed Forces" (NSZ) — and in Yugoslavia by scattered units of the Chetniks. Such activity was based on the calculation that war between the USSR and the United States was inevitable and, in fact, imminent. Gradually, however, these lonely fighters found themselves more and more isolated, with the people tired of war and the West uninterested in the area.

By 1948 most of them had been liquidated and only sporadic and isolated groups carried on.* The second, and largest, group consisted of those who decided to work within the framework of the system and organize democratic parties. Expecting Western insistence on free elections, they calculated that through the democratic process they would succeed in defeating the Communist minority, and they assumed that the USSR would not dare to oppose such powerful democratic states as the United States or the United Kingdom. This course was pursued particularly by the leaders of the various peasant parties. However, the price of open electoral contests was the repudiation of the more violent opposition to the Communists, and hence the anti-Communist camp was split from the start. Finally, the third group was composed of those who felt that collaboration with the Communists was justified because the Communist domestic programs were desirable and because the Communists were a guarantee against the return of "right-wing" governments. Members of this group entertained no illusions about an East-West war or about some Western intervention on behalf of free elections. Recognizing Soviet domination of the area as the determining factor, they conceded that the future belonged to the Communists and that the reasonable thing to do was to join them. Some of them might have also hoped that by joining the Communist ranks they would mollify the more extreme or brutal Communist programs. Much of the left wing of the various socialist parties, as well as radical agrarians, oscillated in this direction.

These general considerations may be briefly examined in terms of some of the individual countries concerned. Conditions in each varied significantly, but three varying patterns of Communist activity may be broadly discerned: (1) consolidation of power already obtained through Soviet occupation by 1945, and the initiation of domestic reforms not necessarily doctrinaire in form; (2) efforts to obtain power through participation in the political process and through active encouragement of internal reform; and (3) consolidation of power obtained by their own efforts, and the launching of a radical totalitarian revolution. There was occasional overlapping, but on the whole the

---

* The scale of the Polish resistance can be seen from the following figures. In the spring of 1947 the Communist regime acknowledged that it was imprisoning 21,176 persons for political reasons; during the "amnesty" period concluded in April 1947 some 55,277 members of anti-Communist organizations stepped forward, handing over close to 15,000 weapons (including, for example, 10 cannons and 904 machine guns); Communist losses amounted to 1,427 security men and 2,000 party members killed in 1945 and to about 30,000 between 1945 and 1948. S. Korbonski, *W Imieniu Kremla* (Paris, 1956), pp. 268, 290; *Po Prostu*, October 14, 1956; *Polityka*, February 15, 1958; *Glos Koszalinski*, May 23, 1956.

first pattern applied to two former enemy states, Bulgaria and Rumania, and also to Poland which the USSR initially treated as if it had been an enemy power (occupation, arrests, deportations). The second pattern applied to Czechoslovakia, and the third to Yugoslavia. Hungary was a marginal case, partially fitting the first and partially the second category. External Soviet protection prevented outside interference from disturbing the unfolding of these patterns and doubtlessly also constituted an element of psychological support to those engaged in furthering them.

The Polish Pattern

There appears to be little doubt that Poland, due to its geographical position, was the primary objective of Soviet policy in East Central Europe. A non-Communist Poland would have resulted in the exclusion of the USSR from Central Europe. The Polish fear of Germany, however, was a major Soviet asset. The overwhelming hatred for the Germans was a legacy of Nazi rule which the Communists could easily manipulate, particularly in terms of the necessity for close Polish-Soviet collaboration. The territorial changes made at the Potsdam Conference, setting the Polish western borders on the Oder and Neisse (Odra and Nysa) rivers, made such an alliance imperative to Poland's future. The Nazi and Soviet extermination policies, which had decimated the Polish intelligentsia, the usual source of the political elite, had badly weakened the nation as a whole, decreasing its capacity for resistance.* The Red Army on entering Poland pursued a policy of wiping out political and military centers controlled by the underground and by the Polish government in exile, and set up its own body, the Committee of National Liberation, controlled by the Communists. The committee represented a fusion of the underground Polish Workers' Party founded in 1942 on instructions of the Comintern with the Committee of Polish Patriots, founded in Moscow

* According to available statistics, about 700 university professors and academic workers were exterminated; about 1000 gymnasium and professional school teachers perished, as did 4000 primary school teachers. About 43 per cent of the various cultural and educational resources were totally destroyed; 60 per cent of the educational facilities. Over 6 million Polish citizens perished as a result of the German attack and occupation; of these 5.3 million died through various forms of terror (executions, pacifications, death camps, starvation or exhaustion in concentration camps) and 0.6 million through direct hostilities. For every 1000 citizens in prewar Poland, 220 perished, a much higher percentage than even in Yugoslavia (108 per 1000) or the USSR (40 per 1000). *Zachodnia Agencja Prasowa*, bulletin no. 3, 1957. To the above totals, about 1.5 million should be added to account for those deported to the USSR and who subsequently never returned, and the 10,000 officers killed by the Russians in Katyn and elsewhere.

in 1941, and it was recognized on January 5, 1945, by its sponsor, the USSR, as the provisional government of Poland. The Czechoslovak government of Eduard Benes followed suit with recognition on January 31. In keeping with the Yalta agreements and following the inclusion in the provisional government of four Polish non-Communists from abroad — including the Peasant Party leader, Stanislaw Mikolajczyk — this body was recognized on July 5 as the government of Poland by the major Western powers. The government, in which the four "imports" were outnumbered by sixteen incumbents from the Soviet-sponsored body, was to hold free elections in which all "democratic" parties were to participate.[5] With most of the important governmental positions under their control, the commitment to elections did not change the fundamental facts of the Communist position, openly stated in October 1945 by Wladyslaw Gomulka, the Communist secretary and former underground head of the Workers' Party. The "commanding heights" of the political system were well in hand.

The Polish Communist Party, dissolved by the Comintern in 1938 and rebuilt in the late months of 1941 and early in 1942 as the Polish Workers' Party, emerged from the war with limited cadres.[6] Its early 1944 membership was between 20,000 and 30,000,[7] but its ranks grew rapidly with the influx of Polish Communists from the USSR and through local recruitment. Apart from the party's self-identification with some of the more important national causes (such as the western frontiers), the very fact that it was wielding power made it more attractive to some elements. By the end of 1945 its numbers grew to 235,296, a year later to 555,888; and by the end of 1947 it numbered 820,786.[8] The majority of the membership at this time was recruited from the workers with whom the policies of industrial recovery, nationalization, and development of the former German enterprises were popular. The proportion of peasant membership was also appreciably higher at this period than after the party had consolidated its power and had launched its collectivization policies. As might be expected, the majority of the peasants enrolled in the party were from among the very poor strata of the peasantry.*

* In December 1945, the social composition of the party was as follows: Workers — 62.2 per cent, Peasants — 28.2 per cent (W. Zaleski, *The Pattern of Life in Poland*, Paris, 1952, p. 56). According to Zambrowski, a member of the Politburo, 68.7 per cent of the peasant membership was composed of peasants owning average or below-average land plots ("On the Realization of the Leading Party Slogan in the Countryside," *Nowe Drogi*, no. 5, 1955, p. 55). There is striking correspondence between these figures and comparable data on peasant membership in the French and Italian Com-

The party at the same time applied pressure on the left wing of the Polish Socialist Party in order to have it join in an electoral alliance against Mikolajczyk and eventually to fuse it with the Workers' Party. The Socialist Party was badly split and handicapped by the absence of able leadership. Its most prominent leaders, well known in the international labor movement, had perished during the war, or were in exile, or under arrest.* The party was in the hands of second-string leadership, less known among the rank and file (which still equaled the Communists in number). Its opposition to Communist invitations was made on two grounds: the question of Polish independence from Russia (much in keeping with the patriotic traditions of the Socialist Party) and that of internal democracy. But the economic programs of the Communists and the need to close national ranks for the purpose of reconstruction could not be opposed. Under these circumstances, and aided by terrorism, arrests, and pressure, the splinter left-wing faction led by such men as Jozef Cyrankiewicz and Oskar Lange gradually was able to assert its control over the Socialist Party and, from the very beginning, to prevent it from supporting the democratic forces led by Mikolajczyk.

The task of liquidating Mikolajczyk's opposition was more closely linked to the international situation. It could be argued that his position was doomed from the very start and that it was only a matter of time before the full measure of Western disengagement in East Europe would reveal the extent of Mikolajczyk's weakness. His only *real* source of power was the assumption widely made by the Poles,[9] and presumably shared even by the Communists, that Mikolajczyk was returning to Poland with some Western guarantees of support in the event Soviet promises to allow free elections in Poland were violated. Beyond that, his political power was almost nothing from the day of his arrival in Poland (as vice-premier of the newly constituted government) to his departure two years later. True, he enjoyed great popularity among the peasantry, and most democratic and even conservative forces considered him their only source of salvation from Soviet and Communist domination. In a free election he most cer-

munist parties. In France, of the peasant membership, 69 per cent come from the average or poor economic level (which can broadly be equated with land ownership); in Italy 88 per cent of peasant membership is recruited from among the tenant farmers and laborers. S. M. Lipset, "Socialism — Left and Right — East and West" (mimeographed, 1958); figures based on P. Williams, *Politics in Post-War France* (London, 1954), and *Italian Political Party Preferences* (New York, 1953).

* Dubois and Niedzialkowski were shot by the Germans; Puzak and Pajak perished in Stalin's prisons; Erlich and Alter were executed by the NKVD; Arciszewski was heading the free Polish government in London.

tainly would have won a sweeping victory, with possibly even the majority of the Communist membership voting for him. But free elections were not likely to occur. In Poland of 1945 (and to a greater extent later), all the levers of power were in Communist hands, the Red Army was on the scene, and the NKVD was active. Mikolajczyk's popularity under these conditions had no political significance, while the growing awareness of the absence of effective Western support made it possible to apply increasing doses of terror against the Polish Peasant Party. In 1947, after the manipulated elections formalized the liquidation of his party, Mikolajczyk escaped abroad.[10] From the point of view of the Communists this concluded yet another chapter in the process of sweeping away the remnants of the preceding historical phase — that of bourgeois rule.

At least as important to the Communist strategy as these political developments were the economic and social measures which the Communists were able to launch. The series of economic and social problems besetting Poland even before the war, and deeply aggravated by the German oppression, gave the Communists a golden opportunity to take advantage of what they themselves considered to be "the objective processes" of history. Seizing the initiative in these fields meant again that all democratic forces which emerged with Western encouragement to compete in the promised free elections had to endorse major parts of the Communist program and to associate themselves with it. The greatest impact of the reforms was felt, naturally enough, in agriculture, where need for land reform was genuine, and in industry, which was badly devastated and which was now more important because of the recovery by Poland of the Silesian basin.

Radical land reform was initiated even while the hostilities were in progress. On September 6, 1944, a decree on the expropriation of landholdings exceeding 100 hectares (247 acres) of total area or 50 hectares in cases of purely agricultural land was announced. No compensation was provided, and in the execution of the land reform properties even below the proscribed maximums were also seized. Since political considerations were paramount, the land reform in the old parts of Poland resulted in the proliferation of uneconomically small landholdings.* The accompanying table gives a statistical pic-

* "This form of parcelling was inexpensive in terms of new investment, because most of the former laborers continued to live in their laborers' quarters on the estate. . . . It did little for the farmers on the old dwarf farms who received additional land, since they could not make a complete living on either the original or the slightly increased holdings. It did not provide a surplus of grain or other food stuffs for the non-farm population." *Report of the F.A.O. Mission to Poland* (Washington, 1948), p. 39; cf. Iwanska, cited in note 8, pp. 468ff.

Size and number of private and public farms

Size of farm (in hectares)	Prewar area of Poland, 1931		Postwar area of Poland, 1949	
	Holdings		Holdings	
	In thousands	% of total	In thousands	% of total
Less than 2	747.1	25.5	962.1	28.7
2–5	1,136.1	38.7	1,084.0	32.3
5–10	728.7	24.8	906.3	27.0
10–50	309.1	10.5	392.6	11.7
Over 50	14.7	0.5	10.3	0.3 [a]

[a] 90 per cent of the land owned by farms over 50 hectares was in state or collective ownership.

Source: *Foreign Agriculture*, no. 7–8 (1953), p. 143.

ture of the situation. In the former German territories, more medium-sized farms — about 60 per cent of all farms were from five to twenty hectares in size — were created for the new Polish settlers through the expulsion of the Germans and the division of former German estates.[11] However, the reform did have the effect of liquidating the formerly influential landowning gentry and of stimulating a measure of class conflict in the countryside. It resulted in the curious paradox of the peasants supporting Mikolajczyk in the hope that he would defend their soil against the Communists and the landowners supporting him in the hope of less radical expropriations.

Nationalization of industry already applied since 1944 through the seizure of former German plants and the setting in motion of frequently abandoned enterprises in the prewar Polish territories, was decreed in the law of January 3, 1946, entitled "Concerning the Seizure of Basic Branches of the National Economy." [12] The decree provided for the seizure "with compensation" of the mines, the petroleum industry, the power, gas, and water works in the public service, all synthetic-fuel industries, foundries for ferrous and nonferrous metals, armament industries, cokeries, sugar factories, flour mills of a given capacity, cold-storage facilities, and printing establishments — as well as any other industrial undertaking "capable of employing more than 50 workers per shift." [13] As Boleslaw Bierut, the Communist leader of the government, explained, since the law really sanctioned the existing state of affairs, compensation was not actually paid to domestic owners affected by the decree. This measure, while enlarging appreciably the role of the state, again was viewed by many as a necessary consequence of the war and dictated by the imperatives of recovery. And the Communists stressed throughout, particularly in the Three Year Plan of Economic Reconstruction (adopted in July 1947 but effective as of January 1), that the Polish economy would be based on the "coexistence" of three fundamental sectors: public, private, and cooperative. In this manner they distinguished Poland from the Soviet model.[14]

The sum total of these measures, launched by a regime already under Communist control and directly sponsored by the Soviet Union, was to create in Poland new patterns of economic and social relations. The foundations for a "People's Democracy" were thus laid through a blend of political and economic policies: through terror and reform, by giving land to the peasants and expropriating the large and medium entrepreneurs, by appealing to Polish nationalism against the Germans and destroying those wishing to assert Polish independence against the USSR. The acquisition of the lands east of the Oder and Neisse rivers and the opportunities created by the availability of ownerless farms, homesteads, and factories gave the Communists unique patronage opportunities, and Gomulka himself took charge of the development of these territories. The consolidation of power was in this manner linked with the initiation of an internal transformation. But both had to proceed at a relatively cautious pace because Western attention was focused on Poland to a far greater degree than on any other country in East Europe. The Communists in Poland were secure enough through Soviet support to be able to afford a certain amount of restraint.

The Bulgarian, Rumanian, and Hungarian Variants

The Polish pattern, involving a party in effect already in power at the conclusion of the war, might be considered as a case example also applicable basically to Bulgaria and Rumania, and partially to Hungary. Some differences, however, must be noted. International complications played a lesser role in Bulgaria and Rumania, both former Axis powers, although the negotiation of peace treaties did give the Western powers the opportunity to express continued interest in the internal affairs of these countries. The case of Hungary, also a former enemy power, was somewhat complicated by its proximity to Austria and Czechoslovakia. In these two states the Communist parties still entertained certain aspirations, and possibly as a result the Hungarian Communist Party moved with greater caution. Also, unlike Poland, the institutions of government had not been destroyed by the war and did not have to be rebuilt in their entirety. In Rumania and Bulgaria the state structure was taken over by the Communists and gradually was being adapted. In Hungary a more drastic break with the past took place through the destruction of the Horthy regime and the establishment of a republic. Nonetheless, here too the Communists had to cope with institutions such as the army or the bureaucracy which, unlike Poland's, survived the holocausts of the war. While not challenging Communist control, these institutional factors did constitute an impediment which the Polish comrades did not have to face. Each party could thus plead a variety of difficulties, external or internal, which delayed or rendered more difficult its rapid consolidation of power.

In Bulgaria, the Communist Party had the advantage of having enjoyed some measure of popularity in the past and was not handicapped, as in the cases of Poland, Rumania, and Hungary, by nationalist anti-Russian feelings. In 1919, the Bulgarian Communist Party succeeded in electing over one fifth of the deputies to the parliament and was, until outlawed, the country's second largest party. Subsequently, operating under the label of Independent Workers' Party, the Communists managed to elect 31 of the 274 deputies in the 1931 elections. During the war they were instrumental in setting up the Fatherland Front, an organization of anti-Fascist parties dedicated to the overthrow of King Boris' dictatorship. When the Soviet Union suddenly declared war on Bulgaria in September 1944, on the eve of a Bulgarian decision to join the Allies, the Fatherland Front seized power. In the coalition government the Communist Party obtained control of the important Ministry of the Interior and played a major role in the "purge" of public officials which was immediately launched. The purge amounted simply to a terror operation, designed to destroy the political cadres of the "bourgeoisie" which had not been decimated by the war (as was the case in Poland). Within six months of the entrance of Soviet troops into Bulgaria, the special courts had condemned 11,667 persons, 2,138 of whom were actually executed.[15]

In July 1946 a decree on "Leadership and Control of the Army" paved the way for a thorough purge of the armed forces. When the elections for the National Assembly were held on October 27, 1946. It came as no surprise that only 99 deputies out of 465 did not belong to the Communist-dominated Fatherland Front. Eleven days later, Georgia Dimitrov, the former head of the Communist International, became the Premier of Bulgaria, having just renounced his Soviet citizenship. The year that followed was marked by the liquidation of the opposition which had refrained from joining the Fatherland Front, most notably the peasant movement under Petkov. Symptomatic of the general caution exercised against a premature union with the socialists (to be distinguished, however, from the close cooperation which was stressed from the start and which was used to split the socialists), it was only early in 1948 that the Bulgarian Social Democrats were formally absorbed into the Communist Party.* [16]

This initial period (September 1944–1947) was highlighted by an economic recovery drive organically linked with social reform. However, unlike the other East Central European states, Bulgaria did not have to cope with large-scale private property either in industry (a minor sector in the Bulgarian economy until the post–1948 industrialization) or in agriculture. Land reform had been carried out already in the twenties, and the postwar decree limiting private land holdings to a maximum of 20 hectares by 1947 affected only 3 per cent of a total of 7.8 million hectares of arable land. [17] Collectivization of the agricultural sector was left on a "voluntary" basis until after the September 1947 peace-treaty ratification removed the Allied Control Commission from Bulgaria.

In Rumania the situation might be considered as already heavily weighted in favor of the Communists by March 1945, when the young Rumanian monarch, acting under duress applied by the Soviet representative, Andrei Vishinsky, commissioned a cabinet headed by Petre Groza, a Communist sympathizer, and dominated by the Communists. The monarchy persisted for two more years, acting as a passive restraint (the Communist daily *Scinteia* even wished the king on November 8, 1946 "a long life, good health, and a reign rich in democratic achievements"), but was powerless to prevent the Communist consolidation of power. The Communists benefited from the Soviet willingness to entertain Rumanian claims to Transylvania, and the Rumanian Communists were able to argue that only they could obtain such Soviet support. "The unhealthy state of Rumanian agriculture, the persistence of extensive cereal cultivation and low level of productivity, the failure of the 1918–1921 land reforms to establish a prosperous peasantry, the persistence of metayage and other semiservitudes, the proletariazation of the poorer peasantry, and the inability of a great number of Rumanian peasants to support themselves on their meager holdings" [18] — all these factors played into the hands of

* In fact, there is reason to believe that Moscow generally discouraged the rapid absorption by the Communists of the local socialist parties on the sound ground that a premature merger might result in Social Democratic predominance. To the more eager Communists, this might have appeared as excessive caution or, at least, as indicating a certain lack of confidence in their ability to handle the situation.

the Communists who decreed an extensive land reform on March 22, 1945, twenty days after the formation of the Groza government.[19] The "war crimes" trials of Rumanian leaders responsible for Rumania's support of the Axis paralyzed the right wing and the officer corps, preventing an anti-Communist coalition with the liberal and peasant groups. By 1946–47 the latter were powerless.

In Hungary the Communists encountered greater difficulty than either in Bulgaria or Rumania, partially because of the strong anti-Russian prejudice of the people and partially because of their greater restraint. The latter (as noted already) was presumably due to the close proximity to Austria and Czechoslovakia, both traditionally sensitive to Hungarian developments. Another element in the picture might have been the strong impression created on the Hungarian Communists by the failure in 1919 of Bela Kun's Soviet Hungarian Republic, which was in part due to excessive revolutionary zeal. In any case, the Hungarian Party, under the leadership of Matyas Rakosi who had returned to Hungary with the Red Army, actually experienced a sharp electoral reversal in the relatively free elections held in November 1945, polling only 17 per cent of the vote as opposed to 57 per cent for the Smallholders' (Peasant) Party. In the Hungarian case, the land reform, carried out in the spring of 1945 and affecting about 33 per cent of the arable land — Hungary's prewar agricultural system was the most antiquated in East Europe — actually worked against the Communists by removing rapidly a legitimate grievance. The Hungarian Communists were also severely handicapped by Hungary's territorial losses, blamed by the people on the USSR, and could not pose therefore as the protectors of the national interest.

The Communist response to this setback was to intensify the terror against "war criminals," broadly interpreting that category, and to sponsor a coalition of the "democratic" parties against the allegedly reactionary Smallholders. A Leftist Bloc was formed, composed of the Communists, the Social Democrats, and the National Peasant Party, the latter comprising rural radicals and the populist writers who had been in the forefront of the anti-Horthy intelligentsia. In 1947, taking advantage of the temporary absence from the country of Ferenc Nagy, the Smallholder Prime Minister, the Communists succeeded in forcing his resignation, and they quickly followed up their advantage by revising the electoral law. In the August 1947 elections, the Leftist Bloc "polled" 60 per cent of the votes, although the Communist share still remained a meager 22 per cent. During this period, nationalization was not actively pushed, and until March 1948 about a quarter of the heavy industry and four fifths of all other industry remained in private hands. In this respect the pattern also varied from that in Poland and more closely resembled the Rumanian example.

Looking at the situation from the perspective of the Polish, Rumanian, Bulgarian, and Hungarian Communists, their goals accordingly had the following priority: (1) creation of an effective political organization, which would contain a hard core of disciplined supporters and an outer rim of allied groups sharing most of the immediate goals even if not the ultimate ends (which were at the time not made explicit); (2) crystallization of a pattern of action designed to undermine the legal opposition usually led by the peasant parties and in Poland tacitly supported by the remnants of the anti-Nazi underground; (3) economic reconstruction on patterns compatible with the political end of consolidating power; (4) social reforms which would be popular and which would weaken the anti-Communist elements; (5) identification of Communism with nationalism through emphasis on popular national issues, typically territorial ones. The cumulative effect of these measures, the Communist leadership probably calculated, would produce a sufficiently profound internal transformation of society to make for a qualitative difference both in the character of the society and in its relations with the USSR.

The Yugoslav and Czechoslovak Extremes

Czechoslovakia and Yugoslavia are the two countries deviating from the broad pattern of Communist action. In both cases the Communist Party had strong indigenous roots and support, and in both cases it came to power largely on its own, although benefiting from Soviet backing. In Czechoslovakia a variety of factors favored the Communist Party. The republic, modeled on the Western type, suffered a disastrous loss of prestige in 1938, and many of the returned leaders were held to have been responsible for Czechoslovakia's fall to Hitler. Many others had collaborated with the Germans. The country was badly split by an intensified sense of nationalism in Slovakia, fed by the wartime existence of a separate Slovak state. Soviet prestige was high, both because the USSR was not blamed for Munich and because of its wartime role. The Communist Party gained further acceptance by exercising great moderation after 1945. At the same time as it posed as a champion of decentralization, the party was able gradually to consolidate its position on the local level by gaining control of the "people's committees" established in December 1944. A special factor in the postwar Czechoslovak scene was the rapid ouster of the Sudeten Germans, as well as portions of the Magyar minority. This operation, carried out ruthlessly, resulted in a considerable shift in property relations, already badly undermined by German expropriations, killings of Jewish owners, and postwar confiscations. Large-scale nationalization was decreed in October 1945, involving banks, insurance companies, and so on.

The rapid growth of its membership (see the table in Chapter 5) soon made the Communist Party the leading party. It justified its claim to this distinction by polling 38 per cent of the vote in the free elections held in 1946. The party's leader, Klement Gottwald, was then asked by President Benes to accept the premiership. The following year was accordingly marked by the consolidation of the Communist influence, particularly in the police, in the army, and in a workers' militia, set up once control had been gained in the Central Trade Union Council. Although the final take-over did not take place until February 1948, on the eve of the national elections, the Communist grip on the instrumentalities of power was by then sufficiently secure to allow Czechoslovakia to join rapidly the other Communist-ruled states in initiating more radical domestic programs and, in time, even surpassing them.

The events in Yugoslavia followed a much more revolutionary pattern, and during the first postwar years Yugoslavia's Communists outdistanced the other parties in their common march toward socialism. Already in the November 1945 "elections," the Yugoslav voters had been presented with a single slate, and this plebiscite was meant to be merely a formal confirmation of the fact that power was firmly in the hands of the Communist-led partisans of Josip Broz-Tito. His partisan movement, deriving its hard-core leadership from the illegal prewar Communist Party (which early in the twenties was able to obtain some measure of peasant support) and ably capitalizing on Croat-Serb animosities, was able to defeat the Serb nationalist and anti-Communist Chetnik forces of General Draja Mihailovic. Power was firmly in its hands by the war's end. The new Yugoslav constitution of January 1946 was unashamedly patterned on the Soviet constitution of 1936, and the regime pushed forward with a radical socio-economic program. Between November 1944 and December 1946 a series of decrees transferred to state ownership all industry, as well as banking and other enterprises, while in the fall of 1945 a land reform was carried out. Shortly afterwards, the regime began to lay the groundwork for collectivization.

These patterns of development in the immediate postwar period were thus in keeping with the fivefold syndrome of Soviet interests in the area, suggested briefly at the outset of this background chapter. That these interests were closely interrelated is cogently illustrated by the fate of the Benes government in Czechoslovakia which was not spared from Communist subversion even though Benes' policies satisfied the first two Soviet *desiderata:* he was prepared to consider East Central Europe as falling primarily within the Soviet sphere of influence, and he was determined to be, above all else, a staunch ally of the USSR. As events proved, that was not enough. In the case of Tito, the determination of the Yugoslav leader to pursue a radical domestic policy, accompanied by a certain hesitation in fully subordinating his state to the USSR, was already in 1947 placing strains on an otherwise warm and close relationship.[20]

Elsewhere, the Communist regimes were highly dependent on Soviet support, even while consolidating their power. The worst Soviet abuses, such as the dismantling of industry and other unfavorable economic measures (see Chapter 6 for further detail), at this time took second place to the paramount objective of cementing power. Dependence on Moscow was further heightened by the relative isolation and inexperience of the Communist leaders; violently hostile to the West, which was giving moral support to their domestic enemies, they also frequently vented their traditional national animosities toward one another, with the result that Moscow was their only rallying point and arbiter. Seeking ways and means to power and then to the fulfilment of many years of waiting, many of the Communist leaders, returning after decades of exile — fighting in Spain, waiting and debating in wartime London, or undergoing disciplined service in the USSR — must have felt somewhat out of touch and must have derived a certain sense of comfort from the thought that they were backed by a central leadership, powerful, purposeful, and experienced. Outwardly united against the common enemy, their various origins necessarily created cliques and competition between the "Spanish" veterans, the London intellectuals, the Moscow *apparatchiki,* the graduates of the German concentration camps (the *Kazetniki*), or the domestic hard core which survived the German occupation. But to all of them Moscow was a common frame of reference.

Within this early pattern of development, there was thus both a broad congruence of interests between the local Communists and Moscow and a considerable range of diversity in action. The diversity meant that, within the framework of Soviet interests, the local Communists were able to make adjustments which to some may have been only tactical but which to others represented a more suitable way of building Communism. The Soviet Union acted as a decisive buttress without which they would fail, but it was not yet fully subordinating local interests to its own. At this stage the Soviet policy, which occasionally even restrained the local Communists against excessive zeal (see Chapter 3 for cases of greater Moscow restraint), seemed to be guided by a sound strategic consideration: "the whole task of the Communists is to be able to *convince* the backward elements, to be able to work *among* them, and not to *fence themselves off* from them by artificial and childishly 'Left-wing' slogans." [21] Thus it is clear that even in this early period problems of theory were being related to problems of action.

CHAPTER **2** —

Problems of Theory

> There is one absolute demand which Marxist theory makes in
> connection with the analysis of any social problem whatsoever:
> that is to place it within its *specific* historical framework and
> then, if the problem concerns one particular country (for ex-
> ample, the national program for that given country), to take
> account of the concrete particular traits distinguishing that coun-
> try from others within the framework of the same historical
> period. — V. I. Lenin

In 1945 a new political and socioeconomic reality was in the making in East Central Europe. To the Communists, who believe that
popular consciousness tends to lag behind changes in material reality
and that their strength lies in keeping up with history, and even in
outpacing it, the critical questions now were: What are the theoretical
implications of the new situation? How does it fit the established categories which guide political action? What practical considerations
does it portend? They noted that, thanks to the decisive factor of
Soviet power, a series of states were about to rise in which they would
have a dominant voice. Yet, for a variety of reasons, these new states
could hardly be classified as Soviet Republics, pure and simple, even
though to have done so would have simplified the theoretical and political issues a great deal. At the same time, the important role played
by the Communists in these new states seemed to suggest some new
and distinctive features which required evaluation as a springboard
for further Soviet action.

The doctrinal problem facing the Communists was to extract from
the existing ideological arsenal of Marxism-Leninism meaningful categories for *analyzing* and *directing* contemporary political dynamics
in East Europe. Assuming that the local Communists also tended to
think in Marxist categories, their immediate purpose was somehow to
provide a program of action which in itself would promote the im-
pending transformation of East Europe into a Communist society but
which would also facilitate the short-range tasks at hand. The task of

the doctrine was, as always, to crystallize a conceptual framework which would provide an understanding of the existing reality and be a useful guide to action for the Communists actually engaged in shaping that reality.

Stalin and his local Communist associates realized that the very presence of the Red Army (as well as the acquiescence of the West) guaranteed the Communists a major voice in the various governments about to be established. They would participate in restoring the ravaged economies, in healing the wounds inflicted by Nazi brutalities, and in setting up political institutions to direct the process of peacetime recovery. Nonetheless, the local Communists and Moscow realized that the situation was not free from complications. As one might have expected from the Marxist-Leninist doctrine, to set up a series of republics on the Soviet model would have meant coming up against other considerations which a Communist, even if only thinking theoretically, could not ignore. Apart from the uncertain element of Big Power relations and the need to mollify the United States and the United Kingdom, it seemed that in East Europe itself, the situation was still not ripe for the duplication of Soviet experience. The bourgeoisie still had its own political forces; the workers were to some extent under the influence of "right-wing" socialists; the peasantry was controlled by peasant parties openly hostile to the Communists. This resistance would have to be undermined and ultimately crushed, but within the framework of the states which the Communists would now help to construct. The implicit necessity of some kind of transitional phase raised serious problems of theory.[1]

According to well-known Marxist-Leninist doctrines, the collapse of the bourgeois states must lead to the setting up of a dictatorship of the proletariat as a prelude to the transition to socialism. Lenin stated in 1920 that "the dictatorship of the proletariat is the fundamental question of the modern working class movement in all capitalist countries without exception."[2] This view was in keeping with his strong conviction that there was no middle ground between the old forms of the dictatorship of the bourgeoisie — the last state form before the revolution — and the dictatorship of the proletariat. While it is risky to prove a "Leninist" position on the basis of Lenin's chameleonic statements, the following citation is characteristic:

The forms of the bourgeois state are extremely varied, but in essence they are all the same: in one way or another in the last analysis, all these states are inevitably the *dictatorship of the bourgeoisie*. The transition from capitalism to communism will certainly create a great variety and abundance of political forms, but in essence there will inevitably be only one: the dictatorship of the *proletariat*.[3]

Stalin frequently reasserted these tenets, maintaining that the dictatorship of the proletariat had to be created by revolutionary violence and that "to overthrow capitalism it was not only necessary to remove the bourgeoisie from power, it was not only necessary to expropriate the capitalists, but also to smash completely the bourgeois state machinery."[4] Clearly, then, the collapse of the "bourgeois dictatorship" had to involve the violent destruction of its institutions, the expropriation of its dominant class, and the setting up of the proletarian dictatorship. As far as the actual form that the dictatorship of the proletariat was to take, Lenin, and later Stalin, maintained that the Soviet type (based on the 1905, and subsequently 1917, experience) was the most suitable and represented a general norm. "The Soviets are a higher form of democracy, and even more they are the beginning of the socialist form of democracy."[5] In turn, according to Stalin, the political essence of the proletarian dictatorship was the rule of the Communist Party: "it could be said that the dictatorship of the proletariat is in essence the 'dictatorship' of its vanguard, the 'dictatorship' of its party, as the main guiding force of the proletariat."[6]

Earlier revolutionary practice outside the USSR had accordingly been grounded on the assumption that the overthrow of the bourgeois state results in the creation of a dictatorship of the proletariat in the form of a Soviet state. No intermediary form was considered possible, either in theory or in practice. When, shortly after the Bolshevik revolution, the Communists succeeded in seizing power in Hungary and in Bavaria (March and April 1919, respectively), Soviet Republics were proclaimed in both cases, and in Hungary land socialization was immediately attempted. This was also the policy adopted in Slovakia where an abortive Soviet Republic was proclaimed in June 1919, and declared to be a dictatorship of the proletariat.[7] Similar doctrinal rigidity characterized attempted Communist coups in the Baltic states during 1918 and 1919, and during the Polish-Soviet war of 1920 a group of Polish Communists also proclaimed a Polish Soviet Republic.[8] The pattern everywhere was to imitate the October Revolution, particularly in terms of doctrinal precepts.

Although the failure of these early endeavors resulted in remarkably little theorizing about the problem during the interwar period,*

* A somewhat more flexible line was suggested by the Fourth Congress of the Comintern which introduced the following gradations of "real labor governments": (1) a government of workers and poor peasants, such as may develop in the Balkans,

it did leave behind a feeling that rigid application of the theory could be harmful in that it failed to take into account the many particular factors varying from country to country.* The post-World War II situation in East Europe certainly appeared to require more elastic concepts than rigid attempts to fit the East European situation into the early Bolshevik categories. The governments created with the assistance of the Red Army were obviously no longer dictatorships of the bourgeoisie. The important role played in these governments by the Communists and their measures of land reform and nationalization excluded the application of the standard categories of analysis derived from the experience of the bourgeois states. On the other hand, for reasons already suggested, they could not qualify as dictatorships of the proletariat. In some of them, the Communists were clearly minority partners in coalition governments — hardly the dominant role which the party is to play in a true dictatorship of the proletariat — and in all of them, "hostile" political forces were still organized and politically active. To the Communists, the "objective" circumstances, and not just the Yalta and Potsdam agreements which spoke broadly of democratic governments, required a reconsideration of standard formulas, and a "creative" application of Marxism-Leninism to the new and complex environment.

Emergence of the People's Democracy

The concept which seemed to answer this need was that of the People's Democracy. The term was apparently first coined by Tito in 1945 at the Congress of the Yugoslav Fatherland Front, and in this early period the term "New Democracy" was also occasionally used. The People's Democracy was to serve as a theoretical insight into the existing phase of development and as a policy plank for the various

---

Czechoslovakia, and so on; (2) a workers' government with the participation of the Communists; (3) a genuine proletarian workers' government, which in its pure form can be realized only by the Communist Party. *Protokoll des Vierten Kongresses der kommunistischen Internationale* (Hamburg, 1923), p. 1017, as quoted in R. Fischer, *Stalin and German Communism* (Cambridge, 1948), p. 213.

* The feeling that the early foreign Communists might have been a little too "sectarian" is conveyed by the *ex post facto* Soviet efforts to rewrite the history of the Lithuanian Communists, making them appear somewhat more responsive to the need of gaining popular support. Thus even the name of the revolutionary Lithuanian regime which in 1920 was describing itself as "the Provisional Revolutionary Workers' Government" (*Politika Sovetskoi Vlasti po natsional'nym delam za try goda, 1917–XI–1920*, Moscow, 1920), in 1954 was changed retroactively to "the Provisional Workers'-Peasants' Government of Lithuania" (A. M. Andreev, *Borba Litovskogo Naroda za Sovetskuiu Vlast*, Moscow, 1954) to stress the need for a broad popular base.

East European Communists and fellow travelers in whose eyes the concept of the Soviet dictatorship of the proletariat was not only theoretically inapplicable but also a political liability. Preoccupation with ideology was clearly linked again with efforts to isolate those elements which would favor the desirable (and hence inevitable) political ends. As a result, and under the benign shield of Stalin's vague remarks about the democratization of East Europe, after 1945 the local Communists provided the impetus for the conceptual development of the People's Democracy as a new form of state organization.

Their new concepts, partially influenced by the wartime alliance between the USSR and the capitalist powers and partially based on observation of domestic processes, stressed the need for a broad democratic front, including the progressive bourgeoisie. This was not only for the earlier purpose of defeating Nazi Germany but also for the construction of new democratic states in which power would be shared with the Communists. As early as the fall of 1941, this was the consensus reached by the surviving Polish Communists in the USSR (Stalin had most of them shot in 1938) in the course of lengthy discussions with Georgi Dimitrov, the Comintern head.[9] As a result, and given the factors of the postwar East European situation as they saw it, the leaders of the local Communist parties were forced to conclude that the hitherto universally valid concept of the dictatorship of the proletariat was inapplicable to the new state forms. Gomulka, the secretary of the Polish Workers' Party, asserted explicitly in November 1946 that the Polish People's Democracy was not a dictatorship of the proletariat and that Poland would reach socialism by avoiding it altogether. "Our democracy is also not similar to Soviet democracy, just as our social system is not similar to the Soviet system," Gomulka explained.[10] It followed logically from this that the Soviet type of state also could not be applied in the new East European context. This point was repeatedly stressed by some of the most prominent Communist leaders, with long Moscow associations. Bierut, the Communist president of Poland, asserted in June 1946 that "this specific order is not based on any existing model. It is not similar to the Soviet socialist order or to the classical economic system of the West." [11] Dimitrov, speaking in Sofia three months later, was even more direct:

Bulgaria will not be a Soviet republic but a people's republic in which the functions of government will be performed by an enormous majority of the people — workers, peasants, craftsmen, and the people's intelligentsia. In this republic there will be no dictatorship of any kind.[12]

Furthermore, the origins of the People's Democracy were not to be traced to the revolutionary consequences of a domestic upheaval, fitting the classical Marxist-Leninist concepts of intensified class conflict leading ultimately to a revolution. It was, first of all, the direct consequence of the presence of the Soviet Army. Thus Gomulka, while stressing that the changes which were occurring in East Europe had "the character of deep revolutionary transformation," acknowledged that they had been effected without a revolution because of the presence of the Red Army, in the face of which "the forces of reaction were inhibited and paralyzed in their activity." [13] Second, the revolutionary processes produced by the dislocations of war and by the presence of the Red forces were still not a true socialist revolution, but rather a "national democratic" one, as the Communists were fond of calling it. The idea of a socialist revolution was not mentioned, and Gottwald, in a confidential speech in May 1945 outlining party tactics to Communist functionaries, warned: "We must continually remind ourselves that in the present phase we are following the line of the national and democratic . . . and not the line of the socialist revolution." [14]

Leninist strictures notwithstanding, the conclusion that the People's Democracy was something entirely new under the sun seemed inescapable. It was no longer the classical oppressive bourgeois state; yet it was not therefore its antithesis, the dictatorship of the proletariat. What was it then? Bierut gave a rather lame explanation: "the People's Democracy is a special form of revolutionary authority which came into being under new relations among classes in the international arena." [15] The very vagueness of the statement is mute testimony to the ideological embarrassment which this old Comintern *apparatchik* must have felt. "A special form of revolutionary authority" does not tell much about such simple issues as whether a state has ceased to be a bourgeois state and is now a proletarian one, or in whose hands the power rests. The issue was stated in a more precise, but also more extreme, fashion by a member of the Hungarian Central Committee. Martin Horvath asserted that "in view of the fact that a People's Democracy does not destroy the right to own the means of production, it can simply be regarded as the most progressive form of bourgeois democracy (or, to put it more correctly, its only progressive form)."*

* *Tarsadalni — andomanyi szemle*, October 1948 (Kardelj, *On People's Democracy in Yugoslavia*, p. 8; Kardelj distorted the spelling of the publication. The correct version was *tarsadalomtudomanyi szemle*). In this state, private property was to enjoy

Unlike the orthodox view of the dictatorship of the proletariat, in which its vanguard wields the effective power, the political power of the People's Democracy was to be shared in a formal sense by national coalitions and in the real sense (if we may use these distinctions of Marx) by an alliance of the working and peasant classes, but with neither exercising a hegemony. The reason, of course, was that in a People's Democracy the former exploiting classes, while no longer enjoying a monopoly on power and gradually losing it altogether, still continued to exist. "In the state of People's Democracy there still exist classes which live by exploiting the work of others; these are the capitalists — various entrepreneurs, well-to-do merchants, factory owners employing a certain number of workers, rich peasants, speculators and other non-workers," explained Bierut.[16] Power is wielded by a broad coalition of the working class, the peasantry, the middle strata of the urban population, the working intelligentsia and a portion of the bourgeoisie,[17] all of whom are said to be opposed by the remnants of reaction. Under these circumstances the usual Leninist concept of a unified, single-class, state authority was both theoretically and practically inapplicable.* "There is nothing more false than accusing the Polish Workers' Party of mono-party tendencies, of the desire to subordinate other democratic parties," Gomulka was frequently assuring the Poles,[18] even adding that "an evolutionary way of social change and an evolutionary transition to a socialist order is entirely possible." [19] A further and consequent tenet in this line of reasoning was the assertion that domestic violence was unnecessary and that it might be possible to avoid it because of the overwhelming power of Soviet support. Stalin's notions about the intensification of class struggle after the seizure of power were discreetly not mentioned.

The crux of this type of evaluation was the frequent insistence of

the benevolent protection of the authorities of the People's Democracy. For instance, Dimitrov: "Bulgaria will be a People's Republic in which private property acquired by labor will be protected by the state authorities." (Chervenkov, as cited in note 12.) Bierut was almost whimsical on the subject of free enterprise; stressing the newness of the People's Democracy, he attributed it to the "specific harmony of the two factors; on the one side the leading role of the state . . . on the other side, the spirit of enterprise, the energy and free initiative of the mass of independent entrepreneurs" (speech in Cracow, June 1946).

* This was explicitly stated by Joseph Revai, one of the leading "ideologues" of the Hungarian party. Cf. his speech quoted in the *Information Bulletin of the Central Committee of the Hungarian Party*, no. 8, 1948. Revai has always been identified as one of the staunchest Stalinists in the committee, and after the October 1956 events he led the struggle for the most severe condemnation of Nagy and Lukacs.

the local Communists that in every situation Marxian policy had to be shaped in accordance with the specific circumstances. These circumstances varied from country to country in 1945, and they certainly also differed from those encountered by the Bolsheviks after the 1917 Revolution. No wonder then that many local Communists stressed the specific character of their individual countries. Rakosi, who was to become the scourge of the "national Communists" during the anti-Tito phase, expressed this rather well:

During the last 25 years the Communist Parties of the world learned that there are several roads which lead to Socialism and accordingly we cannot build Socialism if we do not build our own road, taking into account the special conditions prevailing in the country. We have learned that lesson, and, while we are strengthening the Hungarian democracy, we are not doing this because of tactical reasons or in order to achieve some secret aim, but because of our deep Communist convictions, and we will do whatever we can to fill the frame of the democracy with the largest possible Socialist content. That will speed up the progress which leads mankind into Socialism. We also know that, although Socialism utilizes a multitude of international experiences, our Socialism can be created only as a result of the development of Hungarian history and Hungarian economic, political and social forces. That will be Socialism born on Hungarian soil and adapted to Hungarian conditions.[20]

Quotations to this effect could be cited for Gomulka, Gottwald, and many others.

One must note, however, that a clear-cut, theoretical, and well-reasoned analysis of the People's Democracy, made within the context of Marxian ideology, was not elucidated systematically by the East European Communist leaders. It may well have been that most of them were not, trained as they were in the Stalinist Comintern or in local undergrounds, theoretically equipped or so inclined. In addition to this, they were faced with the many daily tasks inherent in the unfolding struggle for power and could hardly be expected to devote themselves to a serious formulation of an admittedly ticklish subject. Finally, they probably preferred to leave the field of theory, with all its dangerous quicksands, to their Soviet senior colleagues and limit themselves to mere elaborations of formulas shaped in Moscow.

During this initial period, the Soviet leaders themselves also refrained from making any definitive programmatic statements. Stalin's assertions were rather vague and stressed such broad considerations as "democracy," "democratic governments friendly to the Soviet Union," and the like. It was only in the latter part of 1947 (to be dealt with subsequently) that Soviet leaders made public *ex cathedra* pronouncements.* Soviet scholars, however, were less reticent, and it is to them that we owe a more systematic treatment of the theoretical problem presented by the People's Democracy. It may be safely assumed that their reflections corresponded to the broad lines of analysis of the top Soviet leadership and that it was not mere intellectual curiosity that prompted their preoccupation with the subject. It was probably from them, as well as from the informal channels of party communications, that the East European Communists drew their ideological inspiration. Consistency in broad outlook was hence properly maintained.

The view of the Soviet scholars, as developed between 1945 and 1947,[21] may be briefly summarized as follows: The People's Democracy was not to be confused with a proletarian democracy, the latter being essentially "identical with the dictatorship of the proletariat which does not share its power with any other class." [22] This could hardly be the case in Eastern Europe where the class rule of the proletariat was, at best, incipient,† and where the other classes were still economically and politically active. A true Marxist had to conclude, therefore, that the existing order was neither bourgeois nor socialist, although the proletariat was able to influence sufficiently the political organization of society to ensure that a "real democracy" was realized. The theoretical journal of the Communist Party of the Soviet Union (CPSU) accordingly held that:

* In what appears to this writer to be an accurate statement for all the East European parties, Joseph Revai, writing in 1949 about this early period in reference to Hungary, stated: "The Party didn't possess a unified, clarified, elaborated attitude in respect to the character of the People's Democracy and its future development." He also implied that Stalin was not very helpful before the autumn of 1947. "The Character of a 'People's Democracy,'" as translated in *Foreign Affairs* (October 1949), p. 147. See also Chapter 4 for further discussion.

† There seems to have been some disagreement among Soviet scholars on the degree of class rule of the proletariat already in existence. Varga, as cited in note 21, p. 13, spoke vaguely of "the political rule of the toilers," while Trainin (note 21) was inclined to claim that the political hegemony of the proletariat was already operative, although in a somewhat different form than in a Soviet type of state. "The hegemony of the proletariat is expressed in the fact that the proletariat, in the shape of its vanguard — the Communist Party — tends toward finding solutions for these tasks not through the strengthening of capitalism, but through the gradual consolidation of the principles of real democracy, which correspond to the interests of the working class and all working people, that is, the overwhelming majority of the people" (p. 3). Trainin's views were backed by A. Schaff, a leading Polish Marxist theoretician. In his book, *Wstęp do teorii marksizmu* (Warsaw, 1948), Schaff maintained that Poland, while not a dictatorship of the proletariat, already was under the hegemony of the proletariat for reasons outlined by Trainin.

There have arisen in these countries new, higher forms of democracy as compared to the old, bourgeois-parliamentarian democracy. These countries have so developed and expanded democracy as to signify the participation of workers and peasants in the state administration and make the benefits of democracy accessible to the broadest masses. Thus new forms of state polity have been created which are a big step forward in comparison with the bourgeois democratic states and which offer possibilities for further progress by these countries in the economic and political fields.[23]

These new People's Democracies, insofar as their administrative structures were concerned, were to be a hybrid between the forms of the old bourgeois state (presumably with its instruments of class oppression) and the forms of the socialist state as created by the USSR. Academician Eugene Varga, for instance, explicitly stated that the old state had not been demolished in its entirety, but that some of its institutions were being creatively reshaped, through the infusion of new class content, to fit the existing requirements. In an actual institutional sense, the constitutional picture of East Europe was at this time remarkably diversified. Two of the states, Rumania and Bulgaria, were still monarchies. The Bulgarian and Rumanian constitutional structures were not changed, although by 1946 the Communists began to agitate against the "antiquated" constitutions, demanding particularly that a national system of people's councils be established to "democratize" the state. Nonetheless, it was not until after the creation of the Cominform that the old forms gave way to new constitutions. In Hungary, where a provisional government was set up after the expulsion of the Germans, a new constitution was proclaimed on January 31, 1946, and Hungary became a republic. The constitution provided for a president, somewhat on the Western model, and a parliamentary form of government.[24] In Czechoslovakia and Poland the prewar constitutions were essentially retained, although in Czechoslovakia a provisional national assembly was to prepare the groundwork for a constituent assembly which would draft a new constitution. This undermined Benes' claim of legitimacy, replacing it with a "revolutionary conception" of legality.[25] In Poland, the 1935 constitution was ignored, and the government was said to base itself on the 1921 constitution framed on the French model. Only in Yugoslavia and Albania were truly new constitutions adopted.

Varga could thus maintain that in the People's Democracies "the old state apparatus is not destroyed, as was the case in the Soviet Union, but is being renovated with the steady absorption of the followers of the new regime. Those are not capitalist states in the ordinary meaning of the word. But neither are they socialist states. Their development in the direction of Socialism is based on the nationalization of the chief means of production and on the very character of those states." [26] Eventually, it was stated, the capitalist sector was to disappear, but at the same time it could not avoid having some temporary effects on the political scene. Hence, the presence of bourgeois parties associated in the government through coalitions or through national fronts was explained. The specific degrees of adjustment between the socialist and capitalist sectors depended, of course, on the specifics of each country's situation. In brief, what the Soviet theorists were suggesting was a form of permanent revolution in which the transitional phase developed a distinct institutional identity. But if this was the case, then the Communists had to ask in turn: what are to be the relations of this new type of state with the only true socialist state, the USSR?

Relations with the USSR

From the standpoint of international politics, the postwar relationship of East Europe to the USSR was defined in a number of documents usually identified by the name of the location in which each had been signed. The Teheran, Yalta, Potsdam agreements, in one way or another, all expressed the view that postwar East Europe was to be governed by regimes "democratic and friendly" to the USSR. These broad statements of purpose never clearly defined what the link between the two norms (democratic and friendly) was: whether both were of equal importance or whether one was to serve as a basis for the other. Yet it should have been clear that one of the basic assumptions of Marxists, who think in dichotomic terms,[27] was that there exists a basic hostility between capitalist and socialist states. We may therefore conclude that if East Europe was to develop along the lines of "bourgeois democracy" (which Churchill and Roosevelt presumably had in mind), there could be no question that, in the Russian view, its relations with the USSR would have to be fundamentally hostile, even if some form of coexistence were possible. East Europe could be truly friendly to the USSR only if some significant *internal* transformation were to occur, lifting East Europe out of the "bourgeois democratic" orbit, which, as Lenin stressed, was essentially identical with the dictatorship of the bourgeoisie. The People's Democracy was such a transformation. This put the question of relations on an entirely different plane.

Thus, the problem of relations between the People's Democracy and the USSR could be approached from the standpoint of relations between states which were not mutually antagonistic by their very definition. The task of defining the relationship was at least free of this particular complication. However, a major political liability encumbering the Communists in East Europe was the widespread popular belief that their ultimate objective was the incorporation of the area into Russia. This prospect was loathsome to practically all East Europeans, from the conservative to the most progressive, and charges of this type could be supported by documented precedents. The fate of the Baltic republics, once they embarked on the road of "socialist construction," was one striking case in point. The left-socialist faction in Poland, which originally founded the Polish Communist Party, had split away from the Polish Socialist Party (PPS) precisely on that issue: it did not wish to identify itself with the cause of Polish nationalism. This was the case elsewhere in East Europe.[28] The Communists during the war and immediately afterwards had to labor against this apprehension.

There is no doubt that in the past East European Communists had taken a violent stand against nationalism, which they identified with bourgeois rule. They tended to emphasize their international character and their contempt for national traditions and habits. Nonetheless, a careful reading of Lenin and other Bolsheviks [29] reveals that their approach to problems of nationalism and of international relations was purely a *tactical* one, based on certain more general theoretical assumptions. It seems clear that Lenin and others condemned nationalism as one of the many subterfuges designed to obscure the development of class consciousness, to obliterate the international sense of solidarity of the proletariat rooted in its common relationship to the means of production. Thus it was the task of the Communist to struggle against nationalistic feelings — to remove this smoke screen obscuring the vision of the working class. Ideally, a socialist society would be composed of many nationalities living side by side without national animosities.

However, Lenin and others stressed that the attitude of the Communist toward nationalist feelings had to be derived in every case from a proper appreciation of the major factors involved. The setting up of Communist rule, after all, was not an end in itself but only a means to the final end. Therefore, a Communist, while being very careful not to subordinate his class ends to a temporary nationalist zeal, also had to consider the depth of the nationalist feelings in society lest he lose touch with the situation. He always had to bear in mind Marx's warning: "We know that we must reckon with the institutions, the customs and traditions of various individual countries." [30] Lenin elaborated this into a clear principle in his "First Draft Theses Concerning the National and Colonial Question," addressed to the Second Comintern Congress (1920):

the more undeveloped a given country is, the stronger also are its small agriculturists, its patriarchical sentiments, and its backwardness — all of which inevitably give particular strength and tenacity to the most profound small bourgeois prejudices, i.e., the prejudices of national egotism, national narrowmindedness. Since these prejudices can only disappear after the disappearance of imperialism and capitalism in advanced countries and after a radical change of the entire basis of economic life in backward countries, the extinction of these prejudices cannot but be very slow. Therefore the duty of fully conscious communist proletarians of all countries is *to handle with particular caution* and particular attention the remnants of these nationalist sentiments in the case of the countries and nationalities which have been oppressed longest; likewise their duty is *to make certain concessions* for the sake of the quickest possible extinction of these feelings of mistrust and these prejudices.[31]

It follows that an important corollary of this principle was the insistence on the right of secession and self-determination. These rights, again, were still only relative. The idea was that the very granting of the right would take the sting out of much of the nationalist appeal and would thereby permit the workingman to attend to his true interest. As long as the bourgeoisie was able to claim that its dominance was required by some national cause, such as liberation or expansion, the tasks of the social revolution would be delayed.* The Communists were accordingly justified in supporting national emancipation of oppressed nations, thereby linking even the processes of national liberation with social revolution under certain conditions. The long-run objective, of course, did not change, and in each case the question of self-determination, or secession in the case of a multinational state, had to be resolved in terms "of social progress as a whole and the interests of the class struggle of the proletariat for socialism." [32]

In the case of Russia, the Communists felt justified in insisting that the unity of the state be preserved, albeit in federal form. The prob-

---

* "Just as mankind can achieve the abolition of classes only by passing through the transition period of the dictatorship of the oppressed class, so mankind can achieve the inevitable merging of nations only by passing through the transition period of complete liberation of all the oppressed nations, i.e., their freedom to secede." Lenin, "Right of Nations to Self-Determination," *Selected Works* (New York, 1943), V, 271.

lem of nationalism, they felt, was solved by granting the right of secession. But to attempt to exercise it in the Russian context was to go against history. "There are instances," Stalin explained, "when the right to self-determination comes into conflict with another higher right, the right of the working class which attained power to fortify its power. In such cases, it must be stated frankly, the right of self-determination cannot be and must not serve as an obstacle to the realization of the right of the working class to its own dictatorship. The first must recede before the second." [33] The Bolshevik leaders also felt that the Russian federation had shown itself to be a desirable form of expressing relations among socialist states, since presumably in the future they would all have the same institutional form: the dictatorship of the proletariat. However, at best this was the eventual prospect, and in the more immediate future it could be expected that some states might wish to preserve their complete independence. Stalin, in commenting to Lenin on the latter's "Draft Theses," emphasized that a major distinction must be made between nations and nationalities which had been part of the Russian Empire, for which "our own (Soviet) type of federation can and must be considered a suitable way toward international unification," and nations with long traditions of separate statehood. The latter, even if already under Soviet-modeled institutions would, Stalin thought, prefer to maintain their distinct identity, and it would be erroneous to fit them into some federal mold. [34] Communists would have to accept the idea that separate statehood for these states was desirable for the time being.* For this reason separate national Communist parties would have to be maintained, although the Soviet leaders were quick to assert that it was the task of every national party to strive for Communism by giving continuous support to the Soviet state. They categorically rejected any suggestions that there could be a conflict of interest between a national party and the Soviet party and its state.†

In East Europe, as noted already, nationalism was very intense as a result of the war. To ignore nationalism would have been to hand it to the bourgeoisie, who could exploit it for their own class interests. In keeping with Bolshevik notions, to enflame nationalist feelings was a prelude to true internationalism. The brighter the flames of na-

---

* The long-range goal remained, in the words of the Second Comintern Congress, a "World Federation of Soviet Republics." *Kommunisticheskii Internatsional v Dokumentakh, 1919–1932* (Moscow, 1933), p. 88.

† A suggestion to this effect had been made in the German Communist Party paper, *Roter Kurier*, early in 1924 and most violently condemned in a letter from Comintern head Zinoviev. Fischer, *Stalin and German Communism*, p. 395.

tionalism, the sooner they would burn out. Accordingly, the local Communists thoroughly identified themselves with nationalism. Such identification to them did not involve either an ideological zig-zag or a theoretical capitulation. It was, instead, a sensible adjustment to the requirements of the situation, quite compatible with basic doctrinal assumptions. Local Communists became the most vociferous spokesmen for national interests. They took every opportunity to wave the flag (and it was rarely the red one), to associate themselves with any cause enjoying nationalist appeal. Talk of any union with the USSR was condemned as bourgeois slander. The founding declaration of the Polish Workers' (Communist) Party reads almost like a nationalist harangue.[35] The reconstruction and maintenance of independent statehood was one of the chief planks in all Communist programs in East Europe. The new states were to be sovereign — not Soviet. Their relations with the USSR were to be, naturally, "friendly" but founded on mutual recognition of the principles of independence and noninterference in internal affairs.

The Soviets, for their part, also felt compelled to adjust not only to their own international commitments but also to the problems faced by their local agents in East Europe. Moscow's role was to make the process of acquisition of power within the existing framework easier, not through direct help alone but also by assuming the proper ideological stance. In the spirit of Lenin's injunction (quoted at the beginning of this chapter), Stalin was fond of repeating his dedication to the task of reconstructing independent states in East Europe and frequently asserted that the Soviet Union would pursue a policy of friendship and alliance toward them. This friendship was said to be possible due to the internal transformations in process. Federation, or even a confederation (which in 1920 had been considered as an eventual alternative), was not mentioned. Formal ties along traditional lines were established between the USSR and some People's Democracies: state treaties of friendship and alliance on the basis of equality between the cosignatories (see Chapter 6). But beyond this formal equality, a convenient theoretical element of historical inequality was implied in the very definition of a People's Democracy. Since the People's Democracy was only at the threshold of socialist development, the more advanced USSR implicitly enjoyed the position of a guide, even if roads to socialism varied. Thus, within the essential meaning of People's Democracy and the formal nature of official links with the USSR, the seeds of future ideological subordination were planted.

The Dissidents

In the immediate postwar period, which saw both the theoretical and the practical birth of the People's Democracy, all the local Communists save one group labored under the major handicap of having been brought in on the coattails of the Red Army. Many of the theoretical problems inherent in the attempts to define the People's Democracy were due to the fact that the acquisition of power did not quite fit the ideal notions of a genuine proletarian revolution. Difficulties of interpretation were maximized by the international commitments of the USSR and by the presence of domestic forces capable of offering the Communists at least a temporary challenge.

In one country, Yugoslavia, the situation differed radically. The Yugoslav Communist Party, proudly bearing that name and scoffing at those who hid themselves under the euphemistic label of workers' party, had won power through its own resources, though aided in the last stages of the war by the entrance of the Red Army. In the course of their partisan activities the Yugoslav Communists had crushed the bourgeoisie and had thus effected what they considered to be a revolution not unlike the Bolshevik revolution of 1917. In the words of Kardelj: "In view of the fact that our Revolution began to develop in the conditions of the National Liberation War, in its first phase it possessed the form of a People's Democracy, but, in view of its class forces and the internal relationship of these forces, it could in fact only be a Socialist revolution." [36]

There was no reason, therefore, to think that the power wielded by the Yugoslav Communist Party differed in its essentials from the dictatorship of the proletariat as set up in Petrograd some twenty-eight years earlier. Though willing to adopt the label of a People's Democracy, the Yugoslavs asserted that this was merely another form of the dictatorship of the proletariat and very much similar to the Soviet type of republic. The Yugoslav constitution of January 1946 and the Albanian constitution, passed a month and a half later, explicitly broke with the "bourgeois-democratic" forms of state organization, proclaimed the states to be People's Democracies, and unabashedly copied the Soviet constitution of 1936.[37] By adopting a constitution markedly like the Soviet, Tito again rejected the more moderate practices of his Communist neighbors and underlined the fact that the old state had been destroyed in substance and in form. This was another way of expressing what the Yugoslavs felt other East European comrades were neglecting to assert—that the People's

Democracy did not differ in essentials from the Soviet system. Even after Tito's expulsion from the Comintern in 1948, the Yugoslavs heaped scorn on their East European colleagues for the latter's efforts to define the People's Democracy as some new type of state.

Speaking after the 1948 break to the People's Assembly, Kardelj made the following modest claims:

We owe the victory of our People's Revolution precisely to the fact that we nurtured no illusions as to the "new paths in principle" which lead to Socialism. We were the only ones to set out this attitude clearly at the first session of the Informbureau. Contrary to it, the leaders of the Communist Parties of the other People's Democracies constantly made some kind of "discoveries" about their own — in principle — "new path" to Socialism, about various "specific harmonies" between socialist and capitalist elements, and about the especial worth of some vestiges of bourgeois democracy, which they glorified as a singular aspect of a People's Democracy. And all of them were unendingly claiming patents for these "discoveries" of theirs. Then the Soviet professors repeated these phrases in countless variations. That is why the Soviet press always gave more prominence to various opportunistic absurdities from the other People's Democracies than to facts about the new Yugoslavia, *which stood far ahead of the others*. And we, who contended that we had won our Socialist revolution, *that our People's Democracy was of the Soviet type*, we were told that we were narrowminded sectarians and entirely incapable of inventing something new, despite the fact that practically everything that is really new in the present People's Democracy had been created in our country.[38]

The Yugoslav argument was based on Marx's discussion of the transitional period (in his "Critique of the Gotha Programme") during which some remnants of the capitalist era would persist, although eventually giving way to the socialist order. It was the dictatorship of the proletariat which politically expressed this transition. Hence, the Yugoslavs reasoned, the People's Democracies could not be anything but a dictatorship of the proletariat — as developed in Russia in 1917 and in Yugoslavia in 1945, and as should be the case in East Europe also. In the strictest sense, they were probably right but their perspective was rather provincial. Viewing the area through the prism of their own experience they could not help but be somewhat contemptuous of their comrades elsewhere, who were organizing coalitions, talking about a new type of democracy, stressing distinctive patterns of development, even playing court to kings and attempting to stage elections. Impatient and somewhat doctrinaire, the Yugoslavs at this stage were ideologically more Stalinist than Stalin.

The Yugoslav thinking on the nature of their state naturally impinged on the problem of interstate relations within the Soviet bloc. Like their colleagues elsewhere in East Europe, the Yugoslavs endorsed nationalist sentiments and gave free vent to their sense of national pride. They felt justified in doing this because of their wartime struggles and successes. In fact, they most likely felt that their subjective sentiments were in keeping with the objective requirements of the moment. Yugoslavia, like the rest, had to go through the nationalist phase, and Yugoslav Communists, unlike the rest, were fully justified in enjoying the fruits of national pride. However, they never lost sight of the fact that this was to be only a temporary phase. And since Yugoslavia was already a dictatorship of the proletariat, ultimate socialist unity was not as distant as assumed by those who made "erroneous" assertions about the uniqueness of the People's Democracy. If we are to trust the June 5, 1945, dispatches of the Soviet Minister in Belgrade, and they seem to be in keeping with the general tenor of the prevailing Yugoslav thinking, Kardelj considered himself and Tito to be leaders *conscious* of the course that history had to take, their national pride notwithstanding. In the Soviet Minister's words:

We would like, continued Kardelj, the Soviet Union to look at us as representatives of one of the future Soviet Republics, and not as upon representatives of another country, capable of independently solving questions. . . . [They] consider the Communist Party of Yugoslavia as being a part of the All-Union Communist Party, that is to say, that our relationship . . . [should emphasize] that Yugoslavia in the future would be admitted a constituent part of the USSR. Therefore they would like us to criticise them directly and openly, and to give them advice in what way to conduct the home and foreign policy of Yugoslavia in the right direction." *

But even though the Yugoslavs deviated by overinsistence on orthodoxy, they were not, initially at least, viewed as harmful. They represented a higher stage of development to which the other parties could ultimately aspire. Stalin paid special tributes to Tito, and Yugoslav Communists were even convinced that Tito would succeed

---

* *The Correspondence between the Central Committee of the CPJ and the Central Committee of the AUCP(b)* (Belgrade), p. 49. Stalin and Molotov, in their May 1948 correspondence with Tito, gleefully branded these views as "primitive and incorrect." They certainly raised a point on which the Yugoslavs were particularly touchy but which, in terms of dialectical thinking, had not been incorrectly put. Nonetheless, by 1948 Kardelj's early views seemed somehow strangely romantic, naive, and provincial.

Stalin as the leader of the international Communist movement. In the meantime, the responsibility of Communists everywhere in East Europe was to obtain and consolidate a firm grip on power. Since the reigning doctrine stressed a form of harmonious diversity, the occasional Yugoslav outbursts of super-loyalty could be viewed with that benign tolerance which is occasionally granted to a precocious child. It was only when these views began to develop a political import of their own — that is, when they began to affect broader problems of power outside Yugoslavia and to imply theoretical equality with the USSR — that the need arose for Moscow to cope with them. For the time being, however, the People's Democracy was an adequate theoretical reply to the questions asked by local Communists; it was a guide to action sufficiently doctrinaire to maintain overall unity of purpose and elastic enough to deal with the existing diversity.

CHAPTER **3** —

Problems of Diversity

T HE Soviet leadership, surveying the East European scene in 1947, had some cause for gratification. In all the capitals, including even Czechoslovakia's, the most powerful offices of state were occupied by Communists. Democratic forces were everywhere either defeated or very much on the defensive. Internal changes in East European societies were undermining the remaining "hostile class elements," most of which had already been deprived of effective political power. The Western states were implicitly accepting Soviet hegemony over the area, despite occasional verbal outbursts. The Soviet leadership, viewing American disinterest and Anglo-French impotence, could gaze serenely on its new dominions.

The institutional and ideological diversity which characterized the Communist world at this time was the natural outcome of the complex and fluctuating postwar conditions. In 1945 the Soviet leadership could not be certain what limits the West would attempt to set on Communist control and at what point the West might possibly react to excessive and rapid Sovietization of the area. It was not yet clear how strong the anti-Communist forces in the area were. Furthermore, at that time it looked as if revolutionary situations might develop further west. The task of the Communists, therefore, was to act so as not to activate their enemies by excessively peremptory measures. This was the time for caution, for elasticity, for camouflage. By 1947, however, even if the potentially revolutionary prospects in the West were not unfolding quite as rapidly as desired, the stabilization of Soviet control in East Europe was moving apace, and the uncertainties of the initial picture were beginning to give way to a clearer image of the postwar phase of development. A reassessment of this phase was becoming necessary.

The Soviet Scene

Soviet internal developments undoubtedly had something to do with the need for reassessment. In the Soviet Union itself the political aftereffects of the war — the blurring of clear-cut political and ideological lines — had also resulted in a measure of theoretical and institutional diversity. This diversity had been tolerated as a concomitant of the peculiar historical phase in which the USSR had found itself. Some expressions of this phase were purposely tolerated for the sake of the immediate goal of winning the war. Others had sprung up by themselves, as a spontaneous outgrowth of the USSR's engagement in a total conflict. The most serious of these was the decline in party zeal, the lowering of party morale, and the relaxation of the tight organizational bonds so necessary to the efficient operations of a ruling totalitarian party. The war produced a tremendous turnover in party membership — with many hundreds of thousands admitted each year, and almost as many dying each year on the battlefield. The exigencies of an obvious emergency situation meant that normal procedures of training, indoctrination, and discipline had to be suspended. Party membership for quite a few ceased to be a privilege and became mere routine. The consequence was that the CPSU emerged from the war with an organization badly in need of reform and very much in need of new political fervor.

The impact of the war on the party produced another consequence of vital significance to the leadership. The very same factors which undermined the qualities that the Communist leadership considers so central led to the appearance of the army on the Soviet political scene. The army emerged from the war considerably more powerful than it had been at the beginning. While the CPSU went into the war in 1941 with a more disciplined membership, with every indication of being the central organ of the Soviet system, and emerged with these qualities somewhat blurred, just the opposite happened with the army. It went into the war disgraced by the Finnish defeats, still licking its wounds from the great purges, even having to reach into the concentration camps to replenish its depleted command staffs; it emerged blazoned with glory, with a powerful fighting machine, with decorated marshals — the victors of Stalingrad, Budapest, and Berlin. In a May 1 photograph they were shown surrounding their generalissimo, thereby almost symbolizing new domestic realities.

It would be misleading, however, to exaggerate the significance of this development. Despite a certain measure of degeneration, the party still remained the key political instrument and, above all else, its leadership was still the leadership of the country, controlling the secret police. The latter's power was enhanced by the wartime pressures for internal security and the responsibilities of coping with enemies in the occupied countries. The army lacked a political purpose, a "political sense," and a politically oriented leadership. It did not therefore constitute a purposeful challenge to the party's supremacy. It did, however, create strains by its very presence and popularity. It was to these problems that the party leadership had to turn its attention in the immediate postwar period, and it resolved them by downgrading the military and by revitalizing the party.

The symbolic gesture indicating that the role of the military would differ in peacetime was the removal in March 1946 of Marshal Georgi Zhukov from his prominent position in Berlin and his reassignment to an obscure command post. Politically even more significant to those "in the know" in the Soviet political system, though not at the time a matter of public record, was Zhukov's removal in the same year from the party's Central Committee. At the same time, organizational measures were taken in the military forces to activate political controls and party indoctrination.[1]

Insofar as the party machinery and ideology were concerned, the measures adopted involved, first of all, a far-reaching, though unheralded, membership purge in the territories recovered from German occupation. For the upper echelons of the party, and also of the state administration, a resolution of the Central Committee (of August 2, 1946) envisaged a thorough reorganization of the training and indoctrination programs under the direction of the Higher Party School and the Academy of Social Sciences, attached directly to the Central Committee. Similar institutes were to be established on the lower organizational levels.[2] In the realm of ideological concerns the party cracked down on certain publications accused of pursuing a "nonideological, apolitical line." This was followed by similar measures with respect to the theatrical world.[3]

A return to more orthodox patterns also took place in the agricultural sector of the national economy. The war had resulted in the destruction of the collective farm system in the German-occupied parts of the USSR, and this had aroused widespread hope in many peasants that collectivization would not be rigorously applied and might even be given up altogether. In the parts of the Soviet Union not reached by the Germans, the collective farm system operated during the war in a somewhat more relaxed fashion. Possibly due to the weakness of party controls and discipline, to the desire of the regime to obtain the maximum of foodstuffs from the peasants, and possibly also due to the premeditated effort to cultivate the good will of the populace, the Draconic application of existing agricultural regulations gave way to a semiofficial policy of ignoring the growing expansion of private plots and private herds, clearly at the expense of the collective sector. But on September 19, 1946, the Soviet peasant population learned that socialist construction in the countryside was to continue and that the regime would insist on strict adherence to its programmatic goals.⁴ This, together with the measures to revitalize the rural party organizations, marked the return of totalitarian conformity to the Soviet countryside.

By late 1946 and early 1947 the process of coping with the internal relaxation which had developed in the USSR during the war was well under way. The outside world was also beginning to emerge in sharper focus. Major revolutionary upheavals in Greece had been suppressed as early as 1945, although a renewed attempt was made on the fringes of the Greek mountain ranges in 1946–1947. In Italy and France the non-Communist forces had consolidated their position, and the Communist partisans had been disarmed. In May 1946, De Gaulle scored a major electoral victory in France on the constitutional issue, and it was becoming apparent that a seizure of power by the French Communist Party through pseudo-legal means was no longer feasible.

The crystallization of Soviet thinking about the nature of the postwar phase probably occurred in this period.* The peaceful, and indeed friendly, coexistence which had been the recurring theme of Soviet declarations in 1945 began to give way to more and more explicit assertions of the fundamental difference between Soviet socialism and the capitalist world. Stalin himself signaled the shift in a Supreme Soviet campaign speech in February 1946. Forcefully, he extolled the superiorities of the Soviet system and contrasted it with the capitalistic world torn by internal contradictions. Thereafter the Soviet press directed a steadily intensifying campaign against the West. From the Soviet point of view, Churchill's speech in Fulton, Missouri, in March 1946, calling for an Anglo-American alliance in view of Soviet violations of the Yalta Agreement and continued Soviet efforts to expand, constituted capitalism's last-ditch effort to allay

* The Varga debate was one of its later symptoms. Late in 1945 Yevgeni Samoilovich Varga concluded his book *Change in the Capitalist Economy after World War II*. The book was published in the early part of 1946. In it Varga took a sanguine view of capitalism's postwar prospects. Based on Varga's book, three lively debates took place among Soviet economists in May 1947, with the purpose of clarifying the general line for the continuing analysis of the Western economy and of the entire economic and political system of the Western world. As a result of these debates and subsequent discussions, Varga was expelled from most of his posts. However at the beginning of 1949 he announced that he would revise the theme of his book. Finally, in 1953 his new book appeared, *Basic Questions of Economy and Politics of Imperialism after World War II*.

internal contradictions through emphasis on the common enemy, Communism. At the twenty-ninth anniversary celebration of the Bolshevik revolution (November 7, 1946), the restoration of the old dichotomic approach toward world affairs was affirmed by Zhdanov who delivered the main address. Reasserting in most emphatic terms the need for internal discipline and ideological indoctrination, Zhdanov militantly condemned the Western attitude toward the USSR and its East European policies. Not only did he make frequent references to "reactionary circles" in England and the United States; he also made repeated use of such phrases as "the Soviet Union leading the democratic countries," "USSR — the vanguard of the democratic movement," and so forth.[5] Implicit in all of this was the vision of a world rapidly splitting into two fundamentally hostile camps, with the Soviet Union asserting its leadership over one of them.

The People's Democracy: A Transitional Phase

Stalin's and Zhdanov's speeches had special pertinence to the future development of the People's Democracies. The changes in the internal and theoretical character of these states which followed after the founding of the Cominform in 1947 (see Chapters 4 and 5) have consequently led some observers to assert that this entire period of relative institutional and ideological flexibility had been a well-timed hoax. They have been able to point effectively to certain clearly definable stages of development in the Soviet pattern of domination and consequently feel justified in asserting that a plot had been effectively carried out according to a preconceived blueprint, its ultimate objective being the stage-by-stage total subjugation of East Europe.

Some evidence to buttress this type of approach is readily available. It would certainly be rash to take at face value, considering past behavior and the postwar record, Soviet statements about the truly democratic and unique character of the People's Democracy and the Soviet assertions of their dedication to the maintenance of free states in East Europe. Statements of that type could well have been designed to lessen Western suspicions and to pave the way for the processes which subsequently followed. From the very beginning of the Soviet participation in the war, duplicity in speech and action had been faithfully practiced by Moscow. Soviet policy toward Poland is a case in point. On the one hand, in July 1941 Stalin signed an agreement with the Polish government in exile, recognizing it as the legal spokesman of the Polish nation and giving it the power to organize a Polish army on Soviet territory. The army was to be recruited from the Polish

POW's taken during the Hitler-Stalin pact. Almost simultaneously, however, a Union of Polish Patriots was set up in Moscow, composed of Polish Communists and extreme left-wingers. This Union, which rejected the Polish government, was then given broadcasting facilities (the Kosciuszko Station) and, following the Soviet rupture of relations with Poland early in 1943, it began to organize a Polish army under Soviet sponsorship. The subsequent transformation of this Union into a Soviet-sponsored government of Poland is a matter of public record.

In addition to the Union of Polish Patriots, the Soviet Union took measures to reactivate the Polish Communists even while the Nazi Armies were driving on Moscow and Stalin was entertaining General Wladyslaw Sikorski, the Polish Prime Minister. Communist elite groups were gathered together and prepared for parachute drops into Poland. After a short period of training and indoctrination, the first of such groups was ready for an air drop as early as September 1941. Following a special briefing by Dimitrov, the Comintern head, the group proceeded to Vyazma, west of Moscow. However, a plane accident prevented the departure, and the rapid Nazi advance prevented a rescheduling of the flight. The uninjured members of the team were evacuated east of Kuibyshev, to a small locality called Kusharenkovo, just north of Ufa. There they met another Polish Communist group which had been similarly trained at the Comintern school in Pushkino near Moscow and which had also been evacuated. They were headed by Jakob Berman, at the time a Comintern instructor, who now assumed direction over both groups. After the Nazi offensive had been halted, the two groups returned to Moscow and were dropped near Warsaw and some Silesian centers on December 28, 1941, and January 3, 1942, respectively.[6] Their task was to prepare for participation in a postwar Polish regime on the assumption that Poland would be freed by Red and not Western armies.[7]

Similarly, evidence could be cited in support of the argument that from the very beginning the other People's Democracies were mere shams. In the case of those parties which, unlike the Yugoslavs,[8] did not have domestic forces at their disposal, the Polish pattern was followed. For instance, a Hungarian committee was set up to direct the Kossuth Radio (a patriotic name, much like the one selected for the Poles) under the control of Matyas Rakosi who, with several colleagues, was charged with drafting plans for postwar Hungarian policies.[9] The Czech Communists, particularly Gottwald, Sverma, Slansky, and Kopecky, all of whom were destined to play major roles in setting up the Communist regime, also were actively involved in drafting Czech postwar programs. In addition, they directed the propaganda campaign from Moscow and published a Czech-language journal.[10] Planned action designed to seize power everywhere seems evident.[11]

However, there is a danger of distortion present in any *ex post facto* interpretation of events, assigning with the wisdom of hindsight both purpose and foresight which at the time might have been less clear. History begins to acquire a logic which in the immediate perspective it could not conceivably have possessed. Events begin to take on a meaning because of the significance they subsequently acquire. It would be more appropriate, therefore, to inquire into what the Soviet extrapolations of the nature of the postwar period were, irrespective of subsequent events which necessarily infused them with further content. Evidence on this is extremely scanty, but a few tentative judgments can be essayed.

Looking more closely at this particular phase and even at the events preceding it, one notices aspects which suggest that the People's Democracy phase, certainly never an end in itself, *was* considered to be a meaningful political expression of the peculiar relationships of domestic and external forces which the Communists felt would exist in postwar Europe. The argument that Soviet domination was the ultimate objective of the People's Democracy phase does not in itself mean that the People's Democracy did not have content of its own, and it certainly does not prove that this phase had to last the three years that it did rather than one, five, or ten.

It would appear that Stalin and his associates, reconsidering their original idea that the world war was essentially a crisis between capitalist states, initially accepted the notion that the anti-Nazi alliance would have some significant implications for Communist conduct in Europe not only during the war but also afterwards. Of course, they probably continued to assume that events would generally unfold in the direction of an eventual Communist triumph, but that during the war and immediately following it a popular-front political situation would reflect most closely the underlying social and economic conditions. How long these conditions would last no one could tell in advance, but as long as they did, caution, flexibility, and "guided democracy" ought to be the essential qualities of Communist conduct lest the West be prematurely jolted into upsetting the developing patterns.

Soviet commitment to such a policy of flexibility is well expressed in their wartime instructions to the Yugoslav and Polish Communists. Moscow, for instance, criticized Tito on March 5, 1942, for allowing the partisan movement to acquire "a communist character" and for not joining in the common struggle with "other Yugoslav patriots" who were not Communists or Communist sympathizers. On another occasion, Moscow eliminated some pro-Soviet slogans from a Tito proclamation which the Soviets were broadcasting on his behalf.[12] Later in the same year, in November, Tito informed Moscow that he was setting up "something like a government, which is to be called the National Liberation Committee of Yugoslavia." Moscow immediately became concerned that this might smack of a Communist takeover and advised Tito "not to fail" to give this committee a broad political character and not to consider it as a government. The message went on: "Do not put it [the committee] in opposition to the Yugoslav government in London. At the present stage, do not raise the question of abolition of the monarchy. Do not put forward any slogan of a republic." [13] In brief, Tito was enjoined not to deviate from the "democratic alliance" formula which, the Soviet leaders felt, represented the political embodiment of the existing pattern of basic forces.

An almost identical situation arose with the Polish Communists. Those who happened to be in the USSR at the outbreak of the Soviet-Nazi war proceeded to hold discussions among themselves and with Dimitrov about the nature of the existing phase of world affairs. Noting that the USSR had abandoned its earlier assessments and was now a partner in an anti-Nazi alliance, the Polish group decided that the "fundamental principle of tactics of all Communist parties in the occupied countries" must be the achievement of mutual understanding with the progressive bourgeois forces for the eventual democratization of the socioeconomic order. The Polish Communists, accordingly, even favored naming their party the Polish Worker-Peasant Party and it was only after some further discussion with Dimitrov that the label of the Polish Workers' Party (PWP) was adopted as the most suitable. After the Polish groups had been dispatched to Poland, they encountered among the local Communists a more "provincial" orientation, not unlike Tito's. Some of the local Communists, viewing the matter from the standpoint of their own local experience, were rather disturbed by the new line and by the new name. They favored the open restoration of the Polish Communist Party under the old name. To some, the new program, which stressed a democratic state with Communist participation in the government and a peaceful transition to the social revolution, appeared to be "incorrect" and possibly even "some new form of provocation." It was only after a series of lengthy and heated discussions that the local Communists accepted the instructions brought by the parachutists, and the Polish Workers' Party was officially launched on the new platform. To underscore its new character, it did not become a section of the Comintern but an entirely separate party. Shortly after, when the Comintern was abolished, the leaders of the PWP dispatched a telegram hailing this development as a factor which would further aid their work among the Polish masses.[14] It was, however, the Moscow-trained and indoctrinated group which helped to set the Polish party on this course.*

None of the above, of course, could be interpreted to mean that Stalin and East European Communists were forever committed to the new analysis on which, subsequently, the People's Democracy was founded. To a Communist, every situation is fluid — the important thing is to detect the speed and direction of the flow of events. Once a new situation arises, or is in the process of arising, the preceding phase must give way and a new phase, with its own imperatives of action, begins.† It seems clear that in East Europe the policy of caution, pursued in rapidly diminishing degrees as time went on, was predicated on an analysis which stressed both the internal and the external complexity of the picture and which presumably assumed that domestic non-Communist forces would be more powerful and get greater support from the West than actually turned out to be the case.

* Some evidence of wartime tension between the groups in Poland and Polish Communists in the USSR is provided by a recently published text of a report sent by the Warsaw Communist leadership to Moscow on January 12, 1944. The report complains of insufficient support for Communist activity in Poland, and at the same time gently protests the decision of the Moscow Communist group to set up a committee with the powers of a provisional government. Noting that matters pertaining to domestic Polish affairs should be decided in Poland, the Warsaw group offered to consider the Moscow committee as its foreign representative. *Ksztaltowanie sie Podstaw Programowych Polskiej Partii Robotniczej* (Warsaw, 1958), pp. 205–221.

† A good example of this type of thinking is provided by Gomulka's answer in May 1945 to those critics who accused the party of either abandoning or masking its Marxist character by putting main stress on popular democracy: "Our slogans and the political line of our party can be incomprehensible only to those to whom the science and theory of Marxism-Leninism is basically distant and foreign, to whom the concepts of democracy and socialism are incomprehensible. . . . The Polish Workers' Party applies most consistently the policy of uniting all the democratic forces of the nation, precisely because it is a Marxist party. And Marxism is not some soulless dogma and Marxist science is not some Talmudistic petrification. . . . The dialectical Marxist method of analyzing phenomena occurring in human society allows the Marxist parties to apply the most correct evaluation of the situation at every stage of the class struggle and in every historical phase. And the correct line of the party depends on the proper evaluation of the political situation." *W Walce o Demokracje Ludowa,* I, 150.

The wartime policy probably had involved assessments stressing both minimum and maximum Soviet objectives. The minimum Soviet expectations, which grew as the battlefields shifted westward, were predicated on a belief that the postwar European situation would present the Communist movement with certain revolutionary opportunities, either through the direct assumption of power or through participation in democratic governments. Stalin's behavior and his communications to the Yugoslav and Polish comrades, suggest, however, that the Soviet leaders feared that rash actions might precipitate a Western reaction or even induce the West to sign a separate agreement with some "bourgeois" anti-Nazi German elements, thereby depriving the USSR of its rightful share of the spoils of victory. In order to prevent concerted efforts to contain the Soviet Union, the tasks of the Communists outside the USSR were to make themselves an inseparable part of any postwar political structure and to participate in the reconstruction of the occupied states. A form of popular front was the very minimum which the USSR expected in East Europe.

Addressing a closed meeting of the party's agit-prop workers of Budapest in May 1945, even before the term People's Democracy had been devised, Rakosi presented an analysis of world affairs which substantiates the interpretation suggested above. Rakosi, undoubtedly reflecting Soviet thinking, suggested that the postwar phase would be dominated by the collapse of the British Empire and by weakened Anglo-American relations. This would allow, in turn, the gradual expansion of the Communist sphere. However, to prevent a mobilization of capitalist resistance, such expansion would have to avoid a radical, revolutionary character. By the same token, internal policy in East Europe, and Hungary in particular, would have to eschew revolutionary measures and would require a "great compromise" with the middle class and the peasantry. He drew the attention of his audience to Lenin's warnings in *"Left-Wing" Communism — An Infantile Disorder*, and estimated that such a transitional phase might last a decade or more.[15]

The USSR's maximum expectations took on greater significance as the West's fundamental disinterest in the area was revealed and as the westward march of the Soviet armies was creating opportunities for *faits accomplis*. The various satellite organizations sponsored in the USSR gradually ceased being mere candidates for partnerships in postwar governments and became the embryos for such governments. "Revolutionary" manifestations would be certain to arise not only in areas under Soviet control but even beyond, where the popular-front phase would lead to a rapid accumulation of Communist strength. The setting up of Communist-dominated governments in East Europe and possibly even further west was not an unreasonable maximum expectation, given the general international picture as it was emerging in 1944 and 1945. The unresolved question, however, still remained: when, and how?

To the Soviets, the pleasantly surprising factors in the postwar European picture were: (1) the overwhelming Soviet strength; (2) the weakness of the non-Communist forces in East Europe; and (3) the rapid demobilization and disengagement of the West. As long as hopes existed for revolutionary situations elsewhere, and as long as the internal Soviet picture made direct Soviet involvement in the management of East Europe less immediately desirable, the phase of diversity and flexibility was the most rational policy to adhere to. Its very vagueness was its strength, and it also freed the USSR from premature ideological commitments.* By 1946, however, both the international picture and Soviet domestic developments called for a return to a more dichotomic image of the world and to an accelerating revolutionary pace. The transition was to be shorter than originally expected.

The Strains of Diversity: Domesticism

Zhdanov's 1946 evaluation accordingly had ominous implications for the existing pattern in East Europe. True, the initial tasks were yet to be fully accomplished in Czechoslovakia; true, in some countries the remnants of hostile political movements were still on the scene. The substance of the situation, however, pointed to the indisputable

* Wladyslaw Bienkowski, a close associate of Gomulka, was one of the chief theoreticians of the evolutionary patterns of change, based on alliance with other social forces, and it might well have been from him that Gomulka derived some of his views. Bienkowski's views were expressed during the war in Communist underground publications and endorsed by Gomulka who, in his speeches, explicitly referred to the "lengthy" struggle necessary before socialism is achieved, and specifically stated: "The road to socialism is neither short nor can it be simplified. For these reasons the Polish Workers' Party fought and fights for a Democratic Poland." He warned against "gross oversimplifications" which suggest that Poland can pass through the transitional stage rapidly. (Gomulka, *W Walce o Demokracje Ludowa*, I, 155.) Revai's article (cited on p. 30) frequently mentioned as proof of the "plot" interpretation, makes it clear that in the case of Hungary it was not until the Cominform sessions in the fall of 1947 and the summer of 1948 that the Hungarian Communists were "taught . . . that a People's Democracy could not stop at any but the final stage of its destruction of the capitalist elements." This again suggests that Communist thinking was essentially in terms of relative phases and the question was only one of how long it would last.

conclusion that effective power was in Communist hands and that the area was in the Soviet camp. Yet the existing institutional and ideological diversity was by 1946, and even more so by 1947, tending to produce what, from the Soviet standpoint, were disquieting symptoms. These symptoms appeared to be precisely the product of the doctrinal and practical insistence on recognizing the specific requirements of each individual situation. The various Communist leaders, most of whom had been either Comintern or NKVD agents and had always displayed the deepest loyalty to Soviet interests, were now becoming too engrossed in their own domestic tasks. The Soviet leaders, on the other hand, were finding that it was more difficult to run several Communist states than to run one. What had begun as an operation based on the complete identification of Soviet objectives with the objectives of the local Communists was now developing certain, admittedly very minor, but potentially significant, crevices.

This development might be described as involving the onset of a form of parochialism, or, more broadly, a malaise of "domesticism" in orientation and emphasis. Such a domestic perspective was not the same thing as the later phenomenon of National Communism or Titoism.[16] Domesticism is merely a certain implicit perspective which is inevitably acquired by even the most loyal Soviet functionaries when they are assigned to specific tasks within the framework of more loosely defined ideological conceptions. It may involve a frequently unconscious preoccupation with local, domestic Communist objectives, at the expense of broader, international Soviet goals. Absence of direct external purpose, such as struggle against world capitalism, or of direct Soviet involvement in the management of a given country, generates the domestic orientation in many local Communists. But once the issue is obvious and the priorities are again clearly stated, this type of Communist should adjust to the new values without hesitation. In East Europe, the acceptance of transitional diversity was closely linked to the problem of the domestic perspective, for the principle which accepted flexibility implied the need to adjust to the varying internal conditions. The Communist *apparatchiki*, entering with the Red Army, were originally dedicated to what appeared to be, at least conceptually, a simple proposition: to attain and consolidate power in keeping with the ideological insights into the unfolding events (this being linked closely with the interests of the USSR). But as their power began to jell more firmly, some of them began to realize that the task of building Communism is complex, that there is an absence of clearcut, detailed ideological guides to every specific situation, that human inventiveness and initiative must complement the broad ideological framework. Under these circumstances, and given the ideological definition stressing the uniqueness and peculiarities of the People's Democracy, many of them gravitated toward domesticism.

Domesticism expressed itself in a number of ways. The hard-boiled, wholly unsentimental secretary of the Polish Workers' Party, Gomulka – who did not hesitate to exterminate the opposition or to endorse the Soviet deportations of thousands of young anti-German underground fighters – by 1947 found himself defending the nationalist traditions of the Polish Socialist Party against critics upholding the relatively weak Rosa Luxembourg faction in the Polish working-class movement. It is doubtful that Gomulka had become infected by the romantic notions of patriotism, especially since it was clear that Communist efforts to attract the socialists were encountering resistance among the highly nationally conscious proletariat which viewed the Communists with suspicion. Gomulka's appeal, however, does not seem to have been based entirely on expediency. He apparently shared the feeling of many left-wing Poles that the Communist Party had erred in the past by divorcing itself from the mainstream of patriotism, thereby appearing to be purely a Soviet agency. "The fundamental error of the Communists was that, while fully appreciating the question of struggle for the social emancipation of the working masses, they did not sufficiently appreciate the question of independence. . . . The struggle for social emancipation cannot be separated from struggle for national emancipation," Gomulka warned his comrades.[17] Seeing no basic incompatibility between Polish national interests and those of world Communism, Gomulka presumably felt both ideologically and politically justified in his stand.

The commitment to building socialism in Poland by a maximum of domestic effort also affected some of Poland's relations with her Communist-ruled neighbors. In the case of the Germans, where the SED was only in organizational stages, the Polish Communists preached and practiced a fanatical national hatred somewhat out of step with the doctrinal concepts of relations between nationalities. In this they were echoed by the Czechs, while the SED leadership, anxious not to be saddled with responsibility for the Oder-Neisse line, at first even hinted broadly to the Germans that it was not committed in favor of this line.*

* Cf. *Neues Deutschland*, September 14, 1946, in which a lead article, entitled "Clarity on the Eastern Question," quoted Wilhelm Pieck as stating that the frontier is only provisional and that "the necessities of life of our people will be taken into

Relations between the Polish Communist regime, grasping for domestic popularity, and the Czech government of Klement Gottwald, who was to prove himself Stalin's most loyal shield-bearer in East Europe but who was also concerned at this time with enhancing the popularity of the Czech Communist Party, were similarly uneasy. They reached the point that the Communist Prime Minister felt compelled to imply publicly that the two regimes did not quite see eye to eye. In a speech which stressed, above all, Czechoslovakia's friendship for and alliance with the USSR and, secondly, Tito's Yugoslavia, Gottwald expressed the Czech willingness to enter into similar arrangements "with other States with the same interests, if the relations of such States with us warrant it." And then he added: "This applies in particular to Poland. However, it is necessary that our vital interests, which we cannot sacrifice, should find the fullest recognition and respect on the Polish side." [18] (The Czechs at the time were making claims to areas around Kladzko, while the Poles were unhappy about the Cieszyn settlement.*) The relations between the Hungarian and Rumanian Communists were even worse, and at the Paris Peace Conference the two sides had a sharp altercation after which their relations were characterized by marked coolness.[19] The Hungarian Communists had hoped that a nominal concession on the Transylvania issue would improve their domestic position.

The natural preoccupation of the East European Communists with the consolidation of their power within the individual states led some of them to lose sight of the broader international considerations. Again, this was not necessarily a matter of pursuing an independent, "national" line; it was rather the consequence of their instructions to take advantage of the domestic situation and to manipulate it accordingly so that, under the external protection of the USSR, domestic power consolidation would take place. Interpreting this to mean that they should take advantage of every opportunity to build up socialism, the Polish and Czech Communists reacted favorably in July 1947 to the American invitation to participate in the Marshall Plan. They

---

account" if "democratic" Germans represent German interests. The paper also quoted Max Fechner, the leading SED candidate in Berlin: "I would like to declare that the SED will oppose any diminution (*Verkleinerung*) of German territory. The eastern frontier is a provisional frontier and can be fixed only at the peace conference." The SED conducted at the time a whispering campaign to the effect that it, if supported by the Germans, would be more effective in gaining Russian support for a revision of the frontier, a tack very disturbing to the Polish Communists.

* The southern Cieszyn (Teschen) area had been seized by Poland during the Munich crisis; it had been taken by force by the Czechs in 1919, when Poland was embroiled in war with Russia. In 1945 the Czechs regained this territory.

presumably felt that the economic advantages accruing to their countries through such participation would make their political tasks easier, thereby furthering their own and Soviet objectives. They apparently did not read Zhdanov's speech of the preceding November very carefully. The Soviet leadership had developed by then a "deeper" insight into American motives. Accordingly, the Soviet leadership reacted violently, condemning the plan and peremptorily announcing in Moscow that Poland had decided not to participate. In the case of the Czechs, a delegation went to Moscow, and shortly afterwards the Czech position was clarified.[20] The leaderships of the two parties were thus forcefully reminded that in their own domestic pursuits they must not forget the implications of the division of the world into hostile camps.

In some respects, the most glaring example of domesticism in theory and practice was supplied by what appears to have been the most orthodox, the most Stalinist, the most Soviet type of regime in East Europe at the time: Tito's. His domestic orthodoxy, his insistence on considering the Yugoslav People's Democracy as merely a Soviet Republic, led him not only to adopt a rather condescending attitude toward his East European comrades but also to identify the interests of world Communism with his own, rather than the other way around. As a result, Tito became increasingly insistent that the USSR, and presumably the Soviet bloc in general, endorse his territorial ambitions in Austria and Italy, and that they consider them as crucial interests of international Communism as well.[21] This reversal in values must have been somewhat discomforting to Stalin, though possibly, given Tito's wartime behavior, not surprising. Nonetheless, the rather thinly veiled Yugoslav suggestions that the Communist alliance be prepared to go to war against the West for the sake of Yugoslav claims to Trieste — thereby throwing on the scales of history everything which had been built up at such cost through so many years — must have appeared as the height of provincialism. And it could have occurred only within the flexible framework of institutional and ideological diversity.

The Balkan Union scheme, originally encouraged by Moscow and planned by Tito and Dimitrov, can also be viewed from the perspective of domesticism. At first a scheme designed to weld together some of the Balkan states under the hegemony of Dimitrov and Tito, certainly tried and trusted Stalinists, it must have appeared to Moscow as a desirable arrangement, quite in keeping with the ideological assumptions about the ultimate pattern of relations among socialist states. In both countries the Communist parties enjoyed a measure of popular appeal unparalleled elsewhere in East Europe with the exception of Czechoslovakia, while their leaders were unusually distinguished Communists. In fact, according to Dedijer, Tito's court biographer, Stalin whetted Tito's vanity with veiled hints about bequeathing to him, some day, the mantle of leadership of international Communism, and as a token of his esteem (and also as a convenient arrangement) encouraged Tito to dominate Albania, where the Yugoslavs could be trusted to set up an orthodox regime.[22] A Balkan Union would have accordingly constituted a solid unit, self-supporting but loyal, and more able on its own to effectively withstand possible Western pressure.

However, by 1947 a Western challenge was unlikely, and Soviet control over the area was uncontested. At the same time, Tito's and Dimitrov's enthusiasm for the Balkan Union appeared to be dominated more by considerations derived from their domestic concerns and from purely personal factors (for example, Tito's rather flattering image of himself as the second-ranking Communist leader in the world *) than by broader perspectives. There is no doubt that some of the economic difficulties encountered at home in both countries could partially have been resolved through closer ties.[23] Their missionary zeal — Tito made a number of trips to the other neighboring capitals, failing in one instance to inform Moscow about it,[24] and signed treaties of friendship with his former enemy neighbors even before the USSR did † — began to bear fruit: favorable reactions to a Balkan Union, eventually even expanded into an East European one, came from the Poles and the Rumanians. Both Dimitrov and Tito must have viewed this as a desirable and a normal historical development. To both of them, this larger framework seemed dictated both by doctrine and by good politics. It would be the first stage in the construction of a multinational Communist society. To these flamboyant and fiery leaders with rich revolutionary histories, this offered a larger stage on which to gain Communist virtue and to be acclaimed for it. Whatever the motives, in late 1947 the two leaders were furthering the union not only in response to Soviet prodding but with an increment of personal enthusiasm which rapidly transformed the venture into their own private little enterprise.

* Dimitrov, too, given his Comintern position, may have had personal ambitions on this score. Ruth Fischer, for instance, felt that if there should ever be "a Stalinist United States of Europe, one of its principal officers may be Georgi Dimitrov." *Stalin and German Communism*, p. 309.

† With Bulgaria, November 27, 1947; with Hungary, December 8, 1947; with Rumania, December 19, 1947. Cf. table on p. 109, Chapter 6.

By that time, however, the scheme of a more rational and solid organization for Communist-controlled states in the Balkans no longer suited the requirements of the situation as the Soviet leadership probably saw it. In January 1948, after Dimitrov's public press interview in Sofia of January 23 in which he envisaged a future federation embracing even Poland and Czechoslovakia (and Greece, should the Greek Communist partisans succeed), *Pravda* published an explicit critique that left no interpretative doubts. Federation or confederation was not desirable, *Pravda* stressed, and it was much more important to develop internal forces in the individual states "as correctly stated in the known declaration of the nine Communist Parties" (referring to the Cominform declaration).[25] The original imprimatur for the project was thus withdrawn. Following this, both the Yugoslavs and the Bulgarians were invited to Moscow where they were charged with conduct, in Molotov's words, "inadmissible either from the Party or from the state point of view," while Stalin personally castigated Dimitrov for behaving "as if you are still the Secretary of the Comintern."[26] The crux of the matter, however, was again the problem of diversity's having outlived its usefulness and actually creating difficulties. Stalin stated it bluntly: "Mistakes are not the issue: the issue is conceptions different from our own." * [27]

A similar, though less directly political, instance involved the Polish-Czech efforts to establish closely knit economic collaboration, the territorial conflict notwithstanding. The Polish-Czech Economic Collaboration Convention of July 1947 provided for a permanent economic council, with eight specialized commissions, to guide industrial development collaboration in the Silesian basin, jointly develop energy resources, and eventually establish a waterways system linking the Oder with the Danube. Hungary was to be included subsequently, especially in view of its bauxite resources. If effected, such collaboration would have materially strengthened the Polish and Czech position in Central Europe, and its failure to materialize was related closely to the potential political implications.

In brief, what in 1945 and 1946 had been a sensible adjustment to the complexities of the new situation was tending by 1947 to drive a wedge in the community of interests of the Soviet leadership and the East European leaderships. The local Communist leaders were taking

---

* One upshot of this incident was the formal commitment made by Belgrade on Moscow's insistence that Belgrade would consult Moscow before taking any foreign-policy steps. Such a formal arrangement was hardly needed in the case of the other parties, which were much more dependent on Soviet support. Dedijer, p. 324.

their domestic tasks too seriously, and, in their search for the best possible solutions to the problems facing them at home, they were not always sufficiently conscious of broader Soviet goals. Even a Dimitrov
or a Bierut, faced with truly overwhelming burdens not only of political consolidation but also of economic reconstruction, naturally
tended in time to interpret his role in terms of the various forces and
elements that he had to cope with. Considering the Soviet unwillingness to step in and set up open Soviet occupation authorities, and
considering the Soviet insistence that they would supply help only to
prevent a domestic revolt against the Communists and only minimal
help in launching internal Communist operations, the local Communists could not avoid developing a certain domestic perspective in
the execution of their tasks.

Despite various acts of Soviet interference, considerable areas of
initiative were left to the local Communists during this phase. They
had to justify ideologically to themselves and to others the roles they
were playing; they had to build up their organizations; they had to
control the patterns of reconstruction so that they would proceed in
the desirable direction; they had to define the position of their particular states not only vis-à-vis the Soviet Union but also to one another.
The Soviet Union could remove or paralyze the anti-Communist
threat, but the consolidation of Communist power was still in large
measure up to the Communists themselves. Under these circumstances,
a Polish-Czech economic collaboration, or even Marshall Plan aid,
might have appeared to the Communists involved as the most desirable way of achieving their domestic political and economic goals, and
as in keeping with their ideological notions about interstate relations.
"National Communism" was not yet involved: no choice was being
made between the interests of the larger unit and those of the particular state involved. In fact, in every case it was assumed that the larger
unit would benefit from such decisions, since a community of interests
was said to exist on all levels.

The Cominform: An Antithesis

To Stalin, viewing the situation from the perspective of his own
efforts to re-establish totalitarian unity at home and noticing the growing external tensions, the phase of diversity must have seemed to have
reached the stage of its own antithesis: having fulfilled its general
purposes, it now made imperative a greater emphasis on unity. This
unity would be attained through a more conscious perception of the
objectives of all Communist power at home and abroad, through a

common discussion of practices to eliminate the excessive commitment to narrow national interests, and through the drawing of a common ideological line which would de-emphasize the existing diversities in theory and practice.

The founding of the Cominform was the Soviet response to the challenge presented by the phase of diversity. It was to initiate the transition to more common patterns of development for which the necessary basis had been laid by the popular fronts, by national appeals, by the mobilization of the working class and by the beginning of social and economic transformation. Ironically, it was the Yugoslavs, with their distaste for compromise, who, as early as 1945 had first suggested that some sort of international organization be revived to further the "exchange of views and . . . the exchange of the wealth of experience" between Communist parties.[28] It is not difficult to surmise that from the standpoint of the zealous Yugoslavs such an institutional device would have served to assert more violent revolutionary patterns in East Europe. To the Soviet leaders, however, the application of such violent patterns in countries without strong indigenous parties would have meant a more direct and a more costly Soviet involvement in domestic affairs, not to mention international complications. This inhibition was less marked by mid-1946, when Stalin himself broached the issue of a new Communist International to Tito, encouraging him to take the initiative in organizing it.[29] Stalin's logic in choosing the Yugoslavs for this undertaking was commendable: if the phase of diversity was now to give way to its logical antithesis, the Yugoslavs could play a significant role in encouraging the other states to adopt, not only on the Soviet but also on the Yugoslav example, more uniform political and economic patterns. And such community of behavior would necessarily induce a more common ideological perspective in which the primacy of universal goals (equated necessarily with the USSR's) would be asserted. Conversely, the assertion of a common perspective would help establish more common patterns of action. In both, the Yugoslavs were far ahead of the rest and close to the USSR.

After some months of consultations, the formal inauguration of the new International took place in September 1947 at Szklarska Poreba, a small resort town in southwestern Poland. Zhdanov, the chief Soviet spokesman, delivered to the assembled representatives of the ruling Communist parties (except Albania's), and of France and Italy, a broad analysis of the international scene. He indicted the United States on charges of conspiring for world supremacy by exploiting the destruction of its two capitalist rivals, Germany and Japan, as well as by exploiting weakened France and Great Britain. The consequence of this American design was the division of mankind into two camps, Zhdanov noted. For this reason the relations among Communist parties, particularly those in power, must be especially intimate, although, Zhdanov hastened to add, they must be based on "equality and mutual respect." The Soviet spokesman felt further that:

the present position of the Communist Parties has its shortcomings. Some comrades understood the dissolution of the Comintern to imply the elimination of all ties, of all contact between the fraternal Communist Parties. But experience has shown that such mutual isolation of the Communist Parties is wrong, harmful, and in fact unnatural.[30]

This theme was echoed in the first resolution passed by the new Cominform, "Resolution on the Interchange of Experience and Coordination of Activities of the Parties Represented at the Conference":

The Conference states that the absence of contacts among the Communist Parties participating at this Conference is a serious shortcoming in the present situation. Experience has shown that such lack of contacts among the Communist Parties is wrong and harmful. . . . [It was decided to] charge the Information Bureau with the organization of interchange of experience and, if need be, coordination of the activities of the Communist Parties on the basis of mutual agreement.[31]

The other Soviet delegate, Malenkov, devoted a good part of his report to the internal Soviet scene, and his emphasis on the need for internal ideological uniformity in the USSR itself left no doubt as to the close links between domestic Soviet developments and the reassessment of the East European scene. Of the East Europeans, all of whom "informed" one another of their domestic programs and progress, the most assertive tone was taken by the Yugoslavs, who again took the opportunity to assert their ideological orthodoxy, repeatedly stressing the social-revolutionary content of their activities and the great similarity in Soviet and Yugoslav patterns.[32]

There is probably little reason to doubt that to many East European Communist leaders, and not only to the Yugoslavs, the founding of the Cominform was a welcome development. The very process of forced internal change and the sharpening of conflicts was creating increasing pressure toward dependence on the USSR. Those who had originally held to an image of a People's Democracy in which social

PROBLEMS OF DIVERSITY 61

progress and change would be furthered by the cooperation of all
good-willed citizens were rapidly finding that the realities of politics
were shattering their dreams.* For the Moscow-trained *apparatchiki*,
furthermore, there was a certain security to be gained from conformity. Liberated from the tensions and strains of diversity which
frequently served to reveal their own domestic weakness, the East
European Communists could now expect the transitional period of
Soviet noninvolvement to give way to more direct Soviet participation in the "socialist construction." The situation would be much
less blurred. The compromises and conciliatory gestures which the
preceding phase required—and which Stalinist cadets like Rakosi or
Bierut or Gottwald probably found distasteful—could now be jettisoned. They would no longer need to plead for the support of the
"progressive" non-Communist forces while at the same time fearing
being swamped by them. Moderation, which to a fanatic Bolshevik
is a sacrifice greater than any suffering for the cause, could now give
way to class struggle, to violence, to real revolution, the victory of
which would be assured by greater Soviet involvement.

As far as is known, the founding of the Cominform was opposed
by only one prominent leader, Wladyslaw Gomulka. His opposition
did not evaporate into thin air once the line between domestic and
"larger" (hence Soviet) interests was drawn.† He himself subsequently admitted having opposed the organization of the Information
Bureau, and, in the deliberations of the constituent meetings, took a
somewhat deviant position on such matters as collectivization and the
relationship of the Communists to Polish socialists whom Gomulka,
even in his published report, defended by implication.‡ This came at

* Some of the left-wing socialists might have subscribed to this point of view,
and even among some Communists there were those who believed that a maximum of
diversity and a minimum of violence were necessary to build a popular program of
reform. Also, some well-known intellectuals belonged to this category of non-Communist idealists, Czeslaw Milosz for one.

† Gomulka's orientation is revealed by the following statement made at the
First Congress of the Polish Workers' Party: "there are those among the former
members of the Polish Communist Party [i.e., the one abolished in 1938 by the Comin-
tern] who have not been able to feel themselves into the new situation, have not been
able to understand it, have not ceased being narrow sectarians. It is necessary that they
also begin to think with the categories *of the nation, of the state* in which we now
co-govern." *W Walce o Demokracje Ludowa*, I, 323; italics added.

‡ There are striking parallels between Gomulka's behavior here and at the fortieth
anniversary meeting commemorating the Bolshevik revolution, November 1957 (see
Chapter 12). In the words of one of the participants at the Cominform founding
(E. Reale, *Nascita del Cominform*, Mondadori, 1958, p. 35), Gomulka's report "was
most noteworthy for the reservations which the chief of the Polish Party advanced
against collectivization of land in which he underlined the difficulties in a country

a time when, according to Zhdanov, the world was divided into two camps and the socialists were "objectively" the agents of imperialism. Gomulka is also said to have taken the position that no resolution of the meeting should be made public and that the meeting itself be kept secret.[33] With the memories of the Polish Communist Party's dissolution by the Comintern in 1938 apparently still fresh in his mind,* and presumably fearful lest the Cominform give a new, arbitrary shape to his "Polish way to socialism," Gomulka's independent line meant the transformation of his domesticism into the first case of what came to be known as national Communism — that is, the explicit assignment of priority to internal considerations even if openly challenged by those who consider themselves to be the central spokesmen of international Communism.†

The founding of the Cominform, much more than the subsequent break with Tito, meant the end of the phase of diversity and the beginnings of what is most satisfactorily identified as Stalinism — a period of total conformity in the relations among Communist states. For a while afterwards, a certain degree of diversity inevitably lingered on and expressed itself in such incidents as the Balkan Union affair, or the opposition of the Polish Politburo to the June 1948 Cominform resolution enjoining collectivization,‡ but the mounting assertion of the Cominform's control over the Communist power structures meant a rapid acceleration in the direction of uniformity. The problem of Titoism arose as a consequence of this effort to establish hierarchy and coordination. As long as the phase of diversity existed, Titoism — at that time a form of premature Stalinism — could be tolerated. It was no longer tolerable once conformity was estab-

---

such as Poland which is fundamentally agricultural. . . . I was struck by the complete absence of any rhetoric and above all by the absence of these exaggerated fountains of gratitude, expressions of recognition, etc. for the Soviets which characterized the other speeches. I was struck, moreover, by a certain tone of coldness toward the proposition of activating a permanent consultative organization among the various parties, truly a strange thing on the part of those who had, at least officially, taken the initiative for bringing about the meeting."

* This writer was particularly impressed in the course of his conversations with Polish Communists to learn to what extent this single incident colored Soviet-Polish Communist relations.

† The 1948 Gomulka deviation was caused by "his lack of understanding of the essential idea of the mutual relationship between the countries of the People's Democracy and the USSR and the leading role of the All-Union Communist Party in the international front of the struggle against imperialism." *Pravda*, September 9, 1948, accounts of the Resolution of the Polish Workers' Party.

‡ The Polish delegation even opposed the use of the word "collectivization" but finally voted for the resolution. Gomulka was no longer a delegate. See *Nowe Drogi*, no. 10 (1956), p. 90.

lished because the essence of that conformity was a clear-cut institutional and ideological hierarchy. Without that hierarchy, compliance, discipline, and single-minded unity of purpose could not be achieved. The situation can be compared to that of a successful guerilla army which is eventually organized into a professional military establishment. As long as operations are conducted by relatively self-contained units, strategic and, especially, tactical elasticity is essential. Decisions, in keeping with the grand conception of purpose, are made on the spot in terms of the conditions encountered. But once the enemy is on the run and the guerilla units begin to be merged with the professional army which had finally made its appearance on the scene, the bravest, the most successful, and hence the proudest guerilla units may be a far greater source of difficulty than those which have done less or in fact little.

The various incidents cited in the Soviet-Yugoslav correspondence, involving the role of the Soviet ambassador, the Soviet officers, the Soviet efforts to organize spy networks,[34] were expressions of tension inherent in this situation which came to the fore once the processes of unification were launched. It is ironic to recall that the formation of the Cominform had first been urged by Tito himself because of his orthodoxy in behavior and aspirations. What he had forgotten was that imitation within diversity did not imply the same political consequences as imitation within uniformity. In the former, imitation was an act of independent decision made in terms of one's own specific situation. In the latter case, imitation led to subordination to the center and that subordination Tito was not willing to acknowledge. But until the very end of their association with Stalin, Tito and his colleagues trusted that an arrangement providing for their local autonomy could be worked out and that an open conflict with Moscow could be averted. Hence an ideological content in Tito's position was lacking at the time of the break.* Their domesticism, which only Stalin transformed into national Communism by his expulsion of the Yugoslavs from the Cominform, blinded them to the nature of Stalinism, which they had practised domestically, as an international system. They failed to perceive that subordination was an essential quality of Stalinism.

On Stalin's side, the decision to launch the Cominform meant that a new phase in Communist relations was beginning, and that, given

---

* Tito admitted as much in speaking to the Central Committee session which, on April 12, 1948, upheld his resistance to Moscow: "Comrades, remember, this is not a matter here of any theoretical discussion. . . . Comrades, the point here, first and foremost, is the relations between one state and another." Dedijer, p. 338.

the Yugoslavs' devotion to himself and to the Soviet Union, the achievement of Yugoslav subordination would not be a difficult task. He was, therefore, obviously willing to bring the undersurface conflict out into the open on the assumption that the Yugoslavs would submit. But Stalin overlooked — maybe because of Tito's ideological orthodoxy — Tito's independent power. This miscalculation, which was revealed in the aftermath of Tito's expulsion from the Cominform, later sharpened the trends toward conformity in East Europe.

Titoism, however, had not begun the new phase; it was its first symptom. The new phase started because diversity in theory and practice seemed dangerous and no longer properly reflected the times. Domestic consolidation of the Communist parties, which had been the Soviet goal, had required various internal adjustments which necessarily called for some measure of diversity. Stalin's decision to insist on conformity meant that a far greater degree of Soviet involvement would be necessary, with one of its costs being a further decline in the domestic sources of support for the Communist parties. For reasons already sketched, Stalin was prepared to pay this price. Titoism, Stalin's inadvertent creation, added to this calculation a further dimension: that internal practices on the Soviet model did not guarantee loyalty to the USSR and that premature Communist power, even on the Stalinist model, could have a corrupting influence on the Communist leaders. This fear and suspicion of Communist power abroad was what the experience with Tito bequeathed to the Stalinist era, thereby intensifying Stalin's insistence that ideology and power must have a common and undisputed source.

THE SECOND PHASE
1947–1953

STALINISM — INSTITUTIONAL AND IDEOLOGICAL UNIFORMITY

The cult of personality cannot be confined solely to the person of Stalin. The cult of personality is a certain system which prevailed in the Soviet Union and which was grafted to probably all Communist Parties. . . .

The essence of this system consisted in the fact that an individual, hierarchic ladder of cults was created. Each such cult comprised a given area in which it functioned. In the bloc of socialist states it was Stalin who stood at the top of this hierarchic ladder of cults. All those who stood on lower rungs of the ladder bowed their heads before him. Those who bowed their heads were not only the other leaders of the Communist Party of the Soviet Union and the leaders of the Soviet Union, but all the leaders of Communist and Workers' Parties of the countries of the socialist camp. The latter, that is, the First Secretaries of the Central Committees of the Parties of the various countries who sat on the second rung of the ladder of the cult of personality, in turn donned the robes of infallibility and wisdom. But their cult radiated only on the territory of the countries where they stood at the top of the national cult ladder. This cult could be called only a reflected brilliance, a borrowed light. It shone as the moon does.

— Wladyslaw Gomulka, 1956

CHAPTER 4 —

The Theory Reconsidered

Love of the Soviet Union does not tolerate the slightest reservation. The road into the morass of treason indeed begins on the
inclined plane of reservations and doubts regarding the correctness of the policy of the Soviet Union. — *Rude Pravo*, May 25,
1952

THE previous diversity of views and constitutional arrangements
could not be maintained in an era characterized by the omniscience of
a single individual whose views were considered to be a universally
applicable dogma. "So calm, wise, human, sincere and illuminated by
the stars. . . . Behold! This is Stalin!" mused a Czech broadcast.[1]

The imposition of doctrinal uniformity took place over a period
of about two years, from mid-1947 to some time in 1949, although its
aftermath lasted much longer as the new doctrines continued to be
elaborated in fuller detail. The major change, however, was not
merely a matter of asserting Stalin's position of infallibility and universality. While that certainly played a role, the theoretical changes
were also a response to the dictates of the actual situation and a guide
to actions designed to shape the future. In other words, the theory
changed because the requirements of power had changed; but, in addition, the requirements of power changed because the conceptions of
the type of power desirable also changed. Ideology and power again
interacted.

The Reassessment

In time, the new reassessments developed a reality of their own,
particularly since individuals often tend to associate themselves with
certain policies in order also to promote their own interests. Gradually, the very process of shaping a policy begins to affect the individuals themselves and in turn to shape their thinking and actions. When
this happens in an organized group, the impact on thought and behavior is that much intensified. The concept of the class struggle may
serve as an example. Among the East European Communist leaders

there were certainly many whose firm belief in the need of intensified class struggle even after the seizure of power (a classical Stalinist contribution to Marxism-Leninism) was based on a combination of "rational" assumptions about the nature of rapid social transformation and of deep personal animosity toward the former ruling classes. Many of them had been alienated from their societies and harbored bitter hatreds. Some of the Jewish Communists had been exposed to anti-Semitism. The Stalinist notions of the class struggle could, therefore, be quite appealing and provide the justification of historical inevitability for actions which the Communist leaders also might have wished to carry out for reasons of personal gratification. That in waging such class struggle they would be acquiring Communist "virtue" was, of course, gratuitous; and moral problems were resolved by this historical inevitability: "when one chops wood, chips must fly."

During the earlier transitional period of diversity, some measure of differentiation of views among the various leaderships was inescapable. Faced with a variety of postwar challenges, each leadership had to devise its own ideological concepts and political weapons. Within the limits imposed by Soviet sponsorship, this meant a certain amount of creative debate. But once the diversity began to narrow down, the previous divisions of opinion gave some leaders a welcome opportunity to castigate those whose views had least approached the newly established and more militant standard. They could now assert that their own earlier differences in tone had been a method of expressing their misgivings with the policy of neomoderation, and they could now claim credit for having deviated least from a standard which then only potentially existed. Competition in loyalty to the USSR, a vehicle for advancement and the fulfillment of one's own views, thus rapidly developed and accelerated the process of redefining some of the basic domestic assumptions of the East European Communists. A few held to their original views and had to be removed. Some had always viewed the preceding phase with a measure of suspicion and were now triumphant. Some shifted their position out of fear and desire to accommodate. Some shifted because they genuinely believed that the situation itself had changed sufficiently to warrant some new evaluations.

That the domestic scene in East Europe had shifted appreciably in the direction of more common patterns is undeniable, and this, considering the Marxian assumptions about the relation between reality and ideology, was bound to affect the ideology. Between the founding of the Cominform and the expulsion of Tito, the Communist parties completed the elimination of the articulate opposition and were ready to pass from the stage of consolidation to a stage of "socialist construction" (see Chapter 5). The differences between the Communist-ruled states diminished; the similarities became more marked. The Soviet Union was displaying a more active attitude toward the domestic affairs of the People's Democracies, culminating in the establishment of the Cominform. On a larger plane, these shifts and developments were certainly not immune to the growing international tension and the accumulating evidence that Communist parties in France and Italy could come to power only through violent means. A more militant Communist bloc seemed dictated by history.

The initial reconsideration of the meaning of the People's Democracy, and of the pertinent ideological problems, proceeded at an uneven pace. The stimuli which came from the Cominform meeting found the Hungarians and the Bulgarians most responsive. They were gradually joined by the Polish party, while the Rumanians and the Czechs lagged somewhat behind. Apart from the very important consideration that clear ideological guidance was at this time still unavailable, there were the obvious domestic reasons for this initial variety in response. In Rumania, the Communist Party was barely completing the consolidation of its internal power and, shortly after the first Cominform session, had unburdened itself of the monarchy. (A People's Republic was proclaimed on December 30, 1947.) There even might have been some genuine doubt as to whether Rumania had yet become a People's Democracy — Zhdanov certainly implied as much in his first speech to the Cominform when he made a vague distinction between People's Democracies and countries like Rumania which had just "broken with imperialism." In Czechoslovakia, where the Communist Party had been heading the ruling coalition since 1946, it was not until the February coup of 1948 that Communist power was firmly consolidated and the Communist leaders could devote their attention to broader problems. In the meantime, they maintained a cautious silence. In Poland, where the ideological problem was linked with the person of Gomulka, the conflict was sharpened by an internal power struggle which came to the fore immediately after Tito's expulsion.[2]

The patterns of reassessment seem to fall into the following chronological order:

(1) From the 1947 creation of the Cominform to about the time of Tito's expulsion — assertion of certain basic principles common to all People's Democracies.

(2) From Tito's expulsion to late 1948 — negation of the most extreme aspects of the formerly alleged uniqueness of the People's Democracy and the assertion of certain common programs of action.

(3) After late 1948 and in early 1949 — elaboration of a common interpretation of the People's Democracy, of its "constitutional" forms and its pattern of growth.

Although the change can be dated to the 1947 Cominform meeting, that gathering did not lay down an explicit new line for all to follow, other than to stress the need for close collaboration between parties and "exchange of experience." In his report to the meeting, Vulko Chervenkov even repeated Dimitrov's earlier adjurations about the Bulgarian road to socialism and the irrelevance of the dictatorship of the proletariat insofar as Bulgaria was concerned. His remarks, it seems, were still considered perfectly proper and received due publicity. Shortly afterwards, however, once Stalin's two-camp theory had made its impact, a spate of pronouncements appeared in which the first shifts in the existing ideological framework became apparent. The reconsideration of the theory was under way.

Matyas Rakosi and Vulko Chervenkov, the latter soon to become Dimitrov's successor, were at the time the most active discussants of Communist-bloc affairs and frequent contributors to the Cominform journal. Rakosi, an impatient Stalinist *apparatchik*, eager to get on with the job and anxious to take advantage of the avenue opened to him by the Cominform sessions, might have also aspired to Tito's mantle as the most trusted East European Stalinist. For Chervenkov, the question of the ailing and aged Dimitrov's successor was probably not irrelevant, and rapid identification of his fate with the new trends was not likely to harm his prospects. They were aided by occasional hints from the chief editor of the Cominform journal (*For a Lasting Peace, for a People's Democracy*), P. F. Yudin, a CPSU *apparatchik* personally selected for the job by Stalin. Initially, the emphasis was put on two major aspects: the role of the party and the role of the USSR. It was stressed that the Communist Party was the mainspring in the process of "democratization" which East Europe was experiencing and that, therefore, its role must not be equated with that of the "other democratic" parties with which it happened to be collaborating. True, the Communist Party was a member of a coalition, or a national or patriotic front (depending on the given country), but while enjoying equality with the other parties, it stood above them because of its sense of purpose, which went far beyond the more limited perspectives of the other parties.[3] The claim to one-party hegemony was incipient in these views.

The Soviet Model

The growing and articulate emphasis on the leading role of the Communist Party was accompanied by mounting stress on the ideological significance and relevance of the Soviet system itself. The earlier tendency not to stress Soviet experience, which, indeed, most East Europeans did not view with much admiration, gave way more and more to an insistence on the leadership of the Soviet Union.[4] But this aspect was not yet interpreted to mean that ways to socialism may not differ; in fact, some parties continued early in 1948 to stress their own way to socialism while acknowledging Soviet leadership — a balance which was to be re-established only in 1957.[5] That the concept of Soviet primacy, however, had certain theoretical and practical content soon became apparent from several hints dropped by the editors of the Cominform journal. On February 15, 1948, Yudin published a lengthy missive on the occasion of the centenary of the Communist Manifesto, which he used to lay particular stress on the general applicability of the Soviet experience. A month later, an editorial in the same publication, entitled "The Ideological Weapon of the Communist Parties," explicitly called upon the Parties to "generalize" their experience, and severely admonished those party organizations whose leaders "are lukewarm propagandists of Marxist theory" and who, therefore, "inevitably lose all sense of perspective, and from whom one can expect the most extravagant and pseudo-Marxist 'ideas' and 'theories.'" The editorial then flatly asserted:

The Communist Party of the Soviet Union (Bolsheviks), created and educated by the great geniuses of revolutionary theory, Lenin and Stalin, serves as an example to all fraternal Communist Parties of how to approach the development of Marxist theory. . . .[6]

During the summer of 1948 events began to move more rapidly, particularly in view of the mounting tension with the Yugoslavs. The Cominform met and, apart from dealing with the Yugoslav case, established certain general principles for the construction of socialism along the lines of known Stalinist precepts. The meeting adopted the position that socialist transformation cannot be limited to the towns, but must be pushed into the countryside where Soviet experience can fruitfully be applied.[7] At the end of August and beginning of September, the Central Committee of the Polish Workers' Party convened to deal with the problem posed by Gomulka's persistence in holding to his "antiquated" positions (already debated at an earlier July meeting). The full account of this deviation has been presented elsewhere.[8] For our purposes, it is particularly relevant to note that Gomulka was charged with distorting the role played by the party and undermining the class struggle content of the socialist transformation of the countryside. Gomulka was accused of having recommended that the Polish delegation to the Cominform's June meeting refuse to endorse the agricultural resolution and of having refused to support the struggle against the kulak, which was stated to be the very basis of the socialist transformation.[9] The charges pertaining to these domestic errors were buttressed by an accusation which, in years to come, was to have an increasingly ominous ring: inadequate understanding of the role of the USSR, the attitude toward which, "given the increasing polarization of forces in the world between the imperialist and the anti-imperialist camps," is in fact "the test of true internationalism, the test of devotion to the cause of socialism." [10]

The Polish plenum helped to focus more sharply on what the central issues facing the Communists in East Europe were and to spell out the broad outlines of the *correct* position. By bringing the Gomulka case out into the open, the Polish party performed the service of placing in bold relief the borderline between orthodoxy and heresy. From now on, to err by omission would be more difficult. Nonetheless, even the Polish plenum did not achieve the task of a systematic revision of the ideological basis for the People's Democracy. It did not indicate with precision what was and what was not still sacred. The urgency created by the conflict with Tito, and the ideological confusion resultant from the fact that Tito's position in many respects had been ideologically closest to the prevailing Soviet notions, made a more formal guideline imperative. It came forth in two forms: an article by Yudin in the Cominform journal in October 1948,[11] and a speech by Dimitrov in December to the Fifth Congress of the Bulgarian Communist Party.[12]

Yudin's article took as its point of departure the tenth anniversary of the publication of the "Short Course History of the CPSU," authorship of which had been generously credited to Stalin. Hailing this work as "a classical creation of scientific Communism," Yudin stressed that the central themes of the book, which described the Soviet experience with the socialist transformation, were a "universal source of inspiration" to all Communist parties. The article emphasized repeatedly the widespread applicability of the specifics of Soviet experience, castigated leaders like Gomulka (explicitly named) for committing "a big mistake by ignoring the experience of the USSR," and left little doubt as to the dangers inherent in attempting to follow one's own road to socialism. As if to underscore the point, prominent space was also given in the same issue to an article by a member of the leadership of the Hungarian party, Z. Biro (Rakosi's brother), entitled "Learn from the CPSU(b) How to Struggle and Win."

Dimitrov's speech, which became a classic frequently quoted by other leaders, went beyond the questions of the role of the party, the primacy of the USSR, and the universal applicability of the Soviet experience. It was a systematic effort to revise most of the earlier assumptions concerning the People's Democracy. He categorized Bulgarian postwar experience into two phases: the first, from September 9, 1944, to the execution of the peasant leader Nikola Petkov in September 1947, as the struggle of all democratic forces against Fascism in the process of which domestic "malicious opposition" was eliminated; the second, which followed, as the beginning of the socialist transformation. Dimitrov pointed out that in the present phase the People's Democracy was performing the functions of a dictatorship of the proletariat in order to eliminate the remnants of capitalism within the framework of a world democratic coalition headed by the USSR, on whom "the very basis of the existence of People's Democracy" depends. Friendly relations with the USSR were thus a fundamental aspect of the People's Democracy itself.* The general effect of his speech was to initiate a full-scale revision of the concept of People's Democracy. Under the existing circumstances the various leaders hastened forward with their own contributions to the construction of theoretical uniformity.

The East European leaders now had the advantage of generous Soviet ideological assistance. Apart from the programmatic statements of Zhdanov or Yudin's articles, the Soviet scholars themselves elaborated during 1948 and 1949 a new conception of the People's Democracy.[13] Out of these re-evaluations emerged a new theoretical framework which not only shaped and rationalized the domestic policies but which also served as the basis for the new constitutions which followed. For this reason, in discussing the ideological changes effected after Dimitrov's speech it may not be inappropriate also to refer occasionally to one of the most significant collections pertaining to the

---

* Dimitrov's categorization of Bulgarian events survived the various post-Stalin vicissitudes. Thus, for instance, in a discussion of "Our Development on the Path of Socialism" on April 11, 1956, Radio Sofia emphasized the two stages (September 9, 1944–1947: "solution of democratic problems"; 1947 on: "nationalization and building of socialism") and pointed out that the presence of a "coalition" of parties "did not mean that this democracy was basically different from the Soviet form of proletarian dictatorship."

Stalinist notions of the People's Democracy — namely, a three-volume collection of papers, articles, and discussions, amounting to 1589 pages and entitled (in English translation), "The Legal Problems of the Constitution of the Polish People's Republic." The collection was the product of a conference planned early in 1953, but actually held in July 1953, to discuss all the pertinent aspects of Marxist-Leninist thinking on the problems of the state and constitution in a People's Democracy.[14] It represents the quintessence of Stalinist thinking, for the few months which had passed since Stalin's death were too brief materially to affect the views presented and undoubtedly prepared earlier.

On the fundamental questions of internal democracy, democratic coalitions, and the dictatorship of the proletariat, Dimitrov in his speech, Revai in his oft-cited article, and the Soviet theorists [15] all now maintained that the People's Democracy was a new *form* of the dictatorship of the proletariat which, depending on the given historical circumstances, "can mean different qualitative conditions of the state: it can initially be a state building socialism or subsequently a state of victorious socialism." [16] Thus, even in its early stage of historical development, "the content of the People's Democracy is the dictatorship of the proletariat." The People's Democracy, in Yudin's words, is one of the two historically established forms of the proletarian dictatorship, the other being the Soviet form.[17] Among the reasons explaining why the People's Democracy was a different form were cited the favorable conditions under which it had been established which rendered unnecessary the disenfranchisement of the old exploiting classes.[18] At the same time, however, the existence of democratic coalitions meant that the hegemony of the working class was not expressed directly through the one-party system, as in the USSR. The democratic coalitions were said to be the aftermath of the anti-Fascist struggle and, thanks to the presence of Soviet power, they did not constitute a challenge to the role of the party.* As one leading Soviet scholar put it, this was merely a special application to the East

---

* This was stressed by all concerned. Revai: "we must liquidate the concept that the working class shares its power with other classes. In this concept we find the remnants of a viewpoint according to which a People's Democracy is some quite specific kind of state which differs from the Soviet not only in its form, but also in its essence and functions" (p. 150). Sobolev: "A multi-party system is characteristic of the political life of the countries of People's Democracy. . . . Experience has shown that the system of People's Democracy can perform the functions of the dictatorship of the proletariat also under conditions of the existence of several parties, but with this imperative condition, that the leading and directing state power is the vanguard of the working class — the Communist Party" (pp. 94–95).

European scene of Stalin's concepts of the alliance between the proletariat and the working classes. He then noted: "The content of a People's Democracy, as also of Soviet power, is determined by the Marxist-Leninist leadership of the Communist Party." [19]

At the Polish constitutional conference, held several years later, the supremacy of the party was not only firmly asserted but made the basis for the sovereignty of the People's Democracy on the grounds that party leadership guarantees the maintenance of the dictatorship of the proletariat which is the foundation of sovereign national power. [20] The party is not only supreme insofar as the other "democratic" parties are concerned, it also rejects any institutional limits on its power. Separation of powers, which in feudal times was a progressive arrangement, was pointedly criticized as having lost all its progressive character and for serving as a bourgeois device to suppress the people. "In a real people's state there is no room for any 'competition' of organs." [21]

The nature of the East European states was said to reflect a sharp break with the past, a break which involved the complete replacement of old state forms by new ones. Previously, it had been held (see Chapter 2) that the retention of some of the old bourgeois forms constituted one of the unique features of the People's Democracy. This view was now rejected, although it was conceded that the smashing of the old forms had not been performed in one violent sweep, as during the Russian revolution. [22] "It must be openly acknowledged, that from the first moment of the existence of People's Poland we have a completely new form, although one cannot ignore the fact that in specific fragments of our system we temporarily used the old forms which subsequently, through the inflow of the new content, were liquidated in the course of intensifying class struggle," declared a Polish constitutional expert. [23] Even in Czechoslovakia, where the state had not been as disrupted by the war as in Poland and where the Communists took over the machinery of the state almost intact, similar change in *content*, and gradually in form, was alleged. [24]

The class struggle was now held to be a common denominator in the transitional period after consolidation of power. After the Soviet break with Tito, the Yugoslavs and Gomulka as well were castigated for underestimating or ignoring its importance as a "law of development." [25] They were charged with failing to understand that the bourgeoisie cannot be patriotic and cannot cooperate sincerely in the task of national reconstruction. [26] Insofar as the People's Democracies were held to be now entering on the stage of laying the foundations

of socialism, and last-ditch, desperate resistance of the former "op-
pressors" could be expected, this was a particularly serious charge.
The earlier definition of the revolution as a democratic, but not a
socialist, one was accordingly broadened to include a struggle against
world imperialism, thereby making the early stage more "historically
meaningful" than a mere bourgeois revolution and allowing its rapid
transformation into a revolution "of the socialist type." * The class
struggle would be imperative in this phase.

The arrival of the People's Democracies at this higher historical
plateau raised the question of the relation between their development and that of the USSR. They were all forms of the dictatorship
of the proletariat, but admittedly they were not identical. The reason
for that was history. The People's Democracies were still at an earlier
stage of development, and even the process of the complete liquidation of the former exploiters was not finished. The above conditions
notwithstanding, Soviet support was said to have made possible the
creation of the dictatorships of the proletariat under conditions considerably more favorable than in 1917. They could hence pass almost
immediately to the internal fulfillment of the three basic tasks of a
proletarian dictatorship: to liquidate the exploiters, to strengthen the
alliance of the proletariat with the masses, and to lead toward a socialist society.[27]

It would be a grievous error, however, to conclude that because
of more advantageous circumstances the People's Democracies could
pursue a distinct path of their own. While acknowledging that
Leninism requires recognition of "individual characteristics, condi-
tioned by differences in historical development," [28] both the Soviet
theorists and the East European politicians warned against any excesses.
The Soviet scholar, N. P. Farberov, stressed that "it would be incorrect to maintain that 'as many countries as many roads to socialism.' This kind of statement means the negation of the international
significance of the experience of the USSR and of the basic laws of
the transitional period." He therefore felt that "the countries of People's Democracy do not march along some new, distinct road from
that which the Soviet Union took to reach socialism." [29] That his
views reflected the official Soviet thinking is suggested by the fol-

---

* There was some disagreement on whether the two phases together were a
"socialist revolution." See Skilling, p. 28, for a contrast between some Soviet scholars;
for later views, see Sobolev, pp. 91–92, and *Zagadniania Prawne*, I, 352–353, where a
difference is made between mere bourgeois revolutions and "popular democratic"
revolutions, the latter having occurred in East Europe and leading directly into the
proletarian dictatorship.

lowing citation from the theoretical journal of the CPSU, *Bolshevik:*
"The general laws of transition from capitalism to socialism, discovered by Marx and Engels, and tested, put to concrete use, and developed by Lenin and Stalin on the basis of the experience of the
Bolshevik Party and the Soviet State, are binding upon all countries." [30]

The East European leaders, under the existing political pressures,
soon found it necessary to move from mere assertions of the relevance
of Soviet experience to stringent proclamations of blind devotion to
the USSR. Starting with declarations that in all fundamental questions the USSR was a model for the People's Democracies,[31] the various leaders were soon competing in proclaiming their determination
to apply the Soviet example and in minimizing the particularities of
their countries. This was extended to mean that the basic criterion
for judging an individual or a policy was its relation to the USSR, and
that any underestimating of the relevance of Soviet experience was a
bona fide indication of dangerous nationalist or even proimperial-
ist leanings.[32] Soviet classics, particularly Stalin's, were described
as "brilliant" contributions which had to be applied in East Europe
through the adoption of the Soviet type of central planning, collectivization, and heavy industrial development.[33] To remove any last
doubts, the emergence of the new theoretical uniformity, which
served as the basis for policies which characterized the East European
scene after 1948, was said to have been assisted through the personal
contributions of Stalin himself.[34]

Impact on Constitutions

The new theoretical uniformity also found expression in East European constitutions and constitutional thinking. To a Communist, a
constitution is not an intricate legal arrangement organizing and limiting power and expressing certain societal norms. Rather it is a reflection of existing reality and a means of furthering the transformation
of society. It is both passive and active, meaningful only within its
own historical phase, and can be altered when circumstances dictate.
Given the actual environment changes that had taken place, particularly since the formation of the Cominform, and given the recent theoretical reassessments, the emergence of more commonly shared constitutional forms seemed unavoidable. Without going into a detailed
structural discussion,[35] it is noteworthy that in short order all the
states adopted new constitutions.

Bulgaria led the way with a new constitution proclaimed on November 4, 1947. Its provisions testified to the impact of the July Cominform meeting, for they differed significantly from the May 1947 draft.[36] Unlike the earlier version, it was modeled closely on the Stalin constitution and abandoned the planned post of president on the Western model. Rumania followed suit on April 13, 1948; Czechoslovakia on May 9, 1948; Hungary on August 20, 1949; and finally Poland on July 22, 1952. All these states declared themselves in their constitutions to be People's Democracies and drew heavily on the Soviet constitution for their legal, administrative, and local government provisions. This indebtedness was considered to be one of their particular excellences, and the parental relationship was not denied. "All the basic principles and institutions of the people's democratic states bear on them the stamp of the beneficent influence of the Stalin Constitution," one Soviet scholar asserted.[37] Two of the constitutions, those of Hungary and Poland, both products of a more ripened Stalinism (1949 and 1952, respectively), actually praised the USSR in their texts — not a frequent procedure among sovereign states. Although no one would admit it, the People's Democracies had finally reached the stage attained already in 1947 by the Yugoslavs.

The spirit behind the new constitutions was fully revealed in the Polish constitutional lawyers' discussions. The basis for political power was the alliance between the working class and the toiling peasantry, with the former playing the leading role on the basis of the victorious socialist construction in the USSR.[38] The state apparatus was said to express the transformation of the "popular anti-imperialist" revolution into a socialist one,[39] and the restriction and liquidation of exploiters was one of the purposes of the institutional framework. For this reason, such operations as the state budget would serve as one of the means for socialist transformation and elimination of exploiting classes.[40] Similarly, the criminal code had to evolve according to the actual objectives on the political and economic front, "depending on the form and intensity of class struggle." [41] Thus the evolution of the criminal code after the war was said to have gone through three main stages: (1) struggle against imperialism and fascism, against survivals of feudalism; (2) suppression of the resistance of internal class enemies; (3) protection of socialist property.[42] The law, according to the Polish constitution, reflects at all times the interests and purposes of the working class and, for this reason, all acts injurious to socialist property can be equated with sabotage or diversion (article 77). (Czech legal thought went even further and maintained that it can be equated with treason.[43]) These considerations, expressing the dominant themes of established Stalinist thought, as well as the adoption of local institutions modeled on the soviets, gave the constitutions of the People's Democracies a "socialist character," making them "after the great Stalin Constitution, the most progressive and democratic constitutions in the world." [44]

The only exception was East Germany which had been granted a constitution in October 1949 after the West German state had been set up. Up to this point East Germany had not entered into consideration because it constituted an occupied territory, without any pretense of independent statehood. The broad outlines of East German thinking, however, followed the pattern already traced. In 1945 the founding proclamation of the German Communist Party declared: "We are of the opinion that the course of forcing the Soviet system on Germany would be incorrect, since this course does not fit the current conditions of development in Germany." It then stated itself to be in favor of a "parliamentary-democratic republic." [45] Walter Ulbricht expressed similar sentiments on numerous occasions.

The 1949 constitution was based on a draft proposed by the SED in November 1946 and which had been meant for all of Germany. East Germany was proclaimed to be a "Democratic Republic" rather than a People's Democracy. This distinction was emphasized for essentially two reasons: Germany was still divided and the new East German institutions were meant some day to apply to West Germany where capitalism was still supreme; furthermore, internal changes in East Germany were lagging behind those in the People's Democracies. Colonel Tulpanov, the *politruk* of the Soviet Military Administration, used the following striking analogy to draw the difference between the various satellites insofar as their "socialist transformation" was concerned: "Yugoslavia has already reached the other bank [a socialist state]; Bulgaria is taking the last few strokes to reach it; Poland and Czechoslovakia are about in the middle of the river followed by Rumania and Hungary, which have gone about a third of the way; while the Soviet Occupation Zone has just taken the first few strokes away from the bourgeois bank." [46] The GDR was thus said to be a democratic state ruled by an alliance between the workers and peasants. This was no longer a bourgeois type of state, but it was not yet a People's Democracy because power was shared with other social groups. [47] It was not listed among the People's Democracies, although on July 23, 1952, it too significantly revamped its constitutional structure in the Soviet image. The component Laender were deprived of many of their functions, and the central government was given powers of annulment over local enactments of district assemblies, patterned on the soviets. The adoption of the system of hierarchical assemblies was hailed as another step in the process of "democratization."

Thus by 1952 the content of the East German system was very similar to the People's Democracies though the label, for external reasons primarily, was not adopted. The SED openly assumed the posture of the ruling party, thereby paralleling the role played by the Communist parties elsewhere. In Otto Grotewohl's words: "the Workers' and Peasants' Authority in the GDR is the state form of the dictatorship of the proletariat under our special national conditions." [48]

The People's Democracies, together with the "more advanced" Soviet society, were thus in a class by themselves. In the eyes of the Communists they had outstripped other forms of political organization, particularly the Western democratic type, and had attained in short order a higher stage in historical development on the road to the eventual socialist society. Together with the Soviet Union, they were the only countries in the world which were basing their domestic organization on certain conscious insights into the laws of societal development and, armed with that understanding, which were creating a society that was in keeping with history. Recognition of Soviet leadership, given the Soviet Union's more advanced stage of socialist development, was accordingly a natural consequence of this perception of the real state of affairs. Similarly, there had to be intimate friendship with the USSR, given the fact that the People's Democracies were following so closely the Soviet road, a road which was said to lead away from traditions of national hostility, class oppression, artificially stimulated nationalism, and trite territorial ambitions. All of these vices faded, it was claimed, once the internal transformation of the People's Democracies gathered momentum. Friendship with the USSR, which in the earlier stage had been stressed as a matter of policy, now became an *organic* quality of the People's Democracy, maturing and strengthening as the People's Democracy transformed itself.

This "natural" development, inherent in the very process of transformation, was abetted, however, by external stimuli which could not be ignored. The splitting of the world into two camps was to the convinced Communist another proof of the need for maintaining Leninist-Stalinist norms of discipline, not only within each individual party but among them also. It meant that "democratic centralism" had to be applied on the interparty level, that hierarchy of command had to be respected, that the Cominform and ultimately Stalin himself had to be obeyed in every instance. Personal qualms about the ethics of any given policy had to give way in face of the external challenge lest the dreaded Leninist standard be applied: "does the enemy benefit from your stand, view, or policy?" Subjective motives then became irrelevant; the question pointedly raised the issue of the objective consequences of doubting the established line. Even the best domestic cause had to yield if the enemy were to benefit, if the international solidarity of the socialist camp were to suffer. Since the focal point of East-West tensions was the relationship between the USSR and the capitalist powers, the enemy would benefit from anything which could be construed as damaging to the USSR. Since the Soviet leadership would know best what was and what was not damaging to it, the primacy of its views on domestic affairs in East Europe was hence again justified and sanctified. To many Communists this line of reasoning was irresistible and for many years provided the crucible of their attitude.

In fact, the revisions in the ideological conceptions of the People's Democracy, the rapid advances made by them on the road toward "socialism," the emergence of fundamental characteristics common to all of them and to the USSR, and the need to close ranks in face of external threat brought the People's Democracies closer to the USSR than ever before. Given the known Marxist conceptions concerning relations between states and the basis for separate statehood, the stage was now reached when the very purpose of separate statehood could be questioned legitimately. The differences that still distinguished the People's Democracies from the Soviet Union were less significant than the similarities which involved some of the more crucial aspects of the nature of a state or society. The facts that they were already dictatorships of the proletariat, that the party was wielding power, that the "exploiting class" was defeated, were much more important than the specifics of the various temporary adjustments in some of these states. Considering this, and also considering the circumstances prevailing in the Soviet Union (the reassertion of monolithic party control, ideological conformity, industrial drives, and so on), was not the merger of the People's Democracies with the USSR not only theoretically justifiable but indeed dictated by the laws of historical development?

The ideological objections that might have been raised could have stressed a fact which has already been noted — namely, the differences in the stages of development between the satellites and the Soviet

Union. For this reason a union, federation, or confederation would have been premature. But such considerations had not prevented the formation of the USSR itself, with its component units ranging in stages of development from the industrial to the almost prefeudal; nor did they prevent the incorporation of the Baltic states, which had no prior "socialist transformation." Clearly, then, the problem of relative stages was not crucial.

Probably much more important in this question of a merger were the presence of Titoism and the emergence of Communist China. Paradoxical as it seems, it may have been Tito's earlier hints about eventual union with the USSR that now helped to delay what seemed so timely. The Soviet government had gone to considerable lengths to discredit the Belgrade regime as a betrayer of both international Communism and the Yugoslav people. Kardelj's pious hope for a Union of Soviet Socialist Republics including the People's Democracies was ridiculed, reviled, and rejected. Every emphasis was placed on the significance of the sovereignty of each individual People's Democracy even while that sovereignty was being drained away. After 1949, a further consideration might have been the creation of a Communist state in China which probably would not have viewed with enthusiasm the idea that the launching of domestic socialist transformation is tantamount to formal union with the USSR.

Finally, practical considerations were involved. Incorporation, or even federation, would not have increased by much, if at all, the existing ideological and political supremacy of the USSR. But it might have caused domestic complications in East Europe, weakened the Communist appeal abroad, provoked resentment among some East European Communists and caused suspicion among the Chinese, while providing the Yugoslavs and the capitalists with additional ammunition. The dotting of the *i* could well be delayed, for it would have involved no significant gains since relations with the People's Democracies were already based on the ideological principle of the universality of Soviet experience, expressed politically through the acceptance of Soviet primacy. The forms of independence were hence maintained.

The reconsideration of the theory of the People's Democracy, aided by growing Soviet intrusion, ended the most creative period in postwar Communist thought and led to a rapid decline in the importance of theory. The dynamic interrelationship between ideological disputes and political problems, which had been at least embryonic in East Europe, was eliminated. Politics began to dictate ideology and to manifest the general unwillingness to go beyond the limits of already established doctrine. Thus, ideology ceased to be what it had been for those Communists who had been so genuinely motivated by it — a method of understanding reality, thereby creatively guiding and shaping political action while also serving as a source of mass appeal. It became instead the ideology of a state, with its content determined by reason of state or, more correctly, by the interests of specific groups within the ruling class.

But to many East European Communists, dependent for their position and new privileges on Soviet support, the reconsidered theory represented a much less complicated insight into their existence. Reliance on Soviet experience was the safest way of coping with any new problems which might bring on interpretative difficulties and consequent political pitfalls. Those internal problems which flew in the face of the state ideology were viewed as expressions of hostile activity or, at the very least, as manifestations of a lag in social consciousness left over from the bourgeois period. The operational formula was to take a Stalinist dictum or action and apply it rigidly to the domestic circumstance. Sterility in thought and policy was the consequence.

CHAPTER 5

Laying the Socialist Foundations

As the theory was being reconsidered, the construction of the foundations for socialism was beginning in earnest. The situation was no longer obscured by the need to adjust, to compromise, to take one step backward before leaping two steps forward. The internal transformation of society was based on tried Stalinist patterns and reflected Stalin's apparent conviction that the political-economic course he had pursued in the USSR during the thirties had been essentially correct and had saved the Soviet Union. The Soviet dictator, aging and growing more suspicious with each passing day, seemed no longer willing to relate the experience of the past and the perception of what is new to the existing situation. Like many old tyrants, he now sought security in rigidly applying *his* past experience to every new circumstance. He was fortunate in possessing the power to make the new circumstances fit his established and well-tried criteria. Fearing that war with capitalism was a real and immediate possibility, he probably felt that loyalty would be best achieved by duplicating the Soviet structure in East Europe. He believed that in so doing he was creating the material conditions for close liaison between his socialist state and the People's Democracies while eliminating those sources of diversity which might ultimately lead to disunity.

The new pattern, which was to serve as a basis for the relations between the USSR and East Europe and which was applied uniformly to the area, stressed: (1) the implementation of the theory of the Communist Party's political supremacy and the assertion of the dictatorship of the proletariat; (2) the intensification of the class struggle not only to seek out the known hostile classes but also to unmask the enemies which had infiltrated the Communist movement; (3) the carrying of the class struggle into the countryside to break the resistance of the peasants, particularly the more prosperous ones, to the socialist transformation of agriculture without which both effective industrialization and real socialism were said to be impossible; (4) the launching of rapid and large-scale industrialization of each People's Democracy. The result would be a uniformity in existing conditions which inevitably would produce conformity in behavior and interests. The Stalinist formula had the virtues of simplicity and directness.

The Supremacy of the Party and the Dictatorship of the Proletariat

The assertion of the party's supremacy was merely a matter of openly acknowledging the prevailing state of affairs and mopping up the remnants of the former opposition. By 1948 in every People's Democracy the Socialist Party had been absorbed into the Communist Party,* and open opposition had been dispersed, imprisoned, or liquidated.† The Communist parties, which had enjoyed a spectacular growth in membership, by 1948 had reached a plateau in their number (see accompanying table) on which, like the CPSU, they were to remain for the next ten years. In fact, the leaderships had just cause to fear that their efforts to increase memberships rapidly, a political necessity during the earlier stage, had resulted in the influx of many questionable elements. Accordingly, paralleling Soviet postwar practice, they sharply reduced any further recruitment. The non-Communist parties, when not actually abolished, were emasculated and merged in the patriotic or national fronts (National Front in Poland, Czechoslovakia, East Germany; People's Independent Front in Hungary; People's Democratic Front in Rumania, and Fatherland Front in Bulgaria); they were given the task of transmitting to their members and sympathizers the directives of the ruling party. The Communist Party openly assumed state leadership and abandoned the pretense of partnership with the other parties. In Poland, Bierut, the first secretary, also held the office of president and, after that was abolished, that of premier; in Czechoslovakia the first secretary, Gottwald, was also president; elsewhere the posts of premier and first secretary were combined.

There is no need to trace in detail the penetration of each society by party controls. Suffice it to say that the Soviet model was duplicated,[1] and in every factory, enterprise, town, or village it was the party committee which was the source of authority, no matter how trivial the issue, no matter how unimportant the problem. With this accumulation of power the party soon became the source of privilege

* Rumania: February 23, 1948; Hungary: June 14, 1948; Czechoslovakia: June 27, 1948; Bulgaria: August 11, 1948; Poland: December 15, 1948.

† The process, of course, never had a clear cut-off date, but the symbolic end of effective opposition may be set as October 1947 for Poland (Mikolajczyk's flight abroad); October 1947 for Rumania (Maniu's trial); February 1947 for Hungary (Bela Kovacs' arrest); and September 1947 for Bulgaria (Petkov's execution).

Growth of Communist Party membership from the seizure of power to the New Course

	Poland 1956 Pop. 27.5 million	Czechoslovakia 1955 Pop. 13 million	Hungary 1955 Pop. 9.8 million	Yugoslavia 1953 Pop. 16.9 million	Bulgaria 1955 Pop. 7.5 million	Rumania 1956 Pop. 17.5 million	GDR 1950 Pop. 18.4 million
	Dec. 1945 — 235,296	Aug. 1945 — 712,776	May 1945 — 150,000	Dec. 1945 — 141,066	Sept. 1944 — 25,000	Sept. 1945 — 217,000	Feb. 1946 — 511,000
	Dec. 1946 — 555,888	Mar. 1946 — 1,081,554	Sept. 1946 — 653,000	July 1948 — 468,175	Mar. 1945 — 254,000	June 1947 — 710,000	Apr. 1946 — 1,298,415 [a]
	Dec. 1947 — 820,786	Nov. 1947 — 1,281,138	May 1947 — 700,000	Dec. 1949 — 470,379	Mar. 1946 — 500,000 (approx.)	Sept. 1948 — 937,846 [a]	June 1948 — 2,000,000 (approx.)
	Dec. 1948 — 1,368,873 [a]	May 1948 — 2,000,048	May 1948 — 884,000	Nov. 1952 — 779,382	June 1948 — 495,658 [a]	July 1950 — 720,000	Jan. 1949 — 1,773,689
	Dec. 1949 — 1,200,000 (approx.)	May 1949 — 2,311,066 [a]	Mar. 1949 — 1,200,000 [a]	Dec. 1953 — 716,985	Dec. 1949 — 460,000	June 1956 — 580,000	Apr. 1950 — 1,750,000
	Dec. 1953 — 1,226,716	Feb. 1951 — 1,677,443	Mar. 1952 — 880,000	June 1955 — 624,806	June 1950 — 367,000		Sept. 1953 — 1,239,000
	Mar. 1954 — 1,297,000	Aug. 1954 — 1,480,234	May 1954 — 864,607	June 1956 — 635,984	June 1954 — 455,251		Apr. 1954 — 1,272,987 [b]

[a] Following absorption of the Social Democrats.

[b] Figure excludes 140,326 candidates.

Note: We may make the following observations: (1) There was a rapid growth in party memberships during the early phase, preliminary to complete liquidation of the opposition. (2) Following the consolidation of power, the membership remained relatively stable. (3) The parties contained a relatively high proportion of the population, as compared to the CPSU where the total never went above 3.5 per cent of the total population. (4) The more totalitarianized the regimes, the smaller, relatively, the parties.

Sources: For Poland: Iwanska, p. 316; for Czechoslovakia: Hajda, p. 324; for Hungary: Rakosi, *Valsgatott Beszedek es Cikkek* (Budapest, 1953), pp. 60–61, 229, 205; for Yugoslavia: *Komunist*, no. 11–12, 1956, pp. 754–765, no. 7–8, 1956, pp. 495–504; for Bulgaria: *Materiali po istoriia na bulgarskata komunisticheska partiia* (Sofia, 1956), p. 391; for Rumania: S. Fisher-Galati, ed., *Romania* (New York, 1957), pp. 69–76; for GDR: C. Stern, *Die SED* (Germany, 1954), pp. 152–3, and Ulbricht, *Tagesspiegel*, March 5, 1946.

and corruption. With the growing shortage of housing and consumer goods, special facilities for party members were made available, and the heavily curtained stores without names became a source of public scandal and indignation. In time this was to cause serious demoralization, but in the first flush of victory it seemed like justifiable spoils. Subsidiary party organizations were established to embrace the youth, the women, the university students, and so on, much on the Soviet model.[2] Party controls reached into the universities through Communist youth organizations, through the introduction of new curricula (particularly courses on Marxism-Leninism), and finally through appointment of new professors and purges of the old ones. Those disciplines which represented an inherent challenge to the official doctrine, such as mathematical logic, sociology, and psychology, were eliminated altogether. Universities were deprived of their academic independence; promotions were made on the basis of political criteria; the Soviet academic system of *kandidaty* replaced the Western doctorate. By 1952 party controls on education had been imposed in all the states. Yet even after Stalin died, in a typical example of the competition in imitating, the organ of the Czech Party complained that "it is still a frequent phenomenon in our country that while we proclaim in our slogans that the Soviet Union is our example, at the same time we are very often satisfied merely with the proclamation. Therefore it is now necessary to study more concretely and systematically the life of Soviet universities."[3] Within the various states, academic and scientific activity was coordinated by academies of science, modeled again on the Soviet and controlled by the ruling party.*

In other fields of creative endeavor the party also asserted its domination and articulated its expectations. Socialist realism was proclaimed to be the norm in the arts, and at the World Congress in Defense of Peace (August 25–28, 1948) the Soviet spokesman in literature, A. Fadeiev, drew a sharp and distinct line between those who are

---

* In a remarkable exposé published in Poland after October 1956, a distinguished Polish professor revealed that the presidium of the Polish Academy of Science played a purely fictional role and that all power was vested in the scientific secretariat which was an agency of the party's control. In fact, elections of the secretariat's membership were so nominal that once the election of a member to it was announced immediately after the party's Central Committee had made its selection and before the formal vote in the Academy had taken place. Of the Academy's 107 members, only 27 belonged to the party; of its presidium's 26 members, 12 belonged to the party; of the secretariat's 12 members, 10 belonged to the party. The article, by J. Chalasinski, "Ways and Byways of Socialism in Polish Science (1949–1954)," *Kultura i Spoleczenstwo*, no. 1, 1957, is a broad indictment of Communist policies in the field of scholarship and science.

for socialism and those who are against it. In architecture, a field especially important since its achievements cannot disappear as easily as a bad book, particular stress was laid by the Communist parties on emulating the Soviet "gingerbread" style. Architectural journals were filled with discussions of the socialist city, the socialist style, and the Soviet architectural experience. Party ideologues, such as Revai in Hungary, took an active part in urging and cajoling architects to learn from the USSR.[4] In Poland, Bierut himself participated in the discussions on the reconstruction of Warsaw and severely castigated, as "cosmopolitan and bourgeois aberrations," the modernistic tendencies of the Warsaw architects.[5] The symbol of the new era, and of the close Polish ties to the USSR, was the Stalin palace constructed in the center of the city. Statues to Stalin dominated the horizon elsewhere.

The party was to be omnipotent and omnipresent. The pervasiveness of its controls was to leave no doubt that it, the vanguard of the proletariat, was directing the life of society toward the ultimate utopia. The previous emphasis on reconstruction and reform, which in its very essence implies some relation to existing reality, gave way to shrill insistence on the need for revolutionary change — to be effected within and through the institutional framework of the dictatorship of the proletariat which the People's Democracies were now said to be. This insistence was not merely a case of ideological ritualism. The dictatorship of the proletariat was a conception not devoid of political content, and the Soviet and East European leaders must have been fully aware of it. Its implementation was bound to speed up those historical processes which to a Communist must naturally seem desirable and inevitable. At the same time, the fulfillment of such objectives could not help, it seemed, but narrow the gap between the USSR and the People's Democracies in the historical progression toward Communism.

A concomitant development was the decline in importance of state institutions. The most dramatic expression of this trend was the reduction of the assemblies to a purely nominal role, both on the national and the local levels. The popular councils, adopted with so much fanfare as another step forward in "democratization," became at their very inception mere appendages to the local party committees and the instruments of endorsement of administrative *fiats*.[6] The decline in the importance of the administrative structure, however, was not tantamount to a withering away of the bureaucracy. On the contrary, particularly with the large-scale nationalization and industrialization, the bureaucracy grew even as the ultimate decisions slipped from its hands.* The additional factor of fear of "hostile penetration" meant that extensive controls were instituted on all levels, thereby further expanding the bureaucratic apparatus. Cross-checking and interpenetrating organs were designed to exercise "proletarian vigilance" against diversion, sabotage, and other forms of hostile class activity. The atmosphere of the state administration soon lost the character of a public-service organization and became dominated by internal militancy, suspicion, and almost paranoiac secrecy.†

By 1950/1951 the administrative structure of the People's Democracies began to assume what was labeled as the forms of socialist administration. This usually followed the adoption of the new constitutions reflecting the new ideological concepts (see preceding chapter). The ministries were broken down into smaller, more specialized units directing specific economic branches. By 1953 the adoption of long-range planning — Bulgaria: Five Year Plan, 1949–1953; Czechoslovakia: Five Year Plan, 1949–1953; Hungary: Five Year Plan, 1950–1954; Poland: Six Year Plan, 1950–1955; Rumania: Five Year Plan, 1951–1955; East Germany: Five Year Plan, 1951–1955 [7] — made possible the introduction of "the socialist forms of state budget," [8] in which the turnover tax, on the Soviet model, became the most important source of state revenue. [9] These fiscal arrangements of the dictatorship of the proletariat were, however, construed as being primarily designed to facilitate the historical dialectic of the class struggle. For this reason, in the words of an East European planning journal, "in the people's democracies, taxes serve the ends of the dic-

* The prewar size of the Polish state administration was estimated at 172,000 (Spulber, p. 21). In postwar Poland, with its population decreased by 30 per cent, the number of purely state administrative officials was 348,500 (B. Minc, "The Problem of Bureaucracy," *Nowa Kultura*, May 27, 1956). These figures do not include officials of state enterprises or full-time Communist Party functionaries (roughly 15,000 in Poland). In prewar Czechoslovakia there were 345,300 officials, including state officials (200,800), teachers, and officials of state enterprises and monopolies (Spulber, *ibid.*). In 1956, the figure was 792,000 for "public administration and the courts, banks and insurance companies, in social organizations, science, research" (*Predvoj*, February 27, 1958). The prewar Czech ratio of productive workers to administrative personnel declined from 4:1 to 2.32:1 under the Communists (*East Europe*, VII, no. 8). The number of state officials and teachers in prewar Bulgaria was 63,000 (Spulber, *ibid.*). In 1952 the number was 91,000 (*Statisticheski Godishnik na Narodna Republika Bulgariya*, 1956, p. 100).

† The Bulgarian *State Journal*, December 6, 1948, included the following items as military information and therefore state secrets: number and distribution of workers, fulfillment of the Plan in absolute figures, absolute figure on sowing, livestock, and agricultural production, results of research work, and so on. In Polish scientific institutions even geological and botanical findings were classified as state secrets and suppressed. W. Szafer, "On Some Unfulfilled Aims of the Polish Academy of Science," *Kultura i Spoleczenstwo*, no. 1 (1957), pp. 61-62.

tatorship of the proletariat. They are an efficient tool of class warfare and are devised to help in the process of limiting and ousting capitalist elements from the national economy." [10]

The class conflict was broadly interpreted and therefore broadly applied. "The means which the enemies use are varied: from destroying and damaging machines and installations to the systematic disorganization of production through the false preparation of plans, erroneous decisions, misleading accounting, statistical frauds; from premeditated negligence of fire prevention measures, of security regulations and labor hygiene — to the organization of arson and causing catastrophes and accidents in places of employment; from ordinary theft or illegal sale of rationed items to the cutting up for scrap of useful machines." [11] Such a definition of hostile activity on the economic front embraced in one sweep both subjective and objective guilt and made it possible, as frequently became the case, to try for sabotage individuals guilty of a simple mistake. It also resulted in increased security measures at places of employment, with a consequent component of fear and suspicion.

Terror as a form of public policy in the USSR and East Europe is a matter of generally familiar record, and it had an impressive history even during the earlier period when the Communist parties were just seizing or consolidating their power. However, the emphasis on class struggle made organized violence an integral characteristic of the People's Democracy as a social system. It was expressed in a continuous series of public and secret trials of various real and imagined enemies of the system. These ranged from former underground leaders in Poland or the "White Legion" trials in Czechoslovakia [12] — involving, in both cases, manifestations of organized resistance to the system — to a variety of economic sabotage charges, frequently involving people who merely happened to have been engaged in some state venture which failed. The growing number of arrests throughout the area resulted in the establishment of a regular system of concentration camps, usually utilized for purposes of forced labor. For instance, in Rumania, the Danube–Black Sea Canal project employed prisoners; in Poland, special penal battalions were formed for the most exposed and deadly coal shafts in Silesia. The number of *identified* camps suggests the scale of this operation: 124 in Czechoslovakia, 199 in Hungary, 97 in Poland.[13] The first country to institute this procedure, as early as 1945, was Bulgaria. It was then used against former Fascists, but its scope was enlarged in March 1948 to embrace "alien class enemies." Czechoslovakia followed suit in October 1948. Other Soviet police controls were also adopted: between 1950 and 1952, for example, internal passports issued by the police became obligatory throughout the area. Mass deportations from some of the large urban centers were enforced (particularly in Budapest, Bucharest, and Sofia) to eliminate former industrialists, soldiers, and professionals, thereby vacating sorely needed space for the new elite.

But far more important, as the future was to show, in the connection of these regimes to the USSR was the changing relationship between the secret police and the Communist Party. In the USSR, the secret police under Yezhov had run amuck during the great purges, and Stalin finally had to purge it.[14] After the war, the Soviet secret police regained some of its influence, and Stalin seemed to be using Beria as a lever to insure the monolithic unity of the party, occasionally unchaining the police to exact the party's unquestioning loyalty. The Voznesensky case and the Leningrad affair, both tangled and complicated matters of intraparty strife, are still, broadly speaking, cases in point.[15] In East Europe, following the decision to establish conformity through the intensification of class struggle, the secret police inevitably began to assume greater political significance as the "shield of the revolution," defending the People's Democracy against all forms of subversion. Its operations gradually slipped out from under the party's control, and the secret police became semi-autonomous, subject only to direct Soviet control (see next chapter). The police became a state within a state, feared by both the population and the party membership.[16]

Purge Patterns

The stature of the secret police was particularly enhanced by the purges and the purge trials of various party leaders and members. The purges were closely related to the new phase of development, marked by new theories and policies. The East European purges, much like the earlier Soviet ones, were a product of organizational and doctrinal pressures. With power seized, all sorts of elements not identified with the objectives of the movement flocked into the ruling party (see membership table). The absence of competition resulted in internal stagnation, decay, and loss of revolutionary zeal. Various "mutual-admiration societies" developed, sponsoring one another within the movement purely for reasons of self-interest. Power, in brief, corrupts, and a totalitarian system lacks the competitive qualities of democratic party struggle to minimize the corruption. The method of resolving these dilemmas was the purge.

Inherent in these general considerations was the growing Soviet fear of Titoism — both of the "national Stalinism" variety (which might be described as the left wing) and of the more moderate right-wing variety which insisted that existing domestic situations be a primary consideration in shaping Communist policies. As it happened, Soviet fears of the right-wing type of orientation were largely exaggerated — only Gomulka in Poland and Patrascanu in Rumania really fitted this category, and it is extremely unlikely that either Rajk, Slansky, or Kostov could have been accused of plotting a policy geared more to domestic requirements than to Soviet ones. Rather, they seemed to have originally favored a revolutionary policy and, in this respect, reflected the more extreme earlier Titoist position. It may be surmised that the left wing drew some of its inspiration from the Zhdanov policy of ideological and political radicalism. Its liquidation coincided with the purge of the Zhdanovites in the USSR following Zhdanov's death in the summer of 1948.

Whatever the motives, the elimination of alternatives was bound to improve coordination and unity, especially since in East Europe the Communist parties were much less monolithic than the Soviet party. They had only recently acquired power, and it is sometimes forgotten that these parties were initially amalgams of very diverse groups, held together only by a commitment to the usually unarticulated Communist image of tomorrow. After the war all kinds of individuals, ranging from the most hard-boiled party veterans to starry-eyed fellow travelers, came together from many parts of the globe. The new ruling parties were split into a variety of overlapping factions (for instance, the Moscow Communists versus the domestic ones, the Soviet stooges versus "our own road to socialism" believers, the former Spanish Civil War veterans, the wartime London refugees). Held together by common hostility to the non-Communists, they differed on the positive program to be pursued once power was won. Indeed, from the Soviet point of view, these diverse backgrounds were sufficient proof of the "objective" existence of an unhealthy diversity among the ruling groups. In November 1949 a resolution of the Cominform accordingly warned the Communist leaders that they must "increase by all possible means revolutionary vigilance in their own ranks."

The purges were most violent in Bulgaria, Hungary, and, particularly, Czechoslovakia. In these countries some of the leading Communist figures were tried and executed. They were accused not only of ideological deviations; the defendants were also charged with treason. The victims came from diverse backgrounds: some were old Communists, now accused of having been Gestapo agents; some had fought against Franco, now called "cosmopolitan" traitors; many were Jews, now accused of being Zionist infiltrators; some were even Moscow-trained *apparatchiki*, now supposed to have betrayed the movement. The pattern of the Soviet purge of 1936–1938 was thus being closely imitated. With the elimination of such "factions" as the Spanish Civil War veterans who had a special sense of group identity, the party could become monolithic.

The first violent purge took place in Hungary. In September 1949, Laszlo Rajk, Politburo member and Minister of the Interior, a Communist with many years of devoted service, faced a People's Court accused of being an employee of Allen Dulles and Alexander Rankovic (head of Tito's secret police). Sharing the dock were several important party and army functionaries (including, for instance, General Palffy, who engineered the communization of the armed forces). In a trial remarkable for the fantastic content of the confessions (after the Hungarian revolt it was revealed that the defendants had been tortured and promised clemency for confessing), the chief defendants were condemned to death and duly executed by garroting. Rajk's execution and the resulting atmosphere of fear did much to strengthen the hand of Rakosi, who, unlike Rajk, had spent the war years in the USSR. And it made the policy of blind imitation of Soviet forced industrialization and collectivization a matter above discussion. Dependence on Soviet support naturally increased, and any Titoist alternatives (whether such had ever been considered by Rajk is doubtful) were out of the question.

A similarly violent operation was almost simultaneously performed on the upper echelons of the Bulgarian Communist Party. The political picture was complicated by the previous Bulgarian negotiations with Tito about the Balkan Union, which resulted in opportunities among Bulgarian leaders for charging each other with complicity with Belgrade. The undisputed chief, Dimitrov, had been ailing for some time, and this necessarily generated a struggle for succession. In March 1949, Traicho Kostov, a Deputy Prime Minister and Politburo member, was summarily removed from his posts. He had previously been one of the contenders for power and was associated with the rapid economic revolution being pushed in Bulgaria. According to some reports, he became so enthusiastic over his tasks that he tended, despite his known anti-Titoism, to develop a "Bulgaria-first" outlook. His fall was followed by the rapid advance of one of his chief rivals,

Vulko Chervenkov, who succeeded to Dimitrov's mantle. In December 1949, Kostov, together with several high party functionaries, was indicted on charges which might have been borrowed directly from the Rajk trial. The only sensation of the trial was Kostov's sudden repudiation of his alleged confession. Kostov, as a matter of course, was executed, and the official party organ, *Rabotnichesko Delo*, reported that after the sentencing he repudiated his repudiation. His associates received severe prison sentences and the top party echelons were thoroughly purged. Of the forty members of the Central Committee, seventeen were removed.

The most extensive purge swept the leadership of the Czechoslovak party. The purge gradually gained momentum between the years 1950 and 1952. Individual leaders were dropped from their high posts; others then accused them of treason. In turn the accusers were dropped and accused. The first to go, early in 1950, were some high officials handling foreign policy and trade, such as Vilem Novy (editor-in-chief of *Rude Pravo*, the official organ, and chairman of the Foreign Affairs Committee of the National Assembly) and Evzen Loebl (Deputy Minister of Foreign Trade). They were followed by Vladimir Clementis, the Foreign Minister and a high-ranking Slovak Communist, suspected of "right-wing" leanings. The purge then covered the top echelons of the Slovak Communist Party. By late 1950 and 1951 it began to embrace the Czech Communist leadership itself, and finally reached its zenith in November 1951, with the announcement that Rudolf Slansky, a Deputy Prime Minister and formerly the powerful Secretary General of the Central Committee, had been arrested. It is noteworthy that, among Communists, Slansky was considered to have been close to Zhdanov. President Gottwald stated: "new disclosures have proved Slansky guilty of a direct, active and, one might say, leading part in the anti-Party and anti-state conspiracy." [17]

The purge then proceeded to cleanse the secretariat of the Central Committee and the Central Committee itself. Gottwald's primacy was now consolidated. Fifty of the ninety-seven members of the Central Committee and six of the seven members of the Secretariat were removed, and the purge reached deep into the bureaucracy and the army. Insofar as Slansky and Clementis were concerned, their cases were linked even though they appeared to have been at opposite ends of the political spectrum, and a typical Soviet-style show trial was staged. The Minister of Justice drew explicit parallels between the Slansky trial and the Soviet purge trials of the late thirties. The special feature of the trial held in November 1952 was its openly anti-Semitic character, which paralleled the campaign being then waged in the USSR in the form of special press emphasis on the execution of "Jewish speculators" and which culminated in the Doctors' Plot. Since a high proportion of the defendants in the Slansky-Clementis trial were Jews (including Slansky himself), the prosecution repeatedly stressed the alleged links of the defendants with Israel, mocking some of them for their Jewish accents and accusing them of a "cosmopolitan" orientation. Eleven of the accused, headed by Slansky and Clementis, were hanged on December 3, 1952.

Less violent purges occurred in Rumania, Poland, and East Germany. In May 1952, several high Rumanian Communists (including Ana Pauker and Vasile Luca) were dropped from the Politburo, but recourse to violence was delayed until April 1954 when Patrascanu (purged in 1948 for alleged nationalism) was executed. This operation, however, lacked the staging of the Rajk, Kostov, and Slansky performances. Clearly, 1954 was no longer the season, and apparently the Rumanian leadership wanted to get rid of an inconvenient skeleton in its closet. Furthermore, it seems that the dismissed Politburo members did represent an internal clique which in the phase of uniformity was incompatible with Stalinist leadership. No open violence was involved in the purges of the Communist leadership in Poland and East Germany. In 1950 the East Germans removed Willi Kreikemeyer and Paul Merker, and in 1953 F. Dahlem and Else Zaisser paid a political price for the East German domestic difficulties. They, together with Minister of Justice Fechner, were accused of pursuing a "defeatist" or "right-wing" line toward opponents of the regime. One third of the Central Committee's membership of fifty-one was also purged. These moves, however, were relatively *sub rosa* and did not produce any openly significant ideological cleavage or any major show trials. The absence of an explicitly ideological aspect distinguished the German purge from the also relatively nonviolent Polish pattern.

In Poland, the removal of Gomulka occurred in the context of a power struggle between him and Bierut which, under the circumstances, was almost predetermined in favor of Bierut. It also occurred, however, in the context of an ideological cleavage in which Gomulka favored a delay in collectivization as well as greater autonomy, and hence diversity, in domestic policy. The ideological discussions, with Gomulka gradually giving way and being demoted step by step, lasted from the late summer of 1948 to November 1949. Gomulka and his associates were then expelled. The Soviet pattern of development was now obligatory for Poland — Stalinism was the official path. Nonetheless, initially Gomulka was not even arrested (he was taken into custody in 1951) and never tried. No show trials of Polish Communists were staged.

What are the reasons for this distinct pattern in Poland and East Germany (though of course in Germany no one of Gomulka's stature was involved)? No definite answer can be given without access to party archives, but we do know that Stalin had insisted that purge trials be held and that severe methods be used. Polish observers were "invited" to the various show trials abroad and presented with evidence "implicating" Gomulka. At the Eighth Plenum (October 1956), Berman, the Politburo member most responsible for the secret-police terror in Poland, explicitly took credit (with the Politburo) for having resisted Soviet pressures to do away with Gomulka.[18] There is no way of checking Berman's veracity, but since none of his enemies belied him at that session we may assume an element of truth in his account. Why did the Polish party resist Stalin's pressures and, more important, how was it able to procrastinate until his death, thereby saving Gomulka?

The causes might be linked with the fact that the Polish Communist Party labored under the bitter legacy of Stalin's 1938 accusation that the party was an agency of Polish espionage. At that time, the Comintern abolished the Polish Communist Party, and Stalin completed the process by shooting almost all of its leaders, many of whom had served with Lenin. The reconstituted party, according to the accounts of some of its well-informed members, consequently went out of its way to avoid any further executions of its leaders. Furthermore, the openly anti-Semitic character of the Slansky trial might have frightened Berman, the Politburo member directly responsible for such matters. On a more general level, Stalin's pressures for violence were combined elsewhere in East Europe with domestic needs for a purge. The Czech party might have actually needed a violent shake-up of its leadership, once the democratic elements had been crushed. Security tends to breed disunity and factionalism, and Stalinists know only one way of resolving such difficulties. Paradoxically, the relative weakness of the Polish and East German parties might have enabled them to avoid a violent purge by pleading that such violence would further undermine their position and harm the unfinished process of consolidation. (In East Germany there was, of course, the further need to appeal to some left-wing West German elements.) Weakness might have thus been a source of evasion insofar as responding to Stalin's pressure was concerned.

In addition, all of the East European Communist parties adopted during this period broader measures to reassert the monolithic quality of their organizations. These took the form of purging their memberships of real or alleged "unhealthy," "alien," or "hostile" elements, more or less on the basis of the categories established in the purging of the prominent deviationists. Since very large numbers were involved, the degree of violence was less intense than in the more spectacular individual cases. But the scope is suggested by the following data on Communists purged in this period:

Poland	Czechoslovakia	Rumania	Hungary	East Germany	Bulgaria
370,000	550,000	200,000	200,000	300,000	90,000

On the average, about one of every four party members was purged in each of the East European parties.[19]

Transformation of the Material Environment

The reliance on Stalinist experience in the socialist transformation of the People's Democracy also led the regimes into extending the class struggle into the agricultural sector. This policy was one of the most glaring examples of dogmatic application of alien experience. Some of the previously existing social inequities had been resolved by land reform, and most of the land holdings were now concentrated in the small and medium categories, while the large landowners had all but disappeared. The policy of collectivization, adopted in 1948/49 and launched in 1950, was justified by reference to Stalin's "law of

Private agricultural holdings: percentage distribution

Holdings (in hectares)	Czecho-slovakia	Poland	Hungary	Rumania	Bulgaria
Small					
0–2	46.5	28.8	68.6	53.1	29.2
2–5	23.5	32.5	18.9	22.9	38.6
Medium					
5–10	17.1	27.1	8.5	17.9	25.4
Large					
10–20	10.6	10.1	3.4	5.0	6.8
20–50	2.3	1.2	0.6	1.1	—

Source: Spulber, p. 245.

development" which categorically stated that socialist industrialization must be accompanied by a socialist transformation of the countryside.* At the fifth Congress of the Bulgarian Communist Party (1948), Dimitrov stressed that nationalization of land is the inescapable end of the process of socialist transformation,[20] while the Polish constitutional discussions stressed that the persistence of private-land ownership is "the most important factor" delaying "the tempo of social change." [21] It was argued that by reducing the peasant to the status of a hired laborer, the socialist transformation of the countryside would assure state control over food supply, provide surplus labor through the introduction of mechanization, squeeze out of the agricultural sector some of the funds necessary for capital investment, and prevent the peasants from wielding political influence. Since these considerations, abstracted from the problem of their actual social and economic validity, seemed important to the regimes' survival, they felt justified in using the means necessary to achieve the desired consequences.

The policy of collectivization, applied with a considerable amount of coercion, relied on the following devices for inducing the peasants to join either the collective farms or the state farms: heavy taxes, forced state deliveries, moral pressure through repeated visits from party activists, a certain amount of local violence usually pitting the poor peasants or the landless rural proletariat against the richer farmers, punitive expeditions of urban party activists and police whose task would be to "socialize" rapidly a given district. The collective farms as established in East Europe ranged from the pooling of privately owned machinery and property to common ownership of land and machinery. Most, however, were of the latter, more "advanced," type and for this reason provoked a high degree of peasant resentment. Unlike an American farmer, say, who tends to think of his land as a commodity which is a source of income, to the peasant, land has also the properties of tradition and sentiment which vest it with a certain mystical quality. Efforts to deprive him of it were hence considered as measures directed at the very essence of his being. No wonder then that even among those peasants belonging to the party, the majority were unwilling to join the collectives. In Poland, for instance, only 31 per cent of peasant party members had joined by 1953.[22]

Generally speaking, the progress in collectivization was roughly equivalent to the degree of violence applied. The table below suggests

* "To create the economic base of socialism means to merge farming with socialist industry, in one integral economy, to subordinate farming to the direction of socialist industry." *Problems of Leninism* (Moscow, 1940), p. 121.

Per cent of arable land in the socialist sector [23]

	1950	1952	1953	1954	1956	1957	1958
Poland	12	13	17	19	24	14	15
Czechoslovakia	25	24	48	44	45	70	77
Rumania	12	19	21	26	35	50	51
Hungary	19	25	37	32	33	22	23
Bulgaria	44	50	62	60	62	90	92
East Germany	—	5	8	30	33	40	—
Yugoslavia	18	—	24	—	9	—	—

significant differences in the various states in this regard. In fact, it could be claimed that the internal strength of the regime was reflected by its ability to push collectivization forward and overcome internal resistance to it. In every country, with the exception of Bulgaria and to a lesser extent Czechoslovakia, the progress made was considerably slower than in the USSR during the 1930–1938 period. The rate of progress notwithstanding, a consequence of this policy was the rapid alienation of a good part of the peasantry. From the standpoint of larger ideological perspectives, this was not as important as the fact that the People's Democracies were going forward in eliminating what was considered to be the chief block to the socialist transformation. With this transformation progressing, material differences between East Europe and the USSR were lessening and the bonds for a close relationship strengthening.

The launching of the collectivization policy followed the earlier nationalization policy and paralleled the intensified efforts to industrialize the region. The nationalization policy, particularly in industry but also in handicrafts, by 1950 had resulted in the fairly general adoption of state ownership throughout the area, thereby breaking with the former pattern of diversification.* As a result, at the beginning

* The patterns of establishing uniform state ownership in nonagricultural production in East Europe may be briefly summarized as follows. At the end of the war, and following the first nationalization acts, in Czechoslovakia the nationalized sector contained about 57.7 per cent of the industrial labor force. Two years later, just before the February coup, the state sector had grown through minor nationalizations and adjustments to 63.9 per cent of the labor force. The new Communist regime immediately launched further state ownership schemes, and within a year, by January 1949, the state sector had grown to 89.2 per cent. Thus, to all intents and purposes, by 1949 nationalization had been achieved and the regime had attained direct control over the productive processes. In industry it went even further, taking in 96 per cent of the total industrial workers. In the next four years, the Communist regime successfully completed the eradication of the handicrafts and the imposition of its controls over retail trading.

In Rumania, another state in which nationalization had initially lagged, in June of the long-range socialist planning, all the People's Democracies could boast that the major means of production, save the agricultural sector, were in the hands of the proletariat. Socialist transformation was now to be accompanied according to the tried Stalinist experience, by a radical and rapid industrialization of the individual states, unhindered by private enterprise. This industrialization would result, together with collectivization, in a radical destruction of the old ways of life, bring to the cities hundreds of thousands of new laborers, produce extensive urban development, and shatter once and for all the remnants of former habits, traditions, and nonsocialist characteristics. The repetition of the Soviet experience of the thirties would be bound to create an environment essentially like the Soviet environment.

The plans, admittedly prepared with the assistance of Soviet economic advisers,[24] emphasized the priority of the development of heavy industry, to which the major investments would be assigned.* The funds were to be used to expand the existing industrial plants and also

---

1948 a broadly conceived nationalization law swept away most privately owned industries, and by 1949 the state sector included 85 per cent of the total industrial production; by 1952, 95 per cent.

In Hungary, after the postwar nationalization acts, by the beginning of 1948 about half of the industrial labor force was in the state sector and, two years later, upon the launching of the first Five Year Plan, the state could boast that its sector contained 90.5 per cent of the labor force.

In Bulgaria the industrial sector was nationalized in one major act in December 1947, and the state sector as far as production was concerned jumped from 6 per cent to 93 per cent.

In Poland, much of the initial nationalization was dictated by the wartime destruction and geographical changes, and already by 1946 the private sector in industry controlled a mere 11 per cent of the labor force. Two years later it was only 7 per cent, and by 1949, after further nationalization, in keeping with prevailing area trends, it decreased to 4.6 per cent.

Nationalization of domestic trade, which by 1947 had reached the level of 13 per cent in Hungary, 22 per cent in Poland, 42 per cent in Czechoslovakia, and 43 per cent in Bulgaria, moved apace and by 1950 reached 40 per cent in Hungary, 80 per cent in Poland, and about 98 per cent in the other two states. Elimination of private enterprise was thus rapidly accomplished. Based on Spulber, pp. 49-50, 64, 78, 80, 82, 90; Roberts, p. 322; *Wykonanie Narodowych Planow Gospodarczych 1948-1952* (Warsaw, 1952), p. 10; *News from Behind the Iron Curtain*, August 1952, p. 21; *Razvitie Ekonomiki Stran Narodnoi Demokratii* (Moscow, 1958), especially chapters 2-4, 6, 9-11, and the statistical appendix.

* The percentages of total investment assigned to heavy industry according to the national plans were: 34.5 per cent in the case of Poland: 37 per cent in Czechoslovakia, which represented an increase of more than 5 per cent over the initial version of the plan; 47.6 per cent in Hungary, an increase of more than 11 per cent over the initial plan; 44.1 per cent in Rumania; 36 per cent in Bulgaria. Economic Commission for Europe, *Etude sur la situation economique de l'Europe depuis la guerre* (Geneva, 1953), p. 25, as quoted in Marczewski, *Planification et croissance economique des democraties populaires*, p. 200.

to launch several spectacular schemes which were to symbolize the new socialist era and stand as lasting monuments to the socialist order. Each People's Democracy boasted of some such project: the Nowa Huta Steel Works in Poland, the Gottwald Steel Plants in Czechoslovakia, the Stalin Works at Dunapentele in Hungary, and the Dimitrovo Steel Plant in Bulgaria.[25]

Without evaluating the plans and their fulfillment, it is worth noting that within a few years of almost superhuman effort and tremendous social sacrifice, the various countries of East Europe could point to certain genuine achievements. Considerable strides were made in such sectors as steel production and coal extraction, and by 1953, total steel production was roughly equal to West Germany's and about twice as much as before the war. The area's hydroelectric capacity was more than doubled, and by 1953 Czechoslovakia, Poland, and Hungary roughly tripled their engineering production as compared to the prewar level.[26] By 1952, Poland's annual industrial production reached 194.8 per cent of the 1949 level (by comparison, in agriculture the total was only 104.9 per cent),[27] and in Czechoslovakia the comparable percentage was 198.9 per cent.[28] The area, with all its deficiencies and problems, was emerging into the industrial age even though its economies were still largely unintegrated and developed on a semiautarkic pattern.[29]

Internally, the *politically* significant consequence of this process of industrialization was the rapid increase in bringing the nonagricultural labor force into the organized, and hence more politically controllable, industrial process and urban life. According to the most exhaustive study available on the economics of East Europe, "between 1948 and 1953 there was a net increase of the non-agricultural labor force of about 400,000 in Bulgaria, 465,000 in Yugoslavia, close to 600,000 in Czechoslovakia, 750,000 in Hungary, 825,000 in Rumania, and over 1.9 million in Poland."[30] This amounted to an increase of about 33 per cent in the industrial labor force, telescoped into the remarkably short time of five years. During this period the rural population, while remaining generally stable in absolute numbers (with some small decreases), declined in terms of ratios between urban and rural populations as the new industries drained off the rural youth, having previously absorbed whatever surplus town labor had existed (in the form of the unemployed and the female labor force).

The new proletariat, housed in temporary barracks and workers' hotels, with no privacy, individuality, or family ties, was to help build the new tomorrow, the socialist society. The conditions under which

it labored have been best described by the poets and novelists. But to
many of these workers, the new environment did at first offer an improvement over previous conditions, or at least an opportunity of
breaking away from a life which many of them no longer thought
meaningful or desirable. Many of them did not have a clear image of
what tomorrow would bring, but many did have a vague feeling that
today was no longer for them — a feeling which Communist agitation
stimulated. The masses flocking to the cities and industrial work sites
were hoping for something they did not clearly grasp; but by coming
they were helping to weaken the existing social bonds, to undermine
the social institutions of the past which the Communists felt had
to fall. The effect of industrialization was to create a revolutionary
social situation in which the only source of cohesion would be the
party, the only source of direction the leadership's will.

Under these conditions, the Soviet methods of labor discipline and
organization were rapidly adopted. The trade unions were usually
subordinated with the absorption of the Social Democratic parties and
with the nationalization of the last areas of private enterprise. One-
man management assisted by party committees became the norm, and
the factory became merely a unit within a hierarchically organized
industrial pyramid, characterized by the strictest discipline and subordination. Laws of labor regulation, such as penalties for absenteeism
and lateness, and a system of sanctions patterned on the Soviet model
were adopted, together with specified norms, "socialist competitions,"
and premiums. Labor discipline was strictly enforced and labor recruitment subjected to state control. Announcing the introduction of
strict state surveillance over employment, the Czech Minister of Labor
stated:

By this new regulation the entire existing system, which was based on the
voluntary movement of labor under state supervision, will be abandoned,
and a new system applied which will directly control labor recruitment
for the most important sectors of our industry in the same manner as our
entire Socialist economy is directed.[31]

The submerging of society in the state, a process characteristic of
totalitarian development, was accordingly to be one of the major by-
products of the internal transformation.

The application of these new concepts meant that the People's
Democracies were becoming replicas of the Soviet system, though
somewhat less advanced (in the Marxist historical sense). In effect,
they duplicated the Stalinist pattern of "economic war communism,"
that is, a rigid system of limited priorities to be achieved at the cost of

other, less essential, economic sectors, particularly agriculture, housing, and light industry. The previous diversity among East European states was giving way not only to common patterns but also to a fundamental affinity between their domestic patterns and those of the USSR.

At this stage one might again raise the question: which of these changes had been motivated by ideology and which by power considerations? Power alone cannot explain the emphasis put on rapid collectivization unless the peasant is considered by those in power to be an imminent political threat. But if he is, then the very act of such consideration is colored by ideological assumptions about the implications of private enterprise. Industrialization was badly needed by the area — and Communist power was admittedly strengthened by it, initially at least. But the nature of the industrial development, based on Soviet experience, again was affected by the image of the society desired and the forces said to oppose it. In this manner policy reflected the impact of a peculiar normative perspective on reality as well as the assumed existential imperatives of that reality for those in policy-making positions.

As far as relations among Communist powers were concerned, it followed from Marxist thinking that these necessary internal changes were also creating political and economic bonds between the Soviet and East European societies. The result would be a solid, spirited, and single-minded phalanx which would stand together under any circumstances. The parties, by becoming Stalinized, by purging themselves and destroying such sources of deviationism as the Social Democrats, would tend to be more oriented toward the USSR. Terror used against the population at large would destroy any sources of potential opposition to the regime and introduce such fear that compliance with the policies and purposes of the system would be assured. Collectivization would carry the class struggle into the countryside and weed out the normally conservative orientation of the peasants, driving them into collective institutions where they could be subjected to organized political and economic control. Economic transformation through nationalization and, more significantly, through industrialization would create the objective basis for socialism while ripping apart the social fabric to such an extent that the Communist Party — Stalinist and dependent on the Soviet Union — would be the only source of social cohesion, the only organization to which the youth, in particular, could turn for guidance. The revised theory as applied would create the material bases for an internally cohesive socialist bloc. It would serve as a solid foundation for Stalinism as an interstate system.

CHAPTER **6** –

Stalinism: A Pattern for the Communist Interstate System

STALIN never underestimated the historical significance of political power. Entertaining a marked Bolshevik distaste for those Marxists who wished to rely on spontaneous material processes for the achievement of the desired goals, the Soviet leader throughout his spectacular career displayed a remarkable talent for wielding political instruments and employing organizational devices in the promotion of his ends. This was as true in the case of his personal political career as in the broader area of the development of the Soviet state and the "socialist transformation" effected in Soviet society. He unquestionably believed that the role of the state in a socialist society must be that of an indispensable tool for the acceleration of inevitable historical trends and that this positive role of the state deserved ample recognition in Soviet ideological perspectives. The practical expression of such an orientation was Stalin's growing reliance, particularly in his later years, on state institutions and the administrative structure – a reliance symbolized by Stalin's dual capacity as Premier and Secretary General and effected through the appointment of most Politburo members to responsible bureaucratic posts. Following the Second World War, the line pursued in domestic propaganda was to glorify the Soviet state as an almost coequal agent with the CPSU of historical progress.* In theory this meant the assignment to the state – to the political superstructure – of an important, positive, and conscious role.

Stalin's most elaborate statement concerning his views on the func-

---

* This attitude, as was to be expected, was duly imitated in the People's Democracies. In his memorandum to the Central Committee of the Hungarian Communist Party, Imre Nagy noted: "It is well known among Party leaders that when Matyas Rakosi became Premier he alluded to Stalin in voicing the view within the Political Committee that it was necessary to increase the role of the state vis-à-vis the Party; that it was necessary to place the government more in the foreground. . . . He indicated that placing the state and the government more in the foreground and increasing respect for them was an important task of the Party when the Council of Ministers came to the fore." *On Communism*, pp. 251–252.

tions of the socialist state came at the twilight of his career, when his dependence on the administrative structure had placed the state in an exalted position in the Soviet system. In an oft-cited pronouncement, "Regarding Marxism in Linguistics," Stalin restated the basic assumptions of Marxism concerning the relation between change in the socio-economic realm and change in the political sphere:

Every base has its corresponding superstructure . . . the capitalist base has its superstructure, the socialist base has its superstructure. If the base changes and is eliminated, then its superstructure changes and is eliminated after it; if a new base is born, then a superstructure corresponding to it is born after it.[1]

This, however, was not to be interpreted literally. To do so could lead to a dangerous underestimation of the role of the state and, particularly, to erroneous conclusions regarding its historical significance once the socialist changes had taken place. Stalin duly amplified his views, explaining that:

The superstructure is generated by the base but this by no means signifies that it merely reflects the base, that it is passive, neutral and indifferent to the fate of its base, to the fate of classes, to the character of the system. On the contrary, having put in an appearance, it then becomes a *most active* force which contributes vigorously to the formation and consolidation of its base, takes all steps to assist the new order to drive the old base and the former classes into the dust and liquidate them.[2]

It follows from this categorical assertion that for anyone to minimize the role of the Soviet state would be tantamount to a betrayal of the interests of the socioeconomic base — to a betrayal of socialism, in fact. The interests of the Soviet state are hence considered inseparable from the cause of socialism.

Stalin's insistence on the fundamental importance of the state, even for effecting a revolutionary upheaval in the material base, is illustrated by his discussion of collectivization. Pointing out that collectivization was a revolution which had set up a new socialist order in the countryside, Stalin explained that it still did not require, as might have been expected from usual Marxist thought, the creation of a new regime because it had been "a revolution from above" carried out by the state with the support of the majority of the peasantry.[3] The socialist state, established by a revolution, could thus in turn become an instrument of positive reform, creating further changes in the base through political devices. It could do so effectively because, unlike a bourgeois state, it was no longer plagued by internal contradictions which would ultimately spell its doom. The socialist state could be an agent of history without fearing that history would inevitably turn around to devour the state.

The very nature of the Soviet bloc involved similar principles. The People's Democracy as a political institution represented a superstructure resting on an only partially transformed base. The bloc's task, therefore, was to complete the process of the socioeconomic transformation of the base, but it would be rash, or at least premature, to depend purely on a community of patterns in the socioeconomic base for the maintenance of close ties between it and the USSR. For this reason, it was essential that political ties be firmly established as part of the creative contribution which the superstructure has to make in each historical phase to "the formation and consolidation of its base." [4] Stalinism as an interstate system in the existing phase had to be, given Stalin's categories of analysis, an essentially political system.

The construction of the Soviet bloc, however, could not be carried on at a sacrifice to the Soviet state. In fact, since what harmed the Soviet state harmed socialism and what aided it could not help but aid socialism, the construction of the Soviet bloc was only meaningful if it strengthened the USSR. The strength of the Soviet state, in turn, was bound to aid the People's Democracies in their "construction of socialism." This meant, simply, that no conflict of interest was possible as long as a consistent policy of assigning priority to the interests of the Soviet state was pursued. Temporary difficulties caused as a result of this were more than compensated for by the strengthening of the Soviet state; this state in turn would strengthen the states of the People's Democracies which in turn could then proceed to reconstruct those parts of the base which still needed it. According to this neatly circular argument, if temporary difficulties arose as a consequence, for instance, of economic arrangements favoring the USSR, these difficulties were outweighed by the resultant increased might of the political instrumentality.

Stalinism as an interstate system, then, rested on the primacy of the political factor and on the priority of Soviet interests, derived logically from Stalin's concepts of the relation between the material and the political, between the base and the superstructure.

The Formal Devices

The vital political "superstructure" had relatively few formal institutional devices. Much like the Soviet political system itself, the formal arrangements were meaningful only when infused with the more dynamic content of informal leadership, controls, and ideological zeal. Without this content the Soviet government would be a far different kind of system. This is also true in the case of Soviet-satellite relations. Without the informal content, the outward forms of that relationship would be radically different in practice, as the future, at least in part, was to show.

The formal ties binding the People's Democracies to the USSR and to one another were expressed through a series of bilateral state agreements, usually in the form of a treaty of friendship, collaboration and mutual aid, and cultural cooperation agreements.[5] The treaties were all bilateral — no multilateral agreement existed — and, significantly, the Soviet Union refrained from signing cultural cooperation agreements with the People's Democracies although the latter did conclude such agreements among themselves. However, the ties among the various People's Democracies were never as close as between any one of them individually and the USSR. No special political schemes bringing, say, Rumania or Bulgaria closer together, or Poland and Czechoslovakia (which had planned a federation during the war), were implemented in the treaty structure. After the creation of the German Democratic Republic, the People's Democracies signed cultural and political treaties with it, but the latter, since Germany was still formally demilitarized, were carefully called treaties of friendship, not mutual aid (see table, p. 109), and the Soviet Union, still hopeful of exerting influence in West Germany, refrained from concluding such a treaty until West Germany joined NATO.

All of the political treaties emphasized the determination of the signatories to assist each other in case of external attack, with a re-armed Germany or some state allied to it usually singled out for specific mention.[6] The anti-German orientation of the defense treaties effectively played on the vivid memories which most Central and East Europeans had of the German occupation and supplied one of the very few popular aspects of the treaties. This was especially the case with the Soviet-Polish treaty which gave formal protection to the Oder-Neisse line. Similarly, the Polish-Czech treaty, despite the fairly widespread dislike of the respective populations for each other, did contain a genuine element of national interest insofar as the German problem was concerned. When the Polish-East German agreement of 1950 was signed, it was hailed by Polish-German official circles as the first instance of formal German recognition for the new frontier [7] and, despite the known limitations of the East German

regime, it was welcomed by Polish public opinion as another impediment in the way of any future German designs on this territory.

Beyond this persistent concern of the East European states with
the German question, the treaties could hardly be accepted as politically meaningful arrangements reached by equal and sovereign partners and with reference to their own specific national interests. They
did, however, serve as symbolic expression of the Marxist position
that states building socialism cannot harbor aggressive designs against
one another and are, by definition, friendly. States with bitter and
still vibrant traditions of hatred went through the motions of signing
friendship treaties even while unresolved territorial issues were keeping the passions aflame. And certainly the East German Communists
were not helped by Grotewohl's renunciation of the lands east of the
Oder and Neisse rivers, nor was Rakosi's popularity enhanced by his
approval of the loss of Transylvania or parts of Slovakia. The Polish
Communists similarly labored under the handicap of having sanctioned the Soviet seizure of East Poland, although this bitter pill was
made easier to swallow through the Oder-Neisse line and the Soviet
support for it.

The timing of the treaties deserves comment. The accompanying
table suggests that in the initial phase the construction of formal links
applied primarily to the USSR, Czechoslovakia, and Poland. Yugoslavia at that time was also an active treaty partner, having signed a
political alliance with the USSR on April 11, 1945, with Poland on
March 16, 1946, and with Czechoslovakia on May 9 of the same year.
These treaties were abrogated following Tito's expulsion from the
Cominform. At this time, however, Hungary, Rumania, and Bulgaria
were not included in the bilateral network since technically they were
former enemy states subject to armistice arrangements. Following the
1947 Paris Treaty, Yugoslavia was the first to conclude formal treaties
with them (see Chapter 3), thereby beating the USSR to the punch.
In the course of one year, however, these states were included in the
treaty structure while the agreements with Yugoslavia were declared
null and void.

The treaties followed a set pattern. First, they created so-called
defense alliances between the cosignatories and prohibited them from
entering into any coalitions opposing the interests of one of the signatories. Second, they bound the signatories to participate in all efforts
to protect the peace and particularly enjoined them to oppose any
and all aggressive designs on the part of a rearmed German state and
its allies. Third, they made explicit the positive qualities of the friend-

Bilateral political treaties and cultural treaties

	USSR	Poland	Czecho-slovakia	Hungary	Rumania	Bulgaria	East Germany
USSR		FMA 4/21/45	FMA 12/12/43	FMA 2/18/48	FMA 2/4/48	FMA 3/18/48	
Poland	FMA 4/21/45		FMA 3/10/47	FMA 6/18/48	FMA 1/26/49	FMA 5/29/48	F 7/6/50
			CC 7/4/47	CC 1/31/48	CC 2/27/48	CC 6/28/47	CC 1/8/52
Czecho-slovakia	FMA 12/12/43	FMA 3/10/47		FMA 4/16/49	FMA 7/21/48	FMA 4/23/48	F 6/23/50
		CC 7/4/47			CC 10/14/47	CC 6/20/47	
Hungary	FMA 2/18/48	FMA 6/18/48	FMA 4/16/49		FMA 1/24/48	FMA 7/16/48	F 6/26/50
		CC 1/31/48			CC 11/25/47	CC 10/29/47	
Rumania	FMA 2/4/48	FMA 1/26/49	FMA 7/21/48	FMA 1/24/48		FMA 1/16/48	F 8/22/50
		CC 2/27/48	CC 10/14/47	CC 11/25/47		CC 6/20/47	CC 9/20/50
Bulgaria	FMA 3/18/48	FMA 5/29/48	FMA 4/23/48	FMA 7/16/48	FMA 1/16/48		F 8/25/50
		CC 6/28/47	CC 6/20/47	CC 10/29/47	CC 6/20/47		CC 5/5/52
East Germany		F 6/6/50	F 6/23/50	F 6/26/50	F 8/22/50	F 8/25/50	
		CC 1/8/52			CC 9/20/50	CC 5/5/52	

Key: FMA: Friendship and Mutual Aid; CC: Cultural Cooperation; F: Friendship Treaty.

ship existing between the cosignatories by emphasizing mutual respect for sovereignty, noninterference in domestic affairs, and equality in their relations. Fourth, they either provided for future economic cooperation or endorsed it if it had already been established. Finally, in the case of treaties among the People's Democracies, provision was made for cultural cooperation between them.[8] The treaties were hailed as expressing a new type of state relations, confirming Stalin's thesis that new social content seeks new political forms. They were said to represent a community of interests based on common socioeconomic forces as well as a new form of international behavior.

The formal relations between the USSR and the People's Democracies went quite far in stressing the latter's sovereignty, equality, and independence. Nothing in the treaties sanctioned either Soviet leadership or direct Soviet interference in the domestic affairs of the allied states. Soviet supremacy, stressed ideologically, was thus not given a formal basis and could not, in the future, justify itself by any reliance on formal arrangements. On the contrary, the egalitarian forms, once power began to waver, could begin to exert some slight influence of their own — at least a point of departure for those who may have wanted actual relations to be compatible with the formal. The latter declined in importance as the Soviet bloc more and more took on the character of the Stalinist system. During the earlier phase of diversity, the agreements signed with Czechoslovakia, Yugoslavia, and Poland were actually meaningful links in the chain tying these states to the USSR. Yugoslav efforts in the Balkans also took advantage of these more traditional methods. The agreements reached between 1948 and 1950 merely completed the initial process, and there are good grounds for assuming that an agreement of friendship reached between the USSR and, let us say, Rumania in 1948 had far less political significance than did similar agreements signed with Czechoslovakia in 1943 or even with Yugoslavia in 1945. Its value was now essentially symbolic and propagandistic and to some extent required by local Communists who wished to maintain a formal position no less dignified than that of the Poles or Czechs. The treaties also served to regularize the relationships established earlier and internationally symbolized the formal equality of Communist states. However, after 1950 no political treaty of any significance was signed between Stalin and the People's Democracies since there was no useful political task to be served by doing so.*

* A minor but very characteristic corollary of this was the disappearance of traditional diplomatic activity in the Soviet camp. With the exception of periodic foreign

The decline in the importance of what formal ties there were was particularly reflected in the waning of the Cominform's position. It was originally designed to coordinate the most important Communist parties and to arrange for the mutual "exchange" of their experiences. By 1950, however, the problem of exchange had become a matter of one-way traffic, while the failure of the anti-Tito campaign had discredited the Cominform, a primary agent in the campaign. A further factor minimizing the significance of the Cominform as a binding organization was the fact that the recently victorious Chinese party was not included in its membership. (It is not known whether it was kept out by Stalin or whether the Chinese refrained from joining, which they might have done on the easy pretext that the Cominform was essentially a European organization.) The absence of China, the loss of Yugoslavia, and the direct Soviet involvement in East European affairs meant that the Cominform lost much of its original purpose and vitality. Its formal meetings became increasingly rare (the fourth, and last, plenary session took place in Hungary on November 27, 1949 [9]), although its publication continued to appear. In fact, its function became increasingly informational and propagandistic. In its declining years the Cominform was used primarily against the Yugoslavs, and its lessened political instrumentality was symbolic of the predominant Stalinist reliance on informal and indirect devices for keeping the Soviet bloc together.*

The Informal Devices

Stalin himself constituted the most important informal instrument of control. Strange as it may seem in a situation in which socioeconomic processes played such an important role, a single individual was able to exert such influence in the shaping of societies and political systems. Thus it is quite impossible to discuss the pattern of Commu-

---

ministers' conferences called to take a united stand on some issue, politically significant contact was not maintained through diplomatic channels, with the exception of the role played by Soviet ambassadors. The Foreign Ministry was not considered to be an important position in the People's Democracy, and second-rate party politicians were appointed to the post. (Among the more important joint conferences, the following may be cited: the June 1948 Warsaw Conference of the Foreign Ministers of the USSR, Poland, Czechoslovakia, Yugoslavia, Hungary, Rumania, Bulgaria, and Albania, with respect to the creation of a West German state; the October 1950 Prague Conference of the Foreign Ministers of the above countries, without Yugoslavia but including East Germany, on the problem of West German rearmament. Cf. *Pravda*, October 22, 1950.)

* In this an old tsarist domestic practice was perpetuated. This is discussed in my paper, "The Patterns of Autocracy," *The Transformation of Russian Society Since 1861*, C. E. Black, ed. (Cambridge, 1960).

nist interstate relations at this particular juncture without specifically referring to Stalin's role. Stalin as a symbol, Stalin as a victorious leader, Stalin as the builder of socialism in the USSR, contributed to these relations an intangible yet crucial psychological dimension which introduced devotion, fear, and hatred into the policy-making process and made him present in any important discussion. To the Communist fanatic, love and devotion to Stalin were essential ingredients of one's beliefs. To the practitioner, fear made him act like the fanatic even as it induced hatred. And for most Communists, all these elements together created a certain ambivalence, even if not a complete charismatic commitment.

While it would be easy to exaggerate the devotion to Stalin and underestimate the ingredient of fear and hatred (as in the case of the dissolution of the Polish Communist Party), it still would be difficult to explain the impact on many Communists of Khrushchev's revelations of Stalin's crimes unless in fact they entertained this idealized image of him and through him of the system in general. Stalin somehow personalized the conviction that the ends justify the means, and it was not really so much the contents of Khrushchev's revelations that were so shocking but the realization that the "means" had not been really necessary. Yet it is no exaggeration to say, and this has been confirmed by many former East European Communists, that between 1949 and 1953 many (but certainly not all) of the most radical decisions were made not on the basis of direct orders from Stalin but through the application of the principle of "anticipated reaction" — by attempting to do what Stalin might wish done.*

This situation was further intensified by the fact that by this time all the East European leaders had been approved by Stalin personally, and, in his later years particularly, he was not known for approving those blessed with an independent character. As a result, the leaders of the area were usually people who had successfully demonstrated their commitment to Stalinism either early in the Comintern days — Ulbricht, Rakosi, or Dimitrov — through loyal service in the Comintern-NKVD *apparat* — Berman or Bierut — or through demonstrable employment of Stalinist methods in the handling of one's party — Gottwald or Gheorghiu-Dej. While the essence of Stalinism was al-

---

* Rakosi was certainly one such leader, as brought out not only by Nagy but even by Kadar. Another example is Bierut of Poland, whose devotion even Stalin sometimes had to restrain. On one occasion, for instance, Bierut suggested that the Polish national anthem be replaced by a less nationalistic song. Stalin balked at this innovation with a remark, "it's a good song. Leave it for a while." Testimony of J. Swiatlo, a Polish Secret Police defector.

ways the maintenance of a degree of insecurity among local leaders, there was no doubt that to them the sole, albeit by no means certain, avenue of salvation was the intense practice of Stalinism. Stalin's lieutenants in East Europe knew this, and their knowledge constituted a basic factor in the shaping of Soviet-satellite relations.

Stalin's personal prestige was closely associated with the prestige of the CPSU as the original revolutionary party. To outsiders this may appear odd, but to those who were actually committed to the movement the CPSU had a special place by virtue of its unique position and historical role. In time Stalin tended to overshadow it, but even many of those who disagreed with Stalin still had a special, personalized commitment to the Soviet party which they felt could not ultimately err even if it should occasionally stray from the right path. Dedijer's descriptions of Tito's and his associates' reactions to Soviet threats is a case in point.[10] It brings out once again that, because for so many years the CPSU had been the only party actually building socialism, many Communists were unwilling to pit their views against those of the CPSU. The determination of policy on the basis of ideological assessments was thus conceded to be a Soviet prerogative because the CPSU had gained Communist virtue through the baptism of power.*

A pattern of autonomous controls resulted from the factors outlined above. In some respects the controls operated automatically, without continual communication and direction; or they operated merely through indirect hints, such as the aforementioned *Pravda* article condemning the Balkan Union or the January 24, 1955, article by Shepilov praising heavy industrialization (see Chapters 8 and 10). However, neither the East European leaders nor presumably Stalin

---

* S. Bialer, until 1956 on the staff of the Polish Central Committee, in his testimony (*Wybralem prawde*, p. 7) states that even as late as 1955 the standard reply of Berman or Ochab to any doubts raised by their associates was: "We must have full confidence in the Presidium of the Soviet Party." Probably the best summary of the type of reasoning which typifies a self-imposed system of control was given by a high-ranking Yugoslav leader, S. Zhujovich, who opposed Tito's intransigence vis-à-vis Moscow: "the Soviet Union as the offspring of the October Revolution, a country of socialism, the homeland of the proletariat of the whole world, was a state with an administrative organization, with a leadership in the organization of the economy and production that corresponded to the teachings of classic socialism and the postulates of Leninism, theoretically formulated and elaborated by Stalin. Therefore, there was or could be no comment or explanation — only silence . . . the Soviet Party was the parent Party, the only complete and correct interpreter of Marxism-Leninism . . . above all: Stalin, the Leader, the Teacher" (Dedijer, p. 398). This type of orientation, when operative *within a Stalinist system*, can easily result in the most orthodox Stalinist pattern of behavior, divorced from all reality.

seemed satisfied to limit these autonomous controls to an inner sanctum of the top-level leadership. Ultimately, as in the Soviet Union itself, the entire society should have a similar orientation.[11] For this reason, the adulation of Stalin and the USSR as a whole became a matter of purposeful policy designed to induce this broader orientation. The worship of Stalin became part of the daily routine of almost anyone engaged in factory or office work: the pictures on the walls, the incantations at exhortation meetings, the posters, the statues. In every field of human endeavor reference to Stalin was made,* and with streets, parks, factories, and even cities named after him, Stalin personified the close relationship being forged between the USSR and the People's Democracies.

On a more general plane, similar efforts were made with respect to the USSR. In every People's Democracy a society for the propagation of friendship with the Soviet Union was established, both on an elitist and mass basis. Leading intellectuals were enjoined to enroll as members, and recruitment drives were held throughout the countries. In Poland, the membership amounted in 1956 to 7.1 million;[12] in Bulgaria 1.7 million;[13] in Rumania about 5 million;[14] in Czechoslovakia about 2 million in 1953. The societies, usually with branch offices in every town, sponsored Soviet exhibits, featured Soviet movies, held appropriate celebrations on Soviet anniversaries, published their own papers and magazines, arranged for translations of Soviet books and organized Russian-language classes for adults (compulsory for school children).† Their task, in brief, was to eliminate negative conceptions

---

* Some sample press citations: "The teaching of Stalin embraces all the universal principles of nature in its smallest details. He solves all the practical problems of understanding natural science" (*Elet es Tudomany*, December 24, 1952). "Without the special care of Stalin, the present advanced techniques in meat-combines, preserve and sugar plants, fish, and everything else done in the field of food industry would not exist" (*Rabotnichesko Delo*, January 7, 1950). "It is only Stalin . . . who is able to analyze clearly and find with mathematical precision the exact way toward solution of present day problems" (*Rude Pravo*, December 21, 1952). *News from Behind the Iron Curtain*, March 1953, pp. 36–37.

† The teaching of Russian was also used as a medium for instilling devotion to the USSR and to Stalin. For example, the following is an account from a Rumanian newspaper of such a language class held for workers of the Bucharest Post Office: "From the first bench, Comrade Dumitrescu rises and goes shyly to the blackboard. He is now in front of it — he takes the chalk from Comrade Medelcovici and, following the word 'Mir' [Russian for peace], he writes, full of emotion, 'Slava Stalinu' — Glory to Stalin–" (*Viata Sindicala*, January 10, 1952). The scope of the activities of the friendship societies is suggested by the following figures: In Czechoslovakia, before 1947, Soviet publications constituted only 4 per cent of the books published; by 1952, the figure had risen to 50 per cent (*News from Behind the Iron Curtain*, December 1952, p. 40), and the total number of books printed was 21 million. In Poland, the

of Soviet life and instill a positive emotional commitment to the USSR.*

The policy of stimulating a sense of commitment to the USSR was, of course, most seriously applied in the schools and youth organizations. The hope was that ultimately a new spirit of genuine and voluntary identification would emerge as "class hostility" to the USSR was undermined by the socialist transformation. Organized national adulation, and the beginnings of a form of cultural Russification, would in the meantime paralyze any independent responses through the creation of a surface unanimity which very few individuals would ever dare challenge. That day would finally come when diversity would no longer be desired or even conceived of. "If the mind is obligated to obey a word of command, it can at any rate feel that it is not free. But if it has been so manipulated beforehand that it obeys without even waiting for the word of command, it loses even the consciousness of enslavement." [15]

The application in East Europe of radical political and economic measures increased the dependence of the ruling Communist parties on Stalin's support. Without his support, by 1952, it is doubtful that any regime (even including the Czech) could have successfully maintained itself in power. This, of course, gave the autonomously operative controls an additional quality of self-interest insofar as the ruling stratum was concerned. The Soviet rulers, however, were unwilling, and indeed probably unable, to rely entirely on support derived from motivations of conviction and self-interest. For this reason they had elaborated at home a complex system of controls designed to maintain

---

society arranged, during ten years of its existence, for the translation of 5000 Soviet titles with a printing of 100 million copies, and also sponsored 1300 competitions on various Soviet themes (*Trybuna Ludu*, October 6, 1955). In 1954, of all the translations printed, more than 90 per cent were from Russian (Halecki, p. 146).

* Combating negative stereotypes took various forms. An interesting instance of typically totalitarian practice was prohibition of the use of certain words carrying a subconsciously negative connotation. In Poland, the most frequent translation of the word *Soviet* was *sowiecki* (Soviet Union: *Zwiazek Sowiecki*). Since this word had been used during the twenty years of Polish pre-World War II statehood and had acquired a certain value content which was rather anti-Soviet, the word was replaced by another derived from the literal Polish translation of the word *Soviet*, which means a Council, in Polish *rada*. The Soviet Union hence became *Zwiazek Radziecki* (Councillar Union). Another more frequent form of combating anti-Soviet sentiments was the prohibition of the sale of anything which might even indirectly lead to anti-Soviet views. For instance, after October 1956, it was revealed in the legal organ, *Prawo i Zycie* (no. 5, 1957), that a bookseller in Poznan had been sentenced in 1953 to three years' imprisonment for the sale of the official memoirs of a cavalry regiment which had fought against the Soviet forces in 1920.

loyalty and to prevent societal and political relations from acquiring excessive rigidity. This system, presumably for similar reasons, was exported to and imposed on East Europe.

The first link in the informal chain of imposed political control was direct consultation between the Soviet leadership and that of the countries concerned. The second was the permanent supervision of domestic events through reliance on the Soviet ambassadors. The third link was a close contact with various party organs, particularly those dealing with ideological matters, through frequent exchange of experts and visits of Soviet "advisers." The fourth tie was the direct penetration of those governmental institutions particularly important as the instruments of power and force. And the fifth was the isolation of the various Communist states from the rest of the world and from one another. All of this was buttressed by Soviet military might, both in the potential and the actual sense. These controls, unlike the autonomously operative ones, were subject to purposeful Moscow direction.

The direct consultations with Moscow almost always occurred on a bilateral basis, with a given party leadership invited to a conference with Stalin and his associates. No multilateral top-level Communist consultations were held from 1949 until the Nineteenth Party Congress in October 1952. Accordingly, in each instance a party leadership was facing Moscow alone and Stalin was able to assure his visitors that the other parties had already endorsed and were enthusiastically backing the suggested policy. Under such circumstances a visiting delegation had no choice but to endorse whatever was suggested and to do so with enthusiasm and alacrity. The usual procedure was for the Soviet leadership to invite for "consultations" the trusted head of a party and some of his associates who were in charge of matters pertinent to the planned discussions.[16] A visit to Moscow was viewed by those selected as an opportunity to re-establish personal connections and to strengthen individual positions. The delegation would return home with a keen appreciation of the latest Soviet assessments and programs. This in turn would give its members an advantage in any power competition over those who had been left behind. That the range of Soviet intervention reached the most important personnel decisions as well was openly admitted by Imre Nagy in his memorandum prepared in 1955–1956 for the use of Hungarian leaders, and not meant for publication. He revealed that, even after the death of Stalin, the Soviet leaders considered it their prerogative to discuss and decide who ought to head the Hungarian government and what its policies ought to be.*

The second lever of control was the Soviet ambassador. Direct intervention and interference were not always used in this sphere. Given the whole Stalinist complex — the fear of secret police, the internal competitions in loyalty, the genuine desire of some to be true Stalinists — the ambassador's very presence on the scene constituted an important lever of control. Every high party functionary knew that the Soviet ambassador continually reported his assessments of the situation, his evaluations of the "construction of socialism," his estimates of the attitudes and behavior of various important public figures back to Moscow. This is a normal, almost routine, aspect of ambassadorial activity. But in the existing context, considering the *personal* implications that might follow from such reports, all the leaders naturally wanted the ambassador's reports to give the "proper" evaluation of their activity and to correspond to their own reports to the Soviet leaders.[17] An unavoidable consequence was that the less secure a leader, the more anxious he would be to make certain that the Soviet envoy got *his* views of the situation, *his* estimate of the other party colleagues. Such a relationship could not help but develop a certain dynamic which in time established as a matter of regular practice the extreme importance of being on good and very close terms with the Soviet ambassador. The fact that the local leaders normally would not see his dispatches merely increased their uncertainty and diligence. Hence, even without actual meddling, the Soviet ambassador became a central lever of Soviet supervision.

* In May 1953, following the Soviet decisions to establish "collective leadership," Rakosi traveled to Moscow for a major policy discussion. According to Nagy (*On Communism*), Comrade Malenkov pointed out that the Soviets had discussed with Rakosi the personal questions that concerned the separation of party and state leadership. "We asked, 'whom do you recommend as your deputy?' He could name no one. He had objections to everyone whose name was mentioned; he had something against everyone. Everyone was suspect except he alone. This appalled us very much, said Comrade Malenkov" (pp. 250–251). Describing a later Moscow conference, in May 1954, Nagy cites various criticisms of the Hungarian party leadership voiced by Khrushchev, and adds, "Comrade Malenkov, too, found that we were slow in correcting our mistakes in Party leadership and that Rakosi, as Party First Secretary, was not doing the job well." He then cites what might have been the minutes of the meeting and quotes the Soviet leaders as stating, "Comrade Rakosi must take the lead in the fight to correct previous mistakes and to implement the resolutions of the Central Committee. . . . The Party leadership needs Comrade Rakosi, but he must know and realize that he will have to merge into the collective leadership because that is the only way in which he can do his work well" (pp. 280–281). A certain "paternal" relationship is suggested by these comments.

Not all Soviet ambassadors, however, relied merely on the implications of their presence. Some are known to have intervened actively in the domestic affairs of the People's Democracies. The official Soviet position on the role of the Soviet ambassador was explicitly stated in the correspondence between Stalin and Tito prior to the break. A Soviet envoy in a People's Democracy was held to possess the right to gather information on all domestic matters, including the most confidential, and from anyone he pleased. He could do this either through his secret agents or by requesting such information from the most highly placed Communists without having to go through official channels. While reciprocity was not granted in this respect to the envoys of the People's Democracies in the USSR, the privileged position of the Soviet ambassador was claimed on the basis of a true Communist-to-Communist relationship. In Yugoslavia, the Soviet ambassador thus felt justified in intriguing with those Politburo members who opposed Tito. In Poland, according to the testimony of a party defector who had read the transcripts of the July 1955 CPSU Central Committee Plenum, the Soviet ambassadors (V. Z. Lebedev, 1946–1953; G. M. Popov, 1953–1954) were said in this document to have sponsored intraparty intrigues, occasionally abusing the Polish party leaders, treating them as inferiors who could be summoned to the Soviet Embassy whenever the ambassador desired.[18] Lebedev's behavior apparently became so intolerable that after Stalin's death the Polish Politburo prevailed on the Soviet leadership to have him recalled.[19]

The Soviet envoy also acted as a transmitter of important policy decisions when no direct consultations were deemed necessary. At least two significant coincidences seem to suggest this: the arrival in Prague of V. Zorin just prior to the coup of the Czech Communist Party, and the flight of V. S. Semenov from East Berlin to Moscow and the announcement of the New Course in East Germany a few days after his return. The role that the Soviet ambassador played during the era characterized by Stalinism doubtlessly varied depending on the local circumstances, on the degree of actual implementation of Stalinist policies by the local leadership, on the indigenous strength of the regime, and on the personal ties of the leaders with Moscow. Nonetheless, his functions, both passive and active, went far beyond the realm usually prescribed by diplomatic protocol.

The third type of informal controls operated through the maintenance of close contacts between the CPSU Central Committee *apparat* and the Party *apparats* in the People's Democracies. In the first instance, this involved the appointment of Communists with an extensive Soviet or Comintern background, frequently with experience in the NKVD networks, to head the various sections of the central committees. According to one source, the Inspectorate of Party Cadres in the Bulgarian Central Committee was staffed with former functionaries of the Soviet secret police, as was also the case with the Commission of State Control and the Commission of Science, Art, and Culture.[20] In Poland, apart from the two most prominent leaders themselves, Bierut and Berman, who had worked for the NKVD and the Comintern, respectively, even as late as 1956 a member of the Politburo, F. Mazur, was considered to be in the service of the MVD. The same was said to be the case with the Polish ambassadors in Moscow and Peking.[21]

Beyond these glaring, but not infrequent, cases, control was exercised through visits of Soviet party functionaries whose task was to advise the East European Communists concerning the latest Soviet views on matters of interest to them, particularly on matters of ideological thinking. S. Bialer, a defector from the agit-prop section of the Polish Central Committee, reports that he consulted with Professor Alexandrov whose task was the ideological supervision of the Party academies in Poland; other Soviet experts would occasionally be dispatched to consult with Polish philosophers or to discuss and guide the work of the Polish economists, and so on.[22] As a further assurance, the most promising young party activists were sent to study (usually for one year) in the Soviet Party Academy, attached to the Central Committee of the CPSU, where they could drink from the fountains of wisdom, acquire dialectical skills, and master the arcana of politics.

The most institutionalized informal control system involved the direct Soviet penetration of those governmental institutions which were particularly important as instruments of power: usually the secret police and the armed forces. The purpose was essentially twofold: to ensure their absolute loyalty to the USSR and to prevent their control by some local leaders who might then be tempted to oppose the Soviet Union. For this reason, the Soviet leadership felt it desirable to establish the most intimate links between its own secret police, under Beria, and the networks set up in East Europe, as well as between its armed forces and those being created in the People's Democracies. This association became particularly important in the later stages of Stalinism, when the intensity of the party purges all but liberated the police from party control and made it a semiautonomous agency subject, in the final analysis, only to Moscow itself.

According to Colonel Swiatlo of the Polish Security Forces, the Polish Security Ministry only occasionally reported to the Polish Politburo. Swiatlo's assertions were confirmed in 1956 by Berman, the head of the Politburo Committee on Security.[23] The organization of the secret police from the very beginning was carried on with the personal assistance of important Soviet officers. In Poland, General I. Serov assisted in the initial organization, and particularly in the liquidation of the Home Army.[24] The head of the Polish Security Ministry, W. Radkiewicz, had Soviet officers as his personal guards and was advised by General Lalin of the Soviet Ministry of State Security.[25] In the Polish ministry itself, of the twenty departments, eight were headed by Soviet officers directly, three had Soviet "advisers," and of the eleven identified as Poles or Polish Jews at least four were former employees of the NKVD and one a former officer in the Soviet armed forces.[26] That seems to have been the pattern elsewhere as well.* In Bulgaria, for instance, already in 1948 — according to Yugoslav allegations — the Ministry of the Interior was under complete Soviet control,[27] and the Minister of the Interior, Georgi Tzankov, was a product of MVD training.[28]

The Soviet secret police, apart from penetrating and apparently subordinating these agencies, also maintained its own autonomous structure in East Europe and was empowered, whenever Soviet security was threatened, to arrest nationals of the People's Democracies in a People's Democracy. That certainly was the case in East Germany and the former enemy states, and there were also instances of this having happened in Poland. Furthermore, during the purges, the MVD headquarters and even Stalin himself would occasionally dispatch to a national party leadership materials incriminating some party official and would demand that the local security people deal with the situation.[29] In this manner, the Soviet leaders were directly involved in the problem of loyalty and security right up to the top levels of Communist leadership in the People's Democracies.

The armed forces were given similar attention. At the end of the war only Yugoslavia and Poland had sizable military establishments.

---

* Czechoslovakia is a notable exception, although the evidence available is scanty. But studies of the Czech Communist regime do not point to intense Soviet penetration of the main organs of power, and apparently the Czech Communists, with considerable organizational experience behind them, had the situation well in hand. According to reliable Hungarian data, the AVH was advised by twelve to forty Soviet officers (depending on the period).

The Yugoslav army was highly politicized and fiercely loyal to Tito. The Polish army was split into two parts, symbolizing the fate of the country. The armed forces in the west were demobilized and about one half of the soldiers returned home (many were subsequently arrested), the others having chosen exile. The army at home had been expanded from the units organized in 1943 in the USSR through mobilization and occasional incorporation of Home Army units which had escaped deportation to the USSR. After the war most of these forces were demobilized. In the initial period, the Soviet Union did not encourage the development of large-scale military forces in any of the other People's Democracies and, on the whole, those existing were badly equipped and inadequately supplied. After 1948, particularly because of the mounting international tensions, energetic efforts were launched to build up these forces into more modern military organizations. The problem of loyalty, both to the existing governments and to the USSR on whose side these forces would be expected to fight, thus became even more important.

The concern with loyalty was expressed through the appointment of trusted Communists to head the armed forces: in August 1948, M. Farkas, later to gain notoriety in connection with purge brutalities, was appointed Minister of Defense in Hungary; in April 1950, Gottwald's son-in-law, A. Cepicka, Minister of Defense in Czechoslovakia; in Poland, in a most striking case of direct Soviet control, the post was given in November 1949 to Marshal K. Rokossovsky, a Soviet officer. Rokossovsky, also to become a Politburo member, was virtually independent of any party control insofar as military matters were involved and conducted himself on the basis of direct Soviet commands.[30] He was assisted by numerous Soviet officers, who commanded all the major branches of the armed forces[31] and initiated a large-scale purge of the officer corps.[32]

The general pattern of Soviet controls, with some variation, was imposed in the following sequence: During the early stage the armed forces were de-emphasized. The demobilization paved the way to a removal of any prewar officers whose politics were likely to be anti-Communist. In Czechoslovakia, for instance, former officers of the Czech Legion were particularly suspect; in Poland, those who had served with Pilsudski. In the former enemy states, "anti-Fascist" measures included the ferreting out of prewar officers on the grounds of having supported the war against the USSR. Only in Yugoslavia did the army retain its strength, primarily because of the tensions over Trieste and because it was firmly in the hands of the regime. The widespread elimination of many high-ranking professionals made possible the rapid promotion of a number of junior-ranking men whose new status was dependent on the existing political situation and who therefore had a vested interest in its maintenance. The most important posts, however, were filled with Communist officers who either had a Spanish Civil War background, or had served with Communist partisans, or had fought in the Red Army. A system of political and police controls on the Soviet model was established, and intensive political training was made a large part of each prospective officer's curriculum.

In addition, in all the armies, save Czechoslovakia's apparently and Yugoslavia's, Soviet officers served in command or advisory capacities. In Poland, they arrived as early as 1945, and helped to organize the army. After an interlude of about three years, a second wave came with Rokossovsky, paralleling similar developments elsewhere. In Hungary, Soviet military advisers also came in two waves: first, in 1948, to train the army in the handling of new weapons; and then, much more openly, in the fall of 1949 when the modernization of the Hungarian Army was accelerated. The Soviet officers in Hungary were headed by a chief of the Military Delegation and by a political adviser to the Hungarian Army. They set up a system of controls very much like that in Poland and supervised the activities of their Hungarian fellow officers.*[33] The Soviet table of organization was adopted in all the armies, as were the Soviet drill and system of ranks. Only Poland retained its traditional insignia, although it too made modifications in the military uniform to conform with the general pattern. Through these devices, as in the case of the police, loyalty to the Soviet Union was to be ensured by the penetration of Soviet personnel and prevention of direct domestic control.

The Soviet levers of control made certain that purpose, policy, and performance in each People's Democracy were in keeping with the overall Soviet objectives for the camp of socialism. An additional peculiarity of Stalinism as an interstate system was the isolation of each People's Democracy from one another. In terms of relations between parties this expressed itself, as already noted, in Soviet insistence on bilateral dealings between the CPSU and the other parties rather than on multilateral consultations. Until 1948 some of the parties had

---

* According to General Bela Kiraly, by 1951 Soviet "advisory" staffs were operating even on the regimental level; in the General Staff College which he commanded there were fourteen Soviet "advisers," headed by a general, to a total of two hundred officers (from his interview with Professor Ferenc Vali).

been very active in establishing and maintaining close contacts and frequent conferences. They terminated abruptly, and, even for some years after Stalin's death, contact between neighboring Communist regimes was at a minimum.* Nor did the various central committees and their sections exchange views or experiences.[34]

The only times that East European leaders met were at various functions in Moscow on the occasion of some Soviet anniversary, such as May Day or Stalin's seventieth birthday. Moscow was thus the communications center for the Soviet bloc. Otherwise, contact was strictly curtailed and usually limited either to some important propaganda undertaking, such as the joint East German-Polish announcement that the Oder-Neisse line was the "frontier of peace," or to an occasional exchange of delegations. On a more general level, strict travel restrictions were applied, and procedures involving interstate travel were just as complicated as those pertaining to travel to a "hostile capitalist" country. Between Czechoslovakia and Poland a frontier zone existed, and citizens of the respective People's Democracies had to obtain special passes to be able to work in the proximity of a neighboring People's Democracy. (These particular restrictions were lifted only in 1956–1957.)

Soviet domestic experience again seems to pertain. In the effort to create the new society, all traditional bonds had to be dissolved since they constituted impediments to both policy and power. The consequence of these efforts has often been described, with some exaggeration, as "totalitarian atomization." An essentially similar pro-

* In the words of Imre Nagy: "A peculiar People's Democratic provincialism, an intensified estrangement in those efforts that are raising a veritable Chinese Wall, not only between our homeland and the Western capitalist countries but between the Hungarian People's Democracy and other countries in the democratic and socialist camp, is now developing. We have come to the point where Party members, even members of the Central Committee, cannot obtain the newspapers of sister Parties; the statements by Party and state leaders of other People's Democratic countries; the speeches or articles of Comrade Bierut or Siroky, or the resolutions of sister Parties. The same applies to numerous manifestations in culture, art, and literature, to the debates in People's Democratic countries, to the exchanges of ideas, etc. Indeed, we have come to such a point that members of the Central Committee cannot even obtain certain publications of the Communist Party of the Soviet Union. Thus, for example, the agricultural resolution of the Central Committee of the Polish Party is banned in Hungary, and so is the evaluation of this resolution by the official paper of the Party, *Trybuna Ludu*, and so is a study concerning relationships of Polish and Western literature and art, etc. In numerous areas of Hungarian economic, political, and cultural life there is a hermetic seal isolating the problems that friendly countries share in the same areas; this indicates a fear of criticism, and at the same time — and this is more serious — it furthers the intensification of nationalism and of attitudes opposed to the teachings of Lenin on the subject of proletarian internationalism." *On Communism*, p. 240.

cedure was followed with respect to the People's Democracies. Their traditional associations, as well as new ones formed by local Communists (such as the Balkan Union project), were a hindrance to the central leadership. Therefore, they had to be dissolved and, ideally, each party, much like every citizen in the USSR, was to face the Center alone. Its isolation would thus become a source of unity and purposeful cohesion.*

Economic Aspects

Isolation as basis for unity was not only a political feature of the Stalinist pattern but was also vigorously applied on the economic plane. Political bilateralism and isolation were matched by economic bilateralism and autarky. Just as political bilateralism meant in practice Soviet domination, economic bilateralism involved a good deal of exploitation of the area by the USSR in the name of the overall interests of the Communist bloc. At the same time, however, a further objective in the economic field was the integration of the entire "socialist bloc" into an interdependent unit, although the implementation of this goal was not very actively pursued during the Stalinist period and seems to have been subordinated to more immediate Soviet economic interests and to autarkic features of the five-year plans. Integration would have meant foregoing certain profits for the USSR, and, with the prevailing scale of priorities, the economic welfare of the Soviet Union was viewed as more important. As a result, some measure of tension entered into the economic pattern of relations.

The formal foundations for a policy of economic exploitation — a policy which, in the Marxist point of view, could not exist between socialist states — were based on the war settlements imposed by the USSR after the conclusion of hostilities. The Soviet Union required both Hungary and Rumania to make reparations payments, for a period of six and eight years, respectively, to the amount of $200 and $300 million, respectively, *at 1938 prices.* That this represented a sizable portion of the annual expenditures of these two small states is attested by the fact that reparations commitments absorbed 26.4 per cent of the 1946–1947 Hungarian budget and 37.5 per cent of the Rumanian. In the following year the figures were 17.8 per cent and

* But for this reason also the USSR could not go to the other extreme: *divide et impera.* It could not sponsor traditional conflicts between People's Democracies as a method of furthering its rule because these conflicts would become a source of strain and divisive tendencies. Probably only in the early stage could this have been possible, and in some cases appears to have been so used (as with the Rumanians and the Hungarians over Transylvania).

46.6 per cent.[35] In the case of Poland, an allied country, the problem of reparations again served as a useful point of departure. German reparations to Poland were to be handled by the USSR and were to amount to 15 per cent of the total German reparations to the USSR. In its turn, Poland, according to the agreement of August 16, 1945, "undertakes, beginning with 1946, to deliver to the Soviet Union once a year throughout the entire period of the occupation of Germany, *at the special price* agreed upon, eight million tons of coal during the first year of deliveries, thirteen million tons annually in the next four years, and twelve million tons in each of the subsequent years of the occupation of Germany" (italics added). Subsequently the delivery quotas were lowered, but the "special price" meant that by 1956 Polish losses in coal exports to the USSR alone amounted to about two billion rubles or half a billion dollars.[36]

The reparations from Hungary and Rumania were reduced, but not abolished, in 1948 in the spirit of "socialist cooperation." The balance was halved, although the Soviet Union still insisted on receiving payments of the debts incurred by these states toward Germany. The seizure of former German property and the dismantling carried on in the entire area when it was still a war zone, represented still more profit to the USSR. The creation of a number of joint companies, co-owned with Rumania, Hungary, and Bulgaria, was a further feature of the Soviet-satellite economic relationship. (In Yugoslavia it had been terminated by the rupture, while Poland was unwilling from the start to agree to such arrangements and the USSR apparently decided not to force the issue.) The joint companies were set up in the petroleum industry, quartz mining, shipping, and air transport, usually on a fifty-fifty basis. Moreover, much of the Soviet capital came from German assets seized locally, thereby giving the USSR a rather convenient means of financing these undertakings.[37] All in all, sixteen such companies were created in Rumania (Sovromtransport, for instance, controlled most of the larger Rumanian vessels and about one third of the entire tonnage [38]), six in Hungary (40 per cent of the bauxite output was subject to one company [39]), and seven in Bulgaria. Special secret agreements were made with Czechoslovakia and Hungary concerning uranium exploration. The least hesitation was shown in exploiting East Germany, and until 1954, even after the setting up of the GDR, the Soviet military administration continued to operate two hundred formerly German-owned enterprises.

A complete evaluation of Soviet–People's Democracies economic relations is rendered difficult by the secrecy which was maintained with respect to the content of economic agreements. Full and detailed arrangements were rarely published during the Stalinist period and even earlier, beyond the general statistical statements of the overall turnover and warm affirmations of the mutual benefit to be derived from the specific treaty.* The secrecy became particularly marked as war tensions increased and the People's Democracies were required to develop armaments industries. Nonetheless, the November 1956 Polish-Soviet agreement explicitly admitted that "inequalities" in the relationship had existed and were in the process of being corrected. Earlier, these inequalities had been subject to strong Yugoslav criticisms, and the Yugoslav *White Book* cited numerous examples of the joint companies' being used to Soviet advantage. A general estimate of the amount extracted by the USSR from East Europe in the period 1945-1956 would put the total at about twenty billion United States dollars (see Chapter 12, p. 284, note).

A combination of economic and political motives resulted in a marked shift in the direction of trade relations of these states: from the West toward the USSR and one another. As the industrialization of East Europe, including East Germany, proceeded apace, the economic importance of the area to the Soviet camp grew accordingly. By 1953-1954, the combined steel production of the People's Democracies was about 31 per cent of that of the Soviet Union; pig iron, 27 per cent; electricity, 44 per cent; crude oil, 18 per cent; and coal, 103 per cent.

A closely integrated political bloc had to stress, therefore, closer economic ties, especially as the economies of the Communist states were moving forward into the industrial age. For this reason, beginning in 1948, foreign-trade agreements were drafted with reference to the long-range plans of these states, thereby becoming part of the general process of transformation and integration even though national plans were still not integrated.[40] In a short time, the former trading directions of the People's Democracies were reversed and their trade relations with non-Communist states became negligible (see table). Direct trade with the USSR amounted in 1951 to 29 per cent in the case of Hungary (which had practically no trade with the USSR before the war): 58 per cent in the case of Bulgaria; 25 per cent in the case of Poland; 51 per cent in the case of Rumania; and 28 per cent

---

* For instance, *Nowe Drogi*, no. 7 (1953), p. 32, speaks of the "priceless treasure of Soviet experience" in the area of metallurgy which has been made accessible to Poland, and describes it as a "real spiritual wealth." See also *Nowe Drogi*, no. 1 (1953), article by S. Jedrychowski, "The Significance of Soviet Economic-Technical Aid for the Construction of the Foundations of Socialism in Poland."

Trade with the USSR and other People's Democracies
(imports and exports in per cent of total)

	1937	1948	1949	1950	1951
Bulgaria	12	74	82	88	92
Hungary	13	34	46	61	67
Poland	7	34	43	59	58
Rumania	18	71	82	83	79
Czechoslovakia	11	30	45	52	60

Source: N. Ivanov, "The Foreign Trade of the European People's Democracies," *Vneshnaia Torgovlia*, no. 10, 1952.

in the case of Czechoslovakia. In turn, about 80 per cent of all Soviet trade in 1951 was with the People's Democracies.[41] The table suggests that in Bulgaria and Rumania a major shift in the trading pattern preceded the Stalinist phase and was merely accentuated by it. In Hungary, Poland, and Czechoslovakia the Stalinist period sharply affected the trading patterns of these states.

The official economic equivalent to the Cominform was the Council for Mutual Economic Assistance, formed in Moscow in January 1949 as a response to the challenge of the Marshall Plan. Its organization was initially limited to six functional departments (this was expanded in 1955–1956 — see Chapter 12), and its stated purpose was to assist the economic development of its members: USSR, Poland, Czechoslovakia, Hungary, Rumania, and Bulgaria.* Its main emphasis, however, was on coordinating trade within the Soviet bloc, although there is reason to believe that the Council was also concerned during that time with stimulating the development of the armaments industry which grew under Soviet pressure during the Korean War. (It is to be noted that such an industry is particularly unprofitable to underdeveloped but industrializing nations.) While the initial sessions of the Council did lay stress on pooling resources, no overall plan for division of labor or specialization emerged, and industrial development continued on a more or less autarkic pattern.†[42] Proba-

* In 1950 these states were joined by East Germany and Albania; North Korea and North Vietnam subsequently sent observers.

† In the cautious words of the Communist premier of Hungary between 1953 and 1955: "It must be pointed out that, although economic cooperation and mutual assistance between the socialist states brought significant results, the activity of CEMA [the Council] from the point of view of industrial production and development was extremely limited during the period of the First Five-Year Plan. This also contributed to the rise of inequities in work distribution among friendly countries. Despite the fact that agreements were made with some of the democratic countries with a view to assigning work in a way that would promote economic production and work dis-

bly its major accomplishment during this time was the introduction, in 1950, of the ruble as the standard currency for international transactions within the bloc, which made the USSR the ultimate arbiter of the rates of exchange.[43] Related to this was the systematically lower average of unit-value indices of goods sold to the USSR by the People's Democracies as part of the long-term (usually five-year) bilateral trade agreements initiated by the Council.[44]

Other than these measures, the Council apparently did not assume during Stalin's lifetime a major role in the direct management or planning of the economic life of the area. Like the Cominform, which declined into a mere anti-Tito organ, the Council was quite active in sponsoring the economic boycott of Yugoslavia. It thus appears that, as in politics, the pattern of economic relations was characterized by an absence of overall formal arrangements and depended on direct relationships which were usually favorable to the USSR. In large measure these one-sided arrangements conflicted with the domestic aims of the socioeconomic transformation and made it a much more expensive proposition. However, the important dimension in this situation was the strengthening of the USSR in the face of alleged external danger — and Stalinism never hesitated to choose the political gain over the purely economic.

The Special Case of China

Stalinism as an interstate and international system did not have to cope with the specter of a powerful Communist Chinese regime. The problem of crystallizing the relation of the Chinese Communist Party to Stalinism was felicitously delayed throughout Stalin's life. Until the formation of a victorious regime in the fall of 1949, the Chinese Communist Party was embroiled in a bitter civil war and primarily involved with domestic problems. Foreign policy, particularly in terms of the American position, was a function of the civil war in which the USSR played the role of a benevolent, even if formally neutral, spectator. Hence, even in this case relations were dominated by the

---

tribution, parallel manufacturing, especially in the field of machine industry, had an increasingly detrimental effect on our export opportunities and consequently on our foreign trade balance. Parallel manufacturing affected not only trade among the friendly countries themselves but led to an unhealthy competition among them in the capitalist markets as well. The exaggerated trend toward autarky, which manifested itself in the machine industry in the other friendly countries too, was most apparent also in the fields of precision instruments and telecommunications. This was a serious blow to our most developed and most favorably producing export industries." Nagy, *On Communism*, p. 189.

domestic conflict; the Chinese Communist perspective on international Communist problems was of necessity a narrow one, and in essentials reflected the Soviet position. Following the conclusion of the struggle on the mainland, Chinese freedom of action continued to be limited by the Taiwan conflict and, within a very short period, by the Korean War which lasted until the end of Stalin's days. As a result, Communist China restricted its foreign liaison primarily to the USSR and largely abstained from participation in the expanding formal links binding the Communist camp. It was not until April 3, 1951, that a cultural agreement (but not a political one) was signed with Poland, followed by others in subsequent years (May 2, 1952, with Rumania; October 25, 1952, with Bulgaria, and so on). No formal treaties of alliance were concluded with the People's Democracies.

The absorbing Chinese international military undertakings put off an adjustment of the hierarchic and disciplined Stalinist system to the new situation. But the Communist Chinese victory in itself contained the need for somehow defining the status of China in the socialist bloc. Unlike all of the People's Democracies, but very much like the expelled Yugoslav Party, the Chinese regime was, in the final analysis, an indigenous one and its victory, even more than in the Yugoslav case, was the achievement primarily of the party itself. Second, again unlike the People's Democracies but like Yugoslavia, the revolutionary tactics pursued by the party in the course of its struggle had raised some ideological issues on which the local leadership did not see eye to eye with Moscow. The Maoist concept of revolution, through reliance on a standing army and a revolutionary peasantry, had not won the endorsement of the Soviet theoreticians, who tended to underestimate the strength and the potential of the Chinese party.[45] The emergence of Communist China, a great historical event in its own right, thus raised problems for the Stalinist system.

What was now needed was a mutual understanding of the character of the international Communist state system, the role of the USSR in it, and China's new relationship to it. As in the case of the People's Democracies, this involved formal and informal aspects. Insofar as the formal measures were concerned, superficially the relations resembled those between the USSR and the European bloc. Mao Tse-tung, committed to the dichotomic world view, repeatedly stressed his belief that Chinese Communists, given their experience and existing historical situation, must pursue a "lean-to-one-side policy," which he defined in June 1949 as follows:

To lean to one side is the lesson taught us by the forty years of experience of Sun Yat-sen and the twenty-eight years of experience of the Communist Party. We firmly believe that, in order to attain and consolidate victory, we must lean to one side. . . . Not only in China, but in the whole world, one leans without exception either to the side of imperialism or to the side of socialism. Neutrality is a hoax.[46]

His orientation clearly called for the closest links with the USSR, and shortly after the Chinese Communists had formally constituted themselves as the government of China, a delegation headed by Mao Tse-tung himself proceeded to Moscow. There they negotiated a treaty of "Friendship, Alliance, and Mutual Assistance" (February 14, 1950), as well as two subsidiary agreements concerning the disposition of the Changchun railroad, the ports of Dairen and Port Arthur, and a long-term loan to China. The clauses and affirmations of the political treaty resembled the agreements concluded between the USSR and the European bloc, with Japan taking the place of Germany as the potential aggressor and the United States more or less understood as the sponsor of such potential aggression.[47] The subsidiary agreements contained a number of provisions which could be interpreted as favorable to China, such as the transfer of the Changchun railroad in 1952 rather than in 1975 as envisaged in the Sino-Soviet treaty of 1945, an earlier withdrawal from Port Arthur, and a more generous compensation for property seized by the Soviets from the Japanese in China.[48] Of course, Soviet interests were not neglected, and the Chinese delegation also agreed to somewhat less favorable provisions concerning Dairen and compensation for Soviet "improvements" in Port Arthur.[49] Furthermore, the potentially divisive issues of Mongolia and Sinkiang were left in abeyance. While the treaty and the affirmations of friendship generally conformed to the pattern already traced, probably the most striking indication of the somewhat more complex relationship involved was the fact that the treaty negotiations in Moscow lasted over two months, from November 1949 until February 1950.

Any hidden complications notwithstanding, after the treaty relations between the two states seemed to take a familiar course. Soviet military experts arrived to assist in the training of the Chinese army, which was modernized with Soviet equipment.[50] Economic advisers came to help organize and run the metallurgical, coal, oil, chemical, machine-building, and transport enterprises, as well as trade and cooperatives.[51] Chinese trade with the USSR and the People's Democracies, which in 1931 amounted to only 8 per cent of total Chinese trade, increased fourfold between 1950 and 1953 to about 75 per cent of the total.[52] As early as October 1949, a Sino-Soviet Friendship Society was established. By 1951, it counted some seventeen million members and engaged in various cultural-political activities designed to strengthen popular affection for the USSR. As in East Europe, ties with the USSR were explicitly stressed in the preamble to the constitution of 1954 ("indestructible friendship with the great Union of Soviet Socialist Republics") and in the first basic law passed after the 1949 victory, the Common Program.

Chinese leaders also repeatedly asserted that "the path already traversed by the Soviet people is exactly the path we should follow," [53] although they refrained from pronouncing their state to be a dictatorship of the proletariat. Hailing the People's China as a "new democracy," the Chinese leadership adopted the position that this was their version of the People's Democracy, a line in keeping with general Soviet notions. However, the stress on a domestic alliance of the peasantry and bourgeoisie under the leadership, or "the hegemony," of the proletariat clearly implied that China had not yet reached the stage of the dictatorship of the proletariat. After Stalin's death, the Chinese extolled this as a new and creative contribution to the theories of socialist transition, but as long as he was alive this apparent innovation was de-emphasized.[54] Furthermore, on closer examination, one is struck not so much by the obvious differences in the official concepts of the People's Democracy as seen in Moscow and as proclaimed in Peiping, but by the startling similarity between the Chinese position and that adopted by the East Germans, with obvious Soviet blessing.* It would, therefore, appear that in both China and Germany it was more a matter of concessions to international pressures and the great domestic problems than of pointed divergence from the Soviet-sponsored pattern.

These surface relations, and even the apparent subservience, shielded a reality much more complex than the simple Stalinist pattern would suggest. The Soviet military advisers in China could hardly be compared to the overlords in charge of the Polish or Hungarian armies built from scratch by Communist regimes dependent on Soviet support. In China the revolution had been won by a poorly

* Ulbricht, speaking at the Second Party Conference in July 1952, described the East German system as a new order based on an alliance of "the working class and the working peasant element" in cooperation with the intelligentsia. The leadership in the order was said to belong to the "most progressive" proletarians led by the SED. (*Einheit*, no. 8, August 1952, pp. 739-740.) The Germans, however, were evasive on the crucial question of whether they could enter the stage of socialism directly.

equipped, primitive army, but still by a Chinese army which, by 1949, represented a numerically impressive military establishment, led by men with a revolutionary consciousness and, presumably, a justified sense of achievement. In these circumstances, whatever Soviet aspirations might have been, the role played by the Soviet advisers was inevitably circumscribed. In addition, and this applies to economic advisers also, the Soviet and Chinese leaderships both were probably aware of the dangerous parallels between their relationship and that formerly existing between Moscow and Belgrade and, duly forewarned, strove to minimize unnecessary tensions.[55]

By 1949, in spite of Stalin's rigidities, the Soviet leadership must have realized that it had grossly miscalculated in the Yugoslav case and that an indigenous revolutionary movement develops a certain inherent capacity for resistance, even against as hallowed a shrine as Moscow. This is especially true if, in addition to the armed forces, the revolutionary movement controls firmly the security apparatus — as both the Chinese and the Yugoslavs did. Accordingly, the patterns for states like the People's Democracies could not be enforced in China. Indeed, an attempt in that direction would be detrimental since it would tend to obscure the natural community of interests dictated by the presence of the alleged capitalist threat. This was the period of the Formosa conflict, to be followed shortly by a war with the leading capitalist power. Given the international situation, particularly since the summer of 1950 (the Korean War), the lesser degree of actual Soviet control was compensated by the fact that the USSR was more necessary to the survival of the Chinese Communist regime than that regime was to the USSR.

On the eve of the war in Korea, China had just completed a period of almost fifteen years of uninterrupted warfare which had left its economy devastated, its communications disrupted, its administration disorganized and subjected to a revolutionary change. Soviet assistance, in the form of economic aid, was desperately needed if the Chinese Communist regime was to restore a semblance of normalcy domestically and pursue its internal and external objectives. Variations in ideological perspectives or even potential conflicts of interest, either territorial or involving leadership among Asian Communists, could not transcend the fact that common Leninist organizational experience and ideological orientation gave the Chinese leadership no choice but to maintain their association with the leading Communist power. A necessary concomitant of this association, considering the world situation and possibly even Stalin's foibles, was the acceptance of certain

informal obligations which, unlike the pattern in East Europe, operated entirely autonomously through the motivating force of self-
interest. Thus Soviet leadership was recognized, imitation of the
USSR proclaimed, even if not fully practiced, and endorsement of
Soviet policies elsewhere unhesitatingly given.

China, faced by the external war and the violence of internal
changes, particularly in the countryside where a Stalin-like collectivization was forcefully pushed, could not afford, and indeed had
no reason to desire, to become a Yugoslavia. Its relations with the
USSR (and the absence of such relations with the People's Democracies) were dictated by a combination of a common ideological outlook and an overwhelming external pressure for unity, which was
not marred by crude Soviet requirements for subordination. Formal
equality was thus not accompanied by informal control but by informal recognition of relative scales of mutual interest, aspirations,
and power. On the Soviet side, even during Stalin's lifetime, the USSR
had no choice but to tolerate what it had not tolerated with Tito: a
fundamentally Stalinist regime which operated autonomously within
the framework of international Stalinism.

Interaction of Domestic and International Pressures

The external factors, so pre-eminent in the case of China, were
also important in shaping the pattern of events in the Communist
states of East Europe. The split with the West, which by 1949 and
the Berlin blockade had reached the proportions of a war scare, was
intensified by the Stalinist insistence on the dichotomy between the
forces that are for socialism and all others that are therefore "objectively" against it. Suspicion and hostility toward any state outside
the Stalinist system became particularly marked after the successful
Yugoslav stand against the Cominform onslaught. Fear of internal
diversion, either strictly "counterrevolutionary" or of a Titoist
variety (and to Stalin the difference between the two was purely
one of form), accompanied the hostile stance adopted against
the external world; it found reflection domestically in a growing
stress on the class struggle within the nation and the party, on a
more intensive transformation of society, on a greater reliance on
the instruments of violence for the pursuit of domestic objectives.
In this, all of the Communist-ruled states shared, from the USSR
down.

With the outbreak of the Korean war came an even greater intensification of the monolithic pressures inherent in Stalinism. The

threat of a total war, which to an East European Communist implied more dire consequences than to his Soviet colleagues, obscured internal differences and created a unity born of fear. The conflict, no matter who began it, seemed to bear out the Stalinist position that America had been preparing for war against the Soviet camp. If it had not, then why should it intervene in an area which it had previously disclaimed as being of no political or strategic significance? The United States reaction clearly implied, to someone viewing reality from the Communist perspective, that America was seizing an opportunity to engage in active military operation against the "bloc of peace." Malenkov, in the political report addressed to the Nineteenth Party Congress, expressed this point of view in the following words: "The U.S. attack on the Korean People's Democratic Republic marked the transition of the American-British bloc from preparation of aggressive war to direct acts of aggression." [56] Domestic Stalinism frequently resorted to an image of the "enemy" to justify its more violent policies; Stalinism as an international system similarly relied on this technique.

The application of this device was facilitated by the Soviet monopoly of any evaluation of the world situation. This evaluation then served as a basis for the policies of the various People's Democracies, intensifying those tendencies which made for greater reliance externally on the USSR and on repressive measures at home. In the cautious but revealing words of Imre Nagy, writing to a central committee of a party still firmly committed to the USSR:

We never examined the international situation thoroughly in the light of our own country's interests nor from the viewpoint of its effects on our country. . . . This was the reason why changes in the international situation often clashed sharply with internal politics. In the years 1949 to 1952, incorrect evaluations of the international situation, *overemphasis of the war danger*, and *the actions resulting from these assumptions*, played a very serious part in those grave mistakes that were made by our Party leadership with regard to the economic activities of the people. . . . The events in June, 1953, in East Germany, Czechoslovakia and Hungary, and elsewhere clearly show how an incorrect evaluation of the international situation and a resulting unsound foreign policy brought about grave crises in the internal life of the countries mentioned.[57]

It would be erroneous, however, to ascribe primary importance to external factors in the process of shaping the Stalinist international system. Soviet domestic Stalinism, with the expansion of Soviet power, could not help but become the form and content of relations between the new Soviet-dependent Communist states. It is very difficult for any state to conduct its relations with lesser powers in a fashion which drastically differs from its own internal politics. For a while, such divergence can be justified by real or alleged overriding national interest, but in time there must be coalescence in the forms of domestic and external politics.*

However, it is much more difficult for a totalitarian state to conduct anything else than a policy of domination against its weaker neighbors or associates. Not to do so would be to adopt restraints on its behavior wholly out of keeping with the image of the world which guides its domestic conduct and the aspirations which give shape to the sacrifices exacted from the population. Furthermore, a belief in environmental influence tends to exaggerate the importance of a community of views between the various leaders and the identity of institutions and socioeconomic systems. Similarity of material conditions becomes one of the vital guarantees of unity of action, and such similarity can best be established through the duplication elsewhere of the institutions of the dominant power. With *Zhdanovshchina* in full bloom on the fertile soil of Stalinism, with the Soviet dictator apprehensive about a possible decline in the pace of revolutionary change, the application in the People's Democracies of patterns other than the Soviet would have constituted a danger to the structure of Soviet power itself and a deviation from the clear-cut "we versus they" image of the world.

This pattern of institutional and ideological uniformity did much to eliminate divisive tendencies, such as those rooted in the domesticism of some leaders. Nonetheless, under the monolithic surface, some important differences among the various People's Democracies continued to exist even during the height of Stalinism, which could not effectively control *all* aspects of life and foil *all* forms of evasion. Some parties went quite far in imitating Stalinism in all its facets; others did not. The purges in Czechoslovakia, Hungary, and Bulgaria differed sharply from the pattern in Poland, East Germany, and Rumania. Similarly, not all states pushed collectivization forward at an even pace. However, procrastination and even evasion were not enough to constitute a significant deviation from the common pattern.

* In democratic states, the divergence, when it takes place, can only be away from the "democratic" pattern in external relations, but, after a while, internal pressures develop for adjustment. Some recognition of the principles which guide domestic life then follows in the sphere of international affairs. One example of this is the United States' policy toward its Latin neighbors.

To conclude, the Stalinist interstate system was characterized by: (1) The worship of politics. In practice, this meant reliance on identical political "superstructures" and attaching primary significance to political controls and bilateral political contacts as the most reliable means of ensuring unity. (2) The leadership of Stalin and the USSR was openly acknowledged and a special bond of personal allegiance cultivated between Stalin and his chosen leaders for the People's Democracies (except China). Stalin's relationship with the satellite leaders could in effect be described as one of *feudal* subordination and obligation. Within the strict hierarchical pattern some concession was made to the particular position of China, which was usually assigned the second and special place of mention, and with which Soviet relations were only crystallizing. (3) Ideology served as an important source of self-imposed controls, although gradually declining in the course of this phase. No systematic ideological justification for Soviet supremacy was developed. Rather, a series of didactic assertions related to a rejection of alternative ways to socialism were postulated with the ideology providing a means of identifying the enemy. Ideology thus performed the broad function of pointing out the nature of the given international phase – the period of capitalist aggression – while in internal policies it relied on tried Stalinist practices. (4) A superficial framework of state independence, guaranteed by treaties, formal recognition of sovereignty and national equality, masked an informal though effective system of subordination of these states to the center. Soviet intervention in domestic affairs of the People's Democracies operated, however, in most day-to-day instances on the basis of local anticipation of Soviet *desiderata* according to the guidelines of Stalinist ideology and practice. Direct Soviet control was applied mainly through the secret police and the armed forces. The emphasis on indirect controls distinguished the Stalinist system from the Nazi domination. The Stalinist pattern involved a far more extensive reliance on indigenous participation and, unlike the Nazi destructiveness, also stressed social transformation with some positive attributes. Soviet armies, after the initial phase, played a secondary role: staying in the background, it was sufficient for everyone to realize that they would be used when necessary. (5) Primacy of Soviet development justified the economic exploitation of the area even while its rapid industrial development was encouraged. This introduced further economic strains which increased the political dependence of the regimes on the USSR.

Stalinism as a pattern for Communist interstate relations was a system noticeably untouched by innovation and experimentation. In the final analysis, it merely relied on the Stalinist domestic experience and applied it to those areas which were within the purview of Stalin's power. Ironically, but precisely because of that, Malenkov was probably right when he stated in 1952 that "the USSR's relations with these countries set an example of entirely new relations among states, relations never yet encountered in history." [58]

CHAPTER 7

The Stalinist Legacy

> If we cut down the time in which changes have to take place,
> especially in the sphere of social consciousness — such as ideology
> and culture, and in the forms of society, we may fall victim to
> the idealistic view that we can bring about changes in these phe-
> nomena independently of the material conditions which influence
> their formation. — Wladyslaw Bienkowski, "Socialism versus
> Mythology."

THE Stalinist legacy, in the terminology of the initiated, was the
mounting contradiction between the imperatives of the political superstructure and the dictates of the material and social base. The
priority assigned to narrowly defined political considerations meant
that socioeconomic factors which politics were supposed to reflect
were subordinated to the overall political interests of the bloc as defined by its center. This subordination, in turn, had a restrictive impact on creative ideological development by divorcing ideology from
precisely those elements which were said to stimulate its growth and
refine its content. Ideology divorced from reality and rigidly dictating
the established practice of one particular power degenerated into
dogma and lost its dynamic component — its ability to relate itself to
changing society. Even totalitarian ideologies, dogmatic almost by
definition, must respond in some measure to domestic aspirations and
must somehow reflect the existing reality, even while striving to
change it altogether. This certainly was the case initially with the
Nazi doctrine and with the Bolshevik appeal. A static ideology which
reflects an actual and alien model tends to become corrupted, to lose
its vitality, to become a mere rationalization for power. Tito discovered this shortly after the break, and after 1950 the Yugoslavs franti-
cally sought new ideological formulations to take cognizance of the
present and to shape the future (see Chapter 9). The East European
Communists were not as fortunate and rapidly came face to face with
a situation in which politics had few links with reality and in which

their ideology had become a sterile guidebook for dubiously relevant socioeconomic practices.

Communist Testimony

During the later stages of the Stalinist period an increasing number of Communists became aware of the dangers inherent in the established practices. This is evident from a number of statements made after Stalin's death, not designed for "hostile capitalist propaganda" but addressed to the local ruling parties and often favorably received by many party members. The difficulties and shortcomings discussed were clearly the products of the Stalinist era even if the suggested remedies already reflected the post-Stalin atmosphere. Nonetheless, we can get a relatively extensive picture of the Stalinist legacy as seen at least by a portion of the Communist elite from the following: the situations discussed in the summer of 1953 by the plenums of the Hungarian Central Committee and of the East German SED's Central Committee (see Chapter 8); the resolution of the Polish Central Committee's Third Plenum in January 1955; the elaborate statement written by Imre Nagy in 1955 and addressed to both the Hungarian and Soviet leaderships; [1] and a short volume of essays by Wladyslaw Bienkowski, until 1957 a close associate of Gomulka,* entitled *Rewolucji Ciag Dalszy* (The Revolution Continued), published largely before October 1956. Very similar themes run through the depositions of some former Hungarian Communists, interviewed by the Columbia University Research Project on Hungary. [2] One might also consider pertinent the speech delivered by Gomulka to the Eighth Plenum in 1956 upon his restoration to the post of First Secretary. These assessments of leading Communists are more relevant to the problem of Soviet-satellite relations than a general critique of the Stalinist legacy would be, for it was the Communist's perception of the situation that was reflected in the policies first adopted after Stalin's death.

The implicit and explicit themes of such assessments may be broken down into these three categories: political problems, related ideological and ethical issues, and economic difficulties. From the standpoint of the party, the critical issue was the party's increasing subordination to the secret police. Discussing this trend, Imre Nagy, writing during Rakosi's hegemony (see Chapter 10), stated that the secret police, with the "far-reaching aid" of Stalin, was raised "above

---

* Bienkowski, appointed Minister of Education after Gomulka's return to power, shared Gomulka's political eclipse after 1949. In 1957 he became identified with revisionism (Chapter 13) and gradually lost his political influence.

society and Party and made . . . the principal organ of power." [3] This resulted in a "degeneration of Party life" and the partial extermination of the leading cadres of the party.[4] The net result was "Bonapartism," a term used by Leninists to denote a betrayal of the revolutionary ideals once power had been seized, and even "Fuehrerism," a manifestation of distrust for the party rank and file and for the masses.[5] Nagy was ably seconded by Bienkowski. Stating that "responsibility is an institutional matter" which cannot be ignored by merely asserting that one social order is free from contradictions,[6] he charged the Stalinist epoch with having created an abyss between the political leadership and society at large: "the working class and all other social forces were placed in the position of being a potential enemy of the socialist order, the true exemplar and devoted defender of which was the bureaucratized apparatus of power." [7] This fear of the masses in turn led to a fear of individuals, Bienkowski asserted. "Stalin, in a suspiciousness typical of dictators, persecuted first morally, and then physically, not only those who had the courage of their opinion but also those whom he suspected of being able to have it." [8]

A political system structured on suspicion and with a predilection toward personal violence could not develop organizational techniques such as those characteristic of the Weberian notions of a rational bureaucracy. Political controls within the bureaucracy, controls to check the controls, and general bureaucratic hostility toward the masses resulted in a system in which an expanding and rather inefficient bureaucracy lost all concern with human values and showed only occasional spurts of vitality whenever "a class enemy" was spotted.[9] The decline and eventual disappearance of revolutionary fervor within some of the ruling elites is therefore not surprising.[10] Both Nagy and Bienkowski vented their concern with the decline of morale within the ruling circles, a decline which could not be blamed on the vestiges of the pre-Communist past. Servility and corruption were to be encountered everywhere, and the legion of careerists "tends to increase because, instead of denouncing them, the leaders tolerate and quite frequently even pamper them, since their kowtowing flatters the vanity of the leaders, as they will do anything or carry out any orders for them without reservation." [11] Bienkowski, citing Lenin, warned that beyond the corruptive tendencies noted above, bureaucratization breeds a dangerous conservative impediment to social progress by creating a "closed class" of professionals who are professional only in the defense of their vested interests.[12] This development is again inherent in the mistrust of the masses and in the usurpation of the sole right to express the popular will.

A conservative inclination of this kind could not be limited to the administrative apparatus alone. In general, Bienkowski asserted, the socialist revolution was not able to rise above the historical tendency of revolutionary forces to become rigidified and brittle after their victory.[13] The revolutionary ideology becomes (as in the case of Stalinism) a defense of the status quo, too often defined in the narrow terms of self-interest of the new ruling elite. The revolutionary ideals degenerate into a series of pat institutional recommendations, and those in power forget "about living society, about man with his manifold, complicated, individual and social relations, at the crux of which are ethical and moral problems." [14] Certainly not all, in fact probably only a few, Communists were as perceptive as Nagy or Bienkowski. It was largely because of this that the gap between ideology and reality, between aspirations and practice, became so marked in a system in which power was worshiped and its exercise was considered to be the most hallowed ritual.

The Stalinist legacy in economics, as perceived by some Communists, came under equally scathing indictment. Describing it as "lunar economics," Bienkowski charged that the general tendency was to divorce theory from economic practice and to make the former a matter of dogma unaffected by any existential conditions.[15] The consequence was "idealistic voluntarism," which stressed political criteria with a reckless disregard for the complexity of economic processes. The frequent and triumphant citing of advances in specific production fields entirely ignored the simple fact that an economic organism, much like a human being, can have a healthy heart, lungs, or stomach and yet be critically ill. Bienkowski's view was seconded by Nagy, who was particularly disturbed by serious disproportions which developed in planning due to the primacy assigned to industrial development. The situation was made worse by the outbreak of the Korean War; the Polish regime, for instance, according to its erstwhile party First Secretary, "spent millions for the defense industry and transferred its best workers and machines to it." [16]

The impact of the Stalinist notions was nowhere more disastrously felt than in agriculture. Even Communists acknowledged that collectivization was pushed forward without ensuring adequate food supplies for the urban population, while actual food production did

not increase and even declined. The introduction of class struggle
into the countryside was based on the principle "the worse the agricultural situation, the better it is" since it will lead to more rapid socialization.[17] Established methods of good farming suffered accordingly. Ideologically this move was justified as denying "accumulation"
to the private owner, who was considered an enemy of the new system. This policy was based on an artificial division of the peasantry
into three categories: the poor, the medium, and the rich; the "socialist transformation" was to be effected through an alliance of the first
two groups against the rich peasant. The liquidation of the kulak was
to be the actual expression of the class struggle in the countryside,
and was to facilitate a real workers-peasants alliance. But no one really
knew how to determine who was a kulak. Prosperity might be one
criterion, but what was the basis for that prosperity? If it was land
holding alone, then some objective standard might be maintained.
But that criterion was explicitly rejected,[18] and all too often the prosperous peasant was the good peasant, the efficient farmer. The frequent consequence was that the able farmers were made the butt of
the "class struggle," that party posts in the countryside were filled
with the worst rural elements whose only conception of action was
to destroy the better farmer.[19] The existing political atmosphere
merely intensified these tendencies. Agricultural productivity suffered, especially in the public sector,[20] while the myth of Stalinist infallibility was undermined.

The Stalinist legacy, which became a matter of open political dispute within a short period after the dictator's death, involved many
additional factors which even the Communist critics were loath to
acknowledge publicly. The most serious of these was the widespread
impoverishment of the working class, to a great extent due to the
rapid "socialist construction." According to data available, the low
point was reached between 1951 and 1953. The forced social sacrifice,
depressing the standard of living, intensified popular resentment and
strengthened the widely prevailing suspicion that the USSR was also
responsible for the decline. The rights and wrongs of this assumption
notwithstanding, the political consequence was the mounting resentment of the working class and growing uneasiness among party planners.[21] At the same time, the rapid pace of the industrialization resulted in the introduction into posts of responsibility of managerial
and technical cadres with relatively low training standards. This was
particularly true in Hungary and Poland, which lacked an engineering intelligentsia, and applied, to a much lesser degree, in Czechoslo-

vakia and East Germany.* Cohesion necessary to keep the system going was increasingly provided by a resort to administrative pressures, including severe labor laws.

The cumulative effect of the application of Soviet experience resulted in a growing sense of apprehension among the more thoughtful Communists in East Europe. The open soul-searching typical later of the post-Stalin period was at this time limited to gnawing doubt. Personal fear, the sense of commitment, the impact of the Korean War, all tended to push into the deepest recesses of the mind the increasingly important question: is the Soviet model, developed in response to the alleged requirements of the Russian society as it existed in the first decades of the twentieth century, really relevant to the relatively more advanced societies of East Europe in the middle of that century?

At the same time the presence of often undiplomatic Soviet advisers, the suspicions concerning the nature of economic relations with the USSR, the mounting hostility toward the rulers and their Soviet sponsors stored up explosive popular forces which an open party airing of policy dilemmas could only too easily spark. A resolution of these dilemmas could be postponed only as long as Stalin lived, but the delay required a continued and mounting dose of Stalinist procedures to suppress the domestic pressures. The parties themselves were caught by the Stalinist technique of the "dilemma of the one alternative."

The excessive personalization of interstate relations by Stalin himself, his practices and ideas, was a strength only as long as he lived. His legacy would unavoidably involve a political vacuum, a consideration which during his lifetime could not be publicly considered. As a result, Soviet relations with the other Communist states remained perched on a potentially unstable limb. Stalin limited the frequency of direct consultations with the other Communist leaders. These leaders utilized the principles and methods of Stalinism as a guide to their

---

* In Hungary, for instance, 30 per cent of the directors in the Ministry of Metallurgy and Machine Industry, 26 per cent of the directors in the Ministry of Heavy Industry, 50 per cent of the directors in the Ministry of Light Industry, and 50 per cent of the directors in the Ministry of Building Industry had only eight years of secondary school education or even less (*Figyelo*, May 27, 1958). In Poland, in 1956, of the factory directors only 16 per cent had higher education and 45 per cent medium. Of the individuals occupying the ten top factory posts, 16 per cent had higher education and 48 per cent medium. 59 per cent of factory directors held their posts less than five years and 15 per cent less than one year, with the percentage appreciably higher in the responsible technical posts (*Zycie gospodarcze*, February 23, 1958).

domestic action and as a vehicle of internal party struggles. As noted in the preceding chapter, the indirect and informal structure of Soviet controls was not formalized by treaties or fully legitimized by ideology. With respect to China, the formal alliance was reinforced by overriding international pressures, while the autonomous internal position of the Chinese leadership avoided some of the tensions inherent in the Stalinist legacy elsewhere. In East Europe some of the difficulties in Soviet-satellite relations might have been avoided had the Soviet Union been prepared to take a drastic step: to incorporate the People's Democracies into the USSR as Soviet Republics. In 1952 there was little to prevent such a step and, symptomatically, it was predicted in the East European capitals. However, the relatively effective functioning of the indirect controls made such a step seem unnecessary and bound to intensify short-range difficulties. In addition, it might involve international complications, including the loss of badly needed United Nations votes. Forms of independent statehood were accordingly preserved. Yet new circumstances could infuse them with new meaning.

Of course, it would be a distortion of the then-existing state of affairs to picture the Stalinist system as tottering on the brink of disaster and as being kept from toppling over only by the providential power of the aging dictator. The system, while facing difficulties which even some of the ruling elite could no longer ignore, was also characterized by elements of cohesion and strength that Stalin's death per se could not undermine. The first, most self-evident, and decisive was the factor of Soviet power, derived from the USSR's central position in world affairs and from its willingness to use that force for the preservation of its established interests. Efforts to loosen Soviet control, therefore, had to stop short of a provocation likely to induce a violent Soviet reaction. The chain of command and the solidarity of purpose derived from common outlook ensured unity of action, while the reliance on indirect controls freed the Soviet Union from an excessive commitment of its energies to keeping the bloc together. Furthermore, by 1950 the process of internal factional struggles, encouraged personally by Stalin,[22] had weeded out of power those whom the Kremlin did not consider to be trusted and experienced Stalinists.

The degree of that trust, as well as the margin of local autonomy enjoyed by respective Communist leaders, varied from country to country. Since the former involved the matter of personal relationship and the latter was a matter of occasional initiative rather than formal delineation of autonomy, one can only hypothesize about their actual scope. In general, it would seem that by 1950 Stalin could be quite certain that in all of the satellite capitals the heads of the parties were capable of operating on a day-to-day basis without continuing instructions from the center. Beyond this, however, he probably differentiated the Polish and Rumanian leaderships from the others. Stalin might have suspected that the reason for the relative Polish and Rumanian tardiness in implementing the Stalinist programs (collectivization, violent purges, and so forth) was their excessive concern with their internal lack of support and their exaggerated consciousness of anti-Soviet, or traditional anti-Russian, popular attitudes. Stalin might have felt that Gheorghiu-Dej or even Bierut lacked the revolutionary fervor of Rakosi or the more orderly zeal of Gottwald. Polish Communists have repeatedly claimed after 1956 that on the eve of Stalin's death the Polish leadership was coming under increased pressure to intensify the domestic class struggle and that Moscow was showing signs of impatience with Polish suggestions that there were special extenuating circumstances at work in Poland.

By far the most extreme regime was the Bulgarian, which showed its mettle in large-scale violent purges. In some respects during Stalin's life, and afterwards also (see Chapters 12–13), the Bulgarians seemed to enjoy a limited form of inverted autonomy – being more Stalinist than the general norm. In part this was related to the relatively established domestic position of the regime and in part to the fact that Yugoslavia's hostility meant that Bulgaria, fearful of Yugoslav ambitions, had to rely on the USSR. However, no cause-and-effect equation between domestic stability and domestic violence, or conversely between domestic instability and domestic moderation, can be posited. The situation varied considerably from country to country. The relatively consolidated Czech and Bulgarian regimes engaged in considerable internal violence and radical policies. The relatively unconsolidated Polish and Rumanian regimes did so to a far lesser extent. The case of East Germany, while falling by and large into the Polish-Rumanian category, must be considered outside this pattern because of the overriding external factors. Hungary, on the other hand, pursued an extreme domestic policy in spite of the regime's relative lack of domestic support. In this instance, personal, subjective factors, such as the nature of the leadership, its morale, the relatively high incidence of Jewish membership in the Politburo (and the related problem of anti-Semitism), the antiquated social structure – all these factors influenced the situation. However, the point is that East Europe seemed pretty well Stalinized. The system appeared entrenched, too much so to be wholly undermined by Stalin's death.

Stalin could also derive some comfort from the thought that the dispersal of society effected by the twin impact of political violence and rapid social transformation, applied to societies demoralized by war and postwar depravities and largely in a state of social flux,* meant that no cohesive groupings, political or social, remained. Effective opposition to a government which is prepared to suppress all opposition can be organized only if some common bonds remain, preferably of an institutional variety. After 1949–1950 the revolutionary social change and the sustained violence precluded any such resistance; the church as the sole surviving institution could remain simply a sanctuary of alternative philosophical and moral values, not a source of active opposition. It must also be noted that initially, probably until about 1951–1952, the Communist emphasis on the future, contrasted with a reality still bearing the marks of the German occupation, appealed to many, particularly among the younger generation. Even the emphasis on rapid industrialization, albeit destructive in some of its social consequences, was not without its appeal. Communism seemed to offer a key to the understanding of a complex and often brutally unpleasant past and a straight causeway to a socially controllable future. The era of uncertainty bred many who craved such certainty. The Communists seemed to enjoy a monopoly on the tomorrow to which those who opposed them were no longer able to provide any alternative. Thus even the unbelieving were brought face to face with the dilemma of the one alternative — to oppose Communism was to be against everything and for nothing.

Stalin's Testament

Even if Stalin did not fully appreciate the decaying processes within his still smoothly operating system of controls, he was too perceptive a leader to be blinded by surface appearances of monolithic unity. Power and success usually breed a layer of insensitivity to inadequacies, errors, and distortions; in a totalitarian system the power of the leader produces a vacuum around the dictator, making

* For an excellent theoretical treatment of this problem by a leading Polish sociologist, written in Poland after October 1956, see J. Szczepanski, "An Attempt at Diagnosis," *Przeglad Kulturalny*, November 5–11, 1957; see also his *Inteligencja i Spoleczenstwo* (Warsaw, 1957). Szczepanski argues that the "informal ties integrating society" decayed during this period. The situation was most marked in Poland where, in addition to the factors mentioned, over 33 per cent of the population lived after the war in different places than in 1939. (It is to be remembered that this applied to a society still largely rural, and hence not mobile.)

it difficult for him to fully perceive the extent of any developing shortcomings. Considering this, it is indeed a testimonial to
Stalin's perspicacity that in 1952 he was able to display an awareness
of certain potential difficulties in the system he had built and
that he attempted to establish a general framework for coping with
them.

Stalin's political "testament" appeared late in 1952 in the form of a
statement on "Economic Problems of Socialism in the USSR." Most
of it pertained to domestic Soviet issues although some aspects were
also relevant to the People's Democracies directly or, indirectly,
through his analysis of the world situation. The statement reflected
Stalin's continued preoccupation with political techniques, but it also
showed some concern over their possible abuse. In a tedious, pedantic,
and often didactic manner, Stalin appeared to be warning the Soviet
Communists, and by definition therefore the other Communist parties,
against excessive overconfidence in the capability of centralized planning to "create new laws of economic development." At the same
time he also admonished them not to neglect that sense of purpose
which is derived from the "basic economic law of socialism" — that
is, from the efforts "to assure maximum satisfaction of the constantly
growing material and cultural requirements of all of society through
the constant growth and improvement of socialist production on the
basis of the highest technology." [23] Stalin thus seemed to be reminding
his fellow Communists that it would be dangerous to overestimate
the capacity of the Soviet state, even "in view of the special role allotted by history" to it, and to assume that it had reached that historical stage of development in which it could satisfy the popular
cravings inherent in socialist aspirations. Presumably with Voznesensky in mind,* Stalin condemned "rational planners" who had forgotten that the way to socialism is a long one and that it involved
continued emphasis on heavy industrial development. To those Communists in East Europe concerned with excessive industrialization,
this must have seemed a particularly relevant admonition.

What was needed, Stalin seemed to be saying, was a sense of perspective and a common core of doctrine which could be derived only
from a keen appreciation of the dynamic quality of Marxism-Leninism. He reflected:

* N. A. Voznesensky, member of the Politburo and planning chief, disappeared
suddenly early in 1949 and was shot in 1950. Subsequently he was charged with over-
emphasizing the "law of value" in economics and with creating the impression that
economic laws can be created by willful action. See M. A. Suslov in *Pravda*, December 24, 1952.

The point is that we, as the leading core, are joined each year by thousands of new, young cadres fired with the desire to help us, eager to prove themselves, but lacking an adequate Marxist education, uninformed of many truths well known to us, and thus obliged to wander in the dark. They are amazed by the colossal achievements of the Soviet regime, their heads are turned by the extraordinary successes of the Soviet system and they begin to imagine that the Soviet regime "can do anything," that "everything is child's play" to it, that it can negate scientific laws and fashion new ones. What is to be done with these comrades? I think that systematic repetition and patient explanation of so-called "commonly known" truths is one of the best means of Marxist education of these comrades.[24]

The relevance of these remarks was not restricted to the USSR. In fact, Stalin hinted strongly that the situation was even worse in the other ruling Communist parties. To cope with this, the essentials of Marxism-Leninism-Stalinism would again have to be restated, in a single-volume form, especially because "of the inadequate level of Marxist development of the majority of the Communist parties in foreign countries, such a textbook could be of great benefit also to the veteran Communists in those countries who are no longer young."[25] In brief, Stalin was openly fearful that Stalinist political "voluntarism" would be used to justify modifying economic Stalinism. By demonstratively rescuing old-fashioned determinism he was hoping to perpetuate his own Stalinist voluntarism in both economics and politics.

Turning to the world situation and its bearing on the socialist camp, Stalin repeated with firm finality his belief that the capitalist world was torn by internal contradictions which in themselves constituted a threat of war. Noting that the power of the USSR discouraged a direct attack on the Soviet Union (a reassurance needed by the war-weary Soviet people), Stalin warned that international conflicts were inherent in the market competition of the capitalist world and that such conflicts could not avoid generating political warfare among the capitalist states. By drawing analogies with the Second World War, Stalin hinted that in such an event even the USSR could again find itself enmeshed in an international conflict and that the only ultimate protection was the destruction of imperialism. Indeed, the emergence of a common socialist camp inevitably involves a shrinking of the area subject to capitalist exploitation and leads to "the aggravation of the general crisis in the world capitalist system due to disintegration of the world market." However, at the

Nineteenth Party Congress in October 1952, Stalin was careful to remind the other parties that "it would be a mistake to think that our party, having become a mighty force, is no longer in need of support. That is untrue. Our party and our country always have been and always will be in need of the trust, sympathy and support of fraternal peoples abroad. . . . As for the Soviet Union, its interests are altogether indivisible from the cause of world peace." [26]

Stalin's exposition, hinting that "errors" in action and thought were again cropping up in the Communist movement, implied that the aging dictator was not merely concerned with matters of ideological purity but also with behavior which was both deviant and harmful. Not since the mid-thirties had such an ominous warning been issued, and the earlier consequences of similar Stalinist admonitions were still fresh in Communist memories. The *Zhdanovshchina*, by way of comparison, involved issues more narrowly prescribed both in their ideological content and human scope. Stalin's 1952 observations could hardly be considered idle musings: they were preceded and followed by events which suggested a cause-and-effect relationship between his assessments of the situation and the fate of some individuals. The execution of Voznesensky, doubtless linked with internal party intrigues, appeared highly relevant to the views postulated by Stalin in "Economic Problems of Socialism in the USSR." The intensification of domestic vigilance campaigns in the USSR, culminating in the Doctors' Plot,[27] implied that Stalin was seriously contemplating the need to follow up his diagnosis with action. In other words, increasingly suspicious that somehow his system was becoming brittle and static, Stalin was preparing to deal with it the only way he knew how.

Stalin's death, however, in March 1953, left no one able to perform the task, while the protracted search for a successor brought to the surface the internal doubts and difficulties. Whether a recourse to extreme violence could have sealed the gap between the "superstructure" and the "base," between political imperatives and socio-economic realities, is doubtful. A violent purge might have revitalized the Communist movements and further obscured their internal dilemmas. Such a purge probably would have involved the final liquidation of Gomulka and his associates in Poland; it probably would have included the Jewish Communists in the Hungarian and Rumanian Politburos; it very likely would have embraced the top echelons of the CPSU, including the Politburo itself. Its surface consequence would have been an even more intensified dedication to Stalinism, a more rapid imitation of Soviet experience in the other Communist states, and an even further extension of secret police power. But this could only be achieved if the dictator lived for a few more years. Only he could supply the inner drive for the execution of a policy less and less related to reality even as seen by many Communists themselves. This was amply demonstrated by the policies adopted within a few months of his death. Stalin's last-minute effort to infuse Stalinism with a new purpose merely served to intensify the reaction against it.

PART II

IDEOLOGY AND POWER IN RELATIONS AMONG THE COMMUNIST STATES

THE THIRD PHASE
1953 – 1956

FROM THAW TO DELUGE – INSTITUTIONAL AND IDEOLOGICAL DIVERSITY

the roads and conditions of socialist development are different in different countries . . . any tendency to impose one's own views in determining the roads and forms of socialist development are alien to both sides. – Soviet-Yugoslav Declaration, Moscow, June 20, 1956.

CHAPTER 8

The New Course: Stalinism Dissipated

Stalin's death did not lead to the immediate distintegration of the Stalinist system. It did deprive it of the crucial psychological ingredient of personal fear — a fear shared by the subdued populations of East Europe, to whom Stalin was symbol of the Soviet might, and by their Communist leaders trained in the stiff Stalinist school of the Comintern and promoted through the rigorous competitions of the great purges. For the time being, however, the institutions of power remained, particularly the links between the Soviet secret police and the satellite networks, and the Stalinist conception of the relations between the USSR and the Communist bloc as well. The new Soviet leadership groped carefully in the initial stages, seeking to maintain continuity with the past while attempting to develop its own solutions to a variety of domestic and external problems left by the Stalinist legacy. The surgical solution which Stalin might have been contemplating in the closing days of his life now had to give way to a prolonged cure.

Soon both the institutions of Soviet power in the Communist-ruled states as well as the theoretical framework governing their relations to the USSR were subjected to the pressures of changed conditions and new requirements. As the ingredient of power, so dependent on the personal impact of Stalin, gradually, almost imperceptibly, shrank, the Stalinist monopoly of ideology and power in Soviet-satellite relations slowly gave way to a greater reliance on ideology. The dilemma was that Stalinism as an ideology was so dependent on power that by itself it could not cope with the post-Stalin situation in the Communist camp. Under the circumstances, the ideological framework linking the Communist states had to be made more elastic to permit greater variation in domestic policies within the context of overall unity. By 1956 and 1957 the search for new solutions was taking the form of a widespread dialogue between various Communist parties, leaders, newspapers, and intellectuals.* In effect, the Stalinist

* Admittedly, it is difficult to distinguish between ideological conflict which is politically motivated and that which primarily involves pure doctrine, especially when doctrinal positions form a basis for eventual political action. Nonetheless, one can

unity of ideology and power was dissipated within less than four years of his death. What led to this diversity? What were the new problems in the relations among the Communist states? The next four chapters (8–11) will attempt to provide the answers.

Problems of Soviet Succession

Stalin was not merely the Soviet dictator but also the leader of international Communism. Yet, in view of the central position of the USSR, it was only fitting that the succession be resolved, initially at least, within the framework of Soviet domestic considerations. The competition for power produced immediate and broad disagreements on policy, even if only as a function of the succession crisis. In addition, Stalin's death brought to the surface certain dilemmas which had long been obscured by the single-minded purposefulness of Stalinism as long as the dictator was at the helm. Dormant political and economic issues now demanded immediate attention and resolution. Unavoidably, such Soviet domestic preoccupations tended to leave the Communist leaderships in the neighboring states somewhat to their own resources.

Among the most important items on the agenda of the new "collective" leadership were the creation of some stable leadership arrangement which would safeguard the dominant interests of the upper levels of the political elite and prevent a violent and disruptive conflict; a reorganization of the party and administrative structure which had grown too large and unwieldy under Stalin; a diminution in world tensions which were imposing a heavy strain on Soviet and Communist development; and, finally, a review of the Stalinist economic formula which favored heavy capital development at the expense of consumption and agriculture.

Now, it is highly unlikely that, following a devout wake for Stalin, his successors actually sat down and enumerated point by point the problems that they faced and the methods required for solving them. Some of the above issues were spontaneous products of the struggle

---

point to certain ideological disputes in which problems of power are so involved that it is not unreasonable to suspect that the dialogue on theory is a mere sham for a brutal power struggle. The least one can say is that ideology and power have become inseparable at such a juncture. This would appear to have been the case with many of the disputes which developed after Stalin's death among various Communist leaders and parties in East Europe, including the USSR, and also in the case of the positions taken by the Chinese and French Communist parties. There is also, however, the more genuine conflict of ideas in which power plays only a secondary role. This seems to have been the situation with much of the ideological disputes which went on inside Poland, conducted by intellectuals not tied to specific posts of authority.

for power which itself altered the relationships among the various institutions of Soviet power. Other issues arose as the new leaders proceeded to formulate policy and think independently, almost for the first time in their mature lives. Genuine conflict of opinion certainly might have arisen on the controversial issue of heavy capital development versus consumer-goods programs and agricultural growth.[1] Finally, it is quite likely that a review of foreign policy aiming at the reduction of tensions followed logically from Stalin's testament which had posited the intensification of conflicts within the capitalist camp. This testament, therefore, implied that the USSR should not allow the capitalists to obscure their internal contradictions by channeling their aggression against the Communist world. But here again a conflict of interpretation on scope and method was bound to arise and be exacerbated by the absence of a final arbiter. And ambivalence in Moscow, thanks to Stalinism, meant ambivalence in Prague or Warsaw.

The first year and a half following Stalin's death was dominated, within the limits of an uneasy "collective" leadership, by Georgi Malenkov. The initial succession problem which the new regime faced was that of the secret police which had grown powerful under Stalin and which now seemed to be reaching out for total power.* The echoes of the July 1953 announcement of Lavrenti Beria's arrest and the Christmas Eve 1953 execution of the former secret police chief and six of his top associates had particular significance for the East European Communist parties smarting for the preceding few years under police surveillance. The subsequent stress on "socialist legality," though still largely verbal, in itself represented a factor potentially limiting the formerly unchecked interference of the police in party matters. Tackling another of the problems it considered basic, the regime in 1954 took a first tentative step toward decentralization of the Soviet administrative structure,[2] although Malenkov continued the Stalinist practice of a multiministerial Council of Ministers, ruled internally by an inner cabinet of first deputy prime ministers. The measure of duality of party and state administration which had developed under Stalin remained largely unchanged, and, indeed, the effort to avoid a concentration of power in one man's hands resulted in the appointment of different individuals to head the party and the administration.

* At the time many observers were inclined to feel that the secret police was the actual ruler of the USSR. See the remarks by G. Kennan and H. Arendt in C. J. Friedrich, ed., *Totalitarianism* (Cambridge, 1954), pp. 76–77, 82–83.

It was in the sphere of economic policy that the Malenkov period was marked by the greatest innovation. Of course, here again, the position adopted by Malenkov — namely, that of stressing an improvement in the standard of living — in some measure may have reflected a commonly felt need among the post-Stalin leaders to court the people. However, soon it did become an issue in the struggle for power, with the government organ, *Izvestia*, and the party organ, *Pravda*, publicly disagreeing at one point on the policies that ought to be followed,[3] and with Khrushchev finally warning that abandoning the heavy industry priority is "nothing but slander of our Party . . . a belching of the rightist deviation, a regurgitation of views hostile to Leninism." [4] Khrushchev's violent outburst, accompanied as it was by Malenkov's dismissal as premier, was nothing short of a complete repudiation of the Malenkov policy, which had been expounded in a major address to the Supreme Soviet as far back as August 1953. That policy had emphasized a shift in investment toward light industry and trade, as well as increased incomes for collective farmers and a greater availability of consumer goods. To underscore the importance of this program, the issue of *Pravda* which carried the full text of Malenkov's August 1953 address also ran special inside stories which emphasized only those portions of the speech pertaining to an improvement in the standard of living.

In foreign policy, the Malenkov period coincided with a reduction in world tensions, the most outstanding feature of which was the Korean armistice of July 27, 1953. In his August speech Malenkov took credit for a "normalization" in relations with Turkey, Iran, and Afghanistan, and for an exchange of envoys with Yugoslavia. As far as East Europe was concerned, Malenkov stood fast on the position that the People's Democracies were firmly tied to the USSR; much like Stalin earlier, he did not feel compelled to devote more than a passing phrase to them. One might well speculate, on rereading Stalin's "Economic Problems of Socialism in the USSR" that had the old dictator remained alive, Soviet foreign policy would not have been very much different. The Malenkov policy, too, seemed to take the permanence of the Soviet bloc much for granted and to count on growing tensions within the capitalist bloc to undermine the cohesion which had developed in the face of the earlier Soviet threat. In broad terms, the Malenkov policy may be characterized as a general continuation of Stalinism politically, possibly from sheer momentum, balanced by an attempt to reduce the harshness of the Stalinist economic policies. It was an attempt, in brief, to pursue a new course in economics without basically altering the framework of essentially Stalinist politics.

The Malenkov New Course

The Malenkov New Course struck a responsive chord among some of the leaders of the People's Democracies. Without yielding the most important Stalinist positions, it seemed to permit them to reduce somewhat the accumulated economic tensions. Political concessions, such as the introduction of collective leadership, were essentially procedural and, unlike the USSR, did not involve a substantive change in the East European power picture. In formal imitation, the leaders relinquished some of their posts to their associates, but this was of political significance only in Hungary. In some states which had lagged behind the others in Stalinist terror, such as Poland and Rumania, police violence mounted during this period.*

The first state to initiate a new course was East Germany. The mounting internal difficulties of this probably most Soviet-dependent regime forced the German Politburo to turn to Moscow, in April 1953, with an urgent request for assistance and to begin a reconsideration of the Stalinist capital-development policy. This was a particularly bad moment for approaching Moscow with such a request. The Soviet leadership was deeply divided, with Beria apparently favoring a radical political reform program for East Germany. On June 9, four days after the return from Moscow of the Soviet High Commissioner, V. S. Semenov, the SED Politburo made a public statement of self-criticism, admitting "aberrations in the past," and announcing a three-point program for alleviating the most acute hardships. Delivery quotas and taxes were reduced, state loans were made available to private business, and material allocations were increased. The timing of the High Commissioner's presence in Moscow was particularly interesting because it was precisely at this time that the CPSU Presidium was holding talks with Rakosi as the preliminary to a new course in Hungary. This certainly seems to confirm the notion that the Malenkov New Course was a purposeful program of action not for the USSR alone but for the People's Democracies also. Because of this larger perspective, the New Course was not sidetracked by the East Berlin uprising which followed within a week of the SED an-

* For example, in Poland, Cardinal Wyszynski was arrested in September 1953, and, in May, nineteen high army officers with distinguished war records were executed; in Rumania, Patrascanu, purged earlier from the party leadership, was executed in April 1954.

nouncement.[5] Indeed, the outbreak, followed shortly by Beria's arrest, even seemed to confirm the wisdom of the new policy: of political concessions there must be few, while economic concessions are warranted to relieve the political tensions. Following the suppression of the revolt by a show of Soviet strength, another SED Central Committee plenum convened on July 24–26, 1953. The Fifteenth Plenum rejected general criticisms of the party line, branding them as "defeatist and capitulationist," although it did admit that accelerated efforts to construct the socialist foundations had erred in ignoring practical internal and external considerations. The party pleaded guilty to disregarding the fact that a large portion of German public opinion lived under capitalist influence and that its views had to be considered when policy is framed. For this reason East Germany ought to strive for a standard of living higher than in West Germany. This would sound the death-knell for the Adenauer line by making East Germany an irresistibly appealing force.[6]

The main burden of the Fifteenth Plenum's resolutions was accordingly in the economic realm. The previous political line was judged essentially correct, the Ulbricht-Grotewohl leadership was absolved and even hailed, and those party officials who had wavered in the face of the crisis were dismissed.* At the same time, further economic concessions were made. The distribution of investments was altered, with the 1953 sum for heavy industry cut by 1.7 billion East German marks. Wage taxes and prices were reduced in October, and minor offenders were granted a partial amnesty. Simultaneously, however, the party reiterated its commitment to socialization in agriculture, and the percentage of collective and state-farm holdings grew (see table in Chapter 5, p. 99). In general, the easing of the economic situation — further aided by the return, on January 1, 1954, to East German control of German enterprises managed by the USSR and the termination of reparations to the USSR — did result in a marked improvement in the standard of living and relieved some of the political tensions in the country. The Malenkov formula seemed to pass this test of experience.

The next state to adopt a new course was Hungary. The situation there, however, differed substantially from East Germany's. The Hungarian regime had been considerably more violent than the East German (see Chapter 5), and the economic changes adopted by it had

---

* After the uprising, Wilhelm Zaisser, Minister of State Security, Max Fechner, Minister of Justice, and R. Herrnstadt, editor of the party daily, were dismissed. A second wave of dismissals followed in January 1954.

been forced on a country with a much more primitive economic structure. Consequently, the impact of Stalinism had been felt a good deal more sharply. The violence of the purge trials and the executions of many non-Communist leaders were matched by an industrial-development drive which envisaged during the Five Year Plan a 380 per cent increase in the production of producer goods.[7] Extricating the regime from the existing situation, therefore, was bound to be a far more complicated and dangerous task. Soviet initiative again was the decisive factor. In June 1953, a conference convened in Moscow between the heads of the CPSU and a delegation from the Hungarian Politburo, headed by Rakosi. The Soviet leaders apparently spared no words in castigating the Hungarians for *economic* excesses which "had driven the country to the verge of catastrophe." [8] At the conference Mikoyan, Malenkov, and Khrushchev took the lead in insisting on immediate economic reform to prevent unrest, while politically they appeared satisfied with an imitation of the limited Soviet amnesty and of the collective-leadership principle.[9]

In the Hungarian circumstances, the Malenkov adaptation of Stalinism could not avoid having profound political overtones. The critical economic situation, added to a long-term resentment of Rakosi's political practices, produced within the party an opposition to Rakosi strong enough to justify, in Moscow's eyes, Rakosi's resignation from the premiership. The new premier, appointed as a formal concession to the principle of collective leadership, actually happened to be an individual who was personally committed to the principles of the New Course — just as Rakosi was personally against it. Imre Nagy's appointment was thus politically significant for it pitted the combined prestige of a new policy and a new premier against the entrenched power of the First Secretary of the party. The new premier was supported by a minority faction within the Central Committee but, for the first time, this minority controlled an important state post and pursued an official policy blessed by Moscow. The First Secretary could not, therefore, oppose the New Course openly — he had to bide his time and make certain, in the meantime, that his position within the party *apparat*, made loyal to him through the purges and by a common vested interest, was not undermined. The economic part of the New Course in this manner created an ambivalent political situation: Rakosi retained party control and hence the power, but Nagy shaped the program and hence interpreted the ideology.

Nagy's program was officially inaugurated by a major Parliamentary address delivered on July 4, 1953. The initial impact of the New

Course was largely economic even though it did involve measures which sharply reduced the class-struggle atmosphere which dominated the preceding phase. But the economic ills which the New Course was to correct were so deep-seated in the system that efforts to remedy them involved profound criticisms of past policies and implicitly of the entire system. The new premier promised that his economic policy would be guided by the principle of "cut your coat according to your cloth," * and he noted that "the development of a Socialist heavy industry cannot be an end in itself." [10] Nagy then promised to reduce the rate of development and to modify its direction "in conformity with the capacity of the country." He explicitly promised to reduce investments allotted to heavy industry, an act which would have the effect of raising the standard of living. He was particularly scornful of the agricultural policies pursued by his predecessors:

agricultural production has been stagnating and during the past few years its pace has been determined by meager investments, the lack of support offered to individual farmers, the far too rapid development of producers' cooperatives, which is neither economically nor politically justifiable, and has made the peasantry's work insecure.

During the land collectivization program too much bullying was practised. This not only offended the peasant's sense of justice, but also caused serious harm to our economy and played an important part in bringing about the present state of affairs. [11]

Nagy then postulated "the consolidation of legality" as one of the most urgent tasks of his government and promised to abolish the internment camps and to separate the judiciary from the secret police. His program of action may be summarized under the following headings: (1) price reductions, wage increases, reduced compulsory obligations; (2) cancelation of some agricultural deliveries and a 15 per cent reduction in taxes on the peasantry, as well as sanctioned withdrawal from collective farms; (3) greater religious tolerance, abolition of internment camps, and partial amnesty. The program thus closely resembled the Malenkov formula, even though distasteful to the more radical party faction headed by Rakosi. However, unlike the USSR,

* It is interesting to note that at this time there was considerable uncertainty concerning Nagy's position. In the *News from Behind the Iron Curtain*, August 1953, p. 8, he was even described as "a trusted friend of Rakosi." A Communist of many years standing, he had lived in the USSR since 1929 and returned to Hungary only in 1945. After serving in several ministerial posts, in 1951 he was promoted to the party secretariat. According to the literal use of labels, he could have been identified as a "Muscovite."

in Hungary the past policies, applied over a shorter time span and in different circumstances, produced far greater strains, while the division in Hungarian leadership immediately translated such tensions into a political conflict of major proportions. The New Course could not stay within the limits set by the Soviet example and presumably intended by its framers. Soviet-Hungarian relations could not remain unaffected (for further developments, see Chapter 10).

The next three countries to follow suit, but without the resultant political and international strains, were Rumania, Bulgaria, and Czechoslovakia, in that order. In none of them did the imitative application of the collective-leadership principle materially affect the substance of political power.* All of them had suffered the stresses of rapid industrialization but none to the extent of Hungary. In addition, in Czechoslovakia and Bulgaria the economic difficulties were not matched by a violent national hatred of Russia, while in Rumania, with a similar anti-Russian national tradition, economic Sovietization had lagged behind the other states.† Furthermore, in Bulgaria and Czechoslovakia, the Communist parties were much more solidly entrenched than in Hungary and therefore better able to withstand the tensions involved. The Rumanian New Course was initiated by Gheorghiu-Dej's address of August 25; in Bulgaria, by a similar speech delivered by Chervenkov on September 8. In both cases almost entirely economic measures were stressed (but notably with continued collectivization), and these were initiated by known and trusted Stalinists.

The most enthusiastic response to the series of reforms which began in Hungary came from Czechoslovakia. There was good reason for this. Somewhat like East Germany, but without the wartime devastation and postwar reparations, Czechoslovakia suffered least from economic dislocation and social disintegration as a result of the rapid development envisaged in the five-year plans. Thus a policy reversal was possible without serious political consequences, while a reduction in economic pressures was bound to strike a responsive

* It is interesting, however, to note that the pattern of choice of posts varied, with the "strong man" choosing in one case the post of premier, in another that of first secretary. In Poland, Bierut chose the party post; in Czechoslovakia, A. Novotny did likewise, and so did Rakosi in Hungary, Enver Hoxha in Albania, and Walter Ulbricht in the GDR; in Rumania, however, Gheorghiu-Dej chose the premiership as did Chervenkov in Bulgaria.

† In the more industrially advanced Czechoslovakia and East Germany, industrial production by late 1955 was, respectively, 2.4 and 2 times higher than before the war. In the relatively non-industrial Poland and Hungary, the ratios were 4 and 3.5 times respectively. Yet in the case of Rumania, only by 2 times (*Trud*, April 3, 1956).

chord in the population. The summer 1953 riots in Pilsen (prompted by a currency reform) were a warning to the regime of the potential dangers involved in maintaining economic Stalinism, and the regime welcomed the timely, and still relatively safe, opportunity for withdrawal. Accordingly, the Czech response to the Hungarian program was much more openly favorable than in any other East European state; there was greater press coverage of the new Hungarian policy — a sure indication in a Communist-ruled country of official approbation, when not accompanied by derogatory references. Finally, on September 15, 1953, the Czech premier, Siroky, delivered an address in which he stressed the need for "proportionate growth" in Czechoslovak economy and announced a series of reforms in the existing plans. Apart from the usual decreases in taxes, wage increases, and reductions in delivery quotas, a slowdown in the rate of growth in industrial production was promised and limited permission granted to withdraw from collective farms. The last provision was rescinded within a year and collectivization was renewed (see table in Chapter 5).*

In retrospect, it seems that the economic version of the New Course worked well in Czechoslovakia. The reforms reversed any existing trends toward an appreciable lowering of the standard of living without, however, capitulating on the essentials of socialist construction. The continuation of the collectivization policy (after a short halt) indicated the regime's determination to liquidate the last remnants of private ownership in the economy while politically and ideologically maintaining tight control over the country. The economic reforms appear to have stymied the opposition undercurrents within the party, while the finality of the earlier purges removed some of the potential leaders of such an opposition. Indeed, the Czech Communist leadership, partially because of the country's relative prosperity and advanced economy, partially because of the party's strength and greater experience, and partially because of a relatively pliant population, displayed the greatest skill in applying the modified policy and thereby in maintaining ideological and institutional unity with the USSR.

The last to formally adopt the New Course was Poland. It did so on October 29, 1953, at the Ninth Plenum of the Central Com-

---

* Between June 30, 1953, and November 1954, the number of collective farms declined from 7038 to 6530, and the percentage of socialized arable land from 44 per cent to 30 per cent (*Lidova Demokracie*, November 5, 1954). This presumably alarmed the leadership.

mittee of the United Polish Workers' Party. The reforms adopted were minor. In his speech to the Plenum, Bierut, whose power at this time was at its height, stressed the need to improve the standard of living but conceded nothing in the political field. He still called for a struggle against the kulak, although it was admitted that an error had been made in lumping together the rich with the medium peasant. From now on, it was promised, a distinction would be made between the two, and the party was to make a concerted effort to wean the latter away from the former. Only this would assure the final victory of socialism in the countryside.[12] Economic concessions were limited to some price reductions and to tax and compulsory-deliveries relief. The party also promised to reduce the share of accumulation in national income from 25.1 per cent in 1953 to 19.8 per cent in 1955 and to increase the turnover in socialized retail trade by 20 per cent.[13] The chief of Polish economic planning himself admitted that these changes were much more modest than elsewhere, particularly when compared to Czechoslovakia and East Germany.[14]

The political atmosphere remained basically unchanged. Indeed, as noted, some of the most extreme acts of violence took place around this time. Nonetheless, the very fact that Poland lagged in following the example of others and displayed considerable reticence when finally adopting the plan was significant. To some extent this could be explained by the previous policy of caution. Stalinism had been gingerly and timidly distilled in Poland. As has been observed in previous chapters, it involved a little less violence within the party itself, less collectivization and fewer compulsory deliveries for the farmers, and a little more circumspection in outright imitation and adulation of all things Soviet. Furthermore, the general instability of the economy, widespread poverty, and weakness of the party might have convinced the leadership, firmly in the hands of old Stalinists like Bierut or Berman, that a point of no return had been reached and that a sharp reversal would be dangerous. This was especially the case since they had not liquidated all the political alternatives. An admission of fundamental error would have been an implicit recognition that Gomulka, still living and not forgotten, had been right. Caution and restraint in moving away from a domestic policy of economic and political radicalism seemed the soundest political course to follow. The program was presumably cleared with Moscow, and the Polish leaders asserted with specific reference to Malenkov's August 1953 address that "the countries of People's Democracy and their leading force — the Communist and Workers' Parties — get their example and inspiration from the achievements and policy of the peoples of the Soviet Union and the leading force of mankind – the Communist Party of the Soviet Union." [15] Nonetheless, the primacy of domestic considerations seemed inherent in the new policy. This was not without its hidden significance.

During the Malenkov period the People's Democracies, with the Soviet Union leading the way, concentrated their efforts on coping with the economic legacy of Stalinism. However, the reaction of the various parties to Malenkov's new course, while substantially uniform and hence in keeping with the Stalinist formula of unity, already involved varying shades of enthusiasm, timing, and degree of personal commitment. The broad pattern of Soviet controls was still not affected and the habit of obedience was still deeply ingrained, but it was certainly easier for the post-Stalin Soviet leadership to recommend policies which made the domestic tasks of the various party leaderships less difficult. The response of the satellite leaders on the whole was a reflection of their approval, with some qualifications, of the new line. But what would they have done if they had concluded that Moscow's policies would make their job harder or go counter to their personal interests or views?

The very fact that the New Course did take into consideration the peculiar domestic facts existing in each case is a reflection of the change that had taken place in relations in the Soviet world since Stalin's death. The disappearance of Stalin, the destruction of Beria, the signing of the Korean armistice and the resolution of the Indo-Chinese conflict, the Soviet acknowledgment that the February 1954 Berlin conference of foreign ministers of the major world powers had led to "better understanding" of the international situation [16] – all tended almost imperceptibly, but significantly, to alter the existing relationships. With the decrease in external pressures, the excessive personalization of Communist interstate relations, which had been a source of strength as long as Stalin lived, became a source of weakness when he died.

Malenkov's efforts not to disrupt the political structure, while remedying some of the underlying economic grievances,* did in fact achieve certain desirable results in the more economically advanced states and also in the least-developed states. However, in Poland and Hungary the Malenkov formula was insufficient to resolve the di-

* Symptomatic of this approach were the announcements of the transfer of the Soviet share in the jointly owned companies to Rumanian ownership (*Izvestia*, September 25, 1954); to Bulgaria (*ibid.*, October 12, 1954); to Hungary (*ibid.*, November 10, 1954). In each instance, the recipient was to pay off the Soviet share on otherwise unspecified "favorable terms."

lemmas bequeathed by Stalinism without a clear and sustained Soviet involvement. In the Hungarian and Polish reactions to the new pattern there were harbingers, very faint ones, of future diversity. In Poland, the New Course was applied more slowly because of existing internal tensions and earlier caution, as well as potential dangers involved in it; in Hungary, the New Course was applied quickly and extensively precisely because of existing tensions but also because of earlier excesses. In Poland, the presence of a political alternative which had inhibited the leadership and the sense of popular disappointment with the leadership's conservatism in applying the New Course gradually transformed it into a political phenomenon (see Chapter 11). In Hungary, the creation of such a political alternative through Nagy's appointment and the rear-guard struggle waged against the New Course by the Stalinist first secretary of the party immediately made the policy a crucial domestic dilemma (see Chapter 10).

In the Soviet Union itself there was developing a marked ambivalence toward the policies to be pursued. The uncertainties in the Soviet line, which burst into the open through the unprecedented cleavage between *Pravda* and *Izvestia* in December 1954 and which had been a matter of earlier party discussions, could not leave the People's Democracies, and particularly Poland and Hungary, unaffected. The resulting disorientation and lesser Soviet involvement meant that a consideration of alternatives was gradually replacing the single-minded purposefulness of Stalinism as the basis for policy formation. Even if not participating actively in Soviet policy dilemmas, the East European Communists could not avoid taking sides emotionally, intellectually, or politically,* especially as long as the Soviet leaders continued to assert the relevance of the Soviet experience for the People's Democracies.† But even distant and relatively passive participation in Soviet policy dilemmas meant a break with the mechanical acceptance of Moscow programs as "revealed truth."

Khrushchev's Conception of the Communist Camp

During 1954, the Soviet political scene was dominated by the rapid growth in the stature of the first secretary of the party and by

* Bialer (*Wybralem Wolnosc*, p. 12), in the report of his activities while on the staff of the Polish Central Committee, refers specifically to frequently heated discussions among Polish *apparatchiki* on the meaning and implications of various Soviet policy shifts during this period.

† For instance, at the November 1954 anniversary of the Bolshevik revolution, M. Z. Saburov, the Moscow keynoter, stated that "Socialist construction in the USSR is the source of a wealth of experience for all the people who have now taken the path blazed by the Great October socialist revolution." *Pravda*, November 7, 1954.

the increasingly peremptory tone of his pronouncements. As one authoritative observer has noted, "the step-by-step ascent of Khrushchev to a position of undisputed leadership represents a striking recapitulation of the Stalinist experience," [17] and it was accomplished primarily in terms of domestic issues and through the manipulation of domestic forces. By skillfully seizing the initiative in pressing for new and dynamic schemes of internal reconstruction, Khrushchev assumed the role of the Leninist revolutionary struggling against the vested interests of the bureaucrats, and he succeeded in mobilizing the party around him. His insistence, in February 1954, on a new agricultural policy, his shuffles of the party *apparat*, as well as his active interest in the parties of the People's Democracies (demonstrated through personal visits to Poland, Czechoslovakia, and China), made him appear as the dynamic innovator so necessary to keeping a totalitarian system from stagnating. Naturally, this produced resentment from those sections of society interested in stability, but in late 1954 and early 1955, Khrushchev succeeded in gaining the support of the Central Committee of the party on the critical issue of the methods of industrialization and of the rate of development of heavy industry.[18]

In retrospect, it appears that the Soviet leadership was at the time divided into three groups: some Soviet leaders favored relatively "softer" methods on the international front and some domestic economic concessions; others, accepting the proposition that Soviet interests would be best served by a foreign policy somewhat less Stalinist in form though not in content, differed fundamentally on the domestic economic line and insisted on heavy industrial development; still others supported domestic and external policies essentially Stalinist both in form and content. To the degree that it is possible to generalize about as complex an issue as the policy outlook of specific Soviet leaders, it would appear that the first attitude was held by Malenkov, the second by Khrushchev,* and the third by Molotov. It was a combination of the last two that united to remove Malenkov on the issue of domestic policy, although Molotov was apparently unable to carry the day on the international issue. Thus, in international politics, the new Khrushchev-Bulganin team continued the efforts to present the USSR as genuinely striving to settle all international issues, reflecting the reassessments made late in 1952. The Geneva Confer-

---

* Khrushchev, however, already in mid-1954 dissociated himself from Malenkov's willingness to concede that an all-out nuclear war would spell the end of humanity and firmly contended that such a conflict would mean the final destruction of capitalism.

ence held in the summer of 1955 between the heads of governments of the United States, the United Kingdom, France, and the USSR (and with the First Secretary of the CPSU participating) was the culmination of this policy. It is likely that the Soviet leaders hoped that a measure of relaxation would allow the contradictions in the capitalist camp to mature while permitting the USSR and the People's Democracies to press their domestic industrialization unhindered by threats of war. Furthermore, the Soviet and other Communist leaders might have reasoned that such diminution of international tensions, symbolized by the Geneva handshakes with the leaders of the West, implicitly meant the West's acceptance of the status quo in East Central Europe.

In some respects it could be argued that the Communist calculations were well founded. However, the 1955 spell of international good will had a further and unexpected consequence. While possibly extinguishing any lingering hopes of Western "liberation" of East Europe, it also reduced the fears of the Communist ruling elites and undermined the feeling that they must "sink or swim" with the USSR. The internal Soviet ambivalence in policy and the reduction in international tensions produced the belief that the People's Democracies could now afford to frame their policies to fit their domestic requirements. The Stalinist "dilemma of the one alternative" was upset with the fading of the external enemy, while the Soviet return to heavy industrial development immediately put to the test the willingness of the parties — as well as their ability — to emulate the USSR under these new circumstances, even when such imitation imposed domestic strains. The situation was now quite different from the Malenkov New Course period.

That Khrushchev expected the People's Democracies to follow the new Soviet economic policy seems clear. Admitting that some "disproportions" had existed in the past, the Soviet leadership adopted the position that such errors had now been corrected and that correction of errors is not a substitute for policy. *Pravda*, commenting six weeks after the CPSU Plenum which had repudiated the Malenkov line, stated:

It would be incorrect to think that the creation of the material basis for socialism is proceeding without difficulties. Reorganizing the entire technical base of a national economy requires large capital investments, new cadres and great experience. The difficulties experienced by the economies of the people's democracies were manifested first of all by a number of economic disproportions. The decisions of the administrative bodies of the

Communist and Workers' Parties of the people's democracies point out the fact that the rate of growth of agriculture is insufficient to meet the working people's growing requirements. The development of the raw material and power base is lagging behind industry's needs.

In certain of the people's democracies the regrouping of capital investments carried out in order to eliminate these disproportions was interpreted by some as a renunciation of the preponderant development of heavy industry. The Party press in these countries writes that *these views*, which are *basically incorrect* and *harmful* to the cause of socialism, are being severely criticized.[19]

Pravda then commented approvingly on a recent resolution of the Hungarian Central Committee which had condemned such "anti-Marxist, anti-Party, opportunist views." [20] (See Chapters 10 and 11 for Hungarian and Polish developments.)

The Khrushchev formula for the USSR and for the Soviet bloc involved no basic change in the foreign-policy approach of the preceding two years, but domestically it stressed a return to an economic policy of maintaining heavy capital development while at the same time striving to improve agricultural productivity and to revitalize the economy. A by-product was to be an improvement in the standard of living, but without loss in heavy industrial development. However, because of the moderately relaxing effect of the two years' post-Stalin New Course, such an economic reshuffle could not be accompanied by a continuation of political Stalinism, and Khrushchev accordingly attempted to weave together some new fabric of unity and cohesion. By allowing an economic relaxation, Malenkov was able to ignore for the time being the political problem. By insisting on an economic "neo-Stalinism," Khrushchev had to face the political problem squarely. The formula which he apparently developed in the course of the following year involved increasing emphasis on common economic practices while tolerating an undefined and limited measure of political autonomy, unthinkable during Stalinism. Its further concomitant was to be the elevation of those Communist leaders who seemed more acceptable to the people, and Khrushchev made it painfully clear that Jewish Communists like Rakosi or Berman or Ana Pauker were in his judgment handicapping their parties. These efforts to develop some indigenous support for the various Communist regimes were to be matched by closer, formal institutional ties which would fill the vacuum left by the disappearance of the personal Stalinist ingredient, and by greater emphasis on common ideological bonds which would result from similar economic undertakings.

Indeed, allowing for the differences in scale, the Soviet-Chinese relations in the two years following Stalin's death might have served as a basic model for Khrushchev's thinking. (As noted, Khrushchev visited China in 1954.) The Chinese Communists found it much easier to profess strict adherence to the Soviet model of socialism in the absence of the Soviet dictator, and the resulting Soviet search for a successor and a new program relieved them of any fear of actual subordination.* International pressures on China were also lightened, while the Soviet Union acted as China's "honest broker" in the international arena. Internally, the Chinese forcefully pursued a policy of rapid industrialization on, as they asserted, the Soviet model.[21] However, beyond these somewhat ritualistic formulas, the Chinese did insist during this period on "adapting" all of this to specific Chinese conditions, and they even laid claims to having made creative and original contributions to Marxism-Leninism, particularly in the area of the "eradication of capitalism by peaceful methods of Socialist transformation."[22] They were careful, however, to restrict the applicability of this to the unique Chinese experience. The rather different techniques applied to cope with the domestic bourgeoisie, as well as the redefinition of the notion of the dictatorship of the proletariat in the Chinese context,[23] still did not weigh heavily on Soviet-Chinese relations and did not undermine what Khrushchev apparently considered the essentials of ideological unity: the leading role of the CPSU in the Communist camp, the Communist Party's supremacy in the domestic transformation of the various states, rapid industrialization and collectivization as essential components of that transformation.

Observing Sino-Soviet relations and bearing in mind the great dependence of the East European regimes on the USSR, Khrushchev could feel justified in altering the Stalinist formula in the direction of greater reliance on a community of economic patterns and emphasis on ideological uniformity. Such a framework could effectively contain the inherent pressures for diversity, but without the need for continuous Soviet involvement which Stalinism had demanded. In the words of Khrushchev's *Pravda:* "The historical experience of the Soviet Union and of the People's Democracies shows that, given unity in the chief fundamental matter of ensuring the victory of socialism, various ways and means may be used in different countries to solve

---

* In February 1955, the Chinese were even described by Molotov as sharing in the leadership of the socialist camp, and following Khrushchev's visit the joint-stock Sino-Soviet companies were abolished.

the specific problems of socialist construction, depending on historical and national features." [24] In keeping with this, the return of the various states to a policy of rapid industrialization was a qualified one. Everywhere lip-service was paid to the pre-eminence of heavy industry. Nowhere did a full return to the Stalinist rate of industrialization take place.* [25]

With Stalin gone, and the post-Stalin circumstances producing greater diversity, the Stalinist method of informal political ties had to be buttressed through formalization. Khrushchev, even though somewhat of a "vulgar Marxist" in his notions concerning the sources of cohesion between socialist states, was still sufficiently steeped in Leninism-Stalinism to recognize the importance of political bonds. This awareness was no doubt sharpened by certain international factors (such as the inclusion of West Germany into NATO), which made a more formal arrangement desirable. During Stalin's lifetime the independent state forms of the Communist-ruled nations had been emptied of most of their political content, but now there was the danger that such forms could become impediments to real international Soviet unity as the local regimes gradually began to emphasize a more domestic point of view. Since the formal abolition of these states as independent entities was no longer feasible — and, on the contrary, in some cases it was even desirable to increase their number, as was done with East Germany — it was necessary to adopt a solution based on their continued existence and probability of growing importance. The answer to this and to NATO was the creation of the Warsaw Pact and the invigoration of the dormant Council of Economic Mutual Assistance (CEMA).

The creation of the Warsaw Pact was presaged by a conference held in Moscow in November 1954 between the Soviet government, represented by Molotov, and the heads of the Communist governments. The conference took a firm stand against the Western policy of West German remilitarization and warned that the Communist

* These figures have been adapted from Taborsky, cited in note 25:

Percentage increases in the gross industrial output
(previous year: 100)

	1951	1952	1953	1954	1955
Bulgaria	119	118	112	109	110
Czechoslovakia	115	118	110	104	111
East Germany	122	116	112	110	108
Hungary	130	124	111	103	108
Poland	124	120	118	111	111
Rumania	129	123	114	107	114

states would be forced to act jointly if this should come about.[26] The Warsaw Pact was, accordingly, partially an answer to the German development. The pact, entitled "On Friendship, Cooperation, and Mutual Aid," was signed in Warsaw on May 14, 1955, by all the European Communist states and the USSR. It contained a general political agreement and a military convention.[27] The states reaffirmed their unity of purpose and, in the vaguely phrased fifth clause of the agreement, allowed for the disposition of troops under a joint command as deemed appropriate by them and the command for purposes of mutual defense. No further agreements for the stationing of foreign troops on the soil of any one of the signatories was made (a matter regularized only after the Hungarian and Polish events in 1956), but the pact itself represented a formal "legalizing" of the stationing of Soviet troops, especially since the military convention assigned the joint command to a Soviet officer and stipulated that troop disposition would be made according to mutual arrangements of the governments concerned (that is, between the USSR and the country concerned). The official Chinese observer, Peng Teh-huai, the former Korean War commander, associated himself with the pact and promised Chinese support in the case of foreign aggression.

The preponderance of Soviet power in East Europe should not obscure the political significance of the Warsaw Pact. It represented the single most important formal commitment binding the states to the USSR, officially limiting their scope of independent action, and legalizing the presence (and hence the political influence) of the Soviet troops stationed in some of them. The gradual return of "content" to the forms of state independence was in this fashion balanced by a treaty structure which provided for joint consultation on all major issues and Soviet command of all troops, and which did not provide any procedures for withdrawal from such treaty arrangement or for the removal of the Soviet forces.* Finally, since the sharp point of the pact was directed against Germany, which some of the treaty members deeply feared, an element of mutual self-interest was also present.

These formal political ties were to be further buttressed by an

---

* The Political Consultative Committee created by the Warsaw Pact met in Prague in January 1956 and decided to meet regularly not less than twice a year and to create a standing commission for foreign-policy coordination and a standing secretariat. In a sense this meant the abandonment of the Stalinist technique of bilateralism (*Zasedaniia Politicheskovo Konsultativnovo Komiteta*, Moscow, 1956, p. 53). The international military command, however, was not set up; the satellites did not appoint liaison officers to it; and control remained in Soviet hands. This underscored the primary political purpose of the treaty.

increased reliance on the CEMA. After several years of relative in-activity, during which it occupied itself primarily with channeling trade between the Communist states, the CEMA became more vigorous after 1954. Meetings of the Council were held at least annually (see Appendix I), the council's organization was developed and its objectives defined. Its basic goal was to facilitate mutual exchange of experience and techniques; to promote a division of labor and specialization in industrial production; to coordinate investment and the subsequent five-year plans.[28] The division of labor was a departure from the Stalinist notions of an essentially autarkic construction of socialist industrialization,* while the political significance of the economic cooperation was openly stated. "Intensification of the co-ordination of the national economic plans of the USSR and the People's Democracies is needed to strengthen socialism," *Pravda* observed commenting on the activities of the council.[29]

Hand in hand with this stress on economic integration went a growing emphasis on the benefits to be derived from cooperation with the USSR. "The mighty socialist industry of the USSR plays the decisive role in strengthening the great socialist camp. Relying on its economic capacity, the Soviet Union extends to the countries of People's Democracy fraternal assistance in the development of their economies," [30] the Soviets asserted. They were correct in the sense that, by 1954, the industries of some of the states were highly dependent on Soviet supplies. About 70 per cent of Czech iron-ore imports in 1954–1955, 68 per cent of the Polish, and 100 per cent of the Rumanian and Hungarian came from the USSR, as did all manganese, a large part of cotton, and so on.[31] After 1955, the Soviet Union also became a more active source of credit for the People's Democracies,[32] although Khrushchev's boast to the Twentieth Party Congress that the total amounted to 21 billion rubles presumably included very large, secret military credits extended at unknown rates of interest during the Stalinist period. In March of 1956, in a further gesture of close cooperation, all the Communist states banded together in organizing a Joint Nuclear Research Institute to be headed by Professor A. V.

---

* Under the plan, East Germany was to specialize in the production of precision instruments and electrical equipment; Poland: rolling stock, ships, mining equipment, chemicals; Czechoslovakia: machine building, automobiles, engines; Hungary: diesel engines, motor trains, buses; Rumania: oil pipes, drilling equipment. Standing committees, functional in nature and distributed among the various capitals, were also set up. Reflecting the importance of these committees was the fact that the various member states were normally represented by the respective ministers or vice-ministers. R. Fidelski, *Wspolpraca Gospodarcza Polski z Krajami Socjalistycznymi* (Warsaw, 1959), pp. 81–83.

Topchiyev of the Soviet Academy of Sciences and to be situated in the USSR. The member nations were to make proportional contributions to its establishment.[33]

In this fashion the slightly greater measure of political flexibility in the bloc would be balanced by common economic interests and ideological commitment. Indeed, Khrushchev might well have hoped that the last two would more than compensate for any retreat from the rigid Stalinist insistence on political subordination which, in some cases, impeded the development of even "objective" ties. It is symptomatic that, unlike Malenkov's, the burden of Khrushchev's informal criticisms of Stalinist policies in East Europe involved political aberrations rather than economic ones (which in some measure had helped to produce the political).[34] Paralleling Soviet domestic re-emphasis of the party, the excessive Stalinist reliance on controls was giving way to an emphasis on close party links among the Communist regimes in the hope that closer Party relations would also revitalize the common ideological bonds.* While Soviet power remained a crucial background factor, ideology based on economy was to replace power masked by ideology.

The Issue of Yugoslavia

Within this revised framework the conflict with Yugoslavia lost most of its meaning and, indeed, could only impede the implementation of Khrushchev's vision. On *this* score, Khrushchev might have been supported by some members of the displaced Malenkov group. In any case, given the changes in East Europe and recalling Tito's loyalty to the USSR prior to 1948, a portion of the Soviet leadership apparently concluded late in 1954 that the Soviet-Yugoslav rift was ideologically barren and largely a product of the late dictator's pathological hatreds and phobias. Noting that, domestically, Tito had been a forceful Communist, the Soviet leadership appears to have assumed that an arrangement stressing common party bonds while accepting Tito's domestic autonomy would establish a pattern for similarly firm Communist regimes elsewhere. They would be bound together through the rigorous party dictatorships run on similar doctrinal assumptions, reinforced by integrated economic processes. Khrushchev realized he could not wipe out Tito's national Communism, but he hoped to harness it.

* Characteristically, high CPSU officials were appointed as ambassadors to the various Communist states: for instance, in Poland, the appointment in May 1955 of P. K. Ponomarenko, former first secretary in Kazakhstan, and in October 1957 of P. A. Abrasimov, former party secretary of Belorussia.

The decision to improve relations was made sometime in the fall of 1954, but the limits of the projected improvement were left undefined and, in the summer of 1955, caused a sharp exchange of views within the Soviet leadership, particularly between Khrushchev and Mikoyan on one side and Molotov on the other. Initially, however, even Molotov might have approved a "normalization" in relations, for during 1954 the Soviet peace campaign directed against the Western European Defense Community (EDC) went into high gear and the Yugoslav position of "positive neutrality" also involved a rejection of the Western scheme. In the fall of 1954, Soviet newspapers carried several articles citing the Yugoslav views [35] but without the usual derogatory references to Tito, and even quoting verbatim lengthy passages of Tito's criticisms of the EDC and the Atlantic Pact.[36] Following a series of friendly gestures (such as the CPSU Presidium's attendance at the Yugoslav Embassy celebration of the Yugoslav national holiday and laudatory press articles on the anniversary,[37] increased cultural contacts,[38] a limited trade agreement [39]), it was announced that direct talks between the Yugoslav and Soviet leaderships would be held in May 1955. The Soviet press emphasized that the Belgrade talks would end a situation which "had been only to the advantage of the enemies of peace." [40]

Khrushchev strove from the very outset of the talks, which began on May 27, to stress common ideological party issues and to put them on a Communist-to-Communist plane. Even in his apologetic airport speech Khrushchev adhered to this intention, while also revealing the basic assumptions of his thinking:

The strongest ties are established between the peoples of both countries which have as their guiding force Parties that base all their activities on the teaching of Marxism-Leninism. The Parties that take the Marxist-Leninist teaching as their guide achieve complete mutual understanding because they have a common aim — struggle for the interests of the working class and the working peasants, for the interests of the working people.[41]

The agreement, however, that was signed on June 2 was purely a joint declaration of the two states and did not cover party or ideological matters as Khrushchev had wished.* Nonetheless, it explicitly acknowledged that Yugoslavia was a state building socialism and it did contain some implicit ideological concessions to the Yugoslavs. Reference was made to "mutual respect for . . . different forms of

* A Yugoslav ambassador stated to this writer that the agreement was based on a Yugoslav draft.

Socialist development" and, at the end of the eight-point agreement involving state matters (to which the Yugoslavs wished to restrict the conference), provision was made for "the exchange of Socialist experience." [42]

The Yugoslav reserve was understandable. Having gradually emerged with an ideological position and certain institutional arrangements which they considered as their own creative contribution to Marxism-Leninism (see Chapter 9), they feared the new Soviet policy of minimizing ideological and party differences before a clear-cut, un-Stalinist principle of diversity was acknowledged. They might well have been disturbed also by the equivocation of the Soviet leaders on the subject of the 1948 resolution which had expelled Yugoslavia from the Cominform. Even though the Yugoslavs were formally acting as if it had been renounced, the Soviet leaders pointedly rejected only the November 1949 Cominform resolution which had so violently condemned the Yugoslavs as Gestapo spies and such; little was said about the 1948 declaration which had charged them with a variety of ideological sins.* To Khrushchev, however, allowing the Yugoslavs to place a somewhat wider interpretation on the revision of the past, and even having to acknowledge indirectly a tolerance of diversity implied by the agreement, represented a small price to be paid for drawing Yugoslavia back into the fold. Such a step would minimize ideological differences and strengthen the bonds between the Soviet Union and the other People's Democracies in this post-Stalin period. Past Yugoslav experience could even serve to reinforce the argument for the imitation of Soviet experience.

However, the Yugoslav reserve was apparently shared, for other reasons of course, by some of Khrushchev's colleagues, most notably Molotov (for East European reactions, see next chapter). The matter was raised at the July 1955 Plenum of the CPSU Central Committee and led to a thorough airing of the entire problem of Soviet-satellite relations.[43] Opposition to Khrushchev's policy was voiced by Molotov who already, in February of 1955, had expressed misgivings concerning excessive fraternization with Tito.† Subsequently Molotov in-

---

* In 1958, both the organ of the SED and Khrushchev himself asserted, with no direct Yugoslav rebuttals, that the Yugoslav leadership had been told that it was the 1949 resolution only which was being denounced. See *Pravda*, July 12, 1958; *Einheit*, no. 5, 1958. The November 1949 declaration, entitled "The Communist Party of Yugoslavia in the Hands of Murderers and Spies," in effect urged Tito's liquidation.

† This also explains the strange exchange between Molotov, speaking to the Supreme Soviet in February, and Tito, addressing the Skupshtina in March. In his speech, Molotov alleged Yugoslavia's partial responsibility for the abyss existing between the two states, explaining it in terms of Yugoslav deviation from their initial

dicated that he approved normalization of diplomatic relations (presumably for reasons of international grand strategy) but still opposed Khrushchev's ideological initiatives. At the July Plenum, Molotov charged that Tito could no longer be considered a Communist, that he was anti-Soviet, and that accepting him back on a party-ideological basis would be extremely dangerous. Molotov conceded that the 1948 break was unfortunate, but only in the sense that all avenues of resolving the then-existing differences had not been exhausted. He maintained, however, that although the break had subsequently caused complications, it nonetheless had been fundamentally justified since an absence of firm and decisive Soviet action might have caused Poland to follow in Tito's anti-Soviet, "provocative" footsteps. Thus, in a sense, it had been a matter of choosing the lesser of two evils, and Molotov warned against a policy which he felt would again create disruptive tendencies.

He was answered by Khrushchev, Kaganovich, Mikoyan, and Shepilov. Like Molotov's, their answers reflected a concern with holding the Soviet bloc together, but they interpreted the disruptive tendencies differently. Their replies in effect involved a general evaluation of Stalinism as a system of state relations. Kaganovich charged that, during Stalin's life, the Soviet ambassadors appointed by Molotov behaved in a manner calculated to provoke hostility to the USSR, while Mikoyan, in a severe critique of the joint companies and the role of Soviet economic experts, characterized Stalinist economic relations with East Europe as "economic nationalism" which played into the hands of Soviet enemies. He conceded Molotov's allegation that Tito and his associates, particularly Kardelj, were veering in some respects toward a Western kind of socialism. But he reminded his listeners that many of the East European Communist leaders were former Social Democrats — they too may have looser concepts of socialism — and thus it would be particularly important to bind Tito to the Soviet bloc and to influence him ideologically. Khrushchev, while admitting that the 1948 resolution had been fundamentally correct in its evaluation, claimed that unless the Soviet Union adopted a policy of drawing Yugoslavia back into the political and ideological fold, the other Communist states in the post-Stalin phase might be tempted to emulate the

---

postwar position. Tito indignantly rejected this allegation, and *Pravda* (March 12), without discrediting the foreign minister, attempted to smooth over the issue by suggesting that the matter was not really important. It seems, in retrospect, to have been a conscious effort by Molotov to torpedo the rapprochement or, at least, to place it in its proper ideological perspective.

Yugoslav example, thereby causing the USSR unnecessary difficulties. That his view carried the day was duly recorded in *Pravda* which reported that "the Communist Party's Central Committee, which personifies the collective wisdom of our Party, resolved: 'To approve the results of the talks between the government delegations of the Union of Soviet Socialist Republics and the Federal People's Republic of Yugoslavia.'" [44] The paper then added significantly:

The Communist Party of the Soviet Union considers it desirable *to establish contact* and a rapprochement *between the CPSU and the Union of Communists of Yugoslavia on the basis of Marxist-Leninist principles*. The first results have now been achieved and the prerequisites have been established for this contact and rapprochement. It is hoped that rapprochement with the Union of Communists of Yugoslavia will continue and develop on the basis of Marxist-Leninist principles. [45]

The last few months of 1955 were accordingly marked by the gradual falling into line of the other Communist states on the Yugoslav question, although with markedly less enthusiasm (see next chapter). Khrushchev continued to apply pressure on the neighbors of Yugoslavia, and one by one they withdrew from their anti-Titoist positions.

The Twentieth Party Congress

Domestically, Khrushchev was busy consolidating his position. The CPSU's Twentieth Party Congress had been scheduled for February 1956, at which time the official party program was to be expounded and top party posts filled. Domestic issues accordingly occupied the Soviet leadership a good deal. The earlier July session had also discussed current problems of industrialization; in September an amnesty for certain political offenders had been decreed, a press campaign for more effective struggle against illegality developed, and the Stalinist architectural style repudiated. In consolidating his position, Khrushchev was raising the Leninist banner, calling for more revolutionary zeal, and appealing to the antibureaucratic prejudices of the masses. It was not the heavy capital development which was denying them the fruits of Soviet industrialization but the privileged and inefficient bureaucrats who were to blame, he argued, subtly linking his opponents with the bureaucrats. However, his domestic preoccupation did not lead him to neglect foreign policy. The agreement with Tito was followed by the Geneva Conference and, later in the fall, by the triumphant tour of Asia by Khrushchev and Bulganin. The new leadership, by word and deed, was demonstrating to its adherents its determination to cope in an imaginative way with the legacy of Stalin-ism.

In ideological matters, continued stress was laid on the significance of doctrine in the relations among Communist states. A curious episode, probably linked with the July plenum, gave the party's theoretical journal, *Kommunist*, an opportunity to expound on this subject more fully. In September, Molotov, in a published letter, re-tracted a statement made by him earlier in the year to the effect that the foundations of a socialist society had already been built in the USSR. The statement could have implied that a complete socialist society had not yet been constructed in the USSR. In withdrawing the statement as "theoretically erroneous and politically harmful," Molotov did not see fit to repudiate a further part of his original sen-tence, in which he had asserted that the People's Democracies "have made only the first, though highly important, steps in the direction of socialism." [46] A major disproportion in levels between the USSR and the other states was thus implicitly asserted. *Kommunist*'s editorial, commenting on the issue, stated that Molotov's original formulation was harmful because it underestimated the ideological and socio-economic importance of the Soviet system, particularly in view of the "present-day struggle for Communism." The editorial went on to stress the vital need of the party to struggle against the "cult of the personality" which is part "of the struggle of the new with the old," and to stress pointedly the party's intolerance "of the com-placency and conceit of certain leaders and cases of isolation from the masses." [47]

Having used the ideological issue as a point of departure for an attack on the domestic conservatives, *Kommunist* shifted to the in-ternational problem. Restating once again the thesis that the crisis within capitalism was deepening, the editorial charged that those re-sponsible for foreign policy had been neglectful of the Marxist-Leninist orientation. It then noted that domestic construction of socialism in the USSR is inherently linked with the general problem of the socialist camp, or "commonwealth," as the editorial called it, "headed by the Soviet Union," since it involves a continuous search for theoretical formulations to guide the patterns of development, to decide what is general and what is particular, and to bind the socialist states in true proletarian internationalism. Soviet primacy is derived from its advanced historical stage and is accordingly justified ideo-logically. The Khrushchev formulation of the relations between Communist states was then explicitly stated:

A new, socialist type of international relations arose with the formation of the commonwealth of socialist states. These are relations of fully equal rights, genuine friendship, fraternal cooperation in the sphere of politics, economics and culture, and mutual assistance in the construction of a new life. These relations are determined by the nature of the social-economic system of the countries of the socialist camp; by the unity of their fundamental interests and ultimate great aim, the building of communism; and by the single Marxist-Leninist world view of the Communist and Workers' parties. . . .[48]

Khrushchev's notion hence did not abandon Soviet primacy, but attempted to place it on a new and, as he hoped, firmer basis. He thus found himself agreeing with Tito that Stalinism — more as a form of consciousness which lags behind the new reality than as an actual force — was becoming an impediment to the achievement of Soviet domestic and external objectives.

In this light, Khrushchev's performance at the Twentieth Party Congress becomes even more meaningful. His speech on Stalin, a stunning surprise in the vigor of its condemnation, was designed to shake the Stalinist orientation prevailing among many party members at home and abroad. Khrushchev may have been carried away in his delivery, but there is little doubt that the speech was designed to destroy the myth of Stalin's infallibility, which would in turn permit Khrushchev to be more selective in deciding which portions of the legacy could be retained and which portions already represented a moribund past. Notably, the speech contained no references to Stalin's treatment of the People's Democracies — precisely suggesting that Khrushchev was leaving to himself the opportunity to select subsequently those aspects of Stalinism he might still want to retain. The verbalized rejection, however, of Stalin's view that the class struggle intensifies after the Communist seizure of power certainly had immediate relevance for the relatively new People's Democracies. The shattering effect of the speech on the delegates, despite the fact that they had been prepared by an earlier and also violently anti-Stalin speech by Mikoyan, is a matter of historical record. But a proper perspective on the speech should take into consideration that its primary design — to shake the rigid Stalinist attitudes which were impeding the task of adapting the Stalinist legacy — was meant to apply to the entire bloc.

More positive conceptions emerged from Khrushchev's formal, public address [49] and were echoed by some of the other leaders. However, with the exception of the admission that under certain favorable circumstances socialism may be established by nonviolent parliamentary devices and the assertion that war was no longer inevitable due to the power of the Communist bloc, no startling changes in the existing trends were foreseen. Rather, these trends were given a formal, explicit, and coherent form. The disintegration of the "imperialist colonial system" was analyzed and the development of "the zone of peace" noted as contributing to the decline of aggressive imperialism. With respect to relations with Communist states, Khrushchev now verbalized what he had been tacitly conceding since the summer of 1955: (1) ways to socialism may indeed differ and may in the future become "more and more varied" although socialism will presumably be the same; (2) "alongside the Soviet form of reorganizing society on socialist foundations, we have the form of People's Democracy," Khrushchev stated. Hence the two do differ (although his references to substantive differences were limited to the Chinese handling of private industry and trade and to the Yugoslav "unique specific forms of economic management"). There was still a paucity of detail in Khrushchev's speech on what is tolerable and what is not in the construction of socialism. But he did concede that, unlike the USSR, the construction may proceed by peaceful change if the working class shows sufficient strength and with the further stipulation that "in all the forms of transition to socialism, an absolute and decisive requirement is political leadership of the working class, headed by its vanguard. The transition to socialism is impossible without this."

The restrictive clauses notwithstanding, Khrushchev's statement clearly suggested an ideological justification for institutional diversity which Stalin had not been willing to tolerate, and it was so interpreted in at least some of the other Communist states.[50] It must be remembered, however, that in the September 1955 Molotov affair it had been emphasized that the USSR had already constructed a socialist society, a goal toward which the other states were striving. This inherently imposed limits on the degrees of diversity that the other Communist states could adopt, since the ultimate objective was personalized by the Soviet system with the experience of socialist construction behind it. That seems to have been the nuance introduced in the Twentieth Congress deliberations by Suslov's speech, when he cited Lenin's "inspired prediction that while the path to socialism would *essentially be one and the same for all*, the transition of different countries to socialism would not be entirely identical." [51] In citing those parts of Soviet experience which are relevant to other states, Suslov gently implied that intensive class warfare after the seizure of power might be necessary:

Political leadership of the state by the working class is necessary in order that over a shorter or longer period, depending upon the specific conditions, the capitalist class be deprived of ownership of the means of production and that the means of production be made public property, that *all attempts* by the overthrown exploiting classes to restore their rule be repulsed and that socialist construction be organized.[52]

Whether this represented a reasoned difference in view from Khrushchev's position or a new purposeful limitation on the initiative of other Communist leaders is difficult to tell. Nonetheless, the very ambivalence in Moscow meant more room for independent action and interpretation abroad, and a resulting tendency towards more diverse perspectives.

A restoration of uniformity would have required Soviet resources for the subordination and maintenance of Communist regimes, but this was made almost permanently unpopular because of the domestic rigidities it imposed. Such a policy would also have conflicted with the broad international stance adopted by the USSR after Stalin's death and, indeed, with some of the domestic reforms. Limited diversity opened a vista for the emergence of self-supporting Communist regimes but at the price of cohesion of the bloc. Khrushchev's somewhat ambiguous formula attempted to straddle this dilemma by superimposing ideological party unity on an acceptance of some domestic institutional diversity, which in turn he hoped would be balanced by growing economic ties. But this involved a rejection of Stalin the man and Stalinism the dogma, and these had been part of the power element which had buttressed and long since merged with ideology. Dissipating it, Khrushchev placed a tremendous burden on the ideology. At the same time the ideology had to cope with the domestic problems left behind by Stalinism and with the pressures emanating from the independent, but now legitimately Communist, Yugoslav position as well as from developing domestic events in Hungary and Poland. Their effect on relations among Communist states was to prove of critical importance, and the Khrushchev formula was yet to face its test.

CHAPTER **9** –

The Impact of Yugoslavia

KHRUSHCHEV had restored Yugoslavia to the position of an active agent in the politics of the Communist camp. While Stalin lived, the appeal of Yugoslavia's independent position to the other Communist states was mitigated by the prevailing international situation and by the domestic weaknesses of the regimes, while their Stalinist systems required continued manifestations of hatred and doctrinal condemnation of the Yugoslav policy. Tito's regime was equated with the most despised "capitalist imperialists," and any indication of laxness toward him was considered sheer treason.* This dichotomic relationship was abandoned late in 1954, and Khrushchev's subsequent moves restored to the Yugoslav government the stamp of political legitimacy and, after some reluctance, even doctrinal purity. An authentic socialist state was recognized to exist in Yugoslavia, and its independent position was no longer considered an *ipso facto* source of deviationism. As noted in the previous chapter, in rejecting Stalin's earlier conception of the Yugoslav role Khrushchev might well have been drawing on the experience of Sino-Soviet relations in his efforts to eliminate needless sources of ideological conflict.

Faithful to his general concepts, Khrushchev moved rapidly after the Twentieth Party Congress to eliminate any remaining obstacles to the "true" Marxist-Leninist relationship that ought to prevail between the USSR and Yugoslavia. Khrushchev undoubtedly felt that once these obstacles were removed and a unity re-established which recognized Yugoslav autonomy, the central position of the CPSU, its prestige and its Marxist-Leninist experience, as well as Soviet might, would automatically assert Soviet primacy and discourage divisive trends. This would be especially true once the Yugoslav way to

* A by no means extreme illustration of the prevailing attitude are the following excerpts from a 1952 Czech book on Yugoslavia: "Thrown out by the worker parties, thrown out by the people . . . thus one day Rajk, Kostov and Slansky were found on the carcass heap of history. There one day Tito will be found. Their names will figure in history as prototypes of the most filthy treason . . ." (p. 25); "Who are the rulers of the country? It is Tito, a bloody maniac, it is Rankovic who only yesterday was an agent of the Gestapo, it is Moshe Pijade the professional demagogue. In a word a handful of political gangsters who are ruling the Yugoslav nations by fascist terror" (p. 47). From L. Tarantova, *Zrada sidli v Belehrade* (Prague, 1952).

socialism no longer implied the glittering, but of course illusory, image
of distinctiveness and independence. In April 1956 the Cominform
was disbanded — a rather empty gesture since it had passed into obscurity some years earlier, but still a move greeted with approbation
in Belgrade [1] — and in June 1956 Khrushchev again met Tito, this
time in Moscow. The atmosphere of the meeting, quite unlike the
previous one, was characterized by ebullient cordiality. To Khrushchev it meant the culmination of a policy pursued, despite obstacles
and opposition, for a year and a half.

Tito's doubts and reservations of June 1955 no longer barred the
way to an ideological agreement a year later. The Twentieth Party
Congress had dispelled any lingering Yugoslav fears that Stalinism
might still be the norm for relations among Communist states, while
Khrushchev's formal address had clearly accepted what the Yugoslavs
considered to be their own position on the problems of building
socialism. Thus the Yugoslav press reacted with particular enthusiasm
to the congress speeches of Khrushchev and Mikoyan, both of which
made warm references to Yugoslavia. Indeed, the Yugoslavs felt that
both the Twentieth Congress and history in general had vindicated
their 1948 stance. Partly from vanity and partly from their desire to
assist Khrushchev in the struggle against the remnants of Stalinism,
the Yugoslavs were willing to ignore the Soviet equivocation on the
1948 Cominform resolution. It was probably in this spirit, and not
merely as a vindictive and spiteful gesture, that on March 20 *Borba*
published a condensed but accurate version of Khrushchev's secret
speech on Stalin, thereby lifting the veil of secrecy surrounding it.
By destroying Stalin, the Yugoslavs felt, a service was being performed both to international Communism and to those Soviet leaders
who were struggling against the distortive remnants of the Stalinist
myth. The Yugoslavs made no secret of this view, even though no
official Soviet admission of the authenticity of Khrushchev's speech
was made. Prefacing its account of Khrushchev's remarks with a
laudatory comment on the achievements of the Twentieth Congress,
and particularly noting the importance "of Lenin's principles that
transition to socialism be effected in various forms and manners,"
Borba added:

The whole course of the Congress and everything that happened after it
confirms that not only certain theoretical principles are involved but *an
entirely new orientation*, which indeed from the point of view of theory
and practice quite differs from the Stalinist one. The reality confirms that
these theoretical principles are *the expression of a sincere wish and reso-*

lution of the Communist Party of the Soviet Union, headed by Khrushchev, Bulganin and Mikoyan, to realize them in all fields.

This resolution is eloquently proved by the fact that the Communist Party of the Soviet Union has not concentrated its efforts only upon theoretical disclosure of the cult of personality but also upon *concrete unmasking* of its supporter, Stalin.[2]

Khrushchev's public speech denounced the dogma while his secret speech, publicized for the first time by Belgrade, repudiated the man. The abolition of the Cominform removed the last institutional remnant of the past, while Soviet economic offers helped to heal the memories of the former boycott.[3] Convinced of Khrushchev's sincerity and of the depth of the changes effected by the congress, the Yugoslavs were fully in favor of an interparty-ideological embrace.

It was consummated by the June 20 agreement in Moscow. Its key provision was the joint affirmation "that the roads and conditions of socialist development are different in different countries, that the wealth of the forms of socialist development contributes to their strengthening, and . . . that any tendency to impose one's own views in determining the roads and forms of socialist development are alien to both sides."[4] It seemed that Stalinism was giving way to Titoism. And yet, curiously, Khrushchev and others (with the exception of Molotov) appeared to be guilty of an offense which no Marxist should ever commit: allowing their consciousness of reality to lag behind reality itself. For the Soviet bloc which Khrushchev was trying to repair was no longer the bloc it had been before the revelations of the congress. Tito was no longer the Tito of old, and Yugoslavia had also changed — and the changes were both institutional and ideological. Finally, Titoism was no longer predicated on the desire to be an autonomous Soviet-like regime within the Soviet system.

The Yugoslav Road to Socialism

A retrospective glance seems appropriate here. Initially, even after the expulsion from the Cominform, Yugoslavia continued to profess its devotion to a model of socialism which essentially reflected the Soviet, and hence the Stalinist, experience. That, of course, was the most natural response of a leadership whose perspective had been molded in the rigid frames of Stalinist dogma and practice, although its personal allegiance to the center had been shaken. But even on that score, the Yugoslav leaders could not quite bring themselves to believe that Stalin could entertain views about them which the Yugoslavs knew to be incorrect. With their conscience clear of any deviationist notions, proud of their orthodox behavior, their normal reaction was to assume that what had happened had been a most tragic error — and that, therefore, it was merely a matter of time before the reality would win out and amicable relations be restored.

At the party congress in July 1948, which approved Tito's position vis-à-vis the Cominform, the assembled delegates hailed "Tito-Stalin," and the Yugoslav press continued to paint a dichotomic image of international affairs, with the USSR and its allies pictured as the "democratic and peaceloving" states threatened with aggression by the Western imperialists.[5] Speaking plaintively to the Third Congress of the People's Front of Yugoslavia on April 9, 1949, Tito cited press statistics to show that even then the Yugoslav press was "continuing to acquaint our masses with the successes of the workers of the countries of People's Democracy and the Soviet Union," and characterized as "slander" the possibility of United States aid to Yugoslavia.[6] As Adam Ulam, writing in 1951, put it: "One of the outstanding features of the continuing crisis between Yugoslavia and Russia has been the remarkable difficulty the Yugoslav Communists have experienced in reorienting some of their ideas and habits of thought."[7] In comparison to the intellectual debates, to the philosophical dialogue, to the preoccupation with the relation between ethics and politics that engulfed the Polish and Hungarian Communists during the dissipation of Stalinism, the emergence of a Yugoslav road to socialism was markedly unencumbered by intellectual soul-searching. Despite the violence of the break with Stalin and the abuse heaped on the Yugoslavs, men like Djilas and Dedijer were lonely figures. It was the party leadership, retaining dictatorial control over the society, which gradually manufactured the distinctive Yugoslav features and modified the Stalinist model. But they did so gradually, and for about two years after the break Yugoslavia continued to consider itself a dictatorship of the proletariat, with all its concomitants: the primacy of the party, the intensified class struggle, collectivization, the dichotomic vision of the world.

The Yugoslav road to socialism developed as it became apparent that a reconciliation with the USSR was not feasible and that a policy based on this expectation would demoralize the party while preventing Yugoslavia from accepting Western aid, desperately necessary in view of the Communist boycott.[8] This necessarily involved, first of all, a modification of the rigid Stalinist image of the two irreconcilable world blocs. Since it could not maintain indefinitely the stance of a rejected ally, and since Tito could hardly afford to suddenly announce his conversion to capitalism, a redefinition of international affairs was dictated by the imperatives of survival. Positive neutralism was the answer. It was to be based on the principle of coexistence between countries of differing socioeconomic orders, and it explicitly rejected Stalin's view that coexistence was a tactical adjustment not vitiating the fundamental inevitability of war. However, presumably because of the weakness of the Communist regimes in the People's Democracies, the Yugoslavs, while condemning their forcible subordination to the USSR, were rather reticent in suggesting alternative solutions to the Soviet domination of East Europe.

In large measure, the changes in Yugoslav thinking were shaped by the political requirements of the unenviable international position of the Yugoslav regime. In addition, however, Tito, Kardelj, and others, as Marxists, still felt compelled to take cognizance of facts which they could no longer ignore in the name of devotion to orthodoxy. The USSR was not modifying its position; the "aggressive" capitalist world was willing to come to Yugoslavia's assistance even while hostile to its system; Yugoslavia led by a Communist regime was being ostracized by states also led by Communist regimes. All of this did not fit the basic assumptions, and, after a suitable period of time had elapsed during which they had hoped against hope that reality would again reflect their orthodox views, the Yugoslavs found themselves with no alternative but to redefine orthodoxy to fit reality. And, in time, their new conceptions, involving a reasoned rethinking of their beliefs as well as a rationalization of Yugoslavia's position, acquired the rigidity of a new dogma which was to again restrict their freedom of policy (see below and Chapter 13).

A rejection of Soviet premises on international affairs could not avoid impinging on the domestic premises as well. It is a basic contention of Marxist-Leninist thought that the two are inseparable, and Tito and the others still thought of themselves as good Marxist-Leninists. Therefore, in dissociating themselves from Stalin's intransigent foreign policy, they inevitably became involved, willy-nilly, in mounting criticisms of the Soviet system itself. Marxism-Leninism was still their point of departure, but since neither Marx nor Lenin were noted for rigid consistency and since both had been voluminous writers, the Yugoslavs were not hard pressed to find numerous quotations to indict the Soviet system. Stalin was accordingly charged with having reduced the "creative" substance of the theory to a sterile rationalization for his personal dictatorship. This was superimposed on a socioeconomic system which had little in fact to do with socialism. The Soviet party was no longer the vanguard of the proletariat but a bureaucratized clique with a vested interest in its privileged position and periodically subjected to murderous purges by its bosses. The state ownership of the means of production, operative within this context, had lost its progressive social function and had degenerated into state capitalism with all its oppressive and conservative connotations.[9] After 1950, a number of Yugoslav leaders, particularly Kardelj, Djilas, and Dedijer, developed these notions into a vigorous and extensive condemnation of almost every aspect of Soviet domestic policy, ranging from Great Russian chauvinism and the introduction of large-scale social inequality and stratification, to a destruction of the solidarity of the international labor movement and a betrayal of Marxism-Leninism.[10]

Such criticisms in turn had to bear on past Yugoslav domestic reality. To criticize the Soviet system was implicitly to criticize what had happened in Yugoslavia itself, since for a number of years imitation of the USSR was considered the highest virtue. Historical periodization, however, provided the escape-hatch. The development of the Soviet system was broken down into favorable and unfavorable periods, with positive phenomena acquiring at a certain point rigidity and losing their dynamism, thereby being transformed into negative manifestations of bureaucratism and stagnancy. Revolution became reaction. Yugoslavia, however, was said to have avoided this dialectical pitfall of history through the adoption of timely reforms, before positive manifestations were transformed into negative ones. To demonstrate this, the Yugoslav leaders had to abandon some of the old Stalinist policies and adopt new variants and solutions. Theory and practice were again contingent. By the fifties some of the existing policies were clearly leading nowhere and to pursue them was to court disaster. True to their training, the Yugoslav leadership was loath to admit that this was the case, and preferred to pitch their justification for a change on the ideological level. Nonetheless, by 1950 it was apparent that the Yugoslav policy of heavy industrial development within the framework of a highly centralized and over-bureaucratized administrative structure, handicapped by the Soviet boycott, had produced an inflationary spiral made more acute by shortages of essential goods and abandoned construction projects.

The turning point came in June 1950 with the passing of legislation handing "the ownership" of industrial enterprises to the workers themselves, who were to exercise this ownership through the Workers' Councils. This reform, which became the keystone of Yugoslav assertions of ideological originality, was followed by decentralization of the economy and the administration, revisions in the criminal code, and finally in 1953 by a new constitution which broke with the earlier Stalinist model.[11] Even the party did not come out unscathed and, as if trying to live up to his criticisms of the CPSU, Tito decreed that the Yugoslav Communists were no longer to enjoy special privileges.[12] The name of the party was changed to the League (Union) of Communists of Yugoslavia, symbolizing its alleged voluntary and democratic character.

The reforms, some of them important and novel, did not alter the substantive power situation in the country. The Workers' Councils were balanced internally by effective party controls, or League cells, by technical controls wielded by the plant director, and by the norms of the national economic plan. In subsequent years, the degree of the Councils' actual power varied and, on occasions, the regime felt compelled to move in so as to restore what competence remained.[13] But there is no doubt that, whatever the actual scope of the Councils has been, they played an important role internally in improving workers' morale and externally in emphasizing the Yugoslav claim to having established the true Marxist-Leninist method of constructing socialism.[14] The central role of the party was not undermined, and certainly Tito's power was not affected. But it was precisely a corollary of this undiminished importance of the Communist Party that agriculture, the orphan child of Marxist thinking, continued to suffer in the usual way even as the other reforms were being implemented. It was not until 1953 that collectivization was actually suspended, and only after the failure of a renewed drive. Apparently the regime had continued to feel that collectivization was inherent in a socialist society and, despite its 1950 assertions that the principle of volition would be respected, had expected to be able to pursue this line. The March 1953 Decree on Property Relationships and Reorganization of Peasant Working Cooperatives,[15] allowing the peasants to withdraw, sounded the end of the collectivization policy. From now on, the emphasis was on incentives and cooperative development.

Yugoslavia, isolated from the Communist bloc and lacking the self-sufficiency to shape reality in terms of doctrine, had thus to adapt to reality. The doctrine also had to adapt, and this meant still further criticisms of the Soviet model. For instance, the Yugoslav Workers' Councils were seen as proving that the oppressive functions of the state were "withering away" in Yugoslavia, which was said to contrast favorably with contrary trends in the USSR. Asserting that by definition the claim to universality of any one system was bound to lead to "reactionary results," the Yugoslavs insisted that true Leninists had to assert multiplicity of ways to socialism; they characterized their own way as that of "social democracy."

Probably the most explicit statement of the Yugoslav doctrine was made in an Oslo address, delivered in September 1954, by Kardelj. Using alternate paths to socialism as his basic motif, Kardelj elaborated the following propositions: the USSR has exaggerated the role of the state, which has assumed "a very special *economic position* within the system of social relations" (italics his); that in Western Europe evolution toward socialism through the existing political structure is both feasible and is being realized; the Yugoslav revolution had been necessary due to the inability of the Yugoslav bourgeoisie to move forward with history; the first task of the new regime had been to change "the material ratio of social forces in favor of socialism" through industrialization, and hence a measure of internal discipline had been necessary; since then, unlike Stalinism, Yugoslavia had been able to avoid the danger of bureaucratism by initiating the gradual withering away of the state through the strengthening of socialism by means of social ownership, the Workers' Councils.[16] True socialism in Yugoslavia was thus sharply differentiated from the state capitalism said to prevail in the USSR.

Legitimate doubts may be raised concerning the theoretical soundness of the above propositions. Given the political context of the Workers' Councils, the old syndicalist view that "social ownership" through the Workers' Councils is the first step in the withering away of the state seemed to involve a rather artificial conception of the state as well as of the nature of ownership. The justification of initial terror in Yugoslavia, but with an arbitrary line drawn between desirable and undesirable terror, opens the door to claims that, because of alternate ways to socialism, conditions elsewhere might require a longer period of suppression (a position, incidentally, which the Yugoslavs found themselves forced to adopt after the 1956 rapprochement with the USSR). For our purposes, however, it is relevant to note that by 1955 the Yugoslavs had evolved a broad perspective on the nature of their own efforts and on the Soviet system. But experience wedded to doctrine can easily become an impediment to a perception of new phenomena which fit neither the realm of experience nor the framework of the doctrine. It certainly is easier to adapt the new into the categories of the old, thereby seeing the familiar rather than the strange in developing situations.

One sees evidence of this rigidity in the extremely suspicious

Yugoslav responses to the first few changes in the USSR. Admittedly, caution and fear of duplicity were fully warranted, both in terms of past experience and in terms of what subsequently happened in the years 1957–1958. It is, however, interesting that because of their doctrinal position, and their emphasis on broad social-institutional relationships, the Yugoslavs initially dismissed Stalin's death as being of no consequence insofar as the Soviet system or its foreign policy was concerned. Denying that the essence had changed even though tactics admittedly had, the Yugoslavs felt justified in asserting that "it is completely irrelevant to us whether in such a USSR Stalin is or is not alive, and how much earth has been put on the grave of the deceased despot." [17]

The bitterness of the rejected devotee had also in time been sharpened by a reassuring doctrine of his own purity and of the fundamental depravity of the former idol. And since that depravity was said to be grounded in established political and economic institutions, the mere disappearance of an individual leader could hardly change the broad picture. Tito accordingly responded with the greatest caution to Khrushchev's overtures in 1955 and, while willing to accept normal diplomatic relations — a position clearly in keeping with Yugoslavia's policy of "coexistence" with the two blocs — he was unwilling to budge from his doctrinal stance which required a fundamental differentiation between the Yugoslav system, the capitalist system, and the state-capitalist system in the USSR. It was only after Khrushchev gave manifest proof of his desire and capability to deal with what the Yugoslavs considered to be the stagnant bureaucratization of the Soviet system — or Stalinism — that a sufficiently important "objective" change in the USSR was said to have begun to take place. A fundamental compatibility between the Yugoslav and the Soviet systems at that stage could again emerge and a doctrinal and party collaboration was warranted, indeed dictated, by the requirements of this new "objective" situation. The final proof came only with the Twentieth Congress and with the destruction of Stalin. From that moment on Tito considered himself as Khrushchev's first ally in the crusade against the remnants of Stalinism.

The Emergence of the Anti-Stalinist Axis

That the ultimate purposes of the two energetic leaders were not identical should be apparent from the preceding discussion. But the problem of the ultimate objective is always a complex one and liable to lead easily to misunderstandings. However, as long as the methods to achieve them are similar, an alliance can be maintained and the more concrete, immediate goal can obscure the long-range, ephemeral objective. Thus, for over a year, Tito and Khrushchev maintained an uneasy front against those forces which opposed the changes envisaged by Khrushchev and which bitterly despised and feared Tito. The burden of most of the combat fell on Khrushchev's broad shoulders — and reasonably so, since it involved conflicts within the Soviet party itself and in parties subject to the CPSU. Indeed, it was now for the first time since Khrushchev's ascendancy that the satellite Communist leaders were called upon to perform tasks manifestly displeasing to them (see Chapter 8). Their reaction, generally slow and hesitant, was mute testimony to the growing weakness of the Stalinist system without Stalin even before the fateful repudiation of the Twentieth Congress, and to a change in the pattern of relations.

The only party which could afford to emulate the CPSU at no risk to itself was the Chinese party. Its leadership did not feel threatened by the Tito episode and, since it was both powerful and indigenous, it could imitate with good grace the Soviet pattern in this particular instance. At the same time, no outstanding issues required settlement prior to a normalization of relations with Yugoslavia. Diplomatic relations were accordingly restored in December 1955, and trade missions were exchanged. The situation differed radically in the case of the East European Communist regimes. Albania, which as a consequence of the Soviet-Yugoslav rift had freed itself from Yugoslav tutelage, had everything to lose by an improvement in relations; Russian support against Yugoslavia and Greece would have been welcome to any Albanian regime. The Czechoslovak, Hungarian, and Bulgarian leaders, and to a much lesser extent the Rumanian, had consolidated their positions by bloody purges conducted in the name of anti-Titoism, and a shift in their attitude was bound to reawaken dormant issues and bitter memories within their respective parties. In Hungary, the Nagy interlude of 1953-1955 had already created a political problem with which Rakosi, once again in command, was merely beginning to cope. In the case of Bulgaria an added concern might have been a fear of a revival of the Balkan Union as a federative unit within a more loosely structured Communist commonwealth — a scheme which the ambitions of Tito and the unpredictability of Khrushchev might conjure up. The East Germans feared the new policy for the simple reason that any relaxation of bonds with the USSR and any efforts to promote more indigenous regimes immediately raised the question of the very survival of the Pankow rulers.

In Warsaw, the domestic economic difficulties and the mounting intellectual ferment (see Chapter 11) were causing sufficient dilemmas without the regime's having to endorse Tito, since such endorsement indirectly reflected favorably on the "right-wing deviation" of Gomulka. The June 1955 and the later June 1956 Soviet-Yugoslav agreements could not have been viewed by the East European Communist leaders with favor.

The caution and patent discomfort of such leaders were thus understandable. With the exception of Czechoslovakia, and possibly Bulgaria, all of these regimes were still feeling the birthpangs of forced and rapid economic changes and of the consequent alienation of at least part of their party cadres and proletariat. Their position in this respect was quite different from Khrushchev's or Bulganin's. The Soviet leaders might undermine their own positions if their Yugoslav policy failed; the East Europeans stood to lose their positions as soon as the policy was implemented. In addition, the USSR of 1955 or 1956 had a certain measure of internal stability, acquired through forty years and a victorious war. The retention of some forms of Stalinism, and therefore only a partial reconciliation with Yugoslavia, was a *sine qua non* of most of these regimes' political stability.

The regimes accordingly dragged their feet and moved only when under pressure. This pressure came from two sides. Speaking in Sofia immediately after signing the 1955 agreement, Khrushchev specifically linked the People's Democracies with the USSR insofar as Yugoslavia was concerned: "Today we can say that the road toward the development of friendly relations between the USSR and the People's Democracies on the one side and Yugoslavia on the other has been opened." In a secret speech to the Bulgarian leaders Khrushchev, in an apparent effort to undermine their hesitation, launched an extensive attack on Stalinist policies in general and on Stalinist policy toward Yugoslavia in particular.[18] He personally communicated a similar message to the satellite leaders on June 5, in a hastily convened conference in Bucharest.[19] The Yugoslavs, in the meantime, while cautiously maintaining their policy of independence from both blocs, interpreted the agreement to be a repudiation of the entire anti-Titoist phase of the preceding seven years. Speaking eight weeks after signing the agreement, Tito, reiterating his nonaffiliation "with any bloc," hailed the Soviet leaders as "men who wish to follow a new path" and specifically noted that "they saw that Stalin's path was a wrong one." He then charged "certain of our neighboring countries" with practicing terror against those in favor of normal relations with Yugoslavia, slyly suggesting that its victims were merely people wishing to follow a course already charted by the USSR. Finally dropping his reserve, Tito specifically singled out Hungary and Czechoslovakia as having regimes which spilled the blood of innocent Communists and which were lacking "the Communist courage to admit their errors." [20]

In pressing for amends, the Yugoslavs, consistent with their doctrinal position, were unwilling to accept the Soviet interpretation which placed all the blame for the past on Beria and which, therefore, absolved all others of any responsibility. Tito pointedly included Stalin as "the main man," while the juxtaposition of "new men" in the USSR with the leaders of East Europe explicitly suggested that the positive trends in the USSR still awaited duplication in East Europe. Paradoxically, Yugoslavia, as some eight years earlier, was again demanding that East Europe imitate the USSR even though this time Yugoslavia was doing so in the name of diversity and the many ways to socialism. The Yugoslav condemnation of the Cominform — reiterated on numerous occasions after the June 1955 declaration — stemmed from the same roots: it had now become a stagnant and conservative institution which impeded the successful and rapid imitation of the USSR in East Europe, and any efforts to create a single international Communist center were bound to provoke difficulties, given the existing circumstances in the bloc and particularly in view of Soviet-Yugoslav relations.[21]

The East European leaderships, essentially still Stalinist, found themselves in an unenviable position. On the one side, they were being pressed openly by Tito whom they could no longer attack and, on the other, the Soviets were giving Tito at least tacit support.[22] Their desire to maintain an anti-Titoist position — a stance justified by considerations of survival — could be maintained only through firm adherence to the old Stalinist precepts which included a condemnation of Titoism. But a crucial component of Stalinism was also the elevation of Soviet experience into a norm of behavior — and in this instance that behavior required an abandonment of a Stalinist position. For a while, of course, a delaying action could be staged. They could claim that the Yugoslav-Soviet rapprochement represented merely a temporary tactical maneuver and hence need not be imitated because it would shortly be reversed. Apparently, according to Tito,[23] this was the interpretation voiced in Rakosi's Central Committee when the question came up. Another line was to pin all hope on the relatively unsettled conditions in the Soviet leadership and expect a reversal in the Soviet position through the displacement of some existing leaders.

In the fall of 1955 the situation was not wholly clear and the future easily might have appeared to be still in doubt. The defenders of Stalinism, given their calculations and interests, accordingly maintained their orthodox positions, even though this necessarily implied an unorthodox nonconformity in behavior. In a roundabout way domesticism — almost verging on a form of national Communism in the name of Stalinism — was being adopted by the anti-Titoist Stalinists. Their unwillingness to adjust in effect amounted to a denial of a universal norm. For example, in Poland, which originally had delayed even a normalization in diplomatic relations with Yugoslavia,[24] two former ministers, W. Lechowicz and A. Jaroszewicz, purged earlier in connection with the national Communist purges, were tried and sentenced in the summer of 1955. Their fate might have served as a discreet reminder of the regime's attitude. The Hungarian regime, with Tito conjuring Rajk's ghost, responded to the Soviet-Yugoslav agreement only in August through a speech delivered by Rakosi, Tito's chief opponent. Rakosi, absolving himself of responsibility, blamed the past deterioration in relations on Gabor Peter, a former head of the secret police, and promised an immediate improvement in relations.[25] He, and the other Communist regimes, refrained, however, from rehabilitating the Communists who had already been purged, and often executed, as Titoists. The gesture made, the Hungarians refused to go any further, and in a curiously "neutral" fashion, symbolic of the new uneasy diversity, *Pravda* reported on September 27 that the Hungarian-Yugoslav economic negotiations had been broken off, citing first the Hungarian version, which blamed "excessive" Yugoslav demands, and then citing the Yugoslav version, which placed "the reason for the failure of the talks" on Hungarian unwillingness to meet their obligations.

Thus in the six months following the Belgrade declaration of June 1955, the Soviet efforts to establish binding ideological ties and intimate party relations were met first by Yugoslav suspicion, which was exacerbated by their doctrinal notions about the Soviet system, and then by Yugoslav demands that the past be fully repudiated, particularly as it pertained to the anti-Titoist phase in the history of Yugoslavia's Communist neighbors. The latter, on the other hand, were willing to take the 1955 Belgrade declaration only at its face value and restricted themselves to the formal aspects of the new policy: interstate cooperation, trade agreements, cultural and athletic exchanges, border crossing, and minorities arrangements.[26] Indeed, on numerous occasions during the fall of 1955, the leaders of the People's Democracies made plain their willingness to improve only the "quite abnormal relations" that existed between them and Yugoslavia,[27] usually coupling this perfunctory concession with pointedly complimentary references to Stalin and with insistence on the universality of the Soviet experience. At the November 1955 celebration commemorating the Bolshevik revolution, Istvan Kovacs, a member of the Hungarian Politburo, hailed Stalin as "Lenin's best disciple and the perpetuator of his work" and ended his speech with a resounding cry "Long live our ideal, the CPSU and its Central Committee." [28] Stalin was similarly praised in the Czech festivities,[29] while the Rumanians, ignoring both Stalin and their relations with Yugoslavia, merely noted the improvement in Soviet-Yugoslav affairs.[30] The East European leaders were in this devious manner attempting to bridge the developing gap between the maintenance of Stalinist positions and the new Soviet policy. But even on this restricted level, some of them, like Hungary and Albania, were demonstrably slower in adjusting and were thus practicing, for the first time, a limited foreign policy of their own.

Titoism for Export

The aftermath of the Twentieth Party Congress subjected the camp to its severest test. In the course of four months following the June 20,. 1956, Khrushchev-Tito declaration, the full measure of Khrushchev's miscalculation concerning Tito, as well as the capacity of some of the East European regimes to operate beyond the Stalinist framework emerged in startling proportions. In the summer of 1956 Tito seemed to be cast in the role of Khrushchev's nemesis. He not only continued to press for his pound of flesh but, with Stalinism dissipated and a substitute for it absent in the confusion and demoralization that followed in the wake of Khrushchev's pronouncements, also made it eminently clear that Titoism was now a doctrine available for export. The June 20 declaration was based on a Yugoslav draft, and it was the Yugoslavs who took the initiative in formulating the new norms for relations among Communist states.[31] Yugoslav parochialism — their defensive insistence on national Communism — had ended sometime between February and June 1956. In this post-Twentieth Congress atmosphere Yugoslavia's national Communism was national only in the sense that Tito considered many of its forms applicable to every Communist state individually.

Indeed, the Yugoslavs carefully and logically refrained from describing their system as one of national Communism. To have done so would have meant to deny its potential validity elsewhere.[32] On the contrary, the Yugoslav leaders and newspapers repeatedly asserted the need for a sharing of experience among the various Communist parties. In the case of borrowing from Yugoslavia, this clearly meant the adoption of those forms which were distinct from the already existing and available Soviet model. This was coupled with an increasingly vigorous condemnation of those East European Communist leaders who were proving themselves unable to adjust to this post-Stalinist situation, with the operative criterion being their willingness to repudiate their past anti-Titoist activities. The Yugoslavs insisted on this with a firmness which, combined with the apparent willingness of Khrushchev to appease Belgrade, must have been discomforting to the other Communist regimes. Even the disbanding of the Cominform, executed with some face-saving remarks about its formerly positive role "in developing and strengthening fraternal ties and mutual exchange of experience," [33] a phrase repeated with glee by the East European Stalinists, provoked immediate Yugoslav ire. The very next day they responded with a flat assertion that the Cominform (the creation of which they had originally urged) had been an undesirable institution from the very beginning.[34] Under the circumstances no one was prepared to argue the point.

At the same time, Yugoslav pronouncements on the Communist bloc assumed an air of authoritativeness which must have been galling even to those who favored a reconciliation with Belgrade. The Yugoslavs, while somewhat patronizingly congratulating the CPSU on having "rejected the old concepts about obligatory uniformity of ways and forms of socialism," [35] never missed an opportunity to point out that they had been right all along, and had been so by remaining the only true Marxists-Leninists. As M. Stajakovic, a member of the Commission for Foreign Relations of the Socialist Alliance of Yugoslavia pointed out: "It is frequently said that the 1948 conflict with Stalin's hegemony was a 'misunderstanding' which has now been happily surmounted. . . . In this struggle there was no misunderstanding; it was clear that the Yugoslav Communists and the entire Yugoslav nation were defending the fundamental principles of socialist policy." [36]

Belgrade made no secret of the fact that it regarded the Twentieth Congress as having hammered the last nail into the coffin of Stalinism. It welcomed the repudiation of Stalin's executions and arrests of some party leaders with the observation that "in rehabilitated persons, Stalinism has perhaps the most outspoken opponents. . . . Rehabilitation of old Bolsheviks in the Soviet Union represents a very important stage in the reestablishment of the ethical principles of the revolution." In the Yugoslav view, "objective" forces against a revival of Stalinism were being unleashed by the revelations and their impact was not restricted to the USSR. To help these forces a press and radio campaign was launched against the East European anti-Titoists who, unlike some of their West European counterparts,* could not afford the luxury of defending both Stalin and their own anti-Titoist past.

The dissipation of Stalinism occurred at a most unfortunate phase of development in some of these states — in the immediate aftermath of the most difficult stage of industrialization and collectivization but before the new social institutions could take roots — and their capacity to resist the suddenly combined external and internal pressures was severely taxed. Being directly dependent on the USSR, they could no longer ignore the new Soviet policy toward Yugoslavia, nor could they remain insensitive to internal pressures which were gaining the ideological upper hand. While no single formula stands out, it is apparent that the ability of each regime to ride out the crisis depended on the depth of its internal socioeconomic crisis, the degree of alienation of the working class and the intelligentsia from the regime and Communism as well as their revolutionary morale, the extent to which the regime had been involved in anti-Titoist policies, and the availability of alternatives in policy and leadership.

One by one the Stalinist bastions were assaulted. The most disastrous consequences occurred in Hungary and Poland where disintegrative processes had been under way ever since the relaxing effects of the New Course had first been felt. The Twentieth Party Congress pushed these trends further while the sudden prestige of Titoism gave them a more positive sense of direction and legitimization. The implications of the Polish and Hungarian patterns of development are discussed more fully in the next two chapters. But even in the other states, where the socioeconomic tensions had not been sharpened by politically significant events or led by "providential" individuals who transformed the thaw into a deluge, the joint impact

* The most rigid position was adopted by the French Communist Party which not only openly defended and praised Stalin (as in "Quelques questions capitales posées au XX Congres . . . ," *Cahiers du Communisme*, no. 4, April 1956, pp. 391–392) but also openly proclaimed that the 1948 Cominform resolution had been correct (M. Thorez, as quoted in *Cahiers du Communisme*, no. 6, June 1956, p. 776).

of the dissolution of Stalinism and the restored orthodoxy of Yugoslavia was felt deeply.

Posthumous rehabilitations became the vogue. In Bulgaria, the regime at first limited itself to pious editorials in *Rabotnichesko Delo*, such as "For a New Upsurge in Party Work," which condemned the cult of the individual but which also contained a warning against carrying the criticisms too far. "We must resist and unmask all hostile encroachments and unsound and rotten anti-Party misconceptions in connection with the eradication of the cult of the individual," the party paper admonished.[37] This, however, was coupled with references linking Vulko Chervenkov to Stalin and the news that the Central Committee of the Bulgarian Communist Party had convened, with a well-feted Yugoslav delegation in attendance.[38] Chervenkov's fate was sealed when the official announcement of April 14 rehabilitating the hanged Kostov also condemned the premier for having "considered that his word was law."[39] Three days later, Chervenkov resigned and was replaced, in the midst of attacks on his "brutality," by Anton Yugov, a former Minister of the Interior, who in the past was attacked by Chervenkov for his "lack of vigilance."

The Yugoslav delegation, however, apparently was not too convinced that fundamental changes were involved (a matter of some importance, given their earlier reservations), and the Yugoslavs' displeasure was vented shortly afterwards in a purported newspaper report from Sofia, featured in a provincial Yugoslav newspaper.[40] The story alleged that indignation was rampant in Sofia among Bulgarian Communists because the High Party School was still named after Chervenkov and still headed by his wife. It also reported that Bulgarian Communists felt indignant because the April Plenum did not go far enough in condemning Chervenkov and that "energetic" action had not been taken against the secret police.

Whatever the degree of fiction in this newspaper story, it did reflect an element of reality. The shift in the Bulgarian party leadership had not brought to power leaders genuinely well disposed toward Titoism; they were merely another essentially Stalinist faction which took advantage of the situation to unseat the incumbents. T. Zhivkov, for instance, who became First Secretary during the "collective leadership" period, retained his post. In fact, considering the energetic purges in the past as well as certain traditional enmity between Yugoslavia and Bulgaria, particularly over Macedonia, it is doubtful that a faction truly friendly to Belgrade existed, or could exist, on any large scale in Sofia. Dimitrov's earlier plans, after all, were closely associated with his international Communist experience and ambitions, and because of his stature he could afford to consider close ties with Belgrade. In 1956, a Yugov or a Chervenkov was no match for Tito, and the change of guard in the Bulgarian Central Committee did not, therefore, amount to any more than just a change of guard. The old policies went on as before: Yugov and Zhivkov continued the intensive collectivization drive and in July launched a new militant plan designed to expand the collective sector and to make it more attractive by decreasing some of the burdens of the collective farmers.[41]

Nonetheless, the timing of the change in leadership could not avoid having an impact on rank-and-file party members. Discipline inevitably slackened and criticisms of the leadership were heard and openly published.* The party leaders felt compelled to note that "such ideologically disoriented comrades under petit-bourgeois influence have proven themselves unprepared to understand the main problems. Interpreting the spread of internal Party democracy as freedom to speak whatever they wished, some of them expressed wrong political opinions." [42] The Bulgarian party leadership was thus striving to impose strict limits on internal dissent while externally attempting to live up to the strenuous requirements of this trying phase. Its efforts, however, were typical of what the Soviet and Yugoslav moves had wrought in each regime: more flexibility in coping with domestic problems yet with the same obligation of living up to the external uniformity.†

The Central Committee of the Bulgarian party met again in early fall, and its September 19 communiqué (issued exactly a month before Gomulka's return to power in Warsaw and the outbreak of the Hungarian revolution) defined with greater clarity the relevance of anti-Stalinism to the Bulgarian situation. To all intents and purposes,

* For instance, *Rabotnichesko Delo* complained on May 20, 1956, that a treatment of the recent events, "The Lesson," published by *Otechestven Front*, "is directed against the leaders and against the Party and state cadres. According to this article, the Party and particularly the Party leaders have broken off from the people; shortcomings and mistakes are criticized in such a manner that the successes so far achieved are minimized."

† Thus the Bulgarians, while paying lip service to friendship with Yugoslavia, went out of their way to continue stressing the relevance of the Soviet experience for the Bulgarian building of socialism. The second slogan on the Bulgarian Liberation Day (Radio Sofia, August 25, 1956) read as follows: "Eternal gratitude to our liberator — the Great Soviet Union, the invincible pillar of peace and progress throughout the world! Glory to the heroic Soviet Army — our liberator! Long live the life-giving Bulgarian–Soviet friendship! Glory to the Communist Party of the Soviet Union — organizer of the first in the world socialist state, the great, inspiring, and leading force of the Soviet people in their struggle for peace, democracy, and socialism!"

the communiqué, while stressing Bulgarian appreciation for the "profound Marxist-Leninist analysis" supplied at the Twentieth Congress through the criticisms of the "cult of the individual and its consequences," spelled out the notion that domestic circumstances in Bulgaria did not permit the party to allow any substantial deviation from previous practices. Indeed, the burden of the resolution was devoted to pointing out that because of the Twentieth Congress and the subsequent endorsement of many ways to socialism, "attempts have been made to deny or reduce the importance of our great successes in socialist building, to strike at the prestige of the Central Committee, to shake the workers' faith in the Party leadership and its *correct* policy." The resolution abounded in references to "alien," "careerist," "petit-bourgeois, "liberal," elements who criticize the party.[43] The party leadership left no doubt that domestically Stalinism would remain in force — which, in turn, of course, made the Yugoslav-Bulgarian reconciliation a mere formality.

Similarly, in Czechoslovakia the initial response to the Khrushchev-Tito flirtation and the Twentieth Congress was one of caution and suspicion. The Czech Central Committee met in late March, and Party Secretary Novotny's report, devoted to a critique of Stalinism (or, euphemistically, "the cult of the personality"), warned against any minimization of the authority of the party. "We must reckon with the fact that the enemies will abuse the fight against the cult of personality and the disclosure of our mistakes and shortcomings." [44] Lest anyone lose trust in Communism as a result of Khrushchev's disclosures, the membership was at the same time exhorted to resolve all problems of conscience with the simple formula: "have faith in the Party!" [45] Two weeks later, A. Cepicka, a member of the Politburo and Defense Minister, was dropped from the leadership as a token in the struggle against the cult of the personality.* No further important changes in the leadership were made. In May, however, in response to continued Yugoslav promptings and possibly even to Moscow suggestions, came the partial rehabilitation of some of the previously

* At the National Party Conference in June, 1956, Cepicka made a self-criticizing declaration, excerpts of which deserve quotation: "Certain interventions and measures which bore positive results strengthened in me the inclination to act authoritatively and to make authoritative decisions. . . . All this led me to be impatient with people. I now realize that, by gradually adopting Stalinist methods of work, I also developed more and more the characteristics of the cult of the personality. To these characteristics of cult of personality I must ascribe the exhibiting of my photographs, the shouting of various slogans at demonstrations, and the claiming of credit for various achievements through the press. There is no doubt that I became a typical example of the cult of personality." Radio Bratislava, June 15, 1956.

condemned party leaders. V. Siroky, addressing the Central Committee of the Slovak party, asserted that Slansky and Clementis had in fact been justly executed for serious crimes (Slansky for brutality, oppression, and illegal use of the secret police; Clementis for "incorrect attitude toward political problems") but that Slansky's alleged Titoist conspiracy had been a Beria fabrication.[46] But, again, this was accompanied by warnings that enemies might take advantage of such admissions to attack the party.

In this rather conditional fashion the Prague regime strove to adjust to the requirements imposed on it by the new situation. These were limited concessions avoiding any substantial leadership and policy changes. But, as in the case of Bulgaria, in the overall context, they generated the very public reaction which the regime had feared. The Second Congress of Czechoslovak Writers, which convened late in April, featured critical discussions of the Czech political scene and was followed shortly by student demonstrations.* The party leadership for this reason continued its warnings against abuses of criticism, claiming that it could be used only within the framework of party discipline.[47] Efforts to keep the reactions down were coupled with measures to improve the standard of living by cutting prices and improving wages, as well as by official announcements of restraints imposed in the name of "socialist legality" on the operations of the secret police.[48] The economic measures, particularly, were designed to satisfy the working class, thereby isolating the intellectuals and making them politically powerless.

In the other Communist states, East Germany, Rumania, and Albania, a policy of similar caution was pursued after the initial shock had somewhat faded. In Albania, the past anti-Titoist violence was blamed on a purged Politburo member, Koci Xoxe,[49] much as the Soviets had made Beria shoulder the blame. This in turn provoked a Yugoslav attack on the Albanian party chief, Enver Hoxha, as the major source of all past difficulties.[50] Late in June, a joint Yugoslav-Rumanian declaration of solidarity and cooperation was issued,[51] although again no major domestic shifts were involved. The same was

---

* A students' resolution, for instance, demanded "the democratization of public life," abandonment of excessive idolatry of the USSR (such as playing the Soviet anthem at the end of Czech radio transmissions), and raised the problem of the Soviet exploitation of the Czech uranium deposits (*News from Behind the Iron Curtain*, July 1956, pp. 42–43). At the Writers' Congress, according to published reports (*Literarni Noviny*, April 28–29, 1956), officially sponsored candidates for posts in the Writers' Union were rejected, clemency was demanded for imprisoned writers, and the freedom of conscience of each individual asserted.

largely the case in East Germany where the party leadership made only formal acts of obeisance to the new situation, although the initial impact of the Twentieth Congress had prompted Ulbricht to declare that "Stalin cannot be counted among the classics of Marxism." [52] Once composure was restored in East Berlin, the only concession was the late July rehabilitation of Dahlem, Merker, and the other high SED officials previously purged.[53] Again, much as in Czechoslovakia, this produced some reverberations among Communist intellectuals, and the party was repeatedly called upon to issue warnings against excessive abuses of the enlarged range of discussion. As in all of these states, strict adherence to "socialist legality" was promised.

Efforts to contain the situation provoked by the dissipation of Stalinism and by the increased aggressiveness of the Yugoslavs were facilitated by the fact that of all these states only Poland and Hungary had most of the necessary preconditions for a far-reaching change. In Czechoslovakia, East Germany, and even Bulgaria and Albania the socioeconomic crisis had not been, as already noted, quite as acute as in Poland and Hungary. The first two were already fairly well-developed industrial societies while the second two had not yet approached the critical transitional stage of Poland and Hungary. While East Germany and Czechoslovakia had some circles of alienated intellectuals, each lacked the support of the urban working classes, which were politically neutralized by a combination of economic concessions and strict control. Without the support of the urban working class the intellectual ferment could not be translated into successful politics. This same condition vitiated the significance of any discontent in Bulgaria and Rumania, both rural societies without a strong proletariat. Only in Hungary and Poland did real personal alternatives to the party leaders exist, and for the existing leaders to follow a Titoist path might have been disastrous. In most cases domestic Stalinism, with some adjustments and concessions, seemed the wisest course. In addition, Czechoslovakia lacked the religious and national homogeneity necessary for successful resistance, while its former democratic elites were discredited by the twin failures of the Czech Republic (1938, 1948). Together with the Bulgarians, the Czechs were also traditionally friendly to the Russians and, therefore, did not harbor a deep-seated hatred for the "Moscovites." In the case of East Germany, the presence of a Soviet army and the fresh memories of the failure of the 1953 rising precluded any violent change. Indeed, of the Communist states outside of Poland and Hungary, only Rumania might have come close to meeting the necessary preconditions for an upheaval. That it did not take place probably was due to the absence of a political alternative to the regime and the weakness of the urban working class, so necessary to a successful coup. Nonetheless, the other factors made themselves felt and, had the USSR failed to intervene in Hungary, it is likely that Rumania would have joined Hungary and Poland in experiencing a revolutionary outbreak.

With ideological unity dissipated, with the local power of the regimes threatened, with direct Soviet intervention in the domestic affairs of these states lessened, it was the negative sanction of Soviet power — the fear of a military intervention — that provided the backbone for the operation of political containment carried out by the entrenched Stalinists. But for the operation to be effective, a clearer line from the center was necessary to restore a common sense of purpose.

Soviet Second Thoughts

Khrushchev certainly was not interested in presiding over the dissolution of the Soviet camp. Indigenous, even autonomous, efforts to contain internal anti-Stalinist pressures were encouraged in the summer of 1956 by certain indications that the Soviet leadership itself was becoming concerned over the interpretations given the Twentieth Congress and the second Tito-Khrushchev declaration. The endorsement of the Yugoslav position and the approval expressed for extensive Yugoslav contacts with western socialists — which, it was hoped, might "overcome the split in the international working class movement" [54] — had, as Khrushchev came to see it, the unfortunate effect of blurring the clear line which was said to separate Communism from capitalism. Khrushchev's task now was to define the limits of the anti-Stalinist aftermath and posit some common foundations for unity. On June 30 the Central Committee of the CPSU issued a declaration which answered some of the anti-Stalinist criticisms of the Soviet system. It stressed that "Marxist parties of the working class, naturally, must retain and strengthen their ideological unity and international fraternal solidarity in the struggle against the threat of a new war, in the struggle against the anti-people's forces of monopolistic capital striving to suppress all revolutionary and progressive movements." [55]

To bring this about, the Soviet leaders gradually moved in the direction of clarifying the extent to which "different ways to socialism" had to be subordinated to some common core of doctrine — without, however, undermining the new Soviet-Yugoslav friendship which was so important to Khrushchev's image of the post-Stalin Soviet bloc. The urgency of this task was underlined by the Poznan outbreak at the end of June, signaling a merger between the restless proletariat and the disenchanted intellectuals, as well as by the growing political instability in Hungary. The Yugoslav condemnation of the Poznan strike probably served to reassure Khrushchev that bringing Yugoslavia back into the fold would be a positive contribution to the internal cohesion of the bloc; * but, at the same time, the Soviet leadership began steadily to minimize the importance of many ways to socialism and to stress instead the special peculiarities of a common core, worked out through the Soviet experience. Common aims, common outlook, and an available model were hence to be the conditions under which specific adaptations would be tolerated. Addressing the Eighth Congress of the Chinese Communist Party, Mikoyan bluntly observed, "Assuredly, each country has its distinctive features and brings its own specific elements to bear in making the transition to socialism. But, as Lenin pointed out, these features can relate only to what is not most important." [56] The emphasis was again on the fine print, on the reservations made in Suslov's Twentieth Congress speech, noted in the preceding chapter.

The Soviet leadership began to draft plans early in the fall of 1956 for common institutional links with the other ruling parties which would not carry the stigma of the Cominform but which nonetheless would bind them together. The method considered was a theoretical journal. Furthermore, the Soviet leaders felt quite justified in dispatching a circular letter some time in September (the precise date is not known) warning the ruling East European parties against a "mechanical" imitation of the Yugoslav experience in the name of the newly legitimized multiplicity of roads to socialism. The existence, but not the precise text, of such a circular letter was revealed officially by Belgrade,[57] and it apparently claimed that the League of Communists of Yugoslavia was not an entirely Marxist-Leninist organization. This warning, given the increased emphasis on Marxism-Leninism as a binding force, could only serve to discourage, indeed to disapprove, any excessive enthusiasm for domestic Yugoslav experi-

---

* The Yugoslav press spoke darkly about antidemocratic forces which had sparked the armed clash in order to prevent further democratization of Poland. This emphasis on provocation was in line with the Soviet interpretation. In retrospect, however, when one reads these interpretations one is struck by the fact that they could have been equally well aimed at the Stalinists (hence the pro-Soviet elements) in Poland. What the actual intent was is difficult to assess. For a Yugoslav commentary, see *Borba*, July 1 and July 6, 1956.

ments or ideological views. Almost at the same time, two hasty conferences were held between Tito and Khrushchev, beginning with Khrushchev's unheralded arrival in Belgrade on September 11 and followed by Tito's flight to Sochi a week later. The sense of urgency involved in these consultations was understandable since both leaders still had a vested interest in preventing the axis from breaking in two. To Khrushchev, Tito was needed to calm down the Hungarians * and to demonstrate that Khrushchev's original gamble had been justified. An open break at this stage would be an admission of error dangerous to Khrushchev's position, certain to be exploited by Khrushchev's internal opponents. Tito too wanted to keep avenues of contact open because without them Yugoslavia was too weak to exert the influence that Tito craved. As a result, the matter of the circular letter was aired, and the Yugoslavs appeared satisfied that it would not happen again.[58]

The Sochi meeting, however, was not without its disappointments and mutual disenchantments. Khrushchev energetically insisted that Yugoslavia must join one of the two world camps, and that, given her social system, "her natural place" was within the Soviet camp.[59] Tito's persistent unwillingness to abandon the principle, if not quite the practice, of neutrality was interpreted by Khrushchev as an indication that the Yugoslav party had become corrupted during its years of alienation from the socialist camp, especially since Tito, interpreting the June 20 agreement rather more liberally than his cosignatory, was welcoming the growing pressures for change in Poland and Hungary while openly disapproving the measures taken by the other Communist states.†

The difference in the long-range objectives, temporarily obscured

* At Sochi, Tito, without prior warning, was confronted with E. Gero, Rakosi's successor (see Chapter 10), and enjoined to give him his blessing. This Tito refrained from doing until mid-October.

† For example, *Borba*, August 23, 1958, two months before the Budapest uprising, described Imre Nagy's return to the Hungarian Communist Party as an "inevitable" prospect and called for the "rehabilitation of that for which he fought." It is to be remembered that Nagy's 1955 fall seems to have been connected with Malenkov's fall in the USSR.

Symptomatic of the disapproval was the communiqué issued by *Jugopress* on October 9, following the visit to Belgrade, to re-establish party relations, of the head of the Bulgarian party, Zhivkov, which noted disagreements with the Bulgarians on "the substance and forms of cooperation of Communist parties" as well as evidence of continuing "distrust and doubt." Its tone left no doubt as to who should revise their conduct and views before the Yugoslavs were to feel that proper relations existed. On another occasion, *Politika* (October 19, 1956) noted that "the Czechs and Slovaks . . . are asking what happened to all those persons who were sentenced in the period of the anti-Yugoslav campaign only because they were friends of Yugoslavia."

by a short-range communality of method, began to emerge in sharper focus. The Yugoslavs, construing Soviet accommodation as a thorough break with the past, were dreaming of a new ruling trinity: Moscow, Peiping, and Belgrade. To Tito, Communism would spread more effectively if it could operate on the basis of heterogeneity, making it more appealing to the masses of the world. His new contacts with Moscow, which seemed to suggest that "polycentric" Communism was also being embraced by Khrushchev, made Tito unwilling to raise openly the banner of national Communism or to expound openly a doctrine fitting the new circumstances and filling the vacuum created by the denunciation of Stalinism.* The Soviets, conscious of their power position yet wishing to place their leadership on a more reliable basis, were not primarily interested in a division of power, but in a *voluntary* acceptance of their primacy. To Moscow, a common core and a center was a requirement dictated by the instability of the East European regimes and by the hostility of the non-Communist world. Soviet insistence on unity distressed the Yugoslavs, and Tito's unwillingness to accept it strengthened Khrushchev's conviction that, without precipitating a new break with Tito, the narrowest interpretation must now be placed on the relevance in the other states of his agreement with Tito. Alas, by September 1956, Soviet redefinitions could no longer contain the developments nurtured by the dissipation of Stalinism and crystallized by the reconciliation with Belgrade. The thaw was turning into a deluge.

* How seriously the Yugoslavs took themselves is suggested by the following dialogue between them and Khrushchev on the subject of relations among Communist states at one of the 1956 meetings. In Khrushchev's version (not denied by the Yugoslavs), it went like this: "I reminded them of the following well-known popular saying, 'The whole company marches in step and only one soldier is out of step,' and asked who must change, the company or the soldier? Koca Popovic [the Yugoslav Foreign Minister], who was present at the conversation, asked: 'And who is the company and who is the soldier?' " *Pravda*, June 4, 1958.

CHAPTER 10

Hungary: The Test Case of National Communism

THE toppling of Stalin's statue at the height of Budapest's heroic bid for freedom in October-November 1956, while symbolic of Stalinism's end, did not mean the beginning of Hungary's freedom. The dialectic of events did not lead from Stalinism through anti-Stalinism to national Communism, but rather to a reimposition of a Soviet-dependent regime which at first attempted a policy of reconciliation but which gradually moved toward mounting coercion. A Tito-like national Communist regime was found both to be incompatible with the Soviet conception of their own interests and to be lacking in domestic sources of stability.

The tragedy of Hungary began its climactic phase with the ouster of Nagy from the premiership in the spring of 1955. Had he retained power and been allowed to pursue the policies initiated in July 1953 (briefly sketched in Chapter 8), it is likely that no major catastrophe would have followed the Twentieth Congress, the Soviet-Yugoslav declaration, or even the accession to power in Poland of Gomulka. The latter event proved to be the spark that ignited the accumulated tensions in Hungary. Nagy's policy had been one of gradually disarming the buried bomb which Stalinism without Stalin had become in East Europe, and particularly in Hungary and Poland. It is also possible, though less likely, that had Nagy not come to power in 1953 Rakosi's regime might have been able, like its Stalinist counterparts elsewhere, to adapt gradually to the new circumstances and ride out the crisis. However, considering its particular complicity in the anti-Titoist phase and its intensive identification with all the worst features of Stalinism, the reverberations of the dissipation of Stalinism would in all probability have struck at the Hungarian regime directly and would have produced serious tensions. Whatever the course of history might have been, the early Nagy period was particularly significant, for it created a conception of an alternative economic and political policy within the existing framework. Nagy's program was more acceptable than Rakosi's to at least a significant portion of the Com-

munist Party and certainly to the majority of the population. Rakosi's
return to power in 1955 reversed the policy but could not destroy the
knowledge of the alternative.

Power versus Ideology

A segment of the party remained unalterably opposed to Nagy's
policy from the very moment of its inauguration. A variety of factors shaped this attitude. Basically, it stemmed from a distrust of the
masses — a suspicion and fear which was so characteristic of Stalin's
notions and which he injected so effectively into his own apparatus.
The masses were construed as fundamentally unable to perceive the
social significance of the changes that were being effected in society,
and they were therefore easy prey to hostile propaganda. It was vital
in view of this, both for reasons of power — a consideration probably
uppermost in Rakosi's thinking — as well as of ideology — a matter
with which Rakosi's comrade, Revai, was most conversant — that the
masses should be suppressed politically and exploited economically
until socialism was secure and its enemies liquidated. It mattered little
if in the process the masses were alienated from the party and opposition grew in numbers as long as the instruments of power were able to
cope effectively with any impediments to the execution of the regime's policy.

Men like Rakosi or Revai were probably more or less aware of
the various economic tensions, potential disasters, and even disillusionment among the faithful that their policies provoked. But in their
perspective such factors lost their immediate significance and could
safely be ignored or even construed as praiseworthy successes of the
regime since they were part of an unfolding pattern of the march into
the future. To slow down the pace, to make concessions, was to
capitulate before the transitional impediments of today and thereby
betray the tomorrow.

In such a perspective the very factors which made Nagy willing
to engage in the New Course made the unreconciled Stalinists more
determined not to concede one iota. The Nagy faction could note
that the working class had grown rapidly since the war — by about
50 per cent [1] — and it would worry about the prospect of proletarian
alienation from the system, given the rapidly changing conditions and
existing deprivations.* Concessions, it was felt, would prevent the in-

---

* According to Nagy, "industrial development amounted to 158 per cent in
Poland from 1949 to 1955, to 98 per cent in Czechoslovakia during the same period,
to 92.3 per cent in the German Democratic Republic from 1950 to 1955, to 144 per

escapable alienation from developing into violent political hostility. To Rakosi this very same fact would be welcome proof that the exploiting class was disappearing, that the proletariat was becoming dominant, but that temporarily the class-conscious, militant minority must retain tight discipline precisely because of the political immaturity of the new proletariat. The Nagy faction could note that the party rank and file was, on the whole, demoralized, fearful, and shared in the popular antipathy toward the regime's past policies while welcoming the New Course. Rakosi's *apparat*, in reply, would point to the party's expanded membership, amounting to about 10 per cent of the population (865,000 in 1954 [2]), as proof that increased ideological work and the maintenance of firm control were required since it was likely that the party was penetrated by "apolitical" and even hostile elements. Nagy could observe improved morale and productivity in agriculture as a consequence of his concessions and could claim that the rural hostility toward socialism would consequently wane. Rakosi could note that in just one year of Nagy's rule 51 per cent of collective farm members had quit the collectives, causing 12 per cent of the collective farms to be dissolved [3] and the "socialist transformation of the countryside" to be further delayed. To statements that the Stalinist industrialization had been unrealistic and based on erroneous assumptions, the Rakosi reply was that "this does not mean, however, that the mistakes are very significant" [4] when compared to the socialist achievements of industrialization. Finally, to the argument that the New Course was in keeping with the prevailing Soviet thinking, the answer of the Rakosi faction might well have been that (1) it did not represent unanimous Soviet thinking even for the USSR itself and (2) that the USSR had already passed through its critical stage of development, was not infested with enemies within and without the party, and that hence true application of the "creative" Soviet experience required Stalinism to go through its full historical phase in Hungary.

To these considerations, there doubtless was attached a variety of personal motivations and interests. From what little is known of Rakosi, he appears to have possessed all the earmarks of a sadist driven

---

cent in Rumania from 1951 to 1955, to 120 per cent in Bulgaria from 1949 to 1955, and to 210 per cent in Hungary from 1949 to 1953" (*On Communism*, p. 185). The impact of the social change is illustrated by the following figures: in a country of less than 9 million people, during the years 1949–1954 the number of wage earners increased by 1,550,000 and workers in the "cooperative sector" by 710,000. At the same time, individual farmers decreased by 1,300,000 and "capitalists" by 540,000 (*Nepszabadsag*, July 10, 1958).

by a strong urge for power and capable of harboring bitter hatreds. The rebuke he received from Soviet leaders in 1953 was probably a deep humiliation to him, and he might well have nurtured a profound dislike for Nagy who had been handpicked by the Soviet leaders to replace him.[5] Such factors, after all, go far in shaping the patterns of history. Rakosi and his associates, furthermore, might have felt genuinely concerned about their personal positions and consequently had a vested interest in Stalinism. Apparently this feeling was shared by the majority of the Politburo and Secretariat which remained loyal to Rakosi and shared his distaste for Nagy's New Course (as contrasted with the lower echelons *).

In this spirit Rakosi from the very beginning of Nagy's rule attempted to undermine both the ideological basis for and the specifics of the New Course. In August 1953 the Politburo under Rakosi diluted the earlier criticisms of the past and was criticized for it by the October Plenum of the Central Committee.[6] Unwilling to give up, Rakosi apparently decided to make his next move before the party congress convened on April 18, 1954, since an endorsement of the New Course by the congress would be bound to strengthen Nagy's hand. In March, the Congress Theses were published as a preliminary step to the "debates" of the congress, spelling out the party line for the functionaries who would be attending. However, two weeks later, on March 28, it was suddenly announced that the congress would be postponed to May 24. The delay in the congress was apparently linked to the intense dissension within the party on policy matters. Nagy had fallen ill during the spring while the congress preparations were in full swing. Taking advantage of this felicitous event, Rakosi rammed through the Politburo a resolution condemning both the New Course and Nagy personally, and then proceeded to plan a trip to Moscow to lay his case before the Soviet leadership.[7]

The 1954 Hungarian machinations are interesting testimony to the changing pattern in relations between the USSR and the Com-

* Trying to explain in 1956 why the "liquidation of mistakes" had bogged down, that is, why Rakosi was successful in stopping Nagy, Rakosi's successor and close associate, Gero, had this to say: "Finally the uncertainty was also caused partly by the fact that for various reasons *the Politburo did not feel that it could rely on unanimous* support from the Central Committee. They felt that no unanimous views were held within the Central Committee as regards relations to the Politburo or to its individual members, and that on the other hand, there was no full unanimity between the members of the Central Committee as regards the policy to be pursued by the Party" (Radio Budapest, July 18, 1956). According to Nagy, the party at this time was controlled by Gero, Farkas, and Revai, led by Rakosi (p. 278).

munist states. Within a year of Stalin's death, and with all the ear-marks of respect for Moscow's leadership and its general line, Rakosi, a Stalinist par excellence, felt confident enough to attempt a *fait accompli*. Admittedly, he still required Moscow endorsement, but the attempt itself is an indication of the enlarged area of local autonomy, especially if one considers the fact that Nagy's policy appeared to enjoy unqualified Soviet support and, indeed, matched the con-temporaneous Soviet line. Of course, Rakosi probably realized that there was division of opinion in Moscow itself on both foreign and domestic policy, and he might have expected that a *fait accompli* to-gether with the backing of some Soviet leaders (Molotov?) might carry the day. But this too is testimony to the greater scope of do-mestic initiative enjoyed by the satellite leaders.

As it turned out, Rakosi's initiative was premature — but only by one year. The Soviet leadership given its 1954 domestic and interna-tional policy and noting the ambivalent attitudes in the Hungarian party, rebuffed Rakosi's solo venture to Moscow. In 1954 this was still enough, despite the implications of his initiative, to turn the projected coup into a fiasco. A Hungarian delegation, including both Nagy and Rakosi, ultimately traveled to Moscow in May 1954, and both Khrushchev and Malenkov heaped generous abuse on Rakosi's head in the course of the conferences. Rakosi was blamed for past and present inadequacies and "he was obliged to admit both in Mos-cow and before the Political Committee that he had made the Political Committee accept a resolution containing unfounded and misleading statements concerning collective leadership, unity of principle, and Party democracy, and that he had informed the Soviet comrades in this vein." [8]

Although in 1954 the Soviet leadership decided to go along with Nagy, it did not create the circumstances for the complete eradication of Rakosi and his group. It apparently felt that Nagy's policies would tax the Soviet resources less and would create more favorable con-ditions for the fulfillment of ultimate goals, presumably shared in common with Nagy. At the same time, however, the Soviet leader-ship, cautiously feeling its way in the first year after Stalin's death and possibly even restrained by internal disagreements, was apparently unwilling to go the full distance in destroying the Rakosi wing — in-deed, it seemed to be pursuing a policy of not burning all its bridges. The principle of *divide et impera*, whether circumstantial or purpose-ful, made the USSR an arbiter between two opposing but still loyal factions, thereby making up for whatever might have been lost in direct Soviet control over Hungary through the gradual erosion of fear following Stalin's death.

As far as Hungary was concerned, the situation thus remained unsettled. Nagy retained control over shaping the program but was not given sufficient Moscow backing to displace Rakosi's control over the party. Rakosi's power, on the other hand, was paralyzed by his knowledge of Moscow's backing for Nagy's policy. Thus ideology and power, rather than being united in one system merging policy and purpose, were set against each other under a very thin crust of superficial unity. This was evident at the party congress finally held in May. The head of the Soviet delegation, Voroshilov, endorsed the congress program with the cryptic observation that "all of us know that the new tasks of the Hungarian Workers' Party are not easy." [9] Nagy's statements represented a further development of the policies to be pursued within the framework of the New Course: only general references to collectivization which, as a policy, was at a standstill; increase in allocated agricultural investment from 14 per cent in 1953 to 24 per cent of the total in 1954; [10] 16 per cent increase in investment for light industry and the food industry; [11] and a planned decentralization of economic administration to increase the role of local government, hitherto usually by-passed by central organs.* In keeping with this, Nagy also envisaged a shift from external party control of the institutions of local government to greater internal activity of its members as participants within local government. [12] This would overcome the old practice of ignoring the masses, he felt, and overcome the bureaucratic tendencies inherent in the prevailing practice.

One can sense in Nagy's remarks a desire to shake up the party *apparat*, the main impediment to the execution of the tasks designed to place Communism, corroded by a clumsy Stalinism, on firmer Hungarian foundations. In fact, it was revealed at the congress that whereas formerly the party cells had been very active in carrying out their instructions, they had recently grown lax and slow, often ignoring central directives. It was clear that the *apparat* was not for the New Course. Considering the tongue lashing to which Rakosi had been subjected in Moscow, his endorsement of the New Course was

---

* Under the plan, local National Councils would no longer be subject to the Ministry of the Interior but to the Presidium of the National Assembly. The economic departments of the National Councils would direct the economic activity within the localities, and the various central ministries would be expected to deal with them rather than to have a direct chain of command down to the lowest production unit.

not unexpected. He dutifully approved it, condemned past excesses, and outlined reforms for the future in keeping with the general program. Nonetheless, he and his close associates did succeed in introducing a series of observations which could only be construed as veiled criticisms of the year-old policy. Rakosi noted, for instance, an increase in kulak activity and a decline in compulsory deliveries, while secret policeman Farkas, in paying lip service to the notion that the party had not kept in close touch with the people, pointed out that the Hungarian proletariat entertained "backward views" and lacked a revolutionary consciousness.[13] Without being more specific, he seemed to be implying the continued need for class vigilance and presumably, therefore, for the institutional devices for the maintenance of that vigilance. The situation was a stalemate, which could be resolved only by the intervention of some extraneous factor.

The Meaning of the Rakosi Phase

One very important consequence of this situation was the gradual reactivation of those social forces suppressed by unbridled Stalinism. The Nagy-Rakosi semiparalysis meant that something vaguely reminiscent of pluralism began to emerge on the Hungarian political scene, resulting in a conflict of interest groups. This in turn meant that domestic factors were again becoming more important in shaping Hungarian destiny. The party *apparat* and the weakening secret police, somewhat disarmed by Nagy's amnesties, were becoming isolated from the party rank and file, while Nagy's programmatic position was becoming a magnet for hitherto silent intellectual circles. Hungarian life was very gradually taking on the character of that social and political diversity which, by definition, is incompatible with totalitarian dictatorship.

These tendencies in one sense were cut short but, in another sense, given even more vitality by Rakosi's return to power in the spring of 1955. As in 1954, the change in Hungarian leadership appears to have been a domestic initiative on the part of the unreconciled Rakosi, but with certain important differences. A major shift in the locus of power and direction of policy had just taken place in the USSR. The replacement of Malenkov as premier and the abandonment of his policy, accompanied by a vigorous statement in *Pravda* by Shepilov on the necessity of maintaining the priority of heavy industrial investment (see Chapter 8), appeared to undercut the ideological basis as well as the practical source of support for Nagy's program. Shepilov's article, reproduced after a few days of stunned delay in the East

European press, had the impact of a bombshell which threw into panic those elements which favored a redressing of the balance in the old Stalinist economic program.[14]

It seems clear that in these circumstances Budapest was left to its own resources to resolve its party conflict. This in itself might well be a clue to Moscow's attitude, since the Soviet leaders were presumably aware of the relative strength of the Rakosi and Nagy factions. Moscow "neutrality," even if dictated in part by its own domestic complications, was thus a form of negative involvement and even implicit endorsement for Rakosi's harder line. Noninvolvement in Hungarian domestic affairs, since a super-loyal faction did exist, indeed fit in well with Khrushchev's conception of voluntarily pro-Soviet regimes. In these circumstances even indirect hints sufficed to tip the scales in Rakosi's favor. The circular letter sent out by the Soviet leadership to explain why Malenkov had been removed provided such guidance, for it blamed him for introducing certain harmful characteristics into the relations of the USSR with the People's Democracies and specifically cited Hungary as an example.[15] Nagy was hence by implication linked with Malenkov.

The favorable external conditions seized upon by Rakosi occurred simultaneously, as in 1954, with a recurrence in Nagy's illness sometime in February 1955. Using his unchallenged control of the party secretariat (which in making intraparty decisions he had used to by-pass the Central Committee and even the Politburo of which Nagy was a member) Rakosi apparently succeeded in excluding Nagy from the inner party deliberations on the grounds of his illness and proceeded to hold meetings and pass resolutions without informing Nagy of them.* In March Rakosi was able to prevail on the Central Committee to condemn Nagy's policies as "right-wing deviation" and as causing the weakening of the party in favor of the state — a parallel to the Malenkov episode (but also a reversal of the old Stalinist relationship). Presumably out of deference to Moscow, which had originally charted the New Course, and presumably also as a reflection of the changed times which did not permit a full turn of the wheel, the June 1953 resolution was not repudiated, but praised

---

* Nagy (*On Communism*, pp. 290–291) makes reference to "the illegal and irregular resolution of the Political Committee that attempted to isolate and silence me completely on the basis of the medical report composed by the Committee"; he protests against "exaggerated regulations" made "on the pretense of my illness." Rakosi's concern for Nagy's health is a curious parallel to the case of Frunze in the USSR who died under the surgical knife after having been compelled by the Politburo to undergo an operation.

for its "courage." Instead, Nagy was accused of inept and un-Leninist execution of the said resolution. Moscow support for Rakosi became more evident at this stage with *Pravda*'s approving quotation of Rakosi's condemnation of the "anti-Marxist, anti-Party, opportunistic views . . . under the influence of which industry's development was checked, socialist accumulation diminished, and state and civil discipline weakened." [16]

Encouraged, Rakosi moved ahead. On April 18 Nagy was expelled from the Politburo, from the Central Committee, and removed from the premiership. Almost ironically, but possibly to soften the blow, Farkas was simultaneously condemned for past abuses of socialist legality and linked with Nagy, clearly to discredit the latter. Nagy himself was condemned for a variety of offenses, ranging from factionalism — a usual charge against those whose faction has failed — to undermining the party through right-wing deviation, entertaining "anti-Party, anti-Marxist, and anti-Leninist opinions," and forgetting "the most important and supreme prerequisite for the triumph of Socialism — the necessity of steadily increasing productivity." [17] In the foreign-affairs realm Nagy was charged with "overestimating the easing of tension in international affairs," a serious sin according to the Stalinist dichotomic perspective. The shift was followed by a re-emphasis on collectivization,[18] arrests of some kulaks, and a renewed party purge. The most prominent victim of the purge was Nagy himself, who was expelled from the party in November 1955.

But times had changed. Apparently what neither Rakosi nor Khrushchev realized was that processes had been set in motion which now would be difficult to contain and which Moscow's Yugoslav policy, at this time in the early stage of development, was bound to exacerbate. Rakosi's return to power galvanized into bitter opposition those party members and intellectuals to whom the Nagy period had marked the beginning of a new type of Communism, more suited to Hungarian tastes. The abrupt interruption in its development intensified the opposition to the regime, especially as past Soviet support for Nagy and its new Yugoslav line created a certain ambivalence toward Soviet views. More and more Hungarian Communists began to feel that Rakosi was an impediment not only to Communism in Hungary but even to proper relations between a Communist Hungary and the USSR.

In brief, the Nagy interlude was of vital importance both to Hungarian Communists and to those non-Communists whose opposition to Rakosi was muted by fear of the USSR. It provided an answer to the Stalinist "dilemma of the one alternative." Watching Rakosi's return to secret-police terror late in 1955, they observed a growing abyss between the "what is" and the "what is feasible" of a Communist regime. Hitherto, opposing Stalinism had been tantamount to opposing Communism, and this many Communists were clearly not prepared to do. At the same time, the anti-Communists were paralyzed by fear of Soviet might. Nagy, for the first time, seemed to suggest the possibility of change that both groups, even if for different reasons, could welcome. Rakosi's return welded them together.

Crystallization of an Alternative: National Communism

Nagy's program in 1953 had been a product of expediency, Soviet pressure, and existing Hungarian misgivings, as well as of Nagy's own still vague notions on what the policy of a Hungarian Communist regime ought to be. Prior to 1953, he had written a series of articles and delivered a number of speeches dealing with Hungarian economics; consequently he came to power with a background of political practice and ideological reflection. Nonetheless, it was only after his removal in 1955 and his ultimate expulsion from the party that he found himself drafting a more explicit and systematic statement on the practices and norms of Hungarian Communism.* His thinking had been shaped by intraparty polemics, his firmness increased by sharp personal conflicts with Rakosi, and his creativity stimulated by a favorable intellectual climate which encouraged and facilitated the refinement of his own ideas.

Nagy soon found that any consideration of the method of building Communism in Hungary had to face squarely the issue of Communist Hungarian versus Soviet interests. This was the crucial question at the heart of every Communist move, and to it Stalin had given an explicit answer, backed both by ideological concepts of the need for centralized unity and by Soviet might. By 1955–1956, Soviet moves in respect to Yugoslavia, as well as Hungary's limited experience with the New Course, made it clear that Stalin's formula did not possess the finality that he had desired. To Nagy and many others like him, the dilemma again became very real: how to construct within the changing context a coherent and ideologically motivated policy for implementing Communism in Hungary in a manner suited to Hungary. In his effort to resolve this question, by January 1956 [19]

---

* He had hoped to present his writings, or theses as he called them, a rebuttal of Rakosi's charges, to the Central Committee. They were subseqeuntly published in this country as *On Communism*.

Nagy was transformed from a Communist whose practical perspectives were essentially domestic and on broad issues subordinated to general Soviet requirements, into a national Communist willing to put the purposes of Hungarian Communism above the imperatives of Soviet policy. Writing for Rakosi's Central Committee under circumstances of mounting tension, Nagy could not state his thesis explicitly, even though the change in Soviet-Yugoslav relations at least had taken the treasonable sting out of his views. Nonetheless, there can be no doubt as to the meaning of his words.

Nagy realized that the crucible of any policy designed to construct his non-Stalinist brand of Communism in Hungary was the problem of international relations. To a great extent, the policy of subordinating national interests to those of the Soviet bloc — which in practice meant to those of the Soviet Union — was a reflection of the old image of two hostile worlds. Under such circumstances, the need to defend the Communist bloc tended to transform the bloc into an armed camp in which the strongest "fraternal socialist country" naturally played the leading role, defining strategy and assigning tasks and obligations. A small and weak Communist country necessarily was called upon to make great sacrifices which, of course, hampered its own urgent tasks of economic transformation and prevented the emergence of true socialist consciousness among the masses. Nagy felt, however, that since about 1954 a major change in this outlook had occurred, symbolized particularly by the Bandung Conference and the 1955 Belgrade declaration. The first posited the five basic principles of international affairs, subsequently endorsed by the USSR: national independence, sovereignty, equality, noninterference in internal affairs, and self-determination. The contents of the second have already been noted (Chapter 8). Nagy was convinced that the Bandung principles should be applied to the Soviet camp, and he thought he noted signs that this was the attitude of the Soviet leaders also. In any case, their application would only help the cause of Communism, he thought, since they would promote true internationalism by eradicating national tensions. They would make possible the "Marxist-Leninist theory of locally characteristic socialism," a position apparently accepted by the USSR for Belgrade.[20]

Up to this point, Nagy was essentially reiterating the old position that Marxists must recognize domestic circumstances when shaping policy. He went on, however, to assert that the Bandung and Belgrade principles were being opposed by the "remnants of Stalinist autocratic rule" in Hungary,[21] and that such principles did not reflect reality insofar as relations between various Communist parties and the CPSU were concerned. This assertion, stated cautiously in the form of a hope that the implementation of the Bandung and Belgrade principles in East Europe was not too distant, was affirmed further by Nagy's insistence that it was impossible to build socialism without true national independence. Developing his argument, Nagy then stated that true independence, particularly for small states, would be impossible in a world split into hostile blocs. Quite remarkably, he did not discriminate between "good" and "bad" blocs. But how should Hungary extricate herself from existing commitments? His answer, which marks his break with the idea of a priority for international Communist obligations over Hungarian interests, deserves quotation:

The most practicable plan, seemingly, is the *active* coexistence of progressive democratic socialist or similar countries with those other countries having a different system, through a coordinated foreign policy and through *cooperation against the policies of the power groups*, through neutrality or active coexistence.[22]

Nagy was in effect advocating that Hungary adopt a neutral position between the "power groups," since that would be most compatible with the domestic task of constructing Communism. He could now state with equanimity that "it is the sovereign right of the Hungarian people to decide in which form they believe the most advantageous international status will be assured, and in which form they think that national independence, sovereignty, equality, and peaceful development will be attained." [23]

Noting that the assertion of such a right by Hungary was still a matter for future implementation, thereby more than implying Soviet oppression, Nagy called for the liquidation of the legacy of Stalinist subordination, for the shaping of policy which would no longer ignore his country's interests. His national Communism involved him in a rejection of anything that restricted or violated his country's interests as defined in terms of building Communism, which in turn led him to adopt a position which was not only non-Stalinist but even non-Leninist, and much like Tito's: that of neutrality in the conflict between the two large powers and their blocs. He did so by rejecting the fundamental dichotomy which views the world as engaged in continued, dialectical conflicts with one side basically in the right and the other basically in error. Instead he posited the proposition that "we must . . . recognize that we are members not only of the socialist camp but of the great community of nations, to the countries and peoples of which we are bound with countless ties, which we cannot and indeed must not sever, because we do not want to be disbarred from the great community of nations, and also because we could not then successfully progress toward socialism through social and economic improvement." [24]

The Failure of Controlled Transition

The intellectual ferment, the activity of the Petofi Clubs where vigorous debates popularized Nagy's views, the growing contacts between the alienated intellectuals * and the workers, all providing the momentum for the October 23 revolution, are a matter of well-publicized historical record.[25] Within the context of relations among Communist states, it is interesting to note that even though by December 1955 Nagy was emerging not only with an alternative program but was actually consolidating around him a dedicated group of Communists,[26] Rakosi still did not dare to suppress a man chosen by the Kremlin in 1953 to set Hungary's house in order. Possibly Rakosi no longer considered Nagy an active threat once he had been expelled from the party, but that is rather doubtful, especially considering the paranoiac predisposition of this Stalinist party chief. Possibly Soviet efforts to improve relations with Yugoslavia temporarily stayed Rakosi's hand. Whatever the reason, an alternative to Rakosi thus persisted.

For the time being, Rakosi continued a policy of relying on external imitation of the USSR. Soon this proved impossible. The Twentieth Congress, with its downgrading of Stalin, the rehabilitation of Bela Kun, and the continued pressure for the repudiation of the anti-Titoist trials made his situation, especially given his professed ideological position of being the most loyal Soviet lieutenant, increasingly difficult. He was increasingly forced to adopt a policy of compromise which inescapably, in view of the existing alternative, tended to further undermine his position. Thus on March 27, 1956, Rakosi yielded on the Rajk issue and, with an obvious lack of enthusiasm,

---

* A large part of the Hungarian intelligentsia was still the product of the pre-Communist period, but even those who had been elevated into the ranks of the intelligentsia by the Communist system had gradually become repelled by it. A Communist daily, analyzing the role of the Hungarian intelligentsia, has this interesting comment to make: "70 per cent of our intellectuals gained their qualifications prior to the liberation and did not only bring this along with them from the past but also their ideological errors. The remaining 30 per cent, which in certain professions, like those of teachers and engineers, reaches 50 per cent, has been educated in our schools and universities, yet cannot be entirely exempt from the controversial influence produced by the policy of the period preceding the revolution. There is still a considerable gap separating the way of thinking of a number of intellectual workers from that of the working class. . . ." *Nepszava*, June 8, 1958.

rehabilitated Rajk and his associates.[27] Other concessions followed: Archbishop J. Grosz was amnestied [28] (but not Cardinal Mindszenty): in early July a partial amnesty was announced (bringing the total released to 11,398 persons); [29] even Bela Kovacs, a prominent anti-Communist long presumed dead, reappeared from imprisonment.[30] A series of measures designed to invigorate local councils and increase their fiscal authority were announced; [31] calls were issued for better labor relations; [32] and "socialist legality" was to be strengthened by limiting the arbitrary power of the administration.[33] Some of the pressure on the kulaks was to be relaxed, and the regime magnanimously would allow their relatives to join collective farms.[34]

These concessions still represented an effort to effect a limited version of the New Course, but under Rakosi's aegis. However, Rakosi's belated moderation was faced by a new complication: the intensifying ferment among the youth and the intellectuals. His response to this was true to his Stalinist training: the economic concessions were balanced by parallel measures to restrain the "troublemakers." The party press began to attack violently the literary circles for "slandering" the party,[35] and the more outspoken, such as Sandor Lukacsi, were expelled. Some of the writers replied by calling for "an end . . . to this present regime of gendarmes and bureaucrats." [36] The situation was fast approaching the breaking point, while news from Poland (particularly the Poznan outbreak) encouraged the Hungarians to believe that Stalinism was being repudiated throughout the bloc. The structure of dictatorship appears impregnable only until the first brick begins to fall away.

Paradoxically, it was the June 20 Soviet-Yugoslav declaration which prompted Rakosi's last bid for supremacy. He construed it as releasing him from the horns of dilemma on which he had been impaled since his return to power. The declaration proclaimed clearly and explicitly Soviet approval for many ways to socialism. Rakosi could now remain the most loyal Soviet lieutenant *and* a Stalinist without any longer being obliged to imitate Soviet concessions at home. His brand of Stalinism seemed compatible with the newly established principle of diversity. He accordingly moved swiftly to restore his full control of the situation. On June 30 a resolution of the Central Committee stated that:

Gaining courage from the patience of the Party and Communists, the anti-Party elements have launched an attack, which has been gradually increasing in strength, against the policy and leadership of our Party and against our people's democratic system. . . . The open stands against the Party and the People's Democracy are mainly organized by a certain group which has formed around Imre Nagy. The press failed to take a stand against the anti-Party views. Certain newspapers and periodicals . . . have published misleading and unprincipled laudatory reports and occasionally even given space to articles of provocative content. . . .[37]

The party organ followed with an attack on the Petofi Clubs, noting that "it cannot be considered accidental that these opportunist, harmful and anti-Party views were voiced by those who still maintain a close and systematic contact with Imre Nagy, who has been expelled from the Party because of his anti-Marxist views, hostile to the Party and the People's Democracy, and his factionalism. . . . These people turned the debates into scenes of attacks against the People's Democracy." [38] At the Central Committee session of July 12, Rakosi finally announced his decision to liquidate the "Nagy conspiracy" by arresting him and approximately four hundred associates and by closing three literary organs which had been in the forefront of the anti-Rakosi struggle.

He moved too late. The very fact that he had to seek Central Committee approval was evidence of his weakened position and there he encountered unexpectedly stiff opposition with some members appealing (still in the old tradition but in the name of the new Soviet line) to the Soviet Embassy. The June 20 declaration notwithstanding, the USSR had to intervene, and Tito could not but welcome this act. Rakosi's initiative, the Soviets presumably recognized, might not only spark a repetition of Poznan, but undo the wobbling structure of undefined diversity so recently erected by Khrushchev and backed by Tito. Khrushchev's ultimate program for sounder relations among Communist states could thus be harmed by Rakosi's zeal. Rakosi, whose struggle against internal opposition received sympathetic Soviet backing only a few months earlier [39] was obviously becoming a political liability for Soviet external relations, not to mention the prompting of an explosive situation in Hungary itself. The growing disaffection with his rule even reached the staff of the party daily, *Szabad Nep*, and the Soviet Embassy doubtless kept Moscow abreast of all such occurrences. On July 17, Mikoyan arrived in Budapest, and on the following day Rakosi, complaining of hypertension — a justifiable malaise under the circumstances — submitted his resignation for reasons of health.

The Soviet intervention was a halfway measure. It betrayed the Stalinists without satisfying their opponents, or Tito. The new leadership did not mean a return of Nagy, although several formerly imprisoned Communists, most prominently Kadar, Kallai, and Marosan, were elected to party positions in an effort to mollify both Tito and the domestic anti-Rakosi groups. The important post of first secretary went to Gero, a close associate of Rakosi and a bitter opponent of Nagy, who was entrusted with the task of somehow bridging the gap produced by the period between March 1955 and July 1956. His appointment appeared to be a reasoned effort to effect a transition from Rakosi's rule without a violent undermining of the Communist regime. A further factor preventing Nagy's return might well have been his identification with some of Malenkov's policies, making him quite distasteful to the CPSU First Secretary. In any case, the solution seemed to be a compromise designed to contain disintegrative trends while maintaining in power a regime fully committed to the Soviet Union. Gero's line, as stated in his speech to the Central Committee [40] and subsequently reiterated in the Central Committee's resolution,[41] can be best summarized as a promise to wage a struggle on "two fronts" — pledging improvements, admitting inadequacies, restating the party's determination to rehabilitate those unjustly treated, but also emphasizing the priority of heavy industry and the need to continue collectivization, warning against domestic subversion, and finally condemning the opposition elements within the party. Gero's line, not unexpectedly, was thus fully in tune with the Soviets' second thoughts about Titoism and anti-Stalinism, and compatible with their belated efforts to restrict somewhat the meaning of many ways to socialism.

In a revolutionary situation halfway measures are rarely successful. Gero's appointment could not satisfy the masses which were by then craving a *political* reform, an implementation of the alternative which seemed not only feasible but even blessed with a Soviet endorsement. To the uninitiated, the ostensible Soviet policy indeed appeared to call for something rather like Nagy's program. Anti-Stalinism and greater diversity — that seemed to be the meaning of the Twentieth Congress and the June declaration. Gero's appointment thus appeared more and more to be an attempt to hold back the clock, especially since he could hardly acknowledge publicly Mikoyan's sponsorship. Tito's unmistakable distaste for him further intensified this impression.* The new First Secretary, given the unenviable and

* It was to overcome Tito's objections to Gero that Mikoyan flew from Budapest to Yugoslavia and held urgent consultations with Tito, Kardelj, and Rankovic. Tito, however, remained unconvinced and did not change his attitude until after his two

possibly unpleasant task of reforming Rakosi's legacy, found himself
operating without a clear-cut conception of what his policy or even
its basic assumptions ought to be. Moscow itself at this stage apparently lacked such precise notions. In Hungary the practical consequence of such a state of affairs was that ideology, in the sense of
a Communist program of action, was firmly in the hands of the
opposition.

All of this left Gero to rely entirely on the institutions of power.
But these too were rapidly slipping away. The Rakosi period had
accumulated the hostility, had created an antithesis which linked the
masses and a majority of the party in opposing anything short of
Nagy's return. Gero was left with the secret police, the army, and,
ultimately, the Soviet occupying forces. The opposition, lacking
formal organization,* could counter with a popular program, the
passionate loyalty of most party and nonparty intellectuals (a group
traditionally important in Hungarian struggles for freedom), the
students, increasing numbers of urban proletarians, and the passive
support of the vast majority of the peasantry. The party was particularly demoralized by the return from imprisonment of a large
number of party members, purged and mistreated by Rakosi.

The subsequent three months were spent in continued agitation
by the opposition and in desperate efforts by Gero to consolidate his
position. He was granted Soviet financial credit,[42] and, together with
the Soviet leaders, actively campaigned for Tito's endorsement. A
number of concessions were announced,† and even a macabre re-

_____

meetings with Khrushchev in September. For references to the Mikoyan meetings,
see *Borba*, July 23 and 24, 1956.

* According to Hungarian Interview No. 563 (a former well-informed Communist official), Nagy's supporters were divided on the issue of whether to organize
some sort of an opposition nucleus. "One wing of the Imre Nagy camp, though not
Imre Nagy himself, attempted to organize an illegal Party organization. But Losonczy,
Donath, and Ujhelyi opposed this and said that they would not join any such organization. Thus the organization remained somewhat casual, an organization based on
friendships, with a very well developed grapevine. . . . There was a chain linked together by close friendships, the first with the second, the second with the third, etc.,
which functioned very well at all times except during the Revolution. During such
stormy events stronger organization was needed; then the Imre Nagy group fell apart
into its component elements, each of which went his own way. This was because Imre
Nagy's friends were intellectual anarchists and were unable to organize because there
was not one organizer in the whole group. There were only publicists, orators, and
national Weltschmerz artists (*vilagfajdalmas*). They got along very well with Imre
Nagy. Nagy likes to philosophize and these people liked to talk and talk . . ." (p. 74).

† The role of the National Assembly was to be increased, and interpellation and
recall of deputies introduced, although the parliamentary model was explicitly rejected (*Szabad Nep*, July 28, 1956). Officials, including ministers, were obligated to

interment of Rajk's remains staged. This gesture, however, backfired since it gave the opposition an opportunity to dramatically emphasize in human terms the abyss which divided the regime from the people. The popular pressure continued to mount, and at this juncture Moscow apparently advised further concessions. Early in October Gero and Kadar visited the Kremlin and talked to the Soviet officials most directly involved in Hungarian matters, Suslov and Mikoyan.[43] Within a few days of their return, Nagy's reinstatement in the party was announced. Paralleling similar trends in Poland, this must have seemed, even to the most devoted Stalinists, as indicating an imminent triumph for Nagy, and in politics nothing is more likely to assure victory than the apparent inevitability of victory. Cries for his return to power came from all sides.

The army was in a growing state of demoralization. In July, Gero expelled from the party the discredited and hated former Minister of Defense, Farkas. In October Farkas was arrested, following the rehabilitation of several generals previously hanged. Political indoctrination, in all the confusion over the prevailing line, came to a standstill, while the release of imprisoned officers placed in an awkward position those incumbents who had been promoted to replace the arrested commanders. Increasingly, the officer corps and the military cadets identified themselves with the restless intellectuals, even going so far as to take part in the discussion clubs.[44]

The Hungarian revolution began when it appeared that the most important of the remaining two props for Gero's regime was no longer willing to support him. Gomulka's accession to power in Poland, reported in the Hungarian press and radio as an event of "historic significance," was widely interpreted to mean that the USSR was not willing to use force to prevent the removal of Stalinist, or neo-Stalinist, leaders and their replacement by known national Communists backed by the people. At this late stage the literally last-minute October 23 announcement that Tito had finally been persuaded to give Gero his endorsement and that a Yugoslav delegation would visit Budapest to repay the visit which Gero paid to Belgrade on October 15 had lost all its meaning. What Khrushchev had pleaded for with Tito at Sochi (see preceding chapter) came too late. Infuriated by Gero's unwillingness to resign, the crowds started to

---

give instant attention to matters raised by deputies and to receive them immediately (Radio Budapest, September 5, 1956). People forced to leave the frontier zone next to Yugoslavia were allowed to return (Radio Budapest, August 25, 1956), and terror generally abated.

move, and the shots fired by Gero's only remaining source of support, the secret police, sparked the accumulated tension into fury. Gero's new policy was not in time, offered too little, was burdened with too much bitterness, and appeared to lack not only Hungarian but also Soviet support. The controlled transition failed.

The USSR and Ten Days of National Communism

The violence in Budapest put some hard dilemmas before the Soviet leadership. Its acceptance of Gomulka's leadership in Poland, a consideration almost causally related to the Hungarian upheaval, was apparently made on the spur of the moment and with some misgivings, and probably without unanimity in the CPSU Presidium (see next chapter). In Budapest, during the night of October 23, Nagy had been selected by the Hungarian Central Committee, apparently acting without Soviet advice and in desperation, to be the new Premier, although Gero remained First Secretary. In the course of the same night a member of the Hungarian Politburo, G. Marosan, at that time considered to be an anti-Stalinist, a former Social Democrat and only recently released from Rakosi's prison, appealed on the Politburo's behalf for direct Soviet military aid. Clearly, he could have done so only in the name of defending the regime (which now included Nagy *) against the "counterrevolution." The Soviet authorities probably felt that they had no alternative but to intervene, and were probably so inclined in any case since nipping an outbreak in the bud was preferable to dealing with a widespread revolution.

But once the intervention began, it was not clear against whom it was directed. The government was nominally headed by Nagy, the party still by Gero. Nagy continued to appeal for order, promising to follow "a Hungarian road corresponding to our own national characteristics in the building of socialism," [45] while Kadar, more acceptable than Gero as a public spokesman for the party, appealed for vigilance against the "counterrevolutionaries." On October 25 he replaced Gero and joined Nagy in appealing for order, promising magnanimity to the rebels and assuring the people that Hungarian-Soviet relations would be reviewed. Thus, strangely enough, a disavowed revolution was being suppressed by Soviet troops who were protecting a regime which the revolutionaries were striving to set up.

To the Soviets, the situation must have appeared perplexing but

---

* The appeal was formally made in Nagy's name. On October 31 he denied that he had made the request, and after the revolution's suppression Marosan publicly took credit for it.

still not entirely out of hand. Most of the violence was concentrated in Budapest. The Hungarian army, however, remained largely neutral and did not participate on a large-scale or in an organized fashion on either side.[46] Indeed, the Defense Ministry was still under the control of officers loyal to the Soviets, and the chief of staff was able to manipulate the disposition of the troops so as not to help the rebels.[47] The Communist Party leadership, despite the fall of the Rakosi clique and the return of Nagy, still contained people like Kadar or Marosan — the latter had called in the Soviet troops and the former had applauded the Soviet intervention on October 24. At the same time, however, the Soviet participation in the fighting had provoked a state of unrest in Poland, and Polish and Yugoslav messages of sympathy addressed to Nagy and Kadar on October 28 were urging a stop to the bloodshed. Both messages were clear-cut endorsements of the Nagy government which on October 27 was reconstituted to admit several prominent non-Communists, such as Bela Kovacs and Zoltan Tildy. In brief, the situation was too fluid to be viewed with equanimity; but was it sufficiently extreme to warrant an intervention?

The position adopted at this stage by the USSR was highly ambiguous and probably reflected deep-seated uncertainties and conflicts within the Soviet leadership. On October 28 Nagy negotiated a cease-fire, and Soviet troops began to pull out of Budapest on the following day. In the meantime, Suslov and Mikoyan flew to Budapest to reconnoiter the situation. The Soviet press adopted the line that a counterrevolutionary *putsch* in Hungary had been suppressed jointly by the Hungarian government and the Soviet army, claiming that it had been a foreign provocation, and indicated that Nagy and Kadar were the legitimate government, supported by the USSR. According to one source, on October 29 Mikoyan promised Zoltan Tildy that all Soviet troops would be withdrawn shortly.[48]

It was probably in keeping with this hopeful assessment that the October 30 Soviet declaration, "On Friendship and Cooperation between the Soviet Union and other Socialist States," was issued. The declaration was obviously designed to prevent a Hungarian defection from the Soviet bloc and to define the new conditions created by the events in Poland and Hungary. The declaration asserted that "the countries of the great commonwealth of socialist nations can build their relations only on the principle of full equality, respect for territorial integrity, state independence and sovereignty, and noninterference in the domestic affairs of one another."[49] Attempting to dissociate the USSR from Stalinism, it admitted that these principles had been violated, offered to re-examine economic relations prevailing between the USSR and the Communist states and to recall all Soviet economic and military advisers (always a source of major nationalist irritation). In effect, the declaration was no less than a belated equivalent for the orbit of Khrushchev's earlier speech on Stalinism in domestic Soviet affairs.

The declaration then went on to state that the USSR was willing to consider withdrawing its troops from the territory of any member of the Warsaw Pact which so desired but with the following significant stipulation:

In this, the Soviet government proceeds from the principle that the stationing of troops of one member state of the Warsaw Treaty on the territory of another member state of the Warsaw Treaty takes place on the basis of an agreement between all its participants and not only with the agreement of that state, on the territory of which, at its request, these troops are stationed or are planned to be stationed.[50]

This was the last attempt to hold to the line developed in the June 1956 agreement with Tito. It was immediately followed by a Chinese statement, hailing the declaration, reasserting the "five principles," characterizing Polish and Hungarian demands as "entirely proper," and condemning "chauvinism by a big country." [51] (For fuller treatment of the Chinese approach, see Chapter 12.) Nagy's regime thus seemed to have won the endorsement of international Communism.

The tragedy of Nagy's government, however, was that the anti-Rakosi coalition could not stay together once the Rakosi clique had fallen. A great many of the rebels, recalling Rakosi's return to power in 1955 and emboldened by Soviet hesitations, wanted to make absolutely certain that definite institutional guarantees would prevent the return of a dictatorship. They called for a multiparty government. Others distrusted Nagy, especially because of the ambiguous position he was forced into by the events of October 23–28, the date of the announcement of the Soviet withdrawal. All were embittered by the Soviet intervention and called for the complete pull-out of Soviet troops. Nagy in this manner was pushed more and more toward a fundamental revision of the political order and toward an openly national Communist policy.

To those Soviet leaders advocating forceful suppression, the October 30 declaration might have provided the necessary breathing space for deployment of Soviet troops and for taking stock of the situation. In fact, large-scale Soviet troop movements did begin on that day, thereby casting doubt on the sincerity of the declaration. However, events in Hungary itself were strengthening the position of those in Moscow who favored a policy of force. On October 30 a multiparty system was restored and a "revolutionary military council" set up to by-pass the still inactive army command. In addition, even while Mikoyan and Suslov were conferring in Budapest in an attempt to get a firsthand feel of the situation, Nagy stated (on October 31) that it was not he who had originally requested the Soviet intervention and revealed that he was beginning negotiations for Hungary's withdrawal from the Warsaw Pact.* A day later, Hungary's neutrality was officially proclaimed by Nagy's government. National Communism was openly rejecting allegiance to the Soviet camp.

The final Soviet decision to intervene, facilitated by the Anglo-French attack on Egypt,† was probably made after Suslov's and Mikoyan's return to Moscow, sometime on November 1 or 2. Judging from the hesitant military moves, from published Soviet statements, and from consideration of the highly relevant policy of expediency adopted toward Gomulka, it would appear that until the Suslov-Mikoyan mission, the Soviet leadership, even though increasingly fearful of the revolution's spreading elsewhere, was uncertain how to react and was preparing for several contingencies. Military moves laid the groundwork for an eventual suppression by force, while last-minute political consultations and declarations explored the possibility of accepting Nagy, at least temporarily, provided certain Soviet *desiderata* were met — namely, retention of the dichotomic world image and close political-military ties. As of November, the tone of the Soviet dispatches reporting the Hungarian situation changed sharply, and emphasis was put on alleged outrages against Communists.‡ On November 4 Soviet artillery fire signaled the Soviet determination not to tolerate national Communism within the Soviet fold, while the

* According to General Pal Maleter, Mikoyan was informed of this directly on October 31. In response to a question, Maleter stated: "Tildy has informed Mikoyan that we shall repudiate the Warsaw Treaty in any case, and our government demanded that negotiations in this respect begin as soon as possible." Radio Budapest, November 2, 1956.

† The Anglo-French ultimatum to Egypt was issued on October 30, the day of the Soviet statement on relations between Communist states.

‡ That these in fact were very few is shown by the indictment delivered against Nagy in 1958. The indictment, with two years' time to prepare it, charged that 239 Communists were killed during his second tenure of office. Considering the atmosphere generated by the Soviet intervention and the bitterness against Rakosi's regime, the number is surprisingly low. Text of indictment in *New York Times*, June 19, 1958.

failure of Nagy to contain the events demonstrated the inability of national Communism to maintain domestic stability in the wake of brutal Stalinism. Budapest, in its tragic hour, became the graveyard for Tito's hopes and Khrushchev's calculations.

The Soviet suppression of national Communism in Hungary meant that, in the final analysis, the Kremlin interpreted its agreement with Yugoslavia as not applicable elsewhere, but as something which grew unnaturally out of certain "aberrations" in past relations — particularly the militant 1949 Cominform resolution plotting energetic action against Yugoslavia — and which gradually would dissolve as conditions changed. The ideological agreements, which would pave the way to the fading away of the "objective conditions" for national Communism would in the meantime diminish the most attractive element of Yugoslavia's position: its independent distinctiveness in theory and practice. The latter might even persist, but without the former it would not amount to much more than the restricted conception of peculiarities which Moscow was willing to tolerate in the summer of 1956.

Needless to add, such premises excluded any toleration of national Communism in East Europe, since such tolerance would be unhistorical and reactionary: it would be going against the expected trend of events even in the case of Yugoslavia itself, since, ultimately, it was hoped, Yugoslavia too would shed its distinctive mantle. It follows that acceptance of Yugoslav individuality was not meant to imply a general principle. Major domestic shifts from a common, uniform institutional pattern could be allowed in the post-Stalin phase in order to strengthen the local regimes, but not at the price of their losing sight of the limitations to such diversity. The regimes would have to be extremely careful in maintaining ideological unity precisely because of the post-Stalin adaptations, and ideological unity, still given Moscow's pre-eminence, in itself more than implied a retention of the hierarchical pattern of authority within the camp.

Tito's Dilemma

To Tito, the events in Hungary raised a dilemma. In one sense, they represented the fulfillment of both his hopes and his theoretical notions. Stalinism, as a political and economic system, had decayed, even though at one time it had created some of the preconditions for socialism. Subsequently, it had become a brake to the social progress of the countries involved and was therefore doomed to give way to more "progressive" social forces, with the Yugoslav example being highly relevant. The events in Hungary, and in the USSR, seemed to have taken a course compatible with these notions, although the end result had not been the desirable one. But what attitude should Yugoslavia adopt toward the Hungarian upheaval?

Several alternatives were theoretically open. Tito could approve the Hungarian events *in toto*, condemning both Soviet interventions. This would pit him squarely against Stalinism, making him the open champion of national Communism, but it would have the disadvantage of provoking an immediate isolation from the Soviet bloc, cutting Tito's links with those Soviet leaders, like Khrushchev, whom Tito considered to be anti-Stalinist; he would then be forced to wage the anti-Stalinist struggle purely from the outside, which would be inexpedient tactically and doctrinally. Poland had just gained a measure of autonomy, and Tito was anxious to cultivate relations with it, which a sharp break might well prevent. To approve the first Soviet intervention of October 23 and to condemn the second would have made little sense, since it was on October 23 that Nagy came to power and set up a Communist regime basically compatible with Tito's aims. Once the first intervention was approved, there would be even more reason for approving the second. But Tito could not approve both Soviet interventions, since such approval would have meant that Titoism no longer existed and would have sanctioned similar moves against Poland. Tito might have considered intervening himself in order to stabilize Nagy and prevent a collapse of the Communist state,[52] but this he could hardly do without Soviet approval. And to intervene, in effect, on behalf of the USSR would obviously be pointless.

The alternative that was finally adopted, to disapprove of the first Soviet intervention and to approve the second, was worked out gradually as events developed and was clearly designed to promote the continued Yugoslav purposes insofar as the entire Soviet camp was concerned. It had been for the sake of these purposes that Tito finally agreed early in October, in response to Khrushchev's urgent pleas, to back Gero, with the subsequent tragic effect of emboldening Gero on his return from Belgrade on October 23 to take such an intransigent stand. On October 28 Yugoslavia voted in the UN Security Council against placing the Hungarian matter on the agenda; on October 30 Belgrade made its appeal to the Hungarians to stop the fighting and prevent "reactionaries" from exploiting the situation;[53] on November 4 Yugoslavia abstained twice from voting in the UN on the resolution calling for the withdrawal of Soviet troops from Hungary. In his actions Tito appeared to be motivated by a form of dialectical reasoning. The Hungarian events, even if the Soviet inter-vention had set the clock back somewhat and had encouraged the Stalinists, still represented a revolutionary advance in the direction of the disintegration of Stalinism. In the struggle against Stalinism, which was bound to be lengthy, the Leninist principle of one step back and two steps forward had to be applied. Even the program of the new Kadar regime, which seemed to accept many of the policies of Nagy,[54] appeared to be a step forward from the policies of Gero which the Yugoslavs had endorsed on October 23. To prevent the Stalinists from gaining the upper hand, Khrushchev in Russia and Kadar in Hungary ought to be encouraged.

In order to keep Yugoslavia operating within the bloc, Tito was thus prepared to take a small step back: to sacrifice Nagy's national Communism as premature and "reactionary," and to sacrifice Nagy personally as an inconvenient impediment to the higher goals of Yugo-slavia's policy. On November 21 an agreement was reached with Kadar which paved the way for the end of Nagy's embarrassing — and symbolic — sanctuary in the Yugoslav Embassy. While his arrest on leaving the Embassy was violently protested,[55] it did not lead to any serious political consequences. One can even sense a certain feel-ing of relief in Belgrade that an incumbrance had been jettisoned. Nonetheless, since the Hungarian revolution had produced major mis-givings among Yugoslav Communists and since subsequent conduct might have clouded the clarity of Yugoslavia's position, Tito felt compelled to define his policy in the face of the new circumstances and categorically to state again that Titoism was available for export precisely because of Yugoslavia's behavior. His major address de-livered on November 11 at Pula revealed once more the cross-pur-poses involved in the Tito-Khrushchev cooperation. Tito reiterated the Yugoslav belief that the Belgrade and Moscow declarations had been meant for the relations of all Communist states, expressed regret that Moscow, particularly since Poznan, was unwilling to interpret them that way, and suggested that the Soviet unwillingness might be due to lack of confidence in the stability of the People's Democracies once autonomy is granted them. Tackling the Hungarian question, Tito condemned as "absolutely wrong" the first Soviet intervention but, maintaining the balance so necessary to his purposes, he gave qualified endorsement to the second Soviet intervention as a bad thing which might turn into something good. He quite bluntly criticized Nagy for not offering "decisive resistance to the reactionaries" instead of calling "the people to arms against the Soviet Army and [appeal-

ing] to the Western countries to intervene." [56] His condemnation of
the fallen leader of Hungarian national Communism was coupled with
unqualified praise for the new Soviet-imposed Kadar regime ("I
know these people in the new Government and . . . they, in my
opinion, represent that which is most honest in Hungary." [57]) Tito
then noted that because Kadar's popularity had been undermined by
the Soviet intervention, the Yugoslavs must give him backing.[58] To
Tito, Kadar seemed to resemble Gomulka more than he did Rakosi.*

Tito's speech was a compromise designed to keep his influence in
the Soviet bloc (most particularly with Khrushchev, Gomulka, and
Kadar) while continuing the struggle against Stalinism and remaining
the champion of new conceptions for relations among Communist
states. Much of his position was based on the belief that within the
Soviet leadership a split existed between Khrushchev and a Stalinist
faction, and that a sharp break would undermine Khrushchev's position. However, at this point a compromise solution satisfied no one —
for the issues were drawn much too sharply, and the USSR and especially the neighboring Communist regimes violently resented even
Tito's qualified censure. What made matters worse, Tito was still
acting as if he expected Titoism to be formally accepted as the basis
for Soviet-satellite relations and as if he felt himself directly involved
in the internal politics of Yugoslavia's neighbors. The June 1956
declaration, the obeisance paid to him, Khrushchev's praise — all had
tended to give his views undue weight and, from the Soviet point of
view, the time had come to cut Tito down to size. This undertaking
was shouldered not only by Moscow itself but with apparent relish
by those Communist leaders who had the best reasons for entertaining
a strong distaste for him.

The Soviet reply came on November 23 in the form of a lengthy
Pravda article, entitled "To Consolidate Further the Forces of Socialism on the Basis of Marxist-Leninist Principles." [59] Its tone, in view of
the charges made by Tito, was relatively restrained, especially if one

---

* Tito met Kadar while entertaining Gero and was much impressed by him. He
apparently remained convinced that he would be able to influence Kadar's policies,
despite the Soviet suppression of Nagy. Marosan, Kadar's close collaborator, states that
after the suppression of the revolution the new regime was advised by Belgrade "not
to reorganize the Party but to put the ill-famed workers' councils . . . into power.
They even supported this anti-Marxist and anti-Leninist advice with arguments . . ."
(*Nepszabadsag*, July 20, 1958). The Yugoslavs remained hopeful that the new regime
would resemble Gomulka's, and they might have also hoped that Nagy, once in
Kadar's hands, would help it. It is interesting to note in this connection that some of
Nehru's confusion concerning the Soviet intervention in Hungary is explainable in
terms of the interpretations supplied him by the Yugoslavs. (See also Chapter 13.)

considers that the Soviet Union might well have felt that Tito had misled them in pressing for relaxation in East Europe. Without going into too much detail, we may note that the article justified the necessity of the Soviet intervention in Hungary while conceding past mistakes; it accused Nagy of having pursued a two-faced policy; it rejected with greater indignation Tito's allegations about the Soviet system and the cult of personality and finally it passed on to a critique of some Yugoslav aspects. *Pravda* noted critically that the Yugoslav model subsisted on capitalist aid and that such a model could hardly be cited as an example for other socialist states. The statement particularly objected to Tito's propensity to speak authoritatively on matters involving the policies of other Communist parties and suggested that many of the Yugoslav positions showed a marked deviation from "proletarian internationalism." To Belgrade this Soviet inclination to question the virtues of the Yugoslav experience signified, despite *Pravda*'s call for a friendly discussion, a backsliding to the pre-reconciliation atmosphere. Belgrade accordingly replied that the only way to undo the past was to grant to the socialist states full equality with the USSR, for "basically, there are only two roads: a return to Stalinism or the establishment of democratic relations of equality among socialist states." [60]

At this stage the fray was joined by the other Communist powers. Apart from any Soviet promptings, Tirana, Sofia, and the other satellite leaders had good reason for objecting to Tito. Unlike Gomulka, Tito had clearly demanded that personnel changes be made as a price for his friendship. The satellite leaders now felt themselves released from the restraints imposed on them by the earlier Belgrade-Moscow rapprochement. They sprang into an attack on Tito and, more than that, gradually but inevitably into a vigorous defense of Stalinism. In both, either by design or through personal initiative, they went much further than Moscow. Unlike the concurrent ideological criticisms of Gomulka's Poland, the attacks on Tito involved an invective reminiscent of former days. Referring to Tito without the usual prefix of "comrade," the organ of the Albanian party accused the Marshal of spreading "anti-Soviet lies" for the benefit of the imperialists and "the bandit Imre Nagy." At the same time, the paper asserted categorically that the Soviet experience of building socialism had a universal applicability. [61] In December, *Pravda* returned to the argument to take issue with the views advanced by Kardelj, who had stated that in the transition stage of building socialism the bureaucratic features of the dictatorship of the proletariat represented a distinct danger to the eventual withering away of the state. Noting sarcastically that the trial of Djilas "does not indicate that the state is withering away in Yugoslavia," *Pravda* accused the Yugoslavs of opposing the two fundamental aspects of Leninism: the dictatorship of the proletariat and the leading role of the party.[62]

Tito's efforts to hold to a middle line and yet preserve his freedom of action thus largely failed, and anti-Titoist positions remained firm in the East European states, except in Poland and, to a much lesser extent, in Hungary, where the situation was still relatively unstable. Even with Khrushchev himself Tito did not re-establish as close a working relationship as that which had existed for a few short months in 1956. But more serious still was Tito's abdication from the appealing posture of a national Communist. His approval of the second Soviet intervention, his condemnation of Nagy, and the unclear circumstances of Nagy's betrayal to the Soviet secret police meant that national Communism ceased to be an absolute principle for Tito but rather a matter of political expediency. The justification of the second intervention opened the way to Moscow's insistence on its own conception of "unity" and deprived Tito of any ideological arguments against it, or even against the later execution of Nagy. An absolute standard is sometimes more effective in critical situations than relative, and hence ambiguous, conceptions.

Tito's original appeal could never be directed toward the majority of the party *apparatchiki* in East Europe since they feared any break with Moscow. His appeal to the intelligentsia, to the Communist intellectuals, even to the working class, was in the name of independent socialism — of national Communism. His ambiguity on the Hungarian issue took away this appeal; he had failed to recognize that in the immediate post-October–November 1956 situation Communism in Europe was ripe for a doctrine of diversity, of national independence, of sovereign socialism. Nagy was destroyed when he tried to raise that standard; Gomulka could not afford to do so; yet the disaffected and revolutionary-minded Communists were seeking such leadership and such an absolute standard. This was Tito's historical opportunity, but his perspectives had been too narrow and too limited by his own doctrines to seize upon it. A bold and uncompromising stand at that juncture might have made Tito a symbol of change, all the more powerful since the climate for such change had been matured by the Twentieth Congress, the June declaration, and the Polish and Hungarian Octobers. But by conceding values higher than freedom or national independence, namely the protection of socialism, Tito in effect justified the tyranny he professed to abhor. Now any Communist regime could declare the urgent need for its subordination to the USSR in the name of "the defense of socialism," and Tito could no longer call this an error in principle.

Hungary hence marked the defeat of true national Communism.[63] National Communism could now be sought by various states only in relative doses, depending on the circumstances, the place, and the timing. And under such conditions, there could be no doubt that the overwhelming interests and political considerations of the Soviet state would be the determining factor. The Soviet regime, even in the most acute anti-Stalinist phase, had made it quite plain that it would insist on the leadership of its party in Communist counsels, on the maintenance of the dichotomic image of the world with all its political consequences, on the necessity of militant "proletarian internationalism." No Communist regime could be tolerated if it conflicted with international objectives, although sometimes such international objectives could dictate a measure of tolerance for local peculiarities otherwise distasteful. Only within this framework could concessions and adaptations be made, but they would fall quite short of anything resembling national Communism.

CHAPTER 11

The Polish October: The Challenge of Domesticism

THE most far-reaching change in relations among Communist states was caused by events in Poland. The change lacked the drama of Nagy's withdrawal from the Warsaw Pact or the trauma of the street fighting in Budapest. Yet its significance for the Communist states was, in many ways, greater than that of the Hungarian revolution abruptly crushed by Soviet arms. The Polish developments were the product of an evolving pattern which was difficult for the Soviets at any specific point to interrupt justifiably; because of this the foundations of Stalinist controls in Poland were gradually undermined. Indeed, in contrast to Tito's external expediency and internal dictatorship, it appeared, for a few short months after October 1956, that out of this evolutionary pattern a challenging, new form of Polish Communism, combining internal freedom with external independence, might emerge to raise the standard of national Communism. This eventuality did not come about. Instead, Poland remained a member of the Warsaw Pact and of the Soviet bloc, even though the new domestic practices and doctrines shattered the former institutional and ideological uniformity. How did this pattern develop? What were its implications for relations with Communist states, the USSR in particular?

The Controlled Transition: A Summary [1]

In Poland, as elsewhere in the bloc, a New Course had been initiated during the Malenkov period. However, the Polish leadership realized that any excessive departures from established policies would immediately bring up the dormant issue of the "right-wing nationalist deviation" of Gomulka, and for this reason its adoption of the New Course was both delayed and more restrained than elsewhere. The extremely cautious character of the initial reforms, while failing to create a much-needed popularity, did not have the immediate effect of stirring up passions and enflaming loyalties. Poland thus avoided the political difficulties which the New Course initiated in Hungary.

The initial reactions of the population, to the extent that they could be perceived, appear to have been a commingling of suspicion, apathy, and only slight relief. It is to be remembered that the New Course was essentially an economic measure, and that in some respects political terror even mounted in Poland after Stalin's death. To many, all this appeared to be merely an application of the old Stalinist technique of balancing political coercion with economic concessions,[2] and this impression was strengthened by the insistence of the party that the new policies were a reflection of its strength — and woe to those who would interpret it otherwise.[3]

Nonetheless, the leadership soon found it impossible to limit the New Course to economic phenomena. Of paramount importance to the expanding scope of the reform was the liquidation in the USSR of Beria and the consequent weakening of the secret police. The pattern of imitation, still applicable in principle, required emulation in Poland — and within the party there were many who felt that the secret police had grown too strong. This feeling was sharpened by one of those felicitous circumstances that shape history: the defection to the West, in December 1953, of one of the most brutal secret policemen, Colonel J. Swiatlo, whose revelations of police tortures, of depravity within the ruling circles, of Soviet control of the whole secret-police apparatus,[4] were broadcast and airdropped by the Free Europe Committee to Poland, much to the consternation of the upper echelons of the party. This brought home to the party itself the fundamental question of any revolution: at what point does the human cost begin to outweigh the revolutionary ideals? The question, answered easily when the cost is paid by "enemies," takes on a different light when party members themselves become victims.

The current diminution in world tensions also meant that the need for domestic vigilance declined, and the party began to feel that the maintenance of a war Communism atmosphere was a distinct liability. Reflecting this feeling, an article published in the party journal appealed for a two-way dialogue between the party and the nation and criticized the Communist youth organization's concentration on the "unmasking" of anyone who expressed doubts rather than on the intelligent tackling of the more serious problem of "internal emigration" — the passive but hostile withdrawal of the individual from social and political activity.[5] Despite simultaneous warnings against exaggerated departures from the principle of party hegemony, a climate favorable to more outspoken reactions was gradually created, at least within the party. The Swiatlo affair sparked this latent sense of misgiving into an open expression of dissatisfaction at a meeting of the Warsaw central party *actif* in December 1954. In a two-day session, characterized by unprecedented criticisms of conditions within the party, the Politburo for the first time found itself faced by a majority of resentful *apparatchiki*. The existence of the Communist regime itself was not questioned, but the methods of the Politburo were violently condemned. Its leaders were accused of suppressing all initiative within the upper party echelons and of treating the Central Committee as a rubber stamp. The Politburo, taken aback and on the defensive, kept the meeting a secret.[6] Two years later, this episode was described by E. Ochab, Bierut's successor, as having placed the Politburo in actual "isolation."[7]

This isolation forced the leadership to act. On December 7, 1954, much on the Soviet pattern but distinctly more meaningful in the Polish situation, the Ministry of Public Security was replaced by a committee, and significantly, the former head of the Ministry, S. Radkiewicz, was not appointed to head the committee. The party journal simultaneously took notice of "aberrations" in the work of the Ministry.[8] The matter did not rest there. The Central Committee session of January 21–24, 1955, the third Plenum since the preceding party congress, went on record with a much stronger denunciation of the secret police, noting that "with bitterness, with burning pain and shame we learned about facts of brutal violation of people's legality. . . . There were cases of arrests of innocent people . . . shameful, inadmissible methods of investigation."[9] The party leadership was condemned, although in more cautious terms, for inadequate control over the secret police, for allowing the "vulgarization" of the concept of the class struggle, and for lack of contact with the lower party organs. It was publicly announced that a high secret-police official, Colonel Feigin, was expelled from the party and his chief investigating officer arrested. Much more important, but kept secret, was the quiet release from confinement of Gomulka in December 1954. This act, in effect, meant that the party leadership was implicitly shifting its ground on the interpretation of the Gomulka 1948–1949 heresy: while still an ideological deviation, it was no longer considered treasonous. The first major shift, at the time not perceived as such, thus occurred *within* the party apparatus and Central Committee at the end of 1954 and the beginning of 1955. Undisputed leadership of the Politburo was for the first time challenged and tenuous links established between the restless elements in the party and the discontented populace.

Why was this trend not reversed after Malenkov's fall, as was the case in the analogous Hungarian situation? There is no doubt that the circumstances of Malenkov's removal had shaken the central *actif* in Warsaw a great deal, and Shepilov's article on industrialization in January of 1955 (see Chapter 8) provoked a lively debate, with some advocating immediate implementation but with the majority adopting a somewhat independent, critical position.[10] The party leadership took a middle ground, adopting the new Moscow line but justifying the Polish concessions as temporary expedients. At the March Plenum it again adopted an equivocal stand, praising both collectivization and industrialization but not disowning its moderate New Course. This constituted an important step forward in the direction of restoring the primacy of domestic considerations, something unthinkable a year before.

However, under the circumstances, there was little else the leadership could have done unless it was willing, despite the misgivings of its own central *actif*, to reimpose violent Stalinist terror and a radical "leftist" policy. Such a program, in turn, would have forced the leaders to further increase their dependence on Moscow, which no one seemed to desire. From the standpoint of the Kremlin, the Polish regime under Bierut and Berman could not be more loyal, and the only real alternative to them was Gomulka. No repetition of the Hungarian case was hence involved. Active intervention to turn back the clock would not have been in keeping with the prevailing Soviet line on Yugoslavia, the international situation, or Khrushchev's emerging notions on voluntarily loyal regimes.

In this manner, the Polish leadership, not beset by internal splits, became gradually committed to a policy of relaxation which was greeted by the party membership and the people as a whole. The party still recalled the 1938 fate of the Polish Communist Party, and for this reason many members welcomed any opportunity to diminish the party's dependence on the USSR, provided it did not threaten the regime's survival. Nonetheless, as the new policy developed momentum — more in terms of the general atmosphere than in concrete measures — the former Gomulka line appeared less and less heretical. The soul-searching which became so frequent during this period among party members was also prompted by the fact that the membership contained a high percentage of the "working intelligentsia," including officials. Between 1949 and 1956, they grew from 20.3 per cent of the membership (which remained much the same in total number) to 39.5 per cent, or two out of every five members.[11] By the end of 1956, in the crucial Warsaw area, where 28 per cent of the Polish intelligentsia (those with university education) was concentrated,[12] they accounted for 64.7 of the party membership.[13] While not all of them were dedicated to change, a sufficient number were and could make their influence felt. They pressed for a rejection of the former practice of subjecting all cultural and intellectual activity to strict control, and soon influential party leaders themselves were condemning the "vulgar commandeering" in cultural policy.[14]

In spring of 1955, in a small Warsaw apartment, the first spontaneous, still not illegal, organized activity was launched: an intellectuals' discussion club, given the striking name of the Club of the Crooked Circle.[15] The idea proved very popular: by the fall there were twenty such clubs in Poland; during the winter of 1955–56 about forty; by the spring of 1956 almost sixty; by the summer one hundred and twenty; and by the fall over two hundred. The clubs rapidly became the equivalent of what was still forbidden — namely, political assemblies in which the important issues were debated and attitudes crystallized. From their sessions emerged ideas which gradually reached the populace.*

The clubs and the press (even though the latter was still subject to censorship) in this fashion became the breeding ground for a political line which went appreciably beyond the restrained official adaptations of Stalinism. Already as far back as March 1955, some party stalwarts, like W. Mach, felt compelled to denounce various "cultural subversives" who were accused not only of rejecting socialist realism but also "People's Poland." [16] In spite of this, the same literary weekly which had published the denunciations soon published the sensational and bitter poem by Adam Wazyk, "An Ode to Adults," since translated into many languages, which represented a courageous attack on the hypocrisy of the system. By late 1955 and throughout 1956, the Polish writers were asserting with increasing vigor the priority of artistic criteria over political requirements and heaping scorn on the

* For the history of one such club, founded by the graduate students of Cracow University and given the "revolutionary" name of The Club of the Flaming Tomato, and particularly for its activities with respect to the Polish October, see the account in *Tygodnik Powszechny*, October 13, 1957, written by one of the participants. It gives an unusually good insight into the role of the club, the gradual expansion of the scope of its activities, the formation of a mass club, called "Spring 56," to organize broad activities, and finally the last-minute preparations on the eve of the dramatic change-over in October 1956.

"socialist realists." * Even otherwise loyal party members went so far as to reject the Leninist precepts of "partyness" in arts.[17]

After Khrushchev's speech on Stalin in February 1956, the discussions in Poland mounted in intensity and the balance of forces shifted rapidly. The party dogmatists were clearly on the defensive. The void created by the destruction of Stalinism and by violent Polish attacks on Stalin himself led many of those who had previously embraced Marxism to search for some sort of individual statement of beliefs, for a self-defined frame of reference. This was particularly true of the young Marxists who now felt deceived by the past. In their quest they frequently combined a residue of Marxist concepts with hitherto-rejected idealism, humanism, and Polish nationalism. Imitation of the USSR was condemned for having stifled "independence, creative thought and initiative," which could only flourish with a "Polish way to socialism." [18] National feelings were extolled as the highest expression of dedication to the people, and national sovereignty was held up as the only basis for the construction of socialism. The dogmas of the past were now to be replaced by a genuine search for the humanist values of socialism, and one writer went so far as to suggest that the slogan "proletarians of all lands" is meaningless and should give way to a statement of common human aspirations.[19] No wonder that the party ideologue in social sciences, A. Schaff, mused sadly:

We have to admit that in the broad circles of the intellectuals, the authority of Marxist ideology has been undermined. It is not a question of some hostility of the intellectuals toward Marxism, but rather a matter of continuing and serious errors committed by the Marxist camp in the conduct of science and in the ideological struggle.[20]

In this evolutionary pattern, the theoretical basis for the old regime was being washed away. At the same time the working class was

* In the spring of 1956, the Session of Culture and Science criticisms turned into a veritable flood. The statements uttered at the session were striking, especially if one considers that Poland was still under the control of a Soviet-anointed leadership headed by Bierut and Berman. A. Slonimski, a well-known literary figure, is on record in the proceedings of the meeting as declaring that the decline of art began with the 1936 Congress of Soviet Writers: "It was then that Zhdanov, basing himself on the lightheaded opinions of Gorky and utilizing his literary standing, created the theses of socialist realism and handed out this precise instrument for the destruction of the arts to the bureaucrats who with satisfaction and application sharpened by fear, carried on for twenty years this destructive process." For fuller treatment, see my "Communist Ideology and Power: From Unity to Diversity," *Journal of Politics*, November 1957.

brought into the orbit of these discussions, especially in certain key Warsaw factories to which party activists with advanced training had been assigned to supervise party work. These activists, drawn into the activities of the clubs, frequently became the links between the ideological discussions and those who theoretically were the backbone of the socialist state. In the factories, where there were many workers with prewar socialist traditions to provide the necessary leadership, the newly recruited proletariat responded sympathetically to the intellectual currents which seemed to offer an explanation of why the Stalinist oppression had taken place, how it could be overcome, how the workers, alienated from the regime, could begin to feel themselves the owners of the state. Through ideology the movement for change began to create an underpinning of potential power.

The Paralysis of Evolution

The international policy of the USSR and Soviet domestic developments provided precedents in favor of liberalization. Up to the time of the Twentieth Congress it might have seemed possible to the leaders in Warsaw that a policy of gradual adjustment would ultimately strengthen the regime by reducing accumulated tension. In late 1955, the party's theoretical journal, while still defending past policies against "nihilist criticisms" and asserting that the Poles could learn much from Soviet experience, stressed editorially the need for more attention to the particulars of the Polish situation in the construction of socialism. This bow to domesticism was a halfhearted effort to arm the regime with a doctrinal justification more in keeping with the new situation. At no point, however, was the full authority of the party thrown against the developing ferment. The Communist intellectuals were therefore not immediately brought face to face with the old Stalinist equation: either with us or against us. Had they been, it is conceivable that some would not have traveled the tortured journey to a rejection of the dogma. Instead, the party attempted a policy of gradual adjustment and occasional warnings. Events, however, outstripped the Warsaw leadership. The Twentieth Congress had undermined the ideological premises of the regime, and these difficulties were suddenly compounded by the unexpected death, on March 12, 1956, of the firmly implanted Stalinist head of the party, Boleslaw Bierut.

Bierut's death, unsettling as it must have been, served in a way further to reassure Moscow that the situation was relatively well in hand. Khrushchev personally flew to Warsaw, vetoed Roman Zam-

browski, an *apparatchik* of essentially Stalinist orientation, who was
the Politburo candidate for the post of First Secretary, on the grounds
that his Jewish origin would alienate the Poles, and sponsored the
candidacy of another reputed Stalinist, Edward Ochab, a leading
figure in the anti-Gomulka drive.[21] Ochab's selection, on March 20,
had the effect of assuring Moscow that, as in Czechoslovakia or East
Germany, a loyal regime was established in Poland and that the newly
legitimized theory of many ways to socialism would be interpreted
by Ochab in keeping with the broad interests of the Soviet bloc. In
late April this impression seemed to be confirmed by Ochab's article
in the Soviet press branding critics of his regime as "petty bourgeois"
elements guilty of "opportunism and nationalism." [22] A week earlier,
in a sharp speech to the Warsaw *actif*, he had reiterated: "We can
assure our Soviet brethren that no machinations of imperialist ad-
venturers, remnants of reaction, will weaken the alliance and eternal
friendship between People's Poland and the Soviet Union." [23] Ochab
also asserted that Gomulka's condemnation for nationalism had been
fully justified although, significantly, he conceded that the party
leadership had gone too far in interpreting deviation as equivalent to
treason.[24] Ochab's leadership and his avowed loyalty to the Soviet
conceptions thus helped to allay the Kremlin's apprehensions concerning internal Polish developments.

Even so, events were moving rapidly toward eliminating the most
objectionable aspects of the Stalinist legacy. Gomulka's earlier release
was for the first time officially confirmed. In April an amnesty for
some thirty thousand prisoners, including nine thousand political, was
announced and, in early May, Berman was divested of his posts. His
removal was the most important feature in a series of governmental
shifts which had already resulted in the dismissal of the Minister of
Justice, the Prosecutor General, and the Chairman of the State Security Committee. With Bierut dead and Berman discharged, only Minc
was left of the old triumvirate which had implemented the Stalinist
patterns in Poland.

"We must free the people from the fear of making decisions," declared the Prime Minister, Jozef Cyrankiewicz,[25] and to make this
possible many of the functions formerly controlled by the secret
police, such as prisons, border control, and internal police troops,
were transferred to the Ministry of the Interior, while the state-
security staff was cut by 22 per cent, not counting those transferred.[26]
Following a series of published attacks on the trade unions, it was
announced that the Central Trade Union Council had decided to

abolish the practice of confidential reports on employees and that all
existing records would be destroyed.[27] The Sejm (the Polish Parliament) was publicly ridiculed in the party papers for voting unani-
mously on all issues,[28] and it was conceded that "socialist democracy
can have certain aspects in common with parliamentary democracy." [29] This intellectual and political relaxation could not avoid
impinging on economic matters. The most important manifestation
of the new spirit was the criticism to which the views on the primacy
of producer-goods output, restated so firmly by Shepilov in 1955,
were subjected at the Congress of Polish Economists in early June
1956. For the first time it was openly stated that the Polish standard
of living had declined in preceding years. Reforms, departing from
the established Soviet pattern, were demanded. In addition, even in
the party journal, voices were raised against the rigid antikulak line
of the regime, and a more elastic approach, which would ensure the
level of productivity, was demanded.[30]

    All of this, even if followed with growing apprehension in
Moscow, did not seem to call for direct Soviet involvement. Unlike
Hungary, the pattern of gradual change was not interrupted, nor did
it develop a revolutionary character. Even in retrospect it is difficult
to find that particular moment when the Soviet leadership might have
felt that its active intervention was justified. True, the Twentieth
Congress was followed by an extremely intense outburst in Poland.
But the Polish leadership still appeared to be in control of the situation
and, like Ulbricht in East Germany, was setting a sharp anti-Stalinist
tone to the debates.[31] From a dialectical point of view, the developments could have easily been interpreted as a necessary stage which
would eventually lead to a firmer political future of Communism in
Poland. The absence of a top-level party split during this period, the
moderation of the regime's reforms, and the slowly evolving character
of the change thus obscured the growing contradictions within the
regime and failed to create a clear-cut situation justifying, in Soviet
eyes, direct Soviet intervention. It was also at this point that Yugoslavia seemed to be on the brink of rejoining the Communist camp,
and Khrushchev's relations with Tito appeared closer, on a personal
as well as a political plane, than with any other foreign Communist
leader.* On the Polish side, Ochab and his associates, while possibly
uneasy, had no reason to desire Soviet interference, and it may be

    * From the perspective of later quarrels and mutual incriminations, it is hard to
imagine the joyful 1956 scene of Tito, Mrs. Tito, and Khrushchev walking down the
streets of Moscow, hand in hand, licking ice-cream cones.

surmised that they assured Moscow that the situation was well in hand. The formal rehabilitation of the Polish Communist Party, announced after the Twentieth Congress, gave the Polish Communists a new sense of dignity, and direct Moscow involvement in the summer of 1956 seemed unnecessary and "unhistorical."

Gomulka and Power

The situation was changed by Poznan. The late June workers' uprising, suppressed only through the use of the army,* signaled that the ferment had reached the working classes, smarting under oppressive labor conditions. However, the initial reaction of the Polish regime, while panicky, was quite firm and did not appear to require direct Soviet backing. Cyrankiewicz characterized the events as a foreign counterrevolutionary plot, while both Tito and Togliatti praised the firmness of the regime's response.[32] Although possibly both of them were anxious at the time to prevent an active Soviet reversal of the Polish trends,[33] their statements and the initial official Warsaw reaction undercut whatever grounds a Soviet intervention might have had, not to speak of its likely consequences for Khrushchev's domestic position or his broader policies.

The Soviet Union, probably reflecting also the prevailing uncertainties in the CPSU leadership, accordingly adopted a policy of indirect pressure which under Stalin had usually proved effective. Such response was also much more in keeping with the prevailing Soviet-Yugoslav amity and the adjustments then being effected in Hungary. However, it is apparent that the Poznan events were viewed with gravity in Moscow and that the Soviet leaders became more apprehensive about divisive tendencies within the bloc. A lengthy *Pravda* statement was issued to warn against the intrigues of those who "think that if such international working class organizations as the Comintern or the Cominform have ended their activity, then international solidarity is weakening and contacts among fraternal revolutionary parties, adhering to positions of Marxism-Leninism, are being destroyed." While conceding that "transition to socialism in various countries

---

* The use of the army had disastrous consequences on the morale of the military. This writer, visiting Poland one year after the Poznan events, had occasion to observe the deep sense of shame prevailing among the military that they had allowed themselves to be used against their own workers and countrymen. In a published discussion about the October 1956 events, held on its first anniversary, the weekly *Nowa Kultura* (October 20, 1957) cites a colonel of the Polish Army as saying that the use of the military against the workers prompted widespread discussions among the officers and men and brought them closer to the developing ferment.

would not be exactly the same," the paper reminded all Communists concerned that ultimately they "are moving *toward one* goal, toward Communism. It is impossible to move separately or haphazardly toward such a great goal." [34]

It was with this message that a Soviet delegation, headed by Bulganin and Zhukov, traveled to Poland a week later, ostensibly to commemorate the founding of the Communist regime but also to attend the Seventh Plenum of the Central Committee, summoned in the wake of the Poznan outbreak. The message, stressing unity and the need for vigilance, appeared particularly timely since the Poles, once Poznan ceased to be an immediate threat, had shifted their position somewhat and were inclined to replace the "conspiracy" interpretation with admissions that the workers had had justifiable grievances. Arriving in Poland at the time of Mikoyan's sudden flight to see Tito, presumably with a similar message, the leaders of the Soviet delegation stressed the need for unity in the face of hostile efforts to exploit the post-Twentieth Congress atmosphere. "Every country should go its own way to socialism, but we cannot permit this to be used to break up the solidarity of the peace camp, and certainly not under the pretext of respecting national peculiarities or extending democracy," the Soviet premier warned.[35] Simultaneously, in the old-fashioned carrot-and-stick pattern, Bulganin offered to provide Poland with $25 million of consumer goods to alleviate the most acute shortages.[36]

Bulganin's warnings and gifts were somewhat belated. The former solidarity of the Polish leadership, already strained by the period of relaxation and by Bierut's death, was split by the impact of the Poznan violence. The Seventh Plenum, held in late July, became the forum for heated debate. Its official transcript was never published, but the broad outlines of its proceedings leaked out.[37] On the basis of what has become known, the stereotyped division of the "softs" (or liberals), favoring the return of Gomulka, and the "hards," recommending Stalinism, does not appear justified. The picture was much more complex. Everyone involved realized that a crucial factor in the deliberations was Poland's relations with the USSR — that this was the source of the mass demand for democratization and change, as Polish independence euphemistically came to be known. But if Poland were to change its relationship with the USSR, what would happen to socialism in Poland, that is, what would happen to the Polish Communists?

The recommended solutions basically went along two lines, but both in effect skirted the problem of Polish-Soviet relations. The first, advocated by a wing which came to be known as the Stalinist or Natolin * faction, and after October 1956 labeled as "dogmatist," favored the following measures: (1) closest possible external identification with the USSR, a policy bound to intensify domestic tension; (2) restraints on the press to cut down the literary ferment; (3) no major change in agrarian policy and the class struggle; (4) limitation of the number of Jews in posts which are much in the public eye; (5) release of Cardinal Wyszynski; (6) 50 per cent wage increase; and (7) inclusion of Gomulka in the Politburo. It is apparent that the last four were demagogic devices designed to win popular support. In a way, the whole program was an effort to pursue some of the essentials of Stalinism but without Stalinist methods. A corollary of this was the advocacy of rejecting such well-known Stalinists as Berman. Gomulka's inclusion, particularly, would give the regime a much-needed symbol, thereby making up for the unpopularity of the first recommendation. At the same time, Gomulka would not be able to chart the regime's course, since he would be merely appended to the existing leadership and would be expected to disown his past nationalism.

The opposing line was taken by those who stressed that changes in Poland must continue in the direction of institutional reform, both political and economic, designed to liberalize the system, particularly in terms of personal freedom and legality. They may be described as "evolutionists" or, as some of them became known, "revisionists." This group rejected all of the recommendations cited above, either as being demagogic in character (this applied particularly to numbers four and six), or as being devices to avoid substantive change. Paradoxically, it seems that some members of this more liberal wing hesitated about Gomulka's restoration since they apparently feared that such restoration, combined with domestic reform, might strain Polish-Soviet relations too much. They accordingly went to some pains at the Seventh Plenum to disassociate themselves from Gomulka's alleged 1948–1949 nationalism.† At this stage, the group appeared to lack a crystallized program of action. Favoring change, its main source of cohesion was opposition to the Natolin program. Internally, the evolutionists were themselves split into at least two broad orientations. Some of them, particularly the former socialists and some of the intellectuals, saw in the movement for change the harbinger of a fun-

* Natolin is a small palace near Warsaw where the faction held its conclaves.
† This fear allowed the "dogmatists" to accuse their opponents, at the plenum which brought Gomulka to power, of anti-Gomulka attitudes and to demand that the record of the Seventh Plenum be published. Wiktor Klosiewicz, the Trade Union leader and a very effective demagogue, was particularly outspoken on this score.

damental step toward social democracy. Others, and this particularly applied to the *apparatchiki* in the Politburo, men like Zambrowski and Ochab (they came to be known as the Pulawska group, from the street where they held their meetings), recognized that a return to the past was out of the question but had no desire to yield the party's dictatorship. They acknowledged, however, that the Party would have to adopt some bold measures if its domination was to be perpetuated. Both groups agreed that, whatever the future course of the party might be, Polish-Soviet relations and Gomulka's role in the party were the top issues on the leadership's agenda.*

The Seventh Plenum, which Gomulka was allowed to attend, issued a resolution on July 28 which was liberal in its interpretation of Poznan, promised democratization which would limit both the administrative role of the party and the excessive bureaucratization of society, embodied provisions for an emergency program to improve the standard of living, and foresaw increased opportunities for artisans

---

* Gomulka, speaking to a national conference of party activists on November 4, 1956 (Radio Warsaw) after his return to power, confirmed that the divisions between the dogmatists and the evolutionists involved fundamentally the problem of relations with the USSR and that those favoring domestic reforms were not necessarily in favor of his restoration: "The political differences in the leadership of the Party, that is in the Politburo, during the period before the Eighth Plenum and in the Central Committee of the Party, can be reduced to two basic problems: (1) the conception of Poland's sovereignty; and (2) the conception of what should be included in what we call the democratization of our life within the framework of the socialist system.

"Some members of the Central Committee of the Party feared that settling our Party and state relations with the CPSU and the Soviet Union on the principles adopted by the Eighth Plenum would bring unfavorable consequences. While not questioning the need for carrying out certain changes, they were, however, in favor of preserving the previous state of affairs. *This was the main line of division in the leadership of the Party.*

"Differences in the understanding of the context of the democratization of our life were not clear. All the same, they did exist in the leadership of our Party. Irrespective of these basic political differences, there were other problems causing discord in the Party leadership. Among these was the problem of appointments to leading Party and state posts and the question of approaching this problem from the national point of view. Some comrades approached this problem in a very simplified way which could be taken for anti-Semitism.

"In addition to that, before the Eighth Plenum, *many comrades, irrespective of what views they held on problems discussed earlier, differed among themselves on the problem of my return to active Party life.* It was, in this case, a problem not only of my person but of the right evaluation of all phenomena which in the past had been described as right-wing, nationalist deviation from the Party line.

"We can say, comrades, that irrespective of the main line of differences within the Party, there existed in the Party leadership and the actif various other lines of division, which linked some men otherwise divided by the main line of differences." (Italics added.)

and small private-service industries. Gomulka's status was left un-clarified. Return to anything like the situation before Stalin's death was rejected, but the announced program hardly constituted a satis-factory response to the challenge of the situation.

Immediately afterwards, Ochab, accompanied by two members of the Natolin group, Zenon Nowak and Franciszek Mazur, flew to Yalta for consultations with Khrushchev. Ochab's position at this stage was ambiguous. Considered a "hard" Stalinist, Ochab apparently adopted a position at the Seventh Plenum which can best be described as middle-of-the-road: refusing to identify himself with the growing demands for a dramatic change and yet unwilling to back the Natolin-ites. His position was actually closest to that adopted a few days earlier in Hungary and apparently endorsed by Khrushchev. The rea-sons for it are unclear but it may be surmised that Ochab, recalling his 1949 attacks on Gomulka, may have particularly objected to Gomulka's inclusion in the Politburo and thus found himself siding with the evolutionists who feared the disruptive implications inherent in Gomulka as a symbol of national independence. In any case, the fact that the most openly pro-Soviet faction, which heeded Bulganin's warnings about the Polish press and the need for close unity,* was recommending Gomulka's inclusion in the Polish regime had far-reaching consequences. It seemed to convince the Soviet leaders that Gomulka's return to public life was not a challenge to their position in Poland and could even serve the Soviet interests. Viewed from that perspective it even fit into Khrushchev's categories. This was pre-sumably the message conveyed by Nowak and Mazur, and the result was that during the next crucial three months, the increasing likeli-hood of Gomulka's inclusion in the leadership did not provoke an immediate Soviet response.

The Revolutionary Dynamic

The Seventh Plenum merely established a certain pattern; it failed to resolve the problem of Gomulka. Division within the leadership, demoralization within the party, particularly within its youth organi-zation,† and gradual democratization of the system (effected at this

---

* Its public slogan, repeated at rallies, was designed to appeal to the antiintellec-tual and anti-Semitic tendencies among the masses: "two things are responsible for Poland's troubles," they would shout, "the press and the race" (which two words rhyme in Polish).

† A whole chapter could be devoted to the emergence of *Po Prostu* (Speaking Frankly), the journal which became the leading critic of the status quo, and to the disintegration of the party's youth organization. An amazing series of letters from

stage more by stealth than by design), all contributed to a growing
feeling that the Seventh Plenum had not solved the fundamental issues
but had merely postponed them. It became plain that the regime had
neither a defined sense of purpose nor the capacity to suppress the
emerging social diversity. On the other hand, those favoring more
profound changes realized that because of the ultimate Soviet backing
for the regime, such changes could not be effected without the regime.

Pressures accordingly mounted for reform and, thereby, implicitly
for a restatement of the regime's internal and external position. One
of the new party secretaries, Jerzy Morawski, raised the Leninist and
timely slogan, "more bread and more freedom." [38] A former socialist
who was active in the ruling UPWP after the absorption of the
socialists, Julian Hochfeld, while appealing for a reactivation of the
Sejm, also attacked the regime's policy of blaming individual secret
policemen for past bestialities while not recognizing that a more
"fundamental guilt" was involved. [39] (The Supreme Court actually
moved to review the sentences against five of them as being too leni-
ent.) [40] The workers, particularly those in the Zeran automobile
works near Warsaw,* established links with the metropolitan discussion clubs and raised the slogan of workers' autonomy, demanding
the institution of workers' councils. [41] In some places they were set up
by *fiat*. Even the issue of the USSR began to come out. One statement
called for more frank discussions of Soviet reality, asserting that true
friendship cannot be based on sugar-coated paeans, [42] while the youth
weekly *Po Prostu* published a sharp criticism of Soviet collectivization
policies, making it plain that they could not be applicable to Poland. [43]
One of the formerly most violent young Stalinists reminisced in print
about his stay in Moscow during the years 1952–1953, and characterized the period with the words "fascisization, demoralization,

---

disillusioned youth was published at the time in the various papers. After October
1956, some of the internal discussions, revealing the depth of the crisis within the
youth organization, were published in a small volume, *Co sie dzieje w ZMP?* (Warsaw, 1956).

* In a discussion forum held in 1957 to commemorate the October 1956 events,
L. Gozdzik, the young party secretary at Zeran, who had mobilized the workers in
favor of change, had this to say: "The Twentieth Congress came. A discussion began.
First there was panic in the ranks of the Party . . . we discussed all day and all
night . . . we began to reflect. We recalled the days of the October [Bolshevik]
Revolution. . . . We decided that it would not be bad if a Workers' Council was
set up in the factory to administer the enterprise." He added that after the Seventh
Plenum he and his colleagues visited Warsaw University and became convinced that
everyone wished a change. It was then a simple matter to establish contacts with
other plants around Warsaw and throughout Poland. *Nowa Kultura*, October 20,
1957.

careerism." [44] The Warsaw Board of the ZMP (the Polish Young Communist League, literally, the Association of Polish Youth) even made public its demand "for the public release of the contents of the talks initiated by the Party leadership with Gomulka after the Seventh Plenum of the Central Committee," [45] thereby confirming the rumored negotiations between the former leader and the present leadership. More and more, Gomulka, even though his current views were not known, was becoming the focal point of the aspirations both of the radical pro-Soviet faction and of the broad circles of intellectuals, youth, and workers backing the evolutionists. Under these circumstances, his attitude became crucial and both sides were soon conducting parallel negotiations with him.

It is still not clear what role was played in the negotiations by Ochab, the First Secretary. By the middle of September, after his return from a trip to Peiping, he proceeded to identify himself more actively with the evolutionists and, according to various Warsaw informants, his stand was taken to indicate tacit Chinese encouragement. It is conceivable that at this stage the Chinese favored a quiet redressing of the balance in relations among Communist states and might have encouraged the Poles in that direction. But even without such encouragement, Ochab might well have concluded that Polish Communism had reached a dead-end street and desperately needed a fresh start.

The turning point came early in October. In the first few days of the month, it became known that Gomulka's ideas on collectivization, on the interpretation of the 1949–1954 phase of the Polish regime, and on relations with the USSR diverged so sharply from those of the Natolin dogmatists that no arrangement was feasible. The evolutionists, in the meantime, now including both Cyrankiewicz and Ochab, became convinced that a sharp break with the past was imperative. Realizing that the basic issue on which all reforms would either fall or succeed was the problem of Poland's relations with the USSR, they concluded that only Gomulka, because of his symbolic status, could effectively reshape the external relations without undermining Polish Communism. They reached this conclusion in spite of the fact that, as late as September, some of them, particularly Ochab, still entertained major reservations about Gomulka's past and approved the 1949 condemnation. [46] The arrangement reached with Gomulka prompted the resignation on October 9 of Hilary Minc, the architect of the Stalinist economy in Poland, marking the departure of the last prominent Stalinist. The only outstanding questions left concerned the contents of the new program and the composition of the new Politburo.

These final questions were resolved only as late as the weekend of October 13–15. On Saturday, Gomulka attended a regular Politburo meeting and, on Monday, agreement on the composition of the new Politburo was reached, according to some reports, in a friendly atmosphere, with Marshal Rokossovsky, slated for removal, even proposing a toast. In the course of the weekend, however, some members of the Natolin group apparently became concerned with the direction of the proposed policy and personnel changes and, outnumbered in the Politburo, turned to Moscow with urgent warnings.[47] In their dispatches they seized on the proposed removal of Rokossovsky as symbolic of the dangerously anti-Soviet character of the developing situation. Clearly in response to their pleas, the Soviet ambassador issued on October 17 a formal invitation to the Poles to visit Moscow for consultations.

However, even at this late juncture, the situation hardly seemed to warrant forceful intervention. The Soviet leaders expected that political pressure would suffice to contain any negative manifestations and that an accommodation could be arranged. The July 1956 situation in Budapest (see Chapter 10), which was resolved by political pressure, still seemed a good guide. But in Poland the situation had suddenly reached a point of no return. The lengthy evolution had run its course and the breaking point was at hand. The Natolinites became convinced that unless they acted quickly they would be completely cut off from power. They accordingly moved forward to do what Rakosi had successfully done in 1955: to stage a coup in the name of greater loyalty to the USSR. They probably reasoned that in the final analysis Moscow would back them, or, at least, would certainly welcome their leadership once they had been successful. They counted on the presence of Soviet troops in Poland to inhibit resistance, while Rokossovsky's control of the Polish Army would assure them the necessary ingredient of power. Furthermore, the provincial party apparatus was firmly in their hands. Unlike Rakosi, however, they no longer controlled the Politburo or the Central Committee; the international situation in the Soviet camp was distinctly unfavorable to them; and, domestically, the masses were already actively ranged against them. Only speed, as well as some intimidation via Moscow, would give them the necessary margin for success.

The Politburo, sensing the implication of the invitation to Moscow, begged off by pleading that the beginning of the scheduled Central Committee plenum, called to implement the recently concluded agreement with Gomulka, precluded their departure. The pro-Soviet faction then decided to move. On the night of October 18, the eve of the historic Eighth Plenum, the Zeran factory workers, who had been mobilized to back the projected changes,[48] intercepted a list of seven hundred people whom the Natolinites wished to arrest. According to the only official information on these events to have come out of Poland, a radio report of the account given the Gdansk party activists by its provincial leaders:

With the speed of lightning all comrades were warned and not one of them stayed at home. They also prepared pamphlets urging the Army to cooperate, and so forth. These events were followed by the dramatic days of the Eighth Plenum. The security office of Warsaw supported as one man the side of progress. (Applause.) The Internal Security Corps also took the side of progress. (Applause.) In these dramatic days, the Internal Security Corps not only protected the Central Committee but it also occupied the premises of the Polish radio and many other important buildings. Suspicious troop movements started. And again the Zeran workers, who have many cars at their disposal, distributed comrades practically throughout Poland so that our progressive forces in the Central Committee knew all about these troop movements.

The attitude the troops adopted you all know. When orders were issued to staff and political officers, they answered simply that these orders would be ignored. They said that they were with the people and that they would defend the working class.[49]

The domestic resources of the Natolinites thus proved inadequate to the task.[50] What remained to be tested was the degree of Soviet involvement and the capacity of the Poles to resist it.

The Problematics of Intervention

On October 19 a powerful Soviet delegation, including Khrushchev, Kaganovich, Mikoyan, and Molotov, arrived uninvited in Warsaw, determined to hold the consultations which the Poles had two days earlier declined. Their decision to come was a last-minute one and was not cleared with the Poles beforehand.[51] Simultaneously, according to a member of the Polish Central Committee, Soviet armored troops began to move from their bases near Wroclaw in the direction of Warsaw.[52] The Central Committee's deliberations were suspended, despite some opposition from its more hotheaded members, to permit the Polish leaders to consult with their unexpected visitors. The adjournment was voted following the rapid cooptation to Central

Committee membership of Gomulka and three of his associates (Spychalski, Loga-Sowinski, and Kliszko). In addition, Gomulka, whose candidacy for the post of First Secretary was announced by Ochab himself, was included in the Politburo delegation to negotiate with the Russians.

The course of these negotiations was not made public, although anecdotes as to what actually transpired are plentiful.[53] But even judging from the sparse comments made by the Polish participants, it is clear that at the time the Soviet leaders were principally concerned not with Gomulka's domestic program as such but with its consequences for Polish-Soviet relations. This point is important in considering subsequent relations between Gomulka and Khrushchev because, in effect, the Soviets were *a priori* conceding the Poles' right to build socialism in their own way. This concession, however, came with the proviso that it should not conflict with the broader unity of the Communist camp. Admittedly, such a reservation opened the way to varying interpretations as to what does and does not conflict with such unity and hence, depending on the time and circumstance, might still permit Soviet interference in domestic Polish policies.

The task of the Poles was accordingly twofold: to convince the Russians that domestic concessions planned by the Eighth Plenum were designed to strengthen the construction of socialism in Poland, and that the envisaged policy and personnel changes were meant to improve Polish-Soviet relations. From the Polish point of view, much could be done on this score by the Soviets themselves in view of past "aberrations" imposed by Stalin. That the conversations were tense and sharp was openly admitted by the Polish participants. The atmosphere in which they were conducted was described to the Central Committee by Ochab, during an intermission in the talks on October 19, as "matter of fact." [54] Reporting to the plenum on October 21, after the departure of the Soviet delegation in the early hours of October 20, Ochab referred to the conversations as "sincere, difficult and bitter." [55] He mentioned in passing that never before in his life did he have so much "bitterness" to swallow as in recent days and that "unjustified, unheard-of accusations" were leveled against him by "our Soviet friends." [56] No doubt, the Soviets felt that Ochab's position represented a treasonable departure from what had been assumed to have been an ultraloyal standing. His own justification, however, was both audacious and self-critical. Describing post-Stalin domestic policies of the Soviet leadership merely as "probably correct," he categorically rejected them as "certainly . . . not fit to our situation." [57] He asserted that in Poland "the rejection of the past" can and must move forward more rapidly than in the USSR, and he admitted his and the Politburo's culpability in not shaking off sufficiently soon the "traditionally superficial methods" of analyzing events, particularly when dealing with such phenomena as the Poznan outbreak.

His remarks, as well as those of Aleksander Zawadzki, another Politburo member, formerly considered a Stalinist, who sided at this juncture with the anti-Natolinites,[58] shed considerable light on the specific issues raised by the Soviet delegation. Given Ochab's and Zawadzki's Stalinist backgrounds, their versions are all the more noteworthy. Zawadzki, speaking on the morning of October 20,[59] a mere few hours after the 6 A.M. departure of the Soviet leaders, made the following references: (1) the motive of the trip was "the deep anxiety of the Presidium of the CC, CPSU, regarding the development of the situation in Poland"; (2) the Soviet leaders expressed concern with anti-Soviet propaganda in Poland, noting that even in bourgeois Finland such articles could not appear, and lack of adequate party response to it; * (3) the Soviet leaders charged the Poles with not giving them authoritative information on the Polish domestic situation, such as, for instance, the planned personnel changes in the Politburo, and in general with not maintaining close contacts; (4) the tense international situation made the Soviet leaders even more apprehensive about the implications of the above accusations. Zawadzki added that the conduct of the discussions was marked by not infrequent manifestations of "temperament" from both sides.

Still, the situation was at least partially resolved. As Zawadzki stated it, "during our talks with the delegation of the Central Committee of the CPSU . . . we explained to our Soviet colleagues that their anxiety as to the path People's Poland would take were unfounded." [60] On October 20th, the Soviet troop movements within Poland generally ceased, and after the departure of the Soviet guests a communiqué was issued to the effect that further talks would soon be held in Moscow. However, the usual statement about "complete agreement" was not included in the brief announcement. Following the resumption of the Central Committee session, Gomulka delivered a lengthy programmatic statement — his domestic policies are treated in Chapter 14 [61] — and on the next day, October 21, the Politburo

* Ochab, however, in expressing regret, took the opportunity to return the charge, noting that a *Pravda* report on "Anti-Socialist Pronouncements in the Polish Press," published a day earlier and which charged the Polish press with anti-Marxist slanders aimed at undermining socialism, was "unwise, harmful . . . drawing perverted, slanted conclusions." *Nowe Drogi*, p. 114.

elections were held. At this point, however, one of the men un-
reconeiled to the changes, B. Ruminski, possibly acting in the hope
that a sharp posing of the issue of Polish-Soviet relations would bring
about a greater measure of Soviet interference, suddenly nominated
Rokossovsky, not slated for renomination to the Politburo. (That he
would not be nominated had been clearly conveyed to the Soviet
delegation.) The justification for his move was plainly stated: "It is
most important how the masses will interpret the meaning of comrade
Rokossovsky's non-election. In the prevailing atmosphere the masses
will understand that this has an anti-Soviet accent." [62] His arguments
were not openly challenged,* and the Central Committee proceded
to a vote, with the Soviet Marshal included as a candidate. The official
slate of nine candidates obtained a sizable majority (in a secret ballot):
it ranged from 75 out of 75 for Ochab, 74 out of 75 for Gomulka,
down to 56 for Zambrowski (bitterly opposed by the unreconcilables
as a last-minute waverer). Rokossovsky, with only 23 votes, failed
to be elected. Gomulka was then elected First Secretary by a show
of hands, with none voting against him.

No conclusive judgment can be made concerning the reasons why
the Soviets allowed Gomulka to prevail. However, a recapitulation of
the inferences which can be drawn from the above material might
suggest some explanations for the Soviet behavior. It would appear,
first of all, that the Soviet leadership did not go to Warsaw with either
a clear-cut understanding of the situation or a formulated program
to be imposed on the Poles, but rather with a set of specific grievances.
They did not have *a priori* objections to the inclusion of Gomulka
in the new leadership — something which even the neo-Stalinists †

* Except for one illuminating incident. Ruminski asserted that this was a form
of pressure against the USSR and that this was being frankly stated in the back rooms
and corridors. The minutes then show shouts of "who said it, who?" Ruminski answered the interpellator as follows: ". . . comrade Starewicz, now that you are pressing me, I will state that it was you who said so. I spoke with you, I think, a day
after the Seventh Plenum. You told me that Poland cannot be independent because
Soviet comrades do not allow it and interfere in everything. You told me also that
comrade Khrushchev raised the matter of comrade Zambrowski at the Sixth Plenum
and raised the Jewish problem. . . . Comrade Starewicz, do not provoke me as to
who said so because these are your views." He then argued that if Rokossovsky must
go, the people must be prepared gradually for it and that his removal now would be
construed as a manifestation (*Nowe Drogi*, no. 10, 1956, pp. 147–148). Ruminski's
reference to Khrushchev pertains to the selection of Bierut's successor in March 1956
and indirectly confirms the point made earlier.

† There is a continuing problem of labels in all of this. This group might simply
be called Natolin, which, however, is a geographical and not a political or ideological
term. In some ways they can be called Stalinist or neo-Stalinist, particularly as far
as their domestic program was concerned. On the Rokossovsky issue they might be

had advocated — but became disturbed by the implications of Rokos-sovsky's expected removal, probably, in part, under the influence of interpretations suggested by the neo-Stalinists. In the course of con-versations they acquiesced to his removal from the Politburo al-though he was to remain head of the army. During the often heated discussions the Soviet delegation was acquainted with the general out-lines of Gomulka's domestic program, but they apparently refrained from either endorsing or rejecting it.

Thus, matters were left open until further negotiations. Pre-sumably, the Soviets felt that the next few days would test Gomulka's ability to take hold of the situation and that their passive posture did not involve an irrevocable commitment. Certainly, the official com-muniqué had a most tentative character. Finally, it seems that the Soviet leaders conceded that Polish-Soviet relations needed repairs on both sides: the Poles must restrain certain anti-Soviet tendencies, while the Soviets expressed willingness to undo some of the concrete Stalinist abuses of Polish national interest.

But would it not have been better for the USSR to intervene by force of arms? A decision to that effect could not have been made without immediate provocation or without the utmost certainty that it was necessary. Among the factors to be considered there was the danger of undermining by precipitate action the tenuous links with Tito, who only recently had consented to help stabilize the critical Hungarian situation, and there was also the "friendly advice" of the Chinese, urging restraint.* Direct action might have also given imme-diate comfort to those elements in the USSR opposing the de-Stalini-zation campaign. Thus an important domestic consideration was in-volved in Soviet thinking. With the situation in Warsaw unclear and with the Poles postponing the Soviet invitation for them to visit Mos-cow, the Soviet leaders had decided to fly to Warsaw. A decision to

called more pro-Soviet, although it should not be inferred that the others were anti-Soviet. Rather, a different conception of what constitutes "friendly" relations was in-volved here, much as it was also in Moscow. Hereafter, since the Eighth Plenum marks a turning point, if it becomes necessary to use a collective term for the former group, I shall use either neo-Stalinist or dogmatists (the latter in keeping with the domestic Polish usage).

* After two visits to Warsaw in 1957 and 1958 and conversations with many high-placed Polish Communists, this writer is convinced that sometime between Oc-tober 20 (the date of the Soviet delegation's departure from Warsaw) and October 22 (on the evening of which Khrushchev telephoned Gomulka, see below), the Chinese had actually approached Moscow urging patience. One informant even claims to have seen "documentary" proof. There seems to be little doubt that the critical period was after Khrushchev's return to Moscow and before the outbreak of the Hungarian events.

intervene with arms could hardly have been implemented while the Soviet delegation was in the restless Polish capital. Apparently, it was seriously contemplated, since Soviet troop movements began concurrently with the visit. But their stay in Warsaw revealed to them that the Polish leadership was clearly in control of the situation; that it was united in its commitment to Marxism-Leninism and to the desirability of close relations with the USSR, although on a less subordinate basis (with such reputed Stalinists as Ochab, Zawadzki, and Zambrowski backing Gomulka); that the opposing faction was weak; and, finally, that the Polish Army was restive and, in a critical situation, would not obey Rokossovsky.

This was an unprecedented situation for the Soviet leaders. The closest analogy was Yugoslavia in 1948. Yet only a year earlier the Soviet leaders, after much debate, had reached the conclusion that the policy adopted in 1948–1949 against Yugoslavia had been un-Marxist in its impatience, in its unwillingness to prevail upon the Yugoslavs to mend their ways, and in the "subjective" anger which had pushed the situation to a breaking point. Considerations such as these must have been uppermost in the minds of the Soviet leaders as they flew back to Moscow, uncertain of the real meaning of the Polish situation and faced with facts which did not make for simple solutions.* Intervention might have been called for to forestall an imminent catastrophe or if very favorable circumstances made it a relatively simple matter to execute. In the former case, ideology provided a further inducement: counterrevolution must be prevented. In the latter, a facile maximization of Soviet power is always justified. Neither of these two conditions existed, and the absence of a positive set of demands to be presented as an ultimatum to the Poles strongly suggests that an intervention would have had an essentially negative function. This writer is accordingly skeptical of those who suggest that some dramatic Chinese communiqué or the Polish threat to fight was central in staving off the Soviet Army. Rather, it was the factors enumerated

---

* It is noteworthy that among the various accusations hurled by Khrushchev against Molotov after 1957 (including the charge that he opposed Khrushchev's Yugoslav policy), an accusation of having favored active intervention against Poland was not included. Such an accusation, from the perspective of Khrushchev's and Gomulka's friendly relations in 1957 or 1958, would have been quite effective. Its absence suggests that no major Soviet leader favored such a step, at least not immediately. (According to some indications, Marshal Zhukov might have been more sympathetic to such a course; after his demotion, Khrushchev accused him of "adventurism" in foreign policy). And it is more than likely that Khrushchev's personal position demanded that he press for restraint so that a subsequent improvement in Polish-Soviet relations might vindicate his anti-Stalinist campaign.

above which translated the Soviet indecision and absence of program into a policy of wait-and-see.

It was upon Gomulka's triumph that the Polish situation took on a revolutionary flavor. Even as Khrushchev was telephoning Gomulka from Moscow on the night of October 22 to assure him that the Soviet leadership accepted Gomulka's domestic line and to promise him that all Soviet troops would return to their bases, anti-Soviet demonstrations were spreading throughout Poland. Most slogans called for Rokossovsky's complete removal, and there were occasional attacks on Polish-Soviet Friendship Society offices. The demonstrations became particularly intense as events in Hungary developed into a patriotic war against the Soviet Union, and the Poles, traditionally friendly to the Hungarians, openly manifested their sympathy. The Polish Central Committee, in an effort to stabilize the Hungarian situation before it resulted in the complete collapse of the People's Democracy,* publicly endorsed Nagy's government.[63] At the same time, however, the Soviet moves to suppress the Hungarians provided Gomulka with the necessary weapon which could be used to contain his inflammable countrymen. Hungary had thus a triple effect; it created a situation in Poland which could justify Soviet intervention; it gave Gomulka a basis for an appeal for calm and order which the bloodletting in Budapest made very meaningful to all; and, by keeping the USSR preoccupied, it prevented any immediate Soviet measures against Poland. By satisfying the popular demand for the removal of Rokossovsky (he was first given a leave of absence and, on November 13, was altogether dismissed and sent back to the USSR), an issue of rather symbolic significance, and by continuously pointing to the Hungarian tragedy, Gomulka thus succeeded in riding out the most immediate crisis.

In short, the October revolution triumphed because of five interacting conditions: (1) it had been preceded by a gradual and continuing dissolution of Stalinism in Poland in response to the anti-Communist sentiment of the vast majority of the people; (2) power in Poland was retained by the party, which initiated and executed the transfer of authority to Gomulka; (3) Gomulka's past, and the events connected with the Soviet arrival in Warsaw, invested the transfer of authority with a dramatic element of Polish national self-assertion

* According to one unconfirmed report, the Polish leadership dispatched two emissaries to Budapest, A. Starewicz (a Gomulka Man) and M. Naszkowski (a follower of the Ochab-Zambrowski *apparatchiki*), to confer with Nagy. *Imre Nagy: Un Communisme qui n'oublie pas L'Homme* (Paris, 1957), pp. 42–43.

which a mere change in party program would have lacked; (4) Gomulka's program was essentially one of domestic reform without direct challenge to areas of greatest Soviet sensitivity — membership in the bloc and the role of the party; and (5) the pattern of Polish events was such that the Soviet leadership, seeing some analogies to the Yugoslav 1948 break, was tempted to take the path of least resistance and reserve the always risky policy of armed force as a last alternative. Caution on both sides prevented an open conflict.

Conclusion: Domesticism and National Communism

Ideological and institutional diversity thus came to characterize the once monolithic Soviet bloc. Poland joined Yugoslavia in following its own distinct domestic policies. The other People's Democracies practiced and voiced a line essentially Stalinist although tempered by the intervening period of the New Course. The USSR's position toward Hungary clearly evidenced a willingness to employ force when the ideologically viewed political situation created a revolutionary stage. By the same token, the Polish situation warranted manipulation and concessions, despite the reactions of the other Communist leaderships. On November 18, the Soviet leadership warmly received Gomulka in Moscow and signed an agreement with the Poles regularizing the new relationship of "mutual respect, noninterference and sovereignty." Despite Polish unwillingness to endorse Soviet policy in Hungary (and Gomulka could claim that to do so would weaken his party's rule in Poland), Poland was compensated for past economic iniquities by the cancelation of Polish debts to the USSR to the amount of 2.4 billion rubles. A later military convention, while allowing the USSR to retain its troops on Polish soil as part of the Warsaw Pact, at least gave the Poles formal control over their disposition and movement.[64] The Soviet response was clearly one of adjustment.

Soviet behavior, in retrospect, appears to have been justified. A sharp reaction against Gomulka, on the pattern apparently favored by some of the other parties (particularly the East German and the Czech), would have had the effect of forcing him to rally the people around a national standard and to join the ranks of national Communism. There is little doubt that as a last resort Gomulka would have been prepared to do so — in the name of saving Communism in Poland — and that domestic pressures were already pushing him in such a direction. The Soviet leadership, once it had gambled on waiting, certainly must have wished to avoid a situation which would leave the

Polish party no alternative. Following his agreement with Khru-shchev, Gomulka publicly admitted that he had been "nervous" that the Soviet leaders would not "evaluate correctly" the Polish situation and that he was relieved to see that they had.[65]

Gomulka, from the very instant of his assumption of power, coupled all references to independence with assurances of Polish friendship for, and need of, the Soviet Union. In his speeches he never deviated from the basic dichotomic image of world affairs, even if initially toning down the vigor of his attacks on "Western imperial-ism." In domestic matters his references to internal reform and de-Stalinization were qualified by attacks on those who expected that his policy would lead to a "second-stage": to the abandonment of Com-munism. Thus, from the very beginning, the national Communism of Poland, as it was often called by observers, was restricted by Gomulka to domestic affairs, to an insistence on internal autonomy, without translating it into an external ideological challenge or a fundamental revision of Poland's place in the world. The ideological problems that did develop were in part a result of the revolutionary situation, and in part stimulated by the high degree of sensitivity evidenced by the more rigid, essentially Stalinist, regimes surrounding Poland. Go-mulka's attitude still indicated that he had not crossed the Rubicon even if some of his followers were in the process of wading across. Gomulka was neither a Nagy nor a Tito.*

Unlike Tito, Gomulka did not have the backing of a cohesive political movement capable of independently constructing Commu-nism in Poland. In late 1956, the United Polish Workers' Party was at its low point in morale, with the rank and file identifying itself with the broad aims of Gomulka but not clearly differentiating between nationalist reactions against the past and the ideological precepts for the future. The lower-ranking party *apparatchiki* were especially fearful that Gomulka's regime would mean the end of their status and role in society. A complete break with Moscow, of his or Moscow's making, would have either placed Gomulka at the mercy of nationalist and revisionist elements, as Nagy was, or would have forced him into a Kadar-like position. A suspended Soviet threat in the background was thus a strange source of stability, beneficial not only to Soviet interests but also to Gomulka's survival. Moscow's problem was how to maintain the intricate balance of threat and adjustment without

* More will be said in Chapter 14 about Gomulka's ideological views and his re-lationship to the October events, particularly as relevant to domestic development in Poland.

exaggerating the element of threat, which might intensify the tensions, and without diminishing it prematurely, which might encourage those elements elsewhere anxious to imitate Gomulka. The pendulum movement between these two extremes accounted for much of the uncertainty evident late in 1956. It obscured the fact that most anti-Communist Poles were willing to concede that close alliance with the USSR was imperative for Poland's retention of the Oder-Neisse frontier. And no Communist regime in Poland, concerned as it had to be with economic planning, could overlook the degree of Polish economic dependence on the USSR.*

Gomulka's regime, therefore, oscillated from the very start between a very mild form of national Communism and the more restricted orientation of domesticism. With neither the capacity nor the will to become a full-blown national Communist regime, Gomulka increasingly reverted to the earlier pattern of domesticism (see Chapter 3) in which the policy outlook of his regime was characterized by an *inward perspective*, but without making a deliberate choice between the international and national interests. The clash between the two, so characteristic of national Communism in its Titoist and Nagy variety, gave way to a continuing effort to establish some sort of harmony between the demands of Communism as an international revolutionary movement and Communism as a constructive national undertaking. Domesticism was thus a much more complex operation, lacking the clear and absolute criteria inherent in national Communism. For this reason the position of Poland after 1956 required a difficult process of adjustment, though from the start there was no explicit external ideological and political Polish challenge, thereby differentiating Poland from Yugoslavia.

Yet the Polish events had a broader significance. The Soviet decision to tolerate Gomulka, and the even friendly relations eventually established between Moscow and Warsaw, meant that the USSR was gradually, hesitatingly, abandoning its own national Communism and moving toward a greater realization that its leadership in the camp required a more equitable adjustment between Soviet interests and those of the other members. This shift, not without its reversals and cer-

* For detailed data, see *Trybuna Ludu*, May 21, 1956. The Soviet Union imported, in 1955, 95.6 per cent of Polish rolling-stock exports, 63.3 per cent of Polish machinery exports, 33.7 per cent of coal exports, and so on. On the other hand, 34.6 per cent of Polish grain imports came from the USSR, 73.8 per cent of unprocessed cotton, 74.2 per cent of oil, 68 per cent of iron ore, and so on. Given the relative strength of the two economies, there was no question as to which was the more dependent. (For 1957–1958 economic relations, see Chapter 12.)

tainly not made willingly, meant a return to some of the limited diversity which characterized the bloc before 1947. At that time, the diversity was one dictated by the weakness of the Communist regimes and by the uncertainties of the postwar situation. By 1956–1957, however, the new diversity was primarily a function of the diverging national interests of the various Communist regimes once the initial totalitarian revolution, common to all of them, had run its course. A recognition of this state of affairs necessarily dictated a more flexible approach than the old Stalinist formula that what is good for the USSR has to be good for all the members of the Communist camp.

Soviet interests were bound to remain of primary importance in the scale of decision making. Nonetheless, as long as they were not directly affected, some domestic diversity among the satellites could be accepted and not considered as proof per se of treasonable deviation. Even in Hungary things did not return to the former Stalinist pattern after November 1956, and the Kadar regime pursued a socioeconomic policy more liberal than that in Czechoslovakia or Bulgaria. Relations among the Communist states thus increasingly took on these features: the triumph of domesticism operating both in the name of proletarian internationalism (as in the case of regimes still essentially Stalinist) and local considerations (Poland and Hungary); the absence of common ideological norms for these relations; the decline of the active ingredient of Soviet power, except in emergency situations; a greater Soviet preoccupation with its domestic problems related to the Stalinist succession crisis; a growing reliance on top-level bilateral consultations of the various leaderships with Moscow; the increasing stature of China and Yugoslavia, and to a lesser extent Poland, as active agents within relations between Communist states.

In addition to these inherent factors of growth, this new situation was also the culmination of certain errors of analysis in Soviet policy, induced by Soviet ideological perspectives. These errors were essentially fourfold: (1) The underestimation of Tito's ambitions, affecting his attitude toward the USSR and the other states. (2) The overestimation of the influence of socioeconomic changes (such as the creation of "the foundation for the construction of socialism") on the political stability of the East European regimes and, as a result, the underestimation of the extent of alienation and hostility produced by this process, particularly in Hungary and Poland. (3) The failure to comprehend the inherent influence of a mass following on the top leadership, which in the East European circumstances took the form of pressure on the leaders to make domestic conditions paramount in the drafting of further programs. (4) The excessive application of purely Soviet standards in framing those aspects of Soviet policy which would directly affect Communist regimes elsewhere. The most glaring example of this was the attack on Stalinism which, in the Soviet Union, had largely a *shock* effect without undermining the firmly implanted institutions of the system. In the bloc, however, it had a *disintegrative* impact on Stalinist institutions just in the process of construction.[66] Connected with this lack of differentiation was the underestimation of the desirability of external tension for maintaining internal cohesion in the new Communist regimes. The impact of the Geneva conference had little political significance in the CPSU, but in the People's Democracies it opened all sorts of avenues to doubts, to a questioning of the class struggle and even of the role of the USSR — all with fateful political consequences.

Khrushchev, however, in countering the above criticisms of Soviet policy, could at the same time point to certain hopeful signs which the crisis had revealed "dialectically." First of all, the majority of the regimes had successfully adjusted to the new situation, even as the most negative features of Stalinism were being dismantled, while the most dangerous trends in Poland and Hungary had been contained. Inherent in Gomulka's return to power was the likelihood that a more popularly endorsed Communist regime would ensue, even if some of its domestic policies were not to be condoned. Finally, Tito's ambivalence toward Hungary weakened appreciably the ideological impact of the Yugoslav position. In brief, the total picture was more hopeful if one considered the longer-range trends and not merely the crises of the recent past.

To the Soviet leaders of the Communist camp, the immediate problem for the future was how to prevent the new ideological and institutional diversity from exploding into irreconcilable splits. Could this be avoided without strictly limiting the independence of the new Polish regime or abandoning the leadership position of the USSR? Admittedly, the preceding two or three years had shown that the existing formulations and the reliance on past experience were adequate in coping with a challenge such as presented by Hungary but were not sufficiently elastic and perceptive to prevent the dilemma posed by Poland. The Soviet leaders discovered that their doctrine was rich in guidelines for coping with enemies but that it offered little for resolving conflicts and organizing relations among Communist states. Mere similarity of institutions and socioeconomic structures was not enough to guarantee unity. This was a lesson to be pondered by the Soviet leaders, for it revealed a dangerous weakness in a system of ideology and power which, by stressing dichotomic relationships and dialectical conflicts, showed itself too rigid to respond to important changes effected by evolutionary processes. But there could no longer be any question of a return to Stalinism. The Soviet leaders, including even Molotov, had too good a Marxist sense of change seriously to contemplate a return to a system so closely associated with a specific historical phase and a specific individual. The task after 1956 was to establish some commonly held ideological criteria and to forge new bonds of unity to prevent the diversity from becoming political disunity.

THE FOURTH PHASE
1957-1959

THE COMMUNIST "COMMONWEALTH" — INSTITUTIONAL DIVERSITY AND IDEOLOGICAL UNIFORMITY

What do we want? We want unity, closed ranks, and rallied forces. We acknowledge different paths, comrades. But among the different paths, there is one general path, and others are, as you know, like a big river with tributaries. In the same way there are specific peculiarities, but there is only one path, the Marxist-Leninist path. This is the path on which the task of the construction of Communist society must be tackled. — Nikita Khrushchev, Prague, July 11, 1957

CHAPTER 12

The Maoist Reconstruction of the Center

> The experience of the USSR and other socialist countries has fully confirmed the correctness of the tenet of Marxist-Leninist theory that the processes of the socialist revolution and the building of socialism are governed by a number of basic laws applicable in all countries embarking on a socialist path. These laws are manifested everywhere alongside a great variety of historically formed national features and traditions which should be taken into account without fail. — Declaration of the ruling Communist parties, Moscow, November 1957

THE uncertainties produced in the Communist camp by Khrushchev's policy of undercutting the Stalinist myth were only partially dispelled by the Soviet readiness to suppress the Hungarian uprising. The use of force established the outer limits of tolerable diversity. Yet the Soviet willingness to gamble on Gomulka, as well as the continuing endorsement of Yugoslavia as a socialist state, clearly left some key questions unanswered. At what point do gradual quantitative changes become qualitative ones? At what point does a socialist state cease being one under the influence of excessive diversity in ideology and practice? Where is the borderline between the legitimate domestic concerns of a Communist leadership and its higher allegiance to the general interests of the Communist camp? These questions had been answered simply and directly by the Stalinist formula which maintained that only one standard was valid: Soviet experience as the yardstick for policy and as the source of theoretical evaluation.

The Inter-Communist Dialogue

The doubts and the disagreements stimulated by the Twentieth Congress and Khrushchev's Yugoslav policy came to light in the aftermath of the Warsaw and Budapest crises. There was new ideological conflict and definite political diversity. But since none of the states was yet willing to dissociate itself from socialism, the ideological conflict became a method for expressing existing political diversity while maintaining the outlines of unity.

After the Polish and Hungarian events, the following issues seemed to need the most clarification: the definition of socialism and the number of roads leading to it; Stalin, Stalinism, and the Soviet system; the historical meaning of the Hungarian revolution and of the Polish October; the dictatorship of the proletariat and the problem of class struggle; proletarian internationalism or bilateralism; Leninism and revisionism; the Communist camp and the principle of Soviet leadership. These were only some of the major items, but each one touched almost every aspect of the dogma.

The greatest outburst came from Poland. The October assertion of internal autonomy meant that political power, weak and dependent on popular support, had to be more responsive to local currents of thought, even if attempting to contain them. As a result, much of this debate was transferred into the political arena, thereby also becoming, despite Gomulka's efforts to concentrate only on domestic issues, a concern of the other Communist countries. In a sense, the opening shot was fired on October 20 by Gomulka himself, in his report to the Eighth Plenum of the United Polish Workers' Party. Addressing himself to the question of the Polish way to socialism,* Gomulka noted that:

This theory was created by the first classics of Marxism. They never imagined their theory to be complete. . . . What is immutable in socialism can be reduced to the abolition of the exploitation of man by man. The roads of achieving this goal can be and are different. They are determined by various circumstances of time and place. The model of socialism can also vary. It can be such as that created in the Soviet Union; it can be shaped in a manner as we see it in Yugoslavia; it can be different still.[1]

But what of the Stalinist phase which had insisted on uniformity? Did it result solely from a degeneration in the leader's personality, or was it something more basic and related to the Soviet system? The latter proposition was advanced earlier by Togliatti but timidly withdrawn after the Soviet reply of June 30, 1956, which forcefully declared:

Our enemies assert that the personality cult of Stalin was not engendered by definite historical conditions which have already passed but by the

---

* One of the secretaries of the Polish Workers' Party, Wladyslaw Matwin, addressing the trade union plenum a month later, defined socialism as follows: "We still do not quite know what this new socialism will be like. We only know fairly well what it cannot be like, what it ought not to be like; this we know from our own experience. We must do a great deal of work together in order to evolve a model, to lay its foundations, to make it — as a comrade of the Cegielski works said last week — into a kind of socialism one likes." Radio Warsaw, November 18, 1956.

Soviet system itself, by what they consider its lack of democracy, and so on. Such slanderous assertions are refuted by the entire history of the development of the Soviet state.[2]

Gomulka seems to have taken an intermediary position, but his remarks have a dangerous ambivalence to them:

The cult of personality cannot be confined solely to the person of Stalin. The cult of personality is a certain system which prevailed in the Soviet Union and which was grafted to probably all communist parties, as well as to a number of countries of the socialist camp, including Poland.[3]

The Polish position also deviated on the Hungarian issue. The Central Committee of the party characterized as "tragic" the Hungarian request for the first Soviet intervention and went on to add:

We are of the opinion that the problem of the defense and maintenance of the people's power and of the gains of socialism in Hungary can be solved by the inner forces of the Hungarian people, headed by the working class, and not by intervention from without.[4]

Even after the second Soviet attack had crushed the uprising and the USSR had explicitly assumed responsibility for what had transpired, the Poles refused to condemn the uprising as a counterrevolution, refrained from supporting the USSR in the UN, and in the November 18 agreement with the USSR limited themselves to endorsing the new Hungarian regime's efforts "toward the development of socialist democracy and the consolidation of fraternal cooperation with other socialist countries on the basis of *full equality* and regard for *state sovereignty*." [5] The last two points thus again re-emphasized the Polish position that relations among the countries of the Soviet bloc have to be based on these principles. The Polish press, for a time free of censorship, went much further in expressing the feeling that what happened in Hungary was a genuine revolution produced by Rakosi's and Gero's crimes. *Nowa Kultura* and *Po Prostu* ran a series of articles, describing with approval the executions of former AVH members, and even making somewhat unfriendly references to "soldiers with red stars on their helmets," who, according to the correspondents, seemed embarrassed and uncomfortable in their role, surrounded by the seething hatred of the Hungarians.[6]

The Polish position also veered from the established views on the nature of the dictatorship of the proletariat and of proletarian internationalism. The former was hardly mentioned at all, and the process of democratization, referred to so frequently by Polish speakers and writers, was interpreted to mean the broad participation of society

and not just the proletariat in the process of building Polish socialism. This emphasis on the Polish aspect meant that the international
character of the Communist movement would have to be reviewed
critically, since in the past it had been subverted by excessive stress on
Soviet interests. The Poles accordingly displayed considerable sensitivity to the developing Soviet-Yugoslav debate, prompted by mutual
disenchantment and sparked by Tito's Pula speech (see Chapter 10,
section on "Tito's Dilemma"). The weekly of the Polish party described Tito's statement as containing an essentially "correct" analysis
of the relations in the Communist camp,[7] while the Soviet reaction to
it, reflecting a "zigzagging lack of consistency" in the Soviet struggle
against Stalinism, was said to have been caused by the CPSU's historical association with the emergence of Stalinism.[8] More concretely,
references to proletarian internationalism, which to Moscow meant
the principle of unity over any national interest, were coupled with
insistence on full sovereignty and with a marked preference for bilateral party dealings. Thus, paradoxically, in order to avoid being
isolated among more rigidly inclined party leaderships, the Poles were
rejecting multilateral party contacts in favor of directly bilateral
party negotiations, a method previously used by Stalin to maintain his
hegemony.

A more theoretical statement on the problem of relations among
Communist states appeared at this time in the theoretical journal of
the Polish Central Committee. In an article entitled "Crisis of Internationalism?" the issue was stated quite bluntly: in the past the meaning of internationalism had been distorted by the rationalization that
the proof of the "honesty of a Communist is his attitude to the
USSR." This meant that every Communist had to "glorify every act
of the USSR leadership." Since the Twentieth Congress, the search
for the true essence of proletarian internationalism had gone on in
earnest but with the consequent emergence of disagreement in the
working ranks. The author of this remarkably frank article then
noted four key issues on which such disagreement was evident:
(1) the nature of the Stalinist excesses (were they crimes or errors?);
(2) the methods of correcting past abuses (is it enough to condemn
the cult of the personality or should the system be amended?); (3) the
evaluation of the Yugoslav experience; (4) the character of relations
among Communist parties (Togliatti's "polycentrism" versus Stalinism).[9]

Pouring fuel on the fires, the author then noted that lately there
had arisen additional divergences over the Polish and Hungarian

events. He observed that the Chinese, Yugoslav, Italian, Belgian, American, and Polish parties refused to interpret the October 23 uprising in Hungary as a counterrevolution, while *Rude Pravo, Neues Deutschland,* and *L'Humanité* proclaimed it as such. Furthermore, the former merely accepted the Soviet intervention of November 4, while the latter triumphantly welcomed it. He accordingly concluded that theoretical and practical conflicts between Communist states *are* possible and that they must be resolved on the basis of substantive rights and not through the primacy of one or another state. Only then would international socialism achieve its final victory.[10]

What is particularly noteworthy in the above statements is that they appeared in the official party journal which went to print, according to a note on the inside page, on December 14, four weeks after the Moscow Polish-Soviet pact of November 18 which was to resolve past disagreements and about six weeks after a speech by Suslov on the anniversary of the revolution. The disappearance of Stalinism as a guide to Soviet-satellite relations meant that a new line had to be established to take into account the radically changed conditions prevailing as of early November 1956. The Suslov speech of November 6 certainly seems to have been an authoritative Soviet statement made in view of the failure of the Soviet declaration of October 30 to contain disintegrative developments and seemed to suggest that the USSR had realized that its Tito experiment had come to nought. Conceding the importance of specific methods, forms, and rates of development, Suslov attempted to set down what the universal laws of building socialism are for all the socialist states:

first, the establishment of political rule by the working class led by its vanguard; second, the thorough strengthening of the alliance of the working class with the peasantry and other strata of the working people; third, the liquidation of capitalist ownership of industrial enterprises, banks, transport, and communications, the establishment of public ownership; ownership of the basic means of production and the consequent planned nature of the economy; fourth, the resolute defense of the gains of the socialist revolution from the encroachments of the former ruling exploiting classes.[11]

These factors, according to Suslov, suggested that certain features of the Russian revolution had an international, universal significance. Furthermore, the road to socialism was not a matter, as the Poles seemed to suggest, of mere goodwill and a generous dose of experimentation, but also of pursuit of known and established laws.

More explicit criticisms of the Poles appeared in the December 23 issue of *Pravda*, in a long article entitled "On Proletarian Internationalism" by A. Azizian. The *Pravda* writer took issue with a Polish article on Yugoslavia which criticized the former practice of making loyalty to the USSR the focal point of proletarian internationalism. The Polish writer had suggested a new concept of proletarian internationalism, one based on "coexistence" among socialist states and on elimination of national hegemony and the struggle with Stalinism.[12] The *Pravda* article rejected with scorn the idea that a significant aspect of the present meaning of proletarian internationalism was the struggle with Stalinism and suggested that this was a mere mask devised by reaction to fight against Marxism-Leninism. Implying that the Polish writer was falling victim to nationalist tendencies, *Pravda* noted significantly:

The German Socialist Unity Party and the Czechoslovak Communist Party vigorously reject any attempt to form any other platform for the communist movement. All talk about the mythical "National communism," their statement reads, is contrary to Marxism-Leninism. Both parties stress the necessity of unity . . . of a joint struggle. . . .[13]

Pravda was quite correct. Either goaded by Moscow or fearful for their own security, the satellite leaderships of East Germany and Czechoslovakia responded to the anti-Stalinist challenge from Warsaw with far less delicacy and restraint. In Czechoslovakia the regime launched a mass agitation campaign, under the sycophantic slogan, "With the USSR forever," and German and Czech delegations promptly appeared in Moscow to cement the bonds of proletarian internationalism and to re-emphasize the primacy of the USSR in the camp of socialist states. In the latter effort they were joined by Thorez and the French Communist Party. The East Germans were particularly alarmed by Polish claims that a real "October revolution" had taken place in Poland. A revolution against Stalinism could not be a Marxist revolution, Hermann Axen violently proclaimed in *Neues Deutschland*, and he who says so joins the enemies of socialism.[14] Polish talk of "humanistic socialism" was thus admittedly most unsettling to the East German leadership, relying precariously on the support of Soviet arms. For the East Germans, their assertion of loyalty to the USSR and condemnation of the Poles as revisionists was therefore a matter of political survival.

The implications of Polish insubordination were not so immediately dangerous to the Czechs. There the party had succeeded in wielding power without the presence of Soviet troops, and the consideration presumably uppermost in the minds of the Czech leadership was the longer-range implication of the Polish position. For this reason, rather than attacking directly the Polish October, the Czechs, in the words of Novotny, "took a reserved view in evaluating the situation in Poland." [15] However, in emphasizing the need for close cooperation among socialist states, and rejecting bilateralism as a method of interparty relations, *Rude Pravo* strongly criticized the previously cited *Nowe Drogi* article, "Crisis of Internationalism?" and condemned those generalizations which have as their intent a desire "to weaken confidence in the Soviet Communist Party":

it is worth noting that some foreign quarters are expressing doubts as to whether conferences in which more than two communist parties participate are correct and expedient. Views have been expressed that such multilateral talks are inopportune; they carry with them, so it is said, the danger of isolation of communist parties from other organizations of the labor movement, particularly from the socialist parties of the West.

Such conclusions must be flatly rejected. No events of the recent past have altered the need for an expediency of conferences between communist parties, which holds good also for meetings between more than two parties. . . .

With socialist parties it is indeed possible, or rather necessary, to seek an understanding, particularly in questions of unity of action on the basis of working class unity. Yet it is no use blinding oneself to several serious facts. A number of socialist parties have completely abandoned Marxism. In a number of questions, they have adopted the attitude of the bourgeoisie, as was again shown recently during the events in Hungary. . . .[16]

Having thus rebuked the Polish insistence on bilateral dealings, an insistence dramatized by Polish absence from the early January meeting held in Budapest between the Soviet, Bulgarian, Czech, Hungarian, and Rumanian parties (Khrushchev and Malenkov attending), the Czechs proceeded to strengthen their ties with similarly oriented parties. On January 22 they issued the joint French-Czech Party declaration,* and a week later signed a broad economic agreement with the USSR in which the above ideological points were reasserted. Ironically, it was through these bilateral declarations that the Poles were being ideologically isolated for their insistence on bilateralism.

---

* *L'Humanité*, January 22, 1957. Part of the declaration may be cited here: "All attempts to divide the Communist movement into so-called 'Stalinist' and 'non-Stalinist' or 'old' and 'new' camps, as well as the idea that there can be several centers of the international Communist movement, serve only to question Marxist-Leninist principles and proletarian internationalism to which the two parties are attached."

But, as was not the case with the Yugoslavs, the Polish leaders, and particularly Gomulka, were never singled out for attack, and all specific references were directed at individual Polish spokesmen, who were clearly differentiated from the leadership. This was Gomulka's trial period, and Moscow's caution still restrained the extremists in Prague and Pankow.

The Soviets on the whole avoided taking public issue with the Poles in an official way. Indeed, it may be surmised that the outbursts from the local satellite leaders, combined as they were with attacks on Tito, stemmed from a sense of domestic insecurity, which the Kremlin leadership certainly did not share, and from a desire to create such a dichotomic situation that further toleration for the Poles would be ideologically inadmissible and politically inexpedient. Grand strategy for these leaders was hence very much a case of making their own immediate interests the basis for the policies of international Communism. The Soviet leadership was doubtless fully aware of the need to crystallize an ideological conception to fit the situation and to evolve new bonds to replace some of the Stalinist controls. Suslov's November 1956 speech was an effort in this direction, and in December 1956 the CPSU's Central Committee deliberated the matter. Some members of the committee, particularly Molotov, apparently assumed an "I told you so" attitude, while others, especially those charged with economic matters, expressed profound concern with the impact of the political developments on economic planning within the USSR and the camp in general.[17] But in December 1956 a return to the old Stalinist formula seemed to involve too many risks. Most particularly, it would have required an armed intervention in Poland without even the warrant of a clear-cut provocation from Gomulka. A return to Stalinism, furthermore, could not be restricted to the matter of interstate relations in view of the close interaction between Soviet ties with the other Communist regimes and Soviet domestic developments. Khrushchev, who had a personal interest in his gamble on Gomulka paying off, thus succeeded in maintaining his position in large measure precisely because the situation was so unprecedented.

With Moscow wavering, Peiping stepped forward to resolve the dilemma. It is to be recalled that in welcoming the Soviet October 30 declaration, the Chinese suggested that they shared the Polish feeling that Soviet-satellite relations must be critically re-examined:

Because of the unanimity of ideology and aim of struggle, it often happens that certain personnel of socialist countries neglect the principle of equality among nations in their mutual relations. Such a mistake, particularly the mistake of chauvinism by a big country, inevitably results in serious damage to the solidarity and common cause of the socialist countries.[18]

Even after endorsing the suppression of Nagy, the Chinese still seemed to fear that the major problem in Soviet-satellite relations was the danger of a return to Stalinism, and in hailing the November 18 Polish-Soviet agreement the Chinese press * made the interesting observation that the treaty would correct also "whatever was wrong with relations between the Soviet Union and Hungary." [19] By December, however, one could detect signs that the Chinese regime was becoming increasingly concerned over disintegrative trends in the bloc and with the absence of an effective Soviet response. Given its international isolation and its acute hostility to "Western imperialism," Peiping had a special interest in restoring Communist unity. Domestically the country was in a state of transition reminiscent of the violent transformation of Russia in the thirties. Although internal economic shocks were to some extent minimized by Soviet and East European economic assistance, the Polish and Hungarian events had the undesirable consequence of suggesting to some Chinese intellectuals that less radical methods of building socialism existed within the framework of Communism. In their attitude these intellectuals had been encouraged by the initial semiofficial endorsement given by Peiping to the Poles. The Chinese party leadership could hardly tolerate either such internal views or its external sources. In the fall of 1956 the focus had been on a change in the pattern of relations in the Communist camp for the sake of unity. By winter 1956 the emphasis was on unity to improve relations.

Diversity in Unity: The Chinese Solution

The Chinese leadership stepped forward late in December with a programmatic statement concerning relations between Communist states. The declaration, published on December 29 in *Jen Min Jih Pao*, was accompanied by a note that it was a summary of discussions held by the Chinese Politburo. The contents of the declaration were presumably cleared beforehand with Moscow and were immediately re-

* For an interesting commentary, see the November 13, 1956, editorial in *Ta Kung Pao*, "What are the similarities and Differences between Polish and Hungarian Incidents?" The article suggested that in both cases there were legitimate grievances and errors but that in Hungary a mass reform movement was penetrated by the enemy and was poorly led, and hence had become reactionary. At this time, the Chinese press featured many sympathetic articles concerning Poland, including pictures of Gomulka, a sign of tacit approval.

produced in full by the Soviet press.* However, the fact that the statement originated from Peiping instead of Moscow symbolized the degree to which Stalinism had inhibited the Soviet leadership from coping with a new situation. The Chinese statement involved concessions to what the Chinese must have considered to be the imperatives of unity as well as an attempt to define certain areas of independence previously prohibited by Stalinism. In this manner the Chinese hoped to contain the strains of diversity, without, however, making the error of striving to turn the clock back. Their statement accordingly conceded that contradictions between Communist parties were indeed possible although these were "not the result of a fundamental clash of interests between classes but of conflict between right or wrong opinions or of a partial contradiction of interests." It urged patience for the efforts of the CPSU to correct Stalin's mistakes and rejected the thesis linking Stalinism with the Soviet system. Furthermore: "In our opinion Stalin's mistakes take second place to his achievements," the Chinese Politburo decided.[20]

The Peiping statement was categorical in stressing two points concerning the reservations which had been raised by the Poles and the Yugoslavs: the issue of the dictatorship of the proletariat and the question of Soviet leadership. Since the former was related to the general problem of the role of the Communist Party, so recently challenged in Hungary, and also relevant to domestic Chinese problems, the statement minced no words in asserting the importance of the dictatorship of the proletariat for the construction of socialism:

Those "Socialists" who depart from the dictatorship of the proletariat to prate about "democracy" actually stand with the bourgeoisie in opposition to the proletariat . . . they are, in effect, asking for capitalism and opposing socialism, though many among them may themselves be unaware of that fact. . . .

On the subject of Soviet leadership, which was of less vital domestic importance, the Chinese were primarily guided by external considera-

* It has been suggested that the Chinese declaration was merely a trick sponsored by Moscow and designed to utilize Chinese prestige in resolving the existing problems. This in itself, of course, would mean a much greater role for China and an admission of China's position in East Europe. However, given internal disagreements in Moscow, it is more likely that the initiative came from Peiping, and was endorsed by Moscow.

The increased role of China was acknowledged at the time by a Soviet international-affairs publication which stated: "The Soviet Union with the Chinese People's Republic head the united family of the countries of socialism." S. Sanakov and V. Kniazhinsky, "The Leninist Policy of Peace and Friendship among Nations," *Mezhdunarodnaia zhizn*, no. 12 (1956), p. 31.

tions. Given their position of arbiter, the Chinese could stress Soviet leadership in the camp with little fear that its assertion would substantially reduce Chinese freedom of action. Consequently, their Politburo unequivocally described the USSR as the "center of international proletarian solidarity," and Chou En-lai, dispatched suddenly to East Europe in January 1957 on a fence-mending trip, repeatedly made unqualified references to "the socialist countries headed by the USSR." To sweeten the bitter pill, the December statement did reiterate the earlier warning against "big power chauvinism."

In brief, the Chinese seemed determined to set up a pattern of ideological and political unity while recognizing the possibility of limited local diversity. The Chinese statement approved of Poland's new position while Chou En-lai repeatedly, but without success, attempted to obtain official Polish assent to a statement of Soviet primacy in the camp.* Despite their inflexibility on this issue, the Poles apparently did agree in the course of their discussions with the Chinese premier not to air their ideological differences with the USSR, not to attempt to export their views, and to accept the notion that proletarian internationalism and not just coexistence should characterize relations among Communist states. The first implied much closer, supranational, bonds, whereas the second suggested a more formal, distinct relationship. The Polish position was thus markedly different from the Yugoslav insistence on the practical and ideological implementation of many ways to socialism, and it was essentially on this ground that Peiping made its move against Tito:

It is understandable that the Yugoslav comrades bear a particular resentment against Stalin's mistakes. In the past, they made worthy efforts to stick to socialism under difficult conditions. We also agree with some of the points in comrade Tito's speech, but we are amazed that, in his speech, he attacked almost all the socialist countries and many of the communist parties. . . . This can only lead to a split in the communist movement. . . .

* Polish press reports of Chou En-lai's visit to Poland in early January 1957 loyally transmitted the texts of his speeches with the invariable ending, "Long live the unity of the socialist countries with the USSR at their head!" And just as loyally, next to these speeches, would appear remarks by Gomulka, Cyrankiewicz, or Rapacki, stressing variable roads to socialism, sovereignty, equality of rights, and friendship with all socialist countries. See also the text of Chou's speech in Moscow in which he explains his mission as having been of utmost importance in forging new unity in the socialist camp (*Pravda*, January 18, 1957). In an interview in India, Chou openly stated that his trip had "helped to consolidate relations between the Soviet Union and the Eastern European countries." *New York Times*, January 25, 1957.

Clearly, the Yugoslav comrades are going too far. *Even if some part of their criticism of brother parties is reasonable,* the basic stand and method they adopt infringe the principles of comradely discussion.[21]

Following this implied accusation of political disloyalty, the campaign against Yugoslavia snowballed. The satellite newspapers, guided for the first time since June 1956 by a more or less common ideological standard, were filled with articles critical of the Yugoslav position and with indirect warnings to Poland against falling into the "revisionist" pitfall. Like the Chinese, these statements all re-emphasized the ideological verities: dictatorship of the proletariat, proletarian internationalism, primacy of the USSR. The Bulgarian party launched a vigorous campaign against efforts designed to undermine Communist unity by appeals to nationalist feelings,[22] and went explicitly on record as staunchly upholding the principle that "the attitude toward the Soviet Union and the CPSU is the touchstone and the cornerstone of proletarian internationalism." Condemning the Yugoslavs for questioning this, the Bulgarians asserted that the CPSU is "the tactical and theoretical example for all other parties of the proletariat." [23] The least refined attack was launched, as might have been expected, by Tito's old enemies, the Albanians. On February 13, speaking before the plenum of the Central Committee, Enver Hoxha delivered a blistering critique of the Yugoslav line, spelling out in detail the issues on which the Yugoslavs were said to be erring. Hoxha concluded his indictment, which neatly summarized some of the major ideological issues, by calling on all parties to defend Marxism-Leninism against revisionism, expressing his conviction that "with great confidence in the final victory of socialism, our countries, led by the glorious Soviet Union, are marching always forward." [24]

The crux of the matter, however, was clearly the question of Soviet primacy. This was finally stated bluntly by Popovic, the Yugoslav foreign minister, who, explaining the deterioration in Soviet-Yugoslav relations, stated:

ideological differences, in the narrow sense of the term, have not played a decisive role this time. The attitude toward the socialist camp is not an ideological question in the true sense of the word. However, ideological arguments have again served, regardless of whether or not this has been done consciously, as a suitable means for establishment of such interstate relations as the Soviet government considered correct, that is, *convenient* to it.[25]

Although the arguments and disagreements certainly did not end here,[26] enough has been said to illustrate the general pattern of disintegration of the ideological arrangement reached in the June 1956 Moscow agreement. However, since the Poles were in the meantime quietly practicing much of what the Yugoslavs were being loudly accused of, many of the charges against Belgrade were also aimed indirectly at Warsaw.

With the gradual settling of the dust following the explosion prompted by the dissipation of the Stalinist formula, the East European situation began to emerge in clearer focus in early 1957. The Chinese statement of December 29 provided an ideological framework which could accommodate the newly emerged diversified environment. As a result, throughout the early months of 1957 the torn fabric of East European Communism was being mended by weaving together a new formula for Soviet-satellite relations, based largely on the Chinese statement, through a series of bilateral party agreements or declarations * which served to re-emphasize certain common principles: (1) Soviet primacy in proletarian internationalism; (2) the struggle against imperialism internally and externally; and (3) the ubiquity of the concept of the dictatorship of the proletariat. Soviet statements generally relied heavily on quotations from the Chinese declaration, and, while chastising Tito for his open challenge to Communist unity, they seemed satisfied with the absence of direct external defiance by Gomulka.

The picture was thus radically different from the black-and-white dichotomies which so characterized Stalinism in East Europe. Unlike the "monolithic unity" of the past, as of early spring 1957 reluctant lip service was being paid in Poland to the last two principles of the three cited above, although neither of the two was being fully reflected in actual policy or action.[27] The first was simply ignored.†
In the other satellites, official statements were stressing all three prin-

* To list a few: Albanian-Bulgarian (January 29), Soviet-Hungarian (March 28), Bulgarian-Rumanian (March 27), Soviet-Rumanian, Soviet-East German (January 7), Czech-East German, Czech-Soviet (January 29), Czech-French (January 22), Czech-Chinese (March 27), Czech-Italian (April 3), Bulgarian-French (April 15), Soviet-Albanian (April 17), Soviet-Bulgarian (February 21).

† The Polish position, and Chinese acceptance of it, was again shown in the declaration signed in Peiping on April 11, 1957, by Premier Chou En-lai and Premier Cyrankiewicz. The declaration speaks of socialist solidarity based on "the Marxist-Leninist principles of proletarian internationalism and equality among nations." Soviet primacy is not mentioned. It goes on to state that the Chinese party welcomes the changes in Poland since the Eighth Party Plenum (October 1956). Yet, even while Cyrankiewicz was still on his way home, the Chinese were greeting Marshal Voroshilov with statements about the camp of socialism and proletarian internationalism, headed by the USSR. This is a good example of the new flexibility in interstate relations.

ciples but with most emphasis on the first, while domestic policies changed little from the past. The Yugoslavs were stressing the need of adjusting dogma to new situations and, without major departures from past internal policies, were rejecting the stress laid on the above principles as doctrinaire rigidity, replying to charges of revisionism with countercharges of dogmatism. However, in keeping with this greater elasticity, even the anti-Yugoslav campaign declined by early spring 1957. The neighboring and still basically Stalinist leaderships began gradually to realize the new pattern of relations and to perceive the implications of the new ideological conception.* Accordingly, they adopted Moscow's more subdued tone. Chou En-lai touched on the crux of the matter when, reporting on his East European trip, he stated: "Even if no unanimity can be reached for the time being, it would also be normal to reserve the differences while upholding our solidarity." [28]

The Economics and Politics of Unity

The Chinese formula was primarily a stopgap measure, as Chou's remark revealed. It was meant to contain disintegrative trends by focusing on common objectives, allowing time for the repair of more tangible bonds of unity. At this stage ideology was particularly important — especially in the case of Poland, where it buttressed a relationship which only recently had jettisoned the Stalinist controls and was delicately balancing potential external Soviet threats with certain common interests (such as the Oder-Neisse line). A commitment to similar social objectives and a sharing of certain perspectives for viewing reality established a common bond between Gomulka and Khrushchev which, under the circumstances, was important to cultivate. By stressing again and again the points of unity, the divisive tendencies inherent in a situation of diversity might be kept in the background. The Chinese formula also left room for hope that Yugoslavia, despite the tensions and the arguments, might be willing to shift the emphasis of its outlook toward those aspects of Marxism-Leninism which it shared in common with the other regimes. Tito's reaction to Hungary, as we have observed, did not rule out such expectations

* The outward change took place over a period of about one month. On March 3 *Scinteia* published a relatively restrained reply to Popovic's address and it was subsequently reprinted in *Pravda* on March 6, thereby gaining central endorsement, and two days later in *Rude Pravo*. In early April both Khrushchev and Bulganin, on greeting an Albanian delegation in Moscow, went to some pains to indicate that despite ideological differences, Yugoslavia was to be considered on a much friendlier plane than capitalist countries and that fundamentally it too was engaged in socialist construction although not directly part of the socialist camp.

since it indicated again that the institutions of socialism, even if subject to aberrations, were more important to the Yugoslavs than any other principle. It is to be noted, however, that already at this time the Chinese were categorical in drawing a line between legitimate Communist dialogue and treasonable discourse.

While the Chinese were coping with the ideological dilemma and securing the East Europeans' adherence to the new formulations, the Soviet leaders were busily turning to more familiar and less ephemeral remedies: tightening the economic bonds and re-establishing political-institutional ties. The December 1956 CPSU plenum accordingly included a discussion of the economic problems raised by the political changes.[29] The Hungarian and Polish events had many roots in the economic conditions prevailing in the bloc and the Soviet leaders were not unaware of this. In addition, some of them, like Khrushchev, realized that an important substitute for Stalinist coercion was to create such economic interdependence that any separatist temptations would be tantamount to courting national disaster. The fact that Poland's economic dependence on the USSR had helped, among other things, to inhibit Polish aspirations had not been lost on the Soviet leaders, and they accordingly strove throughout 1957 to create an economic equivalent to Stalin's political technique of "the dilemma of the one alternative."

The political events of 1956 had a sharp impact on Soviet economic relations with East Europe. Until then the area had been a source of appreciable economic advantage to the USSR, with an estimated annual Soviet net extract of at least one billion United States dollars.[30] The Soviet admission that past economic policies of the area, largely Soviet-imposed, had courted disaster,[31] the need to bolster the East German regime, to promote the recuperation of Kadar's Hungary, and to stave off a calamitous nation-wide repetition of Poznan in Poland, all forced the USSR late in 1956 and in 1957 to extend credit to these regimes. As a result, Poland, Hungary, and East Germany briefly became economic liabilities.[32] Since, ironically, this meant that less reliable regions were being rewarded, pressure unavoidably arose also to reward the more loyal regimes elsewhere, thereby increasing Soviet economic commitments.* No wonder then

* The February 21, 1957, Soviet decision to suspend the promised $250 million credit to finance aluminum plants in Yugoslavia has to be viewed in the light of these pressures. Soviet credits to East Europe since early 1956 included: 370 million rubles to Bulgaria in February 1956; 1.2 billion rubles to East Germany in July 1956 and January 1957; 200 million gold rubles to Hungary in December 1956; 400 million gold rubles to Poland in September 1956 and 700 million in November 1956; 270 million

that such economically oriented party leaders as Saburov or Pervukhin became increasingly concerned with the implications of Khrushchev's policies and gradually became attracted to those CPSU circles which opposed him on ideological and political grounds.

The loan policy had been adopted to deal with an emergency situation. A broader task, however, was to be performed by the Council
for Economic Mutual Assistance (CEMA), so neglected in the past
by Stalin. Indeed, it is remarkable that the Soviet leadership had
ignored this potentially most promising method of binding the Communist states together. It was again mute testimony to Stalin's dependence on political solutions, and CEMA's reactivation was a compli-
ment to Khrushchev's perceptiveness. Only after Stalin's death did the
council begin to meet regularly, and the year 1957 was especially
marked by a series of moves designed to give it new life and energy.
In June 1957 permanent secretariats to the various specialized CEMA
committees were set up and were empowered to draw preliminary
development plans for some ten to fifteen years ahead.[33] A multi-
lateral-payments scheme, with the state bank of the USSR as the
clearing agent, was scheduled for 1958.[34] It was also agreed that
"broad coordination of the plans of the socialist countries' national
economies" was desirable and would be pursued. In December 1957
a meeting of the economists of the participating countries was held
in Prague to evaluate their foreign trade with "capitalist trade markets" [35] and was followed in January 1958 by a plenary meeting of
CEMA in Moscow, with the heads of government leading the delegations.

The Moscow conference marked a determined bid to integrate
economically that which was proving ideologically and politically

---

rubles to Rumania in December 1956. The November agreement also provided for a
cancelation of Polish indebtedness to the amount of 2.3 billion rubles.

According to the most thorough study available (J. Wszelaki's *Communist Economic Strategy: The Role of East Central Europe*, Washington, 1959), the sum total
of Soviet credits granted to the European Communist-ruled states in 1956–1957 was
$1.3 billion. To this ought to be added $1.8 billion in Soviet credit cancelations, or a
total of $3.1 billion. However, these figures must be compared with the actual net
Soviet gains derived during the 1945–1956 period. Wszelaki's estimates are: $15
billion from East Germany, $2 billion from Rumania, $1 billion from Hungary, $2
billion from Poland — or *a total of $20 billion gained through exploitation* (see
Wszelaki, pp. 68–77). There is also striking evidence that despite the Soviet loan
policy, price discrimination in exports from the area to the USSR and imports from
the USSR continued to favor the USSR during 1957 and in fact increased in comparison to preceding years, thereby offsetting the Soviet loans. See H. Mendershausen,
*Terms of Trade between the Soviet Union and Smaller Communist Countries 1955–
1957* (Rand Corporation, January 1959), published in *The Review of Economics*, May
1959.

divisive. Poland was still interested in foreign, particularly American, loans and was attempting to shift some of its trade Westward, especially coal, its major export item. The conference produced a comprehensive plan of cooperation covering the years 1959–1975, divided into two parts: 1959–1965 and 1965–1975. The first part was worked out in detail while the second part set the broad outlines. Specific tasks for each member were also established, aiming at increased productive specialization of CEMA members. Such specialization, despite its immediate economic merits, in the long run would be bound to restrict the range of economic activity of any one partner, and place all the specializing countries in a relationship of dependence vis-à-vis their major supplier of raw materials and the only member not subject to effective specialization, the USSR. At the same time, the development of such an intimate relationship, particularly given the industrial development of the states, would further increase their economic significance to the USSR's own development plans. For instance, already by 1956 imports of machinery and equipment from East Europe exceeded by about $100 million annually the Soviet exports of similar commodities to the area.[36] Economic ties were indeed outstripping political unity.

In some respects the integration, preceded by intensive industrialization, did open new vistas to East Europe, so long plagued by splinter national economies and so long used merely as a market for Western industrial exports and predatory investments. The transition from a raw material and nonindustrial goods export area into an important source of machinery, particularly for the underdeveloped countries, without doubt represented a major advance for East Europe.* Integration, involving greater technical specialization, offered

* Noteworthy is the shift in the role of finished industrial items, particularly machinery, in the export trade of these states:

	Prewar	1948	1953	1956
Bulgaria	—	0.1%	3.0%	2.7%[a]
Czechoslovakia	6.4%	20.3	42.4	40.3
East Germany	—	31.9[b]	62.6	57.0
Poland	0.7	2.2[c]	12.9	15.6
Rumania	0.1	0.8	8.3	10.1
Hungary	11.4	17.4[c]	38.2	30.3

    [a] 1955
    [b] 1950
    [c] 1949

Source: *Probleme Economice*, no. 5, 1958 (this issue contains a detailed treatment of changes in the structure of foreign trade of the European Communist states).

For a useful summary of economic development in the bloc, emphasizing the positive aspects only, see *Razvitie ekonomiki stran narodnoi demokratii*, N. I. Ivanova et al., eds. (Moscow, 1958).

opportunities for more rapid development of technological skills and for promotion of goods for competition in the world market. However, whatever the long-range material benefits might be, the immediate political consequences were to create more binding ties to the USSR and China. Indeed, the converse result was also of political significance: with Western markets closed, China, absorbing more than half of East European machine exports, became dependent on economic stability in the bloc for the promotion of its own development. Within the pattern of specialization a particular role was to be played by East Germany and Czechoslovakia, the most industrialized and politically loyal states. They were to serve as the key suppliers of industrial equipment within the bloc and particularly to the USSR.[37] In 1957 Czechoslovakia even adjusted upwards her Five Year Plan in order to fulfill the industrial-export obligations imposed upon her, as was frankly admitted by Communist planners.[38] Also in 1957, partly for sound economic and partly for political reasons, the USSR negotiated far-ranging agreements with Czechoslovakia, integrating Soviet-Czech industrial plans,[39] and with East Germany, providing for trade and industrial cooperation, especially in the development of the chemical industry, planned jointly until 1965.[40] According to the plan,[41] Czech export trade will undergo by 1965 the following structural change:

	Capitalist states	USSR	Other Communist states
1957	32.6%	33.8%	33.6%
1965	26.0	41.8	32.2

Soviet economic ties with Czechoslovakia, combining the desirable characteristics of an advanced, highly skilled industrial base and a hyperloyal regime, went beyond any arrangement concluded with other states.[42]

Of the most immediate political significance were the increased economic ties developed between Poland and the USSR. The American loan of $94 million granted in mid-1957 was negligible compared to the total turnover in Polish-Soviet economic relations, which in 1956 amounted to 2,562 million rubles and which grew in 1957 to 2,747 million rubles. According to an itemized breakdown of goods imported and exported,[43] published in detail in order to dissipate public suspicions stimulated by past secrecy, in 1957 Poland was dependent on Soviet supplies for 100 per cent of its oil supplies, 70 per cent of its iron ore, 78 per cent of its nickel, and 67 per cent of its cotton. Particularly important, but advantageous to Poland, was the fact that almost half the Polish exports to the USSR in 1957 (of the total 1,023,600,000 rubles) involved Polish machinery and industrial goods, representing about one half of total Polish machine exports. By way of contrast, only about a fifth of the imports from the USSR constituted industrial goods and machinery, most of it raw materials necessary for Polish industry. Polish leaders could not afford to ignore the potential implications of this economic relationship.

Beyond these purely economic aspects, there was a further consideration involved in the increased zeal of CEMA activities. Since the organization antedated the October 1956 events and, unlike the Cominform, was not branded by Stalinism, the Poles could hardly claim that CEMA was being revived in order to limit their independence. Even during the relatively open anti-Soviet season in the Polish press no significant charges were raised against the council, and all complaints had been aimed directly at Soviet-Polish economic relations. At the same time, however, CEMA's existence presented the Soviet leaders a most opportune and institutionalized forum for *multilateral* consultations where the Poles were bound to be isolated and unable, given their weak economic situation, to wield a veto power. It is no wonder then that, from 1957 on, most of the Communist press, with the significant exception of Poland, sang praises to the role played by CEMA.

The economic measures provided a general underpinning to the more pressing political problems. True, common economic ties and a common economic organization would create centripetal forces so sorely needed. But the Soviet leadership was too steeped in the Leninist-Stalinist tradition to rely merely on gradual economic processes. Its political efforts took three approaches. The first, as already noted, involved bilateral agreements between the most loyal parties reasserting proletarian internationalism, hailing Soviet leadership, and proclaiming certain universal prerequisites for the construction of socialism. The purpose of these bilateral agreements was to underscore those principles which in themselves created pressures for unity. It was hoped that emphasis on recognition of Soviet leadership would effectively undercut the divisive tendencies inherent in "many ways to socialism" and, in a roundabout fashion, restore the old Stalinist prerogative of evaluating and guiding the domestic experience of other Communist states. The declarations, coming as they were from all sides, created pressures on Poland and, to a lesser extent, on Yugoslavia to identify themselves with the stated principles lest their silence be interpreted as negation. They also provided ammunition to the unreconciled neo-Stalinists in Poland who, without fear of being charged with "subversion," could innocently keep prodding Gomulka to identify himself with such praiseworthy principles.

The second method for which the Soviet leadership developed a sudden predisposition was the multilateral conference of Communist leaders in which all disagreements could be ironed out in comradely discussions. The Soviet leaders were obviously not unmindful of the numerical voting strengths that would prevail in such conferences, and they were only too willing to apply the Leninist notion of democratic centralism to them. The application of this principle to international Communism would, they felt, unavoidably strengthen unity and supply a justification for Soviet leadership. With this in mind, the Soviet leaders decided to take advantage of the forthcoming fortieth anniversary of the 1917 revolution to stage an international Communist celebration in Moscow. No true Communist, not even Tito, could refuse to attend.

The third approach aimed at reviving something like the Cominform, an interparty organization which would translate the multilateral conference into a continuing multilateral consultation and guidance. Such an arrangement was in keeping with the former Soviet reliance on the Comintern and the Cominform and thus had the added advantage of being rooted in familiar experience. While ostensibly not clashing with the Chinese formula of unity in diversity, it would grant the Soviet leaders their sorely needed organizational control. But it was precisely the Comintern and the Cominform experience which was calculated to raise the most impassioned Polish and Yugoslav opposition. To the former, the Comintern was a reminder that the Polish Communist Party had been dissolved as a "fascist conspiracy" with most of its leaders shot by the NKVD. To the latter, the Cominform symbolized the very worst features of Stalinism. Unity could hardly be restored by reference to this particular ancestry of international Communism, and even initial Soviet efforts to promote a common interparty theoretical journal were opposed as a portentous revival of the past. These fears in Warsaw and Belgrade were hardly allayed by the clumsy efforts of the Czech party's weekly, *Tvorba*, which while conceding that a revival of some form of Cominform would not be favorable "under present conditions," still seemed to suggest the general desirability of common organizational links: "It would seem that for the sake of firm unity of international Communism roughly the same contacts should be promoted as existed when the Cominform was in existence." [44] During this period, Prague and East Berlin consistently took a more rigid stand than even Moscow.

Yet in the new situation the Soviet regime had to be more responsive to the dominant views prevailing in the Communist world. Soviet power had not declined; in fact, it had grown in every respect. But the new element in the situation was that the power of Communist regimes elsewhere had also grown. The Politburos in Prague and Sofia were no longer staffed by cowed *apparatchiki* intently detecting the significance of the latest Soviet pronouncement, convinced that the center knows best. After the unmasking of Stalin and the October 1956 events, the center's infallibility no longer appeared above question and, indeed, the neo-Stalinist centralists * in the Communist regimes could easily claim that they had perceived much earlier the dangers of the flirtation with Tito or of the tolerance for the Poles. In doing so, they could confidently tell Moscow that after ten-odd years in power they knew best which policies would promote and which policies would undermine Communism in their respective countries. Centralist domesticism thus became a source of pressure on Moscow for more energetic measures to ensure disciplined unity.

Internal considerations also affected the mood of the CPSU Presidium. The record shows that Molotov from the start opposed Khrushchev's experimental approach and favored sticking to established processes. Suslov's formulations at the Twentieth Congress had shown greater caution in endorsing the "many ways to socialism" thesis. And even Khrushchev himself by late 1956 was toasting Stalin as a great leader of Communism. By early 1957 it had become clear that continued maintenance of Soviet leadership would require a greater degree of organizationally structured discipline within the bloc and a common center for defining ideological prerequisites and universals. The year 1956 had taught Khrushchev a priceless lesson in the vagaries of political diversity and in the dangerous ambiguities of Marxism-Leninism as the sole bond for unity.

The Soviet party and the Soviet system were further sources of pressure for a reassertion of unity. The militancy of the movement

* It would be misleading to use the Stalinist and anti-Stalinist categories in this post-October period. The issue of a return to Stalinism as such was no longer really meaningful. Rather, it was mostly a question of the degree of unity and subordination within the bloc necessary for the construction of socialism. By "neo-Stalinist centralists" I mean those leaders who favored the closest links with the USSR even if practicing at home policies not based on the Stalinist principle of abject imitation all that is Soviet. Khrushchev, for instance, could not be described as a Stalinist although by 1957, as we shall see below, he was a centralist.

and its ideology, the desire to recast society, and the belief that life is a continuous conflict – all constituted overwhelming pressures to close ranks. No aberrations of the past could erase the fact that the content of Communist action is progressive and good, and therefore continuously deserving of most intense effort. For many years the Soviet intellectuals, students, and workers had been told that theirs was the most advanced socialist society. Molotov in 1955 had to make a public recantation for ideologically clouding public understanding of the advanced historical stage of Soviet development. Existing limitations on certain freedoms were either denied or said to be a function of the particular phase of development. Yet suddenly some other "less advanced" socialist states were laying claim to their own paths, engaging in reforms, and propagating practices still said to be socialist and yet involving a greater degree of freedom and democracy. One such state, Yugoslavia, was even strongly hinting that its model had a universal socialist validity. Extended official toleration on the part of Moscow for such systems was unavoidably bound to produce responses in the USSR and give ground for similar demands. Such development could affect the regime's power and would certainly diffuse the ideologically defined image of the world, resulting in a desire to diminish internal sacrifices. It could even lead to a form of "ideological relativism," which has dangerous overtones of liberalism for opinions other than those embraced by the official ideology.

Official toleration for diversity beyond a certain point thus had significant domestic implications and was wrought with overtones of disaster for the ruling party. Both ideology and power pointed against it. Ideology, steeped in the Bolshevik tradition, was badly suited to coexist equally with other views which also claimed an insight into history on the basis of Marxism-Leninism and yet which differed on important points. Considerations of power had to reject positions which might lead to significant restraints on such power. Domestic and external pressures clamored, therefore, for the restriction of diversity and for the restoration of a common commitment.

Poland and the Principle of Soviet Leadership

The problem of unity translated into political terms meant coping with two recalcitrant Communist regimes: Poland within the bloc and Yugoslavia on its fringes. The maximum objective, drawing Yugoslavia back into the bloc, was bound to prove the more difficult task, as will be shown in Chapter 13. The establishment of political and ideological ties between Poland and the rest of the camp was the objective for 1957 and, given Poland's ambiguous position, had the greater chance of success.

The Soviet position on Poland remained uncrystallized until sometime in February or March 1957. Soviet fears about the direction of Poland's future course were exacerbated by the rapid collapse of the collective-farm system after October 1956, by the strange alliance between Gomulka and the Roman Catholic Cardinal, by the continuing ideological ferment, and by the unclear situation within Gomulka's party. The neo-Stalinists, highly critical of Gomulka's agricultural concessions and dubious of the consequences for Polish Communism of Gomulka's line on "national sovereignty," were still sufficiently active to warrant the thought in Moscow that a more suitable alternative might still be available. At the same time, however, the Soviet leadership could derive some comfort from a series of reassuring signs. In the course of the January 1957 electoral campaign for the Sejm, which in substance was a plebiscite for Gomulka, some of the more outspoken anti-Soviet candidates were dropped and a Catholic youth organization, with nationalist leanings, suppressed. The elections demonstrated that Poland was willing to support Gomulka's Communist regime as a preferable alternative to the neo-Stalinists who, to rule, would require a more active Soviet support. In the government formed after the elections, Zenon Nowak, a leading member of the Natolin group, was retained as deputy premier. Then in mid-March the regime condemned as one-sided a resolution of the Warsaw Committee which singled out for attack only Stalinism, reminding the committee that the revisionists were also a major danger. To their remarks about national equality the Poles began to add the meaningful phrase "proletarian internationalism." Finally, also in mid-March, Gomulka conceded that the Hungarian revolution ultimately had become a counterrevolution, thereby essentially endorsing the Soviet position.

While it is impossible to pinpoint the date of the Soviet decision to abandon their temporizing attitude and actually to buttress Gomulka's position in Poland, something approaching such a policy decision must have been made prior to the March 25, 1957, agreement granting Gomulka's request for the complete release of many hundreds of thousands of Poles (including many anti-Nazi underground fighters) still under detention in the USSR. Since no previous Communist ruler of Poland had been able to obtain Soviet agreement — and even Bierut had tried after Stalin's death * — Gomulka's success could not fail to increase his standing at home. A few weeks earlier, Khrushchev, speaking of Soviet-Bulgarian friendship, significantly chose that occasion to publicly praise Gomulka's leadership.[45] Gomulka shortly afterwards began to display, for the first time, some vigor in dealing with the Natolin group which had continued its agitation against him. At the Ninth Party Plenum in May, provoked by their criticisms and demands for a formal acknowledgment of Soviet leadership, Gomulka moved sharply against his critics, bluntly rejecting their contentions that his position was weakening socialism. Symptomatic of the Soviet attitude (and certainly not lost on the Polish *apparatchiki*) was the fact that a Soviet Embassy attaché, V. Masennikov, who had criticized the post-October regime, was recalled to Moscow a few days after the plenum.

The Ninth Plenum gave Gomulka an opportunity to restate the meaning of his position in the light of his improving relations with Moscow. Referring to the "Polish (or national) way to socialism," he noted explicitly that Poland's differing conditions required a different way than the Soviet. According to Gomulka only diversity can do justice to proletarian internationalism, and he rejected the view held by "comrades here and in other parties" that Communists must agree on every detail. While stressing the imperative significance of Polish-Soviet ties, Gomulka reiterated his belief that proletarian internationalism would flourish if it tolerated a continuing discussion, based on *common principles*, and with history being the sole judge of who had been right.[46] (For a fuller development of Gomulka's internal policies, see Chapter 14.)

His reference to common principles was significant. It revealed an underlying area of agreement with the Soviets which had been obscured by the openly aired differences and the uncertain political situation. Gomulka listed four such common principles for building socialism:

(1) The organization of a Marxist-Leninist Party of the workers' class and the laboring masses, which governs itself according to the principles of democratic centralism, conducts a policy of alliance of the workers' class with the laboring peasantry;

(2) After the overthrow of the authority of the bourgeoisie — the creation of the dictatorship of the proletariat over the exploiting classes and suppressors of the laboring masses;

* The most that Bierut could do was to obtain in 1955 the release of 6000 individual Poles held in the USSR, many of them veteran Communists arrested during the purges. *Po Prostu*, December 23-30, 1956.

(3) The socialization of capitalist means of production, a gradual reconstruction of productive relationships in the countryside, absorbing the entirety of the national economy into specific frames of central planning and direction;

(4) Conduct of policy in accordance with the Leninist principles of proletarian internationalism, the observance of equality and sovereignty of all states and nations, the uniting of countries and socialist powers to oppose imperialist aggression and to defend peace.[47]

It is noteworthy that Gomulka's first three points embraced all but one of Suslov's "universal laws" as stated in November 1956. The part omitted involved Suslov's justification for resolute class struggle after power had been seized — a position identified in Poland with Stalinism — but the sharpness of this divergence was dulled by Gomulka's inclusion of the dictatorship of the proletariat concept, which could imply much of Suslov's point.

Gomulka's ideological effort also served to underline the areas of recalcitrance, the defense of which he considered vital to his efforts to build socialism in Poland. His "laws" made explicit reference to gradualism in dealing with the peasants (a point further developed in his remarks) and elevated his insistence on national independence and equality to a binding law for socialist construction. This had been a cardinal tenet in his beliefs all along, since he well realized that without it the Soviet Union would have the right to judge his internal policies. Throughout the spring and summer of 1957 Gomulka therefore refused, even when signing joint declarations with the most subservient parties (such as the East German on June 20), to employ any of the standard formulas used to acknowledge Soviet leadership.

Indeed, it was largely to defend his stand on this issue that Gomulka displayed such reluctance to engage in multilateral conferences and, especially, in multilateral organizations. The frequent Polish praise for bilateralism in relations between Communist parties was designed to provide the procedural substructure for the principle of national independence.* In September 1957, following an improvement in Soviet-Yugoslav relations, Gomulka journeyed to Belgrade and the joint Polish-Yugoslav declaration asserted that "both parties consider that today bilateral relations between Communist and workers' parties should particularly be developed."[48] Such an assertion,

---

* On one occasion, when the French Communist Party refused to endorse bilateralism in a joint French-Polish declaration and reference to it was accordingly omitted from their joint statement, the Poles editorially, with tongue in cheek, declared that the Polish-French Communist negotiations had once again proved the profitability of bilateral relations between parties.

issued only two months before the scheduled Moscow multiparty conference, even if accompanied by Tito's concessions to Gomulka's desire not to enflame Moscow,* still reflected Gomulka's continued intransigence on a semantic point pregnant with political significance. The CPSU and the other parties recognized it as such. It was no accident that the May 1957 issue of *Voprosy istorii* singled out the parties of China, France, Germany, Czechoslovakia, and Rumania as the "vivid examples of the consistent and steadfast struggle for the purity of Marxism-Leninism." These were the parties which stressed the desirability of closer ties, with the Czech party's plenum in July calling again for a common interparty journal and even a common commission for political-economic problems.[49]

By the late summer of 1957 two basic formulations of Soviet rule had emerged. The more extreme, espoused by the Czechs, East Germans, Bulgarians, and Albanians, spoke of the "leading or directing role" of the USSR in the Communist camp. The Soviet role was a special one, involving leadership in ideological and political matters and implying in turn its authority even in the domestic matters of other Communist states. These parties also occasionally used the phrase "the socialist camp headed by the Soviet Union," preferred by the Hungarians and the Rumanians and which in January 1957 the Chinese had desired the Poles to adopt. The Soviets tended to use the latter version in their own statements,[50] although also quoting with apparent approval the more "centralist" formulations.

It would be an oversimplification to maintain that the Soviet insistence on this special role was merely a matter of self-interest or power. It was hard for the Soviet leaders not to feel that the October Revolution had blazed a path for all "progressive" humanity and had initiated a new historical phase. This very fact in turn had endowed the USSR with a compelling mission, and all Communists had to realize that their fate was inextricably linked with the Soviet Union. The Soviet experience in building socialism established it as the most advanced socialist state, and a Communist would be guilty of a harsh distortion of reality if unwilling to recognize this. The traditions of the CPSU and its experience inescapably established its right to comment authoritatively on ideological matters, and the scope of such comment could not be limited by such formalistic considerations as national frontiers. Finally, the very fact of Soviet power placed the Communist states in debt to the USSR, because it was Soviet might which made the construction of socialism possible, protecting these

* See Chapter 13, p. 313.

states from the imperialists. Did not all this establish objectively the unique position of the Soviet Union? the Soviet leaders felt entitled to ask. On what grounds, other than crude nationalism, could any Communist question Soviet leadership? [51]

Gomulka accordingly was careful not to go on record as denying the principle of Soviet leadership. He either ignored it or would employ his own formulation which inevitably had the merit of being as vague as it was true. When hailing the Soviet Union he would normally refer to it as "the first and mightiest socialist power," historically and factually correct but without the strong overtones of hierarchy contained in the centralist formulations.* Even at the November 1957 multiparty conference in Moscow, amid repeated incantations to Soviet leadership, Gomulka spoke of "the first socialist state in history, the Union of Soviet Socialist Republics. It takes first place in the democratic family of socialist countries." [52]

But as Gomulka personally discovered in Moscow in November 1957, the pressures for unity within the camp became increasingly difficult to resist. Much of the original Polish confidence, so evident in the summer of 1957,[53] had been rooted in an erroneous analysis of pertinent external phenomena. Two such cases stand out: the meaning of Soviet leadership changes and the attitude of China. In the case of the former, the late June 1957 expulsion of Molotov, Kaganovich, Malenkov, and Shepilov from the CPSU Presidium was interpreted in Poland as indicating the victory of a conception of the Communist camp which would allow considerable latitude for independent action. Gomulka, for ideological as well as geopolitical reasons (especially the Oder-Neisse frontier problem), did not desire to leave the camp, but he did hope that ultimately the camp would be transformed into a commonwealth of essentially equal states. The expulsion of a faction which, at least in part, was held together by past objections to Khrushchev's bloc policies, seemed an encouraging sign, especially as it was followed shortly by renewed Soviet-Yugoslav contacts. Possibly in this interpretation the Poles were right. Khrushchev was certainly preferable to Molotov. But their optimism made them forget that there was still a considerable gap between their views and Khrushchev's. They did not realize that Khrushchev, by not attempting to move the clock all the way back, ultimately might be much more effective. Finally, they did not know that inter-Communist rela-

---

* It may not be too farfetched to suggest that an analogy to the Polish formulation would be if some archbishop in the Catholic Church insisted on referring to the Papacy simply as the "first and oldest bishopric in the Church."

tions were only indirectly involved in the expulsions.[54] The fact is
that Khrushchev's consolidation of power served to free him to respond with greater energy to the problems of unity.

An even more glaring case of exaggerated optimism was involved
in the Polish calculations concerning China. Despite Chou's visit to
Poland, despite his insistence on Soviet leadership, despite the clear
lines drawn between internal autonomy and external obeisance in the
Chinese December 29 statement, and, finally, despite the sharpness of
the Chinese condemnation of the Yugoslavs, the Poles continued to
picture the Chinese as their allies in the struggle against centralist tendencies, particularly against a reassertion of effective Soviet leadership.
Mao's secret speech on "Contradictions within a Socialist Society"
provoked unfounded hopes in Poland that it signified a major shift
toward a greater toleration of diversity, excluding, almost by definition, a center for international Communism and the hegemony of any
one party. His speech was interpreted as relevant "for all countries
which are building socialism"; it was compared to the Polish October
upheaval and was construed as endorsing the Polish position:

We in Poland speak about our "October." The Chinese speak in their own
manner about "a hundred flowers." It appears, however, that between
these two expressions there is a great similarity. It appears that the statesmen heading the Chinese Communist Party favor those changes which
took place in Poland half a year ago. And, what is more, *they are ready to
support our efforts* aimed in the direction outlined in October.[55]

Carried away by their blind enthusiasm, the Poles failed to note
that by the summer the Chinese were stressing that Mao's views were
applicable to China alone, and that the major danger to socialism was
revisionism, not the dogmatism which the Poles identified with the
neo-Stalinist, centralist positions. Even more important, had the
Poles re-examined closely the Chinese statements since October 1956,
they would have noted that their major theme was unity and that
Soviet leadership, particularly since Chou En-lai's visit to Moscow and
East Europe in December-January, was clearly considered to be an
integral part of that unity. Mao's hundred-flowers speech, it seems,
was essentially designed for internal Chinese consumption; the Polish
efforts to represent it as an oblique Chinese redefinition of the character of the camp even might have served to provoke Peiping into
adopting a more unequivocal position.

The Dialectics of Unanimity

The November 1957 Moscow celebration became a testing ground for the Poles' ability to maintain their position. The Poles went to the meeting believing that they would not be required to acknowledge Soviet leadership, and their hopes were raised by the absence of any mention of it in the draft of a resolution to be issued at the end of the conference and circulated beforehand.[56] The major business of the conference was conducted in a special meeting of the governing Communist parties, held at the end of the celebrations. In keeping with this policy, Gomulka pleaded the "special sensitivity of the Polish people to questions of their country's independence and sovereignty" and warned that to ignore it would be "nihilistic dogmatism."[57] His was a lonely stand. (In public speeches only Kadar took a more moderate position, but his domestic weakness made him a doubtful source of support.) From all sides came repeated demands that Soviet leadership be acknowledged publicly in the resolution which would be issued *jointly* at the conclusion of this multilateral conference. To the surprise of the Poles and the delight of the centralists, much of the pressure came from the Chinese. In his speech to the gathering, Mao used the formula "socialist camp headed by the Soviet Union" four times [58] and was quoted as explaining to the Chinese students at Moscow University that "in the socialist camp there must be a head and that head is the Soviet Union. Among the Communist and Workers' Parties of all countries there must be a head, and that head is the CPSU."[59] The open recognition of Soviet leadership by the only party which was in a position to dispute it placed Gomulka in an extremely difficult position. Under these circumstances, his refusal to join in acknowledging Soviet primacy would amount to arrogant defiance which he could ill afford and which, for ideological reasons, he did not cherish. While disagreeing on the nature of the socialist camp, he did not share Tito's more extreme position that the camp itself was expendable (see next chapter).

Gomulka was also faced with two other difficult demands. One was to systematize multilateral party contacts through a joint theoretical journal, reminiscent of the one published by the Cominform, and the other was openly to condemn revisionism as the major danger to international Communism, with its "excessive emphasis . . . on the peculiarities of individual countries."[60] Thus, in a curious case of history repeating itself, Gomulka was replaying the role he had played at the founding of the Cominform (see Chapter 3): opposing the almost unanimous pressure for monolithic international unity which would inevitably limit the domestic freedom of the smaller Communist states. But even though isolated, under pressure from all sides, lacking the support he had expected, even though faced by a conflict between his loyalty to Communism as an international system and his conception of a Polish way to Communism, his situation in 1957 in Moscow was more favorable than in 1947 at Szklarska Poreba. Stalin was gone and the Soviet claim to infallibility went with him. Gomulka was in control of his party and secure in the knowledge that his party's rule in Poland was being strengthened by his stand. The party was no longer entirely dependent on Soviet support, and he realized that, while he could not afford a complete break with the camp, the Soviet leadership preferred to avoid one also. And, finally, he must have felt that despite the unanimity of the views ranged against him he still symbolized a strong current within the Communist movement, a current of change which could be channeled, maybe dammed, but no longer reversed.

The outcome was a partial capitulation by Gomulka and a partial compromise by the others. The planned periodical was not mentioned in the declaration issued at the end of the conference, although the East Germans promptly revealed the conference's decision "in principle" to issue it.[61] (It did come out after some further delays in the fall of 1958, entitled "Problems of Peace and Socialism," published in Prague and edited by A. M. Rumyantsev, a specialist in ideological matters and former editor-in-chief of *Kommunist*). As far as the major ideological issues were involved, the declaration as signed by Gomulka did use the formula "the socialist camp headed by the Soviet Union" *once;* elsewhere it employed Gomulka's version, "the first and mightiest state." On other issues, it is worthwhile to compare some of the points of the theses adopted by the CPSU on the occasion of its fortieth anniversary, which served as the basis for the Soviet position at the conference, with the declaration as issued following the discussions (with Yugoslavia abstaining):

CPSU theses	Declaration of the ruling Communist parties
The views of those who stress the national peculiarities of each country marching toward socialism, and who forget the general basic, fundamental principles of socialist rev-	Disregard of national peculiarities by the proletarian party inevitably leads to its divorce from reality . . . is bound to prejudice the cause of socialism and, conversely, exaggera-

olution, are profoundly alien to Marxism-Leninism.

tion of the role of these peculiarities or departure, under the pretext of national peculiarities, from the universal Marxist-Leninist truth . . . *is just as harmful to the socialist cause . . . both* these tendencies should be combatted simultaneously (italics added).

The ideological subversive activities of the forces of reaction against the Communist movement have lately been reflected in the spread of the pernicious ideas of so-called "national communism," in the spread of all kinds of revisionist attacks within the Communist Parties. . . .
The Communist and Workers' Parties are waging a struggle against the harmful influence of present-day revisionism and giving it a fitting rebuff.[62]

The meeting underlines the necessity of resolutely overcoming revisionism *and dogmatism*. . . .
In condemning dogmatism, the Communist Parties believe that the *main danger at present* is revisionism. . . . However, dogmatism and sectarianism *can also be the main danger*. . . . It is for *each* Communist Party to decide what danger threatens it more at a given time (italics added).[63]

The above suggests that the declaration did not fully assert the centralist position even though Gomulka did join in acknowledging Soviet leadership. The declaration, however, while reflecting the pressures for unity and stressing again and again the areas of common interest and the universal laws of socialist development, left sufficient areas of ambiguity to allow Gomulka room for domestic maneuvering. Indeed, on his return home, Gomulka promptly reasserted his autonomous position by pointedly using his old formula for describing the USSR. In a speech addressed to several thousand Warsaw activists he attempted to balance the need for unity with his insistence on independence for Poland. He left no doubt that, unlike the Yugoslavs, he favored a community of Communist states since such liaison was needed for both ideological and power considerations in the age of imperialism. He thus still displayed a strong predilection toward the Leninist dichotomic vision of the world, even if qualified by his observations that trends in favor of coexistence were also noticeable in the West.[64] At the same time, however, he went out of his way to reassure his listeners that the declaration would not limit the Polish party's internal autonomy and that it was compatible with strict Polish interests.

In the same speech, Gomulka particularly emphasized that multilateral conferences could not dictate the internal affairs of any one party and, while conceding that such conferences were useful in addition to bilateral contacts (which he pointedly praised), he made the curious observation that they ought to be conducted on the basis of an agenda known beforehand to all its participants. Apparently Gomulka desired to protect himself against a repetition of the Moscow situation where demands for an acknowledgment of Soviet leadership and for a common journal were sprung on him without warning and contrary to the original draft resolution examined in Warsaw.

The persistence of some irritants notwithstanding, from the centralist point of view the conference was not without positive consequences. Above all else, it combined the notion of the "Communist commonwealth" with the recognition that such a commonwealth was headed by the USSR. Even Gomulka's insistence on returning to his old formula could not undo the precedent established in Moscow, namely that for the sake of unity he too was willing to concede a principle which had the potential for becoming an operational limitation on his own autonomy. The Soviet commentators clearly suggested that the acknowledgment of Soviet leadership implied the general applicability of Soviet experience elsewhere.[65] Gomulka's grudging concession would make it doubly difficult for him to resist pressures exerted in the name of the camp and buttressed by the authority of the recognized leader. In case of conflict, is not the leader best qualified to decide whether a party is exaggerating national peculiarities? Gomulka's concession thus represented the achievement of the minimum objective: retention of Poland within the camp with at least implied recognition that there were higher considerations than the peculiar requirements of the construction of socialism in Poland. Already the first tangible expression of this was the splitting of the Poles from the abstaining Yugoslavs. The conference helped to clarify — and with Gomulka's assent — the borderline which he could not cross without branding himself a traitor to Communism.

The challenge of evolution was thus met by a clearer proclamation of certain common features which must characterize a state building socialism,* and by the effort to reconstruct a center which could

* The declaration's statement of these "laws" was in effect a combination of the points made by Suslov and Gomulka's assertions, with the word "gradual" making the reference to agricultural socialization palatable to Gomulka: "These general laws are: leadership of the masses of the working people by the working class, the core of which is the Marxist-Leninist party, in bringing about a proletarian revolution in one

authoritatively interpret the common standard. However, neither of these measures, even if satisfying the postulates of the centralists, meant a return to Stalinism. Stalinism did not require objective standards or acknowledgments of leadership as a basis for leadership. Stalinism was based on an enforced claim to infallibility and on the rigid transplantation of its own experience. The centralists merely adopted one of its facets, disciplined unity, but they were otherwise prepared to recognize that blind imposition of Soviet experience was in fact an impediment to that unity. This in itself represented a significant change in the internal relations of the bloc. The issue henceforth was between varying images of the camp and not a return, externally or internally, to the practices and theories of Stalinism.

The method employed to reconstruct the center testified to the new times. Unlike the period of Stalinism, Soviet leadership in the bloc was no longer an autonomous fact due entirely to Soviet power and monopoly of ideological experience. Soviet leadership in November 1957 was contingent in considerable measure on the backing that it received from Communist regimes much weaker than itself but strong enough to be needed if that leadership were to be asserted. China did play a crucial role, but it would be an error to underestimate the importance of centralist support from East Europe. Their vehemence and unanimity had the gradual effect of making Moscow appear Warsaw's best friend, thereby making Warsaw more responsive to Moscow. But, because of that, the Soviet leaders henceforth would have to take into account the more radical attitudes of their supporters in East Berlin or Prague or Sofia. This meant, in turn, that the internal insecurities of the more Stalinist-inclined Czech or Bulgarian leaderships would have to be reflected in the policies framed for the bloc by the Soviet leaders. Although the elevation of

form or another and establishing one form or another of the dictatorship of the proletariat; alliance of the working class with the bulk of the peasantry and other strata of the working people; the abolition of capitalist ownership and the establishment of public ownership of the basic means of production; gradual socialist reorganization of agriculture; planned development of the national economy with the aim of building socialism and communism, raising the working people's standard of living; the accomplishment of a socialist revolution in the sphere of ideology and culture and the creation of a numerous intelligentsia devoted to the working class, the working people and the cause of socialism; the elimination of national oppression and the establishment of equality and fraternal friendship among peoples; defense of the achievements of socialism against encroachments by external and internal enemies; solidarity of the working class of a given country with the working class of other countries — proletarian internationalism."

Soviet leadership to a matter of principle made a farce of the claim
that the Communist camp had become a true commonwealth, the
camp thus did differ significantly from the old Stalinist bloc. The
latter could be compared to a military phalanx in which no one would
even conceive of questioning Stalin's leadership and in which everyone acted with monolithic unity. The "socialist commonwealth" of
November 1957 was much more like a political organization with an
accepted "boss" who could rule almost autocratically but who, to be
effective, always had to manipulate his forces in order to ensure himself the continued support of a powerful majority.

A good example of the new pattern was Soviet behavior at the
November conference. The burden of the attack against the Poles
was carried by the Chinese and the other parties, with the Soviets remaining "neutral." At the end, Khrushchev proposed a "compromise"
involving the points already cited.[66] To some extent this was merely
a maneuver designed to make the Soviet position seem most reasonable, but even so it did mark a new method of leadership in the camp.
The Stalinist bloc of Communist states was in effect one totalitarian
system. The socialist commonwealth emerged as a number of totalitarian states (or, as in the case of Poland, a state ruled by a totalitarian
party),[67] linked together by common goals and political pressures but
still containing the dangerous seeds of pluralism. This was the syn-
thesis which emerged out of the dialectical conflict between extreme
centralism and Gomulka's autonomous domesticism.

A more general lesson taught by this brief phase in Communist
relations was that in a system of states in which considerations of
power are very closely linked with ideological goals, pressures inherently arise either for intense conflict or for ever-tightening bonds
of solidarity and subordination. A loose federation of Communist
states certainly is not precluded by Marxist-Leninist thought, although it would be difficult to conceive of it in practice. Power
when combined with a conception of national interest can result in a
loose association of states for the promotion of certain vague objectives or for the protection of certain interests. Such states, as in
the British Commonwealth, can enjoy a variety of institutional arrangements and subscribe to a variety of basic outlooks. But power
which is cultivated for the execution of tasks determined by ideological perspectives raises issues which inevitably produce conflict.
Matters pertaining to the domestic development of any one state become critically relevant to the purposes of the international association of such states and generate polemic issues of doctrinal purity.

(By analogy, the Catholic Church would find it difficult to embrace national churches not recognizing papal infallibility, for example, or tolerating polygamy.) Belief in one correct path stimulates rigorous condemnation of error. Fear of contamination is then translated into fear that the power of the state will be sidetracked from the correct purposes and historically ordained directions. To avoid this, there must be explicit and binding universal laws. But how can such laws be established, how can they be applied, and how can they be interpreted without creating pressures for discipline and an authoritative center to answer such questions?

Unless there is subordination, the "universal" laws can become a mere disguise for unlimited diversity (as in the case, for instance, of the Protestant movement). Diversity in turn is bound to create weakness and diffuse common purposes. The only way to establish unanimity in purpose and unity in action is to impose a common center and to maintain sharp distinctions between membership and nonmembership, between correct views and treasonable error. The reconstruction of the center and Poland's grudging subordination to it established the former requirement. The struggle against Yugoslav revisionism, which followed shortly, was designed to establish the latter.

CHAPTER 13

Unity Through the Struggle Against Revisionism

let a hundred flowers bloom, let a hundred schools contend! — Mao Tse-tung, February 1957

Weed them out and use them as fertilizer . . . this is . . . the way in which we should beat revisionism. — Lu Ting-yi (Agit-prop Chief, Kianghi), March 1958

THE struggle against revisionism as an aspect of relations among Communist states was rooted in the failure to draw Yugoslavia back into the Communist camp. Poland had raised within that camp the problem of Soviet leadership. The November conference re-solved it by re-establishing the general principle of Soviet primacy. Yugoslavia's position as a "certified" socialist state necessarily raised the question of the unity of the Communist camp. In keeping with the established ideological notions as well as internal pressures for unity, the quest for unity had to be resolved either through the forging of close links or by the drawing of a sharp line. If unity was impossible, this in itself signified to the Communist leaders that within the pattern of their relations with Yugoslavia there was hidden somewhere an ingredient of heresy which had to be unmasked. That ingredient was revisionism.

Revisionism has had a long history in the Communist movement. Conflicts of interpretation, tensions between "spontaneity" and "con-sciousness," reformism and class violence, have plagued the Commu-nists at almost every turn in their quest for power. Bitter controversies and lasting splits were their usual by-products. The distinctive fea-ture, however, of the new outlook which developed in some Com-munist parties following the dissipation of Stalinism and which was labeled revisionism was that it arose within ruling parties which had already effected the primary revolutionary break-through [1] and had created the structural outlines of a "socialist" society. The argument, even when involving doctrinal issues, revolved around the problem of reforming or improving a going concern, a People's Democracy, and not the methods to be adopted to promote the socialist revolution.

Noninstitutionalized Revisionism

Revisionism following the dissipation of Stalinism and the October 1956 events was most pronounced within the Polish party, although all the ruling parties had been infected by it. The loosening of internal party discipline and the initial lack of a sense of direction in Gomulka's Poland led to a lively exchange of views in the course of which many of the tenets of Marxism-Leninism as applied in the USSR were questioned. According to B. Ponomarev, head of the CPSU Central Committee's department dealing with other Communist parties, the seven cardinal sins of revisionism were: (1) minimization of imperialist aggression; (2) denial of CPSU leadership; (3) rejection of class struggle and collaborationism between classes; (4) Social Democratism; (5) denial of Leninist dictatorship of the proletariat; (6) rejection of a centralized, disciplined party; and (7) adoption of national Communism.[2] In many respects, revisionism could be thus identified with the policies of the Polish and certainly the Yugoslav regimes. But revisionism was not merely a matter of political policy. Much of revisionist thought revolved around basic philosophical assumptions which, if adopted, would threaten the entire edifice of Marxism-Leninism.

Among the revisionist writers, the most coherent exposition, and therefore politically the most dangerous, was developed by Leszek Kolakowski, a former Stalinist ideologue and a gifted young scholar in philosophy. His views provoked a violent stir among the more orthodox Communists not only in Poland but particularly among the neo-Stalinists throughout the bloc. Kolakowski's views, not entirely original, were developed in a series of articles which appeared in the Communist literary journal, *Nowa Kultura*. The first of these, "The Permanent and the Transitory Meaning of Marxism," [3] attacked the dogmatization of Marxism. It charged that Marxism had ceased being an intellectual concept and had become an institutional dogma. "Similarly, the word 'Marxist' no longer means a person who recognizes a definite, meaningful view of the world, but a person of a definite intellectual make-up who is distinguished by his readiness to recognize the views established institutionally." Maintaining that Marxism had made creative contributions to social and historical analysis, Kolakowski advocated that its "apparatus of concepts" be revised to keep up with more recent phenomena and warned against excessive commitment to any particular historical interpretation since the very "objectivity" of historical fact is open to question. History is usually politics looking backward, he warned, protesting against historical determinism as scientifically untenable. From these positions, Kolakowski moved against any party interference in scientific and intellectual pursuits, since any such interference is bound to be, by definition, un-Marxist, for Marxism above all else is a continuing rational effort to understand the processes of change in material reality. True Marxists do not need any special camp to protect the monolithic unity of their views.

His philosophical position was expounded later in the same year in four successive weekly issues of *Nowa Kultura*,[4] in essays entitled "Responsibility and History" and subdivided into four parts: "The Conspiracy of Aesthetes," "The Opiate of the Great Demiurge," "Consciences and Social Progress," and "Hope and the Fabric of History." To summarize Kolakowski's position, developed skillfully and with great passion, is not an easy task. In the first essay, constructed as a dialogue between the intellectual and the revolutionary (or, as it is hinted, the *apparatchik*), Kolakowski defends individual judgment as superior morally and more reliable than dependence on history and the social and economic forces that help to shape it. In the other essays, Kolakowski maintains that historical determinism not only fails as a source of moral criteria but is in itself merely a political tool, invested with faith, and not a scientific doctrine. He concludes by calling for an insistent commitment to a program based on *moral* considerations, even if such a program is not immediately feasible, and for an enduring suspicion toward any action commitment lest it become irrevocable while founded on error or ignorance.*

* The following three citations touch upon some of Kolakowski's central points:

"If we are forced to take some immediate attitude to current changes, then we cannot, of course, wait for the uncertain results of historico-philosophical discussions which may remain unresolved for a hundred years. Therefore, our choice will always be best if it is determined by that small particle of certainty which we possess. Lasting moral values, elaborated in the long development of man up to this moment, are the surest support we have if reality demands from us a choice which, ultimately, is also of moral character. In any case, they are more worthy of confidence than any historical science. And this is the reason why, ultimately, I stick to my opinion.

Whatever happens?
Whatever happens. . . ."

("The Conspiracy of Aesthetes" — the dialogue)

"I repeat that it was possible, in the difficult moments during the last war, to expect the laurel of victory to fall to the Nazis. This supposition is, in itself, not subject to moral judgment, but the practical conclusions drawn from it, and the attitude

Not surprisingly, Kolakowski was extensively criticized within and without Poland. His views, it must be admitted, would undermine the very basis of a Communist's subordination to the party and the subordination of the party to any one ideological center. As a result, they could hardly pass unchallenged. The Soviet philosophical journal devoted a full article to him, mixing its refutations with strong doses of invective: "a pitiful compilation of already nauseating attacks on Marxism," "hysterical defamation," "naive," and so forth.[5] Other Soviet journals, as well as the satellite press, followed suit, both in form and content.[6] The brunt of the attack was on the "objective" consequences of such views: "What Imre Nagy did in Hungary in practical politics, the Kolakowskis are doing in theory," Pravda concluded.[7]

Polish revisionism, by provoking reaction elsewhere, became a matter of interparty relations. In the case of the Polish revisionists, however, an important extenuating circumstance tended to contain the centrifugal implications of the revisionist dialogue. Even though Kolakowski spoke as a party member, and even though in the later summer of 1957 he became editor of an important philosophical journal, he did not speak for the party, his views were not endorsed by its leadership, and Gomulka even singled him out for criticism. If Polish revisionism, through its universalist intellectual position, appeared to be on the market for export, it was definitely not sponsored by the party, the leadership of which was just in the process of making its accommodation with the rest of the camp. More and more, as

---

adopted as a result of such a world view, are subject to such judgment. Nobody is free of the moral responsibility for supporting a crime merely because he was intellectually convinced of its inevitable victory. Nobody is exempted from the moral duty to fight against a system of rule, a doctrine, or social conditions which he considers to be vile and inhuman by resorting to the argument that he considers them historically necessary. We protest against such forms of moral relativism in which it is assumed that the criteria or moral judgment of human action can be deduced from knowledge of the *Weltgeist*. . . ."

("The Opiate of the Great Demiurge")

"A philosophy of history worthy of consideration describes only what has existed, the past, and not the creative future of the historical process. For this reason, those who wish to subordinate their own engagement in future processes to the pronouncements of the philosophy of history are only tourists who write their names on the walls of dead cities. Everybody can, if he wishes, interpret himself historically and discover the determinisms to which he was subject in the past. But he cannot do so with respect to the self he has not yet become. He cannot deduce his own future development from the pronouncements of the philosophy of history in which he trusts. To work such a miracle would mean to become the irrevocable past oneself; that is, to cross the river of death which, the poet says, no one ever sees twice."

("Hope and the Fabric of History")

the Polish party consolidated its position (see next chapter), the Polish revisionists became the spokesmen for alienated intellectuals,[8] divorced from power.

The Harich case in Germany was another important case of non-institutionalized revisionism. Wolfgang Harich, like Kolakowski, a philosopher with one-time strong Stalinist leanings, became concerned after Stalin's death with the inability of Communism to adjust to peculiar national conditions [9] and, together with several other East German Communist intellectuals, began holding discussions to crystallize a Communist program of action more in keeping with German traditions. In this he was encouraged by the Soviet policy toward Yugoslavia and particularly toward Poland after October 19, 1956. By November 1956 he and his associates drafted an extensive program, based in some respects on the Polish pattern, and Harich proceeded to make contacts in Poland and with the SPD in West Germany. The latter step proved to be his undoing, for it gave the East German regime easy opportunity for an accusation of treason. Harich was accordingly arrested and sentenced in March 1957 to ten years' imprisonment.

However, unlike those Polish revisionists, who before October 1956 made common cause with the party leaders anxious to restore Gomulka to power, Harich's group had no influential support in the party *apparat* and failed to join with a group of party leaders who were surreptitiously opposing Ulbricht's leadership. This group, crushed by Ulbricht early in February 1958, and composed of K. Schirdewan, E. Wollweber, and F. Oelssner, had already in late 1956 considered the necessity of large-scale concessions and thus leaned in a direction toward which Harich was headed. Harich's program, despite his Leninist protestations, however, went too far in calling for common SPD–SED action and free elections, the consequence of which would be the collapse of East Germany.[10] This was too much for even the anti-Ulbricht elements in the party, just as Kolakowski's views were unpalatable to the practitioners of power in Poland. Noninstitutionalized revisionism could not effectively challenge the institutions of power. Primarily a long-run threat to the party's sway over the intellectuals, its essentially utopian bent made it ineffective as an action program.

The Quest for Unity: Tito Outmaneuvered

The Yugoslav practitioners of power did not permit an ideological dialogue outside the party's direction. To Moscow, this was a reassuring sign. Like Harich, the chief Yugoslav revisionist, Djilas, was rotting in jail. The Yugoslav party tolerated within itself no views other than those endorsed by its leadership, and the latter's firmness against Djilas underscored its determination to crush anyone who undermines the party's ideology and discipline. The ambivalent position taken by Tito on the Hungarian uprising, and the sacrificing of Nagy on the spurious guarantee of Kadar, indicated a fundamental commitment to a common outlook and to common practices which made Khrushchev unwilling to write Tito off as already on the other side of the barricade. Admittedly, the very fact of Yugoslav discipline made the portent of any Yugoslav revisionist views more serious since such expressions could not be differentiated, as in Poland, from the leadership. Nonetheless, Tito, in Soviet eyes, had not burned all his bridges, and the Chinese formula could be utilized transitionally to minimize areas of disagreement, to stress the common outlook and fundamental aspirations, and to promote the maximum objective of the Communist camp for the year 1957: drawing Yugoslavia back into the bloc.

For their part, the Yugoslavs still clung desperately to the views crystallized during their "painful reappraisal" between the two Junes of 1955–1956, in spite of the violent attacks directed at them early in 1957 (Chapters 11 and 12). Just as their own doctrinal perspectives had made them leary of Soviet overtures in 1955, their new outlook made them basically hopeful about relations with the Communist states, the Hungarian events and anti-Tito invective notwithstanding. They dismissed all of these manifestations as hangovers from the past all the more violent since their Stalinist "socioeconomic" basis was said by them to be slipping away. Convinced that Stalinism, and therefore also centralism, was dead — and unable to perceive that the latter was possible without the former — they looked almost benignly on the frothings of Hoxha or the Bulgarians, firm in their belief that such vituperation stemmed from weakness. They were particularly optimistic in their evaluation of the Soviet scene. Here two factors were central. Tito and his associates apparently believed that in the Soviet leadership a continuing struggle was being waged between Stalinists and Khrushchev, the latter dedicated to a more moderate version of Communist relations; and that this power struggle was merely obscuring the fact that Soviet society by 1956 had largely shaken the dominant characteristics of Stalinism. In the long run, the base was bound to affect the superstructure, even if Khrushchev were to lose in the meantime.

However, since they considered themselves to be a socialist (Communist) society and since their actions were bound to affect the

Communist camp, the Yugoslavs thought it unwise to do anything which might prejudice Khrushchev's chances. They felt that his collapse would in turn minimize their role in that camp. Their stand on the Hungarian revolution and their support for Kadar, whom they identified with Khrushchev and, above all else, their support for Gomulka were rooted in this orientation. Khrushchev's consolidation of power following the expulsion of his opponents in June of 1957 was greeted by great enthusiasm in Belgrade, where the Soviet opposition to him was categorized under the all-embracing term of Stalinism. His victory was held to be a vindication of the Yugoslav trust that change in Moscow would have to come.

Undoubtedly, personal and domestic factors played a role in framing this Yugoslav stand. While very little is known about disagreements within the Yugoslav leadership, it appears that, as in Moscow, there were conflicts of interpretation of Soviet-Yugoslav relations. Judging from the public record, it is evident that Kardelj had been most explicit in stressing those aspects of the Yugoslav doctrine which were irritating to the Soviets. Rankovic, Tito's likely successor, on the other hand, was reported to have become concerned over the potential demoralization within the party ranks as a result of protracted Yugoslav isolation, and he therefore favored closer links with the camp. To Tito, an isolated Communist leader on capitalist dole, a return to the status of 1956 would have meant a repetition of his triumph and his restoration as one of the leaders of international Communism. Not surprisingly, after the June Kremlin purge Tito immediately moved in the direction of a rapprochement with Khrushchev who, for reasons noted earlier, was also not inclined to interpret current Yugoslav doctrines as an insurmountable barrier to a stress of common ideological and political commitment. Hoping to restore unity. Moscow accordingly encouraged the Yugoslav attitude:

Our views are identical in the majority [of cases]. Both the USSR and Yugoslavia consider the main task of all peace-loving people to be the struggle for relaxation of international tension, for a general reduction of armaments and for the unconditional prohibition of atomic and hydrogen weapons. . . . Every possibility exists for even broader and more fruitful cooperation between our countries, particularly since the June plenary meeting of the CPSU condemning the anti-Party group of Malenkov, Kaganovich and Molotov, who attempted to destroy the unity of our country and to attack its general line — the historical decisions of the Twentieth CPSU Congress.[11]

Within days of the Moscow shake-up, Tito requested a meeting with Khrushchev.* Such direct contact with Moscow was not only the logical consequence of the Yugoslav position but also fitted in with the Yugoslav procedural emphasis on bilateralism "which includes in itself the struggle against hegemony and centralism." [12] In their enthusiasm, the Yugoslavs apparently were even prepared to ignore those pronouncements of Khrushchev which seemed to run counter to the Yugoslav notion of his *real* views. Within days of a speech by Tito on June 25, in which he had referred to the Workers' Councils as "one of the greatest, indeed it may be said one of the historic acts in the development of Yugoslavia's socialist order," Khrushchev was sneeringly referring to the councils as having been constructed with American funds and warning that there was only one kind of socialism good for all nations.[13] He then laid down in the same speech his conditions for an improvement in relations: "We won't criticize you, and you must not interfere in our affairs. . . . But if you want to criticize us, comrades, we know how to pay back." [14] This would be the message he would give Tito, Khrushchev boasted, promising to point out to him that Western support for Yugoslavia was based on a desire to split the international Communist movement. "What do we want?" he asked rhetorically. "We want unity, closed ranks, and rallied forces. We acknowledge different paths, comrades. But among the different paths, there is one general path, and the others are, as you know, like a big river with tributaries." [15]

Despite the uncompromising tone of these assertions, Tito apparently persisted in his belief that Khrushchev represented a "progressive force," that he deserved all the support he could get, and that his statements still left room for diversity and cooperation. Believing that the phase of upheavals in East Europe had ceased and that the Stalinist faction in the USSR had been routed, Belgrade felt optimistic about a gradual return to the June 1956 principles. However, this time the Yugoslav sights were more limited. No longer interested in precipitating rapid changes in East Europe lest they provoke a repetition of the Hungarian situation. Tito hoped instead to obtain Khrushchev's assent to greater diversity among the existing Communist regimes, an endorsement of Yugoslavia's independent position,

* On July 11, while in Prague, Khrushchev referred to a forthcoming meeting with Tito (*Le Monde*, July 12, 1957) and in 1958 explicitly stated that it had been Tito who requested it (*Pravda*, June 4, 1958). Thus Tito must have made his move almost immediately after the expulsion of the anti-Khrushchev elements.

a halt in satellite censure of Yugoslavia,[16] and renewed economic cooperation. Indeed, a renewal of Soviet aid, suspended in February, was announced on June 30 after an exploratory trip to the USSR by Rankovic and Kardelj. It was within this conflicting framework of cross-purposes and expectations, a curious repetition in reverse of the 1955 and 1956 pattern, that Tito hastened to meet Khrushchev on August 1 and 2 in Bucharest.

According to the limited information available,[17] the conversations resulted in a limited agreement which both sides hoped would pave the way for the fulfillment of their longer-range objectives. Khrushchev apparently reiterated his warning against open Yugoslav attacks on the Communist camp, although agreeing to promote a cease-fire in the camp's anti-Yugoslav campaign. Playing on the "I need you against the Stalinists" theme, Khrushchev skillfully obtained the Yugoslav endorsement of Soviet foreign policy in Europe, particularly in terms of Yugoslav recognition of East Germany and support for the Soviet position in the Middle East, — steps calculated to result in Western resentment against Yugoslavia. The Yugoslavs, furthermore, agreed to participate formally in the forthcoming November 1957 Moscow conference and to help draft the resolution, thereby implicitly signaling their membership in the international Communist movement.[18] To the Yugoslavs, these concessions appeared to be worth the price. The declaration that was issued after the meeting pointedly did not establish proletarian internationalism as one of the key characteristics of Soviet-Yugoslav relations, a point which the Poles had by then conceded, and it reaffirmed the validity of the 1955 and 1956 Soviet-Yugoslav declarations. The stage thus appeared to be set for a return, on a modified basis, to the diversity which the Yugoslavs so desired, and Tito was preparing for his triumphant appearance at the Moscow celebrations as one of the chief leaders of Communism, on a par with Khrushchev and Mao Tse-tung, not to mention Gomulka.

The August conference was the last attempt to bridge the gap between the Soviet efforts to establish a unity based on *belonging* and Tito's insistence, by then limited primarily to Yugoslavia, on unity through association. The solution appeared on surface to have been a substantive agreement on external issues and ideology, but without formal Yugoslav membership and with the Soviet recognition of their independence. The compromise, however, did not bridge the disagreement in basic perspectives. The conflict between the traditional Soviet dichotomic image of the world and the Yugoslav version of an interrelated, world-wide, and largely organic development toward socialism was not resolved. The latter viewpoint necessarily made a more diffuse Communist camp the only intelligible method of operation. The former demanded unity and a center.

The Yugoslavs, much like the Poles, underestimated the pressures for such unity and placed false hopes on the person of Khrushchev. Yet there has never been one iota of evidence that Khrushchev was predisposed toward anything but a firm commitment to a rigidly dichotomic approach. Every one of his speeches, his press interviews, has reflected a commitment typical of a self-taught peasant who has perceived certain immutable laws and will not be shaken from his insight. He has been able to couple this, however, with an elasticity in tactics and a willingness to experiment which apparently made it possible for him to convince Tito that his desire to shake off the inexpedient remnants of Stalinism also involved a departure from the dichotomic vision. But it was only on this tactical level that Khrushchev was willing to adopt occasionally more flexible positions than his more rigid colleagues in the camp. His determination to launch Communism on a new dynamic phase, unencumbered by those features of Stalinism which were only necessary in the "revolutionary" period, did not involve junking the Leninist notions of a cohesive, monolithic movement. The forced wedding of August 1957 could not be consummated.

Tito tried his utmost. Even though Belgrade acknowledged after the meeting that "an abyss" still divided the CPSU from the Yugoslav Communists,[19] in mid-October Tito recognized East Germany, thereby undermining his ties with the West and causing the Western press to proclaim his return to the Soviet camp. He intensified his contacts with Kadar. In mid-September, at Gomulka's urging, possibly in an effort to improve the Pole's position as the "honest broker" between Belgrade and Khrushchev, Tito accepted proletarian internationalism as one of the principles guiding relations among Communist states. "Coexistence of socialist states" was not mentioned, while the usefulness of multilateral contacts, in addition to bilateralism, was endorsed.[20] While not going so far as to accept the Soviet line on unity of Communist states, Tito did endorse the notion that a "strengthening" of relations between Communist states was desirable. Tito basically lived up to his part of the bargain.*

* The full measure of the Yugoslav concessions can be better appreciated by comparison with a later article in *Politika* (December 26, 1957) which restated the original Yugoslav position after a worsening in Soviet-Yugoslav relations and which

To have expected Khrushchev to live up to his commitment to implement the pledges of 1956 involved a thorough misreading of Khrushchev's position. While it might be an exaggeration to maintain that this entire episode had been a cunning plot to isolate Yugoslavia from the West and then to confront it with demands it could no longer afford to refuse, thereby forcing it into the camp, Khrushchev's maneuver was clearly designed to stimulate external pressures on Yugoslavia which would limit its freedom of action. In keeping with this, the draft resolution of the November conference, submitted in advance to Belgrade, did not contain any reference to Soviet leadership, a point which would have been displeasing to Gomulka and absolutely intolerable to Tito. At the same time, however, the draft reiterated the fundamental Communist dichotomic position on world affairs, thereby not only making shambles of the Yugoslav claim to neutrality but also implicitly establishing the binding principle of unity, a mere hair's breadth away from the unarticulated premise of Soviet leadership. The accompanying attacks on revisionism (only subsequently balanced by attacks on dogmatism), while not singling Yugoslavia out, were in effect condemning the very basis for Yugoslav domestic policies. These points Khrushchev had to include. Not to have done so, given the parallel Polish problem (Chapter 12), would have meant the discarding of the principal doctrinal tenets and the destruction of almost the last remaining ideological bonds among Communist states since the dissipation of Stalinism and the resurgence of domesticism.[21] No Soviet leader could do that, least of all when faced with pressure from centralist elements at home and abroad. November, after all, was to be a triumphant celebration of forty years of expansion, hardly the occasion for the public abandonment of the basic concepts of the struggle.

Tito accordingly refrained from making the trip to Moscow and was represented by Kardelj and Rankovic. The fact that a Yugoslav delegation attended in full knowledge that a declaration would be issued suggests that the Yugoslavs still hoped to be able to reach some accommodation to justify their signature on the declaration. Possibly, in addition, they preferred not to leave Gomulka, and even Kadar, prematurely isolated. Nonetheless, at the conference, like the Poles, they were suddenly confronted with demands which went considerably beyond the draft and surprised by Mao's insistence on an unequivocal statement of Soviet leadership. Less surprisingly, Mao

described proletarian internationalism as "nothing but a nice idea" which, however, was used to impose discipline on socialist states.

also was the most adamant in insisting on a severe condemnation of the West with which, of all the Communist states, China was on the worst footing.

Outmaneuvered by Khrushchev and misled by their own evaluations, and with their concessions already implemented, the Yugoslav delegation had only two choices left. They could either capitulate or refuse to sign: the latter move would place them outside the international Communist movement. But even at this critical juncture the Yugoslavs strove to equivocate. They refused to sign the declaration but, so as not to burn all their bridges, then endorsed the Peace Manifesto proposed by Gomulka and signed by all parties. Curiously, however, even though the manifesto was more temperate in its formulation, it still implicitly endorsed the Soviet line and strongly hinted at a world divided into imperialists and anti-imperialists. Disappointed by Khrushchev, outraged by the Chinese, and placed outside the pale, the Yugoslavs still sought to save face. Yet it was precisely their compromising policy and their attendance which strengthened the universal legitimacy of the November conference and which gave Khrushchev a firm basis for warning the Yugoslavs that their actions were inimical to international Communism. A deserter usually provokes greater indignation than an enemy.

Institutional and International Revisionism

The Yugoslav abstinence, following directly on the heels of a series of gestures suggesting that common areas of agreement would finally prevail over points of disagreement, meant that a mere return to the pre-August situation was no longer feasible. Yugoslavia had come so close to the camp that drawing back emphasized all the differences which previously had kept them apart. To the Communist camp, the Yugoslav position translated revisionism from an internal affair of a party into an institutional system with international overtones. The consequence of November was hence to push both sides further apart and to render explict the underlying disagreement.

Of the two sides, it was the Yugoslavs who, in their disappointment and embarrassment, were the more aggressive. In order to justify to their own party the strange zigzags of their relations with the USSR, they were increasingly driven into articulating their position and indicating why the "strengthening" of relations among Communist states, so recently endorsed by Tito, resulted three months later in open defiance of the entire camp. It is to be recalled that the Yugoslav public was not informed by its press of the arrangements made by Tito at Bucharest, which resulted in a certain disorientation. The most reliable way of minimizing it was to raise again the banner of independence and to revive Yugoslav claims to an original and universally valid development of Marxism-Leninism.

It appears further that the November events shook the Yugoslav leaders to the point of their undertaking a broad revision of the perspective developed between 1955 and 1956. The reappraisal led them gradually to the conclusion that they had not only underestimated centralist pressures within the bloc but had mistakenly assigned Khrushchev the label of an anticentralist reformer. They belatedly moved, therefore, to systematize an ideological alternative to the November resolution in order to sum up, in one self-contained message, the scattered and often contradictory Yugoslav ideological pronouncements. Such a document was needed since their earlier statements, while perhaps useful to scholars or analysts, could not be construed by Communists abroad and in Yugoslavia as a sufficiently cogent answer to the dichotomic, centralist argument.* Abandoning any hope of working from within as a bona fide socialist ally, they proceeded to lay the ground for an external ideological challenge. They did so with Khrushchev's warning not to criticize the Soviets openly still ringing in their ears. This in itself is evidence to support the proposition that the Yugoslav position shifted radically after November 1957. In the spring of 1958 the Yugoslavs finally moved to create what they had lacked in 1956: a coherent ideological alternative to the prevailing framework. Unfortunately for them, the political situation was much less in their favor than in October 1956.

The Yugoslav theoreticians accordingly proceeded to cement their claims to being the true Leninists by broadly hinting that Lenin's major contribution to Marxism involved *revisions* of previous thinking (especially on revolution and imperialism) and by asserting that it was Lenin who first recognized the fatal dangers of dogmatism, the antithesis of revisionism. "Once dogmatism nestles within a proletarian party . . . such a party can no longer do anything sensible; life passes such a party by, and the party cannot influence life," they warned, reminding the Communist states that it is idle to assume that

---

* It was also needed because of the prevailing ideological confusion in the Yugoslav Party ranks, caused by the policies of the preceding two years. See the "Circular Letter of the Executive Committee, Central Committee, Union of Communists, to all Organizations and Leading Organs of the UCJ, about Future Tasks of UC in the Struggle for the Elimination of Negative Manifestations in the Political, Economic, and Social Life as well as Elimination of Shortcomings in the Work of UC," Belgrade, February 28, 1958.

all their internal difficulties spring only from "imperialist machinations." [22] In keeping with the revived emphasis on originality, the Workers' Councils, politely ignored even by Tito in his joint declaration with Gomulka, again became fashionable. Writing in the theoretical weekly, a Yugoslav sociologist, M. Hadzi-Vasilev, critically compared the Yugoslav Workers' Councils with the newly instituted Soviet production conferences and reached the not unexpected conclusion that only the councils are capable of resolving the "antagonistic contradictions" which arise as a consequence of "the danger of the bureaucratic usurpation by the state" of all control. [23] Hadzi-Vasilev rejected as merely propagandistic the Soviet contention that their workers, working in a socialist state, were therefore working for themselves, and pointed out the need for each worker to realize that his individual interests are represented in his work. This the Workers' Councils were said to do, while their absence in the USSR, he implied, allowed for the arbitrary identification of "individual interest with the collective and then on that basis building up all economic relationships in the name of a great future." [24] Other Yugoslavs pointed out that by stressing primarily the struggle against capitalism, the dogmatic Communists created a "one-sided" identification of socialism with the state and all its regulations. This was said to be a more primitive version of socialist development than the "higher and complicated" Yugoslav pattern, a statement which more than hinted at Yugoslav ideological primacy. [25] The stage was thus set for the unveiling of the Yugoslav program which would mark the final break with the hopes and calculations of the two preceding years.

Following the November conference the Soviet leadership maintained a restrained position. The Soviet attitude of August 1957 was not incompatible with Khrushchev's public warnings in Prague, and had been premised on the primary goal of forging close unity which would, only if possible and not at any price, also include Yugoslavia. The outcome of the conference, therefore, gave no cause for sudden shifts, even with the Yugoslav abstinence and increasing articulateness. The Soviet illusions concerning Yugoslavia had been gradually fading since October 1956 and, while the Soviet leader was prepared to make one last try in August 1957, he was already coy and waited for the Yugoslavs to come forth. As far as Khrushchev was concerned, Tito was no longer to be treated as a great leader or as a threat. Rather, the policy was to treat Yugoslavia as an unimportant small country, in the meantime consolidating the political unity of the bloc.

Accordingly, the Soviets proceeded in the spring of 1958 to buttress the position won in the November meeting. On March 14 a Prague conference, attended by representatives of the leading European Communist parties, including Gomulka's, made a preliminary decision to publish a common theoretical journal. Poland, increasingly isolated because of the Chinese position and the Yugoslav withdrawal, bowed to these demands, made in the midst of a mounting campaign against revisionism within Communist ranks. What is more, throughout the bloc revisionism was identified with increasing frequency as treason, and "the merciless suppression and liquidation of revisionist views as an important precondition of the triumph of socialism" was postulated.[26] Dogmatism was no longer mentioned, except in Poland, and prominent "dogmatists," such as Vulko Chervenkov, Tito's *bête noire*, were again coming to the fore.[27] The authoritative theoretical journal of the CPSU led the campaign by warning that it had to be expected that the revisionists would intensify their efforts and refine their methods following their rebuff at the November conference.[28]

From the antirevisionist point of view this warning was vindicated by the publication on March 13, 1958, of the draft program for the forthcoming congress of the League (Union) of Communists of Yugoslavia. The contents of the lengthy 100,000-word document signaled both to Moscow and to Peiping that revisionism, not just anti-Stalinism, had become formally linked with the power of the Yugoslav party and that it was being formulated as the latest and most important refinement of Marxist-Leninist doctrine. The program, while emphasizing its particular relevance to the Yugoslav party, reiterated that it "represents the analysis of the contemporary differences in the world . . . expressing the principled views on some of the most essential problems of the contemporary international workers' movement and the development of socialism in the world." [29] Such claims of universality, following in the footsteps of Yugoslavia's November stand, would have caused major irritation, even if the contents of the document had not been objectionable.

But the document was also bound to be irritating. Had the Yugoslav leaders limited themselves in their comprehensive statement to matters clearly within Yugoslav practical purview, they conceivably might have avoided provoking the ire of the Communist parties elsewhere. Since Marxist-Leninist perspectives, however, necessarily involve evaluation of broad international trends, the Yugoslavs could hardly have done so without renouncing their implicit claim to being the true Marxists-Leninists. Indeed, to limit their concepts to Yugoslavia alone would have been a roundabout way of admitting that which the Yugoslavs always reject, namely national Communism. As a result, they felt justified in commenting authoritatively from the Marxist-Leninst perspective on world affairs, on the problematics of the march toward socialism, and on relations among Communist states. Not unexpectedly, these proved to be the most offending passages.

Aware of the charges of revisionism leveled against them, the Yugoslavs' statement went to some pains to define the prevailing deviations from the "true" doctrine and discovered them in "two ideological tendencies": dogmatic revisionism and bourgeois revisionism. The former springs from bureaucratism and etatism, leads toward "pseudo-revolutionary sectarianism and . . . the loss of confidence in the strength of the working class," toward internal violence and terroristic rule, and expresses itself by branding as "revisionism every true effort aimed at really developing the Marxist idea in the contemporary social conditions." The Yugoslavs also rejected bourgeois revisionism, which was said to be based on outmoded "bourgeois-democratic illusions" and which, in effect, provides the dogmatic revisionists with their ammunition. Thus Western social democracy was also explicitly rejected. The Yugoslavs were calling upon all Communists to wage a struggle "on two fronts" in order to preserve and promote socialism, once again establishing themselves as the only legitimate standard-bearers of the Marxist-Leninist ideology.

The Yugoslavs then proceeded to pass judgment on the most vital issues in the Communist world view. Declaring themselves to be simultaneously an integral part of both "the socialist world" and of "the European and world community," the Yugoslavs ascribed most of the prevailing international tension to the existence of "two blocs" which were fathered by the wartime creation of spheres of influence between the major allied powers. Without differentiating between the two blocs, the declaration flatly asserted that "the division of the world into blocs impedes the realization of the idea of coexistence, and is at odds with full independence and sovereignty of peoples and states." The statement, made in the name of Marxism-Leninism, pitted not only capitalism but the Communist camp itself directly against the best interests of mankind.

In addition, the Yugoslavs, taking a broad look at the socioeconomic processes of the contemporary age, rejected the notion that, in the progression toward socialism, the Communist parties were indispensable tools of historical change. Doctrines to that effect were denounced as "theoretically wrong and practically very damaging." The Yugoslavs asserted that even under conditions of capitalism the state, because of the complexity of modern economy and technology, is increasingly limiting the role of private capital and that, while the danger of fascism is incipient in that development, the overwhelming pressures of the increasingly articulate working class are pushing society into the epoch of socialism. "Socialism is more and more becoming the matter of the practice of all nations, it is ever more becoming a universal process and system," the Yugoslavs postulated.

With socialism expanding, the question of relations among the Communist states was all the more pressing. Commenting on it, the Yugoslavs pointed to the pernicious consequences for the international Communist movement of the "bureaucratic-etatistic tendencies" which arose in the USSR because of its retarded prerevolutionary condition and which were encouraged "subjectively" by Stalin. These tendencies were said to have resulted in dogmatism. However, the Yugoslavs noted hopefully, the consequent deformation in the Soviet socialist system had not been fundamental and had been basically shaken by the Twentieth Congress. In the new circumstances produced by it, the various Communist states were able to give more adequate attention to their domestic conditions. But the Communist parties must at all times be conscious of their own national peculiarities, and no party can be allowed to acquire a monopoly of ideological evaluation in the Communist world, even if a specific party, because of its special power, can at some time become the standard-bearer in the struggle for Communism. "Proclamation of the road and form of development of socialism of any country as being the only correct ones is nothing else but dogma, which impedes the process of socialist transformation in the world." Accordingly proletarian internationalism could no longer be defined in terms of one's attitude toward the USSR but in terms of respect and noninterference among all socialist forces. Its true application would not allow a situation in which "it has been possible for a socialist country to maintain in various forms unequal relations with one or several other socialist countries."

In would be inconceivable to assume that the Yugoslavs did not expect a violent reaction to the above theses from the Communist camp. The draft program involved a denial of the dichotomic image so crucial to the role of the Communist camp and the Communist Party, a denial of Soviet leadership, and a theoretical statement which, by attempting to establish a general perspective for the prevailing historical phase, could be construed as the latest and most authoritative alternative to the views crystallized by the November Moscow declaration. Even if the Yugoslav condemnations of the USSR were

somewhat more veiled than at their preceding congress and even if
the program did make some concessions, such as abandonment of "coexistence" as the basis for relations among Communist states, it still
postulated concepts profoundly alien to Soviet thinking and, what is
more, the Yugoslavs must have known it. Past Yugoslav criticisms
could have been discounted as essentially reactions to the "aberrations" of Stalinism. But, in Soviet eyes, there could be no excuse for
such an ideologically divisive move in 1958. The violent reaction
from Moscow and the other Communist capitals was not long in
forthcoming.

In a transparent effort to appear conciliatory once the damage had
been done, and possibly in response to Polish pleas for moderation,
the Yugoslavs, almost on the very day that a lengthy denunciation of
their program was published in the CPSU's *Kommunist*,[30] made certain revisions in their text. Most particularly, they rephrased the part
pertaining to the two blocs to differentiate between NATO and the
"defensive" Warsaw Pact, omitting the discussion of the ancestry of
"spheres of influence." The fundamental theses, however, were not
amended — and hardly could be, once the Yugoslavs had re-evaluated
the internal conditions in the Communist camp and had decided that
a crystallization of an ideological alternative, and not secretive Tito-
Khrushchev arrangements, was the best method of influencing the
pattern of Communist development.[31]

The conflict with the Communist camp, semidormant since November, at once came to life. Speeches by Yugoslav leaders to their
congress, boycotted demonstratively by the Communist parties, further sharpened the disagreement by replying to external criticisms.
The underlying theme of the speeches, starting with Tito's, was
emphasis on Yugoslav independence and a labeling of all criticisms as
interference in Yugoslav affairs.[32] At the same time, stress was laid
on two superficially contradictory propositions: the program's universality was emphasized together with pointed assertions of precisely
those points on which the Yugoslav position differed from the Communist camp. Indeed, as if determined to destroy the Chinese-Soviet
diversity-in-unity formula, the Yugoslavs ignored the points of agreement.

Yet there seems to have been a method in this apparent contradiction. By simultaneously stressing disagreement and suggesting that
their program had universal relevance,* the Yugoslavs were establish-

---

* Yugoslav commentators left no doubt that Tito's horizon did not end on the
Rumanian or Bulgarian frontiers. For instance, N. Pasic in "Socialism as a World

ing their doctrine as an alternative to the established views and were making up for the errors of 1956 when they had allowed themselves to overstress the points of agreement with the camp. In 1958, frustrated in their efforts to work from within and resentful of being ignored, the Yugoslavs were determined to bring existing ideological conflicts into the open. Belgrade remained convinced that underlying social forces working for more heterogeneity within the camp would ultimately prevail and that open exposure would give a sense of direction to and facilitate such processes. In his address to the congress, Tito professed to see signs of this already, as for instance in the greater reliance on bilateralism within the camp [33] (even if, for the time being, not used for the right ends), and the Yugoslavs hoped that ultimately Communist unity would be restored by unanimous acceptance of the principle of diversity.

The Dynamics of Leadership: Hierarchical Contingency

The struggle against revisionism was acquiring concreteness. The vagueness of "the many ways to socialism" period and the difficulties of making a qualitative judgment when faced with evolutionary changes gave way to a concretization of the enemy, to the unmasking of revisionism as not merely an act of revising a sacred tenet but as its actual betrayal. On that score, particularly in view of the possible consequences of revisionism for the less stable Communist regimes, there was essential agreement among the other ruling Communist parties, save that of Poland. There was uncertainty, however, in how best to react against it, particularly the Yugoslav form.

Following November 1957, Khrushchev's apparent remedy was to ignore Tito, thereby denying him status through mutual dialogue and debate. Khrushchev's position led some observers to conclude that Khrushchev's was a more liberal or less dogmatic stand. His past actions and statements (such as his 1957 Prague pronouncements) do not seem to justify such a proposition. Rather, it would appear that the Soviet leaders felt that the Yugoslav initiative in the fall of 1957 had sufficiently compromised Tito and that restraint in reaction

Process" flatly asserts the following: "The Program elaborates and solves the fateful dilemma between war and peace in this atomic century within the framework of a well-developed and scientifically validated conception of active coexistence. . . . The conception of socialism as a world process is the basic view from which the UCJ Program considers and appraises the situation in the international workers' movement. . . . Conscious socialist forces will be much more successful in their struggle if they realize more clearly the world proportion of the process of growth of socialism and the great wealth of its forms." *Nasa Stvarnost,* May 1958.

would implicitly deny the relevance of Yugoslav views outside of Yugoslavia, while maintaining the formula of not stressing differences.* The publication of the draft program, however, must have raised questions about the wisdom of such tactics and presumably placed the Soviet leader under pressure from the centralist elements neighboring on Yugoslavia and most hostile to Tito. The Soviet position accordingly shifted. Until the publication of the program, and despite the November disagreement, all the Communist parties planned to send official delegations to the Yugoslav congress, thereby tacitly confirming Yugoslav status as a regime guided by Marxism-Leninism. On April 5 Belgrade was confidentially informed of the Soviet decision to boycott the congress,[34] but the matter was not made public, presumably in the hope of still effecting some Yugoslav concessions. At the same time, the preparation of an official rebuttal to the Yugoslav program was initiated, and the issue of *Kommunist* containing it was set into print on April 15. Two days later the Yugoslav *Kommunist* printed the minor Yugoslav revisions, which presumably had been communicated to the other parties. On April 19 the Soviet critique was made public, and its text suggests that the Yugoslav revisions had come too late to be considered in the Moscow statement. The estrangement of the preceding few months had become a public matter.

Quite naturally, the *Kommunist* critique attempted to refute particularly those parts of the Yugoslav statement which appeared to undermine the general Bolshevik perspective and which criticized the pattern of relations within the Communist camp.[35] It involved essentially a restatement of familiar Soviet theses. However, considering the importance of some of the Soviet notions that the Yugoslavs were rejecting, the Soviet reply still seemed relatively restrained and designed to preserve some common basis. While occasionally lapsing into harsh language, the article nevertheless expressed the hope that its "comradely comment on a number of questions of principle . . . will be favorably received and considered by the authors of the draft." The *Kommunist* refutation displayed a particular sensitivity to Yugoslav charges that in the past unequal relations had prevailed between socialist countries and rejected the notion that the essence

---

* There is reason to believe that until then the Soviets were toying halfheartedly with the possibility of limited reconciliation. Kadar held an exploratory meeting with Tito on Yugoslav soil on March 27-28, and there are some grounds for suspecting that another Tito-Khrushchev meeting was being considered. Khrushchev arrived in Budapest on April 2 but, with neither side yielding, the meeting with Tito (as far as is known) was not held.

of relations between Communist states is defined by the principles of equality and noninterference said to be the content of proletarian internationalism. "The draft actually defends national communism," *Kommunist* charged. If the Yugoslav line were to be adopted, it could only lead to disunity among Communist states. The statement ended by categorically warning that improvement in relations with Yugoslavia will never be made "by means of concessions at the expense of Marxist-Leninist principles."

Kommunist was both a first shot in the new conflict and a last warning. It reiterated what Khrushchev had been saying in 1957 but which the Yugoslavs, joyfully remembering the June 1956 declaration, were unwilling to understand: that henceforth no ideological ambiguities which might give cause to disunity would be tolerated. However, the Soviet statement was to no avail; the Yugoslavs had passed the point of no return. Their draft program reflected a reasoned reconsideration of their previous views, and in such matters Communists, despite tactical elasticity, do not shift easily from week to week. The congress which convened on April 22 reaffirmed the revised theses.

At this stage, the dynamics of leadership within the Communist camp came into play. Soviet primacy within it, despite the setbacks of 1956, was a matter of sheer fact, given the USSR's military strength and industrial development. But the acceptance of its leadership as a proposition and the actual exercise of that leadership, as differentiated from the *potential* capacity to lead, depended now to an unprecedented degree on the support of centralists in the leaderships of the other states, and particularly in China. While it is extremely doubtful that China could — even were it so predisposed — challenge that leadership, it was in a better position than ever before to exercise pressure and to set a tone which the other centralists could endorse, thereby placing the USSR in the not unfamiliar position of a leader being forced to lead by his following. At the same time, a certain amount of restraint seemed warranted by the gradually improving Soviet-Polish relations.

The problem which faced the camp was essentially a tactical one. There was basic agreement that the Yugoslav program was revisionist, that ideological concessions were out of the question, and that open attacks must not go unanswered. But the degree of condemnation and the sharpness of reply to the gauntlet cast by Belgrade was a matter on which differences of judgment apparently arose. The differences were to a great extent the product of the varying experi-

ence of the leaderships involved. Khrushchev, determined not to repeat Stalin's error, appeared anxious to avoid a repetition of the 1948
break or, if such a break were unavoidable, to let the Yugoslavs effect
it. In addition, to return to 1948 would have meant a repudiation of
Khrushchev's policies of the preceding three years. Accordingly, he
appeared to favor a return to approximately the 1955 situation: maintenance of the normalized state relations but rigidity in party matters.
An added advantage of such a policy would be that Yugoslavia would
not be pushed headlong into "the imperialist camp." The East European centralists naturally favored more extreme measures. The entire
Tito episode had been a threat to them, and a sharp line against him
would also restrict Gomulka, for whom the centralists entertained intense distaste. To the Chinese, the Yugoslavs appeared to be violating
a cardinal rule in Communist ethics by aggressively airing disagreements, endangering the unity so delicately woven at the November
assembly. China, in the midst of internal social revolution and internationally isolated, would rather pay token to Soviet leadership than to
see the Communist camp degenerating into a loose confederation. The
Chinese were hence much more inclined to favor the East European
centralists in their harsh attitude toward the Yugoslavs, and presumably urged Moscow accordingly. The time when Moscow could settle a new line for the camp without consultations was past.

The Chinese inclination toward severity was transplanted into
policy with the publication on May 5 in *Jen Min Jih Pao* of a scathing
critique of the Yugoslav program. Moscow immediately associated itself with it but, at the same time, seemed to suggest that a Yugoslav
recantation would be met with a merciful response from the Kremlin.
Two days after the Chinese statement, as if to underscore the Soviet
attitude, *Pravda* reprinted the text of a Khrushchev telegram to Tito
wishing him success in office and expressing hope for a "strengthening
of friendship between our countries." The telegram made it clear that
Khrushchev was sending it as Soviet Premier and addressing it to the
Yugoslav President.[36] He thus was still maintaining the distinction
between party relations and state relations. But the line adopted by
the Chinese made the maintenance of that distinction increasingly
difficult. The Chinese statement, phrased vituperatively without once
referring to Tito or the Yugoslavs as "comrades," made four basic
points: the Yugoslav program meant the abandonment of socialism;
it fit the subversive plans of American imperialists; the 1948 Cominform condemnation of Yugoslavia had never been reversed by the
Communist parties concerned; and the Yugoslav behavior during the

Hungarian uprising had abetted counterrevolution. Their statement went appreciably beyond the Soviet line, while the waving of the 1948 resolution, immediately and gleefully imitated by the East European centralists,[37] was calculated to drive the Yugoslav leaders to white fury, especially since they had long been implying to their own party that the 1955 and 1956 agreements had involved a repudiation of the Cominform resolutions.

It is to be recalled that at this point these events were occurring within the framework of growing international tensions. The situation was particularly acute in the Middle East. To the Communists, the Western reactions were the confirmation of the old thesis that, when faced with collapse, the imperialists might resort to war. Unity seemed imperative, as did a return to "revolutionary vigilance," to the sharpest demarcation between friend and foe. Given the warm centralist response to the Chinese statement which, as expected, provoked a sharp Yugoslav reply charging the Chinese with returning to "the notorious Cominform declaration," engaging in "filthy insinuations," and interfering in Yugoslav affairs,[38] Khrushchev moved to abandon the distinction between state and party relations. On May 9 *Pravda* published a sharp statement warning Belgrade that such a distinction would be untenable in view of the developing ideological dispute. An official secret message to that effect from the Central Committee of the CPSU was delivered to the Yugoslav party on May 11 by the Soviet ambassador.

Once the 1948 issue had been revived, any fleeting chance of a Yugoslav retraction faded. The Soviet message was therefore merely an empty gesture and might have reflected the persistent Soviet determination to place the onus for any break squarely on Tito's shoulders. With the Yugoslav stance unchanged and with the Yugoslavs still sputtering with rage at the revival of the 1948 Cominform declaration,[39] the Soviet press adopted a more belligerent tone. The Yugoslav position was compared to the "treachery" of Imre Nagy,[40] even though the Soviet leader still expressed the hope that existing Soviet-Yugoslav misunderstandings would be overcome for the sake of "further strengthening the unity of the Socialist forces in the world." [41] That this, however, was considered at best only a remote probability was strongly hinted by Soviet action two days later, forcefully linking the problem of party relations to state relations: the Soviet credit of about $285 million for an important aluminum project was unilaterally "suspended."

The suspension of the credit was followed by two speeches of

Khrushchev, in Sofia on June 3 and in East Berlin on July 11, which bridged the discrepancies between the Soviet and Chinese analyses of the Yugoslav problem.* In Sofia, in a bitter but not entirely consistent outburst (Khrushchev, for instance, occasionally referred to the Yugoslavs as "comrades"), the Soviet leader for the first time openly stated that the CPSU had never retracted its adherence to the 1948 Cominform excommunication of Tito and, secondly, charged the Yugoslavs, just as the Chinese had done, with abetting the Hungarian uprising. While still not accusing the Yugoslavs of acting as United States agents or of betraying socialism, Khrushchev characterized the Yugoslav program as outright revisionism which, in turn, he defined as the Trojan Horse of imperialism. By refusing to subordinate themselves to the unanimous judgment of the other parties, Khrushchev stressed, Yugoslavia was no longer marching in the company of those who guide themselves by Marxism-Leninism.

Khrushchev amplified his views a few weeks later in an address to the Fifth East German SED Congress.[42] In the intervening period, the Yugoslav-Chinese dialogue had become even more violent, with Tito charging the Chinese with aggressive designs in Asia and with courting war. In the course of his defense of Russia's chief ally, the CPSU First Secretary moved even closer to the Chinese position. The two charges made at Sofia, and reiterated in East Berlin, were amplified by ridicule of the Yugoslav system as a kind of socialism which is built on American alms and by a charge that the Yugoslavs, with their revisionist program, were "concurring" in the imperialist attacks on Communism. Khrushchev in this fashion adopted basically the Chinese four-point condemnation of Tito.

The Soviet leader did, however, go to some pains to point out that everything had been done to improve relations with Yugoslavia and that no Communist could feel that he, Khrushchev, had not done his share in this regard. Revealing the Soviet leadership's acute sense of outrage that anyone who considers himself Marxist-Leninist could differ and could refuse to identify himself with the Communist camp, Khrushchev warned that efforts to improve relations must cease "when Yugoslav leaders say that they are Marxists-Leninists, but use

* In addition to the differences in emphasis already noted, the following remark by *Jen Min Jih Pao* (June 4, 1958) suggests possible conflicts of evaluation within the camp: "Perhaps some people feel that even though the Yugoslav Communist League program is revisionist and advantageous to imperialism, it would be best not to point this out in order not to push the ruling group of the Yugoslav Communist League to the side of imperialism . . . to fail to say that they are playing today to imperialism could elicit nothing but a malicious smirk from the Dulleses."

Marxism-Leninism only as cover for misleading trusting people and to turn them from the road of revolutionary class struggle . . . they are then trying to rip out of the proletariat's hands the sharpest class weapon." [43] Both his Sofia and his East Berlin speeches made it clear that it was not the offensive content of the program per se which precipated the reaction (similar views had been expressed by Belgrade before), but the fact that the program posed a "systematized" ideological alternative, that it was timed to pose a challenge, and that Yugoslav "neutrality" through its revisionism was directed against the camp.

By adopting in essence the Chinese charges, Khrushchev abandoned his previous distinction between state and party relations — which, in practice, could have meant a return to the summer 1955 situation. In his East Berlin speech he still reiterated the proposition that the Yugoslavs were the only ones to gain status by an argument with the camp and that, therefore, the CPSU was not inclined to promote Yugoslav megalomania by a continuous dialogue. Minimizing the issue, Khrushchev was avoiding Stalin's mistake of making it a critical concern for the ruling Communist parties, and he was striking home at one of Tito's chief weaknesses, his vanity. The centralist line of simply identifying Tito as a "Judas and renegade," or, in other words, Stalin's 1948–1953 position, was not adopted. Instead, there was to be a return roughly to the mid- and late-1954 relationship, involving a firmly, even violently, stated ideological condemnation and a certain chilly correctness in state relations. It would be as if the preceding four years had never happened. In many ways, that was the most effective way of coping with Yugoslavia.

To cement the new policy there was a need to create a firm landmark which would serve as a lasting reminder to all Communists that the absence of a continuous barrage does not mean that revisionism was no longer tantamount to subversion. Furthermore, there was the need to puncture any lingering Yugoslav hopes of influencing their neighboring Communist states. This requirement was to be met by a human sacrifice. The final act in the restoration of the dichotomy so necessary to unity was to personalize its enemy and then, by destroying him, demonstrate dramatically the line between neutrality which leads to treason and commitment which is the basis of unity. With Tito not available, on June 17, 1958, the execution of Imre Nagy was announced.*

* Executed with him was General Pal Maleter, the hero of the uprising, arrested while negotiating with the Russian command. Nagy's execution was preceded by a

Nagy's execution had the added function of serving as a test case of Gomulkaist Poland's loyalty to the higher interests of the bloc. Despite basic Polish sympathy for the Yugoslav efforts to transform the camp into a looser confederation and a common anti-Stalinist orientation, in several important instances Gomulka was himself inclined to view Tito's opinions with suspicion and to feel that his Yugoslav friend was embracing deviant revisionist positions. Most particularly, Gomulka still basically subscribed to the notion that, given the alternative of belonging to the Communist camp or rejecting it, a true Communist must choose the former, especially in view of the general conflict with imperialism. Gomulka also found it difficult to accept Tito's views on "socialism as a world process" which minimized the imperative role of the Communist parties in effecting the socialist revolution. In brief, while anti-Stalinist, Gomulka remained basically a modified, Polish-style Leninist (see next chapter), whereas many portions of Tito's program recalled Bernsteinian and Bukharinite positions.[44]

For this reason, Gomulka himself probably disapproved of many portions of the Yugoslav program. But, mindful of the past and not wishing to establish any new precedents for Soviet interference, he was cautious and restrained in his reactions. On April 5, his weekly theoretical journal, *Polityka*, reproduced the substance of the Yugoslav program without any comment whatsoever, while Polish Politburo members, Ochab and Morawski, were quietly but vainly pleading with Tito for exclusion of the most offensive portions of his draft.[45] Ten days later, with the Soviet boycott common knowledge, his party's daily printed a lengthy editorial which criticized the Yugoslav views on state capitalism, the program's excessive concern with bureaucratic tendencies in Communist states, and the incorrect assessments of the process of the withering away of the state.[46] However, the paper gave the Yugoslavs credit for their efforts to promote peace, specifically referred to the "errors of 1948" in the camp's relations

---

concerted campaign, linking his "revisionism" with treasonable plans to undermine the Communist camp. For a brief period after his arrest in November 1956, a distinction was made between his motives (not treasonable) and their consequences (objectively treasonable). That distinction was subsequently dropped with the campaign against revisionism mounting. Nagy was identified directly as a traitor. See "The 'Conceptions' of Imre Nagy and the Ideological Preparation of the Betrayal," *Tarsadalmi Szemle*, November-December 1957; "From the History of the Ideological Preparations for the Counter-Revolutionary Rising in Hungary," *Voprosy istorii*, no. 12, 1957. The frequent linking of Tito with Nagy in these statements made it clear that Nagy's execution was not meant to be merely a footnote to the Hungarian tragedy.

with Yugoslavia,* expressed the hope for a friendly, comradely dialogue, and, most important, equivocated on the Yugoslav critique of
past relations between Communist states. The Polish reaction during
April-May represented most closely the actual Polish position: some
ideological disapproval but not ideological disavowal.

Gradually, however, Gomulka's grudging acceptance of Soviet
leadership and his commitment to the bloc, intensified by Polish dependence on Soviet protection of the Oder-Neisse frontier and by
Poland's economic isolation, forced him to elaborate his basic critique
into a more extensive condemnation. Nagy's execution meant that
sides had to be taken, and to be silent in the general chorus of approval was also to take sides. Having already conceded for the sake
of Communist solidarity the principle of Soviet leadership, a point
potentially impinging on his own autonomy, Gomulka must have felt
that to rupture his relations with the bloc for the sake of Yugoslav
views, some of which he disapproved, or for the principles of a man
already dead, even though the Polish leaders privately expressed their
abhorrence of the execution, would be to engage in an idealism which
he as a Polish Communist could ill afford. Accordingly, on June 28,
he finally sided with the camp. In a speech delivered at Gdansk,[47] he
stressed the need for unity and emphasized that Yugoslavia could
build socialism only because the presence of a united Communist
camp prevented capitalist aggression against it. Hence, "objectively"
speaking, the Yugoslav abstinence from that unity, so favored by the
West, was actually aiding imperialism. The same principle he applied
to Imre Nagy, whose execution he described as "severe" (the centralists called it "deserved") and whom he characterized as a revisionist who "step by step moved to capitulation before the counterrevolution, performed its assignments, was destroying the socialist
order in Hungary." Gomulka's only equivocations were not to refer
approvingly to the 1948 Cominform resolution or to argue that revisionism leads to treason, unlike the centralists who equated revisionism with treason.

Gomulka's speech, immediately picked up by the Soviet antirevisionist theorists,[48] was an important element in the restoration of
unity within the camp. It marked Gomulka's second most important

* Gomulka's position in 1948, however, was not unambiguous. Although under
considerable pressure, he still at the time defended his views on other matters while
being quite critical of the Yugoslav position on the grounds that its "narrow nationalism," leading to a break with the camp, would lead to the collapse of Communist
power. See *Nowe Drogi*, no. 11 (1948), p. 42.

concession since October 1956. The principle of Soviet leadership was now solidly coupled with the sanctity of the camp's unity, and the ideological argument for any future Soviet interference was accordingly immeasurably strengthened. Any effort to resist it could be condemned as an act against socialism which, in Gomulka's own words, could only be built through unity. In this connection Gomulka could hardly ignore the fact that already in the anti-Nagy campaign emphasis was put on Nagy's agricultural compromises as proof of his revisionism. Thus, for the time being, the campaign against revisionism did not mean a return to internal institutional uniformity, although it did establish the ideological basis for such a step. Revisionism was for the time being repelled because the revisionist intellectuals had not broken through their isolation from the practitioners of power; and in Yugoslavia revisionism had been compromised by becoming identified with power expediency.

The appeal of Yugoslavia was thus effectively contained. Many of the Communist intellectuals elsewhere, who had previously attached great hopes to Yugoslavia's separate path, became disillusioned by Tito's external Machiavellianism, while the East European *apparatchiki* realized that the adoption of the Yugoslav position would be tantamount to breaking the unity of the camp. To be able to do so, a Communist regime would have to have an indigenous base to maintain itself in power without Soviet support and presumably in spite of the USSR. Most Communists now realize that at the present the Yugoslav position represents an extreme alternative which no Communist regime in East Europe can emulate. This is the significant difference between Yugoslav national Communism or revisionism, and the quiet practice of domesticism. As a result, although the Yugoslav program constitutes a major irritant to the Communist camp, its actual effectiveness is now rather limited.

The summer of 1958 marked the end of a cycle initiated in 1954. While the camp was no longer characterized by the strict Stalinist uniformity and hierarchy, Khrushchev had successfully woven together a new fabric of unity which satisfied the centralists, which isolated Tito, and which gradually subordinated Gomulka. The new fabric combined the old hierarchy with a new sense of contingency. Although this was not the triumphant fulfillment of Khrushchev's 1955–1956 vision, it did involve the reconsolidation of the structure which the events of 1956 had shaken. In achieving this Khrushchev relied much more than Stalin had on the support of the other Communist leaderships. It must also be said that his energy, his elasticity, his tactical sense, his ability to satisfy the centralists and to enlist the anti-Stalinists, deserve a good share of the credit. And he certainly showed a capacity to learn from his errors. By 1957 and 1958 he realized that Marxism's universality as an action program must rely on the elimination of peculiarities derived from efforts to apply Marxism to specific national realities. That had been the strength of Stalinism as an international dogma. Without a common power center jealously to protect certain universal ideological imperatives, Marxism, even Marxism-Leninism, was shown to be inadequate in providing unity for international Communism. Diversity of thought, emerging once the center's controls lapsed, immediately brought to the surface the divisive forces which survived even the heyday of Stalinist unity. National animosities, cultural affinities, territorial claims, specific ideological traditions, all gradually came to the front. All of them could be fit within the framework of the ideology once it became responsive to domestic conditions. Disunity inevitably followed, revealing the ultimate failing of Mao Tse-tung's injunction to "let a hundred flowers bloom, let a hundred schools contend!"

Ideology could thus divide rather than unite. That precisely was why Khrushchev warned that to allow the Communist parties to be fully independent "would lead the Communist and Workers' Parties to contradictory action and, in the final count, to disagreement." [49] The weeding out of revisionism, so necessary to forge unity, was an affirmation of the need for ideological monopoly and a belated expression of distrust in the capacity of ideology alone to promote common action.

CHAPTER 14

The Polish Way to Socialism

VICTORY rarely re-establishes the *status quo ante*. The conflict generated by a direct challenge to existing arrangements is merely a more accentuated manifestation of continuous and often almost imperceptible change. A successful defense of an established order creates an illusory impression of the past's having been recaptured by the present. Yet on closer examination that past turns out to be rather different, maybe not quite as profoundly different as the challenger had desired but certainly unlike what might have been expected if the challenge had never arisen. The restoration of unity and the recognition of Soviet leadership were, in a sense, acts of successful defense of an established order. The Polish way to socialism tolerated within the order was an important new element, highly relevant to the problem of relations among Communist states.

Gomulka and the October Upheaval

Gomulka was the symbol, but not the architect, of the Polish October. The distinction is important to an understanding of Polish developments after October 1956, the internal trends of which this chapter will attempt to synthesize. An architect is the source of much of the form and content of his design. A symbol is shaped to a far greater degree by the events and purposes it is said to represent, though it need not be powerless. If in time, however, the forces which promoted the symbol find it indispensable, it may then acquire an independent position and become a directing force. This was exactly the case with Gomulka.

Gomulka was the indispensable ingredient in the brew concocted by those who made the October Revolution. The intellectuals could create the atmosphere, stimulate the desires, crystallize the general purposes. The students could produce the ferment, the sense of urgency, the passionate commitment. The workers, restive after Poznan, could dramatize the corruption of the ruling party, which ironically bore the name of the United Polish Workers' Party, and at a crucial juncture provide the necessary physical backing to an upheaval. The party activists, even *apparatchiki* like First Secretary

Ochab, could hand over the sinews of power, could immobilize the secret police and arouse the army. But none of these groups could simultaneously effect a change profound enough to satisfy the most embittered while not driving away the most indifferent, produce a sense of *real* change and yet not overthrow the system. As a symbol, Gomulka offered something to everyone. He was a former victim of Stalinism and its recognized opponent. His "right-wing" deviation appealed to nationalist outrage at Soviet domination. He was a dedicated Communist who never wavered in his commitment and who presumably could be trusted not to initiate the dissolution of Communist rule. To the anti-Communists, he was the leader of a movement toward independence; to the revisionists, toward a democratic socialism. To the concerned Communists, he was the saviour of the crumbling Communist rule. His ability to personalize conflicting aspirations, and subsequently to channel them, was another demonstration of the role of the individual in history.

The diverse aspirations of October and the conflicting hopes of the various partisans obscured for a while a factor crucial to an understanding of Gomulka. He was above all a Marxist-Leninist. The son of a disaffected peasant who had emigrated to America only to return disappointed to Poland, Gomulka (b. 1905) was active from his youth in Communist movements.[1] They were to him both a school and a profession. A self-taught Communist whose formal education ended at the age of fourteen, Marxism-Leninism became his only perspective from which to view and eventually shape reality. This did not mean that in every instance a doctrinal precept was the basis for his actions. Gomulka repeatedly showed a keen sense of political realism and undogmatic elasticity. Marxism-Leninism, however, provided him with all his conceptual tools and his sense of commitment. It gave him a broad doctrinal outlook which dictated the ultimate direction, which served as a key to understanding the unfolding course of history, and which justified and necessitated certain actions as both good and inevitable. A sense of self-righteousness tied to historical inevitability can have an enduring attraction, particularly to the self-educated. (It is interesting to note the strong parallels between Gomulka and Khrushchev in this respect.)

Gomulka became the party leader during the highpoint of Moscow's wartime policy of favoring moderate changes in East Europe, expressed through the allegedly distinctive character of the People's Democracy (Chapters 1–3). Unlike some of his more radically doctrinaire colleagues, Gomulka welcomed the wartime policy since it fit well into both his basic Communist commitment and his specific evaluation of the Polish scene. It would be incorrect, however, to conclude from this that Gomulka was characterized by a special sense of liberalism or that he was not fanatically committed to Communism. Indeed, the political opponents of the Communist regime in the immediate postwar period recall that he stood out as one of the most violent and energetic Communist leaders, ruthlessly suppressing the political activity of the opposition and unsparing in his condemnations of the non-Communist Polish underground or of the Polish Army which had fought in the west.[2] Generous in his praise of the secret police, anxious to consolidate his power, he stood solidly with his Moscow-trained comrades in the leadership. But sharing a common purpose is not the same as agreeing on policy. Building Communism is a complex problem involving not only methods, but stages, timing, and coordination of domestic policy with the external interests of Communism as a world movement — or, more specifically, with the interests of the USSR as Communism's center. It is on this level that conflicts are generated, that ambiguities ensue and ideological disputes arise. This was the case in Poland once the primary task of crushing the anti-Communist opposition had been achieved. Gomulka had to comment on many of these issues, and it is testimony to the depth of this man's inner convictions as well as to his intellectual rigidity that in 1956 he re-emerged from obscurity very much the same Communist that he was before 1949.

In studying Gomulka's ideas one finds several themes which appear to be at the core of his thinking and which he has reiterated frequently. To bring out their striking continuity, it might be useful therefore to compare his pre-1949 formulations of certain key issues with his post-October 1956 statements.[3] There is first of all the firm belief that Communism can be built only if there is a monolithically united labor class:

1947	1957
the working class can perform its historical mission of reconstructing of societal relations . . . only when it is monolithic, when in its struggle it utilizes the unconquerable weapon of Marxism. . . .[4]	The indispensable condition for the overthrow of bourgeois power and for the construction of socialism is the direction of these processes by the Marxist-Leninist Party of the working class.[5]

This theme Gomulka verbalized repeatedly after October 1956, even at a time when Soviet pressure was not yet involved.[6] Similarly, before and after his own incarceration he expressed the view that internal violence was necessary and that the secret-police organs therefore perform a positive function:

1946	1956
The Security Organs as a whole are healthy and very dedicated in their work. And as such we will defend them against all unjustified and false accusations. For the Security [Organs] are a sharp weapon in the hands of the Polish democracy in the struggle against reaction. We will not allow this tool to be wrenched from us.[7]	The public security employees have proven that, together with the whole Party and all the progressive forces in our country, they stand unflinchingly on guard over the interests of the nation, that they wholeheartedly support changes in our life, and that they are ready to prevent any attempts aimed against the political line mapped out by the leadership of the Party.[8]

Gomulka, however, did concede that there is a point at which violence becomes a negative manifestation and that it is no longer a major requirement following the defeat of "reaction." Its use to defend the party's monopoly of power was a right still to be reserved, however.

Turning to the central issue of the role of labor in a socialist state, Gomulka's approach, while proclaiming the rule of the working class, has been characterized by a firm insistence that labor's real role in building socialism is to remain disciplined and to increase production. In 1945 he took a firm stand against those workers' demands which took a too literal conception of "the workers' state":

The Plenum [of the Central Committee] has been sharply against the relaxation of labor discipline among the working class and against all sorts of harmful tendencies to limit the scope of the authority of factory directors.[9]

Without raising labor productivity, no one can improve the welfare of the working class.[10]

After October 1956 his attitude toward the spontaneously formed Workers' Councils, which had backed him during the critical period, was one of suspicion and caution — the attitude of a Leninist who jealously protects the political monopoly of the party. He accordingly warned that "the workers' councils are not organs of the political power of the labor class . . . are not links in the administrative apparatus of the people's state," [11] and in outlining the scope of their legitimate activity he pointedly stressed socioeconomic productive goals only.[12]

The post-October Gomulka accordingly still held to his belief in the key role of the party, in the desirability of its monopoly of power, in the justified necessity of occasional violence, and was suspicious of any reforms which might weaken the party's hold. At the same time, however, this orthodoxy was balanced by his unchanged adherence to views which earlier had prevented him from pliantly adjusting to Stalinism. These views, which he firmly restated after 1956, concerned above all his position on the agrarian question, the specifics of the Polish situation, and, especially, Polish-Russian relations. Gomulka seems to have long entertained the opinion that socialist construction is a complicated and involved process requiring not only Stalinist determination but also simple human patience. In 1945 he warned: "The way to socialism is neither short nor can it be shortened. . . . It would be a gross oversimplification to claim that a turn of such fundamental importance to Poland can be immediately, from today to tomorrow, fully and well understood and accepted by the totality of all classes. . . ." [13] His advice applied with particular relevance to the problem of the Polish peasantry, steeped in tradition and religion, land-hungry, and fearful of socialism which to them meant collectivization. In the immediate postwar period Gomulka therefore stressed, as we have seen, that the peasant must be convinced that socialism was a good thing, that it meant land and freedom. Only afterwards, once the peasant suspicions have collapsed, could they be encouraged to undertake cooperative and collective development. Although Gomulka never explicitly rejected collectivization as such, he went far in stressing those peculiarities of Poland which made its adoption in the phase of People's Democracy unacceptable:

1946	1956
We have not the slightest need to follow in the footsteps of Soviet agrarian policy. *We have rejected collectivization, because in the Polish condition it would be harmful economically and politically.*[14]	The road to setting up a vast network of cooperative farms in Poland's countryside is a long one. A quantitative development of producer cooperation cannot be planned because, on the basis of voluntary entry in a cooperative, this would amount to planning the growth in human consciousness, and that cannot be planned.[15]

Gomulka grounded his objections to an accelerated collectiviza-tion program on the general differences between the Polish and Russian revolutionary conditions, a position not acceptable after 1948 and only rather halfheartedly endorsed by Soviet leaders after 1956. He stressed that one of the specific "objective" factors of the Polish scene which had to be considered by any leader was intense Polish nationalism. As a Communist, he felt that to ignore it was to commit an error in evaluation of reality unworthy of a true Marxist-Leninist. To recognize nationalism, he believed, was not to become a national Communist, even if temporarily this might appear to be the case to those who saw only the surface of things. Gomulka argued that a true Marxist-Leninist policy for the construction of socialism had to rec-ognize such domestic specifics, and in recognizing them it must re-spect the autonomy of a given Communist Party to choose the best methods of overcoming them. Equality and independence were thus indispensable to overcoming nationalism.

In 1946, Gomulka pointed to three crucial characteristics of the Russian revolution which he felt were absent in Poland: tsarist op-pression, the strength of capitalism in 1917–1920, and foreign inter-vention.[16] The very same considerations were mentioned eleven years later, in his address to the Ninth Party Plenum.[17] Again, in 1946 he was quite blunt in criticizing his party for underestimating the nation-alist element in the Polish scene: *"The basic error of Communists was that in fully appreciating the problem of struggle for the social liberation of the working class they underestimated the matter of* [national] *independence. . . ."* [18] And eleven years later, writing in *Pravda*, Gomulka repeated the same theme: "a particular trait formed [in the Polish people] in the course of their historical development as a result of age-long foreign oppression and deprivation of freedom . . . is the special sensitivity of the Polish people to questions of their country's independence and sovereignty. The underestimation or denial of national traits and peculiarities in the building of socialism is nihilistic dogmatism. . . ." [19] A proper policy must always strive to balance universal requisites with these profound national specifics.[20] Independence and diversity therefore are not ends in themselves in Gomulka's thinking. They are the necessary, enduring preconditions for true international unity and for the domestic construction of so-cialism. Domestic autonomy and mutual respect must be protected not in order to enshrine independence and nationalism but to create the climate for their eventual transition into a higher Communist brotherhood.

The pattern of post-October political development in Poland becomes more meaningful when considered within the framework of these continuities in Gomulka's thinking, as well as when related to the external factors traced in preceding chapters. Indeed, the only important new element in Gomulka's thinking, but one clearly derived from his general position that in order to change popular consciousness in Poland the factors shaping that consciousness must be appraised properly, was his articulate admission of the importance of the Polish Catholic tradition. In his judgment, the Stalinist period resulted in the unfortunate intensification of religious feelings: "the Party . . . cannot ignore the fact that the former conflict with the Church set millions of believers against the People's Government." [21] An adjustment was thus a necessary concession which would ultimately facilitate the march toward socialism.

Such, in brief, were Gomulka's basic patterns of thought when he came to power. They were, to be sure, tactically elastic, but in substance they had little in common with social democracy or with revisionism. But before they could be translated into the Polish way to socialism they had to survive a confrontation with the post-October political realities.

The Period of Restrained Spontaneity

There was no blueprint for the changes that occurred after October 1956. Gomulka's speech to the Eighth Plenum, elaborated in several public addresses, came the closest to charting a path for "Polish socialism," but it did so only in broad generalities. Indeed, guides for action had to be inferred from the more specific criticism that he made of the Stalinist system previously prevailing in Poland. But such negative instruction was not very helpful in drawing the precise limits to the anti-Stalinist measures that were bound to follow in post-October Poland. As a consequence, the period immediately following Gomulka's accession to power was characterized by a series of spontaneous developments, expressive of a variety of hitherto suppressed aspirations.

In politics, Gomulka's break with the past was interpreted by a large segment of the population to mean a conscious departure from the former totalitarianism, even if not going quite as far as to formally introduce a multiparty system. From the start, therefore, developments in politics were limited by the necessity of recognizing Communist one-party monopoly of power. Still, considerable areas for spontaneous change remained. It can be said that until some time after the January 1957 elections to the Sejm, the Gomulka regime did not actively shape the pattern of Polish life but merely responded whenever a direct challenge to its rule arose. The regime's primary objective at this stage was to win a resounding popular endorsement which would serve to convince the bloc that, in the interests of international Communism, Gomulka ought to be accepted. Abdication of domestic initiative was the consequence of the need to mobilize nation-wide support in the January elections. Given the simultaneous disorientation and demoralization of the Party membership [22] — symptomatically, party members had stopped wearing party emblems in their lapels — and the complete disintegration of the party's youth organization (ZMP), it was not surprising that rapid reactivization of formerly suppressed political elements took place. The two non-Communist members of the National Front, the United Peasant Party (ZSL) and the Democratic Party (SD), emaciated remnants of once-active political organizations,* were revitalized by the release from confinement of many former activists. In the Peasant Party the return to public life of many former pro-Mikolajczyk elements resulted in considerable upheaval. The new party chairman, S. Ignar, elected following a purge of those leaders who had become too identified with Stalinism, by mid-1957 was forced to wage a regular campaign against efforts from below to transform the party into a genuine spokesman for peasant interests.[23] The Communist Party cells in the countryside, with only 125,000 members as against the ZSL's 202,000, remained passive.†

While in the countryside the dissipation of Communist power essentially led to a return to the traditional passive independence of the Polish peasant, the party *apparat* on the district levels initially remained largely untouched by the new political situation. Thus in the medium-sized towns the "spirit of October," either as an intellectual challenge or in the form of new organizations and clubs, was success-

---

* The ZSL was built by combining the original Communist front organization, the Peasant Party, with the remnants of Mikolajczyk's anti-Communist Polish Peasant Party (PSL), after the latter's suppression. Almost entirely inactive during Stalinism, it served to transmit the regime's instructions to the peasantry. The Democratic Party was a haven primarily for those intellectuals and scholars who felt that they had to show some political interest but who could not bring themselves to be card-carrying Communists. Of its members, 68 per cent were from the intelligentsia. *Tygodnik Demokratyczny*, January 23–29, 1958.

† January 1, 1958, ZSL total membership stood at 261,314 members; the Communist membership on September 30, 1958, was 1,023,577. *Zielony Sztandar*, March 30, 1958; *Trybuna Ludu*, December 28, 1958.

fully kept out. The change was more profound in the large urban centers like Warsaw, Cracow, Lodz, Poznan, and so on, where the spirit of rebellion had originally been kindled. The war, the Nazi and Soviet exterminations of the Polish elite, the rapid social transformation produced by the industrialization drives, and the emphasis placed on mass education had radically changed the sociology of Polish urban politics. The postwar Communist dictatorship made a determined effort to prevent the formation of social pluralism and rejected any conception of politics based on the interaction of pluralistic groups. In practice, however, the very process of stressing the role of conscious, planned political activity designed to reconstruct society put a premium on the role of intellectuals * in society and created the basis for their gradual emergence as a politically oriented group. The moment the totalitarian party began to loosen its grip on society, the moment that doubt about the correctness of the regime's program began to be tolerated, the intellectuals were able to assume the leadership in the emerging dialogue to an extent which would have been difficult in prewar Poland, where so much more was left to unchanneled spontaneous action outside of politics. The intellectuals' influence was all the greater because the premium placed on "rational" planned social action meant that the party had to encourage them to join,[24] and after October they again identified themselves as intellectuals first and party members second. Grand designs and programs became the vogue. The "problematics" of development was the theme of post-October discussions. In effect, they involved a search for some measure of politically significant social cohesion after years of Stalinist social atomization.[25] If achieved, this would be bound to become an impediment to the party's rule.

Such efforts were facilitated by the postwar spread of higher education among the masses, which resulted in a large-scale intermediary stratum of so-called working intelligentsia, acting as a link between intellectuals and workers.† The industrial workers, led by prewar socialist activists as well as by their own intelligentsia, responded

* This term is used loosely to denote writers, journalists, academicians, "ideologues," economists, but not professionals such as doctors, lawyers, engineers.

† Between 1949-1950 and 1955-1956 about 700,000 young people, mostly peasants and workers, received higher education. For comparison, we may note that the so-called "mental" workers in all of Poland in 1931, with a population that was larger by a third, totaled 664,000. Among Polish sociologists there is a lively dispute as to whether this new stratum has developed its own character or whether it is essentially adopting the values of its prewar predecessors.

favorably to the search and expressed, through workers' self-government, their own quest for something more than centralized political authority. It was to these Workers' Councils that the intellectuals directed their attention. The so-called intellectuals' clubs, modeled in some respects on the revolutionary Jacobin clubs, were eager to link hands with the Workers' Councils, which seemed to bear some resemblance to the early soviets or even the Paris Commune. With the party vacillating, what stopped the formation of a common front of the restless proletariat and iconoclastic intellectuals?

Three reasons might be advanced. The first, and most important, was self-imposed restraint; the second, absence of a common purpose; and the third, Gomulka. The restraint, evoked by the tragic consequences of the Hungarian revolution, meant that no responsible individual was willing to undermine the precarious structure of post-October Poland, to engage in any activity which might set in motion an irreversible revolutionary chain of events. The example was set by the Catholic Church itself, even though its hostility to the ruling ideology could not be doubted. Indeed, those anti-Communists who were willing to take advantage of the regime's passivity and of the new pluralism to organize some independent political activity did not find much backing anywhere — neither among workers nor the intellectuals nor the Church. The short-lived Union of Democratic Youth, a non-Communist, nationalist youth organization, was suppressed by the regime without provoking popular indignation. The experience of this particular organization showed that while the vast majority of the population remained anti-Communist the circumstances were such that most were prepared to act only as non-Communists.* In the words of a prominent Catholic leader, "it is demagogy to raise slogans which ignore the real conditions and the objective necessity. It would be demagogy to launch now in Poland a program of parliamentary democracy. The problem of a system cannot be resolved abstractly." [26]

The absence of a common purpose was also a powerful factor. Despite the popular rejection of Stalinism and the continuing hatred of Russia, a re-evaluation of the meaning of independence had taken place among many Poles. The futile Warsaw uprising of 1944 had

---

* This, however, did not exclude individual or collective acts of retribution. Gomulka felt compelled to call upon the miners to stop attacking particularly hated administrators, while the militia complained that any intervention by a militiaman immediately earned him the label of a Stalinist and even physical assault. Radio Warsaw, December 3 and 28, 1956.

a shattering impact on the Polish belief in the capacity of Poland to shape its destiny alone. Nationalist romanticism gave way to political "positivism." More and more, the Poles were inclined to concede what they had opposed only a decade before: the necessity of close alliance with Russia, especially with the Soviet support for the Oder-Neisse line (see also Chapter 15). A change in outlook on this point had occurred, and it was, indeed, a profound one. Peasant opposition was disarmed by the collapse of collectivization, openly tolerated by the regime. The support given Gomulka by the Church eliminated, for the time being, religion as a basis of cohesion for a common purpose. The workers gloried in their Workers' Councils and the more active even thought of organizing a nation-wide Workers' Council publication.[27] At the same time, they were handicapped by the presence of many thousands of first-generation proletarians, recruited from the poorer rural elements, lacking in trade-union traditions, demoralized by the new environment, and unable to adjust in a mature fashion to the new responsibilities. As a result, some of them attempted to use the Workers' Councils for short-range gratification, thereby undermining their political significance. The remnants of the middle class, as the fate of the Union of Democratic Youth showed, lacked the cohesion and the economic power to shape an alternative political program.

The past anti-Communist alliance could not be resuscitated. The society, disintegrated by war and by profound socioeconomic changes, rejecting monolithic bonds in a spontaneous and leaderless process, could not create within itself a unified sense of direction. Intellectuals almost by definition are incapable of forging a monistic program of action, but merely can help to crystallize through continuing dialogue a general sense of the desirable, with many specific points left in doubt or subject to conflicting interpretations. Rejecting orthodoxy, they would be the last to adopt a new doctrine. Views such as Kolakowski's (Chapter 13) could not be a concrete program of action. It was only Gomulka who could skilfully fill this vacuum. He never tired of warning the Poles of the dire international consequences of undermining the party's rule, and yet, by avoiding a specific commitment to the future, he remained in the initial post-October period the embodiment of many conflicting hopes. Since any action against the ruling party was also action against its First Secretary, his unique position as the object of mass adulation, probably unprecedented in modern Polish history (Pilsudski included), effectively contained the opponents of the regime at the time of the regime's greatest weakness. In January 1957 Gomulka was given a resounding popular endorsement.*

It was in this context of political stalemate that Polish life moved away from the ideological and institutional uniformity of the Communist camp but without destroying the Communist rule. Some of these changes may be briefly enumerated under the general headings of political, economic, social, and intellectual. In politics, the specific changes were negative ones, that is, reactions to the rejected past: release of prisoners,[28] absorption of the secret police into the Ministry of the Interior and dismissals of parts of the staff, removal of Soviet military advisers, rehabilitation of some formerly dismissed judges, end to the jamming of foreign broadcasts, introduction of some limited debate in the Sejm, and the like. Finally, above all, there was a general popular feeling that the government in Warsaw was a Polish one, despite its ideological views.

In economic life the most striking change was the collapse of collectivization.† Within a few short weeks, only about 1,700 of the 10,600 collective farms were left.[29] Reform was promised in industry, although the nature of large-scale industrial organization precluded any significant alterations. The first step in the direction of change was the demotion of the powerful Central Planning Commission from a super-ministry responsible only to the top leaders to an organ of the Council of Ministers,[30] and the setting up of a competing institution, the Economic Council, charged with drafting a "model" for the Polish economy. Its thinking was well reflected by the following observations of its chairman, Oskar Lange: "The Stalinist scheme of industrialization . . . was not suited to a mechanical transfer to

---

* The elections were, in effect, a plebiscite for national independence, and no contest was involved since a National Front slate was presented and Gomulka urged the voters to vote only for it. However, in voting for the slate, a voter could rank his preferences, and in that limited way express his inclinations. It is interesting to note that the slate's "nonparty" candidates (usually leading intellectuals) had the highest median, followed by the SD, ZSL, and United Polish Workers' Party in that order, although the differences were slight. In terms of the nineteen provinces, the "nonparty" candidates had the highest average in fifteen, the SD in three, the ZSL in one, the ruling party in none. Based on J. Wiatr, "Sejm Elections – A Preliminary Analysis," *Studia Socjologiczno – Polityczne*, no. 1, 1958.

† S. Jedrychowski, Gomulka's planner, made this revealing admission: "Some people, especially bourgeois commentators, believe that the retreat in developing the cooperatives and the dissolving of many of them were the result of Party policy. The truth is that the retreat was caused by the pressure of anti-socialist elements at a time when the Party was not strong enough to counter this pressure." "Socialism on the March," *World Marxist Review* (*Problems of Peace and Socialism*), II, no. 5 (May 1959).

Poland, a country of entirely different economic-geographical conditions. . . . A miniature of Soviet-type industrialization was forced. This miniature also imitated the autarky of the Soviet Union." [31] The council, in addition to favoring decentralization of the economic structure, also leaned toward a limited reintroduction of private enterprise in retail trade, handicrafts, services, and small-scale production.[32] On the factory level, the mushrooming Workers' Councils were regularized through an official decree, although the range of their activities was pointedly restricted to the socioeconomic sphere, and efforts to organize nation-wide links among the Workers' Councils were prohibited.[33] The right to strike was for the time being tolerated and was used by the workers in a number of instances, with success. Probably the most significant act of the regime was the announcement that Western credits would be sought to help Poland through the difficult period of readjustment.

To the average citizen of the Polish People's Democracy, the changes effected during this period of restrained spontaneity were in the less tangible social and intellectual sphere. The restraint and unanimity of the preceding period gave way to a sudden outburst of intellectual vivacity, to the mushrooming of clubs, newspapers, and discussion circles, to large-scale contacts with the West and relatively unrestrained travel abroad. For a short while, the press was virtually in the hands of the "revisionist" intellectuals, and the official censors, bereft of official guidance, in effect stopped functioning. Even articles critical of the USSR were published.* The formerly vilified Home Army was publicly lauded, resulting in large-scale publication of memoirs by non- and even anti-Communist underground fighters, many of whom joined the official veterans' organization (ZBWiD) with some even claiming veterans' status for antiregime activity! Public-opinion polls appeared in many newspapers, often revealing a high degree of hostility to Communism.[34] In the universities banned subjects and ousted professors reappeared, while on the lower levels official text books were withdrawn. Religious instruction within the schools was reintroduced, following the arrangement made between the state and the Church, and Catholic newspapers and magazines reappeared. Such, in summary form, was post-October Poland. But was it a Gomulkaist Poland?

* By no means untypical was an enthusiastic account of a trip to France by a *Przeglad Kulturalny* correspondent, who then described by way of contrast a visit to the USSR, involving the companionship of a boring guide, life in an atrocious hotel, huge profits for the Intourist, and compulsory visits to the "workshops" of Soviet literary "realists" (December 6–12, 1956).

Restoration of Control

A Gomulkaist Poland began to emerge only with the restoration of political control. Constructing socialism, and eventually Communism, was Gomulka's goal. The most obvious problem facing him was that of the party. Without the party the ideological goals could not be pursued. For the time being, Gomulka could maintain himself in power by relying on his popularity as well as on his control of the army, ensured by the appointment of his close associate, Marian Spychalski, to the post of Minister of Defense, and on his control of the police network, headed by S. Moczar. This might have been enough if Gomulka were satisfied to become a traditional dictator, ruling a status quo society by balancing instruments of power and interest groups. However, the state of Polish society urgently required action, while Gomulka's own views and the views of those on whom he depended for support dictated a specific kind of action. His primary task was thus to revitalize the party and to assert his control of it before the self-restraint of the non-Communists gave way to greater political appetite and before the Natolin dogmatists, favoring a radical policy, attempted more violent solutions.

Gomulka could not rely on the "revisionists," who had helped to bring him to power but to whose views he was clearly unsympathetic. To Gomulka, a hard-bitten party leader, the revisionist intellectuals and their socialist labor friends must have appeared as an argumentative, overintellectualized lot, who could discuss but never construct socialism. Yet within the party, which would be his primary instrument of action, he could not count on unqualified support. In the Central Committee, the anti-Gomulka Natolinites could rely on about twenty to twenty-five votes of the total seventy-seven, with the rest primarily in the hands of the professional party apparatus, headed by Zambrowski and Ochab, whose associates also controlled the key party organs. Gomulka could count on the personal loyalty of only a handful of members, as well as on the support of the four-odd revisionists who would always back him against the Natolinites.[35] Thus from the start Gomulka had to associate himself with the dominant group within the upper party echelons. This group eschewed a return to the past but also viewed with the profoundest disfavor the revisionist declarations, which even called for the acceptance of an opposition within the party.[36] Gomulka, who became the First Secretary of the party not to preside over its dissolution but to make its goals compatible with Poland's, accordingly identified himself with a position and an outlook which, for lack of a better label, might be called centrist.

In March 1957 the Gomulka leadership made its first move against the revisionists by stigmatizing their activity as undermining the very foundations of the party and drawing it toward the bourgeoisie.[37] Gomulka's move was well-timed, for it reassured the party *apparat* and undercut the whispering and pamphleteering campaign being waged against him by some of the unreconciled dogmatists. The position of the latter had become weakened in the meantime by rapid changes effected on the provincial party levels, some spontaneously and some by central direction, which resulted in the removal of ten of the seventeen provincial party secretaries and changes in all seventeen committees,[38] as well as a rapid reduction in party staffs.* Gomulka's retention of Zenon Nowak as deputy prime minister also had the effect of conciliating some of the Natolinites. It was around this time that Moscow began more actively to endorse Gomulka (see Chapter 12).

Gomulka's ability increasingly to make himself appear as the chief bulwark of the *apparat's* interests forced the dogmatists to put all their hopes in a frontal attack on Gomulka's policies at the Ninth Plenum in mid-May 1957. Their move was ill conceived. As First Secretary, Gomulka opened the proceedings and placed considerable emphasis on the revisionist threat. The sharpness of his attack, combined with his massive popular support (still strong in mid-1957), convinced the party professionals that without him a serious conflict was almost inevitable. Even at this point the danger of Hungary was not to be excluded, and only with Gomulka at the helm did the party's rule appear more or less secure. Consequently, when some of the dogmatists proceeded to charge the Politburo with failing to recognize Soviet leadership (see Chapter 12), with having betrayed Communism through its policies on agriculture and toward the Church,† their indictment fell on deaf ears and provoked a bitter outburst both from Gomulka and his predecessor Ochab, now in charge of agriculture. Gomulka followed up his two-front offensive

---

* Radio Warsaw, August 7, 1957, reported the transfer of 8,669 party officials to other work. This reduced the party administration from about 13,000 to 5,000 and, carried out rapidly during the height of Gomulka's popularity, strengthened his internal position.

† The leading spokesmen were K. Mijal, W. Klosiewicz, and S. Lapot, members of the Central Committee but not front-rank leaders. It is noteworthy that the former leaders of the Natolin group, such as Nowak and Mazur, were cautious and restrained.

by prevailing upon the Central Committee to elect two of his supporters, Zenon Kliszko and Jerzy Morawski, to the party secretariat. Kliszko, purged in 1949 during the anti-Gomulka campaign, was given the important task of directing the party's organization section, balancing Zambrowski's influence. Morawski, responsible for the section dealing with relations with the other Communist parties, could be relied upon to uphold Gomulka's views on relations within the bloc, and subsequently represented him at the East German, Italian, and Yugoslav party congresses.

The May plenum, unlike October's, was truly Gomulka's personal victory. Although neither the revisionists nor the dogmatists, to use the standard Polish terminology, were fully dispersed, the plenum materially strengthened Gomulka in his "struggle on two fronts." Happily for him, the ideological differences dividing the dogmatists and the revisionists were so profound, and their hostility so intense, that Gomulka could always count on the support of the one group against the other, with the revisionist weakness in the party counsels being compensated by their strong position in the press and among the intellectuals.

The Ninth Plenum was followed by more purposeful moves to unify the party and to isolate the "deviants." Not surprisingly, most of the concrete steps were directed more often against the revisionists than the dogmatists. The latter had been isolated from the people since October and during the period of spontaneity were unable to exercise much influence. The realities of Polish life with which Gomulka was faced in mid-1957 were primarily of the revisionists' doing. For this reason, Gomulka's two-front war was directed more frequently at his former allies than at his current foes.

By the time of the Tenth Plenum, held late in October 1957 on the eve of the Moscow conclave, Gomulka's control was well consolidated. The first revisionist strongholds to fall were those in the press. Between March and May changes were effected in the editorial staffs of party dailies (including a new editor-in-chief for *Trybuna Ludu* [39]), and a warning was issued that freedom of the press did not mean the freedom of party members to agitate against the party. In September press censorship was restored, despite vigorous resistance,[40] and its logical extension was the closing on October 2 of the crusading party youth paper, *Po Prostu*. While the party was formally within its rights in suspending a party paper that was at variance with the regime's policies, the suspension of *Po Prostu*, which had become a symbol of October, provoked a strong reaction in the population, quite unlike the passive acceptance earlier of the dissolution of the Democratic Youth Organization.[41] A majority of the editorial staff was expelled from the party,[42] while some prominent revisionist writers demonstratively resigned from the party.[43]

Gomulka's struggle against revisionism within his party, described by him as a "grippe," did not make him forget dogmatism, which he analyzed as tuberculosis intensified by the grippe.[44] In mid-June, shortly after the Ninth Plenum, some of the dogmatists used the Warsaw party conference as a forum for attacks on two of Gomulka's associates, Zambrowski and Cyrankiewicz. They did so on the grounds that a recent Central Committee decision to expel Berman and Radkiewicz from the party as those responsible for past terror should have also included Gomulka's above-named friends, who held high posts during Stalinism. This demagogic attempt to discredit his regime was accompanied by efforts to seize control of the Warsaw organization. Their efforts were repulsed,[45] and Gomulka quickly followed this up by purging the party *apparat* of the Warsaw-center district, an important party organization in view of its location.[46] Accordingly, when the Tenth Party Plenum convened in October 1957, an exact year after his coming to power, Gomulka could speak with the authoritative firmness of a party leader and not merely as a revolutionary symbol. Declaring flatly that "the Party must be monolithic," Gomulka condemned both revisionism and dogmatism and, warning that there is no room in his party for either, ordered a party purge.[47] His speech was a firm assertion of his determination not to allow any political diversity within the system and marked the effective restoration of one-party rule.

Dangers and Prospects of Gomulkaism

The emergence of a Gomulkaist Poland through the consolidation of political authority also made possible the elimination of those nonpolitical gains of October which did not enjoy Gomulka's favor. Indeed, it was only after the political consolidation that Gomulkaism — or the directed Polish way to socialism — began to appear in sharper focus. While its character was obviously determined to a large extent by the encirclement of Poland by the Communist camp, it should be apparent from the preceding that its roots were also in large measure domestic. Sometimes described as Leninism applied to Polish conditions, Gomulkaism involved an attempt to water down the impatient Stalinist reliance on pure political force and establish a balance between purposeful coercion and gradual change in social consciousness.

The nature of such a balance could not be spelled out with any degree of precision, and only practice could determine its content.

The January 1958 issue of the party journal stated: "The Party can and ought to lead everything." [48] During 1957–1958, censorship was especially intensified in the ideological sector, with the regime suppressing about 50 per cent of the articles in such discussion weeklies as *Nowa Kultura* and *Przeglad Kulturalny*.[49] In October 1957 the party announced that permanent commissions of the Central Committee for control of science, culture, and education, abolished a year earlier, were to be recreated,[50] while a party spokesman explicitly asserted that Poland must have a "cultural policy that promotes the objectives of its system and its ideology." [51] Presumably not irrelevant to these measures were the anti-intellectual suspicions frequently voiced by Gomulka (paralleling similar utterances by Khrushchev). Ideological alternatives would no longer be tolerated even if Gomulka's regime was tardy in stepping forth with its own program.

The reactivation of party rule also meant the gradual limitation of the politically significant right of free association and the quiet reconstruction of the secret-police apparatus. The intellectuals' clubs, survived only in the largest urban centers,[52] and these were forbidden to organize a formal nation-wide assembly. The sixty-odd nonparty members of the Sejm were not allowed to form a parliamentary club, and early in 1958 political control was reimposed on the resuscitated Boy Scouts movement and on the veterans' association. The secret police, incorporated earlier into the Ministry of the Interior, was reorganized into nine departments (to watch the intellectuals, to supervise former underground fighters, and so on) within the ministry, and dismissals from it were halted. By the summer of 1957 its size was reliably estimated at 21,000 men.[53] In November 1957, Gomulka's Minister of the Interior issued a statement stressing the need for security operations against "the reactivation of groups which can be traced to forbidden political parties or reactionary organizations." [54]

In the economy the problem from the very beginning was how to readjust the former Stalinist model without causing widespread dislocation and large-scale decline in production. Furthermore, the low standard of living exerted strong pressures for increased wages which, in turn, threatened to create an inflationary spiral. The economists themselves were split, with two dominant groups evident: those favoring a rather large-scale decentralization, indeed a new Polish economic "model," and those who advocated moderate reforms in the existing structure. The former were in the advisory Economic Council and propagated their views through the economic journal *Zycie gospo-darcze;* the latter were headed by the party economists of the State Economic Planning Commission and of the newly created Economic Committee of Council Ministers, given the special task of evaluating alternative models. It soon became a haven for the more rigid dogmatic planners and was headed by E. Szyr, essentially a dogmatist. On the margins of this dispute was the radical faction which, without an active role in the drafting of economic plans, utilized party plenums to press in general for an intensification of socioeconomic changes in Poland.

The group favoring decentralization submitted its plans in May 1957. In February 1958 a party commission rejected the key recommendations of the Economic Council, namely, the transfer of direct authority (to fix annual plans, to approve investments, and to make decisions on new productions) to the factory or enterprise.[55] However, it did not move back to the rigid Stalinist pattern and urged instead that such authority be entrusted to intermediary complexes or trusts, with provisions for the sharing of a certain percentage of the profit (in the shipping trust, for instance, it was fixed at 17 per cent) with the personnel. More extensive decentralization, on the Yugoslav model, was rejected as unsuitable for the "more advanced" Polish economy.[56] A further consideration, political reasoning apart, might have been the extremely low level of training among industrial cadres (due to rapid industrialization) and hence the dangers of granting them extensive autonomy.* Limitations were also imposed on the right to strike,[57] while the authority of the Workers' Councils, by late 1957 established in the majority of the industrial establishments,[58] was severely circumscribed in April 1958 by the superimposition over them of a so-called Workers' Self-Government Conference. In this, the representatives of a council were outnumbered by delegates of the trade union and the party cell, with the party secretary acting as chairman.[59] The Workers' Councils became essentially grievance boards, although they were still of some importance in articulating the views of the working class.

A special problem which Gomulka had to face in 1957 and 1958 was the question of state-Church relations. The modus vivendi of October 1956 was clearly an emergency solution which could not endure once the party regained initiative. The top party leaders had little desire to return at this time to Stalinist violence which Gomulka had so explicitly condemned. There was, however, growing fear that

* See education and training statistics in Chapter 6, p. 143 n.

the increasing scope of the Church's social activity (organized professional pilgrimages, chaplains assigned by the Church to scouting units, worker-priests, Catholic clubs in the universities) represented an institutional challenge which the political leadership under no circumstances could long tolerate. By early 1958 the regime felt strong enough to launch a press campaign against alleged Church infractions of the existing agreements, and this was followed by occasional trials of priests accused of violating the "tolerance" clause of the Polish constitution (such as a priest's refusal to bury an active Communist in a Catholic cemetery), by an increase in state control of clerics assigned to teach religion in the schools, and by fiscal measures against the Church. However, there was also a special, unpublicized motivation behind the increased vigor of the party's attacks on the Church. The party leadership had become concerned over the general decline of "revolutionary zeal" in the party and decided to use the anti-Church campaign as a method of unifying the membership and, also, to undercut the radical dogmatists. This was quite openly admitted in party circles.[60]

The foregoing discussion points to the conclusion that the retrogression which took place in Poland in 1957–1959, and which is continuing, did not take place merely as a function of external Soviet pressure. Such pressure doubtless existed, and was even manifested by open Soviet criticisms of many aspects of the Polish scene in contrast to its praise for the more orthodox practices of the other Communist states, and by approval of the retrogressive measures described above. However, both the dynamics of one-party rule and of Gomulka's specific views on the construction of socialism would have required such limitation of the freedoms won in October. The question really is not whether the domestic policies pursued during this time were a response to external pressure but rather the extent to which they were aided or handicapped by it. To this question a clearcut answer cannot be given. In one sense, external pressure was indispensable because without the USSR Gomulka could not have carried on. But once that proposition is granted, Soviet pressure could also be construed as a handicap to Gomulka's domestic policy insofar as the very presence of an all-powerful Soviet partner so near to Poland continually forced Gomulka to pay greater heed to domestic aspirations in order to gain and maintain national backing. Thus, curiously, the same external pressures for unity and hierarchy which Gomulka was fearfully opposing to protect his autonomy (see Chapter 12) were making it possible for him to translate his own Communist ideals into domestic policy.

However, just as retrogression fundamentally reflected Gomulka's growing power and not simply Soviet interference, so did the consolidation of certain tangible achievements of October reflect a new political approach within Poland. Despite pointed Soviet praise for those states which collectivize their agriculture, collectivization appears to be postponed in Poland until such time as it becomes economically attractive, with the number of collective farms stabilized at about seventeen to eighteen hundred [61] and the state obligations shouldered by the peasants substantially reduced.[62] Local government was reformed to encourage greater popular participation, which necessarily meant a partial limit on direct party control and active participation on the local level of the two subordinate parties in the National Front.* In the Sejm, where the outcome of the vote still remained predetermined by the artificial Communist majority, the practice of unanimous vote was abandoned, committee work became of some importance in the discussion of issues, and the practice of interpellation was introduced.[63] The press, despite increased censorship, remained lively and undogmatic, occasionally rebutting Soviet criticisms of the Polish scene and carrying stories about the West. The universities, which were freed of practically all political control after October 1956, retained most of their internal freedom, though with growing restrictions on publications, particularly in the sensitive area of social sciences.[64] Leading revisionists were not imprisoned, even if under pressure to desist in their "deviation." Finally, the retrogression that did take place did not involve a full return to the Stalinist past, and it did not undo, even if it did restrict, the relative sense of emancipation evoked by the October outburst. The political climate and the style of life had changed profoundly. The gap between political authority and society had been greatly narrowed.

In effect, Gomulkaism involved an accommodation of the requirements of the Polish reality to the demands of the party, as well as to the interests of the bloc. It was not an easy adjustment, and certainly not one which would permit a static solution. It meant that the

* For example, before October the Peasant Party had only two provincial executive chairmanships (roughly a provincial prefect); in 1957 the number was 5 out of 17. The number of district chairmen grew from 35 out of 321 to 69. This, of course, is not decisive within the framework of a one-party political dictatorship, but it did mean a certain slight decline in the monolithic control of all posts by that party. *Zielony Sztandar*, March 30, 1958.

Gomulka regime would be faced with a continuing problem of recon-
ciling external concessions with domestic recalcitrance and, vice versa,
domestic Communist aspirations with external Communist aid. To do
that successfully, Gomulka had to go out of his way to indicate that
the Polish peculiarities were just peculiarities and that it would be
an error for any other party to attempt to duplicate the Polish experience.[65]

In explicitly rejecting any claims to universality Gomulka was also
mollifying Soviet fears. At the same time, the conclusion of a successful trip in late 1958 to the USSR (Chapter 15), marked by repeated
Soviet endorsement of Gomulka, allowed the Polish leader to turn
with added confidence to the task of liquidating the remnants of the
neo-Stalinist, excessively pro-Soviet faction. This was well demonstrated by the Twelfth Party Plenum in October 1958 during which
the remnants of the old Natolin faction, led by second-stringers
like the economist Szyr and the *apparatchik* Ruminski, attempted to
attack the party's economic plan for 1959–1965 on the ground that it
envisaged an insufficiently rapid development of socialism in Poland.
The plan, stipulating an increase of 49 per cent in industrial production between 1961–1965 (considerably below the 1950–1957 period,
when it grew two and a half times), was described by its proponents
as "the plan of economic stabilization." [66] According to a stenographic
report designed strictly for internal party use, much of the argument
against the plan and for the extremist point of view was based on the
Chinese experience, and Gomulka and his associates could easily dis-
pell it precisely on the grounds of irrelevancy. S. Jedrychowski, a
prominent party planner and Politburo member, firmly concluded
the official rebuttal by stating: "Our pace of economic development
we should define ourselves, on the basis of our own, most conscien-
tious appraisal of our conditions, needs and possibilities. . . ." [67] Another Politburo member, A. Zawadzki, even allowed himself to voice
the thought that the radical Chinese example not only does not prove
(as Szyr argued) that changes in social consciousness can outpace
changes in social conditions but that "the example of China is not entirely convincing" and that it is very doubtful that the Chinese masses
had been won over to Communism.[68]

The plenum itself was an interesting reflection of the growing
consolidation of Gomulka's power. He was solidly supported by the
party's provincial secretaries who simply ignored the ideological arguments of Szyr and Ruminski; no revisionist issues arose; his Politburo

associates spoke out as forcefully as he against the critics; and, finally, it was apparent that the critics had no hopes of displacing Gomulka but were merely striving to push him into a more radical path. This was the last outburst of collective opposition to Gomulka. By way of contrast, the Third Congress in March 1959 was almost dull in its endorsements of Gomulka; the Soviet delegation, including as many as three CPSU Presidium members, was unstinting in its support of the First Secretary; and the new Central Committee was rigorously purged of the remaining neo-Stalinist deviants.* In a symbolic gesture, the 1949 condemnation of Gomulka was stricken from the party records. Gomulkaism was now registered in the sacred rolls of orthodoxy.[69]

Partly for reasons of personal inclination but primarily because of the continuous fear that Polish domesticism could be construed as a threat elsewhere, Gomulka continues to avoid ideological formulations for the Polish way to socialism. The Third Congress, while a personal triumph for Gomulka, contributed nothing in the way of an ideological definition of Gomulkaism. Yet the dangers which face it domestically are to some extent rooted in the absence of a crystallized program of action for this Polish way. The outstanding problems confronting Gomulka, such as the Church issue, the social anarchy, the alienation and frustration of the intellectuals, the loss of the allegiance of the youth (a particularly serious problem for a regime led by aging products of Stalinism),† the weakness of the collective movement in the countryside, all these in the end raise ideological issues which cannot be delayed indefinitely, unless the party is willing to adopt the proposition of "spontaneity," of "automatism" in social change, which clearly it cannot.‡

* Judging by the membership list published in *Nowe Drogi*, no. 4 (April 1959), pp. 761-763, at most only five former Natolinites survived the purge. Mazur was dropped altogether (a former Politburo member and Khrushchev's candidate in 1956 for Bierut's job).

† For instance, the reactivated party youth movement numbered by the end of 1957 only 90,000 members, including "several thousand" students. In the Warsaw Polytechnic, for instance, there were only 12 members out of a student body of 14,000 (*Sztandar Mlodych*, October 23, December 10, 1957). Furthermore, even a rapid increase in their numbers would not be a resolution of the profound problem of ideological skepticism and rejection of Marxism, strikingly revealed by public-opinion polls (in this writer's possession). Especially distressing was the sharp decline in the number of party members of 25 years of age and less. In 1955, 15.9 per cent of the party's membership was in that category; in 1956, 13 per cent; 1957, 10 per cent; 1958, 6.8 per cent (*Nowe Drogi*, December 1958).

‡ It was this that Andrzej Werblan, speaking for the "impatients" in the party,

In agriculture, for instance, the gradual process of splintering of land holdings is bound to produce eventual pressures for some radical change, especially when it begins to affect agricultural productivity.[70] The nation-wide demographic upsurge will pose with increasing urgency the prospect of large-scale unemployment both in the country and in the cities. At the same time, the striking improvement in the standard of living of the peasants raises an acute ideological issue. It must be disconcerting for Communists to note that the only class in the socialist society to enjoy appreciably better living conditions are private landowners, not subject to state planning and operating on an individual basis. No wonder that the Third Congress sounded muted warnings that the party would sometimes have to reconsider its present policy. To mobilize support, to produce revolutionary élan, to build socialism, a sense of purpose is vital and must be stated. Muddling-through, with the silent understanding that it is necessary to avoid foreign interference, cannot be a long-range response to the problem. Both Gomulka and his opponents know it, and this awareness lurked in the background of the Twelfth Plenum discussions and in the dull unanimity of the Third Congress in March 1959.

The Polish way to socialism is thus based on Gomulka's recognition of Polish national peculiarities, including widespread hostility toward Communism, on the specifics of the Polish agrarian scene and the rugged political and social individualism of the Polish peasant, on the more advanced state of industrialization in Poland than at the comparable stage of socialist development in Russia, on a close alliance with the USSR but not on domestic subordination to it, on domestic autonomy without external ideological ambitions. It is hence not comparable to Tito's national Communism or even to China's indigenous Communist regime. At the same time, the efforts of the regime to maintain a measure of independence from the USSR, despite domestic weakness, result in a degree of moderation which did not characterize either Mao Tse-tung or Tito in their revolutionary periods. But these considerations should not obscure the fact that Gomulkaist Poland is a Communist state which is gradually becoming more, and not less, Communist. This direction of change could not be maintained without the presence of the USSR, the interference of which Gomulka rejects. Therein lies the paradox and the inherent weakness of Gomulkaism. In this obvious instability, however, there is an ele-

---

who want action but not necessarily a return to Stalinism (which it might well require in some aspects), attacked in his secret speech to the party Press Commission in May 1958.

ment of negative strength which both Moscow and the Poles seem to recognize: for the time being there is in Poland no workable political alternative to Gomulkaism.*

* Postscript: The foregoing analysis was borne out by the events of October-November 1959. A mounting shortage of meat resulted in growing popular discontent and sharp disagreements within the party. Lack of adequate economic coordination was held to be the main cause for the shortcoming, a vindication of the critical views voiced at the Twelfth Party Plenum. Szyr was promoted to the post of vice-premier and given broad planning responsibilities. Also appointed vice-premier was Julian Tokarski; he had gained notoriety as the minister who had failed to give satisfaction to the workers of Poznan, thereby sparking their revolt in June 1956. (Both Szyr and Tokarski had spent the war in the USSR.) Ochab relinquished his post as Minister of Agriculture, but his stature in the party was maintained by his simultaneous appointment as a party secretary. Szyr's promotion, followed shortly by the politically symbolic dismissals of Bienkowski as Minister of Education and Hochfeld as Director of the Institute of International Affairs (both men were known liberals), signified Gomulka's further evolution in the direction of more rigid party direction over Polish life. However, there was a ray of hope in these developments. The fact that Gomulka was opposed in the Politburo by party secretary Morawski, and possibly others, meant that within the party itself a less rigid alternative to Gomulka was gradually crystallizing, an alternative involving more than simply revisionist intellectuals. Morawski's desire to resign from the Politburo in protest against the new policy also marked the introduction into the procedures of the party leadership of something akin to a sense of personal responsibility in politics.

CHAPTER 15

Problems of the Communist "Commonwealth"

SOME TOPICAL CONCLUSIONS

IN February 1959 the Twenty-first Congress of the CPSU convened in Moscow, three years after Khrushchev's secret speech on Stalin and six years after Stalin's death. It was attended also by the leaders of the ruling Communist parties who took joint stock of the state of their camp. Reviewing the recent past, particularly since their last meeting in Moscow at the November 1957 anniversary of the Bolshevik revolution, they could note two events of primary importance to their camp: the external submission of Poland and the political isolation of Yugoslavia. These two achievements marked the conclusion of the processes launched by Stalin's death and closed a major cycle in the relations among Communist states. Henceforth, the problems that they would face would reflect a new stage in the development of the camp, the stage of ideological and political unity but institutional diversity.

Stalinism, by stressing ideological and institutional unity, sought security in common outlook, behavior, and structure. However, the impact of the Stalinist totalitarian revolution created a revulsion which split the monolithic unity of the orbit shortly after Stalin's death. The subsequent reconstruction of the center and the condemnation of revisionism had restored a measure of unity within the camp. However, several key questions were left unanswered. How was the Polish autonomy to be defined? How could the USSR maintain close relations of friendship and equality with China without being deprived of its status as leader? How could it resolve the old conflict between uniformity and diversity in the affairs of the other European Communist states, all deeply suspicious of the Polish autonomy? Finally, how could the Soviet leadership of the camp be justified in the face of the growing domestic sacrifices that it might entail? All these problems eventually could give rise to serious practical and ideological dilemmas, in spite of the growing effectiveness of economic ties.

Defining the Limits of Polish Autonomy

The problem of Polish autonomy was complicated by the fact that no juridical issues were involved. The formal picture was simple. Poland was a sovereign state, independently shaping its policies, and was an equal member of the "commonwealth." Yet, given the nature of the common ideology and its practical implications, any tangible expression of Polish autonomy was immediately a matter of concern to the other Communist states. Insistence on specific Polish methods, particularly those which were more popularly accepted and required fewer sacrifices and less coercion, raised obvious questions for the rest of the camp.

The problem was hardly solved by Gomulka's assertions of unity or by his reluctant acceptance of Soviet leadership. While laying the groundwork for possible Soviet interference in Polish domestic affairs, such assertions served in the first instance as mere ritualistic requirements to prevent stigmatization as traitor. They granted Gomulka a certain amount of immunity from external attack, in spite of the fact that his very existence was considered a threat by the more rigid Communist states. The Polish pattern seemed to offer a less violent alternative to the established method of building socialism, and hence it was a living refutation of the Stalinist "dilemma of the one alternative." It was no accident that after 1956 Polish newspapers were much in demand, even in the USSR,[1] and that Polish events stirred up lively discussions in neighboring countries, and "not always the right way either," as a critical Czech paper put it.[2] The special appeal of the Polish solution to intellectuals elsewhere meant that, despite Gomulka's immunity, the problem could not be ignored — advocacy of the Polish pattern could well become a sanctuary for revisionists hiding behind the "socialist legitimacy" of Poland.

To cope with the demoralizing implications of Gomulkaism, a twofold approach was pursued on the basis of the Soviet example, even after November 1957. Gomulka himself, his immediate "entourage," and "Polish socialism" in general were not to be attacked, but those specifics of Polish life not clearly identified with a program personally articulated by Gomulka were to be singled out for continuing criticism. This was undoubtedly designed to prevent Gomulka's regime from officially sanctioning them. Furthermore, the Polish leaders were to be subjected to unrelenting but informal and indirect pressure in conferences and meetings, through bilateral declarations of other parties, and the like; this was intended to make Polish Communists deeply aware of their isolation and eventually induce in them a certain amount of Communist soul-searching. A typical example of this was Khrushchev's speech in Sofia on June 4, 1958, in which he stressed collectivization as an important attribute of building socialism and then pointedly praised those states actively engaged in collectivization. In the same speech he attacked Yugoslavia for accepting United States loans; not once did he mention Poland, but the inference was clear. Furthermore, by occasionally forcing the Poles through such indirect means, or even by economic or political pressure, into *declarative* unity, as was the case with Gomulka in November 1957 or with the more violent Polish condemnation of the Hungarian revolution issued finally in April 1958,[3] it was hoped that Poland would be ultimately forced into complete uniformity in action. A good example of the effectiveness of declarative unity was the undermining of Polish resistance to an interparty ideological journal. Once unity and Soviet leadership had been conceded by Gomulka, the ideological arguments against such a publication, based on equality and independence, lost most of their meaning, and the Poles had no choice but to participate in it.

In this fashion, the Polish autonomy was gradually to be whittled down. The press of the neighboring states, partially to immunize its own intelligentsia and partially for the Poles' benefit, tended to concentrate most of their fire on the intellectual and cultural aspects of the Polish scene. Polish revisionists were pictured as wielding considerable influence in the party: "The majority of them do public work and thus have great possibilities to influence the theoretical, political and scientific thinking as well as the preparation of cadres at school," a Czechoslovak journal complained.[4] Polish legal writings advocating the development of the Sejm into a truly legislative organ were interpreted to signify the abandonment of the dictatorship of the proletariat and the return to "bourgeois democracy." [5] The organ of the Czech Central Committee went so far as to publish a black list of Polish journals guilty of propagating revisionism, and suggested that Polish revisionism was a weapon in the imperialist arsenal.[6] It was no mere coincidence that by 1959 Prague was the only important Communist capital, with the exception of the distant Peiping, not visited by Gomulka.

The year 1958 marked a distinct turn for the better in Polish-Soviet relations. Gomulka's domestic policies, as well as his position on revisionism, seemed to vindicate Khrushchev's "confidence" in him and presumably were gratifying to the Soviet leader's self-esteem. At the same time, the greater rigidity demonstrated by the other Communist leaders, including, it seems, the Chinese, helped to create a feeling in Warsaw that within the Communist camp Khrushchev was the only leader with whom the Poles could bargain. That certainly seemed to be the case during Gomulka's prolonged trip to the USSR in October-November 1958. He was received with demonstrable cordiality by Khrushchev, and then, accompanied by the entire Polish delegation, including Cyrankiewicz and Zawadzki, traveled to the major urban centers of the USSR. Gomulka's trip could be interpreted as a coordinated effort, presumably backed by Khrushchev, to "sell" the Polish leadership to the Soviet *apparatchiki* who had always been wary of the Polish experiment.[7] Gomulka accordingly went out of his way to convince the various republican leaders, members of the Central Committee, of his fundamental commitment to the common cause, while also pleading the need for them to understand the special characteristics of the Polish situation. Apparently, as a price, he shifted toward greater uniformity on the still vital issue of Soviet leadership, although just a few months earlier he had rigidly applied his own formula, "first and mightiest," even when visiting the centralist leaderships of Bulgaria, Rumania and Hungary. In the course of his Soviet trip Gomulka devised a new formulation, more submissive but still somewhat vague. He now described the Soviet Union as the "foremost" (*czolowe*) socialist state. The Soviet press at first translated this incorrectly as "leading" or "directing" (*vedushcheie*) but then quickly shifted to the more ambiguous Polish meaning.

In return for these concessions, Gomulka obtained, in the joint Polish-Soviet declaration, a condemnation of dogmatism as well as revisionism and a firm restatement of Soviet support for the Oder-Neisse frontier. It was clear that the Poles had to pay the higher price for the rapprochement that was achieved, but at the same time, however, it served to consolidate Gomulka's position both at home (see discussion of the Twelfth Plenum in December 1958, Chapter 14) and within the camp. At the Twenty-first CPSU Congress in February 1959 Gomulka was recognized as one of the foremost international Communist leaders and assigned the second place of honor. His attacks on revisionism and his support of the Soviet policy on Germany were a welcome proof to the other Communist leaders of Gomulka's loyalty. Possibly also for Gomulka's benefit, Khrushchev emphasized at length that CPSU's "headship" of the camp was essentially a recognition of its historical role and of its strength, and had no other implications. Following the Polish party's Third Congress, in March 1959, in which Gomulka so firmly established his position, the Tass report on the congress decisions even implicitly approved Gomulka's deviant agricultural policy by stating that the Polish party "has secured a faster growth of agricultural production, improved the situation of the village and, liquidating the perversion in the relations between the state and the village, has strengthened the union of the workers and peasants." * [8] Indeed, something even remotely resembling the old Khrushchev-Tito axis seemed to be emerging out of Gomulka's relations with Khrushchev.† [9]

The gradual improvement in Polish-Soviet relations and the domestic consolidation of Gomulkaism makes a return to the pre-October relationship rather unlikely. Indeed, it could be argued that a certain amount of domestic autonomy for Poland is desirable even from the standpoint of the camp. By its very presence and power it absorbs internal pressures and prevents the mobilization of domestic national resistance. In foreign affairs, it can take an occasional initiative such as the Rapacki plan for the "denuclearization" of Central Europe, which felicitously combined Soviet and Polish interests and a general emphasis on the conduct of operations on the international arena in a more "Western" style. Poland also can be used to restrain Tito and can serve as a model for the Yugoslavs after Tito's death.

But the limits to the autonomy are firm, and no Pole can seriously contemplate the likelihood of Polish autonomy's becoming true independence in the near future. The Warsaw Pact, the geographical isolation, the economic integration, the question of the Oder-Neisse frontier, are insurmountable barriers. Observers in the West, noting

---

* The shift in the Soviet position becomes clear when the above statement is contrasted to the remarks made in 1958 by K. Voroshilov, Chairman of the Presidium of the Supreme Soviet of the USSR, after his visit to Poland. Voroshilov bluntly stated: "Of course here we must say frankly that there is much to be done by the Polish people and first, not so much by the State authorities as by the Communist Party, the UPWP. In this respect Polish agriculture has not yet placed itself completely on socialist rails." Radio Moscow, April 26, 1958; omitted in *Pravda*, April 27, 1958.

† After the completion of this manuscript, Khrushchev visited Poland (in July 1959) and roundly condemned the "dogmatists" for opposing "our friend . . . our dear friend and comrade," Gomulka. Khrushchev rejected the claims of the dogmatists that their views coincided more closely to those of the CPSU and advised them to support Gomulka "firmly." Gomulka, in turn, did not hide his feeling that he considered Khrushchev as the Communist leader most friendly toward the present Warsaw regime. *Trybuna Ludu*, July 22, 1959.

Polish hostility toward Communism and Russia, ought not to lose sight of the fact that more and more Poles are beginning to reason along the lines of this argument:

What would Poland mean in the western alliance? . . . It would occupy a lowly place, after England, Germany, France, Italy in Europe and dozens of other states on a world scale. . . . In view of the primary importance to America of Germany it would be the losing party in any Polish-German conflict. . . .

In the socialist camp the proportions are reversed: Poland as the largest People's Democracy is third on the list of socialist states after the Soviet Union and China, and second in Europe.[10]

Barring an upheaval threatening Communist power in Poland or Poland's membership in the bloc, it is likely that Poland will retain an intermediary position between a satellite and a true ally. Its scope of effective autonomy will remain subject to continuous pressures but, at the same time, each passing day will help to consolidate it. The scope of the Polish autonomy and the future character of the Polish way to socialism depend in large measure on further developments in the bloc, and these in turn are not unrelated to the general climate of international politics. An intensification of tensions unavoidably will increase external pressures on Poland, with subsequent domestic repercussions. Any relaxation will increase the domestic options available to the regime. But a great unknown in assessing the future is the degree of dependence of the Polish autonomy on the personal stature of Gomulka and the likely impact of his death. Probably one of Gomulka's close associates, Kliszko, Morawski, or even Ochab, could retain the leadership in Poland and continue to steer Gomulka's centrist course. The years that have passed since October 1956 have seen a gradual reintegration of Polish society, even a certain merging of national interest with the ruling party, which means that any large-scale reversal, any major effort to subordinate internal Polish life to purely external requirements, would encounter broad social and even party resistance.

Externally, however, a successor may find it more difficult to establish himself as a loyal Communist leader in Soviet eyes — not to mention Chinese or Czech — without more concrete proofs of trustworthiness than have been required from Gomulka. It is likely that the successor would be called upon, in some test situation, to yield on some domestic matter as a token of its loyalty and dedication. It could be on the Church issue, or on the agrarian policy, or on contacts with the West (assuming that the Polish contacts remain more extensive than the Soviet). On any number of these issues internal party splits would be likely, and Moscow pressure would have the effect of backing one group against another. Even so, the Polish party would probably realize that the consequent loss of passive popular support would also mean loss of its relative autonomy; it would undoubtedly hesitate to embark on an abrupt change of course, except under extreme external duress. The problem of Polish autonomy is thus likely to persist even without Gomulka.

China: The First Ally

China, the largest ally of the Soviet Union, represents another enduring political problem as well as an immediate strain on the hierarchical organization of the Communist commonwealth. Its very membership raised the question: can a bloc of states bound together by the power of a central state and by common ideological purposes retain its cohesive, hierarchical organization when one of its members ceases to be dependent on the political power of the central state and in fact is able to enjoy a considerable scope of ideological autonomy? Chinese Communist membership in the bloc was certainly not due to a fear of Soviet intervention; rather it was an expression of the ideological aspirations and power of the Chinese Communist leadership. No other bloc member, save the USSR, fully combined both qualities; all bloc members, even Gomulka, needed the USSR to retain power.

In the past the difference in China's relation to the bloc was minimized by Stalin's unquestioned ideological leadership, repeatedly acknowledged by the Chinese, as well as by the very immaturity of the new Chinese regime. By 1958 both factors had ceased to exist. Furthermore, China had gained unquestioned prestige in the Communist camp by its successful domestic consolidation and by its miraculous "victory" over the United States. The post-Stalin Soviet ideological innovations had in some respects backfired, and the Chinese leaders from the autumn of 1956 had been actively intervening on the East European scene to salvage what Moscow had dissipated. The active role played by the Chinese had at first been misinterpreted to mean favoring Polish aspirations almost as an end in itself. However, the disintegrative trends within the bloc and the revisionist reactions among the Chinese intellectuals convinced the party leadership that the most effective manner of dealing with ideological challenges to unity was through ideological rigidity based on an extreme commitment to action. Externally, it meant emphasis on

centralism, on the dichotomic world image, on the explicit acknowledgment of Soviet leadership, and on the anathematizing of the "deviants." Domestically, it meant a rapid intensification in the reconstruction of society.

The external Chinese response had an immediate effect on the
hierarchical scheme of the Communist commonwealth. During Stalinism the East European regimes had no choice but to re-echo the
Soviet line. Following the events of 1956, most of them found it
desirable to imitate the Soviet line in order to contain domestic threats
to their power. Some of them evidently wished that the Soviets had
been rather more forceful toward Poland and Yugoslavia. The qualitatively different Chinese relationship with the bloc meant that
Chinese pronouncements (which took a sterner line against revisionism, say, or against the Yugoslavs) could not be called "sectarianism,"
a device which the Kremlin could easily apply to restrain the East
Europeans. The East European centralists were in this fashion able
to exercise a choice of alternatives which previously did not exist, and
also to apply subtle pressure on their own acknowledged leader,
Moscow.

Advance coordination of the Moscow-Peiping line was hence a
necessity if this choice of alternatives was to be avoided. Otherwise
the Chinese could acquire an excessive aura of Communist virtue by
upholding the more rigid ideological position, which suited the East
European neo-Stalinists. The Soviet leaders, trained by Stalin, were
certainly not unmindful of the old dictator's admonition:

The art of leadership is a serious matter. One must not lag behind the
movement, because to do so is to become isolated from the masses. But
neither must one rush ahead, for to rush ahead is to lose contact with the
masses. He who wants to lead a movement and at the same time keep in
touch with the vast masses must wage a fight on two fronts — against
those who lag behind and against those who rush on ahead.[11]

Indeed, the capacity to take more extreme positions than the USSR,
forcing the USSR to be just as extreme or to negotiate with the
Chinese for mutually acceptable formulas, was the chief source of
Chinese leverage.

That China was dependent on the USSR went without saying. It
needed its presence, if not its backing, for the anti-American policy.
Peiping needed the Soviet Union, and East Europe in general, for
Chinese economic development. The Soviet Union alone, between
1953 and 1957, loaned China 8.5 billion rubles.[12] In May 1958, China

made known to the other states its willingness to cooperate with CEMA. About 75 per cent of Chinese trade was with the other Communist states, with the USSR ocupying the first place in China's total foreign trade (about 55 per cent of the total). Machinery imports from the Communist states took up about 50 per cent of the imports from the USSR, 90 per cent from East Germany, 90 per cent from Czechoslovakia and Hungary, and 60 per cent from Poland. In return, China exported foodstuffs and raw materials and, significantly, by the end of 1958, Chinese repayment of Soviet loans and supplies gave the USSR an import balance in trade to the amount of 2.4 billion rubles in exports to 3.6 billion rubles in imports.[18] Stability in the Communist camp was therefore in the Chinese interest, and on that point complete agreement existed between Moscow and Peiping.

Chinese economic dependence, however, did not give the USSR a onesided political advantage. The hypothetical argument that the USSR could cut off all aid was not entirely meaningful, because the Kremlin could not use this lever without risking a disintegration of the bloc. The blackmailing effect of an eventual denial of economic aid posed a greater dilemma for the party, which was in a position to wield such a threat and, therefore, would have to shoulder ultimate responsibility.

China accordingly raised two long-range problems for the Communist camp. Both of them involved China's future potential as a great power (and in our age, our consciousness of the future affects the present to an unprecedented degree) as well as the specific internal changes launched in China in 1958, following the 1957 "rectification campaign" designed to subdue restless intellectuals. The first of these was the old problem faced by Stalin in 1947: can the bloc remain homogeneous if its uniformity is *only* ideological? Can there be a centralized bloc in which domestic practices vary appreciably from state to state, particularly if the two leading powers differ substantially in their practice even while professing ideological unity? Secondly, how long would the Soviet leadership, based in part on the voluntary consent of its dependents, endure if it leaned too heavily on the endorsement of another large power which might eventually differ with it on major issues?

A historic date in international Communist development was the Chinese Central Committee's announcement on September 10, 1958, launching a nation-wide program of People's Communes. This was much more drastic than the earlier Chinese stress on "the people's democratic dictatorship" in preference to the dictatorship of the proletariat,[14] which was only gradually redefined to be "in its essence" like the latter concept.[15] The announcement marked a turning point of fundamental ideological significance. In the words of the resolution, "Concerning the Creation of People's Communes in the Village":

It seems that the realization of communism in our country is already not something far away. We must actively use the form of the people's commune and through it find the concrete road of transition to Communism.[16]

In two brief sentences the Chinese leadership established itself on the threshold of Communism — something which no other Communist state had yet done.

The new communes laid the ideological basis for Chinese preeminence. The Soviet position of leadership, apart from the admittedly vital consideration of power, rested on the claim that it was in Russia that the socialist revolution had first taken place and that it was there that socialism had first been constructed. Just as the Molotov recantations of 1955 had underscored the more advanced stage of Soviet socialist construction, so the Chinese statement suggested that China might be the first state to realize Communism. In view of this, whether the Chinese leadership wished it or not, its claim meant that China was placing itself on a more elevated historical plane, an indispensable ingredient to ideological primacy.

No wonder then that a measure of Soviet chagrin was evident under the cloak of official approbation. Soviet press coverage of this important event was remarkably sparse, and, in one instance, the reference originally cited on "the realization of communism" was translated as "the realization of the communes." [17] The Soviet press referred to the people's communes as a "new low-level form of organisation of socialist society in China," [18] while the Soviet ambassador to Peiping, in a speech commemorating the October Revolution, pointedly reminded his audience that the USSR is "now entering on the stage of communist construction on a tremendous scale" and referred to China as marching "along the road of building socialism." [19] The Soviets were presumably concerned that the Chinese emphasis on the rapidity of their changes, so out of tune with the general vagueness of Soviet references to a *gradual* transition to Communism, was emphatically linked with Mao Tse-tung's ideological direction, thereby establishing him as the only Communist leader since Stalin's "Economic Problems of Socialism in the USSR" to be tackling the problem of the transition to Communism. "It is obvious that under the direction of Mao Tse-tung's thought, under the banner of Comrade Mao Tse-tung, and at a time when the national economy and culture are developed at such a rate that 'twenty years are concentrated in one day,' one can visualize the gradual transition of our country from socialism to communism," proclaimed one Chinese statement, blandly linking the standard formula of "gradual transition" with "twenty years in one day." [20]

Furthermore, the Chinese transition to Communism apparently was to be characterized by features unique to China. The scheme of people's communes involved a socioeconomic and political transformation which was to combine, within a few years, all administrative and economic functions within a commune, thereby marking the withering away of the state. "The function of the state will be only to deal with aggression from external enemies and will not operate inside," Mao explained. [21] In addition, the new societal framework and production relations were expected to stimulate the growth of productive forces and create the conditions of plenty, or the conditions of Communism. This indeed was straying away from the prevailing Soviet emphasis on increasing productivity as the necessary pre-condition for entering into Communism. The Chinese could not hope to outstrip the Soviets in industrial production in the foreseeable future, and as long as that was the basis for entering Communism, the Soviets could confidently expect that the foundations of Communism would be constructed first in the USSR. But the Chinese method neatly disposed of the economic aspects and represented a convenient shortcut for China.

The many-roads-to-socialism concept had caused the Communist camp considerable discomfort. The Chinese, preaching unity and hailing Soviet leadership, seemed to be implicitly confirming the validity of the many-roads principle, and it was noteworthy that the Poles quickly pointed to this as again validating their stress on autonomous domestic patterns. A potential ideological challenge to Soviet leadership as well as the implicit reassertion of the varieties of domestic Communist construction were thus posed by the presence of China in the "commonwealth."

The Chinese, however, had no desire to precipitate a conflict, and it is conceivable that the rashness of their September statement was engendered by the application of purely domestic perspectives. The cool Soviet reaction may have helped to restore a certain balance between their own domestic prerequisites and their interest in the unity of the camp. In any case, in December, the Chinese leadership issued a further declaration, "On Some Questions Concerning the People's Communes," warning against the danger of becoming "dizzy with success." A gradual transition to Communism was referred to no less than 211 times in the 10,000-word document,[22] making it quite clear that China had to complete the construction of socialism before any realization of Communism might be contemplated. At the same time, however, the specificity of the Chinese road was maintained, even though the processes of socialist construction were to take another fifteen to twenty years.[23] This retreat was followed by explicit Chinese acknowledgment at the Twenty-first CPSU Congress in February 1959 that the USSR was entering the stage of the construction of Communism and by unqualified praise of Khrushchev's contribution to the "treasure house" of Marxism-Leninism. Since the Soviet leader's ideological elaborations concerned the problems of transition to Communism (see below), the Chinese recognition placed him at least on a par with Mao Tse-tung as the only living leaders who have made contributions on that matter. In return, the Soviet Union undertook to loan China further technical and industrial aid, officially estimated at five billion rubles, although it was clear from the agreement that a loan and not assistance was involved.[24]

The Twenty-first Congress and the Chinese December plenum again emphasized ideological unity while maintaining Chinese individuality in domestic processes. It would probably be idle to expect an open break between the two states in the foreseeable future, given their common ideological aspirations, the Soviet commitment to an expanding Communist world and the Chinese commitment to rapid industrialization, and their mutual hostility to the external world. At this stage much more binds them together than divides them. In some respects, one could draw an analogy to Anglo-American relations, which have survived repeated strains and disagreements. This is not to deny that there appear to be several significant parallels between the Soviet-Yugoslav relations of 1945–1948 (see Chapters 2–3) and the Soviet-Chinese relations in 1958–1959. Both China and Yugoslavia were more radical in their policies and ideological views than the Soviet leadership thought opportune or correct. Both states were headed by leaders with great personal stature, victorious in spite of Soviet advice. Both states seemed to desire the Communist camp to back their territorial ambitions (Trieste or Taiwan and Ladakh), and both apparently resented the lack of active Soviet support. However, the difference in scale between Yugoslavia and China is likely to induce greater Soviet restraint, while the mutual Soviet and Chinese *consciousness* of the dangers involved in an open split is also an important binding element. Thus Sino-Soviet conflicts will probably occur repeatedly and may force readjustments, possibly painful ones, but such readjustments will most likely take place within the framework of the camp. Western hopes to exploit such strains tend to overlook the fact that the camp is bound together by a combination of power and ideology, and one cannot promote a heresy within a church to which one does not belong.

Of much more immediate importance, however, is the gradual diffusion of Soviet authority effected by China's presence in the camp. No matter how often the Chinese proclaim Soviet leadership or insist on the obedience of others to Moscow, the very presence in the camp of a power which is *de facto* independent and which pursues its own domestic policies is a denial of the monolithic and hierarchical character of the international Communist system. No empire or church has ever maintained itself with two capitals. Moscow and Peiping have to ponder the fate of Rome and Byzantium.

Neo-Stalinism in One Country

The centralist Communist regimes embodied still another expression of the new internal diversity of the commonwealth. These ultra-orthodox regimes continue to be deeply hostile toward any fundamental innovation. Indeed, one could even surmise that, in view of the unfortunate 1956 consequences of Khrushchev's Yugoslav policy, the advocates of the more rigid program might have felt that they knew better than Khrushchev how to construct socialism and Communism in their own countries. Despite their proclamations of fealty, even to them Soviet infallibility was a thing of the past.

The new sense of domestic self-confidence of these regimes was masked by persistent assertions that the path they were pursuing was the universal, Soviet-tested way, and that their domestic efforts were based on the generally binding concepts of Marxism-Leninism. Realizing that their security depended on the closest links with the USSR, they returned to the pre-Twentieth Congress stress on the importance of the Soviet experience. One Hungarian enthusiast even claimed that past difficulties were due not to "the fact that we took over too many experiences from the Soviet Union; on the contrary, these are far too few in number. And if there were mistakes, it was not because we used these experiences but that we applied them superficially." [25] Similar themes were stressed elsewhere.

The verbal emphasis on uniformity was reflected in some important areas of action. First among these was the domestic response to the challenge of revisionism through the full reassertion of the party's control over the intellectual sphere. Throughout East Europe the antirevisionist campaign involved a reversion to ideological orthodoxy,[26] buttressed by terror. As was to be expected, the most extreme repression took place in Hungary, where the regime boasted that "we not only liquidated the Writers' Association which turned counterrevolutionary but also managed to put an end to the organized hostile activity of certain writers' groups which, even as late as summer 1957, reaction inside and outside the country tried to utilize."[27] In Bulgaria, the return of Vulko Chervenkov to the Politburo, after serving as Minister of Culture, was closely related to the intensified campaign against "hostile views" which were said to have penetrated the cultural front and even the Karl Marx Institute.[28] The theoretical monthly of the Czech Central Committee warned that "the experience of the international Communist movement shows that the slogan 'freedom of criticism,' unlimited freedom, has always been the watchword of anti-Party elements and of the enemies of socialism."[29] In March 1959, a national conference of the Union of Czechoslovak Writers condemned the "harmful opinions" expressed by Czechoslovak writers in 1956 and elected a new presidium composed of more orthodox and politically minded Communist writers (including Ladislav Stoll, former Minister of Culture, who was attacked by the more liberal writers in 1956 for his dogmatism).

The policy of enforced ideological orthodoxy, so reminiscent of the Stalinist pattern, was accompanied by a partial return to economic Stalinism. Heavy industrial development was again given the highest priority, and the post-Stalin criticisms of overconcentration on capital investment were no longer mentioned. The gradual trend toward the reassertion of heavy industry, already marked since 1956,[30] found full expression in the plans announced by some of these states in 1958. At the Eleventh Czech Party Congress, the party leadership announced its 1965 economic goals (closely linked to CEMA obligations), and their meaning was unmistakable: industrial production was to increase by 90–95 per cent, electric consumption by 115 per cent, steel production by 77–87 per cent, chemical production 150 per cent, machinery 130 per cent, while consumers' purchases by a mere 45 per cent and agricultural output by 40 per cent (compare with parallel Polish plans, Chapter 14).[31] Similar trends could be observed in the Hungarian Three Year Plan announced in May 1958,[32] and in the East German "Economic Tasks up to 1960."[33] An interesting change, however, took place in Bulgaria where the 1958 plan was suddenly revised upward in the agricultural sector, with the announced purpose of tripling production by 1961. At the same time, however, the regime reiterated that in the effort "to reach rapidly a period of gradual transition to Communism," heavy industrial development remained all important, and assigned to it was 61.7 per cent of total investment, a ratio higher than during 1953–1956.[34] (The Bulgarians significantly described their efforts as a "great leap," a phrase coined by the Chinese to describe their own rapid development.)

The verbal insistence on unity and uniformity did reflect a considerable measure of underlying reality.. It was also designed, however, to mask a growing diversity among even the relatively Stalinist states. This diversity their leaders were unwilling to acknowledge even while practicing it. Yet the increased scope of their initiative forced them to recognize problems which previously they could ignore. For example, the Czech and the East German industrial administrative reorganizations, announced in February and March 1958 respectively, even though outwardly based on the Soviet pattern,[35] were much more conservative than the Soviet in scope and retained hierarchical pyramids of industrial control cutting across territorial lines. Nonetheless, it was claimed that "our approach is identical with that of the Soviet Union." [36]

Diversity in practice among the relatively Stalinist states was especially evident in agriculture. Despite almost universal protestations that socialization of agriculture was one of the general laws for building socialism, so forcefully restated by Khrushchev in his 1958 visits to East Europe, both Rumania and Hungary lagged notably behind the others in implementing the principle. Socialization was pushed forcefully in Bulgaria: by 1958 about 92 per cent of the arable land had been socialized,[37] and "outside the collective farms there remain only the inhabitants of the mountainous and some semimountainous regions." [38] Next in line were the Czechs with 71.5 per cent socialized land by mid-1958,[39] with the regime pressing an energetic campaign to eliminate "the class enemy" altogether.[40] On the other hand, in Rumania, despite much verbal collectivization, only 12.2 per cent of the arable land was in collective farms, while the state farms, based on former estates, absorbed 36 per cent. Rumanian authorities, while advocating the principle of socialization, openly expressed concern over the uneconomic character of many of the state farms.[41] Similarly, in East Germany collectivization lagged, with the 1961 objective being 50 per cent of arable land in collectives and state farms. The regime avoided a concrete commitment as to when full socialization would be achieved.[42] The Hungarian regime initially also pursued a cautious policy despite verbal extremism. As of January 1958 the "socialist sector" embraced only 23 per cent of the land,[43] and the number of collective farms was less than one half of the pre-October 1956 total.[44] Much as in Poland, the regime was stressing the desirability of giving the medium peasant an opportunity to raise his productivity and urged the party members to find the "necessary patience." [45] Finally, none of the regimes showed any inclination to follow in Khrushchev's footsteps and abolish the machine tractor stations.[46]

A second important manifestation of diversity was the response to the revisionist challenge in its Polish or Yugoslav shape. The East Germans, the Czechs, and the Bulgarians, not to mention the distant Albanians, reacted much more forcefully than either the Hungarians or the Rumanians. On the Yugoslav issue, the Czechs pointedly remarked that they had correctly drawn "basic conclusions" about Yugoslav deviationism back in December 1956,[47] and the Czech, East German, and Bulgarian responses were closer to the Chinese than to the Soviet tone (compare Chapter 13).[48] The Hungarians, echoing some of the violent anti-Yugoslav attacks, were much more restrained in their references to Poland. The Rumanians, who had gone the furthest in improving relations with Tito, were the slowest in working themselves to a fever pitch of hatred, and their initial reaction to the Yugoslav draft program was relatively mild.[49] Similarly, Rumanian reporting of the Polish scene avoided the sharp criticisms so typical of the other states.* [50]

Within the centralist states ideological conformity thus masked practical diversity. Indeed, in some ways, ideological orthodoxy might have been a compensatory substitute for what the various leaderships realized to be an inevitable trend of growing domesticism. The ruling

* The Polish press made strikingly frank references to this. A Gomulkaist weekly noted: "in the Rumanian press, in contrast with that of other countries, we do not find the slightest critical reference to the current political trend of events in Poland. A similar independence — since silence can also be a sign of independence — is also evident in the attitude to the Yugoslavs, although there is not such a noticeable sympathy for Tito as for Gomulka. 'We believe that you can take care of yourselves, but for God's sake keep your nerves; do not let your imagination run away with you; and carefully calculate your strength. Our fate depends on how you will succeed.' Various people told me this. . . ." *Polityka*, July 24–31, 1957.

elites were gradually aging,* and the new cadres that were emerging in terms of local issues, external subordination notwithstanding, were necessarily different from the old Comintern Stalinist *apparatchiki*. Stalinism was no longer a universal method but rather a set of goals which required some common methods as well as domestic adjustments. In brief, it was "neo-Stalinism in one country."

Accordingly, despite the new unity and the Soviet leadership, a bloc within a bloc existed in the Communist camp. The most orthodox centralist states were Czechoslovakia, East Germany, and Bulgaria. Hungary was pursuing a zigzag course, essentially radical in politics, initially moderate in economics and in external policies toward Poland and Yugoslavia. Rumania was also orthodox verbally, but slow in its agricultural revolution and in industrialization.† Within all these states there was evidence of a persisting uncertainty about methods of building socialism. The Hungarian regime was clearly beset by internal conflicts, with Kadar occupying a middle position, attempting to combat both the "revisionists" and the "sectarians." Early in 1958 he launched a vigorous attack on the sectarians but ap-

---

* The process is naturally slower in the neo-Stalinist parties than in Poland where the leadership was drastically revamped after October 1956. Striking differences in age, length of tenure in office and education between the Polish leadership and some of the other leaderships, rigidly resisting change and aging, are illustrated by the table below:

Politburo and Secretariat
(jointly)

	Poland (15)	Bulgaria (16)	Czechoslovakia (20)
Age			
55–65	1	9	10
45–55	11	5	5
Under 45	3	2	5
Years Spent in Politburo			
Total membership in Politburo	12	10	13
Over 5 years:	7	6	10
Including over 10:	3	3	2
Under 5 years:	5	4	3
Education			
University compl.	8	1	1
incompl.	3	1	2
Gymnasium compl.	—	7	1
incompl.	1	2	1
Elementary school or less:	3	5	15

Based on Radio Free Europe mimeographed studies, March 31, May 14, June 9, 1959.

† It may have been just accidental, but it is noteworthy that Czech trade relations grew appreciably with the other centralist states between 1953 and 1957 while decreasing with Poland and Rumania. *Nova Mysl*, June 1958.

parently without too much success; for in December, after a protracted debate, the sectarian position on collectivization, urging its reintroduction, was adopted, although watered-down to avoid extensive
terrorism.[51] It is likely that in time similar factional conflict will become more prominent elsewhere and will be able to take advantage
of any divergent Soviet and Chinese approaches. However, in the
more industrial states, particularly Czechoslovakia and East Germany,
the Chinese position on any given issue will have essentially ideological significance only, since Chinese domestic practice, derived from
a primitive economy, could hardly be applicable. Certainly, the varying reactions of these states to the Chinese people's communes reflected this diversity. The Czechs and the East Germans saw in them
further proof of the need for revolutionary and radical measures, and
for this reason hailed them ideologically but without domestic imitation. The Bulgarians initially went further in stating that the people's
communes might be relevant to the Bulgarian scene and even proceeded in one case to label their newly amalgamated collective farms
as a people's commune. However, on the eve of the December 1958
Chinese reconsideration, the Bulgarians announced that "it is incorrect
to think that the Chinese experience is being transferred to our country" and reasserted again their full loyalty to the Soviet pattern.[52]
The Poles in their reaction took advantage of the opportunity to stress
that the Chinese experience confirmed once more the general proposition of a variety of methods in the march to Communism.

Despite the undoubtedly earnest professions of centralized unity
and respect for Soviet leadership, the gradual consolidation of differentiated neo-Stalinist patterns is a divisive force which creates its
own vested interests and its own specific orientation. The awareness
of this danger was presumably behind the concerted effort launched
early in 1959 by several countries to erase the persistent inequality between them in the extent of socialization of agriculture. Hungary
moved forward with particular force and by April 1959 was claiming
that 50 per cent of arable land had been socialized. The Rumanian
leadership, neatly combining state farms, collective farms, and collective associations, was laying claim to 60 per cent. The likely consequence of these policies, if applied with the vigor necessary for
their success, would be a return to internal violence and greater external orthodoxy. But even so, neo-Stalinism in one country creates
a strain on the internationalist priority which the camp must maintain if it is to keep its cohesive quality.

The Price of Primacy

There is little reason to doubt that the expansion of the Soviet sphere of influence following World War II met with the general approval of the Soviet people. The creation of new Communist states, formally friendly and in fact subordinate to the USSR, gave the average Russian a greater sense of security in a world portrayed as dominated by anti-Soviet imperialist forces. To those motivated by nationalist feelings there was the additional element of pride involved in the expansion of Russia. To the "faithful," the new situation gave cause for deeper ideological satisfactions. The emergence of a camp of Communist states was tangible proof that their doctrine was well founded, that their historical perspectives were in tune with the pattern of historical change. The growing number of Communist states, as well as the increasing ferment in Asia, the Middle East, and Africa, irrefutably bore out the most optimistic expectations voiced by the Soviet leaders. Beyond all this, there were even material blessings in the new relationships. "To the victor belong the spoils" was the operational principle of the millions of Red Army men pouring through East Europe or Manchuria in 1945. Victory and primacy were expressed in tangible, personal ways. The official Soviet policy of dismantling and reparations was another very tangible manifestation of the new, economically beneficial relationship.

Gradually, however, a change took place. After Stalin's death, the allied Communist states began to appear less and less as tributaries and more and more as claimants to Soviet resources. The Soviet regime, anxious for reasons of international prestige to appear as a benefactor, was unable to reveal openly to its own population the fact that economic relations with the People's Democracies had been to the Soviet advantage. On the contrary, even during the Stalinist phase of acute exploitation of the neighboring states, the Soviet population was led to believe that the USSR was selflessly aiding the other Communist states. After 1956 the Soviet government was compelled to revise its economic relations with the bloc, and Soviet credits were granted to obtain political benefits. Indeed, thereafter the Soviet regime was constantly pressed for credits. The Poles demanded and obtained them as compensation for past iniquities. The Hungarians got them to help Kadar restore control. The Chinese got them to push forward their economic planning. The East Germans received them partially to alleviate the dislocation caused by Polish export readjustments and partially to make it appear that the Poles were not being rewarded for their recalcitrance (see Chapter 12, pp. 283–84). To the average Soviet citizen this appeared to be merely a further extension of the policy of economic generosity. With the Soviet regime still unwilling to state that relations in the past had benefited the USSR considerably and continue to do so, many Soviet citizens, as noted by some visitors, began to resent such generosity, especially as the people were being called upon to make sacrifices. Primacy, in this respect, became a burden. Admittedly, such sentiments could have little direct consequence for Soviet policy. They do, however, become part of the amorphous climate of opinion which even a totalitarian leadership must weigh.

Primacy also had its political price. The Soviet leadership was said to reflect the advanced stage of the Soviet Union's transition to Communism as well as of its industrial and military might. To protect its ideological claim, the USSR had to be wary of excessive innovation elsewhere lest it render Soviet experience inapplicable. The Soviet social and economic institutions had to reflect the pioneering role of the USSR in the construction of socialism. They could not therefore allow themselves to become historically dated or outpaced by any other Communist society. Social and institutional changes and industrial primacy were among the essential prerequisites for the retention of leadership. Yet Soviet society no longer benefited from the advantages of "backwardness" — it was no longer in a state of flexibility. As a result, social and political changes were becoming more difficult to carry out than, for instance, in Bulgaria or China. It was becoming increasingly harder for the Soviet leaders to announce transitions to new, higher historical phases through dramatic reforms or revolutionary undertakings. The new Communist states could now do what the USSR in the past was able to do economically: borrow foreign experience, telescope it, and change faster than the original model. Leap-frogging need not be merely the prerogative of delayed industrialization; it may also be a characteristic of ideological emulation.

Entering the second decade of the Communist camp, the Soviet leadership is thus likely to continue striving to assert its primacy, not only because of tangible advantages to the USSR but also because, in Soviet eyes, there is no other alternative. Without such Soviet primacy, the camp could easily become disorganized and unable to challenge the capitalist world. China, geographically as well as economically, is in no position to claim the mantle of leadership. To maintain its direction the Soviet society will have to continue making sacrifices, especially so that Soviet industrial might, the most tangible manifestation of the advanced "historical" stage of Soviet society, remains pre-eminent within the camp. The Soviet emphasis on the development of productive forces as a precondition for the entry into Communism can ensure the Soviet leadership only as long as the Soviet Union itself maintains unquestioned industrial superiority.

The Twenty-first CPSU Congress in February 1959 gave the Soviet leadership an opportunity to state once again the grounds for claiming its primacy and to clarify the problem of building Communism. Primacy was claimed through the gigantic development schemes and industrial advances envisaged in the Seven Year Plan which, according to the Soviet leadership, meant that the Soviet Union had already entered the stage of accelerated construction of Communism. The other states were said to be only completing their construction of socialism. Turning to the problem of "passing to Communism," Khrushchev developed a new thesis, one for which he was hailed by the Chinese and which combined the virtue of compromise with its implicit claim for continued Soviet primacy. It is to be recalled that the September 1958 Chinese plenum had raised what amounted to an ideological challenge by suggesting that China might enter soon into Communism. The first Soviet response was to hint that European Communist states, because of their more advanced economies integrated by CEMA, would be the first to enter jointly into Communism, followed subsequently by the Asiatic Communist states.[53] However, the Chinese withdrawal of December made it possible for the Soviet leader to postulate a new formula, namely that all the Communist-ruled states will be able to enter Communism simultaneously. This eliminated the possibility of any one Communist state again raising the claim that it would be the first to enter into Communism; and Khrushchev's justification for the simultaneous transition — that the more advanced Communist-ruled states would assist the less advanced ones — meant that Soviet economic advances remained the chief guarantee of Soviet supremacy. Khrushchev could confidently expect that Soviet economic leadership in the camp was not likely to be challenged in the foreseeable future. Soviet industrial indexes were Khrushchev's most potent instrument for laying this ideological issue to rest.[54]

It is to be expected therefore that in the foreseeable future Soviet society will again undergo radical socioeconomic reforms, thereby justifying the Soviet claim to primacy within the camp. The widespread discussion in the Soviet Union of the meaning of the transition to Communism has indicated clearly that such changes will involve profound exertions on the part of the Soviet people. According to Soviet theorists, the first stage of the building of Communism will presently involve the following measures: (1) the elimination of the existing differences between town and village life through the absorption of socialist property into state property, through the liquidation of private plots in the collective farms, and through the absorption of collective-farm property into state ownership; (2) the abolition of classes through the elimination of differences between a rural and an urban worker, and by decreasing the differences in rewards for physical and mental work (this process has already begun); (3) the creation of a new "Communist personality" by reducing national distinctions within the USSR and by an intensified educational-ideological campaign; (4) an increase in the directing role of the party as the internal functions of the state are passed over to so-called public organizations. A precondition for all of this is the surpassing of the United States in per capita production. Soviet society has thus been forewarned that changes do not cease with the construction of socialism.[55]

Khrushchev's remarks to the congress, cited widely by the Communist press, in one stroke established him as the leading theorist on a question which will be of increasing importance to the Communist camp. At the same time, however, they highlighted a problem peculiar to dictatorial systems: that of succession. Soviet history suggests that Khrushchev's death is likely to reopen a number of controversial policy issues in the struggle for the leader's mantle. In such a struggle, the various competing factions would have to take into account to a far greater degree than ever before the wishes and aspirations of the non-Soviet Communist leaders, more self-confident and increasingly assertive. It took Khrushchev several years to establish his own standing, and it is to be recalled that, at first, he was viewed with considerable contempt among international Communist leaders. His eventual successes notwithstanding, his relationship with a Novotny or a Ulbricht, not to speak of Gomulka, could never be compared to the relationship between these same men and Stalin. The longer it takes for a new Soviet leader to emerge, the worse for Soviet primacy and the higher the price the internally competing Soviet factions will have to pay to their external allies. Soviet domestic politics will thus gradually become increasingly responsive to pressures from without.

All of these problems reflected the growing pains of the still relatively young Communist empire. Its outwardly monolithic organization merely shielded from prying eyes a continuing process of inward change and adjustment. A comparison between the Communist camp at the time of Stalin's Nineteenth Party Congress in October 1952 and at the time of Khrushchev's Twenty-first Congress in February 1959 might suffice to illustrate that persistent evolution. Toward the end of Chapter 6, five broad characteristics of the camp were noted. Six years later the same camp was characterized by (1) a continued reliance on political ties, but with multilateral conferences becoming a frequently used method for ensuring unity between political regimes alike in the sense that they were all Communist but increasingly subject to growing differences in domestic methods and outlooks. Indeed, unlike Stalinist uniformity, the bloc in 1959 contained regimes such as the Polish and even Hungarian, which were pursuing domestic policies somewhat "rightist" in character (some compromise and concession), and more "leftist" radical regimes in East Germany, Czechoslovakia, Bulgaria, China, Rumania, and the USSR, with the Soviet and Rumanian regimes displaying rather greater tolerance for the Polish pattern. (2) The former feudal relationship had given way to a structure of hierarchical contingency, with the USSR occupying the undisputed first place * but necessarily displaying greater

---

* It is interesting to note that in the "socialist commonwealth of equal states" there is a very definite and revealing hierarchy. It is strikingly illustrated by the order in which the heads of the delegations from the ruling Communist parties have addressed important Soviet party gatherings, as shown below:

Nineteenth CPSU Congress *October 1952*	*Twentieth CPSU Congress* *February 1956*
1. B. Bierut, Poland	Chu Teh, China
2. Liu Shao-ch'i, China	B. Bierut, Poland
3. K. Gottwald, Czechoslovakia	A. Novotny, Czechoslovakia
4. M. Rakosi, Hungary	W. Ulbricht, East Germany
5. Pak, Chon-ae, Korea	G. Gheorghiu-Dej, Rumania
6. V. Chervenkov, Bulgaria	V. Chervenkov, Bulgaria
7. G. Gheorghiu-Dej, Rumania	M. Rakosi, Hungary
8. E. Hoxha, Albania	E. Hoxha, Albania
9. D. Damba, Mongolia	Choe Yong-kun, Korea
10. W. Pieck, East Germany	Tru'o'ng Chinh, Vietnam
11.	U. Tsedenbal, Mongolia

Fortieth anniversary *November 1957*	*Twenty-first CPSU Congress* *February 1959*
1. Mao Tse-tung, China	Chou En-lai, China
2. W. Gomulka, Poland	W. Gomulka, Poland
3. A. Novotny, Czechoslovakia	A. Novotny, Czechoslovakia
4. W. Ulbricht, East Germany	W. Ulbricht, East Germany
5. C. Stoica, Rumania	G. Gheorghiu-Dej, Rumania
6. T. Zhivkov, Bulgaria	J. Kadar, Hungary
7. J. Kadar, Hungary	T. Zhivkov, Bulgaria
8. Ho Chi Minh, Vietnam	Kim Il-song, Korea

responsiveness to the often conflicting aspirations of the other states, particularly China. (3) A concerted effort was made to revitalize ideological bonds by greater clarity in defining the universals of building socialism and Communism, by an effort to legitimize ideologically the special Soviet position, and by limited concessions to the impact of domestic conditions on these ideological prerequisites. (4) Soviet controls, while still relying on the potential threat of military intervention, largely gave way to combined political, economic, and ideological pressures and to a greater dependence on a balancing of conflicting interests of the various regimes, most of which had a continued interest in maintaining Soviet leadership, being dependent on its support. (5) Economic relations, a matter of considerable long-range importance, were developed in the direction of increasing interdependence and specialization, with only the USSR and China free to pursue an autarkic policy. Economic unity was to be the foundation-stone of political uniformity. Direct Soviet exploitation declined, although individual states were still called upon to make sacrifices for the "common weal." [56]

The evolution in the Communist camp progressed more rapidly than possibly even its own leaders fully realized. Most of them still tended to speak with the single-minded unity of old. Nonetheless, a gradual change had taken place in the direction of greater diversity, especially as the individual Communist regimes became more concerned with the complex task of building the future and less with simply destroying the past. The occasional spurts and leaps ahead provoked counterreactions which resulted in some curbing of the diversity. In the immediate future it is likely that a *continuing compression*, emphasizing both institutional and ideological uniformity, will characterize the domestic scene in most of the Communist states.

Fortieth anniversary	*Twenty-first CPSU Congress*
November 1957	*February 1959*
9. Kim Il-song, Korea	Ho Chi Minh, Vietnam
10. E. Hoxha, Albania	E. Hoxha, Albania
11. D. Damba, Mongolia	U. Tsedenbal, Mongolia

(In 1957, Kardelj, speaking for Yugoslavia, followed immediately after Zhivkov and preceded Kadar.) There is too much regularity to this whole pattern for it to be a matter of chance. To some extent it may reflect the special standing of some of the speakers as individuals, but, on the whole, it does establish a certain persistent sequence which is based in part on size but also in part on political standing (for instance, the shift of the East Germans). A sequence reflecting population would have been in the following order: 1. China; 2. Poland; 3. East Germany; 4. (Yugoslavia); 5. Rumania; 6. Czechoslovakia; 7. Vietnam; 8. Hungary; 9. Bulgaria; 10. Korea; 11. Mongolia; 12. Albania.

But the *status quo ante* was not restored, while a persisting measure of diversity bred new problems, as described in this chapter. These new problems will in turn stimulate more diversity and at the same time help to consolidate it. Communist leaders, used to viewing the non-Communist world from a perspective which stresses change, might find it difficult to adjust to the notion that relations among Communist states are also in a state of flux. On their ability to adjust graciously to such change depends the unity of the Communist camp and eventually its very survival.

CHAPTER 16

SOME GENERAL IMPLICATIONS OF

Ideology and Power in Relations Among Communist States

Friendship is real and strong when people share the same views about events, about history, about life. If you do not share the philosophy of the Communist Party because you have your own principles and your own views, then it is possible to maintain good relations with Communists but it is difficult to achieve a deep friendship as we understand it. — Nikita Khrushchev, March 1958

Nikita Khrushchev was speaking of the role of ideology in relations between individuals and among nations. His remarks make it clear that he was addressing himself essentially to the question of political friendship, to that state of affairs in which diverse parties have concluded that there exists among them a sufficient community of interests to justify political collaboration. To a Marxist-Leninist, however, politics requires not only purposeful action to achieve particular objectives but also the conscious awareness of how that action relates to existing reality. Hence we can understand Khrushchev's emphasis on history, on philosophy. In brief, he was suggesting that politics, the exercise of power, cannot be viewed independently of ideology, the source of political purpose.

The importance of the close relationship between power and ideology to Communist practice has been stressed in the preceding chapters. On the basis of the foregoing analysis it now might be appropriate to attempt some tentative generalizations about the role of ideology and power in relations among Communist states, defining at the same time somewhat more precisely the nature of modern ideology. The discussion which follows, while perhaps wide-ranging, might help to bring out the underlying assumptions of what has preceded and provide the basis for evaluating some possible trends in the future.

The importance of ideology in contemporary politics is closely related to the spread of literacy, the increasing pace of socioeconomic change, and the growing political awareness of the populace, all of which have made politics a matter of much broader popular concern. The mass character of modern politics typifies not only the democratic systems but also the contemporary totalitarian movements which engage in mass indoctrination and attempt to channel the growing political consciousness of people. Political power has accordingly become much more dependent on the successful mobilization and manipulation of the masses. This development, in turn, has resulted in a new kind of responsiveness between the ruler and the ruled. In democratic societies the emergence of party systems with certain programs of action has been in large part a response to this social development. In many parts of the world, however, intense social dissatisfaction with the status quo, a sense of political frustration, the weakening of traditional bonds induced by economic change, have resulted in the emergence of a new type of political action which is nondemocratic but which also requires the mobilization of popular support. The continued spread of literacy and industrial technology has at the same time resulted in an optimistic expectation that social engineering based on certain theories about the nature of society can resolve the existing social, economic, and political dilemmas. The bond between those wishing to reorganize society through political action within the context of real or imagined deprivation and the masses whose support is necessary to such action has usually been supplied in modern times by a revolutionary ideology embodied in a political movement. Unlike the more implicit and relatively unarticulated ideological outlook of the stable democratic societies, the ideology of a revolutionary movement is overt, its logic is exposed, and its relationship with political action not only evident but crucial.

Modern revolutionary ideology is essentially an action program derived from certain doctrinal assumptions about the nature of reality and expressed through certain stated, not overly complex, assertions about the inadequacy of the past or present state of societal affairs. These assertions include an explicit guide to action outlining methods for changing the situation, with some general, idealized notions about the eventual state of affairs.

Modern revolutionary ideology thus combines five elements which make it qualitatively different from social consensus and philosophical traditions which characterize, for instance, the American way of life.

1. Such ideology is based on certain *stated* assumptions. In other

words, it is normally an explicit statement to which reference can be made for purposes of inspiration, guidance, or indoctrination.

2. Precisely because ideology serves in part as a link between the political leaders, their movement, and the masses, such statements cannot be excessively complex, and at least parts of the written doctrine must be available in the form of relatively simple, dogmatic tenets, often combining elements of myth with a certain rationality (the latter required by the spread of literacy and technology). Lenin's *Imperialism* or Marx's *Communist Manifesto* — as contrasted with other, essentially philosophical Marxist writings which play a greater role in influencing the more educated and intellectually oriented groups — would be typical examples.

3. Ideology attempts to place the blame for existing inadequacies on some identifiable object, be it a special class, state, or race, thereby concretizing to the masses the nature of their dissatisfaction.

4. It is a guide to action in that it offers specific methods for changing the existing situation, for destroying the identified enemies, and for satisfying mass cravings.

5. Finally, ideology defines generally the nature of the future society in which the existing dissatisfactions will be absent, although in this respect ideology usually tends to be imprecise insofar as specific, concrete, institutional aspects are concerned. The ultimate ideal state tends to be a myth and an aspiration, sufficiently general to satisfy most individual wants.

The preceding definition groups both Communism and Fascism or Nazism under the general heading of revolutionary ideology. The case is not so clear-cut with nationalism since, by definition, there is no universal nationalist ideology, except in the general sense that all nations are entitled to their political independence and sovereignty. Nationalism can be seen as the most basic, even the most primitive, modern ideology, the first to mobilize mass support for purely political purposes, namely to create or strengthen a nation-state. Nationalism planted the seed of political consciousness among the people without which contemporary ideologies would find it difficult to flourish; and the rise of modern revolutionary ideology is, accordingly, closely related to the emergence of the "politics of mass consciousness," that is, politics which are based on the assumption that all members of society should identify themselves with the political process (although not necessarily direct it), and that all members should consciously acquiesce in the officially stated purposes of that political activity. The politics of mass consciousness rejects the notion that society is a spontaneously developing entity, but emphasizes the need to perceive the nature of social change and the feasibility of steering and even shaping such change. That change is said to lead to the victory of virtue over vice, both viewed in absolute terms.[1] Although future-oriented, a revolutionary ideology might become also the source of a defense of the status quo after the ideologically oriented movement has seized power. However, it is very doubtful that the leaders of the movement would then claim that the final stage of fulfillment has been reached. Even after power has been seized, the ideology would continue to serve for purposes of mobilizing support — claiming that Today's is the best possible world but that Tomorrow's will be better yet.

Policy and Ideology

The relationship between ideology and power, as some of the preceding thoughts suggest, involves several facets. Ideology in some respects is inherent in power, as when it serves to raise morale or to stimulate fanatical convictions. Ideology also shapes the purposes for which power may be used, helping to determine the direction in which power is applied; it often serves to rationalize power, to justify it, thereby in effect becoming part of it while implicitly transforming power into authority. For purposes of clarity, we might define power, either in its substantive or relational meaning, as simply the ability to obtain a desired action from others, or to produce a desired event. Ideology might be considered under certain circumstances as a factor of power (just as wealth is), and generally its locus is likely to correspond to that of power. For instance, in the early stages of the Communist camp it was sufficient to know Soviet views or ideological assertions concerning a particular subject to predict the behavior of the other Communist leaderships. Since power, however, involves a reciprocal, and usually asymmetrical relationship (that is, the power wielder is also influenced, but to a lesser extent, by the objects of the exercise of power), the role of ideology in affecting the reactions and shaping the expectations of both the subject and object, either as individuals or as states, becomes relevant. A widespread expectation of a mode of behavior might even help to induce such behavior and thereby become a factor of power relationship.[2] Power, however, is not necessarily equivalent to *authority*, which can attain results similar to those produced by the use of power by being accepted as legitimate or wise, and therefore obeyed even if the actual force to impel compliance is lacking. In time, ideology, by justifying power and transforming it into authority, can diminish the amount of power which must be applied to achieve compliance or to produce the desired effect.

In brief, then, the relationship between ideology and power is viewed here not as causal but as contingent, with ideology being essentially a doctrine of political power which simultaneously defines the ends, outlines the methods for their fulfillment, and mobilizes support for them. Under certain conditions, the imperatives of power may affect the ideological concepts, but it could be argued that the tenets so affected were fundamentally operational ones — those outlining the methods of achieving the ultimate goal — and so may occasionally change without affecting the final ends.

The preceding comments might be clarified if a distinction is made between those portions of the ideology which can be called *doctrine* and those which might be referred to as its *action program*. Although doctrine and action program cannot always be neatly compartmentalized and will often overlap, basically the doctrine involves the philosophical assumptions, the broad historical laws, the ultimate ends — in brief, the *a priori* assertions which form the foundation stone of the ideology. The doctrine remains basically unchanging. The action program, derived from the doctrinal principles, involves the purposeful process of fulfillment of that which is held to be immanent. It can change if need be, and the success of the change in itself establishes a new contingent truth. The question of socialism in one country, or of many versus one way to socialism, is of this variety. Without the doctrine, ideology would be equivalent to mere pragmatism; relying on doctrine alone, ideology would be just a static dogma. Doctrine linked with action program gives modern ideology its religious fervor, its sense of constant direction, as well as its freedom of maneuver in the use of political power to achieve that which must be.

Ideologically motivated power, while forcing occasional practical adjustments, also creates pressures for the fulfillment of the ideology. The maintenance of political power precludes static situations and continuously requires action and policy. The political power of an ideological movement stems from and then requires a response to a situation of stress, of social unrest, or of promised utopia. Since an important ingredient of the movement's power is the element of explicit and proclaimed purpose which furthers its seizure of political power, the fulfillment of major portions of the ideologically stated objectives becomes a necessity dictated by power, by the inner dynamic of the movement itself. It is therefore doubtful that Hitler could have survived without gradually increasing the scope of the National-Socialist revolution in Germany, or that Stalin and his regime could have maintained the New Economic Policy without ultimately losing power. But a mere "power analysis," postulating that the maximization of power is the basic political impulse of these regimes, would be inadequate to an understanding of German and Soviet developments. They only become meaningful when ideology, while considered an element of that power, is at the same time seen as a substantive and residual element in its own right. Purpose and policy thus constantly interact and are inseparable.

There is a further consideration to be taken into account. The exercise of power is in itself a matter of judgment, and ideology accordingly influences the choice of alternatives for action. Ideology as a method of organizing the perception of reality provides certain categories for determining the meaning of an era, the nature of the era's dominant forces — it distinguishes between broad trends and mere passing episodes. It helps to clarify the various observable contradictions and conflicts, and through this provides a sense of purpose and a clarity of direction which involve a long-range commitment transcending the short-range crises. In this respect it is a source of confidence, even blind confidence. As one commentator recently stated: "our empiricism dooms us to an essentially reactive policy that improvises a counter to every Soviet move, while the Soviet emphasis on theory gives them the certainty to act, to manoeuver and to run risks." [3] This too may have its shortcomings, but the question here is not its effectiveness but the matter of the nature of commitment and its relation to power.

To dismiss ideology as an irrelevant criterion to an understanding of the political conduct of Soviet or Nazi leaders [4] raises another problem. To do so would be to assume that it is possible to build up a large organization ostensibly dedicated to certain explicit objectives, in which individuals are promoted on the basis both of their professional ability and their demonstrable ideological dedication, but in which an inner sanctum operates, makes decisions with a complete disregard of the ideological principles of the movement, indeed remains immune to the constant pressures for ideological justification, and cynically disregards the official creed. However, it is a matter of historical record that many of the Soviet leaders suffered personal hardship in the name of their ideological commitment, were educated through the absorption of well-defined concepts, in turn contributed to their further elaboration, and subsequently educated others in the arcana of the ideological thinking. Once in power, they tended to view the world, particularly the outside world, in categories of thought shaped by that ideology and made political decisions on the basis of information forwarded to them by bureaucrats who were either indoctrinated with that ideology or who knew well that their leaders subscribed to it. As a result, the information flowing to the leaders in itself contained interpretations bound to reinforce the doctrine. These leaders, in turn, being intensely concerned with the use of power for the sake of pursuing their ends, made ideological faith a basic criterion of membership within the movement, and subsequently of advancement within it.

A skeptical leader would run a serious risk of undermining his power if he were to allow himself to question the ideology. It is very doubtful that even Stalin could have done it — although this is not to exclude appeals to other than ideological sentiments (such as his wartime nationalist appeals). So much of Stalin's power, however, involved his special position as the creative and sole interpreter of Marxism-Leninism that for him to denounce the ideology would have meant to deny himself an important source of strength. Of course, in shaping policy he might have dismissed it altogether, although the very implementation of that ideology through the recreation of society made the concepts part of the conditioning environment. Indeed, it could be said that as ideology ceases to live in the hearts and minds of the revolutionary "ideologues," it is reborn in the institutions of the new society.

All this suggests that even if Stalin's chief criterion of action was "will this increase or limit my power?" he still had to phrase his policy ideologically; he still employed ideological categories which imperceptibly shaped his thoughts; and he consequently was acting as if committed to it. His operational language and concepts in their turn affected the processes of communications and of information. Given his power, this very fact forced his lieutenants to respond in keeping with the ideological categories, thereby creating a chain reaction downward, emphasizing to the lower minions the importance of ideology. They would accordingly strive to demonstrate *their* ideological fidelity. Echoes of this ideological orthodoxy within the institutions of power would subsequently be heard at the top, making it difficult for the leaders to act in open disregard of the ideology, or at least forcing them to justify their acts in terms of it. However, since the ideology, as observed previously, does not involve the same amount of doctrinal complexity for all the members of the movement, a considerable element of flexibility is retained at the top, especially since changing situations may be said to dictate new departures and solutions. In a way, such flexibility is reassuring evidence to the devotees that their ideology is living and is "creatively" linked with the changing reality.[5]

Communist Ideology and External Relations

Possibly this line of argument may be further challenged by the assertion that even if totalitarian leaders believe their ideology, even if that ideology is inseparable from their power, and even if the ideology becomes an inherent part of the society they have constructed, it still does not prove that ideology is important to understanding their political *conduct* toward other states. Another way of raising this point would be to ask this question: "Do the leaders of ideologically oriented movements in the final analysis behave differently from other power-oriented individuals placed in a similar international context?" The answer to that is yes, with the added stipulation that there is no such thing as a "similar context." A political context is nothing more than the evaluation of the nature of the factors at play, of the relationships between other factors, and of the discernible trends in the situation. A political leader's evaluation of the situation determines his context and also his choice of alternatives. To be in a truly similar context to a Communist is in effect to be a Communist.

Still, could not one argue that the critical factor in relations among Communist states is their respective power and the interests of the various leaderships? But, again, both power and interest involve judgments, purposes, and assumptions. When Molotov was furiously attacked in 1955 (see Chapter 8) for underestimating the historical stage of socialist construction in the USSR (and hence undermining the exalted status of the USSR among the other Communist states), the Soviet regime was illustrating the close interconnection between domestic developments, ideology, and the USSR's paramount position in the Communist camp. The fact that so much importance was attached to the doctrinal issue not only suggests that actual conviction is involved but that the existing system is ideologically oriented and that ideological issues, since they have the capacity to lead people astray, are more than mere rationalizations. If neither Molotov nor his colleagues actually believed that there is an important difference between saying that "the foundations of a socialist society have already been built" in the USSR or that the USSR is now in the stage of "the gradual transition from socialism to communism," [6] they must have at least thought that many others in the system did. And by acting on that assumption they were actually cementing the place of ideology as an aspect of the existing system, not only internally but also in terms of the Communist camp in general.*

The unwavering Soviet insistence on the radical internal reconstruction of states falling under Communist control is also in keeping with this interdependent relationship of ideology and power. Even if the reason for enforcing dramatic, indeed revolutionary, changes in East Europe was merely the desire to strengthen Soviet power over the area and not to construct Communism per se, the mere fact that the method of strengthening that power was conceived in terms of large-scale socioeconomic changes shows the underlying ideological basis. One could certainly argue that a more moderate program would have created much less resistance and hence would have favorably affected the Communist power situation. The standard Communist answer — that Communism is not safe without creating a social upheaval that uproots the existing interest groups — in itself reveals an approach to problems of political power that is strongly tinged with ideological assumptions. This approach then dictates Communist strategy and tactics.

Perhaps the foregoing can be made clearer by a brief summary of the basic assumptions and operational questions relevant to a Communist definition of a political context. However, no effort will be made to treat systematically the actual content of Marxism-Leninism since that has been done elsewhere.[7] Communists, first of all, share the conviction that their ideology has successfully identified the ultimate ends of history and that these ends are absolutely good. These ends must be promoted consciously through action designed to gain hold of political power and then through the use of that power to reconstruct the existing society. The purity of the ideology is preserved by strict organizational unity, which in practice often means that organizational unity (within a party and between parties) becomes *prima facie* evidence of such purity, theoretical or practical departures notwithstanding. The Marxists-Leninists are unrestricted in the choice of means, since all actions are legitimized by the final ends and since all acts sanctioned by the organized movement are said to reflect the ideology. This liberates its members of those restraints on human be-

---

* "The questions of the construction of Communism in the USSR cannot now be considered in isolation from the problems connected with the existence and development of the growing camp of peace, democracy and socialism," *Kommunist* commented critically on Molotov's statement (no. 14, September 1955).

havior derived from the society's traditional norms. Since material
reality changes continuously through the clash of antagonistic contradictions, constant change is said to be the essence of life. This
means that any political arrangement is, by the very nature of things,
transitional and that any arrangement is binding only until it ceases to
interpret accurately that reality. A forward-looking perspective liberates the Communist from the shackles of the past and the present. For
this reason, no long-range commitment to the status quo can be contemplated except in terms of communicating with those accustomed
to think in terms of the present and who regard the changing reality
as part of a vaguely definable, free-flowing, and gradual historical
process.

The preoccupation with change results in a continuing concern
with the question, "at what point do quantitative changes become
qualitative?" Communists have not always been successful in answer-
ing it, but there is at least a persistent awareness among them of the
problem. As a result, in any given situation, the preceding considerations lead to the following sequence of questions raised by the Communists when defining their policy: what is the nature of the present
historical phase? What is the meaning of the relationships prevailing
between economic forces and political institutions? What direction
are they taking? Who is our major enemy? Is the enemy subjective or
objective (for instance, Japan at one time was "subjectively" hostile
in its policy while "objectively" a progressive force since its industrialization was subverting the feudal order)? Who are our allies, subjectively and/or objectively? At which point will we part with our
allies? What ought to be the pace of our efforts to stimulate further
change?

At almost every important turning point in Communist policy,
such questions have come to the forefront and have often resulted in
heated debates and conflicts. But once understanding and evaluation
have been achieved, the debate ceases and policy is set. Understanding, evaluation, action — these are the stages of policy formulation.
Such was the case, for example, with the concept of the People's
Democracy (see Chapters 2 and 4). Applied to specific instances, ideology, as stated earlier, serves first of all as a formulation of ultimate
purposes to which policy must aspire. In that sense it has remained
basically unchanged throughout Communist history. Second, it makes
possible the understanding and evaluating of various historical phases
which serve as stages on the way to the final goal. In policy making,
these phases are not as broad as the general Marxist historical stages,

such as feudalism or capitalism. Rather, they identify the basic character of a specific phase within the present epoch, as, for instance, a
revolutionary phase, a quiescent phase, a phase dominated by aggressive imperialism, or a phase in which the essential force changing
history is the liberation struggle of the colonial peoples. Once properly understood, the nature of a particular phase reveals who the
main enemy is and what measures ought to be adopted. The phases
are transitional in essence: they may be re-evaluated and adjusted
accordingly. They are part of the action program of the ideology.
Out of them emerges strategy which always is in keeping with the
ultimate objective but which is adjusted according to the given
phase. One such recent example is Stalin's 1952 statement, "Economic
Problems of Socialism in the USSR" (see Chapter 7). Finally, within
phases there are specific tactical moves to be made. On this level,
ideology is merely the frame of reference rather than the guide to
action.

Preoccupation with proper "phasing" reflects a distinctive kind of
continuous and conscious effort to identify, dissect, and reconstruct
reality. It also makes clear that while the concept of "national interest"
may not be irrelevant to an understanding of Communist foreign
policy, to be useful it must be linked to the ultimate ideological objective. As far as Communist leaders are concerned, Soviet national
interest is that which increases the power and the capability of the
USSR to promote Communism. Similarly, it should follow from this
that the concept of national interest cannot be the key to an understanding of the behavior of the Communist movements which have
come into power within several states. Indeed, it can be readily seen
from recent history that the power interests of an ideological movement may be different from the national interest of a nation-state.[8]
It would be better to focus on the ideological objectives of such
regimes, on the relation of these objectives to the concrete policies
considered necessary for the retention of power and for the eventual
fulfillment of the ideological objectives, and on the interaction between the institutions embodying the same ideology in different national contexts.

This does not mean, of course, that Communist behavior is therefore predictable or that Marxism-Leninism is a subject fit for simple
exegesis. We can expect, for instance, that in their domestic policies
Communists will continue pursuing policies designed to change drastically the existing socioeconomic order and will continue to stress
rapid industrial development, reflecting their doctrinal compulsion to

overtake and surpass the non-Communist world. These factors in turn will continue to create pressures for evaluating the world in dichotomic terms, to stress internal homogeneity and monolithic unity, in accordance with the polarized view of the world as seen through ideological prisms. But such considerations, clearly, are not helpful in predicting short-range Communist behavior. To do so, one would not only have to estimate the nature of the Communist responses to the questions indicated earlier, but also to possess much more specific knowledge of the attitudes and personalities of Communist leaders as well as of the nature of the information which serves as the basis for their decision making. The same difficulty does not exist insofar as longer-range Communist policies are concerned, as clearly suggested by a careful reading of the proceedings of the Soviet party congresses, or of some of the Comintern congresses in the 1930's, or of Stalin's postwar pronouncements, or of Khrushchev's recent speeches. The fact that the Soviet leaders consider the present era to be characterized by the struggle against imperialism suggests the categories of analysis which they apply and which are reflected in their policies toward anticolonial nationalisms.

The progressive channeling of ideology, from a general world view down to everyday tactical actions, permits the Communist leadership to feel that Communist policy, even when forcibly stimulating change, is in keeping with a natural historical process. A midwife is not interfering with a natural process. A Nazi experimenter, tying the legs of a woman in labor, was. So, in their eyes, is the West in opposing Communist policy. Khrushchev was most probably deeply sincere when he said to Adlai Stevenson: "you must understand, Mr. Stevenson, that we live in an epoch when one system is giving way to another. When you established your republican system in the eighteenth century the English did not like it. Now, too, a process is taking place in which the peoples want to live under a new system of society; and it is necessary that one agree and reconcile himself with this fact. *The process should take place without interference.*" [9]

In such a view, the emergence of Communist-ruled states and the forcible transformation of their societies is part of the historical process. The realization of unity among such states is a necessary attribute of such a process and, in turn, a proof of ideological validity. Without it, the forces resisting change might prevail. Paradoxically, however, the extreme emphasis on unity constitutes a threat to the major source of that unity — the common ideological commitment. The suppression of diversity and the forceful imposition of unity almost inevitably result in excessive reliance on force. The consequent danger inherent in an overcommitment to violence is that the ideological factor will ultimately disappear. Maintaining a balance between ideological unity and a recognition of domestic diversity is an intricate operation, and it has shaped much of the history of the formation of the Communist camp and of the relations among its members.

Patterns of Inter-Communist Relations

Perhaps these relations can be best described as integral relations. The rulers of the Communist states subscribe to certain common ideological assumptions about the nature of social change; they have fundamentally similar utopian conceptions of social engineering; they have been exposed to similar operational and ideological training; and, finally, they share a self-righteous hostility toward a mutual enemy. In brief, even without assuming that their ideology always influences their policy, there is a common and explicit faith linking the rulers of these states. The lowest common denominator of that faith, joining such diverse leaders as those from Peiping and from Prague, can be reduced to several core assumptions: (1) that capitalism is inevitably doomed to collapse and that socialism (Communism) as a form of political socioeconomic organization must prevail in its place; (2) that the social processes dooming capitalism must be promoted purposefully through disciplined organization, action, and class conflict; (3) that in societies ruled by Communists internal social change must be stimulated through rapid socialization and industrialization, the latter also of critical importance in altering the balance of force between capitalism and Communism; (4) that, because of domestic resistance and external threat, political power must be firmly held by the Communist Party and that Communist parties must make certain that their external unity is maintained through centralized leadership, common agreement on the ideological principles, and basic similarity in action. It can be readily seen from the foregoing that the sequence of these central assumptions leads from the general to the more specific. Taken together, they provide a unity of outlook which helps to bridge the great national and cultural gaps in the multinational, Euro-Asian Communist camp.

Relations among the ruling Communist parties are integral in the sense that the policies of any party are derived interdependently from its power purposes and ideological concepts, neither of which regards any aspect of society as outside its purview and both of which are related to a "universally" valid process of historical change. Since a

Communist Party not merely struggling for power but already engaged in the construction of socialism comes under great pressure to adjust to domestic circumstances, only a continuous "consultation" between the various ruling parties can maintain the cohesion so essential to the universal victory. Any political decision related to the core assumptions said to originate from a single source, Marxism-Leninism, necessarily becomes relevant to the political decisions made by other Communist regimes. As a consequence, a policy of a given regime either helps to validate the policy of another regime or, if at variance with it, constitutes a threat to its legitimacy and ideological orthodoxy. Accordingly, and especially because the total social impact of revolutionary change makes almost every activity a potential policy, the traditional international-relations principle of noninterference in the domestic political affairs of one sovereign state by another is inapplicable to relations among Communist-ruled states.*

A sort of Communist "general will," based on both self-interest and ideology, requires a frame of reference which is free of narrow national perspectives. To that end a "legislator" is necessary. Thus, another vitally important factor promoting the development of integral relations is the special role played by the Soviet Communist Party. For several decades the Soviet Union was the only state engaged in implementing policies said to be derived from Marxism-Leninism. Many of the tactical or strategic questions with which other Communists were faced after coming to power, even if under substantially different conditions, had been experienced by the Soviet party. Its leaders naturally felt qualified to comment authoritatively on the domestic policies of the new regimes.

But more important still was the political dependence of the new regimes on the power of the USSR and the personal training of the new leaders by the CPSU. Most of the Communist leaders have been exposed to international Communist activity, either as Comintern agents or as revolutionary leaders, in an era dominated by Stalinism. As a result, among otherwise very diverse nations the ruling elites shared a similar schooling, similar patterns of experience in organizing and viewing reality, and, finally, similar operating and bureaucratic methods. In this respect they suggest an analogy with the various national leaderships of the Catholic Church. Furthemore, faced in their respective countries by almost universal hostility, the newly installed leaders must have felt much like the Christian missionaries on pagan

---

* It must be here conceded that the use of the word *state* in describing relations among Communist regimes is imprecise.

soil. How many concessions could they make before compromising the faith? How many should they make to promote its acceptance? The Jesuits, for instance, under the energetic leadership of Robert de Nobilibus, attempted to convert India during the seventeenth century through adapting to local conditions. Posing as Brahmans, adopting existing customs and rituals, although claiming that the latter were merely civil rites, they made thousands of converts, despite growing apprehension in the Vatican.[10] However, to the East European Communists, directly dependent on Soviet power, the problem of adjustment was not merely one of ideology but also of power. Thus from the first Moscow was in a position to maintain a continued and direct involvement in the political decisions of the new Communist regimes.

China and Yugoslavia were the exceptions to this pattern, and integral relations were maintained essentially on the basis of the special Soviet ideological standing. The fact that the Communist regimes in these two states were basically indigenous diminished their power dependence on Moscow, although their common subscription to the doctrine made close ties with the USSR possible. Soviet efforts to ensure the political subordination of Yugoslavia tested the durability of such an arrangement, with known results. Yet once the political pressure was lifted, Yugoslavia soon revealed its ideological preference, even if with some reservations, for the camp "building socialism." In the Chinese case, Moscow was satisfied with Chinese ideological acceptance of the Soviet model, and both parties avoided a situation which could subject their ties to a severe test. No doubt, the political isolation and the economic weakness of China created additional bonds, making for something approximating political dependence.

The special role played by the USSR, even if resulting initially in nonreciprocal integral relations, helped to establish the principle that the political practice of one Communist state is materially relevant to another, and that each Communist state must continually refer its practice to the general practices of the camp. The unity of theory and practice should never be confined to narrow national frontiers. Over a prolonged period of time, however, that general principle could not be applied with regularity and uniformity. Many varying factors inevitably affected the actual application of the principle to relations between ruling Communist parties. In the course of this study, four basic phases in such relations were noted, each resulting in differing degrees of involvement of one Communist Party (usually the Soviet) in the affairs of another ruling party.

An examination of these four phases strongly suggests that the unity of the camp, and hence the special character of the relations among its members, requires the ideological commitment of the party leaders to be buttressed by the power of the leading party — by its capacity to force specific actions on those otherwise not disposed toward undertaking them and to define, whenever necessary, the meaning of the ideology. That ideology, however, remains an important binding element, translating to some degree the power of that central state into authority. The views of the central state are accepted as authoritative because they either automatically reflect the common interest or spring from greater wisdom and experience, neither of the two conditions being violated by occasional errors committed by the central party. Without such central power, or eventually authority, the unity rooted in ideology could disintegrate under the impact of time, change, specific interests, and differing conditions. The fate of the Protestant churches, once they split from the recognized authority of the Papacy, might be a case in point, as already noted. Therefore, ideology must have an institutional source of sanctioned interpretation and a built-in ideological justification for the existence of that source. This goes considerably beyond a mere reliance on the similarity of socioeconomic conditions and institutions to guarantee identity of view and unity in action.

Within the four broad phases noted in the preceding chapters, it may be observed that during the first the element of Soviet political power provided the general protective shield under which action was undertaken by the various Communist parties to capture and consolidate their power. Relations among Communist parties during this period formally resembled the traditional pattern of interstate relations. The preliminary nature of their activity in itself allowed for greater diversity, which was also justified by the international situation and Soviet preoccupation with reconstruction and consolidation. Integral relations developed in the second phase, during Stalinism. This phase was characterized by the central power's insistence that its experience in building socialism be the slide rule for all domestic calculations of the ruling Communist parties. Ideology declined in importance as a unifying element and became essentially the translation of past Soviet history into current Communist practice. In the third phase, Soviet efforts to reintroduce the core assumptions of the ideology as an active unifying element, together with the actual decline in direct Soviet power and the unsettling consequences of the Soviet policy toward Yugoslavia, created a situation in which domestic developments in the various Communist states began to interact, leading to a dissipation of the uniformity. A divisive interparty dialogue developed out of the varying blends of specific national conditions and universal requisites. The fourth phase saw the continued reliance on common ideological commitment being buttressed by a concerted effort to rebuild and legitimize a common center within the camp. In this phase integral relations became more reciprocal, with the central power's domestic policies more responsive to the domestic policies of the other ruling parties.

The methods used to organize relations among the Communist regimes changed with each of the four phases. These methods can be divided into state treaties, both bilateral and multilateral, interstate economic relations, bilateral and multilateral party dealings, and finally supranational organizational ties, both on the state and party basis. During the first phase bilateral state treaties played a role in organizing and consolidating the politics of the bloc, with such agreements as the Soviet-Czech or the Polish-Soviet or the Yugoslav-Polish actually expressing and strengthening the political status quo. These were thus comparable to regular bilateral treaty relations elsewhere. Similarly, the Yugoslav-Bulgarian interstate ties were of considerable political significance, although essentially in the planning stage. At this juncture, no multilateral interstate ties existed, although some were planned – as, for instance, the possible accession of Rumania to the Yugoslav-Bulgarian federation, a scheme ultimately condemned by Moscow. Interstate economic relations were both bilateral, in the sense of trade treaties and reparations arrangements, and multilateral in that regional economic ties were planned, such as among Poland, Czechoslovakia, and Hungary. Party dealings moved from bilateral ties, existing initially between each party and the CPSU, in the direction of multilateral "consultation," institutionalized in the Cominform, through which the CPSU exploited the weakness of the parties to ensure unity in doctrine and practice.

In the second Stalinist phase, all state treaties declined in importance, and were only used to formalize a relationship of strict hierarchical, almost feudal, subordination. At the same time, the previously planned schemes of political collaboration on a regional basis were abandoned under Soviet direction, and each regime essentially dealt with the USSR only. Significantly, only the Chinese-Soviet political treaty could be regarded as of any consequence during this period, suggesting that Soviet-Chinese relations in 1949–1950 were in a stage similar to, for instance, Soviet-Yugoslav relations in 1945–1946;

this also reflected, of course, the special relationship existing between Moscow and the strong and confident Peiping regime. Economic relations among the states similarly involved bilateralism, with the central focus being the USSR, while autarky was the operational principle for each state. Interparty contacts became infrequent and involved primarily relations between individual parties and the CPSU.

The third phase, one of rapid change and crisis, saw an effort to revitalize the importance of formal interstate ties through the Warsaw Pact, a multilateral political-military treaty. However, more restricted regional political ties were not developed, partly because of the different internal trends within the Communist-ruled states and partly because such a development would certainly have been discouraged in Moscow. In economic relations, the new recognition of the desirability of formal multilateral political ties was matched by the creation of a standing economic organization. Interparty contacts grew in frequency, and interparty declarations of understanding were issued more often than before on a bilateral basis, primarily between the USSR and the respective parties.

The fourth phase, the reconstruction of the camp, involved a renewed importance of bilateral interstate relations. The Polish-Soviet agreements of November and December 1956 played such a role. In brief, interstate relations again took on the shape of the more traditional patterns of international affairs. This development was paralleled by a successful effort to increase the importance of the permanent multilateral economic organ, ultimately shaping the *economic interdependence* of the bloc. Party ties during this phase were cultivated with unprecedented intensity, with more bilateral declarations of common understanding and purpose issued than during the preceding three phases together. The parties striving to protect their autonomy favored bilateralism in view of the relative decline of Soviet power, while Moscow and the centralist parties used bilateral declarations to promote multilateral contacts. Several multilateral conferences were actually staged and used by Moscow to subdue the recalcitrant parties through the combined pressure of the camp's membership.

The Image of the Future

From the preceding summary it would appear that, whenever there was a subordination of ideology to the power of the center, there was a greater tendency to rely on bilateral party relations and state relations, although the latter declined in their importance. When ideology was freed from the tutelage of one power, greater reliance was placed on multilateral consultation and formal devices to restore unity in the camp. It is, therefore, likely that in the near future the USSR will desire to institutionalize multilateral party contacts as a method for rebuilding internal unity. Elements unsympathetic to such centralism will, as a consequence, continue to favor bilateralism in party and state relations. But once cohesive unity is established, there might well be a return to greater emphasis on bilateralism. Economic trends are less likely to shift dramatically in response to such political shifts, although the increased emphasis on the CEMA is likely to favor the political power of the most economically powerful states. In the foreseeable future, therefore, particularly in view of the emergence of a hierarchical contingency within the camp, it is very likely that a concerted effort will be made to institutionalize a *common political organ*, a form of regular "Commonwealth Politburo," to ensure the maintenance of a universal perspective and of integral relations among the ruling parties.

Such a superior interparty political organ might become especially necessary in view of the continued trend within the camp toward alternative approaches to the domestic problem of constructing Communism. The emergence of "right-wing," "left-wing," and "centrist" orientations, noted in the last chapter, bodes ill for the camp's unity and calls for some effective method of continually re-examining and integrating not only economic but also political decisions. The mounting importance of the CEMA is a step in that direction: the integration of economic decisions is bound to be reflected on the political plane. In a very significant speech addressed to the East Germans early in 1959, Khrushchev revealed the extent to which he was relying on economic integration to achieve the *political* union of the Communist world. This was his image of the future:

Communist society, which will have an abundance of material and spiritual wealth, is capable of satisfying the needs of every individual as well as of every nation. . . .
In these conditions the old concepts of borders as such will disappear. With the victory of communism on a worldwide scale, state borders will disappear, as Marxism-Leninism teaches. In all likelihood only ethnic borders will survive for a time and even these will probably exist only as a convention. Naturally these frontiers, if they can be called frontiers at all, will have no border guards, customs officials or incidents. They will simply demarcate the historically formed location of a given people or nationality in a given territory. . . . The foundations for communist relations among

peoples have been laid in the Soviet Union and in the entire socialist camp. . . . Extensive cooperation in all spheres of economic, social, political and cultural life is developing among the sovereign countries of the socialist camp. Speaking of the future, it seems to me that the further development of the socialist countries will in all probability proceed along the lines of consolidation of the single-world socialist economic system. The economic barriers which divided our countries under capitalism will fall one after another. The common economic basis of world socialism will grow stronger, eventually making the question of borders a pointless one.[11]

To rely on economic ties alone, however, would be the economic determinism long since thrown overboard by Marxists-Leninists. The growing consolidation of Communist regimes with their home-grown personnel raises with increasing urgency the question of nationalism and poses the threat that creeping domesticism can be transformed in the long run into national Communism. The fanatic, highly intelligent Stalinists of 1945, men like Dimitrov, Rakosi, or Bierut, have gradually given way to hierarchically trained, pseudo-intellectual party *apparatchiki*, primarily interested in their own power; these leaders in turn are coming under pressure from the younger generation of technically trained intelligentsia, concerned with the domestic development of their countries. There is a growing tendency therefore for a ruling Communist Party to view the Communist camp from the standpoint of domestic interests and to evaluate it in terms of the camp's capacity to satisfy these interests. In domesticism there is always the latent danger that the basic question of Soviet versus national interest will ultimately be raised, even if that national interest merely means the most efficacious methods for the domestic construction of Communism and even if for the time being the power interests of the ruling elites dictate the closest ties with the USSR. Moscow must hence periodically seek some reassurance of the continued primacy of the universal perspective which economic integration alone cannot ensure.* Only a situation of ideological stress and of hostility

* After the completion of my book, I read A. Zauberman's study on "Soviet Bloc Economic Integration," *Problems of Communism*, July-August 1959, which makes a similar point, but more strongly. Zauberman concludes that "the process of integration will be fully consummated only if and when the orbit economies are directed as a single unit in accordance with a single plan drawn up and implemented from a single center of authority. This would practically make the forging of an *organic political entity* a necessary precondition for full-fledged economic integration. . . . In this writer's view, the experience of CEMA lends strong support to the proposition — theoretically evolved by the well-known American economist, Professor Jacob Viner — that it is far more difficult to integrate centrally-planned socialist

to the outside world can prevent such a process from materializing rapidly. Only such stress can hold out a vision of a Poland ultimately returning to greater domestic orthodoxy or of the Yugoslav Communists, once Tito dies, being forced through a polarization of the world to choose the camp which is still construed by the Yugoslav Communists to represent the wave of the future.[12]

The need for a centralized political authority resting on Soviet power may also be stimulated in time by changes in Soviet military primacy within the camp. A crucial ingredient of that might is the Soviet nuclear monopoly. Pressure on Moscow for the sharing of that monopoly is inevitable, and the arguments which may be advanced on behalf of this sharing will not be easily refuted. Starting from the formal premise of equality and true friendship among socialist states, the Chinese, say, might demand nuclear weapons. The Czechs, pointing to their record of political and ideological orthodoxy, could request them to counterbalance the West Germans. The Poles, fearful of the Germans, could similarly claim them. Even the East Germans could request nuclear weapons on the grounds that they cannot effectively compete with West Germany if the West Germans appear to enjoy greater trust among their allies than Ulbricht and Pieck do in Moscow.

It is doubtful that the USSR would be inclined to accommodate such requests. The Soviet leadership probably remembers the recklessness of Tito in wishing to precipitate a war over Trieste, and it might even fear that the Chinese could embroil the camp in a war. The Chinese boast that after the next war there will be "twenty million Americans, five million Englishmen, fifty million Russians, and three hundred million Chinese left" could hardly be reassuring to the Kremlin.[18] After many years of leadership Moscow's sense of responsibility for the fate of the entire camp has presumably matured. As a result, the Kremlin would most likely prefer not to give up its nuclear monopoly, which would further diffuse the center of authority. In time the USSR may find it necessary to "lease" nuclear weapons and Soviet technicians to its allies, which might satisfy their craving for a nuclear status without undermining Soviet production and employment monopoly. The Soviet Military Command of the Warsaw Pact would be a further guarantee of effective Soviet control within such allied "sharing," while a common political authority, in charge of

economies than market economies, without the suppression of national identities. Herein lies the fundamental dilemma of the Soviet planners in Eastern Europe" (italics in original).

framing basic policy and preserving a common outlook, would miti-
gate any possible unilateral adventures by a Communist state.

Future trends within the camp and in relations among Communist
states depend too much on unpredictable factors to allow for much
meaningful discussion. There is, first of all, the changing character
of the cold war and of the external pressures on the Communist camp.
There is the problem of the nature of the domestic changes in the
Communist states and particularly the USSR and China. There is the
question of the balance of industrial and technological strength between the East and the West. The matter of Khrushchev's successor
might result in an appreciable alteration in relations between the
USSR and the Communist states, and particularly between Russia
and Poland. The emergence of new ruling elites in the Communist
states will affect the picture. In Polish-Soviet relations the personal
element seems particularly to play an important role, and the eventual
disappearance of both Khrushchev and Gomulka will inevitably require new adjustments and might produce new tensions. This is also
true in the case of Tito, although the appeal of Yugoslavia in the bloc
has been largely dissipated by Yugoslav policy.

Similarly, the future character of the camp also depends on the
options available to some of its members. For example, the continuing
fear that Germany will desire to reclaim some of its lost territories,
as well as a certain identification in Central European thinking of Western policy with the German rejection of the Oder-Neisse line, places
Poland in a position of dependence on the USSR, regardless of ideological issues. National interest and geography thus serve to buttress
the existing ideological bonds among the party leaderships. On a more
general level, it should be noted that the basic outlines of a socialist
welfare society seem to have taken root in East Europe, which has
not had the most fortunate of experiences with either free enterprise
or foreign capital. For this reason, in any future development the alternatives open to the Communist-ruled states ought never to be discussed in terms of socialism and Soviet domination or free enterprise
and independence.

Given the fact that some of the European Communist-ruled states
identify themselves with European culture and resent the abyss dividing them from Western Europe and driving them further into the
Euro-Asian bloc, efforts to promote the closest all-European links,
without directly challenging the power of the regimes and, even more
important, the basically socialist organization of their societies, might
have the effect of undermining the Communist image of the world. If

the Communist states in Europe were to be continuously invited to join in all-European undertakings of a social, economic, and political character, such Western overtures could eventually have some effect. The present Communist regimes might be expected to reject such invitations out of hand, but they would be likely to prove appealing to the new generation of Communists less exposed to the Soviet dichotomic perspectives and traditional suspicions. Not irrelevant to the attractiveness of such Western initiatives is the considerable gap in the standard of living between the West and East. In any such policy a particularly important role could be played by West European Social Democrats who would be in a strong position to guarantee that Europeanization does not mean de-socialization. Indeed, one might well expect that the advent to power in West Europe of Social Democratic regimes would place the East European parties under greater pressure and might induce Moscow and its centralist supporters to initiate a more violent "leftist" policy to counteract the Western appeal. While such a turn could place the "rightist" policies of Gomulka and, to a much lesser extent, Kadar in great jeopardy, a sudden switch to greater radicalism inside a framework lacking the homogeneity of Stalinism and already exposed for several years to somewhat more domestically oriented policies could have serious consequences within the ruling parties and lead to new crises.

The Threat of Ideological Erosion

However, regardless of any Western policy designed to exploit the divisive forces in the Communist camp, there has been a steady diffusion of the camp's cohesion. This has taken place in spite of the continuing economic integration of these states. Economic integration alone is not capable of overcoming the persisting awareness of national distinctiveness, an awareness sharpened by the unequal relations which have prevailed in the bloc. The alternate waves of liberalization and retrogression have led to a considerable diminution in the directing power of the central party, despite the setbacks suffered by the Poles, the Yugoslavs, and revisionism in general. Indeed, one might postulate that with the increasing maturity of the Communist regimes, relations among ruling Communist parties could evolve from integral into international, thereby reasserting the basic importance of the nation-state within the bloc.

The fact that some of the members of the bloc can claim to be cultural and economic peers, or even superiors, of the dominating nation would be likely to accelerate such a centrifugal process. The first stage of internal dissolution could take the form of the gradual emergence of *two* Communist camps, the more industrially advanced European-Soviet and the industrially retarded but rapidly industrializing, violently anti-Western Sino-Asian complex of Communist states. Khrushchev was probably not unmindful of such a potentiality when he so categorically insisted that all Communist-ruled states would enter Communism together and rejected the notion of some Soviet theorists that the European Communist states might do so before their Asian allies (Chapter 15). Finally, one could also speculate that empire building reflects social disintegration within the imperial society,[14] and that the gradual emergence of social stability within the USSR will be conducive to an eventual waning of Soviet interest in the continued maintenance of a tightly knit hierarchical bloc. A concentration of power requiring growing sacrifices but deprived of the justification of insecurity could lose its social appeal.

The preceding thoughts, however, have neglected one very important consideration. Any evaluation of the possible direction that the gradual evolution of the Communist camp might take must go beyond the analogies between it and the imperial systems so familiar to our civilization; it must take into account the special role played in that camp by its ideology or at least the common assumptions of its political leaders. In spite of a tendency of the Communist parties to become institutionalized, and hence to develop a particular existence of their own, their common dedication and their common conviction that history and Communism are marching together are important unifying elements. The Communist camp is at one time an empire and a church, and this combination results in a type of relationship which is deeply binding. The closest analogy to it is the Islamic world, in which the political leadership at the same time was the effective chief religious authority (not unlike the position won by Khrushchev at the November 1957 conference). But unlike the Islamic world, the modern Communist world also dispenses the latest technology and industrial methods and equipment — further insurance that internal changes within its far-flung dependencies follow a common revolutionary pattern and create a socioeconomic structure firmly linked by political, economic, and ideological ties.

The measure of diversity which gradually emerged in the Communist camp after Stalin may take on a different meaning when viewed in the light of a system which is not merely political, like the imperial structures, but also ideological. The new diversity need not be, therefore, an augury of approaching doom but may act as a shock absorber, or a safety valve, for the tensions which necessarily develop in any large-scale organism and which Stalinism merely attempted to suppress. A measure of elasticity can make the system even more enduring. Such elasticity may allow the gradual development of Soviet power into Soviet authority, a more stable condition not unlike the transformation of the Papacy. That authority can only remain effective, however, if an ideological justification persists. Without the common belief, the authority would cease to function effectively or would have to revert eventually to a reliance on sheer force, a retrogressive step which each passing day would make more difficult to execute. The ultimate danger to the Communist camp is, therefore, not the potential waning of Soviet power but the gradual erosion of the common ingredient of ideological commitment.

That erosion might ultimately occur through a continuing confrontation of ideology with reality. Unlike religion where the ultimate sanction is supernatural, material reality is said to validate the ideological assumptions of Communism. But if Communism fails to expand fast enough, if increasing concessions to the requirements of a particular national situation result in domestic adjustments shattering the basic universal assumptions of that ideology, if the dichotomy said to exist between Communism and the Western world is revealed to be in the final analysis only political and therefore, in Communist terms, artificial, then such erosion might well take place within individual ruling parties. Factors largely pertinent to the relationship of any given Communist-ruled nation to the camp are thus likely to be the source of the erosion of the common ideological commitment.* The bloc's unity requires central ideological and political leadership, as revealed by the various phases of its development. Yet such unity cannot encompass all the diverse aspirations of the several ruling regimes, and their specific interests must bow before the "universal" interest of the camp.

The varying stages of socioeconomic development and the special international interests of the USSR and China might be especially conducive to the emergence of varying ideological emphases. Short

* It seems less likely that urbanization and industrialization will bring about this erosion. These forces in themselves strengthen the ideology in several important ways: they institutionalize an environment which is based on the ideological aspirations and which in itself in time begins to act as a buttress for that ideology; second, through a very tangible sense of achievement they create a widespread acceptance of the ideology which, even if lacking its original revolutionary zeal, becomes even more pervading; third, the nature of a modern industrial society based on social ownership, and which has severely limited individual initiative, requires a continued articulation of societal goals to help preserve a broadly accepted sense of purpose. For fuller discussion, see my "Totalitarianism and Rationality," *The American Political Science Review*, September 1956.

of subordination based on force, any such variation would have to result in a weakening of the ideology or in ideological conflicts. This might occur as the ruling elites begin to see the camp as a brake to the domestic fulfilment of their societal goals, although these varying goals might still be identified domestically under the catch-all of Communism. The general commitment to Communism, and even to its domestic dictatorship, might thus continue, but the common universal perspective will have fallen victim to the processes of erosion. The Communist camp might still persist in form but no longer in content. That at least has been the historical experience both of Christianity and of Islam as state systems, as well as of movements which were based on militant secularist, nationalist, or ideological doctrines.

Revisionism was such erosion's harbinger. Its apocalyptic significance was to break through the integrating but distorting myth of the official ideology. The revisionist intellectuals, like the *politiques* in the sixteenth century, were too divorced from power and from the power wielders to avoid defeat in a direct political contest. But politics has a way of catching up with intellectual insight, and someday even the practitioners of power may realize that their unifying ideology has become a liability. This may take a very long time, especially since political faith is nurtured by success, of which Communism has had ample share in recent years. Communist faith, increasingly relying on outpacing capitalism in the volume of industrial output, is thus likely to draw additional comfort from Khrushchev's confident prediction that the Communist camp soon will be producing more than half of the world's industrial output, thereby tangibly demonstrating its "historical superiority." [15]

If an ideological erosion does take place, it will probably begin with doubts about the general desirability of a cohesive bloc and of similarity in action, both of which would lose their urgency once the enemy ceased to be a threat. It may then lead to doubts about the basic, antagonistic dichotomy between the Communist and non-Communist worlds and ultimately may point to the conclusion that social change is an organic, interrelated process which has no winners or losers. In brief, the process of erosion is likely to begin with the specific core assumptions, lead to skepticism about the general doctrine, and finally result in the Soviet bloc's sharing the fate of other imperial systems. For this to take place, however, the ideology must first be denied both victories and enemies, a difficult and paradoxical task since denial of one can be construed as the manifestation of the other.

The Impact of the Sino-Soviet Dispute

Somebody has raised the question as to who is the one who determines what is truth, and what complies with the principles
of the Marxist-Leninist doctrine. — Walter Ulbricht

THE Sino-Soviet dispute dominated bloc affairs during the years
1959–1961.[1] The dialogue between the two major Communist powers
revealed that Khrushchev's formula of ideological uniformity and institutional diversity could be successful only as long as one power
center and one ideological arbiter prevailed within the bloc.

It seems in retrospect that the Soviet leadership, usually so attentive
to the meaning of history, did not fully grasp the historical significance
of the 1957 Chinese intervention in East European matters. While the
Chinese helped to restore unity within the bloc, they also conclu-
sively broke their ages-long political restriction to the Asian continent.
In 1957 China intervened decisively in Eastern Europe, and the
Peiping leaders no longer saw China merely as a regional power. Having helped the Soviets in their internal bloc difficulties (see Chapter
12), they were quite willing to assist in the formulation of the bloc's
global strategy, thus laying claim to the status of a world power.
Khrushchev's formula for bloc unity had made no provision for more
than one center of political and ideological guidance, and even less
for the eventuality of major disagreements between any plurality of
such centers.

The great significance of this development obscured a simultaneous
process of abatement of tensions in Eastern Europe. The revolutionary
wave, which had reached its crest in 1956, had receded. Soviet hopes
were again high, stimulated by Soviet space achievements and by a
growing Soviet conviction that the West was gradually adjusting to
the notion of the peaceful emergence of global Communist supremacy. Khrushchev's domestic popularity had never been higher,
and it was stimulated also by marked improvements in the Soviet
standard of living.

In 1960 two dreary visits to Warsaw, marked by public coolness
but political correctness, symbolized the mutual adjustment of Go-

mulka and his Communist neighbors. In March, Warsaw was visited by Janos Kadar, the First Secretary of the ruling Hungarian Party. To most Poles, he was the killer of Imre Nagy as well as a reminder of what might have happened to them had Gomulka failed in 1956. Relatively few Poles realized that in Soviet bloc affairs Kadar was striving to associate himself with the more moderate Gomulka position and that domestically he was opposed by the more rigid neo-Stalinists. Nonetheless, the visit to Warsaw of the man who betrayed the Hungarian Revolution was not without its meaning. In September, the First Secretary of the Czechoslovak Party, A. Novotny, who is reported to have pressed for Soviet intervention against Gomulka in 1956, also traveled to Warsaw. His visit, even more than Kadar's, marked Gomulka's full readmission to "the club," for which he had been earnestly sponsored since 1958 by Khrushchev. To the Poles, a special motive for closer relations with Prague was the desire to obtain Czech credits for industrial development.[2] To the Czechs, the containment of Polish "deviationism" had obvious political advantages, while the warmth of Khrushchev's relations with Gomulka inevitably thawed the frigidity that had prevailed between Prague and Warsaw.

Domestically, in Poland, the accent during this period was on economic development, rationalization of bureaucratic organization and procedures, and greater labor discipline. Most of the old labels of Natolinites or Stalinists, Revisionists and Gomulkaists (see note, page 256) lost their meaning. Gomulka had consolidated his policies, and Poland's new relationship with the Soviet Union, combining domestic autonomy with greater Soviet realization of the *Soviet* interest in not pressing the Poles too hard, had gained a measure of resigned Polish social acceptance. "Organic work"—quiet efforts to develop Poland, but abstinence from active politics—became the slogan of many Poles. Even the return to positions of responsibility of some of Gomulka's former opponents (including the notorious Ruminski and Witaszewski) could not be interpreted as a victory for the anti-Gomulkaists. Rather, it symbolized their belated recognition that Gomulkaism did not mean anti-Communism or anti-Sovietism, and that there was no way of undoing what had transpired in the aftermath of the Eighth Plenum in October 1956. In agriculture, the regime still held to its 1956 pledge not to introduce collectivization by force, while pressing the peasants to adopt the so-called "agricultural circles," a form of cooperative pooling of skill and resources. The reimposition of political controls over arts and sciences continued,[3] although largely without administrative repression. The most visible source of tension was the state-church relationship; and the harassment of the church, together with persisting economic difficulties, were the chief causes of the considerable drop in Gomulka's personal popularity.

Yugoslav relations with the other East European states and the Soviet Union remained correct but cool. In general, they followed the pattern set by Khrushchev: normal state relations, but no fraternization by the ruling parties. The Yugoslav Party was not invited after November 1957 to the various Party celebrations held in the bloc, although Yugoslavia was generally referred to as a state engaged in some form of socialist construction. However, the Albanian and the Chinese regimes continued, and intensified, the anti-Yugoslav polemics initiated in the spring of 1958 and refused to consider Yugoslavia as a socialist state. The maintenance of correct relations with Belgrade by the other Communist states did not mean in any way the reintroduction of Yugoslav influence into bloc affairs. This Belgrade itself realized, and Tito increasingly saw his role no longer as one of the leaders of a polycentric international Communism, but rather as a leader of a new "neutralist" third force of African and Asian powers. Yugoslav influence in Eastern Europe took the form primarily of economic appeal; Yugoslav agricultural experiments, cooperative economic undertakings, improvements in the standard of living, etc., attracted much interest in the neighboring states.[4] But, for the future, the question of Tito's succession and its consequences inevitably give rise to growing speculation: Will Yugoslavia be able to steer its course without the Marshal, or will the more diversified non-Stalinist Soviet bloc seem like the safer and no longer incompatible haven for a weaker but still Communist Yugoslav regime? It may be presumed that one of the several reasons why Moscow has avoided burning all its bridges to Belgrade has been its thought that perhaps the latter alternative is not to be altogether excluded.

Elsewhere in Eastern Europe, the political scene remained basically unchanged. Kadar continued his policy of mixing political repression with some tolerance for arts and sciences, of simultaneously improving the lot of the city-dweller and implementing agricultural collectivization. While opposed within the Party by more extreme elements, and hated throughout the nation for his odious role during and after the Revolution, he was buttressed by Khrushchev's personal support; and, in view of East European complexities, it is not surprising that he was apparently regarded by both Gomulka and Tito as the least objectionable of the possible Hungarian leaders. The push for general collectivization continued throughout the bloc, despite major agricultural difficulties in Hungary in 1959–1960. Poland was the only laggard (see table below, and compare with the one on page 99). In 1960, Czechoslovakia proclaimed itself to have become a "socialist" state, thereby being the second Communist-ruled country to have done so, while the East Germans stated early in 1959 that they expected to do the same by 1965.

Socialist sector in agriculture, 1959–1960

USSR	99.9
China[a]	99.1[b]
Poland	13.2
Czechoslovakia	85.2
German Democratic Republic	96.0[c]
Hungary	71.3[c]
Rumania	81.3[c]
Bulgaria	97.4
Albania	86.0
North Korea	100.0
North Vietnam	72.7[c]
Mongolia	99.7[d]

[a] Data for 1958.
[b] Number of peasant households.
[c] In June 1960 (North Vietnam in October 1960).
[d] According to the number of arat households.

This outward stability—as well as the intense efforts to promote close economic, political, and cultural integration of the bloc, which moved apace after 1957 (see Appendix I)—shielded a number of grave problems. Marxism-Leninism as a vital ideology was badly shaken by the post-Stalin crisis, and it had not recovered. Revisionism failed as a political substitute,[5] but at the same time many of its assumptions had penetrated, informally and "by the back door," some of the ruling political elites, not as a formal ideology but rather as part of the prevailing climate of political opinion. As an amorphous force, revisionist views became more difficult to uproot and began to merge with the decaying structure of the official Marxist-Leninist doctrine. The approaching crisis of generations—the wartime gap between the ruling elite of men in their fifties and the rising careerists in their thirties—accentuated the problem, since revisionist thinking seemed to reflect more closely the aspirations of the more youthful East European pretenders to the mantle of leadership. At the same time, the majority of the young people were becoming increasingly "privatized" and avoiding all political entanglements.[6] This development, related closely to the general influence of West European traditions and culture on Eastern Europe, threatened to increase further the gap between the East European Communist states and their zealous, revolutionary Asian counterparts, still experiencing the initial impact of the confrontation of their retarded but restless social environment with an all-embracing ideology of change, modernization, and dichotomic hostility to the rest of the world. Dying in Eastern Europe, feverishly oscillating in Russia, the ideology was being resuscitated in Asia.[7]

The Silent Split

It is difficult, probably impossible, to pinpoint precisely the beginning of the Sino-Soviet dispute. In some respects, it can be dated back to the 1920's, when Moscow directives led the Chinese Communists into the jaws of destruction.[8] In terms of more contemporary issues, there is reason to believe that the Chinese Communist victory in 1949 was neither expected in Moscow nor achieved by methods advocated by Stalin.[9] Following the victory, there were hints that the Peiping-Moscow relationship was not the warmest, and it was only after Stalin's death that the Soviet leadership began to cultivate more affirmatively its Chinese allies (see page 169). The Kremlin probably felt that its efforts were rewarded by the energetic support given it by the Chinese in the aftermath of the Polish and Hungarian revolts (see Chapter 12). At the same time, it was precisely this engagement that produced in the Chinese an acute crisis of confidence in Khrushchev's leadership of the bloc, encouraging them to take a more active part in shaping the bloc's overall line.

In 1960, when the disagreements between the two parties became public knowledge, they were reliably reported to have exchanged strong mutual criticisms and, in so doing, to have attempted to date the beginning of their conscious and actively expressed disagreements.[10] It is revealing to note that Khrushchev adopted the position that it was only after the November 1957 meeting (see pages 297 ff.) that the Chinese began to deviate from the common line. In effect, Khrushchev was claiming that the Chinese started to strain the unity of the bloc just after it had been reconsolidated and that it involved a conscious, "subjective" Chinese act. The Chinese, however, went to some pains in stressing that the Sino-Soviet divergence began with the reckless and unilateral launching by Khrushchev of the anti-Stalin campaign in 1956 and that it was subsequently reinforced by the indecision of the Soviet leadership during the October–November 1956 crisis.* They also harped on earlier differences, dating back even to 1926. The Chinese, in effect, were saying that the dispute was rooted, "objectively," in the transformation experienced by the bloc after Stalin's death and that it was an inevitable consequence of the failures of Soviet leadership.[11]

There is truth in both versions, although it would seem that neither party had "creatively utilized" its Marxism-Leninism in analyzing the origins of the silent split in their world outlook that developed between 1956 and 1959, erupting into an open dialogue in 1960. Both "subjective" and "objective" factors played a role, and it would be useless to attempt to separate them. Basically, the Sino-Soviet divergence can be said to have been rooted in the interaction within the Soviet and Chinese contexts of three elements: domestic developments, their relationship to bloc affairs, the interaction of the two with world affairs—all as perceived within the jointly shared Marxist-Leninist outlook of the two parties.

The years 1957–1958 saw in China a marked shift toward greater political and economic radicalism, while in the Soviet Union they were marked by Khrushchev's triumph over the remnants of Stalinism and a considerable domestic material improvement. The Chinese during this period increasingly became convinced that a repetition of the 1956 crisis, the domestic dangers of which their own "Hundred Flowers" campaign had amply demonstrated,[12] could only be avoided by a unity of all Communist states based on militant action against all bloc deviants. To the Soviets, the period of crisis had passed, while to Khrushchev his improved relations with Gomulka and correct relations with Tito were a useful reassurance against neo-Stalinist hostility elsewhere. The preceding factors were closely related to a divergence in the assessments made after 1957 of the international scene, and particularly of the existing opportunities for further expansion of Communism. To the Soviets, a certain balance of terror seemed to make indirect expansion possible (through economic aid and political intercourse with potentially pro-Communist elements), while to the Chinese the missile gap seemed to be the basis for more explicit linkage of political and military tactics. Thus, here as elsewhere, ideology and national interests were interacting. The Chinese concern over Formosa and Ladakh provided the underpinnings of

---

* In this connection, the Chinese took credit both for the Soviet decision not to intervene against Poland and for the intervention against the Hungarians. According to the Chinese, the Soviets first wanted to intervene against Poland and then shifted to the opposite extreme in respect to both Poland and Hungary.

national frustration, but the Chinese involvement in Algeria and Cuba could hardly be interpreted purely in terms of national interest. Inescapably differing Soviet and Chinese domestic experiences and interests affected their world-wide Communist aspirations and perspectives. In effect, the interaction of these elements created a dilemma: "how the existing differences in ideology and in material situation can be transmuted into ideological and material uniformity. What are the dialectical processes through which uniformities may be developed from dissimilarities?" [13]

The Chinese domestic scene during the years 1957–1961 was dominated by the following characteristics: (1) an apparent shift to the left in the Communist leadership; (2) a revolution on an unprecedented human scale in agriculture, carrying with it significant ideological implications for the Communist bloc and a challenge to Soviet ideological primacy (see pages 366 ff.); (3) a general "Great Leap Forward" in all economic sectors, but one accompanied by mounting economic difficulties, especially an agricultural crisis in 1959–1960, as well as by natural disasters (floods, etc.); (4) the awakening of a fantastic sense of national pride and energy among 650 million Chinese, hitherto politically pliant but now fascinated with industrialization. In effect, the domestic scene involved the simultaneous merging of Communist, industrial, and nationalist revolutions—a combination hitherto not experienced anywhere.

The belated discovery that revisionism had found a fertile soil among Chinese intellectuals created profound misgivings in Peiping. The Hundred Flowers campaign that began in 1956 was brought to an abrupt end in mid-1957, and it was followed by a vigorous "rectification." [14] The National People's Congress in July 1957 was highlighted by a series of abject confessions by "rightists" who had gone too far in criticizing the regime. These confessions set the mood for an assertion within the ruling elite of a tougher, more radical line. For some years subtle alignments of a "conservative" and "radical" character (but not in the form of factions) apparently had existed within the top Party echelons, and the radicals succeeded in placing their stamp on domestic policy in mid-1957 and on foreign policy subsequently. This became more evident in 1958 with the launching of the People's Communes; but already in late 1957 extravagant, radical statements concerning the agricultural policy, the class struggle, and the transition to Communism began to dominate the Party press, while the Party cadres were urged to undertake manual labor. But it was characteristic of the internal stability and cohesion of the Chinese

Communist leadership that the shift did not involve any purges at the top; Chou En-lai, who has often been considered as leaning toward moderate policies, remained in a key position, and the "rightist" alignment may still represent a potential future alternative.[15]

The Great Leap Forward was initiated by Liu Shao-chi's speech to the Party Congress on May 5, 1958 (published on May 31), in which he related the change on the international scene—now said to favor decisively the forces of "socialism"—to domestic Chinese affairs and explained the necessity of proceeding with "the uninterrupted Chinese revolution." Mass enthusiasm and total mobilization of human energy were to be substituted for material-technical development, thereby paving the way for rapid advance into the stage of Communism.[16] After the negative Soviet reactions to this claim (see Chapter 15), the more extreme ideological assertions were toned down, and the subsequent economic and natural calamities of 1959 and 1960 forced the Chinese leadership to moderate some of their targets and their grandoise projects of rapidly reorganizing Chinese society into a series of industrial and agricultural People's Communes.*

It would be rash to conclude, however, that the replacement in April 1959 of Mao Tse-tung by Liu Shao-chi as the formal head of state signified a basic withdrawal. In fact, Liu has been associated

* The Central Committee Plenum of August 1959, which met in Lushan, made substantial reductions in the production targets, and the rationalization of the People's Communes was urged (e.g., *Hung-ch'i*, no. 7, 1959). See the analysis by H. F. Schurmann, "The Communes: A One Year Balance Sheet," in *Problems of Communism*, September–October 1959. More recently, a Yugoslav account stated that since 1958 the People's Communes "have gone through the stage of 'the transition to Communism' and the conversion of cooperative property into all-national—that is, state—property; in the most extreme cases, the very kitchen stoves were transferred to all-national ownership, and finally, at the end of the third year, they reached a state where they differ little or almost not at all from the old and 'obsolete' cooperatives.

"In the course of last year it was definitely stated that the production brigade, and that means the former cooperative, would remain for quite some time to come the main bearer of the right of ownership, of the organization of production, and of the system of distribution in the People's Commune. It was also stated that the period of raising the communes to the next higher grade, in which ownership would be totally vested in the commune, would be put off far beyond the prospects envisaged and forecast as late as 1959. The renewed indication of the need to adhere to the principle of remuneration according to work and the introduction of some measures envisaging material incentives for the initiative of the agricultural producers in the communes are only one more sign, against this whole background, that the administrative and ideological-political factors failed to solve satisfactorily the problem of the further advance of China's agricultural production." B. Bogunovic, "The Difficulties and Problems of the Chinese Economy," *Borba*, February 26, 1961. See *Borba*, March 5, 1961, on "the little liberties" campaign in China's rural areas restoring to the peasants the privilege of eating at home, etc.; see also the table on page 418 for the comparative pace of Chinese development.

with the more ideological, radical wing, and the change may rather be related to some preliminary preparations for Mao's succession (he is sixty-eight). The step thus could be designed to assure continuity in present policies.[17] Indeed, radicalism continued to dominate the domestic scene (as well as to provoke Soviet uneasiness over its ideological implications), and it was reflected also in the international arena. The adjustment in perspectives reached with the Soviets at the Twenty-first CPSU Congress, especially over the all-important ideological issue of the transition to Communism (see pages 367, 378), which had already led to a Chinese challenge to Soviet ideological primacy, was soon strained by international events. These, in turn, intensified the domestic mood of enraged Chinese nationalism.[18] The March 1959 suppression of the Tibetan rebellion soon led to a crisis in relations with India. Russian failure to back China with respect to Chinese territorial demands on India must have produced strong reaction in Peiping,[19] reawakening earlier distress over the Soviet failure to back China during the offshore-islands clash with the United States in August–September 1958. At the same time, Soviet determination to explore the possibility that a Soviet-American *détente* might open indirect opportunities for Communist expansion stimulated growing Chinese fears both of political isolation and of a Soviet betrayal of the revolution. Khrushchev's visit to the United States was viewed with almost open suspicion and hostility; the coolness of the reception given him in Peiping at the October 1959 anniversary of the Chinese revolution reflected accurately the prevailing mood within the Chinese leadership.

By the fall of 1959 it was eminently clear to the Chinese and to the Soviets that they differed profoundly on a number of issues and that they had failed in resolving their differences. While still muting their dispute, they had already differed both on bloc matters and on the bloc's external strategy. The Chinese persisted in their violent antagonism to Tito (adopting even the ominous phrase of "the Tito clique," which harked back to the 1948–1949 period), in part because they genuinely rejected his ideological conceptions, in part because they thought that by forcing all the bloc regimes into militant hostility toward Yugoslav revisionism, they would be welding the bloc together. Their attacks on Tito soon were linked with the divergence between their view and that of the Soviets on neutralism. The Chinese rejected the Soviet calculation that the neutralists could be both courted and aided, and they feared that the Soviet policy would play into Tito's hands, given the Yugoslav efforts to stimulate a

Comparison of selected economic statistics during the "big push"
in the USSR and Communist China

Steel (million metric tons)				Coal (million metric tons)			
USSR		China		USSR		China	
1928	5.0	1954	2.0	1928	38	1954	80
1929	5.2	1955	3.0	1929	44	1955	95
1930	5.6	1956	4.5	1930	50	1956	150
1931	5.5	1957	6.0	1931	57	1957	200
1932	5.6	1958	8.0	1932	64	1958	275
1933	7.0	1959	13.0	1933	82	1959	347.8

Electricity (billion kilowatt-hours)				Cement (million metric tons)	
USSR		China		USSR	China
1928	5.0	1954	12.0	Average annual rate of increase 1928/29– 1937 11.5%	Average annual rate of increase 1954–1959 25%
1929	7.0	1955	13.0		
1934	21.0	1956	18.0		
1940	48.3	1957	22.0		
		1958	28.0		
		1959	41.5		

neutralist "third force" in world politics. They felt that the purpose of the Communist policy should be to stimulate a dynamic flow of the neutralist countries into an openly anti-imperialist bloc built around the Communist parties.[20] Although by 1960 it had become clear even to Peiping that the Chinese line had become counterproductive, and the Chinese had begun to improve their relations with the Southeast Asian states, Peiping continued to place primary stress on the necessity of developing "the imperialist rear into an active anti-imperialist front,"[21] and in so doing the Chinese asserted the general relevance of their revolutionary experience.

These divergent Sino-Soviet views were related to far more fundamental disagreements. The launching of the first Soviet ICBM in the fall of 1957, followed by the Sputnik, and then the 1958 recession in the United States convinced the Chinese, in the words of *Jen Min Jih Pao*, that "U.S. imperialism already has one foot in the grave and can with as much justice be described as a 'rotting bone in a graveyard.'"[22] It is quite evident that in the course of the recent period the Chinese have been acting on the assumption that there has been a fundamental and decisive turning point in international affairs in favor of the Soviet bloc and that the West no longer has any choice but to compromise, either willingly or by being forced.[23] Having challenged the Soviets on the pace of the domestic march to Communism, the Chinese were also pressing them with respect to external efforts for the attainment of a world-wide Communist victory. The policy implications that they drew from their assessment were, in turn, closely related to their more general interpretation of our era as "an epoch of imperialism, wars, and revolutions." [24] Given that, as well as their appraisal of imperialist strength, their policy prescriptions naturally followed.

In effect, the Sino-Soviet "war and peace debate" of 1959–1960 (more open in the latter year) can be reduced to the following exchanges: The Soviets to the Chinese—"You overestimate the ability of the imperialists to initiate a war, hence war is not inevitable; you underestimate the destructiveness of war and our deterrent capabilities; you underestimate the danger of a total war developing out of local conflicts; you underestimate the world-wide appeal of socialism as a powerful force and the global significance of the economic power of the world socialist system." The Chinese to the Soviets—"You overestimate the destructiveness of war; you overestimate the willingness of the imperialists to make peaceful concessions; you underestimate the militant revolutionary opportunities and the dangers of coexistence to the revolutionary zeal of the international Communist movement; you underestimate the ability of the socialist camp to win local wars or to force the imperialists to desist when they start one. Finally, you underestimate the possibility of the imperialists plunging the world into war, either out of despair or duplicity, and hence, there is a continuing danger of war." [25] The Chinese never argued for war as such; they believed that greater activism and even local wars need not lead to a real war.

The issues already discussed were not the only ones. There is reason to believe that the Chinese resented the Soviet Union's failure to supply them with nuclear weapons,[26] and they displayed some coolness to Soviet initiative on behalf of "an atom-free zone . . . in the Far East and the entire Pacific Basin." [27] Subsequently (in January 1960), the Chinese went on record as not considering themselves bound by any international agreements concerning disarmament unless they are a direct party to them, even if the Soviet Union should reach a suitable agreement with the United States. Other tension points included some persisting ambiguity on the matter of delineation of the Sino-Soviet frontier,[28] evidence of a marked decline in

Sino-Soviet cultural contacts,[29] certain testiness in off-the-record official Soviet comments about the Chinese. If the year 1958 was one of shadow-boxing and 1959 one of a steady testing of grip and muscle, the stage was clearly set at the beginning of 1960 for open grappling.

Divergent Unity

The formal Soviet position throughout the period was that there was no disagreement. This was a proper and tactically wise stance for the acknowledged leader and most powerful state in the bloc to adopt. Ignoring the Chinese assertions seemed far more effective than responding to them and thereby being drawn into a debate.[30] The Chinese, on the other hand, seemed to rely on their domestic techniques for handling problems: They seemed convinced that "non-antagonistic contradictions" with Moscow would ultimately lead to unity, through their internally tested process of "unity-criticism-unity." However, by early 1960 it became clear that China's national ambitions, as well as the general world outlook of its highly ideologically oriented Communist leaders, were incompatible with the insistence of the Soviets on playing the game of international affairs purely in terms of their own estimates and interests.

The Chinese, the weaker partner, brought the dispute out into the open. By forcing the issue—in effect, by practicing brinkmanship (i.e., letting the situation get somewhat out of their control)—they could hope to put the Soviets on the defensive, to force them to respond. At the same time, being more radical, they actually increased their leverage within international Communism since their radicalism inevitably served to reassure all Communists of their honest revolutionary intentions. Finally, by openly straining their unity with the Soviets and acting as if they were willing to risk this unity, they put the burden of protecting the unity on the Kremlin, thereby compensating for their economic-military weakness and equalizing the Sino-Soviet bargaining situation. Unity thus became a hostage in the relationship.[31]

By mid-1960 the increasingly open dispute assumed grave proportions and the "hostage" was in some danger. The Chinese apparently abandoned any lingering hope that Khrushchev might be displaced, and rather than wait for a change in the Soviet line, they decided to force one. Furthermore, the Chinese must have felt that in the course of the year 1959 they had been reasonably successful in gaining support among the Communist and revolutionary movements and that, no longer alone, they could more effectively pressure Moscow into changing its policies. Peiping was probably especially gratified by the increasingly intimate contacts with the Algerian rebels and by closer relations with the leftists in many of the Latin American countries. Furthermore, at the Tenth Chinese Anniversary in October 1959, visiting East German, Czech, and Albanian delegations spoke in such warm terms of the Chinese Party that the Chinese leadership could have construed their remarks as indicating support.[32] Last, but certainly not least, the Chinese probably feared that the forthcoming May 1960 summit meeting in Paris would lead to the international isolation of China. For domestic, for bloc, and for external reasons, the Chinese felt that the issue had to be joined.

Even then, however, the Chinese did not abandon the indirect-dialogue technique—i.e., attacking the revisionists for things the Soviets had been saying, or failing to emphasize certain propositions that the Soviets considered essential. To have acted differently would have meant an open ideological split, and in a relationship in which an overt ideology is one of the important binding elements, an open accusation of ideological betrayal would have amounted to an open break. This consideration restrained the Chinese in their otherwise almost overt attacks on the Soviet positions.

Given the intensity with which the Sino-Soviet exchanges were followed by the Western press, there is no need to quote the two sides in detail.[33] Furthermore, overconcentration on the exchanges without seeing them within the general framework of a dynamic bargaining relationship, involving two partners who agree on the ends but differ on the means, is somewhat analogous to examining a marital relationship purely on the basis of an overheard quarrel. The vehemence of the dialogue sometimes reflects uncontrollable passion; sometimes, and this is more often the case with politics, it is a means of scoring points.

The first half of 1960 saw two successive Chinese outbursts. The first took place at the Moscow meeting of the Warsaw Treaty members, which a Chinese delegate attended. In his bristling speech of February 5, the Peiping representative failed to associate himself with a general endorsement of the forthcoming summit meeting and, instead, attacked American imperialism, stressing the danger of a Western-initiated war.[34] His speech was ignored by the Soviet and East European mass media, in line with the Soviet tactic of avoiding a dialogue.[35] Shortly afterward, on the occasion of the April anniversary of Lenin's birthday, the Chinese followed with more extensive criticisms. An article by Yu Chao-li, "On Imperialism as the Source of War in Modern Times, And On the Way for All Peoples to Struggle for Peace,"[36] warned against mistaking tactical changes in imperialism "for changes in the nature of imperialism" and quoted Mao Tse-tung as saying, "If the imperialists insist on unleashing another war, we should not be afraid of it . . . if the imperialists should insist on launching a third world war, it is certain that several hundred million more [people] will turn to socialism." The article asserted that only by actively pressing "imperialism" and isolating it could a war be averted, and only then could local wars started by it be ended at a disadvantage to the imperialists. Using Lenin as his authority, Yu Chao-li emphasized that national liberation wars are "inevitable" and that it is dangerous to conclude "that imperialism will no longer make war."[*]

This was followed by an even more vehement Chinese outburst in June 1960, after the failure of the Paris summit meeting. Determined not to let Khrushchev decide the bloc's line, and proceeding from the premise that "our epoch is one in which the forces of socialism prevail over the forces of imperialism," Chou En-lai urged Communists "to make full use of the present most favorable situation" to defeat U.S. imperialism.[37] The occasion was a general meeting of the WFTU, and its Chinese vice-president, Liu Chang-sheng, went even further. He ridiculed the recent disarmament negotiations (citing passages remarkably similar to some Soviet proposals), emphasized "inevitable" and "just" revolutionary wars, and warned that those who do not share these views "deprive the oppressed peoples of their fighting spirit."[38] Almost every issue of *Jen Min Jih Pao* and *Hung-ch'i* re-echoed these sentiments.[39] The late spring and early summer were thus the period of the big Chinese push,[†] which was felt acutely not only in the bloc but also among the Communist parties of the underdeveloped parts of the world, where the Chinese mood and in-

---

[*] Speaking to a mass rally in Peiping on April 22, Liu Ting-yi warned against those "revisionists" who "develop from fear of war to fear of revolution, and proceed from not wanting revolution to opposing other people's carrying out revolution," and he added that "well-intentioned persons . . . have some incorrect ideas." For a relatively restrained Soviet reply, see O. V. Kuusinen, in *Pravda*, April 23, 1960.

[†] The Chinese also criticized the Soviet argument that Communism shall be built through the development of productive forces. "Some people hold that transition to Communism seems to have no concern with enhancement of people's Communist ideological consciousness and moral qualities, and requires only efforts in building up the material technical base, relying mainly on individual 'material stimulations' to the masses in developing productive forces. Obviously, this view is absolutely wrong. Merely leading the masses to take serious consideration of individual loss and gain and to consider personal, immediate interests more important than state and collective interests is to extend the backward thinking of the masses and to confuse the ideological demarcation of the proletariat and the bourgeoisie. This thinking is practically a reflection of bourgeois thinking in the working people class, or a kind of demonstration of thinking of 'economism' under socialist conditions." Lin Feng, addressing a cultural-intellectual conference, Radio Peiping, June 1, 1960.

terpretation seemed more in tune with the local Communist impatience and frustration.

Moscow painfully realized that ignoring the Chinese simply would not do. The criticisms were too pointed to pass unanswered, and continued silence was creating ambiguity in international Communism and could cause a gravitation in the Chinese direction. A certain ambivalence among the East European neo-Stalinists (reflected in the October Chinese anniversary speeches) prompted Khrushchev to use the February 1960 Warsaw Treaty meeting to make the East European regimes line up solidly behind his forthcoming expedition to the West. The Poles were already firmly pledged to Moscow, so the occasion was used to obtain the open commitment of the other leaders to a posture that the Chinese could not favor.* Isolated and perhaps uncertain of the degree of Chinese opposition, even the Albanians seemed to go along, while the other regimes depending on Soviet support could hardly have acted differently. By the summer, praise of the Chinese, which had been a prominent feature in the East German, Czech, and Hungarian press ceased almost completely. The problem was more complex in the case of the Asian ruling parties, not to speak of those outside the bloc. The continuing tension in Laos, as well as the division of Vietnam, made the Vietnamese Party especially fearful of Chinese absorption, but at the same time it was attracted to policies urging the rapid expulsion of the "imperialists" from Southeast Asia. In July 1959 Ho Chi Minh visited Khrushchev (on his way back through China he did not meet with Mao Tse-tung), but the Vietnamese press, by and large, continued avoiding siding with either Moscow or Peiping. In August the Soviet leader was visited by Tsedenbal, the Mongolian leader, who also paid a state visit to India, with whom Peiping was badly at odds. The Mongolians, who might have been incorporated into the USSR if first World War II and then the Chinese Communist victory had not intervened,†

---

* Symptomatically, in the February 1960 meeting of the International Union of Students, held in Tunis, Chinese attacks on the Yugoslavs were not supported by either the Poles or the Bulgarians.

† A revealing observation was made in this connection by I. G. Yur'yev (in "Laws and Characteristics of the Transition to Socialism in Socially and Economically Retarded Countries," *Vestnik Moskovskogo Universiteta*, no. 1, 1959), who, after arguing that aid "given within the framework of a single multinational socialist state is more effective and speeds up the rate of the transition from feudalism to socialism," hastily added that "from the analysis from the economic side of the question, however, we must not conclude that it is necessary for the Mongolian People's Republic to become part of the Soviet Union or the People's Republic of China, because, *in the complex international situation*, political factors play a far from minor role." (Italics added)

had received sizable Soviet credits in 1958 (Soviet generosity seemed to increase in direct proportion to analogous Chinese efforts) and, still thoroughly under Soviet control, were unlikely to side with the Chinese.[40] The outside parties were a more difficult matter since overt pressure could easily become public knowledge; the Soviets thus preferred to keep them out of internal bloc affairs.

In the early summer of 1960, the Soviets responded more openly to the Chinese criticisms. The summit fiasco (and the U-2 incident) had given the Chinese an opportunity to point the finger at Khrushchev and adopt a "We told you so" attitude. Perhaps somewhat concerned, Khrushchev struck back. On June 12, *Pravda* carried a very strong attack on "leftists," with its central theme appropriately built around Lenin's *"Left-wing" Communism—An Infantile Disorder*.[41] The article stressed that on the domestic road to Communism stages in material development could not be skipped and that "only reckless adherents of the cold war" did not fully approve the Soviet line. Given the theme of the article, it was clearly directed at someone *within* the international Communist movement and was meant to safeguard continued Soviet freedom of action in the international arena.

An even more direct confrontation took place on the occasion of the Rumanian Party Congress in June 1960. Apparently without warning, the Soviet delegation circulated among the other bloc parties a strong criticism of the Chinese views and called upon these parties to endorse the Soviet position. Although the formal speeches and the concluding communiqué stressed unity, Khrushchev openly provoked the Lenin-quoting Chinese by asserting that Lenin's views should be reviewed in the light of the times. He also used an ingenious argument to refute the Chinese assertion that the U-2 incident proved the correctness of their analysis of international affairs: On the contrary, he asserted, to change the Soviet policy "would mean being lead by the imperialists . . . it would be the equivalent of giving them an award for their provocative actions." He then firmly restated the Soviet view of the existing political and economic opportunities for Communist expansion backed by the deterrent capability of Soviet military force, and added, "I hope you understand why it is necessary for me to repeat known truths."[42]

According to some reports,[43] the two parties exchanged not only violent and often personal accusations but also lengthy documents sharply critical of each other's position.[44] They differed on the nature of imperialism, on the meaning of our epoch, on the inevitability of war, on the relationship of local wars to total ones, on the meaning of coexistence, on relations with the national bourgeoisie, on the national liberation struggle, on the stages of building socialism-communism, on Soviet accountability to the bloc for Soviet foreign policy, and on Soviet toleration of domestic Polish and Hungarian "revisionist" practices. Moreover, perhaps emboldened by these differences, the Albanian Party now openly sided with the Chinese;* the East Germans and the Czechs, however, were forced to cease equivocating and to support Moscow openly. Although all the parties issued a joint communiqué reflecting basically the Soviet position, the Soviets and the Chinese disagreed on the procedures to be used in subsequent discussions. The Soviets, understandably, preferred to limit them to the bloc; the Chinese preferred to include outside parties in the name of "proletarian internationalism," and it was difficult for the Soviets to refuse this suggestion. The forthcoming October Soviet anniversary was thus to serve as a major forum for an international Communist discussion.

The post-Bucharest period was one of intensive maneuvering. The Soviets followed up their June charges with further correspondence with the other bloc parties in August. The Chinese Party continued its anti-Khrushchev polemics, issuing a circular letter in September and even using some of its bloc embassies to disseminate among middle-level Party members excerpts from secret Bucharest protocols designed to embarrass Khrushchev. This, not surprisingly, irritated the leaderships concerned and alienated them further from the Chinese. The Soviets also seemed increasingly willing to adopt more extreme measures. In August, Soviet technicians began to leave China,[45] and there were even hints that the Soviets were preparing to force the Chinese either to break or to bow. One well-informed source[46] reported that it was only after consultations with French and Italian Communists and with Gomulka that Khrushchev decided not to force the Chinese to make a choice but rather to attempt some adjustment in the hope that ultimately the common objectives as well as continuous all-round emphasis on Communist unity would resolve the differences. At the same time, Moscow continued its efforts to cement the bloc; for instance, in September, on the occasion of the Third Vietnamese Party Congress, the Soviet delegation delivered

* As late as April 27, Enver Hoxha had echoed the Soviet line and praised Khrushchev's foreign initiatives, including his American trip. See *Pravda*, April 27, 1960.

sharp attacks on "dogmatists" who "put narrow or national interests" over "proletarian internationalism." They also offered sizable aid to the Vietnamese.*

Both the Chinese and the Soviets also engaged in characteristic jockeying for the "centrist" position in the hope of making the antagonist seem to be the deviationist. On the eve of the Bucharest meeting, the Soviets attempted to dissociate themselves from the Yugoslavs by sharply criticizing them, and early in the fall they took advantage of an extensive Yugoslav attack on the Chinese position[47] to again plant themselves in the middle, rejecting both unnamed "leftists" and the Yugoslav arguments.[48] In response, the Chinese theoretical organ *Hung-ch'i* asserted that Mao had always struggled against "left" and "right" and that the Chinese position is the correct response to these two deviations.[49]

During the fall, the CPSU prepared a programmatic draft to be submitted to the forthcoming Moscow conference. (Suslov, Kuusinen, and Ponomarev apparently constituted the drafting commission.) Probably for this reason—and also simply as a result of all the dialectics with the Chinese—Soviet ideological formulations became a little more precise than heretofore. One may suspect that the vagueness that characterized earlier Soviet pronouncements on such matters as the nature of our times, which wars were or were not inevitable, etc., was due in part to Khrushchev's own temperamental predisposition to sweeping assertions, and in part to a Soviet tactical preference not

---

* P. J. Honey (in "North Vietnam's Party Congress," *The China Quarterly,* October–December 1960) argues that in September 1960 Ho Chi Minh decided to support the Soviets after receiving a large Soviet commitment to aid Vietnamese industrial development. In the past, however, China was the major source of credits to Vietnam and its major trade partner, and in February 1961 Peiping made a further economic undertaking to help Hanoi (141,750,000 rubles on a long-term basis). For data showing Chinese economic preponderance, see *Entwicklungshilfe innerhalb des Ostblocks* (Frankfurt a/M, 1960) especially pp. 97–101. Also, on September 2, 1960, the Vietnamese Ambassador to Peiping delivered a speech over Radio Peiping using the Chinese terminology on the subject of war, while at the Albanian Party Congress in February 1961, the Vietnamese delegation seemed to echo the Chinese line. On the other hand, the Soviet aid given to the Laotian rebels can be viewed as manifesting Soviet presence, and might have been welcomed by the Vietnamese as a counter to Chinese domination. The Vietnamese Party developed under French Communist tutelage, and *L'Humanité* is still an authoritative source in Hanoi. This influence, too, would help to counter excessive identification with the Chinese. Thus continued tightrope walking seems to be a more accurate assessment of Ho Chi Minh's performance. For an Indian account of the Hanoi Party Congress, see *Link,* October 16, 1960. (According to the Vietnamese News Agency, April 19, 1961, new agreements provide for 430 million old rubles in Soviet aid and 630 million old rubles in Chinese aid.)

to be tied to precisely defined general and strategic concepts. During the fall, a series of articles appeared that more systematically developed the Soviet line, clearly in preparation for the forthcoming debate.[50] It was interesting to observe how Khrushchev's ideological views became more and more precise under the Chinese hammering. From purely an academic point of view, Khrushchev's intellectual development made impressive progress during the period.

By the time the leaders and delegates of eighty-one Communist parties began their deliberations in Moscow in early November,* some preliminary redrafting of the statement prepared by the CPSU had taken place. In October a commission representing twenty-six parties (including the twelve bloc parties) had reviewed the Soviet draft, but unanimity had not been achieved.[51] The debates lasted into early December, and even official Communist sources made it clear that there were major differences among the parties.[52] The Soviet-Chinese divergence was perhaps the basic line of division, but not the only one. Apparently, some of the Latin American and Asian parties objected to parts of the projected declaration dealing with anticolonial struggle; some of the East European neo-Stalinists might have been sympathetic to a more violent anti-Yugoslav statement; the Albanians strongly supported the Chinese on most issues and even apparently urged that a Yugoslav Communist party "in exile" be set up. While one estimate has as many as twelve parties of the eighty-one opposed to the Soviets,[53] it is unlikely that all twelve would have lined up with the Chinese if the issue had been forced, even though probably more than twelve were sympathetic on this or that score to the Chinese line. Perhaps it was to overcome this dilemma that the Chinese apparently considered forming a faction *within* international Communism and argued that there were precedents for it. However, even more significant are the facts that many leaders actively debated and that the Soviets welcomed the aid they received from Gomulka and some of the other European Communists.

During the conference the Soviet delegation apparently opposed both the setting up of a new form of the Comintern and the formal labeling of the CPSU as the leader. In adopting this position the Soviets might have been anticipating the opposition of others. It may also be surmised that in both cases the Soviets felt that the Chinese pressure, as well as the Chinese efforts to formalize party relations were designed to enchain the CPSU, and they might have now pre-

* Mao Tse-tung did not go, and the Chinese delegation was headed by Liu Shao-chi. Togliatti also did not attend.

ferred both the more informal device of irregular inter-Party consultations and the vaguer label of "vanguard." In the latter case, the
emphasis put in the declaration on Soviet experience still meant Soviet
primacy within the camp, and, as Khrushchev put it in his January
6 address, "the Communist parties must synchronize their watches.
When someone's clock is fast or slow, it is regulated so that it shows
the correct time. Similarly, it is necessary to check the time of the
Communist movement." The emphasis in the statement of the conference on the fundamental importance of the CPSU's experience left
no doubt that its clock was to be the "Greenwich time" of international Communism. Indeed, by emphasizing the primacy of the Soviet
Party and its role as vanguard, stress was put on the *objective* fact
of the Soviet Union's being the first and mightiest power, thus providing the basis for continued Soviet leadership. Nonetheless, the absence of a formally designated leader capable of acting as arbiter is
bound to complicate further the internal situation in the Communist
camp, even if it makes the camp look more "democratic" to the rest
of the world.

The declaration issued on December 6 involved a studied adjustment to the divergent perspectives of the various parties, even while
reflecting in the main the basic Soviet outlook.* The Chinese signed
it, and Liu Shao-chi toured the Soviet Union proclaiming Chinese
fidelity to Sino-Soviet unity and praising Khrushchev. Perhaps Chinese economic calamities had something to do with weakening their
bargaining position. But the Chinese probably consoled themselves

---

* If, in terms of the crucial issues, the statement of the eighty-one parties is carefully compared with earlier Soviet and Chinese pronouncements (e.g., O. V. Kuusinen's important work *Foundations of Marxism-Leninism* [Moscow, 1960] and the
Soviet and the Chinese statements on the occasion of Lenin's anniversary in 1960),
one finds that by and large the Soviet formulations have prevailed, with some adjustments to meet Chinese objections. It may be surmised that the greater emphasis on the
dangers of war and on the aggressiveness of American "imperialism," on the relevance of China to the revolutions in Asia, Latin America, and Africa, on the militant
character of national liberation struggles, and on the direct condemnation of Yugoslav
revisionism all involved adjustments to the Chinese point of view. But on a larger
number of equally or even more important issues, the statement bears greater resemblance to earlier Soviet positions. This is so with respect to such matters as the decisive character of economic development and the role of "the socialist world system"
in shaping our age, the destructiveness of war (its horrors were explicitly reiterated
despite objections), the significance of peaceful coexistence and the possibility of the
prevention of war, the importance of the twentieth and the twenty-first CPSU congresses, the universal significance of Soviet experience, the peaceful transition to
socialism, the character of "national democracy," and the evils of dogmatism. This is
corroborated by Ulbricht's unusually frank account in *Neues Deutschland*, December 18, 1960.

with the thought that through the sheer process of protracted debate they had achieved one of their central purposes: a limitation on unilateral Soviet foreign initiatives. They also probably realized that an open split at that moment would have isolated them from international Communism, thereby decreasing their leverage. Biding their time, even while conceding formal points to the Soviets, was the better strategy.

A few weeks after the conclusion of the conference (on January 6, 1961) Khrushchev delivered a major speech dealing with international affairs. The text showed that through the mere process of making explicit his ideological position the Soviet leader was forced to admit that certain types of war, namely the national liberation struggle, are not only "just" but also "inevitable." However, his apparent ability to explore the possibility of disarmament talks with the new Kennedy Administration, as well as the postponing of unilateral Soviet actions in Berlin and elsewhere, suggested that he had not lost all his freedom to maneuver. His emphasis on the economic factor as the crucial one in shaping the future, and his great stress on the destructiveness of a thermonuclear war, suggested that the pre-conference Soviet line was still guiding Moscow,* although it can safely be assumed that any weakness on the part of the West would always be fully exploited by Moscow, with or without the Chinese pressure.

Thus the Sino-Soviet unity remained a divergent one, even though the press of the two countries began to give favorable coverage to each other's activities.† The Chinese comments on the conference declaration, no longer as critical of Moscow as in the past, still stressed the need for activism against imperialism while implicitly claiming Chinese ideological primacy by asserting that the principles of peaceful coexistence had been formulated by Mao Tse-tung as far back as 1950.[54] Although the dispute was limited by the conscious realization by the two parties of the overriding importance of their unity, by their common realization that they had to deal with each other since they could not displace each other, and by a careful Chinese effort not to challenge directly the special Soviet position in the Communist

* Ulbricht's report made it clear that the extremists did not want any explicit mention of war damage; Khrushchev's speech did exactly that and concretely quantified the number of possible victims.

† However, persisting Soviet irritation over the Chinese attitude toward India was expressed publicly by a *Pravda* article, written by an Indian Communist leader who blamed the frontier dispute for harming the cause of Communism in India. A. Ghosh, in *Pravda*, April 5, 1961.

bloc, their divergent unity itself produced opportunities for further clashes, especially since a rapidly changing world continuously creates situations requiring complex assessments and policy commitments. In effect, since the two partners realized that they could only win together, and hence should not split, they lost together at Moscow. China did not achieve united militancy. The Soviet Union was forced to bargain with its allies. Each went home to interpret the common document as it saw fit.

Albania: Unity with Options

The Sino-Soviet divergent unity had a special consequence for the bloc which the Albanian case quickly brought to light. The open support given the Chinese by the Albanians, followed by an unprecedented public attack by Ulbricht on the Albanian leaders,* meant that for the first time in the history of the bloc the smaller parties could exercise options against the Soviet Union, that their leaders could clash publicly and still remain *within* the bloc.

The Albanian episode was revealing in two other respects. First, it meant that the third of the four Communist parties that had come to power largely by their own efforts had mutinied against central control. Judging by the Yugoslav, then the Chinese, and now the Albanian experience (the fourth Party is the Vietnamese), it seems that defiance of the Moscow center is a malaise to which indigenous Communist regimes (small and big alike) are especially susceptible. Secondly, it is noteworthy that in all three cases the defiance took the form of adopting postures more extreme than those favored by Moscow. Tito was more radical domestically and externally in 1948 than Stalin thought opportune. Mao Tse-tung also differed with Khrushchev on this score. In short, Jansenism seems to be the contagious malady of the indigenous Communist regimes and the point of their departure from Soviet direction. Gomulka's domestic moderation does

---

* Perhaps to eliminate any suspicion that he was still wavering in his support for Moscow, Ulbricht charged: "At the meeting of the Communist and Workers parties, especially the Albanian representative developed a dogmatic and sectarian concept ... we can say that the dogmatists ignore creative work and content themselves with using old quotations wherever possible and repeating them time and again." *Neues Deutschland*, December 18, 1960. To which the Albanians replied: "They call us sectarians, because we are not opportunists, because we do not call our enemies our friends as they do, and because we do not allow the 'Trojan horse' to enter our house. They call us fanatic nationalists, because we are consistent internationalists. They say we are a people who do not understand a thing about Marxism, because we reject their anti-Marxist, revisionist theories." Premier Mehmed Shehu addressing the Albanian Congress on February 17, 1961.

not disprove this case, since it was only possible because of Soviet toleration for Gomulka in view of the lack of domestic Polish support for Communism. Greater extremism is a logical posture for a party defying the center to adopt, since it allows the deviate to be "more Catholic than the Pope," thus protecting the deviant party from the immediate charge of treason.

While the Sino-Soviet divergent unity created the opportunity for the Albanian self-assertion, its roots went back at least to World War II.* The Albanian Party developed during the war under Yugoslav tutelage, and between 1945 and 1948 Albania was a Yugoslav satellite. On at least one occasion, Stalin encouraged the Yugoslavs to incorporate the country,[55] and it was actually the Stalin-Tito break that saved the Albanians. The Albanian leaders immediately instituted a series of violent purges, and no less than fourteen out of the thirty-one Central Committee members and thirty-two of the 109 Assembly deputies were liquidated. The leadership was firmly consolidated in the hands of Enver Hoxha and his lieutenant, M. Shehu. In many ways it resembles a clan: In the present Central Committee of forty-three members, there are said to be ten married couples and fifteen other relatives.[56]

The post-1955 Soviet-Yugoslav relations prompted strong misgivings on the part of the Albanians, and they responded enthusiastically to any signs of Soviet-Yugoslav tension. Although Tirana greeted Khrushchev with almost unprecedented deference as late as June 1959, the Albanian leadership was increasingly echoing the Chinese anti-Yugoslav strictures. In the early summer of 1960, the Albanians sided openly with the Chinese; in their February 1961 Party Congress they spoke darkly of having defeated a foreign plot sometime in the early summer of 1960, and it is possible that pro-Soviet elements in the Albanian leadership had indeed attempted one. In any case, two Party leaders, Liri Belishova and Koco Tashko, were unexplainably fired, and the Albanian naval command, which was in close liaison with the Soviet naval base in Albania, was purged.

Following the Moscow conference of November 1960 and Hoxha's pro-Chinese (and violently anti-Khrushchev, anti-Gomulka) stand, the Soviets began to boycott the Albanian leadership: no personal messages, no "Comrade" prefix, no references by name to the Albanian leaders. The Albanians responded with a campaign designed

---

* Even further back in the case of the Albanian leader Enver Hoxha. Apparently he had been refused admission to a Yugoslav-run Communist Balkan club in Paris in the 1930's on the grounds that he was a fascist spy.

to rally the Albanian Party around Hoxha, and they effusively praised
the Chinese. At the February 1961 Congress the Albanians proclaimed
their fidelity to the Soviet Union (much as Tito had immediately
after the break in 1948), religiously repeated the many points of
agreement with Moscow, and then restated the familiar Chinese arguments concerning imperialism, war, and particularly the Yugoslav
revisionism. Hoxha put it quite bluntly: "It is a crime against world
peace; it is a crime against the socialist camp; it is a crime against the
socialist countries of the Balkans, and, in particular, it is a crime
against Albania not to denounce publicly the aggressive plans of the
Titoists." The Congress cheered Stalin and heaped praise on Hoxha,
ignored Khrushchev, explicitly approved the conduct of the Albanian
delegation during the Moscow conference, emphasized both unity
with the camp and "the correct" Albanian interpretation of Marxism-
Leninism, and stressed that no summits were possible without Chinese
participation.[57]

The Albanian Congress revealed a great deal about the attitude
of the various parties. The Soviet delegation, headed by Pospelov,
warned against any "arbitrary interpretations" of the common line
and condemned "opportunists," "renegades," and "people who have
betrayed Marxism-Leninism" and who criticize the CPSU. Even
more direct criticism was delivered by the Polish delegate, who laid
great stress on the general relevance for the bloc of the anti-Stalin
Twentieth CPSU Congress.* Both parties also warned against dogmatism, and neither stressed the Yugoslav deviation; they were supported
by the other East European parties. By way of contrast, the Chinese
delegation—which, unlike the Soviet one, received a standing ovation
—praised Hoxha, extolled the "correct" leadership of the Albanian
Party, attacked the Yugoslavs, and stressed activism against the
"imperialists." Particularly revealing was the fact that these views
were echoed by the Vietnamese and the North Koreans, as well as
by the Malayan and Indonesian parties (see table on page 433).

According to Yugoslav sources, immediately after the Congress,
two officials of the Albanian Foreign Ministry were arrested for
bringing to the Soviet Embassy the minutes of a meeting of the
Albanian Central Committee on the subject of its relations with Moscow. The CPSU and the other parties of Eastern Europe were re-

---

* There may have been a touch of irony in Gomulka's selection of the former
second-rate Stalinist Roman Nowak as his delegate. Apparently, at the Moscow conference, the Albanian delegates violently attacked the Poles, charging that Rapacki,
the Polish Foreign Minister and a Politburo member, was an imperialist agent.

	War can be and should be averted	Imperialism and war threat emphasized	Revisionism in general attacked	Yugoslav revisionism singled out	Dogmatism attacked	The Twentieth CPSU "anti-Stalin" Congress endorsed	Positive references to Khrushchev?	Positive references to Hoxha	Praise of the "correct" leadership of the Albanian Party
Malayan Party: Greeting	O	O	ER	ER	O	O	O	2	S
Japanese Party: Yonehara	O	F	F	ER	F	O	O	O	O
Indonesian Party: Supit	O	O	O	ER	F	O	3	3	S
China: Li Hsien-nien	F	S	S	S	S	F	O	2	ER
Poland: Nowak	ER	O	F	O	F	ER	2	O	O
Czechoslovakia: Barak	S	O	F	F	S	S	1	O	O
Vietnam: Duy Trinh	O	O	O	S	O	O	O	1	ER
East Germany: Axen	S	O	F	F	F	S	2	O	O
North Korea: Kum-chol	O	S	O	S	O	O	O	1	ER
Rumania: Voicu	S	O	F	O	F	O	2	O	O
Bulgaria: Velchev	F	O	F	F	F	S	1	O	O
USSR: Pospelov	ER	O	S	F	S	S	4	O	O

Some of the major issues disputed at the Albanian Congress

Code: ER—emphatic, repeated assertions; S—strong assertion; F—formal assertion; O—no mention.

ported to have exchanged letters on the subject of the Albanian position. It was clear that the situation was far from stabilized and that explosive events might even be expected.

The Albanian case thus brought to light persistent differences within the camp. While the main line of division was drawn between the Soviets and the Chinese, it was clear that many of the parties occupied intermediate and sometimes changing positions. For instance, while the East Germans solidly supported Khrushchev, they could be suspected of sympathy for a strong line against revisionism, and they might be susceptible to Chinese suggestions that a more active line be pursued with respect to Berlin. Similarly, the Bulgarians and the Rumanians might favor Khrushchev's emphasis on the prevention of war while also being sympathetic to antirevisionism as well as to anti-Americanism. The North Koreans certainly were susceptible to strong anti-American appeals.[58] The Vietnamese probably, above all else, feared a sharp drawing of the line that would force them into either complete isolation or acceptance of Chinese tutelage.

The Yugoslavs, responding to the Congress, tried to take advantage of these differences by demanding that the bloc commit itself on the question of whether Yugoslavia is or is not a socialist country. Since the Chinese and the Albanians had charged that Belgrade had betrayed socialism, the Yugoslavs launched a press campaign designed to prove that Soviet and East European silence on this question merely played into the hands of the radicals.[59] In a special report to the Yugoslav Central Committee, the Yugoslav leadership stated that Soviet and East European efforts to minimize their differences with the more radical Chinese and Albanians were actually harmful to the international Communist fraternity. "The question being posed today more and more insistently is whether it is necessary, in the interest of the cause of socialism and the ideological education of the working class, to conceal these differences at all," an authoritative Yugoslav statement asserted,[60] launching a campaign designed to force the Soviets and the East Europeans to clarify their positions.

The Albanian case thus highlighted the opportunities that the Sino-Soviet divergent unity created for the smaller parties to "play the game" of international politics within the camp.[61] It likewise showed that Sino-Soviet disagreements were also being fought out "by proxy." Gomulka's new prestige in the bloc reflected his special position (gained at Bucharest and Moscow) as Khrushchev's closest ally. This, in turn, gave the Poles a little more room for external maneuvering and consolidated their post-1956 domestic autonomy.

The Soviets, at the same time, were constrained from energetic efforts to suppress the Albanians, for fear the Chinese could immediately raise the charge of "big-nation chauvinism" and take that charge to some new international Communist gathering. The availability of these alternatives was not tantamount to the disappearance of bloc unity (see Appendix I for a discussion of efforts to strengthen it). Indeed, the year 1961 began with concerted Sino-Soviet efforts to reassure all concerned that their unity would persist despite divergencies.* The common commitment to an ideology and the common interest in unity remained the overriding consideration. But the possibility of opting against the Soviet Union and still remaining a bona fide member of the bloc—unity with options—was a new and important feature in the continually changing pattern of bloc relations.†

From a Soviet Bloc to a Communist Camp

In analyzing this changing pattern, one should avoid the prevalent tendency toward extremist conclusions. Talk of a Sino-Soviet conflict, leading even to a Soviet-American alliance against the "Chinese peril," merely illustrates a profound misconception of the essence of the historical phenomenon of Communism, which, while affected by traditional national considerations, has from its very beginning reflected a conscious emphasis on supranational perspectives. Similarly, change within the Sino-Soviet bloc should not be viewed as presaging either its imminent disintegration or, conversely, its eventual consolidation into a single Communist state. The tendency to see the bloc in such extremes simply obscures the important, if less dramatic, changes within it.

Stalinism had given a certain political stability and security to the various ruling elites within the bloc. There was a sense of direction

---

* The flow of delegations between the two states seemed to increase; mutual press coverage became more frequent; praise was exchanged; anniversaries were observed with more emphasis; etc.

In April 1961 a new Sino-Soviet trade agreement was negotiated. Chinese repayments of Soviet loans were to be delayed because of China's economic difficulties. The agreement, which posed an increased burden on the USSR and humbled the Chinese by openly showing their economic dependence, was a further demonstration of alliance as well as of its economic and psychological costs. See *Pravda*, April 9, 1961.

† The wheel of history had indeed turned a full cycle: Ten years earlier, Communist leaders were being executed for allegedly putting their national interests above those of the Soviet Union (see pp. 92–96); in May 1961 the Albanian regime, a member of the bloc, was able to execute some of its high-level officials for allegedly putting the Soviet Union ahead of Albania—and still remain (at least for the time being) a member of the bloc.

and a clarity of purpose. Khrushchev had undermined that stability on the grounds that Stalinism no longer provided adequate answers for either domestic or external Soviet realities. However, many of the bloc's national elites were unprepared to accept Khrushchev's somewhat more elastic conceptions of both domestic matters and the international situation, and the period from 1955 on produced in them a profound insecurity. The hostility generated by this insecurity was often directed at Khrushchev himself, as shown not only by recent Chinese and Albanian reactions, but also by earlier East German and Hungarian ones. A translation of this hostility into overt conflict was avoided because the imposition of Soviet-type Communism on weaker states meant that both unity and diversity were made possible in the relations among very strong and weak Communist regimes. What Harold Lasswell called "restriction through partial incorporation" applied particularly to the Chinese (and more recently to the Albanians): By adopting basic Stalinist patterns, they used the earlier "Soviet national Communism" against the Soviet leaders.[62] The achievement of true Communist internationalism under Soviet direction was thus paradoxically inhibited by the spread of earlier Soviet methods: "The specific process by which the universal was parochialized was that of partial adaptation and countersymbolization."[63]

It is unlikely that the Communist leaders who in 1960 listened to the Chinese and Albanian attacks on Khrushchev, and often defended him against them (knowing that Khrushchev needed their defense), will have the same personal sense of deference toward the Kremlin that they had in the past. Furthermore, some of them—especially those who in the past were most obeisant to the Soviets—have already manifested a psychological condition of "ecstatic emancipation" from their former mentors that often turns to violent hostility. This was very much the case with the Yugoslavs after 1948;[64] today the Albanians are doing the same thing; tomorrow it may be the Bulgarians or the Czechs. A succession crisis either in Moscow or even in Peiping, especially if matched by heightened insecurity in the Soviet or Chinese ruling elites, could spark those latent feelings into more direct policy clashes. For instance, an anti-Soviet faction in Peiping engaged in a struggle for succession could even deliberately attempt to worsen Sino-Soviet relations in order to strengthen its domestic position. Needless to add, a simultaneous succession crisis in both Moscow and Peiping could lead to even greater dangers and spark similar reactions in the other Communist capitals.

The developments since 1956, particularly the Sino-Soviet divergent unity, have thus changed the nature of direct Soviet power in the bloc. In most cases, that power today could be defined as "a last-contingency power"—i.e., the Soviets would be almost certain to intervene by force to keep a Communist state from defecting to the "imperialist" side, but they no longer have at their disposal the more intricate combinations of power, authority, and consent or the direct and indirect channels of control that Stalin wielded for the purpose of preventing most of the national elites from taking even a limited step that displeased him. Economic levers, political displeasure, and induced isolation are all means that Moscow can still apply, but in each case it must now weigh the possibility that pressure can be counterproductive and that a party can turn to the Chinese, or even to the West, for help (particularly if economic levers are used). The Soviets can still intrigue within a ruling elite, taking advantage of factions, but Gomulka's and, more recently Hoxha's, experiences suggest that this is not always an effective lever. Furthermore, such a maneuver puts a premium on united leadership in Moscow; a disunited Kremlin would find it hard to play the factional game. Thus the problem of succession is again directly relevant to bloc affairs.

In politics one change has a way of leading to another. At the November 1960 conference the Soviet Union commanded the loyalty of the vast majority of the parties, and even those favoring the Chinese probably would have sided with the CPSU if the chips were down. But at some future conference the CPSU may be faced with more opposition. And what will happen if someday a majority of the Communist parties rejects a Soviet draft defining the line of international Communism? * The Moscow conference has already indicated that the Soviet conception of the Soviet interest is no longer the automatic guideline for the other Communist parties. It no longer follows that what is good for the Soviet Union is automatically accepted as good for international Communism or the bloc. Furthermore, the attitudes adopted by the various parties on a variety of conflicting issues suggest a trend toward a certain polarization between the more developed and the less developed Communist states and between the nonruling parties in those states (e.g., Europe versus Asia), bringing to mind the possibility that each side might charge the other with subordinating "proletarian internationalism" to its own interests. Uneven develop-

* Or conversely, suppose the majority opposes the very idea of a "general line." According to Ulbricht, already at the Moscow meeting in 1960 "there were objections to the formulation of a 'general line.' However, if we abandon this principle of 'general line,' vacillations may occur in complicated situations."

ment linked to an uneven intensity of revolutionary expectation could subject the Communist ideology to a great strain.*

The Soviet bloc is thus changing into a far more complex Communist camp[65] that may soon be said to include within it several constellations: the solid Soviet bloc, composed primarily of the East European elites; the Chinese-Albanian alignment, which enjoys some popularity within the Bulgarian, Czech, East German, and perhaps other East European ruling circles; the Vietnamese and the North Koreans, who are the "Communist neutralists," carefully steering a middle course between Moscow and Peiping; and finally, given internal bloc complications, the nonruling parties. At some future point, Moscow may have to consider also the views of "fellow traveler" states such as Cuba or Guinea in shaping the bloc's general line.

The Soviet leaders, who presumably consider themselves as shouldering the main burden of protecting the unity of the bloc, thus face increasingly difficult dilemmas.[66] Since all the Communist elites presumably wish to avoid open splits, which would benefit only the common enemy, they will strive to find some basis for unity and some acceptable formula. However, this means that the more obstinate and radical parties will exercise great leverage on policies, since it is they who must be accommodated. Hence, radicalism—the main source of danger to unity—is likely to be nourished by efforts to protect Communist unity. Unlike the extremists of the past who were forced by Stalin to leave the bloc and were then compelled by circumstances to become moderate (i.e., Yugoslavia), the radicals of today within the camp can have their cake and eat it too—they can be more radical and still be "united." Unlike the moderates, they cannot be charged with defecting to the imperialist camp. This, in turn, makes radicalism more convenient to some of the ruling elites, and they may take advantage of some future instability in Moscow to shift over to the radical viewpoint. Even today, one cannot be too certain of the depth

---

* A Polish-Russian social theorist and revolutionary, W. Machajski (1866–1926), developed the theory that the revolution would produce not a true proletarian democracy but merely the dictatorship of the more skilled workers and the disaffected intellectuals over the working masses. Thus continuous pressure from below would be necessary even after a successful revolution for the achievement of true social justice. The ruling parties of the less developed and more aggrieved states could begin to feel that Machajski's theory might apply to the bloc; its inclination to express the interests of the more developed states seems analogous to the danger of the revolution being managed purely in the interest of the intelligentsia, as Machajski warned. For the Soviet point of view, minimizing internal "contradictions" and stressing unity of interest and practice, see M. Mitin, "Unshakable Unity of Socialist Countries," *Kommunist*, no. 2, January 1961.

of conviction in the East German, Czech, or Bulgarian support for the Khrushchev line.[67]

Leaving aside the matter of defections of Communist regimes to either the Soviet or the Chinese position, the very existence of the Sino-Soviet divergent unity stimulates pressures for factional struggles within the ruling elites and immediately gives a focus to such struggles. To avoid stigmatization as a deviant, a faction challenging the prevailing leadership will be likely to use Soviet or Chinese arguments on its own behalf. Others might simply argue that the Sino-Soviet dispute allows greater domestic control over the shaping of each regime's policies.* The same consideration applies to parties outside the bloc. In both cases, furthermore, there is a "feedback" from such factional conflicts to the Sino-Soviet relationship, increasing the divergence in it unless the two parties can somehow resolve all their major difficulties and present a united front.

In addition, since it is unlikely that either the CPSU or the Chinese Party would allow its future to be guided by a majority vote of the bloc or of the international movement as a whole, both will find it necessary to seek some sort of consensus when divergent formulations create tension. This may have a double effect. First of all, given the interdependence of ideology and power (see Chapter 16), even divergent tactical issues lead quickly to ideological differences within Communism, while the conscious striving to analyze the meaning of broad historical phases—not a mean intellectual task in itself—almost inescapably stimulates disagreements once power is no longer in the hands of a single arbiter. Since the interests of the ruling Chinese and Soviet elites cannot always be identical, these differences are bound to occur even if the elites consciously strive not to disagree. Such disagreements, in turn, force each party to define its views with greater precision, but by so doing they even strengthen the conviction of each party that *its* views are correct.

The second effect may be to cause both parties to emphasize more loudly their ideological unity. Within a democratic framework, action is normally derived from some weighing and adjusting of all interests involved. Within a nondemocratic context, united action can be derived either from the application of power by one group against

* There were hints early in 1961 that problems of this nature were beginning to beset the Bulgarian Party. Its journal published a strong attack on alleged factionalists, and there was a sudden flurry of attacks on revisionists, subsequently balanced by counterattacks on dogmatists. See *Partien Zhivot*, March 1961, as well as *Narodna Armiya*, March 15, 1961, for an apparently related attack on revisionism; also see *Narodna Armiya*, March 21, 1961, for an attack on dogmatism.

another or from some other way of minimizing the differences among the various units—be they individuals, groups, or states. In the Communist camp, with the relative decline of the direct role of Soviet power, insistent emphasis on the common Marxist-Leninist ideology, almost in the form of loud incantations, is a way of not only shielding existing differences but also trying to achieve united action. But different stages of socio-economic development, varying social senses of urgency for modernization, and differing relationships of Communism to nationalism (ranging from a linkage of the industrial, national, and Communist revolution in China to a sharp conflict of the last two in Eastern Europe) are bound to produce even on the conscious level different Marxist-Leninist brews. Thus the Marxist-Leninist consensus, as an antidote for the Sino-Soviet divergent unity and the internal bloc options might produce a relativization of the Marxist-Leninist doctrine.*

In the history of ideas, relativization of an absolute doctrine is the first stage of the erosion of the vitality of the doctrine.[68] That is why a situation of prolonged Sino-Soviet divergent unity is so ominous for the Communist world. The dialogue between the two parties has resulted in the crystallization of the ideological views of each, thereby jelling their previously more fluid, less conscious differences. Ulbricht highlighted this dilemma when he reported that at the November 1960 conference "somebody has raised the question as to who is the one who determines what is truth, and what complies with the prin-

---

* It is already an open question whether a Soviet Marxist-Leninist has more in common with a Hungarian Marxist-Leninist or with the Chinese. In turn, one may speculate that the Hungarian has more in common with the Pole than with the Soviet. Finally, the Polish Marxist-Leninist may be suspected of feeling more at home in Paris than in Budapest. Similarly, in terms of Marxist-Leninist "symbols," the image of "imperialists" certainly invokes varying mental reactions throughout the bloc. At the sound of the word, a Polish Communist may conjure up an Englishman or an American who, for "objective historical reasons," is indeed an imperialist, but whom the Pole knows and with whom the Pole finds culturally or intellectually much in common. To a Russian Communist, the image is presumably much more negative, but perhaps this is somewhat offset by his conviction that soon the imperialist will fade and the USSR will dominate. To a Chinese Communist, the image is doubtless even far more negative and provokes a sense of frustrated rage and impatience. These different responses, in turn, tend to weaken the positive unifying impact of the self-identification of the various elites as Communist. Until now, the fate of a Communist state may be presumed to have elicited a basically similar response from all Communist elites. In time, however, strong internal divergencies can give rise to strong internal antagonisms, with the further effect of undermining that common identification. The fate of a Russian Communist may not evoke similar reactions in Peiping or even in Prague. This, in turn, could also lead to varying identifications with the outside world, thereby undermining the Marxist-Leninist dichotomic world image.

ciples of the Marxist-Leninist doctrine." At the same time, since the parties are simultaneously convinced that they are right and also fearful that splits between them may aid the cause of "imperialism," they are forced to undertake consciously the task of arriving at some adjustments and compromises among themselves. Changes in doctrine are thus no longer a matter of one elite's (or even of one ruler's) making conscious (and sometimes unconscious) adjustments with reality while still believing that the universal doctrine remains absolutely right; increasingly, it becomes necessary for several elites or rulers *consciously* to fuzz ideological formulations, even while each firmly believes that its own interpretation is the correct one but that it cannot be expressed because of the higher imperative of unity. In turn, these compromises, with their cynicism and manipulation and consequent relativization, cannot avoid threatening the domestic elite's conviction in the ideology.

In some respects, the Communist camp may be able to capitalize on this greater internal diversity. By appearing more flexible, the Communists may support more effectively the quasi-Marxist regimes in Cuba or in Guinea. Sharing with them some common views (on imperialism and capitalism, for example), the Communists can point to their internal diversity as proof that the new states need not fear Communist imperialism. The Soviet Union has already made some gains from appearing to be more flexible and reasonable than the Chinese, and perhaps it has done so purposely, trying to derive some advantage from this particular difficulty. Even so, the new external strategy is likely to further internal processes of change within the camp. One may expect Soviet allies helping nations like Cuba or Guinea eventually to seek a "most-favored-nation" clause from the Soviet Union, much the way the East Germans did when the USSR was courting Gomulka's Poland in 1956, or the way Latin American states have recently done with the United States, after watching Marshall Plan aid go to Europe. This is all the more likely because of the new opportunities created for internal maneuvering by the various parties for greater self-assertion. And these opportunities will probably increase when China acquires a nuclear capability.

More broadly, the transformation of the Soviet bloc, and particularly the impact on it of the increasingly complex Sino-Soviet relationship, can be viewed as part of a fracturing process of the post–World War II political polarization of the globe. The Western world was the first to experience this break-up, especially with the emergence of the post-colonial neutral states. Yugoslavia signaled the Soviet bloc's susceptibility to this phenomenon, and more recent events suggest that the process is continuing, although not necessarily in as overt a manner as it manifests itself in the more open non-Communist world.

The Communist leaders, many of whom are doubtless aware of much that has been said above, may calculate that the present diversity in the bloc is an inevitable price of their success. They may feel that in the foreseeable future their concerted efforts to protect their unity, as well as the increasing pace of economic and institutional integration of the bloc,[69] will suffice to contain the process of differentiation that all large-scale social organizations inevitably experience. At the same time, they may calculate that the pace of external socio-economic revolutions will bring closer the "inevitable" Communist victory and that continued external successes may rekindle internal ideological enthusiasm, subsuming their various divergencies. In effect, the internal processes of change, differentiation, ideological relativization and erosion, pointing toward Communist polycentrism, are engaged in a race with the external expectations of the Communist elite. For this reason, the future of the bloc also depends increasingly on the attitudes and actions of the West. It is no consolation to think that *after* a world-wide Communist victory, Communism would suffer from many internal strains. Although the changes that have taken place were not of the West's doing, the West could *now* strive to devise policies that would create a favorable climate for the further polycentric growth within the Communist camp.[70]

APPENDIXES
NOTES
BIBLIOGRAPHY
INDEX

Appendix I

The Organization
of the Communist Camp[1]

THE Communist camp is composed of twelve states: the Soviet Union, China, Poland, Czechoslovakia, East Germany, Rumania, Hungary, Bulgaria, North Korea, North Vietnam, Albania, Mongolia. Jointly, the Communist-ruled states account for about 38 per cent of the world's population, 24.2 per cent of the world's area, and approximately one-third of the world's industrial output. During Stalin's lifetime the Communist bloc operated essentially through a relatively simple subordination of the various units to the dictator's will, generally expressed by indirect methods of police and party control. This somewhat informal organization reflected in part the old dictator's specific political style; in part it was a function of the relatively immature stage of the bloc's development. As a result, the "maturation" of the bloc coincided with the difficult post-Stalin period of transition within the USSR and was marked by major upheavals and tensions. By 1958-1959, however, the crisis had subsided, and a new and more complex image of the bloc became apparent. While the Soviet Union continued to exercise leadership, acknowledged at the November 1957 conference of the Communist parties and buttressed by Soviet international and technological prestige, the camp had developed more elaborate mechanisms and processes of cohesion that also contributed to its unity. Some of them dated back to the Stalinist days, but were now infused with new vitality. Others emerged during the post-Stalin phase.

For analytical purposes, these mechanisms are treated in this article under two general headings: formal institutional aspects, including the multilateral and bilateral framework of the camp; and the dynamic aspects, including the various processes of unity, such as party contacts, contributions to the inter-party ideological organ, patterns of trade, and cultural contacts. The focus of the study is on the organization of the camp, and not on the relations or conflicts within it. A

[1] Reproduced from *World Politics*, Vol. XIII, January 1961; permission is gratefully acknowledged.

concise but inclusive treatment is provided of the various institutions and emerging processes that buttress and/or increase the political unity of the camp and organize the relations among its members. In the concluding pages, some of the broader implications of the changing character of the camp are discussed.

I. Formal Institutional Aspects

The formal institutional ties both for maintaining unity and for defining relations among the Communist states have become much more prominent since Stalin's death. They may be examined in terms of the following four general categories: multilateral ties, bilateral political treaties, bilateral economic agreements, and cultural pacts.

At the present time there is no multilateral party organization resembling the Comintern or the Cominform. These organizations, discredited by Stalinism, have not been resuscitated, although efforts have been made to replace them by frequent *ad hoc* multilateral meetings of party chiefs and by a theoretical inter-party journal, both of which are discussed in part II of this study. The two most important multilateral organs binding some of the Communist states together are the Warsaw Treaty Organization (WTO) and the Council for Economic Mutual Assistance (CEMA). There is, however, no organ officially including all the Communist states. It is symptomatic of the post-Stalin diversity in the orbit that efforts to create a new supra-party bloc organ were resisted by some of the leaderships in and out of the bloc, and that the unity of the bloc has had to be promoted through the utilization of institutions which existed prior to 1956. In recent years both the WTO and CEMA have increased in importance as agencies for the articulation of common purposes and for the isolation and eventual subordination of those Communist leaders who were suspect of being unduly influenced by their own national perspective in the shaping of policy.

The WTO is both a political and a military organization. Established formally on May 14, 1955, under the Treaty of Friendship, Cooperation, and Mutual Assistance, it is composed of eight of the twelve Communist States, with China "associated" but not a member, and North Korea, North Vietnam, and Mongolia remaining outside of the pact. It is thus primarily a European organization, serving externally as a counter to NATO, internally as the formal device for the perpetuation of close ties between the Soviet Union and its European satellites. In fact, to this day it constitutes the single most important formal commitment binding the European Communist states to the USSR, officially limiting their scope for independent action by precluding their participation in other alliance systems (Art. 7).

The founding meeting of the WTO provided for a Political Consultative Committee which was empowered to establish supplementary multilateral organs. The Committee exercised this power in its January 1956 Prague meeting by setting up a regular secretariat, with representatives from member states, and a standing commission for foreign policy co-ordination.[2] The meeting also decided that the Committee was to meet not less than twice yearly. However, when Khrushchev addressed the next consecutive meeting, he had to concede that "more than two years have passed since the Political Consultative Committee last met in Prague in 1956."[3] Since the Committee did not convene again until February 1960, it appears that the 1956 decision has lapsed. Two hypothetical explanations may account for this: the resistance of the Poles to such meetings; or (what is more likely, since the Poles could hardly prevent them) the unwillingness of the Soviet Union to push the development of the WTO too far lest it become a genuine consultative organ.

At the present time, meetings of the Political Consultative Committee serve primarily as forums for the articulation of a common stand on important international issues and, in effect, for implicitly delegating the USSR to be the spokesman of the bloc in dealing with the West.[4] The May 1958 session was primarily devoted to an analysis of the international situation, with special emphasis on the program which the Soviet leaders would submit at a summit meeting with the Western powers. Particular stress was put on troop reductions within the bloc as proof of the bloc's stability and peaceful intentions. The 1960 meeting in effect served to endorse the position which the Soviet leadership was to adopt at the expected May 1960 summit meeting, with the only discordant note coming from the Chinese observer, who attended the meetings in keeping with China's status as "associated" with the WTO (see part II).

Judging from the three sessions—the second and third lasting merely one day—it appears that the Political Consultative Committee does not serve as an active policy-making agency, comparable to some of the multilateral meetings of party chiefs, noted in part II. The

[2] *Izvestia*, January 29, 1956.
[3] *Izvestia*, May 27, 1958.
[4] This does not, however, exclude a certain division of labor in dealing with the outside world: e.g., the Polish initiative in the form of the Rapacki Plan; the East German scheme for a Baltic Peace Zone; the Rumanian-Bulgarian plan for a Balkan treaty, etc.

political importance of the WTO is that (1) it provides a formal framework binding the various states together, (2) supplies the juridical basis for limiting the exercise of their sovereignty, and (3) serves as a useful forum for the articulation of unanimity, expressing ritualistically the bloc's support of Soviet foreign policy initiatives. It is significant that one of the charges most often cited against Imre Nagy was that he violated the unity of the bloc through his unilateral decision to leave the Warsaw Pact.

The essentially static, restrictive function of the WTO is evident also in its military aspects. The original agreement provided for a Unified Command of the armed forces of the signatories, and, indeed, the signing of the treaty was followed immediately by a communiqué announcing that a joint command had been set up. Soviet Marshal I. S. Konev was appointed commander-in-chief, another Soviet officer became joint chief of staff, and the command headquarters was to be situated in Moscow. Defense Ministers of the participating states have attended ostentatiously the three sessions of the Political Consultative Committee and Marshal Konev (recently replaced by Marshal Grechko) delivered reports to these sessions on the military situation. Probably some strategic "division of labor" has also been made. However, to the extent that it can be determined, this exhausts the military aspects of the WTO. The international military command has not been set up. The various states have not delegated their ranking officers to serve on it, nor have liaison officers been appointed. In this case, the Soviet Union's fear of arousing new anti-Soviet sentiments was combined with its desire not to share Soviet military secrets with its allies. Since the uprisings of 1956, the stationing of Soviet troops in East Europe has been regularized by bilateral agreements which used the Warsaw Treaty as their point of reference (see below), but they could have easily been concluded independently of such a treaty.

A much more active, positive role is played by the multilateral Council for Economic Mutual Assistance (CEMA), originally set up in January 1949, but activated only after Stalin's death, and particularly after the disruptive events of October-November 1956. The founding members were the USSR, Poland, Czechoslovakia, Hungary, Rumania, and Bulgaria. Subsequently they were joined by East Germany and Albania. These states together have about 300 million inhabitants, or 11 per cent of the world's population. They cover about 17 per cent of the world's surface and produce nearly 30 per cent of the world's industrial output. Although not members, China, Mongolia, North Korea, and North Vietnam have in recent years been sending observers to the Council's sessions.[5] In its initial stage, CEMA resembled the Warsaw Pact: primarily restrictive in purpose, it was designed to keep the European Communist states out of the Marshall Plan.[6] Following its founding session, CEMA held only two more plenary meetings during Stalin's lifetime: one in August 1949 and a secret session, presumably sometime after the outbreak of the Korean War. During this early period, the organization concentrated primarily on redirecting the trade of its members toward each other and it may be surmised that it co-ordinated the development of their armaments industries during the Korean War. After Stalin's death, plenary sessions became more regular and increasingly more important. At first primarily formal gatherings, they gradually developed into working sessions at which common decisions were formulated.[7]

Formally, all members of CEMA are equal and all decisions must be unanimous. This provision, however, is meaningless if the relative economic strengths of the various participants are considered. Indeed, given the often conflicting interests of the various members, it is difficult to conceive how CEMA could operate if this provision were adhered to rigidly. The preponderant economic superiority of the Soviet Union in all instances serves as the determining factor, although this does not mean that the Council is merely a rubber stamp. On such issues as Polish coal, specialization, and prices, vigorous disputes have developed. Formally, the decisions of CEMA are not binding until approved by subsequent bilateral or multilateral formal agreements between the parties involved.

The steady growth of CEMA's bureaucratic machinery has been a concomitant of its increasingly active integrative role. It is headed by a permanent secretariat, located in Moscow, currently directed by a Soviet chairman and Polish and Czech deputy chairmen, with representatives from each of the participating states. The secretariat is

[5] China since 1956; North Korea since 1957; North Vietnam and Mongolia since 1958. See the excellent treatment, "The Role of the Comecon," *East Europe* (New York), VIII, No. 11 (November 1959), pp. 3-11, which describes more fully the operations and organization of CEMA.

[6] See Imre Nagy, *On Communism*, New York, 1957, p. 189, for a concise statement of the essentially negative role of CEMA.

[7] For a description of the CEMA organization and a discussion of its operation, see *East Europe*, VI, No. 11 (November 1957), and IX, No. 4 (April 1960). See also *Voprosy vneshnei politiki stran sotsialisticheskogo lageriia*, Moscow, 1958, pp. 21-23 (hereafter cited as *Voprosy vneshnei politiki*). The December 1959 CEMA meeting took the important formal step of adopting a Charter and a Convention on Competence, Privileges, and Immunities, which was said to contain "provisions that are generally accepted in international practice." For fuller treatment, see *Vneshanaia torgovlia* (Moscow), No. 2 (February 1960).

paralleled by a conference of deputies whose task is to maintain consultation among the member states while the Council is not in session. The sessions of the Council rotate among the capitals of the participating Communist states, to underline the equality of CEMA's members. In addition, there are thirteen permanent, specialized, multilateral commissions, each for a major branch of the economy (subdivided into even more specialized subcommissions) and each located in the capital of the country with the predominant interest in that particular branch.[8] On an average, the commissions meet approximately twice a year.

At the present time, CEMA is doubtless the single most important organ for actively shaping policies designed to promote the camp's unity.[9] In the difficult post-1956 period, it provided a sorely needed forum for multilateral consultation from which the Poles could not absent themselves,[10] and in the subsequent period of stabilization it has been the source of numerous policies designed to mold a "world socialist market" as the basis for the camp's political and ideological unity.[11] Khrushchev underlined the importance attached to this work

[8] Although ostensibly an international organization open to other nations, CEMA operations are shrouded in secrecy. On a recent trip to the bloc, this writer was denied permission to visit its Moscow offices, while Sofia officials even denied the existence of a CEMA commission in Sofia. For a list of these commissions, see *East Europe*, IX, No. 4 (April 1960), p. 4. For a somewhat more recent treatment, see *Tygodnik Powszechny* (Krakow), February 28, 1960. For an interesting account of the operations of one such commission, see I. Pramov, "For some results of co-operation in the field of rural economy between the countries participating in the Council of Economic Mutual Assistance," *Mezhdunarodnyi Sel'skokhoziaistvennyi Zhurnal* (Sofia), No. 4 (1958).

[9] This is openly admitted by Communist commentators—e.g., V. Kaigl, "Co-operation with the countries of the socialist camp is one of the main conditions for the completion of socialist building of the CSR," *Nova Mysl* (Prague), June 1958, who says: "Apart from political and ideological aspects, economic shortcomings helped to a considerable degree in the upsurge of bourgeois nationalism and revisionism in the fall of 1956. Following these experiences, the Communist and worker's parties in the member states of the Council drew the only right conclusion, namely, to strengthen the unity of the socialist camp *through increased economic unity*, and through a higher standard of its planning. The Council of Mutual Economic Assistance decided at its eighth planning session in June 1957 to work out co-ordinated, long-term plans for the development of national economies of the member states covering the period until 1975. The foundation of this co-ordination is to be the mutually heightened approved specialization of the individual countries which would make them into a *truly homogeneous, economic unit*" (italics added).

[10] See my study, *The Soviet Bloc: Unity and Conflict*, Cambridge, Mass., 1960, chap. 12.

[11] E.g., a multilateral payment scheme was set up in 1959, plans were developed for statistical analyses of national incomes, the problem of pricing was tackled, etc. For more detailed treatment, see A. Zauberman, "Economic Integration: Problems and Prospects," *Problems of Communism* (July-August 1959); H. Mendershausen, "Terms of Trade Between the Soviet Union and Smaller Communist Countries, 1955-1957," *Review of Economics and Statistics*, XLI, No. 2 (May 1959), pp. 106-18; O. Hoeffding, *Recent Efforts Toward Coordinated Economic Planning in the Soviet Bloc*, The RAND

when he remarked that "Extensive co-operation in all spheres of economic, social, political, and cultural life is developing among the sovereign countries of the socialist camp. Speaking of the future, it seems to me that the further development of the socialist countries will in all probability proceed along the lines of consolidation of the single-world socialist economic system. The economic barriers which divided our countries under capitalism will fall one after another. The common economic basis of world socialism will grow stronger, eventually making the question of borders a pointless one."[12]

Two other multilateral bloc organizations should be briefly mentioned. The first of these is the Danube Commission set up in August 1948,[13] which includes the Soviet Union, Bulgaria, Czechoslovakia, Hungary, Rumania, and Yugoslavia. Its purpose is to ensure normal navigation on the Danube as an international waterway. The Paris peace conference of 1946 provided for such an organization, but the United States, the United Kingdom, and France refused to sign the August 1948 agreement on the grounds that it violated the provisions and intentions of the Paris agreement. The Danube Commission held its first session in November 1949 and since then has met twice a year, usually in June and December—failing, however, to meet in December 1956. Since the Commission from the very start contained a participant from outside the bloc, it cannot be viewed as primarily an institution for the promotion of the bloc's political unity. However, during the Stalinist phase it did serve, under Soviet directorship, as an agency for the promotion of Soviet bloc objectives in the campaign against Yugoslavia. (The May-June 1951 and the December 1952 sessions were preoccupied with mutual recriminations.) A major change took place shortly after Stalin's death: the Soviets manifested

Corporation, 1959; and S. J. Zyzniewski, "Economic Perspectives in Eastern Europe," *Political Science Quarterly*, LXXVI, No. 2 (June 1960), pp. 201-28. That the problem of pricing has been a source of major difficulty in interbloc planning has been openly admitted by Communist economists. See, for instance, M. Cizkovsky, "A New Stage in the Cooperation Between the Countries of the Socialist Camp," *Rude Pravo* (Prague), March 5, 1959; or V. Ciernansky, "Prices in Trading with Foreign Countries," *Predvoj* (Prague), June 11, 1959; or *Voprosy ekonomiki*, No. 2 (1960), for a discussion of the prevailing pricing system within the bloc. The most recent CEMA venture is a huge oil pipeline, linking the oilfields of the middle Volga basin to Poland, East Germany, Czechoslovakia, and Hungary. Construction began in the summer of 1960 and is to be finished in 1963.

[12] *Pravda*, March 27, 1959. Presumably a further step in that direction would involve the co-ordination of investment policies of the member states. See Gomulka's criticisms of CEMA's failure to do so in *Trybuna Ludu* (Warsaw), June 21, 1960.

[13] *Izvestia*, August 19, 1948. For a recent discussion, see David T. Cattell, "The Politics of the Danube Commission under Soviet Control." *American Slavic and East European Review*, XIX, No. 3 (October 1960), pp. 380-95.

an increasing willingness to pass control over to the Danubian powers; also, since June 1956 the European Economic Commission has been participating in the sessions as an observer, and since June 1957 both Austria and the German Federal Republic have attended as experts. As a result, the Danubian Commission has increasingly become an international technical agency, not restricted to the camp alone. Its technical character makes it similar to such organizations as, for instance, the Organization of Co-operation of the Socialist Countries in the field of communications, set up on Soviet initiative by the 1957 conference of ministers of communications of all the "socialist" countries.[14]

The other multilateral Communist organization to be noted here is the Institute for Nuclear Research set up in March 1956. In part, its establishment reflected the internal pressures on the Soviet Union to share its nuclear monopoly with its allies. The original founding agreement was signed by all the Communist states save North Vietnam, which joined in September of the same year. The agreement appears to have been the outgrowth of the Soviet decision of January 7, 1955,[15] to undertake collaborative research efforts with China, Poland, Czechoslovakia, Rumania, and East Germany, countries which supplied the USSR with uranium and which could be expected to entertain scientific ambitions. Curiously, however, Hungary did not appear on the list, even though it was known to be an extractor of uranium. The January 1955 decision was followed by a series of bilateral agreements concluded by the USSR and the aforementioned states in April 1955, providing for the supply to these states of limited quantities of fissionable material, experimental accelerators, and atomic piles, relevant equipment, and documentation.[16] This was followed shortly by an identical agreement with Hungary in June 1955. (Possibly Nagy's fall from power eliminated doubts that might have existed earlier in Moscow.)

The preceding agreement laid the basis for the March 1956 conference of eleven Communist states which resulted in the creation of the Joint Institute for Nuclear Research. The Institute was located at Dubno, just north of Moscow; it was to be headed by a director and two assistant directors. In practice, the former has always been a Soviet scientist, while the latter have represented the participating

---

[14] *Svet Sovietu* (Prague), No. 24 (1959).

[15] *Pravda*, January 8, 1955.

[16] The agreements are listed in R. Slusser and J. Triska, *A Calendar of Soviet Treaties, 1917-1957*, Stanford, 1959, pp. 326-27. For fuller treatment, see George Modelski, *Atomic Energy in the Communist Bloc*, New York, 1959.

states. Dues for the maintenance of the Institute were apportioned among the participating states on a graduated basis. The Institute was subdivided into specialized laboratories, each apparently also headed by a Soviet scientist. Thus, by and large, effective Soviet control has been maintained even though the Soviet Union did meet at least part way the desire of the other bloc members to share in nuclear development and to acquire the basis for training cadres of their own. Over 100 non-Soviet scientific workers were said to be working in Dubno in 1959, with the Czechs being the most numerous.[17] The Institute as a multinational organization can be seen as combining elements of control with some adjustment to the demands of the members of the bloc.

This multilateral framework is buttressed by a web of bilateral agreements. Of these, the most important are the friendship and mutual aid agreements. They are usually directed against a specific outside threat—either Germany or Japan, and their possible allies—and they contain pledges of mutual support. In that sense, an effort is made to relate the alliance to a concrete danger, activating deeply felt anti-German or anti-Japanese popular feelings existing within some of the Communist-ruled states. However, it would be specious to argue that a treaty of friendship and mutual assistance between, let us say, Rumania and the Soviet Union represents a meaningful partnership. Rather, the treaty is essentially a cloak for a relationship of political subservience, with the juridical fiction of equality serving both to mask this relationship and to perpetuate it.[18] Quite another matter is the Soviet-Chinese treaty of alliance. Here, the two contracting partners have in effect formalized a relationship of alliance and have expressed it in terms which impose meaningful obligations on both sides.

The Soviet Union has entered into friendship and mutual aid treaties with all but three of the Communist states—East Germany, North Vietnam, and North Korea, all divided nations. It seems likely that the Soviet Union does not wish to create a juridical situation which could impede the unification of these nations under Communist auspices, and premature ties might possibly constitute such an impedi-

[17] V. Svanev, "Science and Technology in the Multi-national Family of Scientists," *Pravda* (Bratislava), January 10, 1959.
[18] For a fuller discussion, see P. S. Wandycz, "The Soviet System of Alliances in East Central Europe," *Journal of Central European Affairs*, XVI, No. 2 (July 1956), pp. 177-84; E. Korovin, *Nerushimaia druzhba narodov SSSR i narodno-demokraticheskikh stran*, Moscow, 1955; *Voprosy vneshnei politiki, op.cit.*: and Brzezinski, *The Soviet Bloc, op.cit.*, for listings with dates.

ment. Furthermore, in the past at least, the Soviet Union may have
considered the possibility that ties of alliance could involve the Soviet
Union in local conflicts which might easily erupt (or be provoked)
between the opposing sides of the divided nations. However, it is
likely that in the foreseeable future the Soviet Union will conclude
treaties with these states so as to eliminate an anomalous distinction
between them and the other members of the camp, a distinction increasingly less necessary with the apparent consolidation of the outer
limits of the camp. East German membership in the WTO and
attendance of its sessions by North Vietnamese and North Korean
observers would seem to augur this. At this stage, the East European
states, while bound to one another by treaties of mutual aid and
friendship, do not have such treaties with any of the Asian states;
rather, the expedient of the vaguer friendship and co-operation treaty
has been used. Symptomatic of certain political affinities noted in
part II, China has concluded such friendship and co-operation agreements only with East Germany (December 25, 1955) and Czechoslovakia (March 27, 1957).[19]

All of the mutual aid treaties were concluded by 1950—i.e., in Stalin's
lifetime. It is noteworthy that the treaties did not provide a juridical
basis for the stationing of Soviet troops on the territory of the members of the camp. A provision for Soviet bases abroad was contained
in the multilateral WTO, and even that agreement was very general
in its wording. In a way, therefore, the most substantive bilateral
political agreements concluded among the Communist states were
those which for the first time formalized and rendered explicit the
basis for the presence of Soviet troops on the soil of the other Communist-ruled states.

The model for such agreements was the Polish-Soviet treaty of
December 17, 1956 (ratified by both parties in February 1957), concerning the status of Soviet troops "temporarily" stationed in Poland.
This treaty reflected the new situation created by the changes that
took place in Poland in October 1956, and was designed to meet long-
standing Polish grievances. The political foundation for it was laid
by the agreement reached by the Soviet and Polish government and
party leaders in a conference held in Moscow in mid-November, and
expressed by the joint declaration of November 18, alleviating many

---

[19] Czechoslovakia also concluded such a treaty with Outer Mongolia on April 9,
1957. I am indebted to Dr. Tao-tai Hsia of the Library of Congress for the information
about China. Chinese sources include *Chung hua jen min kung ho kuo t'iao yueh chi*
(Ministry of Foreign Affairs, Peking), Vols. I-VIII, 1949-1959; *Jen min shou ts'e*
(Peking), 1955-1959.

past Soviet abuses and explicitly defining the principles which govern the status of Soviet troops in Poland. The declaration imposed severe restrictions on any unilateral Soviet activity, explicitly prohibited the use of Soviet troops for political purposes in Poland, enjoined the Soviet command to co-ordinate their disposal, transportation, and numbers with the wishes of the Polish government, and made their personnel and dependents subject to Polish law. These provisions were reaffirmed in the formal treaty and a mixed Polish-Soviet commission was established to settle any disputes that may arise.[20]

The Soviet-Polish treaty, while perpetuating Soviet military presence in Poland, marked a definite step forward for Poland and the negotiation of this treaty did involve a measure of bargaining and definite Soviet concessions. Even the subsequent consolidation of Soviet influence within the bloc, which necessarily gave the Soviet Union new opportunities for exerting pressures (any formal limitations notwithstanding), did not undo this arrangement. Furthermore, the concessions won by Poland could not be denied to the other, more loyal Communist states. As a result, a mere three weeks after the signing of the Polish-Soviet treaty, a Soviet-East German declaration (of January 7, 1957) announced that a formal agreement regularizing the presence of Soviet troops on German soil would soon be concluded. Such an arrangement had been prefigured by the Soviet-East German treaty of September 20, 1955, defining the relations between the two countries, and granting East Germany "full freedom" as a sovereign state. However, it seems clear that it was the change in Soviet-Polish relations which prompted the execution of this commitment, and on March 12, 1957, a formal agreement was signed between the USSR and the DDR (East Germany), regularizing the presence of Soviet troops in East Germany.[21] Similar agreements were concluded shortly thereafter with Hungary (the March 28, 1957, joint Soviet-Hungarian political declaration laid the basis for it, and the formal agreement was signed on May 27, 1957),[22] and with Rumania on April 15, 1957.[23] The Rumanian and Hungarian agreements were similar to the one concluded with Poland, except that they did not cede control to these states over entry and exit of Soviet forces. The agreement with East Germany was even more restricted, in that it did not involve the restrictions cited in the Polish case, although asserting East German "sovereignty." The greater concessions made to the Poles

[20] See *Pravda*, November 19, 1956; *ibid.*, December 18, 1956.
[21] *Izvestia*, March 14, 1957.   [22] *Ibid.*, May 28, 1957.
[23] *Ibid.*, April 17, 1957.

reflected the relatively involuntary character of the Soviet adjustments.

Insofar as Poland and Hungary are concerned, the joint Polish-Soviet and Hungarian-Soviet governmental and party declarations of November 18, 1956, and March 28, 1957, respectively, represent the most important bilateral agreements concluded within the bloc. The first of these made it possible for the Polish Communist leadership to remain within the bloc while pursuing policies of relative domestic autonomy, some of which were at the time obviously displeasing to the Soviets. Nonetheless, the granting of compensation for past Soviet economic exploitation, the withdrawal of Soviet overseers from Poland, the acceptance by the Soviets of the Gomulka regime, and the restrictions imposed on the Soviet troops in Poland all were substantive measures designed to normalize and improve Polish-Soviet Communist relations.[24] In the case of Hungary, the March 28 declaration was also designed to improve Soviet-Hungarian relations and involved economic concessions and promises of aid. However, unlike the Polish case, the declaration was much more a unilateral effort on the part of the Soviet government to improve the domestic position of a satellite regime recently imposed on the population by the force of Soviet arms, than an agreement between two states. Nonetheless, it did involve a step forward for the Hungarians as well, especially when compared with the earlier period. Generally speaking, the agreements subsequent to October-November 1956 can be seen as reflecting a recognition on the part of the Soviet leaders of the need to regularize the semi-colonial pattern of relations prevailing between the Soviet Union and most of the other Communist states. An expression of this recognition was the declaration issued by the Soviet Union (and prompted directly by the Hungarian revolution) on October 30, 1956, promising to liquidate the most obnoxious aspects of the Stalinist pattern of Soviet-satellite relations.[25]

Bilateral trade treaties also serve to unify the camp and are meant to create a common and enduring interest in its preservation. Since about 1957 these treaties have been designed to express in more detail and in a binding manner the recommendations of CEMA. Given overall state control of the economy, such treaties govern the totality of trade among its members, and since most of the foreign trade of the Communist states takes place within the camp (see Table 6, part II), these agreements have an important bearing on the future livelihood and development of the signators. In recent years, there has been

---

[24] For extended treatment, see Brzezinski, *The Soviet Bloc, op.cit.*
[25] See *Pravda*, October 31, 1956.

a veritable flood of statistics on the volume, composition, direction, etc., of trade between and among the Communist states, and there have been many valuable discussions of the degree of discrimination practiced by the Soviet Union against its weaker neighbors. There can be no doubt that such relations in the past did favor the Soviet Union and there is some evidence that they continue to do so. However, since 1956, the Soviet Union has become more actively engaged in issuing credit to the bloc states, and this has offset some of the still-prevailing discrimination and, at the same time, has constituted an important bond.[26] There is no need to cover the same ground here. Insofar as the trade agreements are concerned, it should be noted that they are usually concluded for relatively long-term periods, varying from two to seven years. In the early stages of the bloc, annual trade agreements were favored, since long-term planning co-ordination had not yet been effected.[27]

The long-term agreements include a protocol valid for one year, providing a much more detailed breakdown of items to be traded. The protocol is usually renegotiated for subsequent single years and sometimes a price adjustment is made. In some cases, the agreements also outline a longer-range "perspective," sketching out the anticipated volume of trade over a longer period than the actual agreement; on occasions the agreements envisage co-ordination of capital investment and co-operation in production, as well as credits.[28] This enables the contracting parties to plan several years ahead and to remain reasonably confident both of their supply and of their external markets. This is particularly important to states, like Poland, which are just developing certain branches of their industry—for instance, ship-building—and which would find it difficult to compete on the

[26] See Mendershausen, op.cit.; Hoeffding, op.cit.; Zauberman, op.cit; J. Wszelaki, Communist Economic Strategy: The Role of East Central Europe, Washington, D.C., 1959. For some figures concerning Soviet credit in the crisis period of 1956-1957, see M. Choluj, "Soviet Credit Aid to Socialist Countries," Predvoj (Prague), November 7, 1957, in which the figure of 5,776 million rubles is cited as being granted to Eastern Europe by the Soviet Union between December 1955 and February 1957, 58 per cent of which went to Poland, Hungary, and Yugoslavia. Vneshnaia torgovlia has also provided some data.
[27] See G. Radulescu, "Ten Years of Comecon Activity," Rominia Libera, April 29, 1959, for a partial list of long-term Rumanian agreements; Izvestia, November 20, 1955, for aspects of Soviet-Mongolian agreements of 1950-1954 and 1955-1957. See also Slusser and Triska, op.cit., for list of Soviet trade agreements; and J. Dolina, "Poland's Foreign Trade Agreements," Polish Review (New York), Autumn 1956 and Winter-Spring 1958, for the most complete listing, including brief statements of major provisions.
[28] E.g., the Czech-Polish agreement for 1961-1965, signed May 17, 1958; see Rude Pravo, May 15, 1958. For Soviet-Czech agreements, see Pravda, January 15, 1957, and October 16, 1958; and Izvestia, March 7, 1959.

world market against the more advanced industrial states. However, at the same time the dependence of the more industrially developed Communist states (Czechoslovakia and East Germany) on Soviet supplies of raw materials, and of the less developed states (e.g., China) on Soviet machinery, is even further intensified by such long-term commitments.[29] A corollary of these trade agreements is an extensive exchange of scientific knowledge and scientific cadres,[30] and numerous bilateral arrangements between the various national institutes and academies as well as the bilateral commissions for scientific-technical collaboration established not only between the Soviet Union and the other Communist states, but among the People's Democracies as well.

The final link in the formal web of ties that deserves brief mention is provided by the cultural agreements concluded between the Communist states. Since art, culture, and science are subject to state control under the Communist system, all cultural contacts between the various members of the camp must be regulated through official and formal channels. During Stalin's lifetime, however, such contacts were very much limited and only began to develop with the gradual lifting of the internal iron curtains by which the old dictator had isolated each Communist state. Thus, although European Communist states concluded cultural collaboration treaties with one another and also with China quite early in the history of the bloc (1947-1948, except for China and East Germany, which concluded such treaties in 1951 and 1952, respectively), cultural contacts remained essentially dormant until the middle 1950's.[31]

The Soviet Union displayed ostentatious contempt for such arrangements, and refrained (with only one exception[32]) from concluding such cultural collaboration agreements until the mid-1950's. This abstinence, however, did not prevent the Soviet Union from conclud-

---

[29] A good example of this dependence was provided by the panic caused in these capitals by the recent and unconfirmed report to the effect that the Soviet Union would severely cut down its delivery of raw materials to Poland, East Germany, and Czechoslovakia in 1965 (see *New York Times*, April 4, 1960, for a report from Warsaw that at the February 1960 CEMA meeting, the Soviet Union indicated that it no longer wished to deliver unprocessed raw materials).

[30] For statistics, see N. I. Ivanov, *Razvitie ekonomicheskikh sviazei evropeiskikh stran narodnoi demokratii*, Moscow, 1959 (hereafter cited as *Razvitie*).

[31] For instance, when the vice-president of the Rumanian Institute for Cultural Relations with Foreign Countries contributed a commemorative article to a Polish newspaper on the occasion of the tenth anniversary of Rumanian-Polish cultural relations, everything he cited dated back to the pre-1939 period (O. Livezeau, "Ten Years of Co-operation," *Zycie Warszawy*, February 28, 1958; see also Imre Nagy, *op.cit.*, p. 240).

[32] Mongolia, agreement of February 27, 1946.

ing a whole series of limited agreements with the members of the bloc, providing for the training of their citizens in Soviet institutions of higher learning, for "co-operation" in radio programing and subsequently also in television, and finally for collaboration between their respective Academies of Science. It was only in the wake of the attack on Stalin and within the context of very hurried efforts to improve and normalize Soviet relations that the Soviet Union concluded cultural collaboration agreements with all the Communist states.[33] These agreements provided for expanded contacts in education, art, music, literature, the theater, films, press, radio, television, sports, and even tourism. In effect, they were meant to establish a broad social basis for contacts with "the first country of socialism," hitherto sealed off hermetically. In all but four cases, the agreements were to run for five years; in the case of Mongolia, half-absorbed by the USSR, and of Soviet-controlled Korea and what was still Rakosi's Hungary, they covered ten years; and in the case of Vietnam, only three. In an effort to remove obvious discrimination, in the course of 1956-1957 the Soviet Union set up friendship societies with China, Bulgaria, etc., to match analogous friendship societies with the Soviet Union which had existed in the other states since the late 1940's. During 1957-1958 friendship societies also were established among all the Communist states.

The fact that these formal institutional aspects have in the majority of cases been developed or given substance in the post-Stalin phase of the camp's history is not without meaning. It would seem to suggest that these various devices, in spite of their original propagandistic purposes, have become more important to the Communist, and particularly the Soviet, leaders as instruments for the preservation and expression of their camp's unity. Indeed, as if to underscore this development, the old word "camp" (*lager* in Russian) now has a new equivalent: *sodruzhestvo* or, roughly, "commonwealth."[34] This

[33] At the same time the Soviet Union hastened to return to some of the European Communist-ruled states a portion of the art treasures which it had seized in the course of various hostilities. For instance, on June 12, 1956, *Pravda* announced that the Soviet government was returning to Rumania art treasures held in the USSR since World War I; on July 8, 1956, *Izvestia* announced the return of Polish art treasures, seized by the USSR during World War II. Insofar as cultural co-operation agreements are concerned, they were signed in the following sequence: with Rumania—April 7, 1956; East Germany—April 26; Bulgaria—April 28; Albania—May 3; Hungary—June 28; Poland—June 30; China—July 5; North Korea—September 5; Czechoslovakia—January 12, 1957; North Vietnam—February 15, 1957; also a renewal of the ten-year agreement with Mongolia on April 24, 1956.

[34] See Kurt L. London, "The 'Socialist Commonwealth of Nations,'" *Orbis*, III, No. 4 (Winter 1960), pp. 424-42, for a detailed analytical treatment of the origins of the new term and of its broader implications.

in itself suggests a degree of maturation within the bloc, its growth from a relatively simple, informal combination of personal dictator-ship and "big nation" imperialism, to a more complex pattern which preserves the privileged position of the dominant state but expresses this relationship through a more formal institutionalized set of arrange-ments.

II. Dynamic Aspects

The formal institutional aspects provide a broad framework for the organization of the unity of the Communist camp. This unity, however, is given content by the continuous interaction of its mem-bers, resolving conflicts, shaping policies, developing close trade con-tacts, engaging in exchanges and, of course, responding to the demands of the camp's most powerful state. This section will consider the various forms which these processes of unity take within the camp, often revealing the degree of cohesion that exists between the various groups of member states. Again, it is to be noted, Soviet power, the dependence of most of these states on the USSR, and the common ideological outlook of their regimes are taken for granted.

The most important dynamic aspect of the camp's unity is pro-vided by frequent contacts between the top leaders of the various ruling parties. This practice is a relatively recent development and involves an important change in the political style of the bloc.[35] During Stalin's domination, contacts between party leaders were rare and usually in-volved bilateral dealings with the Soviet leaders. In recent years, how-ever, and particularly since October-November 1956 (which can be considered as a sort of watershed in the bloc's history), relatively frequent bilateral and multilateral consultations between the party leaders have taken place. Even more important, Soviet leaders journey frequently to the other Communist states and necessarily have be-come much more conscious of the problems that the other ruling parties face. While not all of these meetings are of actual policy-making importance, they do help to keep the various party leaders better informed about current difficulties and they invariably involve a measure of discussion. Since at such meetings the Soviet leadership can muster the overwhelming support of the other regimes, the multi-lateral meeting is a useful forum for articulating common principles and for forcing recalcitrant parties (until about 1958, the Polish;

[35] A recent Soviet volume devoted to the foreign policy of the bloc (*Voprosy vneshnei politiki, op.cit.*) states: "A form of developing and tightening the unity of the socialist nations, in addition to concluding bilateral and multilateral agreements, are the meet-ings and the consultations between the leaders of the socialist countries" (p. 9).

more recently, the Chinese) into declarations of unity. The most recent example of this was provided during the Rumanian Party Congress in June 1960, when the Chinese were in effect faced with the choice of endorsing the Soviet line or being isolated through open disagreement.

The most important policy meetings—i.e., meetings at which positions and principles were actually hammered out—took place in the wake of the 1956 crisis. These involved, as already noted, many Polish-Soviet meetings, meetings between the Chinese and the various ruling European parties, meetings between the more orthodox ruling parties, such as the East German, Czechoslovak, and Bulgarian, and multilateral conferences initiated by the November 1957 Moscow meeting. The relative surface stabilization of the bloc during 1958-1960 did not diminish the policy importance of subsequent party meetings, and certainly not their informational-declarative value. Soviet-Chinese and Soviet-Polish meetings in 1958 and 1959 dealt with (not merely dictated) important domestic and external issues, while meetings of leaders of the other ruling parties among themselves and with the Soviets and the Chinese defined common stands on such issues as revisionism, collectivization, and foreign policy matters. The party congresses held in the USSR, East Germany, Bulgaria, Poland, Hungary, and Czechoslovakia, as well as the Chinese tenth-anniversary celebration, also created opportunities for frequent top-level multilateral meetings. In addition, as noted earlier, the Communist chiefs were brought together on the occasion of some of the CEMA and WTO sessions. All of these multilateral meetings took place after the November 1957 meeting, which overcame the Polish objections to multilateral gatherings.[36]

Tables 1 and 2 indicate the pattern and the intensity of party meetings at the Politburo level within the bloc. A few observations derived from them might be relevant here. Until the November 1957 Moscow meeting, the top CPSU leaders did not engage in extensive travels, but instead played host to frequent delegations from abroad. (It is to be remembered that during this period there was an intense conflict within the Soviet leadership.) At that time Moscow was visited by the top leaders of every Communist state, with some of them coming several times: Kadar three times, Gomulka twice, Zhivkov

[36] In the period November 1957-March 1960 there appear to have been no less than ten multilateral meetings attended either by the first secretaries and/or Politburo members of the ruling parties, not counting the two more restricted top-level mulilateral meetings in January 1957 (the five-party meeting in Budapest, and the Soviet-Chinese-Hungarian meeting in Moscow).

TABLE I. POLITBURO-LEVEL MULTILATERAL AND BILATERAL
MEETINGS OF DELEGATIONS IN THE PERIODS NOVEMBER 1956-NOVEMBER 1957
AND 1958-1959*

		USSR	CHINA	POLAND	CZECH.	E. GERMANY	RUMANIA	HUNGARY	BULGARIA
		COUNTRY MAKING THE VISITS: READ DOWN							
COUNTRY VISITED; READ ACROSS	USSR		5—3	5—5	3—5	2—5	2—4	5—4	3—5
	China	2—2		1—1	1—1	0—2	0—1	0—2	1—1
	Poland	0—5	1—2		0—1	1—2	0—1	0—2	0—2
	Czecho-slovakia	1—1	2—2	1—1		1—2	0—2	0—2	1—2
	E. Germany	2—2	1—2	1—1	1—2		1—1	0—3	0—2
	Rumania	0—1	1—1	0—1	1—0	—		0—1	1—0
	Hungary	1—3	1—3	0—3	2—1	2—1	2—1		2—1
	Bulgaria	0—2	1—2	0—2	0—1	1—1	1—1	0—2	

* The table probably shows the minimum figures, since doubtless many unannounced meetings were held. The first figure in each box represents meetings held in a given country between November 1, 1956, and November 15, 1957; the second figure represents the meetings held in 1958-1959. E.g., China was visited by Politburo-level Soviet delegates twice in the first period and twice in the second; on the other hand, the Soviet Union was visited by the Chinese 5 times in the first period and 3 times in the second. Thus the total Soviet-Chinese meetings amount to 12 (4 times in China, 8 times in the USSR); see Table 2.

twice, Siroky twice. Of the 31 Politburo-level meetings attended by the Soviet leaders between November 1956 and November 1957, 25 were held at home (see Table 2). In the course of this "stabilization" period, Budapest, East Berlin, and Prague were also focal points for such top-level activity (21 home meetings, as compared with only two in Warsaw). In general, worthy of note is the somewhat relatively higher incidence of meetings of East German-Bulgarian-Czechoslovak representatives, whose parties enjoy a neo-Stalinist reputation.

By way of contrast, in the post-1956 "stabilization" phase, the Chinese party was quite active externally, more so than in the subsequent post-1957 period. (A Chinese Politburo delegation was sent twice to tour Eastern Europe in an attempt to resolve the existing differences between some of the East European and the Soviet regimes.) During this phase, Sino-Soviet contacts were most frequent, presumably reflecting a common concern with the prevailing instability within the bloc. In the post-1957 period, the initiative passed into Soviet hands. Soviet activity increased greatly, and Khrushchev undertook a series of personal visits to all the Communist capitals (something which Stalin never did). After the November 1957 conference,

TABLE 2. TOTAL MEETINGS BETWEEN POLITBURO DELEGATIONS
IN THE PERIODS NOVEMBER 1956-NOVEMBER 1957, 1958-1959, AND BOTH COMBINED*

	USSR	CHINA	POLAND	CZECH.	E. GERMANY	RUMANIA	HUNGARY	BULGARIA
USSR								
China	7—5=12							
Poland	5—10=15	2—3=5						
Czecho-slovakia	4—6=10	3—3=6	1—2=3					
E. Germany	4—7=11	1—4=5	2—3=5	2—4=6				
Rumania	2—5=7	1—2=3	0—2=2	1—1=2	1—1=2			
Hungary	6—7=13	1—5=6	0—5=5	2—3=5	2—4=6	2—2=4		
Bulgaria	3—7=10	2—3=5	0—4=4	1—3=4	1—3=4	2—1=3	2—3=5	
Total meetings with bloc Politburo delegations	USSR 31—47=78	China 17—25=42	Poland 10—28=38	Czech. 13—21=34	E. Germ. 13—25=38	Rumania 9—13=22	Hungary 15—27=42	11—23=34
Of these, at home	25—31	5—10	2—14	5—10	6—12	3—2	10—11	3—10
Abroad	6—16	12—15	8—14	8—11	7—13	6—11	5—16	8—13

* The first figure in each column refers to the period November 1956-November 1957; the second to 1958-1959; the third to the two combined. Thus the Soviets and the Chinese met 7 times during the first period and 5 during the second, for a total of 12.

which marked Gomulka's formal subservience to the principle of camp unity, Polish-Soviet meetings became frequent and Polish activity within the bloc increased greatly. It should be noted, however, that although more than half of the meetings registered in the tables involved first secretaries of the ruling parties, until October 1960 Gomulka and Novotny had never exchanged formal visits (which presumably had something to do with the latter's behavior in October 1956).

Every meeting normally concludes with a statement of principles, reaffirming a common ideological commitment and warning against various dangers to Communist unity. These meetings also serve to symbolize the equality that is formally said to prevail within the Communist camp. At the same time such gatherings provide their participants with convenient arenas for the exercise of subtle pressure. Thus the 1957 meetings were used by the East Germans, the Czechs, and the Bulgarians to assert the fundamental importance of Soviet leadership within the camp and to scourge revisionism. Similarly, in 1959 the Chinese tenth-anniversary meeting gave these party leaders an opportunity to praise effusively the Chinese domestic program and the relatively Stalinist ideological stand of the Chinese, thereby quietly indicating their hope that the other party leaderships would follow suit. The Moscow session of the WTO in February 1960 presented the Chinese delegate with a chance to assure the other party leaders that the dangers of war are still acute and that the camp ought to avoid excessive reliance on "peaceful coexistence."[37] These top-level unity meetings thus involve important doses of "esoteric communication," which would not have been possible in Stalin's day.[38]

The top-level contacts, although frequent, still operate on an *ad hoc* basis. In 1957 there was some pressure from the Soviets and the other centralist leaders (East German, Czechoslovak) to re-establish some regular, institutionalized channel of inter-party contacts. Owing to the resistance of some parties (primarily the Polish, and possibly the Chinese also), this proposal was not implemented. Rather, two substitute methods were developed. First, the Soviet Union began to rely primarily on experienced party leaders, usually of a rank equivalent to a republican or *oblast'* first secretary, as its ambassadors to the other Communist states. In this way, Moscow assured itself of a degree of continuous party contact on a responsible level, subject directly to the CPSU Central Committee's department for dealing with bloc affairs.

Secondly, according to a decision reached at the November 1957 conference, an inter-party political-ideological magazine was established. Its editorial offices were located in hyper-loyal Prague and a high-ranking CPSU specialist in international Communist affairs, A. Rumyantsev, was appointed as its head. It was entitled the *World*

[37] A full text of the vigorous statement by a Chinese observer, significantly ignored by the Soviet and East European press, is contained in *East Europe*, IX, No. 3 (March 1960).

[38] This communication takes the form either of reiteration of certain key and meaningful formulas or of ostentatious omission of certain key concepts. Thus, for instance, the repetition of the formula "proletarian internationalism" as the basic principle guiding relations between the Communist states was directed against the Poles' emphasis on the need to respect their own road to socialism; similarly, the insistence on hailing Soviet leadership was meant to combat the concept of full equality of Communist states. Repeated attacks on revisionism (and silence on dogmatism) were directed against those parties and party members who were pressing for anti-Stalinist reforms. Similarly, attacks on dogmatism were often aimed at the USSR and, in 1959-1960, at China. The recent Chinese emphasis on the innately aggressive character of imperialism, as shown by Lenin, is a form of subtle pressure against those Communist leaders who are willing to concede that war is not inevitable even while capitalism still exists. Finally, exaggerated praise for the policies of one party can be a form of pressure against another; e.g., praise of China can be directed at the USSR, or praise of Bulgaria for rapidly collectivizing can be aimed at Poland, etc.

Marxist Review in its English edition, and *Problems of Peace and Socialism* in its Russian edition. (The editions include the twelve languages of the bloc and seven others: English, French, Spanish, Italian, Dutch, Swedish, and Japanese.) Although distribution of the review is not restricted to the bloc, it was clear from the outset that one of its tasks would be the consolidation of a common ideological-political line for the bloc. Precisely because of that it was hailed by the East Germans[39] and met with silence in Warsaw.

Since publication of its first issue in September 1958, the magazine has appeared once a month. Although it does not seem to have lived up to expectations as the vital organ for the crystallization of ideological and political unity in the bloc, it is the only inter-party publication on ideological-political matters, and in some ways a successor to the Cominform journal, *For a Lasting Peace, For a People's Democracy*. Apart from occasional editorials, it usually contains several major feature articles dealing with sundry problems of foreign policy, ideology, economy, or bloc affairs. A second section, which appears irregularly, is devoted to shorter "exchanges of views" between the various Communist parties. The third section contains brief notes on party activities.

An examination of twenty-six issues (September 1958-October 1960) shows that the magazine's contributors are by no means restricted to the bloc alone. The proportion of bloc contributions is highest among the major feature articles—95 out of 191; in the briefer "exchange of views" category, the proportion is 52 out of 157; in the short news items, 59 out of 238. However, given the origins of the magazine and the fact that it is presently the only open inter-party forum, it is an important and revealing source of information concerning inter-party dynamics within the bloc. Tables 3, 4, and 5 provide a breakdown of the various contributions from the parties belonging to the Communist camp.

The tables seem to warrant the following conclusions insofar as the camp is concerned: (1) Not unexpectedly, the leading role in the magazine is played by the CPSU. (2) More striking perhaps, however, is the domination of the magazine by three parties—the Soviet, the Czech, and the East German. Of the 95 major bloc contributions, they account for 60; of the 52 "exchange of views" in the second table, the Soviets and Germans alone account for 25; of the 59 informational items, the three parties account for 25. (3) It is also noteworthy that these three parties monopolize almost entirely the

[39] *Neues Deutschland* (East Berlin), November 30, 1957.

TABLE 3. FEATURE ARTICLES IN "WORLD MARXIST REVIEW," SEPTEMBER 1958—OCTOBER 1960*

(Total number of articles, 191; Soviet bloc contributions, 95)

COUNTRIES	ARTICLES BY BLOC	EXTERNAL ISSUES				BLOC ISSUES			DOMESTIC ISSUES		
		FOR. POL. GEN.	FOR. POL. NAT'L.	ECON. ISSUES	IDEOL. ISSUES	POLIT. ISSUES	IDEOL. ISSUES	ECON. ISSUES	POLIT. ISSUES	IDEOL. ISSUES	EC. & SOC. ISSUES
Albania	—										
Bulgaria	7				1		1		1	1	3
China	6								1	2	3
Czecho.	15	1		2	2		2	3	2	1	2
E. Germany	11		2		1	3			2	1	2
Hungary	6				1				3	1	1
Mongolia	—										
N. Korea	3	1									2
N. Vietnam	2										2
Poland	8	2	1					1	1	1	2
Rumania	3		1						2		
USSR	34	7	1	3	7		3	3	3		7
TOTAL	95	11	5	5	12	3	6	7	15	7	24

* (1) Not included are unsigned articles of indeterminate character as well as editorials. Included is one supplement on economic development in the bloc. (2) Arbitrary or borderline categorizations include several articles on purely cultural developments (e.g., an article in the April 1960 issue, "A Playwright on Lenin"); such articles have been included under the heading of economic and social issues. An article on science and social issues, in the October 1960 issue, which focuses on the scientific achievements of the USSR and briefly compares them with those of the United States, has been listed under the domestic social-economic heading. An article by G. Obichkin, "Lenin and the Party" (May 1960), dealing with Lenin's theory of the party, has been included under external ideological issues—USSR, on the assumption that it is valid for all CP's, not just for those of the bloc. Otto Kuusinen's article, "Perspectives of Monopoly Capital" (April 1960), is also listed under external ideological issues—USSR, on the grounds that the topic is more than purely economic.

TABLE 4. EXCHANGE OF VIEWS IN "WORLD MARXIST REVIEW," SEPTEMBER 1958–OCTOBER 1960*
(Total number of articles, 157; Soviet bloc contributions, 52)

COUNTRIES	ARTICLES BY BLOC	EXTERNAL ISSUES				BLOC ISSUES		DOMESTIC ISSUES	
		FOR. POL. GEN.	FOR. POL. NAT'L.	ECON. ISSUES	IDEOL. ISSUES	POL. & IDEOL. ISSUES	ECON. ISSUES	POL. & IDEOL. ISSUES	EC. & SOC. ISSUES
Albania	2							1	
Bulgaria	4					2		2	
China	5					1		3	1
Czecho.	3				1	1	1		1
E. Germany	13	1		7	1	1		2	1
Hungary	3				1	1		1	
Mongolia	1					1			
N. Korea	—								
N. Vietnam	2					1		1	
Poland	3					1	1	1	
Rumania	4				1	1	1	1	
USSR	12	4		4	1	1	1	1	1
TOTAL	52	5		11	3	12	4	13	4

* Under this heading is included not only a section labeled "Exchange of Views," which is usually a forum on such questions as "What Are the Changes in the Structure of the Working Class?" (May and September 1960), but also a monthly feature entitled "Communications and Comment," reports on international congresses, and an occasional feature called "Pages from History." Items were excluded if their authorship could not be determined.

APPENDIX I

serious discussion of bloc affairs and dominate heavily most of the
comments on external issues. (4) By the way of contrast, the contributors from the other ruling parties seem to restrict themselves to
their own domestic problems. (5) Very striking is the limited participation of the Chinese party: in feature articles, it is less than that

TABLE 5. ARTICLES HEADED "IN THE COMMUNIST AND WORKERS' PARTIES,"
IN "WORLD MARXIST REVIEW," SEPTEMBER 1958—OCTOBER 1960

(Total number of articles, 238; Soviet bloc contributions, 59)

Albania	4	Mongolia	2
Bulgaria	4	North Korea	3
China	3	North Vietnam	—
Czechoslovakia	8	Poland	8
East Germany	7	Rumania	2
Hungary	8	USSR	10

of Czechoslovakia, East Germany, or Bulgaria, and no greater than
that of Hungary; its share in the other categories is similar. (6)
Not less striking is the small total of contributions from the Asian
countries: instead of contributing roughly one-third (4 countries out
of 12), they contributed little more than one-ninth of the camp's
feature articles, one-sixth of the "exchange of views" contributions,
and one-eighth of the activities items. This seems to have a further
implication: insofar as the camp is concerned, the journal is primarily an organ of Soviet orthodoxy, designed to articulate on *major
issues* the line developed by the Soviet leaders and their most devoted
lieutenants, the East Germans and the Czechs. The other parties either
shun the magazine or are pushed into a relatively narrow, domestically
oriented background. This "in-group" seems to parallel the one noted
in regard to leadership contacts.

Little can be said without access to classified data concerning the
dynamic side of military relations within the bloc. However, certain
facts do stand out. Since 1956, the Soviet Union has striven to remove
the most overbearing aspects of its military domination of Eastern
Europe, a domination to which the Soviet leaders had to admit during the critical days of October 1956.[40] With the recall of most of the

[40] "In the process of the rise of the new systems and the deep revolutionary changes
in social relations, there have been many difficulties, unresolved problems, and down-
right mistakes in the mutual relations among the socialist countries—violations and
errors which demeaned the principle of equality in the relations among the socialist
states" (from the October 30, 1956, declaration by the government of the USSR).

Soviet advisers (Hungary excepted), and with the highly publicized treaties governing the presence of Soviet troops in other Communist states, the most glaring irritants were removed. At the same time, the Soviet Union ensured the availability to its forces of certain strategic areas: e.g., Polish and Rumanian ports as well as frontal positions in East Germany and Hungary. However, these adjustments do not amount to close co-operation and/or military integration. In fact, it would appear that on the military level, the Soviets, possibly anxious to protect their military secrets and hypersensitive to security matters, prefer to avoid tight military integration. Apart from providing some of the satellites with the technical information necessary for the production of Soviet-type weapons (thereby alleviating delivery pressures on the USSR), and general standardization of weapons within the camp, military co-operation tends to operate primarily at the top political-military levels, through exchange of visits and a general definition of broad strategic tasks, but without real military integration or frequent and regular joint maneuvers of the various Communist forces.

The Soviets' determination to protect their military preponderance within the bloc is particularly evident with respect to nuclear weapons. Unwillingness to share them has been expressed through such maneuvers as the scheme for an atom-free Asia (coolly received by the Chinese) and by continuing equivocation in response to requests for greater nuclear assistance from the other "socialist" states, particularly China. It was presumably with this in mind that, according to Radio Peking of June 8, 1960, a Chinese leader, Liu Chang-sheng, made this veiled criticism of the Soviet stand: "We hold that the utmost efforts must be made to reach agreement on the banning of nuclear weapons and to prevent the outbreak of a nuclear war in the world. Soviet mastery of nuclear weapons has now deprived U.S. imperialism of its monopoly of such weapons. The Soviet Union and the other socialist countries should continue to develop their lead in the sphere of atomic energy and, at the same time, the people throughout the world should wage a more extensive struggle against imperialism and against nuclear weapons. Only in these circumstances can such agreement be reached." In other words, the best way to get a nuclear ban would be to share nuclear weapons with China and the other Communist-ruled states.

With respect to the matter of diplomatic relations among the Communist states, considerable regularization is to be noted. In the course of 1957-1958, the Soviet Union concluded a whole series of consular conventions with the other members of the bloc, defining consular competence and clarifying such still outstanding issues as dual-citizenship, problems of mutual legal aid, and civil, criminal, and familial legal issues.[41] However, the Soviet Union still retained its traditional reticence concerning the opening of foreign consulates on Soviet soil; the Poles, for instance, were unsuccessful in their efforts to increase their consular representation in the Soviet Union. At the higher diplomatic level, as noted earlier, the trend in the Soviet case has been toward the appointment of party officials as ambassadors to the other Communist states.[42] However, this does not necessarily mean that the ambassadorial role has actually increased. In some cases, such appointments were made in the wake of the domestic disgrace of the individual concerned (e.g., Molotov and Pervukhin), and in general it may be seen as part of a trend to improve inter-party contacts through the development of a sense of *partiinost* in common dealings, while leaving the determination of more important issues to higher-level party meetings which, as already observed, have become relatively frequent. In this connection, quite suggestive is the increase in the frequency of Soviet ambassadorial shifts in those states which during Stalin's time were almost ruled by the Soviet ambassador. During the Stalinist phase six Soviet ambassadors in Hungary, Poland, Rumania, and East Germany, served a total of 26 years, or roughly four and a half years for each appointment. In the post-Stalin phase, 12 ambassadors served out 26 years, or just over two years each. Apart from domestic Soviet factors involved in such changes, one may well suspect that the relative decrease in the role of the Soviet ambassador as the direct superior of the domestic leaders of the countries involved may have had something to do with this.

These various high-level forms of relations testify to a steadily intensified contact between the ruling regimes. The number of visits of various ministers, deputy ministers, regional party secretaries, assembly deputies, technical and scientific delegations, youth activists, etc., runs virtually into the hundreds.[43] These, too, compare notes

[41] See Slusser and Triska, *op.cit.*

[42] On the basis of recent listings, nine out of eleven Soviet ambassadors to Communist-ruled states appear to have been former senior party functionaries. During Stalin's lifetime, they appeared to come primarily from among the technical-police groups that staffed Molotov's Foreign Ministry.

[43] E.g., in 1957, the USSR sent out 1,116 such delegations; in the first half of 1958, 587. In the same periods, Czechoslovakia sent out 503 and 250; Poland 472 and 263, etc. More than half of these, however, were technical and sports groups. See Ivanov, *Razvitie, op.cit.*, pp. 112-13, for data on exchanges of specialists.

and sometimes engage in subtle communications.[44] Recent years have also seen a marked increase in personal contacts among the several Communist states, something not possible during Stalin's era. The gradual development of tourism means that each year tens of thousands of private citizens of one Communist country visit other Communist countries. (In 1959, for instance, about 60,000 Bulgarians, 70,000 Czechs, and 70,000 Poles traveled within the orbit.[45]) However, in this respect some striking differences among the various states have to be noted. Of the Poles, almost as many visit non-Communist as Communist states, whereas in the case of the other bloc members the total going west is at the most one-fourth (Czechoslovakia) and usually less. Furthermore, the greatest exchange of tourists seems to be among East Germany, Czechoslovakia, and Bulgaria; this is easily explainable in terms of Bulgaria being a genuine tourist attraction, but other considerations would appear to be involved in the case of the large number of Czechs or Bulgarians visiting East Germany, but not, for instance, Poland. Among the many other forms of intensified contacts, one should also note an increasing student exchange, especially between the USSR and China,[46] special conferences of bloc scholars,[47] collaboration agreements between the several national academies of science (e.g., the December 1957 and January 1958 scientific and technological agreements between the respective Chinese and Soviet institutions), and circulation of bloc literature and newspapers (particularly Soviet) among the various states. For instance, the year 1959 saw meetings of the orbit's publishers, economists, film producers, even circus directors. The film producers decided, *inter alia*, to emphasize *partiinost* in their productions, close

[44] For instance, the head of the Polish parliamentary delegation to Rumania emphasized in his account of the meetings with Rumanian parliamentarians the fact that the Rumanians expressed great interest in the ratio of governmental decrees to legislative acts in post-1956 Poland. When he told them that for 76 parliamentary acts passed in Poland in 1958, there was only one governmental decree, the Rumanians admitted that in their case the ratio was almost reversed, but said they were also struggling for a change (*Zycie Warszawy*, October 16, 1958).

[45] *Lidova Demokracie* (Prague), January 7, 1959; *Rude Pravo* (Prague), February 10, 1959; for the most complete treatment, *East Europe*, VIII, No. 7 (July 1959).

[46] For Sino-Soviet student exchanges, see M. S. Kapitsa, *Sovetsko-Kitaiskie otnosheniia*, Moscow, 1958, p. 379. However, the Soviet Union is not actively engaged in sending its students abroad; in 1958 there were, for instance, 1,040 Czechoslovak students in the USSR and only 124 Soviet students in the CSR (*Svobodne Slovo*, Prague, July 19, 1958). Similarly, in Poland the largest number of foreign students from within the bloc came from the Asian countries (*Zycie Warszawy*, October 8, 1958).

[47] For instance, see J. Kowalski, "At the International Conference of Historians of the Communist Movement," *Nowe Drogi* (Warsaw), January 1958, for an account of the three conferences held for party historians of the bloc.

ties with reality, and "the unmasking of revisionism in aesthetics."[48] All of these measures are designed to foster a sense of community, a sense of common identity in "the camp of socialism."

The extensive efforts to promote unity, so lacking during the Stalinist phase of the camp's development, has two further aspects which deserve mention. The first is the matter of trade, the second that of the literature of unity. The importance of close trade ties as a factor of interdependence was recognized much earlier than the need for co-ordinated planning and for the activization of the dormant institutions of CEMA. However, with specialization, trade has assumed an even more important role in shaping a "socialist world market," distinct from the capitalist world and fully self-sufficient. Table 6 shows not only the degree to which trade patterns have been channeled primarily within the bloc, but also the intensity of trade among the various Communist states. In addition to the obvious point that trade with the USSR is of central importance to all of the states, whatever the level of their economic development, it would appear that China depends also to a great extent on supplies from East Germany and Czechoslovakia, thus paralleling the particular ideological affinities of these regimes for one another. While it would be incorrect to claim that there is a causal relationship between trade patterns and ideological orientations, it is a fact that states like East Germany and Czechoslovakia, which entertain a centralistic conception of the bloc, do happen to play an important role in the general economic life of that bloc. Their economic strength thus buttresses their political orientation and gives them greater influence in such organs as CEMA.

In general, in the eyes of the Communist leaderships, the emerging economic interdependence is said to have not only economic but great political and ideological significance. It is quite evident that in the thinking of the Soviet leaders, the consolidation and growth of a "socialist world market," and eventually its preponderance over the "capitalist" market, is one of the determining factors shaping the present epoch.[49] The economic growth and integration of the camp

---

[48] G. A. Mozhaev, *Mezhdunarodnye Kulturnye Sviazi SSSR*, Moscow, 1959.

[49] This theme is often repeated by Khrushchev. See also E. Varga, "The Capitalism of the 20th Century," *Kommunist*, No. 17 (November 1959), and particularly his prognosis for the next ten to fifteen years. Probably the most elaborate and sophisticated development of the expected international and political consequences of the growth of a "socialist world market" is contained in T. Lychowski, *Stosunki Ekonomiczne Miedzy Krajami o Roznych Ustrojach*, Warsaw, 1957, pp. 590-605, where he argues that the existence of such a market will profoundly alter the present pattern of relations between the industrialized Western nations and the developing nations.

TABLE 6. INTRA-BLOC TRADE PATTERNS*
(in per cent of total)

COUNTRIES	BULGARIA		CHINA		CZECH.		E. GERMANY		HUNGARY		POLAND		RUMANIA		USSR	
	1957	1958	1957	1958	1957	1958	1957	1958	1957	1958	1957	1958	1957	1958	1957	1958
Bulgaria			.04		3.0	2.7	1.9	2.1	1.8	1.5	1.2	1.6	2.5		4.5	4.7
China	1.0	2.5			5.0	7.0	6.0	9.4	5.2	6.9	3.7	4.7	4.2		15.4	17.5
Czech.	11.5	10.5	5.7	5.7			7.6	11.3	13.9	13.1	6.2	7.3	6.7		11.2	11.1
E. Germany	8.0	9.3	7.5	6.6	10.1	11.0			11.0	11.0	13.0	11.5	7.5		19.5	18.7
Hungary	2.6	2.4	2.2	2.7	5.4	5.8	3.6	4.3			2.4	2.7	3.3		4.3	4.1
Poland	3.5	4.9	3.2	3.2	10.0	11.0	7.4	10.4	4.9	5.1			4.2		8.3	7.4
Rumania	1.8	1.5			2.3	2.1	1.8	2.0	2.5	2.3	1.5	1.1			5.3	5.6
USSR	52.0	53.3	50.0		34.0	33.1	45.0	43.0	29.5	27.0	30.6	26.2	47.6			
Total share intra-bloc trade	85.0	85.9	75.0	75.0	69.8	72.7	73.3	82.5	70.2	66.3	58.6	55.1	76.0		68.5	69.1

* Read down for the trade of any particular country.

are thus becoming central factors in the Communist perspective on world affairs.

The final aspect to be registered involves the literature of unity that is mushrooming within the bloc and particularly in the USSR. By this is not meant the trite, propagandistic, and largely sterile treatments of the often illusory advantages for the various Communist-ruled countries of friendship with the Soviet Union. Such publications have been available for a long time. In the last two or three years, however, there have been signs that more serious thought is being given in the various states, and particularly in the USSR, to what might be called the problematics of the Communist camp. Apparently it became evident to all concerned that the emergence of a series of Communist states created problems and issues which had specific characteristics and which could not be answered by the standard political, ideological, and economic literature written primarily for Soviet domestic consumption. Furthermore, it became evident that the experience of the other ruling parties often raised issues which could be disturbing to the CPSU membership.

As a result, by 1958 and 1959 even important Soviet publications appeared to be drafted with at least one ear cocked toward possible bloc reactions and domestic echoes of bloc problems. The recently published *Istoriia KPSS*, or the most up-to-date formal statement of the ideology, *Osnovy Marksizma-Leninizma*, edited by O. V. Kuusinen, not only were clearly intended for domestic Soviet consumption but attempted to address themselves to problems that face the other ruling parties. The realization that Stalin had erred in insisting that almost every aspect of Soviet experience was relevant to "the construction of socialism" elsewhere meant that serious thought could be given to the task of defining which parts of this experience were and were not relevant. The efforts of the CPSU's new official history to define the universal laws of "socialist construction" was a response to this need.[50] Similarly, Kuusinen's book was in large part an attempt to provide an up-to-date, authoritative, and serious statement of the doctrine, refuting both the revisionist and the dogmatist views penetrating some of the ruling parties, including the CPSU.[51]

[50] *Istoriia Kommunisticheskoi Partii Sovetskogo Soiuza*, Moscow, 1959, especially pp. 672-74.

[51] To this writer, Kuusinen's volume is the most important Soviet attempt to define Communist ideology since Stalin's statement of 1952. Clearly meant to be a guide to international communism on all political-ideological aspects, including such matters as patterns of the socialist revolution, the issue of war, and the nature of a Communist society, the volume is particularly striking in its de-emphasis of the Chinese experience. While primarily relying on Marx-Engels-Lenin for doctrinal citations, it cites Mao Tse-tung

In addition, within the last two years a spate of books devoted to bloc affairs has been published in the USSR.[52] As the partial listing below suggests, their primary emphasis appears to be on the theme of economic collaboration and on the emergence of a "socialist world market." Occasionally they contain useful comparative materials on the economic development of the various Communist-ruled states and on the stages of their "socialist construction." There are, in addition, two other kinds of general treatment: volumes primarily devoted to the negative task of rooting out "revisionist" tendencies within the ruling parties,[53] and more general political-ideological discussions of the camp's affairs. The latter category supplies perhaps the more interesting examples of the developing literature of unity. One may cite, for instance, the symposium sponsored by the Philosophy Institute of the Academy of Sciences, entitled *The Commonwealth of Socialist Countries* (*Sodruzhestvo Stran Sotsializma*). This 300-page book addresses itself to such issues as the generalities and specifics of the building of communism, the impact of the October Soviet revolution on the development of the concept of People's Democracy (a matter which was once actively discussed in the bloc), a discussion of the peculiarities of building socialism in China, etc.[54] While often simplistically dogmatic in its approach (this is particularly true of a chapter dealing with "proletarian internationalism" in relations between the Communist states), such literature is

---

only twice in the course of 750 pages; Khrushchev, by way of contrast, is cited sixteen times, but Stalin also only twice.

[52] E.g., N. I. Ivanov, *Razvitie Ekonomiki Stran Narodnoi Demokratii*, Moscow, 1958; A. K. Kozik, ed., *Ekonomicheskoie sotrudnichestvo i vzaimopomoshch mezhdu Sovetskim Soiuzom I Evropeiskimi Stranami Demokratii*, Moscow, 1958; Ivanov, *Razvitie, op.cit.; Voprosy vneshnei politiki, op.cit.; Sodruzhestvo Stran Sotsializma*, Moscow, 1958; O. Butenko, *Osnovnye cherty sovremennogo revizionizma*, Moscow, 1959; *Protiv sovremennogo revizionizma*, Moscow, 1959; D. D. Bytakov, ed., *Finansy Stran Narodnoi Demokratii*, Moscow, 1959. In addition to these general works, there is an increasing number of books dealing with specific problems of individual Communist states—e.g., V. Zhamin, *Sel'skoe khoziaistvo Kitaia*, Moscow, 1959; *Problemy novoi sistemy planirovaniia i finansirovaniia cheskoslovatskoi promyshlennosti*, Moscow, 1959; and many others. This reawakened interest in the "problematics" of bloc affairs harks back to the 1946-1949 period, during which time there were many active discussions and publications pertaining particularly to the question of the nature of "People's Democracy" and its relationship to Marxist-Leninist doctrine. Such centers as the Institute of World Economy and International Relations, or the Institute of International Relations, seem to be particularly interested.

[53] E.g., Butenko, *op.cit.*, or *Protiv sovremennogo revizionizma, op.cit.*

[54] Its lead article was contributed by M. B. Mitin, member of the Academy of Sciences and of the Central Committee of the CPSU, in the past a Soviet delegate to the Bulgarian and Hungarian Party congresses and, last but not least, in 1955 the editor of the Cominform journal, *For a Lasting Peace, For a People's Democracy.* A more recent example is the recently published volume, *Obshche zakonomernosti perekhoda k Sotsializmu i osobennosti ikh proiavleniia v raznykh stranakh*, Moscow, 1960.

a modest step forward in the direction of at least recognizing some of the problems involved in building "socialism" on the basis of a common ideology but within the context of several societies, ranging from the technologically most advanced to the most primitive.[55]

III. Some Conclusions

Insofar as the organization of the Communist camp is concerned, recent years have seen concrete efforts in the direction of (1) the regularization of relations among its members; and (2) the intensification of such relations. Many of the earlier sources of tension were due to the essentially informal and indirect system of Stalinist controls, to the blurred lines between central authority and domestic autonomy, to the air-tight compartmentalization of the camp's members, each surrounded by an iron curtain and beholden only to Moscow. The regularization of these relations, and their concomitant intensification, have been designed to reduce the number of tension points, and to liquidate the earlier ambiguities in the division of power between the center and its dependencies and/or allies. While foreign affairs, military affairs, and ideology still remain primarily in the Soviet domain (excepting the special case of China), a limited measure of autonomy in regard to the tempo and specific character of domestic social and economic policies is gradually developing insofar as the other Communist states are concerned. Although the Soviet Union yielded to this development with hesitation and often painfully, the regularization of relations and their simultaneous intensification were both necessities dictated by this concession and responses to the new situation. Most of the organizational aspects of the promotion of unity treated in the preceding pages became important only in the last few years.

This greater emphasis on the organizational aspects of the camp has certain implications for its general character. For one thing, since its unity now involves much more conscious effort on the part of the various ruling elites than was the case earlier, one can note something which could not have occurred in Stalin's day—namely, the appearance, albeit still very timid, of constellations or "in-groups" within the camp. On a number of important issues, it

[55] Literature of this broader sort has also been making its appearance in the satellite states, although perhaps even more timidly. One may cite, for example, *Mezinarodni delba prace v socialisticke svetove soustave*, Prague, 1958; G. Tsonkov, *Obshchoto i spetsifichnoto v razvitieto na sotsialisticheskata revoliutsiia*, Sofia, 1959; or the more general work by T. Lychowski cited in note 49.

would appear that the East German and Czechoslovak leaderships share similar approaches, and quite often they seem to enjoy Bulgarian support. (This corresponds to some of the factual evidence noted in part II of this study.) Furthermore, on occasions they have displayed more sympathy for some of the Chinese attitudes, both on ideology and on foreign policy. For the time being, the Poles, the Rumanians, and the Hungarians have been closer to the Soviets with respect to international affairs, even though the Czechs and the East Germans are relied upon by Moscow to promote the internal line of bloc unity.[56]

Finally, the regularization and intensification of relations within the camp, and the abandonment of the relatively informal Stalinist pattern, have revealed a striking differentiation in the formal institutional structure of the camp insofar as the Asian group of Communist states is involved. They are not in the formal alliance system nor in CEMA, and their contacts with the other parties appear to be less intense. Furthermore, since much of the Soviet hope for the future political and ideological unity of the camp is based on the present drive for closer economic interdependence, an autarkic Chinese development means that in the years to come Chinese unity with the rest of the camp will rest almost entirely on the ideological-political plane. While this is not tantamount to disunity, it does reflect a somewhat less homogeneous reality than the Communist leaders would have the world believe.

This leads to two further points. The history of the camp can now be evenly divided into the Stalinist and the post-Stalinist periods, each lasting about seven years. From a historical standpoint, these are very short phases indeed. What is striking, however, is the difference between them. In the first place, the camp no longer seems as monolithic and as invulnerable to change as during Stalin's lifetime. Because of that, the alternative to it seems less likely to be violent upheavals. Today, in some ways the camp is better equipped to absorb the strains which occur in any multinational organization, and particularly in one dominated by a single national group. By suppressing such tensions through terror, accompanied also by economic exploitation, Stalin created the preconditions for a revolutionary situation. This no longer appears to be the case. On the other hand, because of the greater elasticity which now absorbs the strains and

---

[56] As one highly placed East European Communist said to the writer: "You have your mad dogs of capitalism [paraphrasing a Stalinist statement]—namely, Adenauer; we have our mad dogs of communism—the East Germans and the Czechs."

prevents an explosion erupting from stored-up frustration, the danger of a gradual erosion of the camp's ideological unity seems greater than ever before. Even the small measure of diversity which now exists, even the formal steps taken to regularize and improve relations, can gradually become impediments to the maintenance of the Leninist-Stalinist type of internal organizational discipline, so necessary to the unity of a camp founded on a doctrinaire ideology. This is particularly the case since the camp is still undergoing evolutionary change requiring a continuous adjustment of the ideology to varying and often conflicting national circumstances. Furthermore, to the degree that the Soviet leadership finds it necessary to mobilize the support of other Communist regimes in opposition to some Chinese stands,[57] the relationship of political power between Moscow and the other capitals becomes increasingly less asymmetrical.

Secondly, it seems fair to note that the camp in its first phase was in effect a national empire, centrally directed and run largely to the advantage of the dominant Soviet party. In some ways, if one for a minute overlooks the ideological elements, it was much like the Roman or French or English empire in their earlier days. Precisely because of that, it did not require elaborate machinery. The present development within the camp is increasingly transforming it into an international Communist empire, dominated by various Communist elites, bound together, to be sure, by Soviet power but also by common interests and aspirations. While united in their efforts and in their vested interest in keeping their ideologically oriented empire together and their populations suppressed, they increasingly find it necessary to express their unity through various organizational devices. The need for such organizational devices is felt to be particularly great because in the current Communist thinking "socialist" and subsequently even Communist countries will continue to exist as separate entities until a world-wide Communist society emerges.[58]

[57] For a recent treatment of Sino-Soviet differences, see D. Zagoria, "Strains in the Sino-Soviet Alliance," *Problems of Communism* (May-June 1960). For the argument that the Sino-Soviet alliance involves a dynamic relationship of "divergent unity," see this writer's "The Pattern and Limits of the Sino-Soviet Dispute," *ibid.* (September-October 1960). For a discussion of the problematics of ideological "relativization" and then "erosion," see my "Communist Ideology and International Affairs," *Journal of Conflict Resolution*, IV, No. 3 (September 1960), pp. 266-91.

[58] The fullest and most recent Soviet ideological statement, the thick volume *Osnovy Marksizma-Leninizma*, Moscow, 1959, edited by O. V. Kuusinen, speaks of economic co-operation among Communist countries (not just "socialist") as preliminary to the eventual emergence of a single global "Commonwealth" (pp. 749-51). It is interesting to note that the new "socialist" constitution of Czechoslovakia (which is said to be no

During this transitional, but probably lengthy period, unity between the ruling parties is to be cemented through continuing efforts to develop ever closer political and economic ties among the countries ruled by them. To the extent that such ties do establish normative principles (if only in theory), particularly the principle of equality and independence, they will gradually consolidate the transition from a national to an international empire. By preserving state forms but emptying them gradually of their content, the ultimate hope is to surmount the traditional forces of nationalism and to create in effect an interlocking supra-society. While many obstacles still remain and others may arise, particularly with the further development of China, the West would do well not to underestimate the importance of the organizational development of the Communist camp.

---

longer a People's Democracy) states in chapter I, article 1, that "The Czechoslovak Republic belongs to the world socialist system . . ." as a matter of constitutional law.

Appendix II

Selected Statistics for the Communist Bloc, 1959

	Population at end of 1959	Geographic area (square miles)	Coal production, hard coal (metric tons)	Steel production (metric tons)	Electrical output (millions of kilowatt-hours)
Albania	1,600,000	10,629	290,000	—	174 (approx.)
Bulgaria	7,800,000	42,796	7,900,000	230,000	3,900
China (Mainland)	669,000,000[a]	4,264,467	347,800,000	13,400,000	41,500
Czechoslovakia	13,600,000	49,330	58,700,000	6,100,000	21,900
GDR	17,300,000	41,645	74,400,000	3,200,000	37,200
Hungary	10,000,000	35,911	11,800,000	1,800,000	7,100
Mongolia (Outer)	1,000,000 (approx.)	614,350	790,000[b]	—	70[d]
North Korea	10,000,000 (approx.)	42,633 (approx.)	8,900,000	450,000	7,800
North Vietnam	15,900,000	63,360	2,100,000	—	193 (approx.)
Poland	29,500,000	120,442	103,600,000	6,200,000	26,400
Rumania	18,400,000	92,000	3,500,000[c]	1,400,000	6,800
USSR	212,300,000	8,590,000	435,000,000	60,000,000	265,100

	Communist camp		Rest of world	
Population	34.6%	1,006,400,000	65.4%	1,898,600,000
Geographic area	24.2	14,006,237 sq. mi.	75.8	58,333,000 sq. mi.
Coal production	49.1	1,054,780,000 metric tons	50.9	1,090,020,000 metric tons
Steel production	30.5	92,780,000 metric tons	69.5	211,320,000 metric tons
Electrical output	19.9	418,317 million kwh	80.1	1,673,183 million kwh

[a] 1958.
[b] Planned output for 1960.
[c] In terms of heat units, 1 unit 7,000 calories.
[d] Planned output for 1960.

Sources: *World Marxist Review*, vol. IV, no. 1, January 1961. Supplement: "Economic Development of the Socialist Countries." *Monthly Bulletin of Statistics*, February 1961. Statistical Office of the United Nations, New York. *Mirovaia Ekonomika i Mezhdunarodnye Otnosheniia*, no. 6, June 1960. "*Perspektivnye Plany Razvitiia Narodnogo Khoziaistva Sotsialisticheskikh Stran*." Vietnamese News Agency. Report on Vietnamese production issued by the General Statistical Department, February 22, 1961.

PREPARED BY T. BERNSTEIN.

Notes

Preface

1. Probably the best is H. L. Boorman, A. Eckstein, P. Mosely, and B. Schwartz, *Moscow-Peking Axis* (New York, 1957). A well-documented and provocative account of later developments is contained in A. Whiting's "'Contradictions' in the Moscow-Peking Axis," *The Journal of Politics*, February 1958, reprinted as a chapter in J. H. Hallowell, ed., *Soviet Satellite Nations* (Gainesville, 1958).

1. The Political Background

1. For a thorough discussion of some of the Western assumptions about Soviet conduct and revealing the extent to which Roosevelt was inclined to believe that a major change in Stalin's thinking could be achieved by a policy of conciliation, see H. Feis, *Churchill, Roosevelt, Stalin* (Princeton, 1957). For a more specific treatment of the Polish aspects which played a crucial role in Anglo-American relations with Stalin, see E. Rozek, *Allied Wartime Diplomacy* (New York, 1958). Revealing materials are contained in the wartime correspondence among the Big Three. See the two volumes entitled *Correspondence between the Chairman of the Council of Ministers of the USSR and the Presidents of the USA and the Prime Ministers of Great Britain during the Great Patriotic War of 1941–1945* (Moscow, 1957).

2. Already by the summer of 1945 the worth of this equipment was officially estimated at half a million United States dollars. *Rzeczpospolita*, August 27, 1945.

3. For a provocative study of the appeal of Marxism to East European intellectuals, see C. Milosz, *The Captive Mind* (New York, 1953). Those who feel that events of 1956 disprove Milosz ought to remember that he was discussing this early period.

4. It is to be remembered that even in prewar East Europe the extent of public ownership and governmental control of economy was considerable and generally accepted. See also Chapter 5.

5. For an interesting account by one of the former underground leaders and a prominent peasant party chief during this period of open struggle with the Communists, see S. Korbonski, *W Imieniu Kremla* (Paris, 1956). For the background of the diplomatic maneuvers leading up to the setting up of this government, see Rozek; and for the particulars of the Communist organization, see M. K. Dziewanowski, *The Communist Party of Poland* (Cambridge, 1959).

6. For some recent revelations, see M. Malinowski, "In the Stormy Era"

NOTES TO CHAPTER 1

("W Wazkim, burzliwym okresie dziejow"), *Polityka* (Warsaw) December 21, 1957; for detailed treatment, see Dziewanowski, *passim.*

7. O. Halecki, ed., *Poland* (New York, 1957), p. 108. For detailed data, see the collection of documents, *P.P.R.* (Warsaw, 1959), pp. 291–292.

8. A. Iwanska, ed., *Contemporary Poland* (Human Relations Area Files, 1955), p. 316.

9. Cf. Korbonski.

10. For his own story, see *The Rape of Poland* (New York, 1948).

11. N. Spulber, *The Economics of Communist Eastern Europe* (New York, 1957), p. 232. This is the best treatment of the subject.

12. *Dziennik Ustaw Rzeczypospolitej Polskiej*, no. 3, item 17, 1946.

13. Spulber, p. 59.

14. Cf. H. Minc in *Zycie Warszawy*, January 3, 1946; *Plan Odbudowy Gospodarczej* (Warsaw, 1947); J. Marczewski, *Planification et Croissance Economique des Democraties Populaires* (Paris, 1956), esp. pp. 111–117.

15. L. Dellin, ed., *Bulgaria* (New York, 1957), p. 121; S. Kertesz, ed., *The Fate of East Central Europe* (Notre Dame, 1956) p. 278. For the most comprehensive treatment, see H. Seton-Watson, *The East European Revolution* (New York, 1956).

16. *Pravda*, January 27, 1948.

17. Y. Gluckstein, *Stalin's Satellites in Europe* (London, 1952), p. 15.

18. H. L. Roberts, *Rumania: Political Problems of an Agrarian State* (New Haven, 1951), p. 291. The best study on the subject.

19. *Ibid.*, pp. 294–298.

20. For the Yugoslav account, amply illustrated by alleged conversations between the Soviet and Yugoslav leaders, see V. Dedijer, *Tito* (New York, 1952). See also Chapter 3.

21. V. I. Lenin, *"Left-wing" Communism — An Infantile Disorder* (New York), p. 862.

2. Problems of Theory

1. I benefited a great deal from two excellent studies of this problem: H. G. Skilling, " 'People's Democracy' in Soviet Theory," *Soviet Studies*, July 1951; and R. J. Medalie, "The Policy of Take-Over," *Public Policy*, VII (Cambridge, 1956), originally submitted to my graduate seminar on comparative totalitarianism at Harvard University.

2. *Selected Works* (New York, 1943), VII, 241.

3. "State and Revolution" in *Selected Works*, p. 34 (italics his).

4. *Problems of Leninism* (Moscow, 1940), p. 660.

5. Lenin, p. 341.

6. Stalin, p. 135.

7. See P. A. Toma, "The Slovak Soviet Republic of 1919," *The American Slavic and East European Review*, April 1958.

8. *Kommunisticheskaia Partiia Polshi v borbe za nezavisimost svoei strany* (Moscow, 1955).

9. Malinowski, "In the Stormy Era," p. 2.

10. "People's Democracy: The Way to the Peaceful Development of Poland," *Glos Ludu*, no. 330, 1946. See also W. Bienkowski, "The Practice and Theory of the People's Democracy," *Nowe Drogi*, January-February 1948.

11. Quoted in E. Kardelj, *On People's Democracy in Jugoslavia* (New York, no date), p. 14.

12. Quoted in V. Chervenkov, "The Activities of the Bulgarian Workers' Party," *For a Lasting Peace, for a People's Democracy*, no. 3 (December 15, 1947), p. 2; see also T. Dragoicheva, *Politicheska, Organizatsionna i Stopanska Deinost* (Sofia, 1955).

13. W. Gomulka, *W Walce o Demokracje Ludowa* (Warsaw, 1947), I, 303.

14. K. Gottwald, *Deset let* (Prague, 1947), p. 284, as quoted in P. Zinner, *The Strategy and Tactics of the Czechoslovak Communist Party* (unpublished Ph.D. thesis, Harvard University, 1953), p. 127.

15. Bierut, quoted in Kardelj, p. 29.

16. Bierut, *ibid.*

17. This is actually a paraphrase of Gottwald (as quoted in Zinner).

18. Gomulka, I, 199.

19. *Ibid.*, p. 305.

20. Address before the Second Congress of the Hungarian Communist Party, as quoted in Kardelj, p. 9.

21. The following were the most authoritative discussions: E. S. Varga, "Democracies of a New Type," *Mirovoie Khoziaistvo i Mirovaia Politika*, no. 3, 1947; I. P. Trainin, "Democracy of a Special Type," *Sovetskoie Gosudarstvo i Pravo*, nos. 1 and 3, 1947; A. Leontiev, "The Economic Bases of the New Democracy," *Planovoie Khoziaistvo*, no. 4, 1947. Varga's articles represent a reconsideration of some of his views pertaining to East Europe advanced in his book, *Izmeneniia v Ekonomike Kapitalizma v itoge vtoroi mirovoi voiny* (Moscow, 1946), chapter 15.

22. Trainin, no. 1, p. 3.

23. *Bolshevik*, no. 6 (1947), p. 23.

24. L. Gelberg, ed., *Nowe Konstytucje Panstw Europejskich* (Warsaw, 1949).

25. A. Prochazka, "Changes in the Philosophy of Czechoslovak Law" (Microfilm, Library of Congress), pp. 11–12.

26. *Democratie Nouvelle*, September 1947, p. 463. In his book cited above Varga listed the economies of the People's Democracies as part of the capitalist world.

27. For an interesting comparative discussion, see S. Ossowski, *Struktura Klasowa w Spolecznej Swiadomosci* (Wroclaw, 1957).

28. See Seton-Watson, *The East European Revolution*.

29. Cf. Lenin, "Critical Remarks on the National Question" (1913), "Right of Nations to Self-Determination" (1914), "Revolutionary Proletariat and Right of Nations to Self-Determination" (1915), "Preliminary Theses on National-Colonial Question" (1920); Stalin's *Marxism and the National and Colonial Question*.

30. *Sochineniya*, XXXI/2, 660.

31. *Sochineniya*, 3rd ed., XXV, 290 (italics added).

32. Lenin, quoted in M. Djilas without specific source, "Lenin on Relations between Socialist States," *Komunist* (Belgrade), September 1949.

33. *Sochineniya* (Moscow, 1947), V. 265, from speech to the Twelfth Party Congress.

34. Lenin, XXV, 624.

35. See Malinowski.

36. E. Kardelj, "On People's Democracy in Yugoslavia," *Komunist* (Belgrade), July 1949; English translation in pamphlet form, cited in note 11, p. 4. This cited view was held from the very beginning and, after the break, the Yugoslav leaders were fond of reminding their Stalinist comrades in East Europe that in the initial period the East Europeans had deviated from true Leninism.

37. *Sluzhebni List*, February 1, 1946; Gelberg.

38. Kardelj, pp. 19-20 (italics added).

3. Problems of Diversity

1. Cf. Z. Brzezinski, ed., *Political Controls in the Soviet Army* (New York, 1954).

2. For the full text of the pertinent resolution, see *KPSS v Rezoliutsiiakh i Resheniiakh S'ezdov, Konferentsii i Plenumov TsK*, III (Moscow, 1954), 476-484.

3. *Ibid.*, pp. 485-494.

4. *Ibid.*, pp. 495-501.

5. *Pravda*, November 7, 1946.

6. Malinowski, "In the Stormy Era."

7. See M. Rutkiewicz, "On the 15th Anniversary of the Polish Workers' Party," *Kalendarz Robotniczy 1957* (Warsaw, 1957) for the recollections of a participant in the flight.

8. For an account, see S. Clissold, *The Whirlwind* (New York, 1949) or A. Ulam, *Titoism and the Cominform* (Cambridge, 1953).

9. A comprehensive study of the Hungarian Communist Party is being prepared at Harvard University by C. Stastny. For an informative memoir, see G. Paloczi-Horvath, *The Undefeated* (London, 1959).

10. Zinner, *The Strategy and Tactics of the Czechoslovak Communist Party*, p. 84.

11. For the East Germans, see the account of W. Leonhard, *Child of the Revolution* (Chicago, 1958).

12. All these messages are cited by M. Pijade, *About the Legend that the Jugoslav Uprising Owed its Existence to Soviet Assistance* (London, 1950), 11.

13. *Ibid.*, esp. pp. 9, 10, 20.

14. For a fuller discussion, see Malinowski. My interpretation of this period differs from that in Dziewanowski, *The Communist Party of Poland*. For an informative account of the ideological confusion that prevailed in the Soviet sponsored Polish army and of the frequent clashes with the more orthodox Communists, see I. Blum, *Z Dziejow Aparatu Politycznego Wojska Polskiego* (Warsaw, 1957).

15. J. Schoeplin, "The Hungarian Communist Party's Road, 1945-1950," *Latohatar* (Munich), 1955, VI, 241-242.

16. For a fuller discussion of the latter, see Ulam, *Titoism and the Cominform*.

17. *Trybuna Wolnosci*, December 22, 1944.

18. K. Gottwald, *Statement of Policy* (Prague, 1946), p. 54.

19. I. Nagy, *On Communism* (New York, 1957), p. 239.

20. See H. Ripka, *Le Coup de Prague* (Paris, 1949).
21. *The Soviet-Jugoslav Dispute* (London, 1948).
22. Dedijer, *Tito*, pp. 272, 303.
23. Dedijer, p. 317.
24. *Ibid.*, p. 305.
25. *Pravda*, January 28, 1948.
26. Dedijer, pp. 316–318.
27. *Ibid.*, p. 317.
28. *Ibid.*, p. 291.
29. *Ibid.*, p. 292.
30. *For a Lasting Peace, for a People's Democracy*, no. 1, November 10, 1947.
31. *Ibid.*
32. See speech by E. Kardelj, *ibid.*; good commentary in Ulam.
33. Dedijer, p. 297.
34. Cf. the correspondence between the two Central Committees, published either by the RIIA in London, or the Belgrade publications, and also the discussion by Ulam.

4. The Theory Reconsidered

1. Radio Prague, December 21, 1952.
2. For the treatment of the ideological dispute, see Ulam, *Titoism and the Cominform;* for historical background, Dziewanowski, *The Communist Party of Poland.*
3. Cf. *For a Lasting Peace, for a People's Democracy*, speeches by V. Chervenkov, "Leading Role of Bulgarian Workers' Party (Communist) in Building the People's Democracy," June 15, 1948; speech by M. Rakosi, April 15, 1948; and Gheorghiu-Dej, March 1, 1948, and so on.
4. Cf. Rakosi's address to the Third Party Conference, *ibid.*, February 15, 1948; and Gheorghiu-Dej, "Consolidating the People's Democracy in Rumania," *ibid.*, January 1, 1948.
5. For example, Chervenkov to the Second Congress of the Fatherland Front, *ibid.*, February 1, 1948.
6. *Ibid.*, April 15, 1948.
7. Revai, p. 147.
8. See Ulam, Dziewanowski.
9. H. Minc, speaking at the Central Committee session, *Nowe Drogi*, no. 11 (1948), p. 57.
10. Bierut, *Nowe Drogi, ibid.*, p. 24. See also B. Bierut and J. Cyrankiewiez, *Podstawy ideologiczne PZPR* (Warsaw, 1952).
11. October 15, 1948.
12. Text in *Pravda*, December 21, 1948; see also M. Rakosi, "What is a People's Democracy?" *Szabad Nep*, January 16, 1949.
13. For the fullest treatment of the Soviet contribution, see H. G. Skilling, "'People's Democracy' in Soviet Theory"; for a chronological discussion of similar processes in East Europe see R. J. Medalie, "The Policy of Take-Over." The section to follow owes much to both these excellent studies.
14. *Zagadnienia Prawne Konstytucji Polskiej Rzeczypospolitej Ludowej,*

I–III (Warsaw, 1954); hereafter cited as *Zagadnienia Prawne*. For an orthodox statement of the legal aspects see also S. Rozmaryn, *Polskie Prawo Panstwowe* (Warsaw, 1951).

15. Among the most authoritative Soviet statements are: N. P. Farberov, *Gosudarstvennoe Pravo Stran Norodnoi Demokratii* (Moscow, 1949); A. Sobolev, "People's Democracy as a Form of Political Organization of Society," a lecture delivered at the Moscow Party Training Center and published in *Bolshevik*, no. 19, 1951 and *Nowe Drogi*, no. 5, 1951; E. Burdzhalov, "Concerning the International Significance of the Historic Experience of the Bolshevik Party," *Bolshevik*, no. 17, 1948; cf. also sources cited in Skilling, pp. 17–19.

16. Farberov, p. 27.

17. *Pravda*, April 27, 1949; Skilling, p. 133.

18. *Zagadnienia Prawne*, II, 58 and I, 251.

19. Farberov, p. 35.

20. *Zagadnienia Prawne*, I, 166.

21. *Ibid.*, II, 85.

22. Farberov, pp. 21–24.

23. *Zagadnienia Prawne*, II, 136.

24. See H. G. Skilling, "The Czech Constitutional System," *Political Science Quarterly*, June 1952.

25. Farberov, "On the Character of the People's Democratic State," *Nowe Drogi*, III (1949), 57–58.

26. *Ibid.*

27. *Zagadnienia Prawne*, I, 354.

28. Farberov, p. 37.

29. Farberov, *Nowe Drogi*, III, 158.

30. *Bolshevik*, no. 17, 1948.

31. Revai, p. 147.

32. See particularly Gheorghiu-Dej, "Betrayal of Revolutionary Marxism," a violent diatribe in *For a Lasting Peace, for a People's Democracy*, July 1, 1948; and V. Kolarov, "Struggle against Nationalism in the Bulgarian Communist Party," *ibid.*, May 15, 1949. It is noteworthy that at the time Kolarov was competing against Chervenkov for leadership in the party.

33. Sobolev, p. 96.

34. *Ibid.*, p. 95.

35. See *Zagadnienia Prawne*, I, II; *Nowe Konstytucje Panstw Europejskich;* the Mid-European Studies Center volumes on the countries of East Europe; and S. Sharp, *New Constitutions in the Soviet Sphere* (Washington, 1950).

36. See *Proiekt za konstitutsia na narodna republika Bulgaria* (Sofia, 1946). For the later version, see Sharp.

37. Farberov, *Sovetskoe Gosudarstvo i Pravo*, no. 4 (1950), p. 83 (above translation taken from Skilling, p. 144). See also Farberov's book for similar assertions, for instance, p. 42.

38. *Zagadnienia Prawne*, I, 115.

39. *Ibid.*, I, 351.

40. *Ibid.*, II, 134.

41. *Ibid.*, I, 256.

42. *Ibid.*

43. *Ibid.*, III, 194. For some broader problems, see M. P. Kareva, *Pravo i Nravstvennost v Sotsialicheskom Obshchestve* (Moscow, 1954). For the revision of the Bulgarian code on the Soviet pattern, see *News from Behind the Iron Curtain*, April 1952, p. 11.

44. Farberov, p. 43. See also his comparisons with bourgeois constitutions, pp. 43–45.

45. *Chronologische Materialien zur Geschichte der SED* (Berlin, 1956), p. 7.

46. From his address in April 1948 to the Party Academy in East Berlin, cited by W. Leonhard, *Die Revolution Entlaesst Ihre Kinder* (Berlin, 1955), pp. 483–484; English translation: *Child of the Revolution* (Chicago, 1958).

47. Otto Grotewohl in *For a Lasting Peace, for a People's Democracy*, March 1, 1949.

48. *Einheit*, no. 4 (1957), p. 400. For some Soviet views on this subject, see D. Melnikov, *Borba za edinuiu, nezavisimuiu, demokraticheskuiu Germaniu* (Moscow, 1951); Akademia Nauk SSSR, *Voprosy stroitelstva edinovo demokraticheskovo germanskovo Gosudarstva* (Moscow, 1951); for an analysis of the earliest period, see M. Croan, "Soviet Uses of the Doctrine of the 'Parliamentary Road' to Socialism; East Germany: 1945–1946," *American Slavic and East European Review*, October 1958.

5. Laying the Socialist Foundations

1. See M. Fainsod, *How Russia Is Ruled* (Cambridge, 1953).

2. The following studies, prepared by the Mid-European Studies Center (all New York, 1958) contain special chapters dealing with these matters: S. Skendi, ed., *Albania*; L. A. D. Dellin, ed., *Bulgaria*; O. Halecki, ed., *Poland*; V. Busek, ed., *Czechoslovakia*; S. Fisher-Galati, ed., *Romania*; E. Helmreich, ed., *Hungary*; R. F. Byrnes, ed., *Yugoslavia*.

3. *Rude Pravo*, June 28, 1953. For further treatment see *News from Behind the Iron Curtain*, October 1953, pp. 37–46.

4. J. Revai to Budapest architects, *Tarsadalmi Szemle*, September 1951.

5. J. Skrzeszot, *Nowe Drogi*, no. 5, 1953.

6. For a statement of the Communist point of view, see S. Zawadzki, *Rozwoj Wiezi Rad Narodowych z Masami Pracujacymi w Polsce Ludowej* (Warsaw, 1955). The allegedly advanced democratic character of the councils was based on a claim to broad popular representation with each deputy representing a relatively small number of electors. This was compared critically with the Western model and cited as proof of real democracy. However, the consequence was that these huge councils were structurally unable to make policy, not to mention the external pressures for their subservience.

7. For a compact collection of all the plans and some official accomplishment reports, see *Plany Razvitiia Narodnovo Khoziaistva Stran Narodnoi Demokratii* (Moscow, 1952).

8. E. Drozniak, "For Improving and Lowering the Costs of the State Apparatus," *Nowe Drogi*, no. 2, 1955.

9. Spulber, *The Economics of Communist Eastern Europe*, p. 126.

10. *Zycie gospodarcze*, no. 15, 1950.

11. *Zagadnienia Prawne*, II, 281.

12. *Lidova Demokracie*, December 23, 1952.

13. R. Carlton, ed., *Forced Labor in the People's Democracies* (New York, 1956): for a Polish Communist account of the use of forced labor in coal mining, and of abuses thereof, see *Trybuna Ludu*, June 6, 1956, p. 4.

14. Z. Brzezinski, *The Permanent Purge* (Cambridge, 1956).

15. *Ibid.*, for an extended discussion; also note on p. 147, Chapter 7.

16. In Poland, the secret police even prepared "dossiers" on Politburo members, according to former Politburo member, J. Berman; *Nowe Drogi*, no. 10 (1956), p. 93.

17. December 6, 1951, as quoted in P. Korbel and V. Vagassky, *Purges in the Communist Party of Czechoslovakia* (Radio Free Europe, mimeographed, 1952).

18. *Nowe Drogi*, no. 10, pp. 85–95.

19. *Moscow's European Satellites* (U.S. Department of State, 1955), p. 16; also speech by F. Jozwiak-Witold, *Nowe Drogi*, no. 3 (1953), p. 53, and *News from Behind the Iron Curtain* for the period.

20. *Seria Filozoficzna* (*Nowe Drogi*), II, no. 2 (1949), 24.

21. *Zagadnienia Prawne*, I, 21.

22. *Nowe Drogi*, no. 6 (1954), p. 19. See also S. Skrzypek, "Agricultural Policies in Poland, 1950–1954," *Journal of Central European Affairs*, XVI, no. 1 (1956).

23. See *News from Behind the Iron Curtain*, July 1952, p. 27 and May 1953, p. 31; *Nowe Drogi*, no. 1 (1956), p. 106; Spulber, pp. 254, 261; McVicker, *passim*.

24. B. Bierut, "Poland on the Road to Socialism," *Bolshevik*, no. 21 (1950), p. 23.

25. For a laudatory description of each of the above undertakings, see V. P. Maksakovsky, *Stroiki Sotsializma v evropeiskikh stranakh narodnoi demokratii* (Moscow, 1952).

26. Spulber, pp. 326–327; J. Wszelaki, "The Rise of Industrial Middle Europe," *Foreign Affairs*, October 1951.

27. H. Minc, "On the Proportions in the Development of the National Economy," *Gospodarka Planowa*, December 1954.

28. J. Hajda, ed., *A Study of Contemporary Czechoslovakia* (New Haven, 1955), p. 487.

29. A good graphic illustration is a series of comparative tables on some production items in Spulber, pp. 367–380.

30. Spulber, p. 384. See also Marczewski, cited in Chapter 1, note 14, pp. 202–206.

31. *Rude Pravo*, January 15, 1952.

6. Stalinism: A Pattern for the Communist Interstate System

1. *Pravda*, June 20, 1950.

2. *Ibid.* (italics added).

3. *Ibid.*

4. *Ibid.*

5. For a good survey, see P. S. Wandycz, "The Soviet System of Alliances

in East Central Europe," *Journal of Central European Affairs*, XVI, no. 2 (July 1956). See also G. A. Deborin, *Mezhdunarodnie Otnosheniya i Vneshnaiaia Politika Sovetskogo Soiuza, 1945–1949* (Moscow, 1958), esp. Chapter 3; *Zagadnienie Bezpieczenstwa Zbiorowego w Europie* (Warsaw, 1955), particularly the contribution by C. Berezowski, "Mutual Aid Treaties and the Collective Security System"; E. Korovin, *Nerushimaia Druzhba Narodov SSSR i Narodno-Demokraticheskikh Stran* (Moscow, 1955).

6. Wandycz makes the point that only the Bulgarian-Rumanian treaty spoke of aid against any aggressor.

7. *Zagadnienia Prawne*, II, 546. On October 12, 1949, Otto Grotewolh's government announced its acceptance of this frontier, but it was a unilateral declaration. In January 1951, a final settlement of frontier delimitation was made by the two regimes (I, 146).

8. For an official discussion, see *Zagadnienia Prawne*, II, 540–599.

9. Dates of formal Cominform meetings: (1) September 22–23, 1947; (2) late January, 1948; (3) around June 20, 1948; (4) November 27, 1949. *Ost-Probleme*, no. 27 (1952), pp. 827–833.)

10. Dedijer, *Tito*. See also Chapter 3.

11. For organized Soviet efforts, see A. Inkeles, *Public Opinion in Soviet Russia* (Cambridge, 1950).

12. Halecki, *Poland*, p. 147.

13. Dellin, *Bulgaria*, p. 227.

14. Fisher-Galati, *Romania*, p. 80.

15. A. Gide, *Return from the USSR* (New York, 1937), p. 56.

16. J. Swiatlo, testimony no. 13, "How Poland is Really Ruled" (unpublished mimeographed material).

17. Nagy again, *On Communism*, cites specific instances of Hungarian "reports" to the CPSU (for instance, p. 75).

18. S. Bialer, *Wybralem Prawde*, RFE (New York, 1956), pp. 11–12.

19. Swiatlo.

20. *News from Behind the Iron Curtain*, March 1952, p. 5.

21. Col. Lewikowski and Col. Kuryluk respectively. Information is based on conversations with Polish Communists. Kuryluk is a former Soviet parachutist.

22. Bialer, p. 11.

23. *Nowe Drogi*, no. 10 (1956), p. 88.

24. S. Korbonski, *W Imieniu Rzeczypospolitej* (Paris, 1954), chapter 23.

25. Swiatlo.

26. Based on Swiatlo, *Za kulisami bezpieki i partii*, RFE leaflet, pp. 22–25.

27. Dedijer, p. 328.

28. *News from Behind the Iron Curtain*, March 1952, p. 5.

29. Berman, p. 88, cites the case of incriminating materials arriving from Moscow against his personal secretary and others.

30. Swiatlo, *Za kulisami . . .* , p. 4.

31. For the most extended treatment, see I. de Sola Pool, ed., *Satellite Generals* (Stanford, 1955); for material on Soviet officers in the Polish army, p. 150.

32. In 1956, after his expulsion, nineteen high officers, all with outstanding war records, were posthumously rehabilitated in Poland. They had been shot

several years earlier on trumped-up charges of conspiracy. *Kultura i Spole-czenstwo*, no. 1 (January 1957), pp. 276–277.

33. See recollections of General B. Kiraly, *News from Behind the Iron Curtain*, March 1958.

34. Informal conversations of the author in East Europe.

35. Spulber, pp. 180–181. For an evaluation of the East German, Rumanian, and Hungarian payments, see V. Winston, "The Soviet Satellites — Economic Liability?" *Problems of Communism*, January 1958.

36. This figure is derived from the settlement made by the USSR on November 18, 1956.

37. For a list of properties seized, see Spulber, pp. 207–223.

38. *Ibid.*, p. 191; Roberts, *Rumania: Political Problems of an Agricultural State*, p. 320, observes that "These concerns clearly gave the Soviet Union a controlling position at key points in the Rumanian economy."

39. Spulber, p. 188. See also Columbia Hungarian Interview Project, Interview 202.

40. H. Minc, "The Fruitful Cooperation of the Free Nations," *Zycie Gospodarcze*, no. 20 (1951), p. 1101.

41. Ivanov; *Rude Pravo*, January 1, 1953; Minc; *News from Behind the Iron Curtain*, September 1952, p. 33.

42. For a general discussion, see *News from Behind the Iron Curtain*, September 1952, pp. 28–32.

43. Spulber, p. 430.

44. *Ibid.*, pp. 438–439.

45. See B. I. Schwartz, *Chinese Communism and the Rise of Mao* (Cambridge, 1952).

46. "On the People's Democratic Dictatorship" (Hong Kong, 1949), as quoted in H. Wei, *China and Soviet Russia* (New York, 1956), p. 264.

47. This was explicitly asserted by covering press editorials: for example, *Jen Min Jih Pao* of February 26, 1950, and *Pravda*, same date.

48. Wei, pp. 269–273.

49. *Ibid.*, pp. 273–274.

50. In W. W. Rostow, *The Prospects for Communist China* (New York, 1954), p. 208, M. X. Hsieh's unpublished study is cited for the estimate of 7,000 Soviet military advisers. For the role of Soviet advisers in training the Chinese Air Force see de Sola Pool, *Satellite Generals*, p. 136.

51. Rostow, p. 194.

52. *Ibid.*, p. 192; Boorman, p. 70.

53. Mao Tse-tung, *Jen Min Jih Pao*, October 8, 1949; Wei, p. 292.

54. For a treatment of this topic see B. I. Schwartz, "China and the Soviet Theory of People's Democracy," *Problems of Communism*, III, no. 5 (1954).

55. On alleged equality of status between Soviet and Chinese technicians, see Wei, p. 292.

56. *Pravda*, October 6, 1952.

57. Nagy, pp. 38–39 (italics added).

58. *Pravda*, October 6, 1952.

7. The Stalinist Legacy

1. Published in the United States under the title *On Communism* (New York, 1957).

2. Materials cited from this project are listed under the interview number. Interview 563 is particularly interesting since it contains testimony of a party official active in the daily organ of the Central Committee and exposed to the process of disillusionment with the Stalinist legacy as discussed in this chapter.

3. Nagy, pp. 50, 221; see also Hungarian Interviews 152, 563.

4. Nagy, p. 51. See also statement by J. Berman, *Nowe Drogi*, no. 10, 1956, where he pleads guilty to having fallen under the spell of "suspicion psychosis" and concedes the moral degeneration of the secret-police personnel. See also Hungarian Interview 502.

5. Nagy, p. 279.

6. Bienkowski, *Rewolucji Ciag Dalszy* (Warsaw, 1957), p. 36. This is a collection of essays published earlier.

7. *Ibid.*, p. 6.

8. *Ibid.*, p. 20.

9. *Ibid.*, p. 21.

10. The Hungarian Interview Project shows ample evidence of this. Similarly, many statements made in the East European press during 1956 and in China during 1957 refer to this phenomenon.

11. Nagy, p. 60.

12. Bienkowski, p. 146.

13. *Ibid.*, p. 98.

14. Nagy, p. 44.

15. Bienkowski, p. 82.

16. E. Ochab, Radio Warsaw, August 16, 1956; this remark was not reproduced in the *Trybuna Ludu* text of the speech.

17. Bienkowski, p. 61.

18. M. Pohorille, "On the Antagonistic and Nonantagonistic Contradictions between the City and the Countryside," *Nowe Drogi*, no. 5 (1951), p. 57.

19. Bienkowski, p. 48, states this explicitly.

20. For detailed data see Gomulka's address, *Nowe Drogi*, no. 10, 1956; for comparative productivity of the public and private sectors, see Gomulka, *ibid.*, and Spulber, pp. 261–263.

21. For such data, see Economic Commission for Europe, *Economic Bulletin for Europe*, VIII, no. 2, based on cost of food baskets. For a discussion of prevailing concerns among the planners, see the account by F. Schenk and R. Lowenthal, "Soft Goods vs. Hard Goods," *The New Leader*, January 5, 1959. Schenk is a former East German planner. For an extensive critique of the centralized planning system, of the unreliability of the index figures, of the bonus system, of the mishandling of consumer-goods production, of the dogmatic Stalinist planning (pp. 170–171), see the study by a Hungarian economist, J. Kornai, *A Gazdasagi Vezetes Tulzott Központositasa* (Budapest, 1957).

22. For example, testimony of J. Berman, *Nowe Drogi*, no. 10, 1956.

23. J. V. Stalin, "Economic Problems of Socialism in the USSR." *Bolshevik*, September 1952; I use here the translation of L. Gruliow, ed., *Current Soviet Policies* (New York, 1953), p. 9.

24. *Ibid.*, p. 2.
25. *Ibid.*, p. 10.
26. *Pravda*, October 15, 1952, as quoted in Gruliow, p. 235.
27. The Doctors' Plot involved the arrest of a number of prominent Moscow doctors, mostly Jewish. They were charged with plotting to do away with leading Soviet statesmen. *Pravda*, January 13, 1953.

8. The New Course: Stalinism Dissipated

1. For Soviet reference to a serious lag in the agricultural sector, see M. P. Kim, ed., *Istoriya SSSR* (Moscow, 1957), p. 681.
2. See J. N. Hazard, "Governmental Developments in the USSR since Stalin," *The Annals of the American Academy of Political and Social Science*, January 1956.
3. December 21, 1954.
4. *Pravda*, February 3, 1955.
5. For an account of the uprising, see S. Brant, *The East German Rising, 17th June 1953*, translated and adapted by C. Wheeler (New York, 1957).
6. This was reiterated at the Twenty-eighth Plenum three years later. *Neues Deutschland*, August 12, 1956.
7. *Economic Survey of Europe since the War* (United Nations, no date), p. 29.
8. Nagy, p. 66.
9. According to Nagy's account, pp. 106–107, the Soviet leaders concentrated their criticisms mainly on the economic aspects of the Hungarian scene.
10. *News from Behind the Iron Curtain*, August 1953, p. 47. (Major parts of the speech are translated in that issue; for a broad justification of these policies, see Imre Nagy's book.)
11. *Ibid.*
12. J. Jaroslawski, "Struggle on Two Fronts in Party Work in the Countryside," *Nowe Drogi*, no. 12 (1953), p. 19, cites data with tables on the class distribution of the peasantry in Poland, showing that the medium farmer was the backbone of the peasantry.
13. S. Jedrychowski, "The People's Democracies in the Struggle for a More Rapid Increase in the Standard of Living of the Working Masses," *Nowe Drogi*, no. 11 (1953), p. 16.
14. *Ibid.*
15. Jedrychowski, p. 16.
16. *Pravda*, February 20, 1954.
17. M. Fainsod, "The CPSU Since Stalin," *Problems of Communism*, January-February 1958, p. 8. For a detailed analysis of Khrushchev's rise, see Fainsod's "What Happened to 'Collective Leadership'?" *Problems of Communism*, July-August 1959; also M. Rush, *The Rise of Khrushchev* (Washington, 1958).
18. See *Pravda*, December 21, 1954 (article by V. Kruzhkov) and January 24, 1955 (article by D. Shepilow) for good statements of the Khrushchev position.
19. *Pravda*, March 21, 1955 (italics added).

20. *Ibid.*

21. For instance, Hsiueh Mu-chiao, "China on the Path of Socialist Industrialization," *Pravda*, June 22, 1954; Liao Lu-yen, "Along the Path of Socialist Transformation of China's Agriculture," *Pravda*, July 11, 1954.

22. Boorman, p. 131 (B. Schwartz).

23. See the discussion of this in Chapter 6; and Boorman et al., p. 128.

24. *Pravda*, July 16, 1955.

25. See E. Taborsky, "The 'Old' and the 'New' Course in Satellite Economy," *Journal of Central European Affairs*, January 1958, esp. pp. 383, 387–391.

26. *Moskovskoe soveshchanie* (Moscow, 1954), for the official speeches and communiqué.

27. For texts and speeches, see *Varshavskoe Soveshchanie Evropeiskikh Gosudarstv* (Moscow, 1955); for a semiofficial Communist evaluation, L. Gelberg, *Uklad Warszawski* (Warsaw, 1957).

28. Cf. V. Siroky, "Economic Cooperation on the Level of the Growing Tasks of the Socialist States," *Pravda*, April 6, 1956; R. Fidelski, *Wspolpraca Gospodarcza Polski z Krajami Socjalistycznymi* (Warsaw, 1959).

29. *Pravda*, July 27, 1956.

30. *Ibid.* See also *Trud*, April 3, 1956, for a detailed account of the capacity of enterprises allegedly constructed by the USSR in Eastern Europe.

31. Spulber, p. 432.

32. *Ibid.*, p. 435; See also *Promyshlenno-ekonomicheskaia gazeta*, January 1, 1957. Fuller treatment in Chapter 12.

33. *Trybuna Ludu*, March 28, 1956.

34. For instance, Nagy, p. 143.

35. For instance, *Pravda, Izvestia*, September 17, 1954, citing *Borba*.

36. *Ibid.*, September 22, 1954. For Tito's views on the EDC, see R. B. Farrell, *Jugoslavia and the Soviet Union, 1948–1956* (The Shoe String Press, 1956), p. 163; also *Pravda*, April 22, 1955.

37. *Pravda*, November 29, 1954.

38. *Ibid.*

39. *Izvestia*, January 6, 1955.

40. *Pravda*, May 18, 1955.

41. *For a Lasting Peace, for a People's Democracy*, May 27, 1955.

42. *New York Times*, June 2, 1955; *Pravda* explicitly mentioned the points quoted above in its commentary on the agreement.

43. Our information is based in part on the testimony, written and oral, of S. Bialer, a former member of the Polish Central Committee's staff, who was shown the transcripts of the Moscow proceedings (*Wybralem Prawde*, part 1, pp. 9–16); in part on subsequent Soviet developments, for instance, the July 1957 purge of Molotov, and on pertinent speeches to the Twenty-first CPSU Congress in 1959.

44. *Pravda*, July 16, 1955.

45. *Ibid* (italics added).

46. *Kommunist*, no. 14 (1955), p. 127.

47. *Ibid.*

48. *Ibid.*

49. Text in *Current Digest of the Soviet Press*, VIII, no. 4, 1956.

50. See *News from Behind the Iron Curtain*, April and May 1956, for some reactions; also Chapter 9.

51. *Current Digest*, VIII, no. 8 (italics added).

52. *Ibid.* (italics added).

9. The Impact of Yugoslavia

1. For example, comments of Radio Zagreb, April 18, describing it as the outmoded appendage of Stalinism.

2. *Borba*, March 20, 1956 (italics added).

3. Early in 1956 Yugoslavia had been granted $110 million credit. *Tanjug*, Feb. 2, 1956.

4. *New York Times*, June 21, 1956.

5. For example, *Borba*, October 3, 1948; for a doctrinaire, anti-Western statement, charging the United States with plotting against the USSR and asserting that the forces of peace are headed by the USSR, see E. Kardelj's report, *The Communist Party of Yugoslavia in the Struggle for New Yugoslavia, for People's Authority and for Socialism* (Belgrade, 1948).

6. Text of speech in Farrell, *op. cit.*, 107.

7. Ulam, p. 138.

8. For comprehensive treatments of the Yugoslav system, see A. Dragnitch, *Tito's Promised Land* (New Brunswick, 1954); C. P. McVicker, *Titoism* (New York, 1957); F. W. Neal, *Titoism in Action* (Berkeley, 1958). The last two are more inclined than Dragnitch to stress the distinctive, less totalitarian features of the Yugoslav system.

9. For instance, M. Bace, "On Critique and Auto-critique in the USSR," *Komunist* (Belgrade), no. 6, 1949.

10. For instance, J. Broz-Tito, *Workers Manage Factories in Jugoslavia* (Belgrade, 1950), pp. 12, 26; or E. Kardelj's speech to the Sixth Congress of the CPJ, quoted in Farrell, esp. p. 138; or M. Djilas, *On New Roads of Socialism* (Belgrade, 1950).

11. Cf. McVicker for a thorough survey.

12. Sixth Congress, Zagreb, 1952.

13. For instance, E. Kardelj, *Borba*, December 9, 1956.

14. L. Stoyovic, "Seven Years of Experience," *Politika*, June 25, 1957; Benj. Ward, "Workers' Management in Yugoslavia," *The Journal of Political Economy*, October 1957.

15. *Borba*, March 20, 1953.

16. E. Kardelj, "Socialist Democracy in Yugoslav Practice," *Borba*, January 1, 1955; part 5 of McVicker, pp. 245–305, is devoted to an exposition of the official Yugoslav view.

17. Z. Brihta, "One Year Since Stalin's Death," *Vjesnik*, March 4, 1954.

18. Evidence for this is cited by R. Lowenthal in his letter to *The New Leader*, February 9, 1959.

19. A communiqué noted merely that "satisfaction was expressed" by Gheorghiu-Dej, Novotny, and Rakosi at this turn of events. *For a Lasting Peace, for a People's Democracy*, June 10, 1955.

20. *Borba*, July 28, 1955.

21. For example, Radio Zagreb, August 6, 1955.

22. For example, Tito's speech, including critical references to the East European states, was reprinted in *Pravda*, July 30, 1955.

23. *Ibid.*

24. Tito's speech of October 25, 1954, in Farrell, p. 171.

25. Radio Budapest, August 8, 1955.

26. For details, Radio Zagreb, November 3, 1955; *Politika*, November 1955; *Mlada Fronta*, December 3, 1955.

27. For instance, Radio Sofia, September 8, 1955, speech by Georgi Chankov, the Bulgarian Deputy Chairman of the Council of Ministers.

28. Radio Budapest, November 6, 1955.

29. Radio Bratislava, November 7, 1955.

30. Radio Bucharest, November 6, 1955.

31. This was claimed by Tito personally. See K. Zilliacus, *A New Birth of Freedom* (London, 1956), p. 135. Confirmed to the author by a very high-ranking Yugoslav official.

32. *Borba*, for instance, even stated on April 20, 1957, that "national Communism" was a term invented by Western journalists.

33. *Pravda*, April 18, 1956.

34. *Borba*, April 19, 1956.

35. *Borba*, February 26, 1956.

36. Radio Zagreb, July 26, 1956.

37. *Rabotnichesko Delo*, April 9, 1956.

38. Radio Sofia, April 8, 1956; on friendship with Yugoslavia, see *Rabotnichesko Delo*, April 6, 1956.

39. Radio Sofia, April 18, 1956.

40. *Nova Makedonija*, April 26, 1956.

41. Cf. the data in a *Rabotnichesko Delo* editorial, May 17, 1956, which reported that 282,000 farmers had joined in "the past few months"; also *ibid.*, July 13 and August 9, 1956.

42. "Let Us Study and Apply the 20th Congress Decisions of the CPSU and the April Plenum Decisions of the Bulgarian Communist Party," editorial, *Rabotnichesko Delo*, June 9, 1956.

43. Radio Sofia, September 19, 1956 (italics added).

44. Radio Prague, April 9, 1956.

45. *Rude Pravo*, editorial, "The Force of Truth," April 11, 1956.

46. *Rude Pravo*, May 11, 1956.

47. *Rude Pravo*, September 6, 1956.

48. Full texts, Radio Prague, March 30 and June 15, 1956.

49. Radio Tirana, May 25, 1956.

50. Radio Belgrade, May 28, 1956.

51. *Borba*, June 28, 1956.

52. *Neues Deutschland*, March 4, 1956.

53. *Ibid.*, July 31, 1956.

54. "Useful Contacts," *Pravda*, May 4, 1956.

55. *Pravda*, July 2, 1956.

56. *Current Digest of the Soviet Press*, VIII, no. 38. I am indebted to Miss Gail Warshovsky of Radcliffe College for drawing my attention to this quotation.

57. *Borba*, October 12, 1956.

58. *Ibid.*

59. This was reported by Zilliacus as having been confirmed to him by both Khrushchev and Tito separately (pp. 135, 102–103).

10. Hungary: The Test Case of National Communism

1. *Pravda*, May 26, 1954.
2. See membership table, Chapter 5.
3. *News from Behind the Iron Curtain*, July 1954, p. 53.
4. *Szabad Nep*, July 22, 1953.
5. Nagy's selection by Soviet leaders was admitted by Nagy himself, p. 252.
6. Nagy, p. 283.
7. *Ibid.*, p. 282.
8. *Ibid.*, p. 282; also pp. 280, 281.
9. Quoted in *Research Report: Hungarian Party Congress, May 24–30, 1954* (mimeographed, Radio Free Europe), p. 5; hereafter referred to as *Hungarian Party Congress*.
10. *Ibid.*, p. 24.
11. *Ibid.*, p. 25.
12. *Ibid.*, p. 30.
13. *Ibid.*, pp. 6–10.
14. See testimony of S. Bialer (*Wybralem wolnosc*), who recalls the panic and confusion in Warsaw when the article made its appearance. See *Pravda*, January 24, 1955, "The General Party Line and the Vulgar Marxists"; *Neues Deutschland, Rude Pravo*, January 29, 1955.
15. S. Bialer, "The Three Schools of Kremlin Policy," *The New Leader*, July 29, 1957 (allegedly based on actual reading of the said document while working for the Polish Central Committee).
16. March 21, 1955.
17. *Szabad Nep*, Radio Budapest, April 18, 1955.
18. *Szabad Nep*, May 12 and 13, 1955.
19. The date of his thesis dealing with international affairs.
20. Nagy, pp. 26, 28.
21. *Ibid.*, p. 29.
22. *Ibid.*, p. 33 (italics added).
23. *Ibid.*, p. 33; see also p. 244.
24. *Ibid.*, p. 41.
25. For a detailed treatment, see F. Fejtö, *Behind the Rape of Hungary* (New York, 1957) and T. Meray, *Thirteen Days that Shook the Kremlin* (New York, 1959). Hungarian Interviews 563 and 152 provided helpful information on attitudes prevailing in the party, as did a mimeographed study prepared for the Hungarian Project by G. Heltai, entitled "Hungary 1953–1956."
26. For some of their attitudes, see *Proceedings of the Writers Union*, November-December 1955.
27. See *Szabad Nep*, March 27, 1956; Radio Budapest, March 31, 1956.
28. Radio Budapest, May 11, 1956.
29. *Ibid.*, July 9, 1956.
30. *Ibid.*, July 3, 1956.

31. *Szabad Nep*, June 15, 1956.

32. *Ibid.*, June 28, 1956.

33. Radio Budapest, July 7, 1956.

34. *Szabad Nep*, May 28, 1956.

35. *Szabad Nep*, April 13, 1956.

36. *New York Times*, July 9, 1956.

37. Radio Budapest, June 30, 1956.

38. *Szabad Nep*, July 3, 1956.

39. For instance, attacks on the anti-Rakosi literary circles were reprinted by *Pravda*, December 11, 1955.

40. *Szabad Nep*, July 19, 1956. For a purported, and dramatic, account of the Central Committee session (including, for example, Rakosi's vain telephone calls for aid from Khrushchev), see Hungarian Interview 563, pp. 81–82.

41. Zinner, P., ed., *National Communism and Popular Revolt in Eastern Europe* (New York, 1956), p. 346.

42. *Pravda*, October 5, 1956 (100 million rubles, including 40 per cent in cash).

43. *Szabad Nep*, October 7, 1956.

44. Cf. General B. Kiraly's account, "Hungarian Army — Its Part in the Revolt," *East Europe*, June 1958.

45. Speech of October 24, quoted in Zinner, pp. 409–410.

46. Kiraly, p. 7.

47. *Ibid.*, p. 14.

48. Hungarian Interview 152, pp. 88–91. Cf. *Pravda*, "Collapse of the Anti-People's Venture in Hungary," October 28, 1956.

49. *Pravda*, October 31, 1956.

50. *Ibid.*

51. Zinner, pp. 493–494.

52. R. Lowenthal claims that Belgrade considered such a move. See his "Tito's Affair with Khrushchev," *The New Leader*, October 6, 1958.

53. *Borba*, October 30, 1956.

54. Text in *New York Times*, November 5, 1956.

55. *Borba*, November 24, 1956.

56. Text in Zinner, p. 527.

57. Speech in Zinner, p. 527.

58. *Ibid.*, p. 534.

59. For full translation see *New York Times*, November 24, 1956, and *National Communism and Popular Revolt in Eastern Europe*, pp. 541-562.

60. *Borba*, November 26, 1956.

61. *Zeri i Popullit*, editorial, "In Connection with the Speech Recently Delivered by Josip Broz-Tito," November 23, 1956.

62. *Pravda*, December 19, 1956, "Who Stands to Gain by This? — On the Speech of Comrade E. Kardelj."

63. For a concise analysis of the Hungarian revolution per se and for its historical background, see P. E. Zinner's excellent piece, "Revolution in Hungary: Reflections on the Vicissitudes of a Totalitarian System," *Journal of Politics*, March 1959.

11. The Polish October: The Challenge of Domesticism

1. For much more detailed historical treatment, see relevant chapters in Halecki and Dziewanowski; also F. Lewis, *A Case History of Hope* (New York, 1958).

2. For good theoretical treatment see O. Utis, "Generalissimo Stalin and the Art of Government," *Foreign Affairs*, XXX, January 1952; for application in practice, see my *The Permanent Purge*.

3. For instance, *Nowe Drogi*, no. 10 (1953), p. 110.

4. For a partial text in English, see *News from Behind the Iron Curtain*, March 1955.

5. *Nowe Drogi*, no. 10 (1954), pp. 43, 13. See also no. 5, pp. 13–14, for examples of past cultural controls, such as the setting of quotas and themes for painters by a Warsaw office.

6. For a participant's account, see S. Bialer.

7. *Nowe Drogi*, no. 10 (1956), p. 115.

8. *Ibid.*, no. 12 (1954), pp. 10, 12–14.

9. *Ibid.*, no. 2 (1955), p. 2.

10. Bialer, p. 8.

11. *Nowe Drogi*, no. 7 (July 1957), p. 126.

12. D. Zablocka, "Notes on the Intelligentsia," *Nowa Kultura*, September 7, 1958.

13. *Nowe Drogi*, no. 7 (1957), p. 126.

14. S. Zolkiewski, "On Current Literary Discussions," *Nowe Drogi*, no. 6, 1955.

15. For a general account of the clubs, see E. Bryll and J. Garztecki, "Boiled, Burst and Extinguished," *Orka*, November 29, 1957.

16. *Nowa Kultura*, March 6, 1955.

17. J. Siekierska, a lecturer at the Central Committee's Institute of Social Sciences, in *Przeglad Kulturalny*, no. 8, 1955.

18. *Zycie Warszawy*, April 19, 1956.

19. Z. Florczak in *Nowa Kultura*, October 1, 1956. See also W. Godek and R. Turski, "Is this the Decline of Marxism?" *Po Prostu*, June 24, 1956. Their title is suggestive of the prevailing mood.

20. *Aktualne zagadnienia polityki kulturalnej w dziedzinie filozofii i socjologii* (Warsaw, 1956).

21. Based on personal sources in Warsaw. According to my information, Khrushchev's first choice was F. Mazur (reputedly an agent of the MVD), and Ochab was a "compromise" choice.

22. *Pravda*, April 29, 1956.

23. Radio Warsaw, April 21, 1956.

24. *Ibid.*, April 6, 1956; Warsaw Voievodshi Activ conference.

25. *Trybuna Ludu*, April 24, 1956. Cyrankiewicz, a former socialist, survived all the policy shifts of the regime and retained his post under Gomulka.

26. *Ibid.*, June 17, 1956.

27. Radio Warsaw, May 19, 1956.

28. *Trybuna Ludu*, March 31, 1956.

29. *Zycie Warszawy*, May 29, 1956.

30. For instance, *Nowe Drogi*, no. 2, 1956; J. Rasinski, "A Few Observations on Class Relations in the Countryside," *Nowe Drogi*, no. 5, 1956.

31. For instance, the bitter article by J. Morawski, a party secretary, "The Lessons of the 20th Congress of the CPSU," *Trybuna Ludu*, March 27, 1956; also W. Ulbricht, "Concerning the 20th Party Congress of the CPSU," *Neues Deutschland*, March 4, 1956.

32. *Izvestia*, June 30, 1956; *Pravda*, July 4, 1956.

33. See note on p. 204, Chapter 9, regarding the possible ambivalence in the Yugoslav statement.

34. July 16, 1956 (italics in original).

35. *New York Times*, July 22, 1956.

36. This was preceded by a protocol, signed in February 1956, revising in Poland's favor the Polish-Soviet trade agreement. J. Kobryber, "Polish-Soviet Trade Agreements," *Gospodarka Planowa*, no. 4, April 1956.

37. Information based on personal sources in Warsaw.

38. Radio Warsaw, August 21, 1956.

39. *News from Behind the Iron Curtain*, October 1956, pp. 46–47.

40. Radio Warsaw, August 13, 1956.

41. *Ibid.*, September 22, 1956.

42. *Ibid.*, September 19, 1956.

43. *Po Prostu*, September 30, 1956.

44. *Nowa Kultura*, no. 13, 1956 (W. Woroszylski).

45. Radio Warsaw, September 24, 1956.

46. For Ochab's September objections, see *Nowe Drogi*, no. 10 (1956), p. 112.

47. F. Mazur, one of their leaders and considered in Warsaw to be in the service of Soviet secret police, was at the time in Moscow.

48. For an account of the three-day alert at Zeran, of the numerous Zeran delegations spreading throughout the country to mobilize the workers, and so on, see *Swiat*, November 4, 1956.

49. Radio Szczecin and Gdansk, October 26, 1956.

50. For detailed accounts of the October events, sprinkled liberally with so-called direct quotations from various closed meetings, and such, see K. Syrop, *Spring in October* (New York, 1958), and Lewis, *A Case History of Hope*.

51. According to Ochab, *Nowe Drogi*, no. 10 (1956), p. 16. This issue contains the proceedings of the Eighth Plenum with its startling debates, comments, and rare personal insights. An unusual documentary on the power and ideological processes of a ruling Communist body operating under stress, its publication in English is well merited.

52. *Ibid.*, p. 18.

53. Syrop's book contains the most thorough account (pp. 94–95), based in part on the reports of P. Ben, the *Le Monde* correspondent in Warsaw.

54. *Nowe Drogi*, no. 10 (1956), p. 11.

55. *Ibid.*, p. 113.

56. *Ibid.*

57. *Ibid.*, p. 116.

58. A preferrable designation for this particular moment in view of the diverse elements backing Gomulka; see also Chapter 14.

59. *Nowe Drogi*, no. 10 (1956), pp. 12–18.

60. Radio Warsaw, November 6, 1956.

61. Full text in Zinner, pp. 197–239.

62. *Nowe Drogi*, no. 10 (1956), p. 147.
63. Text in Zinner, pp. 270–284.
64. Full text in *New York Times*, December 19, 1956.
65. *Ibid*, November 19, 1956.
66. The East European leaders apparently did not expect the attack on Stalin, despite Khrushchev's speech in Sofia in 1955. Thus the East German SED theoretical journal *Einheit* was still praising Stalin in February of 1956 as Khrushchev was delivering his condemnation.

12. The Maoist Reconstruction of the Center

1. *Nowe Drogi*, no. 10 (1956), p. 38.
2. *The Anti-Stalin Campaign and International Communism* (New York, 1957), p. 294.
3. *Nowe Drogi*, no. 10 (1956), p. 39.
4. *Trybuna Ludu*, November 2, 1956.
5. *Pravda*, November 19, 1956 (italics added).
6. For example, M. Bielicki, "Conversations on Politics," *Po Prostu*, December 2, 1956; or the poem by A. Wazyk, "Qui Tacent Clament," *Nowa Kultura*, November 25, 1956.
7. *Trybuna Wolnosci*, November 25, 1956.
8. R. Jurys, "Poznan and Budapest," *Zycie Warszawy*, November 23, 1956.
9. J. Wiatr, "Crisis of Internationalism?" *Nowe Drogi*, nos. 11–12 (November-December 1956), esp. pp. 109–113.
10. *Ibid*.
11. *Izvestia*, November 7, 1956.
12. M. Bibrowski, "Yugoslavia: The Beginning of the Great Debate," *Nowa Kultura*, December 9, 1956.
13. *Pravda*, December 23, 1956. For the Polish follow-up, see note 27.
14. *Neues Deutschland*, November 27, 1956.
15. *Rude Pravo*, December 8, 1956.
16. *Rude Pravo*, editorial, "Shoulder to Shoulder for Peace and Socialism," January 8, 1957.
17. See particularly the illuminating series in *The New Leader*, February 5, 12, and 19, 1959 by F. Schenk and R. Lowenthal, "Politics and Planning in the Soviet Empire."
18. Radio Peiping, November 1, 1956.
19. *Jen Min Jih Pao*, November 21, 1956.
20. Quotes from Russian translation, *Pravda*, December 30, 1956.
21. *Pravda*, December 30, 1956 (italics added).
22. For instance, *Rabotnichesko Delo*, January 31, 1957, an article on "Bourgeois Nationalism — Banner of Imperialist Reaction," stated: "The imperialists are trying to drive a wedge into the unity of the world workers' revolutionary movement through various bourgeois ideas which they conceal in a slogan for national independence and equality of rights, or in the term 'anti-Stalinism.' . . ."
23. Both quotations are from P. Avramov, "The Attitude Toward the Soviet Union and the CPSU — Cornerstone of Proletarian Internationalism," *Rabotnichesko Delo*, February 8, 1957.

24. Radio Tirana, February 17, 1957.

25. Radio Belgrade, February 26, 1957 (italics added).

26. For instance, the violent comment on Popovic's speech by *Pravda*, March 11, 1957; replies of *Borba* and *Politika*, March 12; *Rabotnichesko Delo*, March 4, 1957, article on "Guiding Light for World's Proletariat"; Moscow speeches by Bulganin and Kadar on March 27, 1957, strongly condemning the Yugoslavs particularly on the Hungarian issue; and the Yugoslav reassertion of Soviet responsibility for the uprising, *Borba*, April 5, 1957, in a direct reply to Bulganin, and so on.

27. Indicative is the Polish reply of February 10, 1957, to the *Pravda* December 23 article on proletarian internationalism cited earlier: M. Bibrowski, in his "On Internationalism, Stalinism and other Disputed Matters," *Nowa Kultura*, reasserts his previous theses, again attacks Stalinism, gives *Pravda* a lecture on Leninism, and suggests that Azizian, the *Pravda* writer, start practicing true internationalism by ceasing to call those who disagree with his views "bourgeois nationalists," "reformists," "renegades."

28. *Current Background* (translation), no. 439; statement of March 5, 1957 (italics added).

29. See the Schenk and Lowenthal articles.

30. V. Winston, "The Soviet Satellites — Economic Liability?" *Problems of Communism*, January-February 1958, esp. note 15.

31. I. T. Vinogradov, "The Building of Socialism in the European Countries of People's Democracy," *Voprosy istorii KPSS*, no. 3, 1957.

32. Winston; on Soviet loans, see *Mezhdunarodnaia zhizn*, no. 12 (1956), p. 27.

33. "Long Term Planning and Cooperation in Eastern Europe and the Soviet Union," *Economic Bulletin for Europe*, November 1957; see also R. Fidelski, *Wspolpraca Gospodarcza Polski z Krajami Socjalistycznymi* (Warsaw, 1959), esp. pp. 78–90.

34. *Pravda*, July 14, 1957.

35. *Ceteka*, December 14, 1957.

36. For data and tables, see *Vneshnaia Torgovlia*, no. 11 (1957), esp. p. 46.

37. "The GDR and the CSR are the chief exporters of industrial equipment to the USSR. In 1956, approximately 55 per cent of all the imported equipment and some 75 per cent of the equipment imported by Soviet Russia from the socialist countries was from Czechoslovakia and the GDR." *Zahranicny Obchod*, January 1958. For ideological as well as economic justification, see V. Keigl, "The Place of Czechoslovakia in the Division of Labor and Economic Cooperation of the Socialist States"; and G. Kolmei, "The Role of Industry and Foreign Trade of the German Democratic Republic in the World Socialist Economic System," *Mirovaia Sotsialisticheskaia Sistema Khoziaistva* (Moscow, 1958).

38. *Probleme Economice*, no. 1, 1958.

39. Text in *New York Times*, January 30, 1957.

40. Moscow Protocol of July 7, 1958.

41. *Rude Pravo*, July 7, 1958.

42. For a detailed treatment of Soviet-Czech trade, with itemized listings, see *Nova Mysl*, June 1958; *Hospodarske Noviny*, July 8, 1958.

43. The most detailed information is contained in two extensive tables in

Zycie Gospodarcze, October 19, 1958. Other data in *Sztandar Mlodych*, November 6, 1957, and in an interview given by the Polish Minister of Trade, *Przyjazn*, January 19, 1958.

44. "In Unity Lies Strength," *Tvorba*, no. 3 (1957), p. 1.

45. *Pravda*, February 20, 1957.

46. *Nowe Drogi*, no. 6 (1957), pp. 5, 52.

47. *Ibid.*, p. 8.

48. Text in *New York Times*, September 18, 1957.

49. *Pravda*, June 21, 1957; *Rude Pravo*, June 19, 1957.

50. For instance, *Mezhdunarodnaia zhizn*, no. 5 (1957), p. 49. For an extensive Yugoslav critique of this concept, as well as analysis of the different formulations, see V. Vlahovic, "The Idea and Substance of Proletarian Internationalism," *Socijalizam*, October 1958. (Vlahovic is a Politburo member.)

51. For Khrushchev's own justification of Soviet leadership as being "objectively" dictated by history, see *Pravda*, July 12, 1958.

52. *Trybuna Ludu*, November 7, 1957.

53. This writer had an opportunity to observe at the time the strange mixture of optimism, make-believe, and wishful thinking prevalent in Warsaw.

54. As confirmed by the Twenty-first CPSU Congress speeches which revealed that domestic Soviet issues were paramount in the attempted anti-Khrushchev coup.

55. *Zycie Warszawy*, April 23, 1957 (italics added).

56. See speech by Khrushchev, *Pravda*, July 12, 1958.

57. *Pravda*, November 5, 1957.

58. *Pravda*, November 7, 1957.

59. *Pravda*, November 22, 1957.

60. Account of F. Ebert, East German participant, *Neues Deutschland*, November 30, 1957.

61. *Ibid.*

62. *Pravda*, September 15, 1957.

63. *Ibid.*, November 22, 1957.

64. *Trybuna Ludu*, November 29, 1957. This reference was omitted from *Pravda's* coverage of his speech, November 30, 1957.

65. For instance, *Izvestia*, December 28, 1957.

66. Personal East European sources.

67. For the distinction, see my "Poland – A Political Glimpse," *Problems of Communism*, no. 5, 1957.

13. *Unity through the Struggle against Revisionism*

1. For a development of this break-through stage of totalitarian development, see C. J. Friedrich and Z. K. Brzezinski, *Totalitarian Dictatorship and Autocracy* (Cambridge, 1956), chapter 27.

2. *V Pomoshch Politicheskomu Samoobrazivaniu*, no. 12, 1957. See also the Collected Essays by V. I. Lenin, *Protiv Revizionizma v Zashchitu Marksizma* (Moscow, 1959).

3. *Nowa Kultura*, no. 4, 1957.

4. Nos. 35–38, 1957; partial translations in *East Europe*, December 1957, February, March, and May 1958.

5. "Old Tunes in a New Key," *Voprosy filosofii*, no. 4, 1957.

6. For some translated condensations, see *Current Digest of the Soviet Press*, IX, no. 38, pp. 3–8, and in no. 52, p. 24.

7. February 5, 1958.

8. Attacks on Polish revisionists always distinguished them from Gomulka. However, this immunity did not extend to those domestic ideologues in Poland who, in supporting the attacks against Kolakowski, themselves appeared to be straying from the fold. For instance, J. J. Wiatr and Z. Bauman, Gomulkaists openly critical of revisionism, were severely admonished for alleging that in the later stages of Stalinism Marxism as science was dominated by Marxism as ideology. "Is this Marxism?" *Voprosy filosofii*, no. 4, 1957.

9. See his call for "democratic patriotism" in *Deutsche Zeitschrift fuer Philosophie*, March 15, 1953.

10. For Harich's program, see "Die politische Platform Harichs und seiner Freunde," *SBZ-Archiv*, March 25, 1957; for an account of his activities, see the *Neues Deutschland* account of his trial, March 9 and 10, 1957. (I am indebted to my graduate student, L. G. Stauber, for these references.) The *Neues Deutschland* account was not refuted by West German sources.

11. Radio Moscow, August 4, 1957.

12. *Politika*, May 1957; quoted by S. Lyon, *Czechoslovak-Jugoslav Relations* (mimeographed, Radio Free Europe, no date).

13. *Le Monde* correspondence of Khrushchev's speeches on a visit to Czechoslovakia, July 12, 1956.

14. Radio Prague, July 11, 1957.

15. *Ibid.*

16. On the eve of the Tito-Khrushchev meeting both *Borba* and *Politika* published sharp attacks on the Czech and Bulgarian regimes (July 27, 1957).

17. The most complete accounts are provided by Khrushchev's speech in Sofia, reported in *Pravda*, June 4, 1958, and not refuted by Belgrade.

18. *Pravda*, July 12, 1958; no Jugoslav denial.

19. *Komunist*, August 9, 1957.

20. Text of declaration in *New York Times*, September 17, 1956.

21. Typical was the immediate reaction of the East Germans to the August meeting. *Wirtschaftswissenschaft*, an economic journal, in its October-November 1957 issue, strongly criticized the Jugoslav model, pointing out its inapplicability elsewhere.

22. *Komunist*, January 1, 1958 (views of R. Colakovic, Politburo member).

23. *Ibid.*, January 10, 1958.

24. *Ibid.*, December 13, 1957. Soviet polemics by A. Sobolev in *Kommunist* (Moscow), no. 2, 1958.

25. *Nasa Stvarnost*, January 1958 (views of M. Popovic, head of Yugoslav planning).

26. Hungarian-East German Party Declaration, March 26, 1958.

27. At a Moscow meeting attended by the Bulgarian party delegation he was given a greater ovation than even the First Secretary of the Bulgarian party (*New York Times*, February 20, 1958).

28. *Kommunist*, no. 1, 1958.

29. All quotes from the draft based on *The Joint Translation Service Bulletin*, March 24, 1958.

30. Translation available in *Current Digest of the Soviet Press*, X, no. 16.

31. The final version of the program is available in English, *Jugoslavia's Way*, trans. S. Preibechevich (New York, 1958).

32. Radio Belgrade, April 22–24, 1958, speeches by Tito, Rankovic, and Kardelj.

33. As quoted in *New York Times*, April 23, 1958.

34. *Borba*, April 20, 1958.

35. *Current Digest of the Soviet Press*.

36. *Pravda*, May 8, 1958.

37. For example, *Einheit*, no. 5, 1958; *Ceteka*, citing Novotny, June 18, 1958. For a collected volume of such attacks, see *Protiv Sovremennogo Revizionizma* (Moscow, 1958).

38. *Komunist*, May 9, 1958.

39. For example, *Politika*, May 15; *Borba*, May 16, 1958.

40. *Krasnaia zvezda*, May 17, 1958.

41. Telegram to Tito on his sixty-sixth birthday, May 26, 1958.

42. Text in *Pravda*, July 12, 1958.

43. *Ibid.*

44. For comparative purposes, see E. Bernstein, *Gesellschaftliches und Privat-Eigentum* (Berlin, 1891) and N. Bukharin, *Oekonomik der Transformationsperiode* (Verlag der kommunistischen Internationale, 1922), esp. chapter 8: "System der Produktionsverwaltung in der Diktatur des Proletariats," pp. 138–149.

45. Personal information.

46. *Trybuna Ludu*, April 15, 1958.

47. *Trybuna Ludu*, June 29, 1958.

48. *Pravda*, June 30, 1958; P. Pospelov in *Kommunist*, July 1958.

49. *Pravda*, June 4, 1958.

14. The Polish Way to Socialism

A condensed version of this chapter appeared in *Problems of Communism*, June-July 1959.

1. For biographical data, see Dziewanowski, p. 340, note 13, or the preface to his collected postwar speeches, *W Walce o Demokracje Ludowa* (Warsaw, 1947), pp. 7–9.

2. S. Mikolajczyk, *The Rape of Poland* (New York, 1948); Korbonski, *W Imieniu Kremla*.

3. An excellent comparative treatment is to be found in J. Nowak's "Analysis of Developments in Poland since October 1956," (Radio Free Europe, mimeographed, June 1958).

4. Gomulka, *W Walce*, II, 260.

5. Gomulka, *Przemowienia* (Warsaw, 1957), p. 271.

6. Zinner, pp. 233–235.

7. *W Walce*, II, 24.

8. *Przemowienia*, p. 86, translation in Zinner, p. 303.

9. *W Walce*, I, 163.

10. *Ibid.*, p. 185.

11. *Przemowienia*, p. 272.

12. *Ibid.*, pp. 278–283.

13. *W Walce*, I, 155.
14. *W Walce*, II, 162 (italics his).
15. *Przemowienia*, pp. 33–34, translation in Zinner, p. 222.
16. *W Walce*, II, 156.
17. *Przemowienia*, pp. 264–271.
18. *Ibid.*, p. 126 (italics his).
19. *Pravda*, November 5, 1957.
20. *Przemowienia*, p. 269.
21. *Ibid.*, p. 305.
22. See *Trybuna Ludu*, December 7, 1956, for a discussion of "fear" among the members.
23. For example, *Zielony Sztandar*, October 20, 1957, October 27, 1957; March 31, 1957.
24. Chapter 11, pp. 239–240.
25. For an excellent discussion of the social disintegration produced by Stalinism and the war, see J. Szczepanski, "An attempted diagnosis," *Przeglad Kulturalny*, September 5–11, 1957.
26. S. Stomma, one of the leaders of the independent Catholic laymen and deputy to the Sejm, *Przeglad Kulturalny*, no. 43, October 25–31, 1956.
27. To be called *Fakty*, quickly prevented by the party.
28. For data on rehabilitations, see *Zycie Warszawy*, June 26, 1957.
29. *Chlopska Droga*, October 17–20, 1957; *Trybuna Ludu*, May 21, 1956.
30. Cf. interview with its chairman, Radio Warsaw, January 2, 1957.
31. *Trybuna Ludu*, December 5, 1956.
32. For a good insight into the thinking of the Polish economists, see Edward Lipinski, *Rewizje* (Warsaw, 1958); essentially a collection of his articles during late 1956 and early 1957.
33. *Dziennik Ustaw*, November 24, 1956.
34. This writer has been collecting some of them and hopes to publish a short analysis.
35. For some estimates, see my "Poland – A Political Glimpse," *Problems of Communism;* Nowak, "Analysis of Developments in Poland since October 1956"; and R. Staar, "New Course in Communist Poland," *Journal of Politics*, March 1958, p. 76.
36. For instance, L. Kolakowski, "The Ideological Sense of the Concept of the Left," *Po Prostu*, February 24, 1957.
37. Politburo member J. Morawski (closely identified with Gomulka) in *Nowe Drogi*, no. 3, 1957; Politburo member R. Zambrowski (described in Warsaw as spokesman for the central apparat), in *Zycie Partii*, no. 3, 1957.
38. Nowak, p. 54.
39. Leon Kasman, appointed editor, was reported to be a Zambrowski centrist; for a lengthy list, see Nowak, p. 59.
40. For instance, "Again a 'Cultural Policy?'" *Nowa Kultura*, June 16, 1957.
41. Apart from a street demonstration by Warsaw youth, other evidence is suggested by an unpublished analysis of public opinion concerning these events conducted by the Polish Radio (in this writer's possession).
42. For an informed account, see K. Jelenski, "The Rise and Fall of *Po Prostu*," *The New Leader*, December 2, 1957.
43. Specifically, J. Kott, M. Jastrun, P. Hertz, J. Andrzejewski.

44. Speech to the Tenth Plenum, *Trybuna Ludu*, October 26, 1957.

45. Based on personal observation in Warsaw.

46. Account in *New York Times*, August 22, 1957.

47. The purge, conducted without clear ideological guidelines, resulted in the dropping of 200,161 members, of whom only 27,255 were actually excluded, the others being struck from the rolls. The party descreased by 16 per cent, and the vast majority of those dropped had nothing to do with deviation, but had been inactive, or, as in the case of most of those excluded, were guilty of economic offences. *Sztandar Mlodych*, May 15, 1958.

48. "A Few Remarks on the Leading Role of the UPWP," *Nowe Drogi*, January 1958.

49. As stated by A. Werblan in his secret speech to the Central Committee's Press Commission, May 6, 1958.

50. *Trybuna Ludu*, October 17, 1957.

51. *Ibid.*, October 21, 1957 (Professor A. Schaff).

52. At the end of 1957, this number was estimated at about twenty (*Orka*, September 29, 1957).

53. Nowak, pp. 57–58.

54. *Trybuna Ludu*, November 13, 1957.

55. *Express Wieczorny*, February 15, 1958.

56. Personal interview with a cabinet minister.

57. Speech by Gomulka, *Glos Pracy*, April 18, 1958.

58. In 1492 of 1936 industrial enterprises eligible. *Glos Pracy*, September 20, 1957.

59. *Rada Robotnicza*, no. 12, June 18–20, 1958; for the negative reaction of the Workers' Councils, see *Glos Pracy*, June 17, 1958.

60. Confirmed to the writer by a highly placed member of the Central Committee; explicitly asserted at the Twelfth Plenum in October 1958 by W. Matwin, as recorded on p. 44 of an edited stenographic report designed purely for internal party use.

61. *Biuletyn statystyczny*, no. 4, 1958.

62. For a comprehensive analysis, see P. Collins, "The Post-October Agricultural Policy of Wladyslaw Gomulka" (RFE, mimeographed, October 1958).

63. Between 1952 and 1955 only one interpellation had been made. In 1957, fifty-one interpellations were introduced and, it may be noted, only eleven of them came from Communist Party members. *Trybuna Ludu*, November 12, 1957.

64. That distinction was made by Professor T. Kotarbinski, head of the Polish Academy of Sciences. *Trybuna Literacka*, December 1, 1957.

65. For instance, *Przemowienia*, p. 273.

66. S. Frenkel, "The Plan of Economic Offensive," *Przeglad Kulturalny*, November 6, 1958.

67. Confidential transcript, *XII Plenum Komitetu Centralnego* (Central Committee, Warsaw, 1958), p. 198. It is noteworthy that the plenum revealed important defections from the dogmatists' camp, most particularly T. Gede, the ambassador to Moscow.

68. *Ibid.*, pp. 160-161.

69. The Congress proceedings were published in a 764-page issue of *Nowe Drogi*, no. 4, April 1959.

70. For a detailed examination of the various alternatives facing Polish agriculture, see the collected essays *O Nowy Program Rolny* (Warsaw, 1957).

15. Problems of the Communist "Commonwealth"

1. *Trybuna Ludu*, July 30, 1958.
2. *Nova Svoboda*, December 20, 1957. In the summer of 1959 this writer had considerable difficulty in finding Polish papers in Czechoslovakia.
3. *Trybuna Ludu*, April 4, 1958.
4. *Predvoj*, April 3, 1958.
5. *Tvorba*, December 19, 1957.
6. *Rude Pravo*, January 1, 1958.
7. This writer, in the course of his visits to Poland, was repeatedly told of continuing suspicion on the part of the Soviet rank and file toward Gomulka. That suspicion apparently also existed within the Central Committee and the central *apparat*.
8. *Sovetskaia Litva*, March 22, 1959.
9. For *unusually* warm personal references to Gomulka by Khrushchev (such as "our friend whom we know well and cherish deeply"), see *Pravda*, October 26 and 28, November 4 and 5, 1958.
10. *Slowo Powszechne*, March 21, 1958.
11. J. V. Stalin, *Problems of Leninism* (Moscow, 1940), p. 60.
12. For extensive documentation, see "Sino-Soviet Trade," *Soviet Studies*, October 1958; M. I. Sladkovsky, *Ocherki ekonomicheskikh otnoshenii SSSR s Kitaiem* (Moscow, 1957); *Vneshanaia Torgovlia*, no. 8, 1957.
13. *Ibid.*, no. 7, 1959; also R. Moorsteen, "Economic Prospects for Communist China," *World Politics*, January 1959.
14. B. Schwartz, "China and the Soviet Theory of People's Democracy," *Problems of Communism*, no. 5, 1954; "On the People's Dictatorship" in C. Brandt, B. Schwartz, and J. Fairbank, *A Documentary History of Chinese Communism* (Cambridge, 1952), p. 456.
15. B. Schwartz, "New Trends in Maoism," *Problems of Communism*, no. 4, 1957; *New China News Agency*, September 16, 1956.
16. *Jen Min Jih Pao*, September 10, 1958.
17. *Izvestia*, October 1, 1958.
18. *Leningradskaia pravda*, October 23, 1958.
19. *Hsinhua*, November 6, 1958.
20. *Hung-ch'i*, July 16, 1958.
21. *Ibid.*, August 14, 1958.
22. According to the count of M. Gammarnikow, Polish desk, Radio Free Europe, Munich.
23. *Hsinhua*, December 18, 1958.
24. *Pravda*, February 8, 1959. For a rosy assessment of Sino-Soviet relations, see M. S. Kapitsa, *Sovetsko-Kitaiskie Otnosheniia* (Moscow, 1958), esp. chapter 9.
25. G. Fono, "Those From Whom We Can Learn Most," *Nepszabadsag*, October 22, 1957.
26. The Czechs even renewed the publication of Stalin's writings. *Glos Pracy*, September 12, 1958.
27. *Nepszabadsag*, December 15, 1957; see also J. Revai, "Comments on the World Significance of Soviet Culture," *Nepszabadsag*, November 7, 1957.

28. *Rabotnichesko Delo*, February 16, 1958; for conflict with the writers see *Literaturen Front*, November 28, 1957.

29. Editorial, *Nova Mysl*, no. 4, 1958. To ensure unity of thought an Institute for Advanced Study of Marx-Leninism was opened at Charles University. *Vysoka Skola*, no. 10, 1957.

30. See Taborsky.

31. *Rude Pravo*, June 19, 1958.

32. *Nepszabadsag*, May 18, 1958.

33. *Neues Deutschland*, October 22, 1957.

34. *Statistica*, no. 6, 1957; *Rabotnichesko Delo*, December 11, 1957 and April 18, 1958, which states that the increase in "the production of the means of production" is to be 77 per cent by 1962. See also *New York Times*, February 15, 1959.

35. A. Nove, "Problems of Economic DeStalinization," *Problems of Communism*, no. 2, 1957.

36. *Obrana Lidu*, December 4, 1957; see also "Industrial Reorganization in Czechoslovakia," *East Europe*, April 1958 and *Three-Monthly Economic Review of Eastern Europe*, August 1958.

37. Premier A. Yugov, party congress, June 2, 1958.

38. T. Zhivkov, First Secretary, *Rabotnichesko Delo*, October 20, 1957.

39. *East Europe*, August 1958, p. 47.

40. For instance, "The Influence of Kulaks must not be Underrated," *Novy Zivot*, September 14, 1957; also *Rude Pravo*, December 20, 1957, and others.

41. *Agricultura Nova*, December 31, 1957. It is to be noted that many of the collective farms were in fact "phony" organizations, essentially loose associations of peasants and not true collectives.

42. *Neues Deutschland*, November 15, 1957, March 5, 1958. See also statement by Erich Mueckenberger, Politburo member, urging "patience" in persuading German farmers to join (*Neues Deutschland*, October 24, 1958), The 1958 figure stood at about 30 per cent, but in 1959–1960 an intensive collectivization drive was launched.

43. *Nepszabadsag*, January 21, 1958.

44. *Magyar Nemzet*, October 23, 1957; *Nepszabadsag*, July 10, 1958.

45. *Magyar Nemzet*, June 10, 1958. See also the discussion in B. Csikos-Nagy, *Arpolitika Az Atmeneti Gazdasagban* (Budapest, 1958).

46. For example, *Mlada Fronta*, February 4, 1958; *Neues Deutschland*, January 26, 1958; Radio Budapest, March 21, 1958.

47. *Tvorba*, April 24, 1958.

48. *Pravda* (Prague), July 24, 1958; *Rude Pravo*, June 19, 1958; *Novo Vreme*, July, 1958.

49. For instance, speech by L. Rautu, Politburo member, *Agerpress*, April 22, 1958.

50. For instance, *Romania Libera*, May 11, 1958; *Scinteia*, May 13, 1958.

51. For a strong attack on sectarianism, see *Nepszabadsag*, February 9, 1958; for the agricultural debate, see *Tarsadlami Szemle*, January 1959.

52. See *New York Times*, February 18, 1959, for some Bulgarian applications; also *East Europe*, February 1959.

53. T. A. Stepanian, "The October Revolution and the Formation of the Communist System," *Voprosy filosofii*, no. 10, 1958.

54. For a discussion of Khrushchev's views and an explicit rejection of Stepanian's (as cited in note 53), see P. Fedoseyev in *Pravda,* February 9, 1959. Stepanian has long specialized on the subject of transition to Communism, which thus makes the rebuke administered to him all the more significant. See Stepanian, *I. V. Stalin o stroitelstve kommunizma v SSSR* (Moscow, 1950); and "V. I. Lenin on the Building of Communism," *Kommunist,* no. 6, 1954. For emphasis on the difference between Communism, as involving a higher level of industrialization and high productivity, and socialism, as involving a socialist organization of property relations, see *Sovetskaia Moldaviia,* March 17, 1959.

55. For some Soviet discussions, see L. Leontiev, "The Creation of the Material-Technical Basis for Communism," *Pravda,* February 11, 1959; G. Obiedkov, "Theoretical Problems of Communist Construction," *Pravda,* July 31, 1959; B. Ponomarev, "Theoretical Problems of Communist Construction," *Pravda,* March 6, 1959.

56. For some estimates of continued Soviet exploitation, see Chapter 12, p. 284. The growing importance of the "socialist world market" has given rise to special literature dealing with the economic as well as the ideological aspects of this integration, as, for instance, T. Lychowski, *Stosunki Ekonomiczne Miedzy Krajami o Roznych Ustrojach* (Warsaw, 1957); *Sodruzhestvo Stran Sotsializma* (Moscow, 1958); *Mirovaia Sotsialisticheskaia Sistema Khoziaistva* (Moscow, 1958).

16. Ideology and Power in Relations among Communist States

1. For some of its intellectual antecedents, see the discussion by J. L. Talmon, *The Rise of Totalitarian Democracy* (Boston, 1952); for some of the psychological aspects of modern dictatorship, see Z. Barbu, *Democracy and Dictatorship* (New York, 1956). For a discussion of the implications for the intellectual of such ideology, see W. Kula, *Rozwazania o Historii* (Warsaw, 1958).

2. I have found the following very useful: H. D. Lasswell and A. Kaplan, *Power and Society* (New Haven, 1950); and, especially, H. A. Simon, "Notes on the Observation and Measurement of Political Power," *Journal of Politics,* November 1953.

3. H. Kissinger, *Nuclear Weapons and Foreign Policy* (New York, 1957), p. 425.

4. For instance, S. L. Sharp, "National Interest: Key to Soviet Politics," *Problems of Communism,* March-April 1958.

5. V. I. Lenin, *Certain Features of the Historical Development of Marxism* (Moscow, 1955), p. 8.

6. *Kommunist,* no. 14, 1955; for fuller discussion, see Chapter 8.

7. Among some of the very useful works on this subject are A. G. Meyer's two studies, *Leninism* (Cambridge, 1957) and *Marxism* (Cambridge, 1954). N. Leites attempted to extrapolate from such principles a systematic analysis of Communist political norms in his *The Study of Bolshevism* (New York, 1953).

8. Hans Morgenthau himself makes the point that "national interest" is meaningful only in terms of how it is perceived by the national leaders. "An-

other Great Debate: The National Interest of the United States," *American Political Science Review*, December 1952, pp. 966, 972.

9. *New York Times*, August 28, 1958 (italics added).

10. J. W. Kaye, *Christianity in India* (London, 1859), pp. 20–21, 30–32.

11. *Pravda*, March 27, 1959 (italics added).

12. That Yugoslavia will eventually have to choose one or the other camp was openly stated by Gomulka to the Third Congress, *Trybuna Ludu*, March 11, 1959.

13. Reported to this writer by a high-ranking Communist as a remark made by Chou En-lai to Koca Popovic, who repeated it to the informant.

14. See A. J. Toynbee, *A Study of History* (New York, 1947), pp. 336–349.

15. *Pravda*, January 28, 1959.

Epilogue: The Impact of the Sino-Soviet Dispute

1. In addition to Boorman, et al., and Whiting, see D. A. Barnett, *Communist China and Asia* (New York, 1960), chapter 12. For a discussion of the Sino-Soviet alliance in the context of the Korean War, as well as for an analysis of the Soviet influence and Chinese interest in North Korea, see A. Whiting, *China Crosses the Yalu* (New York, 1960).

2. On January 9, 1961, Poland obtained $125 million in Czech credits, and nine days later $64.2 million from Ulbricht.

3. For a detailed and scrupulous analysis, see Z. Jordan, "The Situation in Polish Learning," *Kultura*, no. 3 (Paris, 1961).

4. This author can testify to that on the basis of personal experience when visiting Yugoslavia's Communist neighbors, both in 1959 and in 1960.

5. See W. E. Griffith, "What Happened to Revisionism," *Problems of Communism*, no. 2, March–April 1960; see also chapter 13 of this book.

6. For a discussion of this phenomenon of "privatization" in Western Europe, see Otto Kirchheimer, "German Democracy in the 1950's," *World Politics*, January 1961.

7. For a discussion of the problem of ideological adaptation, see Brzezinski, "Communist Ideology and International Affairs," *The Journal of Conflict Resolution*, no. 3, September 1960.

8. For discussions of the earlier relations, see B. Schwartz, *Chinese Communism and the Rise of Mao* (Cambridge, 1952); C. Brandt, *Stalin's Failure in China* (Cambridge, 1958); C. McLane, *Soviet Policy and the Chinese Communists* (New York, 1958).

9. See V. Dedijer, *Tito*, pp. 321–322.

10. On February 12, 1960, *The Observer* (London) carried a lengthy summary of the 1960 formal exchanges between the CPSU and the CPC, written by Edward Crankshaw and based on a "report, which contains detailed summaries of hitherto secret correspondence" between Moscow and Peiping. Judging from circumstantial evidence, the account seems to be, in the main, accurate.

11. For evidence of Chinese uneasiness over the Khrushchev line toward Yugoslavia in June 1955, compare Khrushchev's reference to Yugoslav socialism with Mao's noncommittal phrases; cf. New China News Agency, June 30,

1955, and *Shih-chieh Chih-shih*, July 20, 1955; discussion in R. Hofheinz, "China Joins the Bloc," unpublished research paper (Harvard, 1960).

12. For discussion, see R. MacFarquhar, *The Hundred Flowers Campaign and the Chinese Intellectuals* (New York, 1960).

13. H. D. Lasswell, *World Politics and Personal Insecurity* (Glencoe, Ill., 1950), p. 128.

14. See MacFarquhar; also T. Chen, *Thought Reform of the Chinese Intellectuals* (Hong Kong, 1960). For a Soviet account, see V. Lazarev, "The Struggle Against the Rightists in the CPR—the Struggle for Socialism," *Kommunist*, no. 5, April 1958.

15. R. MacFarquhar, "Communist China's Intraparty Dispute," *Pacific Affairs*, no. 4, December 1958; Chao Kuo-chaun, "Leadership in the Chinese Communist Party," *The Annals*, January 1959.

16. See Choh-Ming Li, "Economic Development," *The China Quarterly*, no. 1, January–March 1960; Wang Kuang-wei, "The Big Leap in China's Economy," *World Marxist Review*, no. 6, June 1960.

17. For a discussion of the political implications of a vast personality cult of Mao, see R. L. Walker, "Chairman Mao and the Cult of Personality," *Encounter*, June 1960.

18. See R. C. North, "Peking's Drive for Empire," *Problems of Communism*, January–February 1960.

19. The Chinese could hardly take the view that "proletarian internationalism" justified the Soviet statement that the USSR "maintains friendly relations both with the People's Republic of China and the Republic of India." *Tass*, September 9, 1959.

20. For a perceptive analysis, see A. Halpern, "The Chinese Communist Line of Neutralism," Rand mimeographed study (July 1960), p. 2026; D. Zagoria, "Sino-Soviet Friction in Underdeveloped Areas," *Problems of Communism*, no. 2, March–April 1961. The Chinese blamed the Soviets for past failures in this connection and were unwilling to let the Soviets dictate the line for the national liberation struggle. Late in 1959, for instance, the two parties adopted sharply divergent positions concerning De Gaulle's Algerian proposals; the Soviets approved them, the Chinese labeled them as a smoke screen for French imperialism. They also differed on who should lead these struggles, the bourgeoisie or the CP.

21. Halpern, p. 30.

22. *Jen Min Jih Pao*, November 19, 1958; lengthy translation in Halpern, pp. 19–20.

23. See Brzezinski, "The Challenge of Change in the Soviet Bloc," *Foreign Affairs*, April 1961.

24. For a subsequent critique of this interpretation, presaging the December 1960 declaration by the eighty-one parties, see T. Zhivkov, "Peace: Key Problem of Today," *World Marxist Review*, August 1960.

25. For an analogy with the earlier Menshevik-Bolshevik debate, see Brzezinski, "Communist Ideology and International Affairs," p. 279. For a lengthy statement of the Chinese position, see Yu Chao-li, in *Hung-ch'i*, no. 7, 1960; also Liu Chang-sheng, Radio Peiping, June 8, 1960.

26. A. Hsieh, "Communist China and Nuclear Warfare," *The China Quarterly*, no. 2, April–June 1960.

27. Khrushchev's address to the Twenty-first CPSU Congress, January 27, 1959.

28. Perhaps not accidentally, *Voprosy istorii* in its July and September 1960 issues carried a book review and an article, respectively, both reasserting very firmly the historic Russian claim to the present Russo-Chinese border, which Chinese leaders, including Sun Yat-sen, have claimed as unfair to China. See also A. Whiting, "Sinkiang and Sino-Soviet Relations," *China Quarterly*, July–September 1960.

29. See L. Schapiro, "The Chinese Ally from the Soviet Point of View," presented to the Third Sovietological Congress, September 1960.

30. For instance, the Soviets simply ceased citing the Chinese in their press. See also Appendix I, tables 3, 4, and 5.

31. See Brzezinski, "The Pattern and Limits of the Sino-Soviet Dispute," *Problems of Communism*, September–October 1960; this article appears in a revised form, entitled "The Problematics of Sino-Soviet Bargaining," in K. L. London, ed., *Unity and Contradiction* (New York, 1961).

32. For East European comments, see *East Europe*, March 1960. For a discussion of Chinese relations with East Europe, see the symposium on "China and the Soviet Satellites," *China Quarterly*, July–September 1960.

33. A good summary is in Zagoria's "Strains in the Sino-Soviet Alliance," *Problems of Communism*, May–June 1960.

34. An English translation appears in *East Europe*, March 1960.

35. On October 31, 1959, Khrushchev spoke in general terms about Trotsky's notorious line of "neither peace nor war"; that was perhaps the sharpest public reaction to date.

36. *Hsinhua*, no. 7, 1960; translated in *East Europe*, June 1960.

37. Radio Peiping, June 6, 1960 (italics added).

38. *Ibid.*, June 8, 1960. A few days earlier, General Hsiao Hua, Deputy Director of the Political Department of the Chinese Army, mocked those who minimized the possibility of war because of Soviet deterrent power, saying, "After all, we are not the chief of the general staff of the imperialists," Radio Peiping, June 3, 1960.

39. For example, *Hung-ch'i*, no. 12, 1960; *Jen Min Jih Pao*, June 21, 25, and 26, 1960.

40. For background, see R. Rupen, "Outer Mongolia since 1955," *Pacific Affairs*, December 1957; Rupen, "Outer Mongolia, 1957–1960," *Pacific Affairs*, June 1960; as well as Rupen, "Mongolian Nationalism," *Royal Central Asian Journal*, Parts I and II, April and October 1958. See also G. Friters, *Outer Mongolia and Its International Position* (London, 1957).

41. N. Matkovsky, "The Ideological Weapon of Communism," *Pravda*, June 12, 1960.

42. *Pravda*, June 22, 1960.

43. On the basis of interviews conducted in the summer of 1960 in Bulgaria, Yugoslavia, and the Soviet Union, the Crankshaw article and B. Osadczuk, "Conflict China-Russia," *Kultura* (Paris, 1961), no. 1–2, 161, seem well-informed.

44. According to Crankshaw, the formal exchange was initiated by an 80-page Soviet letter; Osadczuk has the Chinese reciprocating with a 120-page memorandum.

45. *Borba*, August 13, 1960.

46. Personal interview; Osadczuk also makes this point.

47. In the form of a book by E. Kardelj, *Socialism and War* (Belgrade, 1960).

48. See *Pravda*, September 2 1960, "The Latest Revelations of a Revisionist"; cf. "The Leninist Theory of Socialist Revolution and Our Times," *Kommunist*, no. 13, September 1960.

49. As reported by *The New York Times*, November 7, 1960.

50. See especially T. Zhivkov (Bulgarian First Secretary), "Peace: Key Problem of Today," which develops many of the points subsequently included in the Moscow declaration; A. Shapiro, "The Contemporary Epoch and Its Characteristics," *Mirovaia ekonomika i mezhdunarodnie otnosheniia*, no. 11, 1960; A. Arzumanyan, "On the Character of the Contemporary Epoch," *Kommunist Vooruzhennykh Sil*, no. 2, October 1960.

51. On the very eve of the conference, the Chinese published a major ideological statement, "A Basic Summary of Experience Gained in the Victory of the Chinese People's Revolution" (*Hsinhua*, November 2, 1960), restating again the more radical Chinese position and labeling as "stupid" the failure of someone to understand that parliaments are a mere sham and that therefore it is idle to speak of a "parliamentary way" to socialism.

52. See Walter Ulbricht's report, in *Neues Deutschland*, December 18, 1960; H. Matern, in *Neues Deutschland*, December 23, 1960; Crankshaw; Osadczuk; and personal interviews.

53. Osadczuk, p. 133. He does not list them, but they may have included the Albanian, Vietnamese, Malayan, Spanish, West German (criticized in 1960 for "leftism"), Indonesian, Cuban, Venezuelan, and Peruvian parties. A credible text of Hoxha's vituperative attack on the Soviet position appeared in *The Daily Telegraph* (London), June 9, 1961.

54. "A Great Anti-Imperialist Call," *Hung-ch'i*, December 15, 1960; cf. "Under the Invincible Flag of Marxism-Leninism," *Scanteia*, December 7, 1960; "The Roadmark of the Communist World Movement," *Nepsabadsag*, December 11, 1960; "The Decisive Factor in the World," *Rude Pravo*, December 10, 1960.

55. Dedijer, pp. 321 ff. See also the penetrating study by R. V. Burks, *The Dynamics of Communism in Eastern Europe* (Princeton, N. J., 1961), which casts much light on the background of Balkan Communist politics (Albanian in particular). For an excellent analysis of the background of the Albanian-Soviet tension, see W. E. Griffith, *Polycentrism in Practice: The Peking-Tirana Axis*, mimeographed study, May 1961. (Unfortunately, it became available when this Epilogue was already in print.)

56. *Borba*, February 22, 1961. For ethnic, as well as clannish, ties in Albanian politics, see Burks, particularly for the discussion of the relationship between the richer Tosks and the more militant and fewer Ghegs. The Tosks had been oppressed by the Turks and feared that any union with Yugoslavia might alter their domestic relationship with the Ghegs since many Ghegs reside in the Kossovo region. Hoxha and his associates are Tosks.

57. Speeches by E. Hoxha and M. Shehu on Radio Tirana, February 13 and 17, 1961.

58. For a discussion of the domestic North Korean situation, see P. Ru-

dolph, "North Korea on the Path to Socialism," *Pacific Affairs*, no. 2, June 1959. For a pro-Albanian North Korean statement, see *Nodong Sinmun*, May 3, 1961. (I am indebted to Dr. Griffith for drawing my attention to it.)

59. The Yugoslav press, in response to Albanian attacks, began a series on the gruesome history of the Albanian Party. See *Borba*, March 19, 20, 21, and 22, 1961, for many hitherto unknown aspects, especially pertaining to the 1956 unrest in Tirana.

60. V. Vlahovic, *A Step Backward*, a report submitted to the Executive Committee of the League of Communists of Yugoslavia on February 10, 1961 (Belgrade, 1961), p. 69.

61. For an earlier distinction between "integral politics" and "international politics" within the bloc, see pp. 395, 405. For an interesting effort to construct a model for Soviet-bloc politics, although somewhat diluted by an inclination toward semantic hairsplitting, see George Modelski, *The Communist International System*, Research Monograph no. 9 (Princeton, N. J., 1960).

62. Lasswell, p. 122.

63. *Ibid.*, p. 121.

64. See chapter 9, as well as discussion in Lasswell, pp. 103–108.

65. For an evaluation of how the Soviets might hopefully construe the the meaning of the change, see K. L. London, "The Socialist Commonwealth of Nations," *Orbis*, no. 4, 1960.

66. For a perceptive analysis, see A. Whiting, "Conflict Resolution in the Sino-Soviet Alliance," Rand study S–2029, 1960, read at the Third Sovietological Congress, September 1960.

67. For evidence of open splits into radical and moderate factions in non-bloc parties, see Zagoria, "Sino-Soviet Friction in Underdeveloped Areas," pp. 10–11. In April 1961, the Indian Party openly argued the merits of the Soviet line of "broad national unity" and of the Chinese line favoring more radical activism by the ICP.

68. See Brzezinski, "Communist Ideology and International Affairs," especially pp. 275–290, for a discussion of the forces promoting and resisting ideological erosion.

69. Most recently, foundations were laid for a CEMA-coordinated twenty-year general plan for the economic development of the participating states. According to *Borba*, March 25, 1961, the Poles have been especially anxious to get some pooling of investments within CEMA. See also Appendix I.

70. A policy discussion would not be relevant here. For this author's discussion of some policy implications, see Brzezinski, "The Challenge of Change in the Soviet Bloc," *Foreign Affairs*, April 1961; "Political Developments within the Sino-Soviet Bloc," *The Annals*, July 1961; and, with W. E. Griffith, "Peaceful Engagement in Eastern Europe," *Foreign Affairs*, July 1961.

Bibliography

Periodicals

Agricultura Nova. Semiweekly publication on agriculture, issued by the Ministry of Agriculture and Forestry. Bucharest.

The American Slavic and East European Review. Quarterly journal of the American Association for the Advancement of Slavic Studies, Inc. New York.

Bellona. Quarterly of military history. London.

Biuletyn Statystyczny. Monthly reports issued by the Central Statistical Office. Warsaw.

Borba. Daily organ of the Communist Party of Yugoslavia. Belgrade.

Cahiers du Communisme. Theoretical and political monthly review of the Central Committee of the French Communist Party. Paris.

Ceteka. Reviews of the daily press and selected topics on domestic events, issued by the Czechoslovak News Agency. Prague.

Chlopska Droga. Weekly periodical of the Central Committee of the Polish United Workers Party. Warsaw.

Current Background. Communist Chinese publication. Peiping.

Current Digest of the Soviet Press. Weekly publication of the Joint Committee on Slavic Studies. New York.

Deutsche Zeitschrift fuer Philosophie. Organ of philosophic research and discussion of the German Democratic Republic. Berlin.

Dziennik Ustaw Rzeczypospolitej Polskiej. Gazette of laws issued by the Council of Ministers. Warsaw.

East Europe. A weekly bulletin of seven East European Countries, susperseded *News from Behind the Iron Curtain.* New York.

Economic Bulletin for Europe. United Nations Economic and Social Council, Economic Commission for Europe.

Einheit. Theoretical journal of scientific socialism. Berlin.

Elet es Tudomany. Weekly paper of the Society for Social and Natural Sciences. Budapest.

Express Wieczorny. Daily of the Workers' Publishing Cooperative. Warsaw.

Figyelo. Weekly publication publicizing economic policy. Budapest.

For a Lasting Peace, for a People's Democracy. Organ of the Cominform, originally published in Yugoslavia. After 1948 published in Rumania. Discontinued after 1956.

Foreign Affairs. An American quarterly review. New York.

Foreign Agriculture. UN Publication of the FAO.

Glos Koszalinski. Daily of the Voivodeship Committee, Polish United Workers' Party. Koszalin.

Glos Pracy. Periodical of the industrial unions, published every other day. Warsaw.

Gospodarka Planowa. Organ of the State Commission for Economic Planning. Warsaw.

Hospodarske Noviny. Weekly publication on economics. Prague.

L'Humanité. Organ of the French Communist Party. Paris.

Information Bulletin of the Central Committee of the Hungarian Communist Party. Budapest.

Izvestia. Organ of the Union of Workers Deputies of the USSR. Moscow.

Jen Min Jih Pao. Organ of the Chinese Communist Party. Peiping.

The Joint Translation Service Bulletin. Press translations, sponsored jointly by the United States and British Embassies.

Journal of Central European Affairs. Quarterly journal. Boulder, Colorado.

Journal of International Affairs. Semiannual journal of the School of International Affairs, Columbia University. New York.

Journal of Politics. Issued quarterly by the Southern Political Science Association in cooperation with the university of Florida. Gainesville.

Jugopress. Yugoslav Press Agency. Belgrade.

Kommunist. Theoretical and political journal of the Central Committee of the CPSU. Moscow. Previously published under the title *Bolshevik*.

Komunist. Organ of the Central Committee of the Communist Party of Yugoslavia. Belgrade.

Krasnaia Zvezda. Central organ of the Ministry of Defense of the USSR. Moscow.

Kultura i Spoleczenstwo. Quarterly of the Sociological and Cultural History Division of the Polish Academy of Sciences. Warsaw.

Latohatar. Semimonthly political and literary journal issued by a group of exiles. Absorbed *Egesz Latohatar*. Munich.

Leningradskaia Pravda. Daily. Leningrad.

Lidova Democracie. Daily of the Czechoslovak Populist Party. Prague.

Literarni Noviny. Weekly on cultural, political, and artistic questions. Prague.

Literaturen Front. Weekly issued by the Bulgarian Writers' Union. Sofia.

Magyar Nemzet. Daily of the Patriotic People's Front. Budapest.

Magyar Vilag. Independent Hungarian daily. Budapest.

Mezhdunarodnaia zhizn. Monthly scientific-political journal. Moscow.

Mlada Fronta. Daily of the Czechoslovak Youth League. Prague.

Le Monde. Daily. Paris.

Nasa Stvarnost. Monthly journal issued by the Central Committee, League of Communists of Yugoslavia. Belgrade.

Nepszabadsag. Central Daily of the Hungarian Socialist Workers' Party. Budapest. Up to November 1956 this newspaper appeared under the title *Szabad Nep*.

Nepszava. Daily of the Central Council of Hungarian Trade Unions. Appeared as *Nepakarat*, November 1956 to January 1958.

Neues Deutschland. Organ of the Central Committee of the SED. Berlin.

The New Leader. Weekly publication of the American Labor Conference on International Affairs. Stroudsburg, Pa.

New Times. Weekly journal published by *Trud*. Moscow.

New York Times. Daily. New York.

Nowa Kultura. Weekly literary journal. Warsaw.

Nova Makedonija. Daily of the Socialist Alliance of Working People of Macedonia. Skopje.

Nova Mysl. Review of Marxism and Leninism. Prague.

Nova Svoboda. Daily of the Communist Party of Czechoslovakia, District Committee of Ostrava. Ostrava.

Novy Zivot. Semiweekly of the Communist Party of Czechoslovakia, District Committee of Presov. Presov.

Nowe Drogi. Theoretical and political monthly organ of the Central Committee of the Polish United Workers' Party. Warsaw.

Obrana Lidu. Daily of the Czechoslovak Army. Prague.

Orka. Polish weekly journal. Warsaw.

Ost-Probleme. Weekly periodical dealing with questions of world Communism. Bad Godesberg, Germany.

Otechestven Front. Daily of the Presidium of the National Assembly and the National Council Fatherland Front. Sofia.

Po Prostu. Weekly journal of students and the young intelligentsia. Warsaw.

Politika. Daily, Politika Printing and Publishing Enterprise. Belgrade.

Polityka. Weekly review on the policy and action of the Polish United Workers' Party in domestic and international fields. Warsaw.

Pravda. Organ of the Central Committee of the CPSU. Moscow.

Prawo i Zycie. Biweekly publication on law, state administration, and socioeconomic problems, issued by the Polish Lawyers' Association. Warsaw.

Predvoj. Weekly publication on politics, culture, and economy, issued by the Central Committee of the Communist Party of Slovakia. Bratislava.

Probleme Economice. Monthly journal of the Economic Institute of the Academy of the Rumanian People's Republic. Bucharest.

Problemy Pokoju i Socjalizmu. Monthly theoretical interparty journal, Polish edition. Warsaw.

Problems of Communism. Bimonthly journal published by the United States Information Agency. Washington, D.C.

Przeglad Kulturalny. Weekly of the Council for Culture and the Fine Arts. Warsaw.

Przyjazn. Organ of the Soviet-Polish Friendship Society. Warsaw.

Rabotnicheske Delo. Organ of the Central Committee of the Communist Party of Bulgaria. Sofia.

Rada Rabotnicza. Trade union journal. Warsaw.

Rominia Libera. Daily of the People's Committees of the People's Republic of Rumania. Bucharest.

Rude Pravo. Central Organ of the Communist Party of Czechoslovakia. Prague.

Rzeczpospolita. Daily of the Czytelnik Educational Publications Cooperative. Warsaw.

Slowo Powszechne. Daily of the Workers Publishing Cooperative, *Prasa.* Warsaw.

Sluzbeni List. Official federal gazette. Belgrade.

Soviet Studies. Quarterly review of social and economic institutions of the USSR. Oxford.

Sovietskaia Litva. Daily organ of the Central Committee of the Lithuanian Communist Party, the Presidium of the Supreme Soviet of the Lithuanian SSR, and the Council of Ministers of the Lithuanian SSR. Vilnius.

Sovietskaia Moldavia. Organ of the Central Committee of the Communist Party of Moldavia and the Supreme Soviet of the Moldavian Republic. Kishinev.

Sprawy Miedzynarodowe. Bimonthly bulletin of the Polish Institute of International Affairs. Warsaw.

Studia Socjologiczno-Polityczne. Sociological-political journal. Warsaw.

Swiat. Illustrated weekly. Warsaw.

Szabad Nep. See Nepszabadsag.

Sztandar Mlodych. Daily of the Central Committee, Polish Youth League. Warsaw.

Tarsadalmi Szemle. Theoretical Periodical of the Hungarian Workers' Party. Budapest.

Three-Monthly Economic Review of Eastern Europe. Publication of the Economist Intelligence Unit Ltd. London.

Trud. Organ of the All-Union Central Soviet of Professional Associations. Moscow.

Trybuna Literacka. Literary supplement of *Trybuna Ludu.* Warsaw.

Trybuna Ludu. Organ of the Central Committee of the Polish United Workers' Party. Warsaw.

Trybuna Wolnosci. Weekly issued by the Central Committee of the Polish United Workers Party. Warsaw.

Tvorba. Weekly Journal for politics, culture, and economics. Prague.

Tygodnik Demokratyczny. Periodical of the Polish Democratic Party. Warsaw.

Tygodnik Powszechny. Weekly Magazine for Catholics on religion, social problems, literature, and arts. Absorbed by *Kierunki,* May 1953–November 1956. Volume numbering resumed December 1956 repeats that of 1954 and subsequent years of earlier issuance. Krakow.

Viata Sindicala. Daily of the Central Council of Trade Unions. Bucharest. At present issued under the title *Munca.*

Vneshnaia Torgovlya. Monthly statistical publication. Moscow.

V Pomoshch Politicheskomu Samoobrazivaniu. Journal of the "Popular Library of Marxism-Leninism." Moscow.

Voprosy filosofii. Journal appearing three times annually, published by the Philosophical Institute of the USSR Academy of Science. Moscow.

Voprosy istorii. Monthly of the Historical Institute of the USSR Academy of Science. Superseded *Istoriicheshii zhurnal.* Moscow.

Vysoka Skola. Monthly journal of the National Educational Publishing House. Prague.

Wirtschaftswissenschaft. Bimonthly economic journal of the German Democratic Republic. Berlin.

Zachodnia Agencja Prasowa. Press agency. Warsaw.

Zahranicny Obchod. Organ of the Ministry of Foreign Trade. For economic information. Prague.

Zeri i Popullit. Daily publication of the Central Committee of the Albanian Workers' Party. Tirana.

Zielony Sztandar. Semiweekly issued by the United Peasant Party. Warsaw.

Zycie Gospodarcze. Biweekly journal of the Economic Community. Warsaw.

Zycie Partii. Organ of the Central Committee of the Polish United Workers' Party. Warsaw.

Zycie Warsawy. Daily of the Czytelnik Press Institute. Warsaw.

Documents, Collections of Documents, Speeches

A Magyar-Szoujet Baratsag Diadalutja. Collection of speeches. Budapest, 1958.

The Anti-Stalin Campaign and International Communism. New York, 1957.

Bass, R., and E. Marbury, eds., *The Soviet-Jugoslav Controversy, 1948–1958: A Documentary Record.* New York, 1959.

Bialer, S., *Wybralem Prawde.* Radio Free Europe. New York, 1956.

——, *Wybralem Wolnosc.* Radio Free Europe. New York, 1956.

Bierut, B., and J. Cyrankiemicz, *Podstawy Ideologiczne PZPR.* Warsaw, 1952.

Chervenkov, V., *Otchetnyi Doklad TsK BEP VI S'ezdu Partii.* Sofia, 1954.

Chronologische Materialien zur Geschichte der SED. Berlin, 1956.

Columbia University Hungarian Interview Project. Interview texts.

Confidential transcript, *XII Plenum Komitetu Centralnego,* Central Committee of the Polish United Workers Party. Warsaw, 1958.

The Correspondence between the CC of the CPJ and the CC of the AUCP (b). Belgrade.

Czechoslovak Ministry of Foreign Affairs, *Statement of Policy of Mr. Gottwald's Government.* Prague, 1946.

Economic Treaties and Agreements of the Soviet Bloc. Mid-European Studies Center, 1952 (mimeographed).

Eighth National Congress of the Communist Party of China. 3 vols. Peiping, 1956.

Farrell, R. B., ed., *Jugoslavia and the Soviet Union, 1948–1956.* New York, 1956.

Gelberg, L., ed., *Nowe Konstytucje Panstw Europejskich.* Warsaw, 1949.

Gheorghiu-Dej, G., *Stati i Rechi.* Moscow, 1956.

Gerö, E., *The Position of the Hungarian National Economy in 1952*. Budapest, 1952.

Gomulka, W., *Przemowienia*. Warsaw, 1957.

——, *W Walce o Demokracje Ludowa*. Warsaw, 1947.

Gottwald, K., *Deset Let*. Prague, 1947.

——, *Izbrannie Proizvedenia v Dvuch Tomach*. Moscow, 1957.

Gsovski, V., ed., *Legal Sources and Bibliography of Hungary*. New York, 1958.

Kardelj, E., *On People's Democracy in Jugoslavia*. New York, 1949.

——, *The Communist Party of Jugoslavia in the Struggle for New Jugoslavia, for People's Authority and for Socialism*. Belgrade, 1948.

Kommunisticheskii International v Dokumentach, 1919–32. Moscow, 1933.

KPSS v Resoliutsiach i Resheniach S'ezdov, Konferentsii i Plenumov TsK, III. Moscow, 1954.

Kszaltowanie sie Podstaw Programowych Polskiej Partii Robotniczej. Warsaw, 1958.

Left-Wing Sectarianism and the New Course. Radio Free Europe. New York, 1954.

Lenin, V. I., *Certain Features of the Historical Development of Marxism*. Moscow, 1955.

——, *Selected Works*. New York, 1943.

——, *Sochineniya*. Moscow, 1947.

Moskovskoe Sovieshchanie Evropeiskich Stran po Obespecheniu Mira i Besopasnosti v Evrope. Moscow, 1954.

Pieck, W., *Izbrannie Proizvedeniia*. Moscow, 1956.

Pijade, M., *About the Legend that the Jugoslav Uprising Owed its Existence to Soviet Assistance*. London, 1950.

P.P.R. Warsaw, 1959.

Protokoll des Vierten Kongresses der Kommunistischen Internationale. Hamburg, 1923.

Rakosi, M., *Wir Bauen ein Neues Land*. Berlin, 1952.

——, *Valsgatott Beszedek es Cikkek*. Budapest, 1957.

VII S'ezd Bolgarskoi Kommunisticheskoi Partii. Moscow, 1958.

Soveshchanie Predstavitelei Kommunisticheskich i Rabochich Partii Sotsialisticheskich Stran. Moscow, 1957.

Stalin, J. V., "Economic Problems of Socialism in the USSR." Moscow, 1952.

——, *Marxism and the National and Colonial Question*. New York, 1935.

——, *O Stroitelstve Kommunizma v SSSR*. Moscow, 1950.

——, *On the Great Patriotic War of the Union*. Moscow, 1946.

——, *Problems of Leninism*. Moscow, 1940.

Swiatlo, J., testimony no. 13, "How Poland is Really Ruled." Mimeographed, unpublished material.

——, *Za Kulisami Bezpieki i Partii*. Radio Free Europe leaflet.

Tito, J. B., *Borba za Mir*. 3 vols. Belgrade, 1954, 1956, 1957.

——, *Borba za Sotsialistichku Demokratiju*. 2 vols. Belgrade, 1955.

——, *Workers Manage Factories in Jugoslavia*. Belgrade, 1950.

Varshavskoie Sovieshchanie Evropeiskich Gosudarstv po Obespecheniu mira i Besopasnosti v Evrope. Moscow, 1955.

Walka o Jednosc Niemiec. Polish Institute of International Affairs. Warsaw, 1953.

Zagadnienia Prawne Konstytucji Polskiej Rzeczypospolitej Ludowej. 3 vols. Warsaw, 1954.

Zagadnienie Bezpieczenstwa Zbiorowego w Europie. Warsaw, 1955.

Zasedania Politicheskogo Konsultativnogo Komiteta Chrezhdennogo v Sootvetstvii s Varshavskim Dogovorom. Moscow, 1956.

Zinner, P., ed., *National Communism and Popular Revolt in Eastern Europe*. New York, 1956.

History, Background, General Works

Agrarian Problems from the Baltic to the Aegean. RIIA. London, 1944.

Almond, G. A., *The Appeals of Communism*. Princeton, 1954.

Amery, J., *Sons of the Eagle: a Study in Guerilla War*. London, 1948.

Andreev, A. M., *Borba Litovskogo Naroda za Sovietskuiu Vlast*. Moscow, 1954.

Barbu, Z., *Democracy and Dictatorship*. New York, 1956.

Bartlett, V., *East of the Iron Curtain*. New York, 1950.

Beck, J., *The Last Report*. New York, 1957.

Benes, E., *Svetova Krise*. Prague, 1946.

Bernstein, E., *Gesellschaftliches und Privateigentum*. Berlin, 1891.

Betts, R. R., ed., *Central and Southeast Europe, 1945–1948*. London, 1950.

Black, C. E., ed., *Challenge in Eastern Europe*. Rutgers University in association with the Mid-European Studies Center of the Free Europe Committee, 1954.

——, *Readings on Contemporary Eastern Europe*. New York, 1953.

Borkenau, F., *European Communism*. London, 1953.

Brandt, C., B. Schwartz, and J. Fairbank, *A Documentary History of Chinese Communism*. Cambridge, 1952.

Braun, J., *German Eastern Territories*. Goettinger Research Committee. Germany, 1957.

Bregman, A., *Najlepszy Sojusznik Hitlera*. London, 1958.

Brzezinski, Z. K., *The Permanent Purge*. Cambridge, 1956.

——, ed., *Political Controls in the Soviet Army*. New York, 1954.

Buell, R. L., et al., *New Governments in Europe*. New York, 1937.

Buell, R. L., *Poland: Key to Europe*. New York, 1939.

Bukharin, N., *Oekonomik der Transformationsperiode*. Verlag der kommunistischen Internationale, 1922.

Busek, V., ed., *Czechoslovakia*. New York, 1957.

Byrnes, R. F., ed., *Jugoslavia*. New York, 1957.

Cabot, J. M., *The Racial Conflict in Transylvania*. Boston, 1926.

Ciechanowski, J., *Defeat in Victory*. New York, 1947.

Clissold, S., *The Whirlwind*. New York, 1949.

Correspondence between the Chairman of the Council of Ministers of the USSR and the Presidents of the USA and the Prime Ministers of Great Britain during the Great Patriotic War, 1941–1945. Moscow, 1957.

Dellin, L. A. D., ed., *Bulgaria.* New York, 1957.

Douglas, D., *Transitional Economic Systems: The Polish-Czech Example.* London, 1953.

Fainsod, M., *How Russia is Ruled.* Cambridge, 1953.

——, *International Socialism and the World War.* Cambridge, 1935.

Feis, H., *Churchill, Roosevelt, Stalin.* Princeton, 1957.

Fejtö, F., *Histoire de Democraties Populaire.* Paris, 1952.

Fischer, L., *Russia Revisited.* New York, 1957.

Fischer, R., *Stalin and German Communism.* Cambridge, 1948.

Fisher-Galati, S., ed., *Romania.* New York, 1957.

Fisher, H. H., *The Communist Revolution: An Outline of Strategy and Tactics.* Stanford, 1955.

Fotich, C., *The War We Lost.* New York, 1948.

Friedrich, C. J., ed., *Totalitarianism.* Cambridge, 1954.

Friedrich, C. J., and Z. K. Brzezinski, *Totalitarian Dictatorship and Autocracy.* Cambridge, 1956.

Garthoff, R. L., *Soviet Strategy in the Nuclear Age.* New York, 1958.

Gluckstein, Y., *Stalin's Satellites in Europe.* London, 1952.

Gross, F., *European Ideologies.* New York, 1948.

Gyorgy, A., *Governments of Danubian Europe.* New York, 1949.

Haines, G. C., *The Threat of Soviet Imperialism.* Baltimore, 1954.

Hajda, J., ed., *A Study of Contemporary Czechoslovakia.* New Haven, 1955.

Halasz, N., *In the Shadow of Russia.* New York, 1959.

Halecki, O., *Borderlands of Western Civilization: A History of East Central Europe.* New York, 1952.

——, ed., *Poland.* New York, 1957.

Healey, D., *The Curtain Falls: The Story of the Socialists in Eastern Europe.* London, 1951.

Helmreich, E., ed., *Hungary.* New York, 1957.

Hogye, M., *The Paris Peace Conference of 1946: The Role of the Hungarian Communists and of the USSR.* Mid-European Studies Center, 1954.

Hunt, C., *The Theory and Practice of Communism.* London, 1950.

Inkeles, A., *Public Opinion in Soviet Russia.* Cambridge, 1950.

Iwanska, A., ed., *Contemporary Poland.* Human Relations Area Files, 1955.

Jordan Z., *The Oder-Neisse Line.* London, 1952.

Kechekian, S. F., and G. I. Fedkin, *Istoria Politicheskich Uchenii.* Moscow, 1955.

Kerner, D. J., *Czechoslovakia.* Berkeley, 1940.

Kertesz, S., ed., *The Fate of East Central Europe.* Notre Dame, 1956.

Kim, M. P., ed., *Istoria SSSR.* Moscow, 1957.

Kolarz, W., *Russia and Her Colonies.* New York, 1953.

Kommunisticheskaia Partiia Polshi v Borbe za Nezavisimost Svoiei Strany. Moscow, 1955.

Komorowski, Y., *The Secret Army.* London, 1957.

Korbonski, S., *W Imieniu Rzeczypospolitej.* Paris, 1954. English translation: *Fighting Warsaw.* New York, 1956.

Kula, W., *Rozwazania o Historii.* Warsaw, 1958.

Lasswell, H. D. and A. Kaplan, *Power and Society.* New Haven, 1950.

Leites, N., *The Study of Bolshevism.* New York, 1953.

Leonhard, W., *Die Revolution Entlaesst Ihre Kinder.* Berlin, 1955. English translation: *Child of the Revolution.* Chicago, 1958.

Lukacs, J. A., *The Great Powers and Eastern Europe.* New York, 1953.

Macartney, C. A., *A History of Hungary, 1929–1945.* Edinburgh, 1956–1957.

——, *Problems of the Danube Basin.* Cambridge, Eng., 1944.

Mackiewicz, J., *The Katyn-Wood Murders.* London, 1951.

McLean, F., *The Heretic.* New York, 1957.

Meissner, B., *Das Ende des Stalin-Mythos.* Frankfurt, 1956.

Meyer, A. G., *Leninism.* Cambridge, 1957.

——, *Marxism.* Cambridge, 1954.

Mitrany, D., *Marx Against the Peasant.* Chapel Hill, 1951.

Morgan, O. S., *Agricultural Systems of Middle Europe.* New York, 1933.

Neumann, F., *The Democratic and the Authoritarian State.* Glencoe, 1957.

Nyaradi, N., *My Ringside Seat in Moscow.* New York, 1952.

Oktiabrskaia Revólutsia v Rossii i Mirovoie Osvoboditelnoie Dvizhenie. Gospolitizdat, 1957.

Ossowski, S., *Struktura Klasowa w Spolecznej Swiadomosci.* Wroclaw, 1957.

Politika Sovietskoi Vlasti po Natsional'nym Delam za Try Goda, 1917–X–1920. Moscow, 1920.

Roberts, H. L., *Rumania: Political Problems of an Agricultural State.* New Haven, 1951.

Rostow, W. W., *The Dynamics of Soviet Society.* Cambridge, 1953.

Rozek, E., *Allied Wartime Diplomacy: A Pattern in Poland.* New York, 1958.

Schwartz, B. I., *Chinese Communism and the Rise of Mao.* Cambridge, 1952.

Seton-Watson, H., *From Lenin to Malenkov.* New York, 1953.

——, *The East-European Revolution.* New York, 1956.

——, *The History of World Communism.* New York, 1953.

——, *The Pattern of Communist Revolution.* London, 1953.

Sharp, S. L., *New Constitutions in the Soviet Sphere.* Washington, 1950.

Skendi, S., ed., *Albania.* New York, 1957.

Starbinger, W., *Grenzen der Sowjetmacht.* Wuerzburg, 1955.

Swarup, R., *Communism and Peasantry.* Calcutta, 1954.

Talmon, J. L., *The Rise of Totalitarian Democracy.* Boston, 1952.

Taracouzio, T. A., *War and Peace in Soviet Diplomacy.* New York, 1940.

Thomson, S. H., *Czechoslovakia in European History.* Princeton, 1953.

Towster, J., *Political Power in the USSR.* New York, 1948.

United States Department of State, *Moscow's European Satellites*. Washington, 1955.

Walker, R., *China Under Communism*. New Haven, 1955.

Wandycz, C. S., *Czechoslovak-Polish Federation and the Great Powers*. Bloomington, 1956.

Warriner, D., *Revolution in Eastern Europe*. London, 1950.

Wiley, A., *Tensions Within the Soviet Captive Countries*. Senate Committee on Foreign Relations, 1954.

Wiskemann, E., *Germany's Eastern Neighbours*. Oxford, 1956.

Wolff, R., *The Balkans in Our Time*. Cambridge, 1956.

Zagorski, W., *Seventy Days*. London, 1957.

Zaleski, W., *The Pattern of Life in Poland*. Paris, 1952.

Zamyslova, Z. A., *Kommunisticheskii Internatsional i Ego Rol v Istorii Mezhdunarodnogo Rabochego i Natsional'no-Osvoboditel'nogo Dvizheniia*. Moscow, 1957.

Political and Ideological Developments since 1945

Akademia Nauk SSSR, *Voprosy Stroitelstva Edinovo Demokraticheskovo Germanskovo Gosudarstva*. Moscow, 1951.

Armstrong, H. F., *Tito and Goliath*. New York, 1951.

Beke, L., *A Student's Diary*. New York, 1957.

Bienkowski, W., *Rewolucji Ciag Dalszy*. Warsaw, 1957.

Blum, I., *Z Dziejow Aparatu Politycznego Wojska Polskiego*. Warsaw, 1957.

Boorman, H. L., et al., *Moscow-Peking Axis*. New York, 1957.

Brant, S., *The East German Rising, 17th June 1953*. London, 1955.

Co sie Dzieje w ZMP? Warsaw, 1956.

Cretzianu, A., *Captive Rumania*. New York, 1956.

Culbertson, W., *Liberation: The Threat and Challenge of Power*. Atlanta, 1953.

Czechoslovak Academy of Science, *Otazky Narodni a Demokraticke Revoluce v CSR*. Prague, 1955.

de Sola Pool, I., ed., *Satellite Generals*. Stanford, 1955.

Deborin, G. A., ed., *Mezhdunarodnie Otnosheniia i Vneshniaia Politika Sovetskogo Soiuza*. Moscow, 1958.

Dedijer, V., *Tito*. New York, 1952.

Delany, R. F., ed., *This is Communist Hungary*. Chicago, 1958.

Deutschlands Ostproblem. Goettinger Arbeitskreis, Germany, 1957.

Djilas, M., "On New Roads to Socialism." Belgrade, 1950.

——, *The New Class*. New York, 1957.

Dragnich, A., *Tito's Promised Land*. New Brunswick, 1954.

Dragoicheva, T., *Politicheska, Organizatsionna i Stopanska Deinost*. Sofia, 1945.

Draskovich, S. M., *Tito, Moscow's Trojan Horse*. Chicago, 1957.

Duhnke, H., *Stalinismus in Deutschland*. Cologne, 1955.

Dziewanowski, M. K., *The Communist Party of Poland*. Cambridge, 1959.

Ekonomika i Polityka Jugoslawii. Collection of essays. Warsaw, 1957.

Esti, B., *Tanulmayok a Magyar Nepi Demokracia Tortenetebol*. Budapest, 1955.

Farberov, N. P., *Gosudarstvennoe Pravo Stran Narodnoi Demokratii*. Moscow, 1949.

Fejtö, F., *Behind the Rape of Hungary*. New York, 1957.

Friedrich, C. J., ed., *The Soviet Zone of Germany*. New Haven, 1956.

Gabor, R., *Organization and Strategy of the Hungarian Workers Party*. New York, 1952.

Gadourek, I., *The Communist Party of Czechoslovakia in the Post-Stalinist Period*. Chicago, 1957.

——, *Political Control of Czechoslovakia*. Leiden, 1953.

Gelberg, L., *Uklad Warszawski*. Warsaw, 1957.

Gindev, P., *Kum Vuprosa za Kharaktera na Narodno-Demokraticheskata Revoliutsia v Bulgariia*. Sofia, 1956.

Gruliow, L., *Current Soviet Policies*. New York, 1953.

Hallowell, J. H., ed., *Soviet Satellite Nations*. Gainesville, 1958.

Halperin, E., *The Triumphant Heretic*. London, 1958.

Hammond, T. T., *Jugoslavia Between East and West*. New York, 1954.

Hildebrandt, R., *The Explosion*. New York, 1955.

The Hungarian Situation and the Rule of Law. The Hague, 1957.

Hungarian State Publishing House, *The Trial of Josef Mindszenty*. Budapest, 1949.

Justice Enslaved. International Commission of Jurists, The Hague, 1955.

Kanapa, J., *Bulgarie d'Hier et d'aujourd'hui*. Paris, 1955.

Kapitsa, M. S., *Sovetsko-Kitaiskie Otnosheniia*. Moscow, 1958.

Korbel, J., *Tito's Communism*. Denver, 1951.

Korbel, P., and V. Vagassky, *Purges in the Communist Party of Czechoslovakia*. Radio Free Europe, mimeographed, 1952.

Korbonski, S., *W Imieniu Kremla*. Paris, 1956. English translation: *Warsaw in Chains*. New York, 1959.

Korovin, E., *Nerushimaia Druzhba Narodov SSSR i Narodno-Demokraticheskich Stran*. Moscow, 1955.

Kovacs, I., ed., *Facts About Hungary*. New York, 1958.

Lane, A. B., *I Saw Poland Betrayed*. Indianapolis, 1948.

Lasky, M. J., ed., *The Hungarian Revolution*. London, 1957.

Lewis, F., *A Case History of Hope*. New York, 1958.

Lyon, S., *Czechoslovak-Jugoslav Relations*. Radio Free Europe, mimeographed, no date.

Maksakovski, V. P., *Stroiki Sotsialisma v Evropeiskich Stranach Narodnoi Demokratii*. Moscow, 1952.

Markham, R. H., *Rumania Under the Soviet Yoke*. Boston, 1949.

Materiali po Istoriia na Bulgarskata Kommunisticheska Partiia. Sofia, 1956.

McVicker, C. P., *Titoism*. New York, 1957.

Melnikov, D., *Borba za Edinuiu Nezavisimuiu Demokraticheskuiu Miroliubivuiu Germaniu*. Moscow, 1951.

Meray, T., *Thirteen Days that Shook the Kremlin*. New York, 1959.

Mikolajczyk, S., *The Rape of Poland*. New York, 1948.

Milosz, C., *The Seizure of Power*. New York, 1955.

Monin, D. D., *Federatsia ili Edinoe Germanskoie Gosudarstvo*. Moscow, 1947.

Nagy, F., *Struggle Behind the Iron Curtain*. New York, 1948.

Nagy, I., *On Communism*. New York, 1957.

Imre Nagy: Un Communisme qui n'oublie pas L'Homme. Intro. by F. Fejtö. Paris, 1959.

Neal, F. W., *Titoism in Action*. Berkeley, 1958.

Nettl, J. P., *The Eastern Zone and Soviet Policy in Germany*. Oxford, 1951.

O Narodnoi Demokratii v Stranach Evropi. Moscow, 1956.

Pod Znamenem Proletarskovo Internatsionalisma. Moscow, 1957.

Prebeichevich, S., tr., *Jugoslavia's Way*. New York, 1958.

Prochazka, A., "Changes in the Philosophy of Czechoslovak Law." Microfilm, Library of Congress, Washington.

Proiekt za Konstitutsia na narodna Republika Bulgaria. Sofia, 1946.

Protiv Sovremennogo Revizionizma. Moscow, 1958.

Reale, E., *Nascita del Cominform*. Milan, 1958.

Reisky-Dubnic, V., *The Communist Propaganda Methods in Czechoslovakia*. Ph.D. thesis, University of Chicago, 1959.

Research and Publications Service, *The Pattern of the Purge*. New York, 1952.

Research Report: Hungarian Party Congress, May 24–30, 1954. Radio Free Europe, mimeographed, 1954.

Ripka, H., *Czechoslovakia Enslaved*. London, 1950.

——, *Le Coup de Prague*. Paris, 1949.

Rostow, W. W., *The Prospects for Communist China*. Cambridge, 1954.

RIIA, *The Soviet-Jugoslav Dispute*. London, 1948.

Rozmaryn, S., *Polskie Prawo Panstwowe*. Warsaw, 1951.

The Satellites in Eastern Europe. The Annals, vol. 317, May 1958.

Schaff, A., *Wstep do Teorii Marksismu*. Warsaw, 1948.

Schmidt, D. A., *Anatomy of a Satellite*. Boston, 1952.

Seydewitz, M., *Niemiecka Republika Demokratyczna*. Warsaw, 1955.

Sharp, S., *New Constitutions in the Soviet Sphere*. Washington, 1950.

Sobolev, A., *Chto Takoe Narodnaia Demokratia*. Moscow, 1956.

Sodruzhestvo Stran Sotsializma. Collection of essays. Moscow, 1958.

Sovietization of the Czechoslovak Judiciary. Research and Publications Service, New York, 1953.

Stepanian, I. V., *Stalin o Stroitel'stve Kommunizma v SSSR*. Moscow, 1950.

Stern, C., *Die SED*. Germany, 1954.

Stypulkowski, Z., *Polska na Progu 1958 R*. London, 1958.

Sulzberger, C. L., *The Big Thaw*. New York, 1956.

Syrop, K., *Spring in October*. New York, 1958.

Tarantova, L., *Zrada sidli v Belehrade*. Prague, 1952.

Tomasic, D., *National Communism and Soviet Strategy*. Washington, 1957.

Ulam, A., *Titoism and the Cominform*. Cambridge, 1952.

UN Special Committee for Eastern Europe, *Report on the Problem of Hungary*. New York, 1957.

United States Department of State, *Moscow's European Satellites*. Washington, 1955.

Valev, L., ed., *Bolgarskii Narod v Borbe za Sotsializm*. Moscow, 1954.

Walka Ludu Polskiego o Wolnosc i Socjalizm. Warsaw, 1953.

Wei, H., *China and Soviet Russia*. New York, 1956.

White, L., *Balkan Caesar: Tito versus Stalin*. New York, 1951.

Zawadski, S., *Rozwoj Wiezi Rad Narodowych z Masami Pracujacymi w Polsce Ludowej*. Warsaw, 1955.

Zilliacus, K., *A New Birth of Freedom*. London, 1956.

Zinner, P., *The Strategy and Tactics of the Czechoslovak Communist Party*. Ph.D. thesis, Harvard University, 1953.

Zofka, B., *La Constitution tchecoslovaque*. Chicago, 1956.

Economic and Social Developments since 1945

Aktualne Zagadnienia Polityki Kulturalnej w Dziedzinie Filozofii i Socjologii. Warsaw, 1956.

Alton, T. P., *Postwar Economic Planning in Poland*. New York, 1955.

Bouvier, C., *La Collectivisation de L'Agriculture, URSS-Chines-Democraties Populaires*. Paris, 1958.

Buhler, N., and S. Zukowski, *Discrimination in Education in the People's Democracies*. New York, 1955.

Carlton, R. K., ed., *Forced Labor in the People's Democracies*. New York, 1955.

Chalasinski, J., *Przeszlosc i Przyszlosc Inteligencji Polskiej*. Warsaw, 1958.

Csicsery-Ronay, I., *Russian Cultural Penetration in Hungary*. Mimeographed, Research and Publications Service, VI, 1950. Vol. II, 1951; Vol. III, 1952.

DeWar, M., *Soviet Trade with Eastern Europe*. London, 1951.

Dyskusja o Polskim Modelu Gospodarczym. Collected Essays. Warsaw, 1957.

Economic Commission for Europe, *Etude sur la situation économique de L'Europe depuis la guerre*. Geneva, 1953.

Economic Survey of Europe Since the War. UN publication, no date.

Feireabend, L., *Agricultural Coops in Czechoslovakia*. Mid-European Studies Center, 1951, mimeographed.

Fidelski, R., *O Radach Rabotniczych*. Warsaw, 1956.

——, *Wspolpraca Gospodarcza Polski z Krajami Socjalistycznymi*. Warsaw, 1959.

Foreign Trade in the People's Democracies of Central and Eastern Europe. Research and Publications Service, mimeographed, November 1952.

Gabensky, I., *Bulgarian Economy*. Research and Publications Service, mimeographed, 1951.

Gertsovich, G. B., *Razvitie Mirnoi Ekonomiki v Germanskoi Demokraticheskoi Respublike*. Moscow, 1954.

Goldmann, J., *Planned Economy in Czechoslovakia*. Prague, 1949.

Hlasko, M., *The Eighth Day of the Week*. New York, 1958.

Hungarian Investment Policy Under the New Course. Radio Free Europe, New York, 1954.

Ivanova, N. I., et al., eds., *Razvitie Ekonomiki Stran Narodnoi Demokratii.* Moscow, 1958.

Jahasz, W., *Hungary's Bolshevized Pedagogy in 1951–1952.* Research and Publications Service, New York, 1952.

Jahasz, W., and A. Rothberg, A., eds., *Flashes in the Night: A Collection of Stories from Contemporary Hungary.* New York, 1958.

Kalendarz Rabotniczy 1957. Warsaw, 1957.

Karra, V., *Stroitel'stvo Sotsialisticheskoi Ekonomiki v Rumynskoi Narodnoi Respublike.* Moscow, 1953.

Kornai, J., *A Gazdasagi Vezetes Tulzott Kozpontositasa.* Budapest, 1957.

Kracauer, S., and P. Berkman, *Satellite Mentality.* New York, 1956.

Lerski, J., *The Economy of Poland.* The Council for Economic and Industry Research, Inc., Washington, 1954.

Lipinski, E., *Rewizje.* Warsaw, 1958.

Lychowski, T., *Stosunki Ekonomiczne Miedzy Krajami o Roznych Ustrojach.* Warsaw, 1957.

Marczewski, J., *Planification et Croissance Economique des Democraties Populaires.* Paris, 1958.

Mayewski, P., ed., *The Broken Mirror.* New York, 1958.

Mendershausen, H., *Terms of Trade Between the Soviet Union and Smaller Communist Countries, 1955–1957.* Rand Corporation, January 1959.

Meyer, P., *The Jews in the Soviet Satellites.* Syracuse, 1953.

Milosz, C., *The Captive Mind.* New York, 1953.

Mirovaia Sotsialisticheskaia Sistema Khoziaistva. Collection of essays. Moscow, 1958.

Nikolitch, R., *Land Reform and Land Tenure in Jugoslavia.* Mid-European Studies Center, mimeographed, 1951.

O Nowy Program Rolny. Collected essays. Warsaw, 1957.

Plan Odbudowy Gospodarczej. Warsaw, 1947.

Plany Razvitia Narodnovo Khoziaistva Stran Narodnoi Demokratii. Moscow, 1952.

Pounds, N., and N. Spulber, eds., *Resources and Planning in Eastern Europe.* Bloomington, 1957.

Przedsiebiorstwo Samodzielne w Gospodarce Planowej. Warsaw, 1957.

Report of the FAO Mission to Poland. Washington, 1948.

Rocznik Statystyczny. Polish Statistical Yearbook, Warsaw.

Sanders, I. T., ed., *Collectivization of Agriculture in Eastern Europe.* Lexington, 1958.

Satellite Agriculture in Crisis. Free Europe Committee, Inc., 1954.

Shuster, G. N., *Religion Behind the Iron Curtain.* New York, 1954.

Sladovsky, M. I., *Ocherki Ekonomicheskich Otnoshenii SSSR s Kitaiem.* Moscow, 1957.

Slusser, R., ed., *Soviet Economic Policy in Postwar Germany.* New York, 1953.

Spulber, N., *The Economics of Communist Eastern Europe*. Cambridge, 1957.

Stankiewicz, W., and J. Montias, *Institutional Changes in the Polish Economy*. New York, 1955.

Statisticheski Ezhegodnik Rumynskoi Narodnoi Republiki. Bucharest, 1957.

Statisticheski Godishnik na Narodna Republika Bulgariya. Sofia, 1956.

Szczepanski, J., *Inteligencja i Spoleczenstwo*. Warsaw, 1957.

Tomasevich, J., *Peasants, Politics, and Economic Change in Jugoslavia*. Stanford, 1955.

Tomasic, D., *Personality and Culture in Eastern European Politics*. New York, 1948.

Varga, E., *Izmienienia v Ekonomike Kapitalizma v Itoge Vtoroi Mirovoi Voiny*. Moscow, 1946.

——, *Basic Questions of Economy and Politics of Imperialism after World War II*. Moscow, 1953.

Wszelaki, J., *Communist Economic Strategy: The Role of East Central Europe*. Washington, 1959.

Wykonanie Narodowych Planow Gospodarczych, 1948–1952. Warsaw, 1952.

Index*

* Entries for the new material added to this revised edition (Epilogue and Appendix I) appear in an Index Addenda beginning on page 542.